33RD EDITION

TWO-YEAR-OLDS OF 2017

33RD EDITION

TWO-YEAR-OLDS OF 2017

STEVE TAPLIN

Foreword by Roger Varian

FRONT COVER: Fair Eva winning the Princess Margaret Stakes at Ascot in 2016. Copyright © Racing Post/ Edward Whitaker.

BACK COVER: Roger Varian (left) and Steve Taplin (right)

Published in 2017 by Raceform
27 Kingfisher Court, Hambridge Road, Newbury, Berkshire, RG14 5SJ

A catalogue record for this book is available from the British Library.

ISBN: 978-1-910497-28-9

Designed by Fiona Pike

Printed in Great Britain by CPI Group (UK) Ltd, Croydon, CR0 4YY

Contents

Foreword

Steve has been producing this marvellous volume for nearly as long as I have been alive, so I am honoured to write the foreword to the thirty-third edition of *Two-Year-Olds*, which is undoubtedly the market-leading resource for assessing juvenile talent and potential throughout the Flat season.

The reputation of this encyclopaedic work continues to grow in stature, even in its fourth decade of publication, and the importance of the book to racing fans, punters and professionals is testament to Steve's dedication and skill, as well as the excellent rapport he has built with professionals from across the industry.

Steve's publication has many functions and uses. Trainers are able to gain a sneak preview into the merits of the opposition, punters can look to find an underestimated bet, while the media can scour the pages for an early indication into those youngsters likely to generate hype and excitement when they first set foot on the racecourse.

However, the beauty of *Two-Year-Olds* surely lies in its longevity. Readers can use the work to formulate an early opinion of a juvenile before tracking the worthiness of that opinion when the form becomes known and established throughout the year. Hence, *Two-Year-Olds* is as useful in November as it is in May, while its importance in gauging horses that are likely to improve significantly as three-year-olds should not be underestimated either.

As we all know, reputations and impressions can change quite considerably over a short period of time, particularly with juveniles. Sometimes we trainers get it right – I was very proud to have nominated Cursory Glance as a five-star selection prior to her Group 1-winning campaign in 2014. It does not always work out so well, but it certainly pleases the trainer, owner and reader when things fall so neatly into place.

Steve's chapter charting the opinions of leading bloodstock experts is a unique insight from those who spend their lives assessing the merits of juveniles, while *Two-Year-Olds* is also a fine reflection of Steve's analytical and perceptive way of thinking. The Fifty To Follow section regularly produces a hatful of winners, while the catalogue of Bargain Buys is a fine starting point for weighing up the form of median and maiden auction races.

Two-Year-Olds has stood the test of time in a way few, if any, of its competitors can boast, which is surely the most ringing endorsement of any publication. I am certain this edition will continue to build on the success of its predecessors and I look forward to regularly referencing the work throughout the year.

Roger Varian

Introduction

Thirty three years and still going strong. It's a long time since this book was in its infancy and just a compilation of some of the best-bred two-year-olds in training without trainer comments. These days I try to be as comprehensive as I possibly can be. My pedigree research begins in September by ploughing through all the yearling sales catalogues for potential entries for the next book. That continues until the spring when my trainer interviews take over and I wonder how I'll ever manage to interview over 70 trainers in a little over three weeks and type up the comments.

For those new to the book let me explain that *Two-Year-Olds* aims to highlight the best juvenile racehorses in training in Britain and Ireland. Many of them will win this year, others will be better as three-year-olds in 2018. So the book can be used as a work of reference next year too.

Newmarket trainer Roger Varian, now settled in at his new yard Carlburg Stables, was kind enough to write the foreword for me. Roger began his training career at Kremlin House Stables where he took over from his mentor, the legendary trainer Michael Jarvis. At Carlburg he's taken over from another well-known and popular trainer, Clive Brittain. The amount of support given to Roger from owners from all over the world is testament to his ability, dedication and friendly nature.

As usual this year I've received the help of over 70 trainers in Britain and Ireland who have all granted me interviews to discuss their young horses. New trainers to give me interviews for the book this year are Archie Watson, Simon Crisford, Tom Clover, Charlie McBride, Martyn Meade and Henry Spiller.

The Living Legend Racing Partnership (my racing syndicate) has moved on this year to the Cheshire yard of Tom Dascombe, who's been charged with providing us with another winner or two in the shape of the two-year-olds Magnus (by Makfi) and Queen Of Salsa (by Havana Gold). I'm not dusting my top hat off for Ascot just yet, but if you're not full of hope in the spring when can you be? If we end up at rather less auspicious racecourses than Ascot then so be it, but in this game you never know when it'll be your turn to pop open the champagne.

My wife Gillian and I went to Seattle and Oregon on holiday last year. One trip we made was to Snoqualmie Falls and of course as a flat racing fan it brought to mind the horses of British owner-breeder Jeff Smith. Their names often include 'Seattle' or 'Snoqualmie' and they've raced with great success. I was visiting trainer David Elsworth this spring and explaining this story to him when who should walk into the office but Dave Bowe, Jeff Smith's racing manager. Quite a coincidence! It was very nice to meet him as I've always had a soft spot for Jeff's horses and you'll see plenty of them in this book.

Regular readers will be aware that each year the book has a number of horses to follow lists, such as the 'Fifty To Follow' and the 'Bloodstock Experts Mark Your Card'. They are always useful for those who want to follow a select number of horses. The 'Bloodstock Experts' always do well and last year they tipped 45 individual winners of 58 races. We mustn't forget either that in 2014 Malcolm Bastard nominated two colts (Golden Horn and Make Believe) that would go on to classic glory the following year. Now that really was quite a feat – well spotted Malcolm!

The big priced winners amongst the 'Trainers' Bargain Buys' no doubt make it a particular favourite section for lots of punters. The Star Two-Year-Olds included very good horses like Thunder Snow (albeit renamed from Super Talent), Fair Eva, Global Applause and Swiss Storm.

As usual, the two-year-olds in the book are listed under their trainers and my aim is to choose those horses most likely to be winners. You'll notice a 'star rating' for each of the two-year-olds, so take note in particular of those with three stars or more. There are no star ratings for those two-year-olds without any comments from the trainer. I think to give them a rating based on the pedigree alone is too speculative.

The following is a rough guide to my description of the ability of family members mentioned in the pedigree assessment of every two-year-old, based upon professional handicap ratings. Please note that these descriptions are standard throughout the book in the vast majority of cases, but there are instances where I rely on my own judgement of each horse's rating.

Below 60 = moderate
60 – 69 = modest
70 – 79 = fair
80 – 89 = quite useful
90 – 99 = fairly useful
100 – 107 = useful
108 – 112 = very useful
113 – 117 = smart
118 – 122 = very smart
123 – 127 = high-class
128 – 134 = top-class
135 and above = outstanding

To make it easier to find a specific horse the book is comprehensively indexed. So you'll find an index of the horses, their dams and their sires.

The book is divided into the following sections:

- Fifty To Follow.
- Ten to Follow in Ireland.
- Star Two-Year-Olds. This system gives an instant appraisal of the regard in which a horse is held. Those horses awarded the maximum of five stars are listed here.

- The Bloodstock Experts Mark Your Card. Bloodstock agents and stud managers suggest potentially smart two-year-olds bought or raised by them.
- Bargain Buys. A list of relatively cheaply bought two-year-olds the trainers feel will turn out to be good deals.
- Two-Year-Olds of 2017. The main section of the book, with each two-year-old listed under the trainer. Trainers' comments (when given) are in italics after the pedigree assessments. Readers should bear in mind that all the trainers' comments come from my interviews which took part from late March to mid-April.
- Stallion Reference, detailing the racing and stud careers of sires with two-year-old representatives in the book.
- Stallion Index.
- Racing Trends. An analysis of some juvenile events that regularly highlight the stars of the future. It includes a list of three-year-olds to follow this season.
- Index of Two-Year-Olds.
- Index of Dams.

Inevitably there are some unnamed horses in the book, but please access my website www. stevetaplin.co.uk throughout the season for updates on those horses named after the book was published.

Researched and compiled by
Steve Taplin BA (Hons).

Fifty to Follow

ALBA POWER (IRE)
b.c. Fast Company – Shehila (Zamindar). *"A smart, speedy colt. He looked like a Royal Ascot type when we bought him and having done a couple of pieces of work he still does. He's a good size, strong, forward-going and I've found nothing I dislike yet".* Hugo Palmer.

ARTHUR DALEY
b.c. Camelot – Nasanice (Nashwan). *"He's a beautiful horse, very good looking, athletic and with a very good temperament. A very exciting horse, he finds it all easy and I couldn't be more complimentary about him, he's very special at this stage".* George Scott.

BE MY ANGEL
b.br.f. Dark Angel – Mullein (Oasis Dream). *"She looks really nice. Growing at a tremendous rate at the moment but she's a lovely mover and I should imagine she'll be ready to run in June or July. She'll be a six furlong filly and I like her for sure".* Henry Candy.

CHARMING GUEST
b.f. Kodiac – Na Zdorovie (Cockney Rebel). *"She goes well. She's a nice filly and I can see her being out in May or June. When she's sharpened up we think she'll be pretty good, so we'll see how we go.* Mick Channon.

CHILLALA
b.f. Requinto – Positive Step (Footstepsinthesand). *"A nice filly that cost quite a lot of money, I like her a lot. She's quite rangy but she shows plenty of speed and I see her starting over six furlongs in May".* Harry Dunlop.

CHOOKIE DUNEDIN
b.c. Epaulette – Lady Of Windsor (Woods Of Windsor). *"A big, strong colt, he's working really well and I like his attitude because he's a lot more straightforward than his half-brother Chookie Royale. A strong-topped colt with good bone".* Keith Dalgleish.

COGITAL
b.c. Invincible Spirit – Galaxy Highflyer (Galileo). *"He's a lovely horse, oozes quality and it's a great family. He's well-built, 16 hands, moves well and he's by Invincible Spirit out of a Galileo mare, so he's got every chance".* Amanda Perrett.

CORINTHIA KNIGHT (IRE)
ch.c. Society Rock – Victoria Lodge (Grand Lodge). *"He's a very nice little horse, everything he does is straightforward. He's pleased us from day one and definitely has the ability to win races at two".* Archie Watson.

COWBOY SOLDIER
b.c. Kodiac – Urgele (Zafonic). *"A very nice horse, he's an early type and will probably be running in April. He looks sharp, has a lot of speed and is very straightforward. An out and out 2-y-o type".* Robert Cowell.

DARK ROSE ANGEL
b.f. Dark Angel – Roseraie (Lawman). *"I'd like to get her started as soon as we can although she's not quite as forward as we first thought. A very nice filly that's doing everything right, she'll come into her own over seven furlongs".* Simon Crisford.

DUTCH MONARCH
b.f. Dutch Art – Regal Heiress (Pivotal). *"She'll be one of the earlier ones. We had her full sister, Dutch Heiress, who won a couple of 2-y-o races over seven furlongs and this would seem to be a similar sort".* Sir Mark Prescott.

ENSIGN EWART
ch.c. Lope De Vega – Caerlonore (Traditionally). *"A very nice horse. He goes well, and it looks like he could be speedy enough for six furlongs. He'll develop into a really nice horse...I'm looking forward to him".* Andrew Balding.

ERTIYAD
b.f. Dark Angel – Lily Again (American Post). *"A really nice filly, she'll be early and might be an Ascot 2-y-o. She's got a bit of scope, a bit of size and a bit of ability too. A quality filly".* William Haggas.

FINNISTON FARM
b.c. Helmet – Logic (Slip Anchor). *"I think he could be one of the nicer ones we've got. He moves beautifully, he's aggressive and we're probably thinking of setting him off in the second half of May over six furlongs. He looks a really lovely 2-y-o".* Tom Dascombe.

FLAMENCO
b.f. Showcasing – Astrantia (Dansili). *"A nice filly, she moves really well. Big and scopey, I think she's got a chance to be a classy filly this year".* William Haggas.

FOUR WHITE SOCKS
ch.f. Lope De Vega – Peppermint Green (Green Desert). *"A very attractive filly, she's from a good family and appears to be going well. I don't think she's particularly precocious but I can see her starting in mid-summer over seven furlongs".* Luca Cumani.

GLOBAL TANGO (IRE)
gr.c. Zebedee – Beautiful Dancer (Danehill Dancer). *"On the forward march and he's starting to please us. He's got a good attitude and he loves his work, he's certainly a 2-y-o and one to follow I'd say".* Charlie Hills.

GOLD TOWN
b.c. Street Cry – Pimpernel (Invincible Spirit). *"A mature, fast, strong individual. He's very forward going in his work but will be better seen stepping up to six and seven furlong. Has a fast, early pedigree".* Charlie Appleby.

HADDAF (IRE)
b.c. Dawn Approach – Deveron (Cozzene). *"A medium-sized, very strong 2-y-o type. He'll start at five furlongs and then we'll take it from there. He goes very well".* James Tate.

HERMOSITA
b.f. Exceed And Excel – Honorlina (Linamix). *"She's a lovely filly and could be quite smart. She has a good action, it's a good family and she's a six furlong 2-y-o that will probably stay seven in time".* Roger Varian.

IBRAZ
b.c. Farhh – Wadaa (Dynaformer). *"He really is a nice horse. He moves well, very athletic and we like what we've seen so far. A nice prospect, I was tempted to make him my 5-star pick".* Roger Varian.

IMMORTAL ROMANCE
br.c. Society Rock – Sundown (Polish Precedent). *"A particularly good mover, this horse is mature looking for his age and we like him. He's quite sharp and certainly looks like he'll do himself justice at two".* Michael Bell.

INDIAN WARRIOR
b.c. Sepoy – Night Gypsy (Mind Games). *"I like this colt. There's a lot of speed on the dam's side, he has a very good temperament, goes well and will be one of the earliest 2-y-o's. Much more precocious than the previous ones I've had by Sepoy".* Ed Dunlop.

IT'S A WISH
b.f. Invincible Spirit – Sun Bittern (Seeking The Gold). *"I'm quite excited by her at the moment, she's really filled out and muscled in every direction and everything I see about her looks nice. She looks to me an out-and-out 2-y-o".* Hugo Palmer.

JELLMOOD
b.c. Acclamation – Emotif (Giant's Causeway). *"He's very strong, looks a 2-y-o and he's taken the fast work we've given him really well. He has speed, so we're hoping if all goes well we'll probably have him on the track by the end of April".* Marco Botti.

JOE'S SPIRIT
b.c. Swiss Spirit – Dimensional (Dansili). *"He may well have run before this book goes to print. He goes well, he's very speedy and every inch a 2-y-o. I think he's a good ambassador for his sire and he has a proper pedigree".* Michael Bell.

LA MAQUINA
b.c. Dutch Art – Miss Meltemi (Miswaki Tern). *"A lovely horse for May or June. He's the*

apple of a few people's eyes here". George Baker.

LEVANTE PLAYER (IRE)
b.c. Kodiac – Isolde's Return (Avonbridge). *"A lovely colt, going really nicely and I like him. He reminds me a lot of Roudee who was a decent 2-y-o and got better with age. I'm sure this horse will be the same".* Tom Dascombe.

LUBINKA
gr.f. Mastercraftsman – Petite Nymphe (Golan). *"A very nice filly, she goes really nicely and does everything right. A quality filly, she'll probably prefer a bit of ease in the ground and she's one I like a lot. She could be very good".* Peter Chapple-Hyam.

MICHAEL CORLEONE (IRE)
ch.c. Declaration Of War – Needles And Pins (Fasliyev). *"Physically I think this is one of our nicest horses, he looks superb, he's really strengthened up and has dealt with everything. I think he'll be a really good racehorse".* Martyn Meade.

MIDNIGHT GUEST
b.f. Acclamation – Midnight Martini (Night Shift). *"This filly has bags of potential. I'll be surprised if she's not up to her dam's class. She's not small, but racy and a proper 2-y-o filly. I'm really looking forward to her".* George Margarson.

MIQYAAS
b.c. Oasis Dream – Fawaayed (Singspiel). *"A nice type and a forward colt, I like him and I'd hope to have him out in late April/early May".* John Gosden.

MOQARRAB
b.br.c. Speightstown – Grosse Pointe Anne (Silver Deputy). *"Probably the most precocious and forward going of our 2-y-o's at present, he's very sharp and he could be our first runner. He's not just an early type either – he looks to have a bit of quality".* Saeed bin Suroor.

MRASEEL
b.f. Sir Prancealot – Suffer Her (Whipper). *"Likely to be our first 2-y-o runner, she's smallish, strong and very much a 2-y-o type. The dam has already bred three 2-y-o winners and this will be another".* James Tate.

NATURAL (IRE)
b.f. Kodiac – Catch The Sea (Barathea). *"She cost a bit of money but she's a lovely filly. One for the middle of the season, she's showing all the right signs at the moment and we couldn't be more happy with her".* Richard Hannon.

OPTIMUM TIME
b.c. Manduro – Mypreciousblue (Peintre Celebre). *"A lovely horse that goes surprisingly well for one with a pedigree that suggests he ought to be backward now. He's beautifully put-together and there's no reason why he shouldn't win as a 2-y-o".* Eve Johnson Houghton.

QUEEN TOMYRIS
b.f. Declaration Of War – Caphene (Sakhee). *"She's a gorgeous filly, I love her. She's a good size, has a good step to her and a sweet temperament. A thoroughly likeable filly and we like her".* William Jarvis.

RAJASINGHE
b.c. Choisir – Bunditten (Soviet Star). *"He's a well-balanced colt and a nice size with a great attitude. He's bred to do well, he has every chance and he'd be one of my picks".* Richard Spencer.

REBEL STREAK
b.c. Dark Angel – Siren's Gift (Cadeaux Genereux). *"So far this fella has been 100% straightforward and being by Dark Angel is no bad thing obviously. One to look out for".* Andrew Balding.

REMA AL KUWAIT (IRE)
b.f. Kodiac – Relinquished (Royal Applause). *"She's done a couple of easy bits of work and she's a nice, straightforward filly with a good temperament. I like her and she should be out in May over six furlongs".* William Knight.

SHAHEEN
b.c. Society Rock – La Chicana (Invincible Spirit). *"I couldn't say anything but nice things about this lad. He's a very good mover,*

everything seems to come naturally to him and in the couple of bits of work he's done he's shown natural ability". John Quinn.

SOLID MAN
b.c. Lord Kanaloa – Maruka Sawayaka (Sunday Silence). *"This is a nice horse, he's very forward, a horse we think a fair bit of and I would expect him to be winning his maiden and then going on from there. He goes very well".* Ralph Beckett.

SOUND AND SILENCE
b.c. Exceed And Excel – Veil Of Silence (Elusive Quality). *"This colt is a natural 2-y-o with plenty of pace and he's one that will be out early in the season".* Charlie Appleby

SPOOF
b.c. Poet's Voice – Filona (Motivator). *"He goes really well, he was an early foal and he's well-built too – so he's got the scope to train on. He's a man already and at the minute he's the standout".* Charlie Hills.

VERANDAH
b.f. Medicean – Palatial (Green Desert). *"She goes well and she's a nice type of filly for July/August time. Very likeable".* John Gosden.

VITAMIN
b.f. Camelot – True Verdict (Danehill Dancer). *"She's a lovely filly with a great attitude, a hell of a mover and plenty of substance and size to her. She looks like she could be very nice and we're really happy with her".* Richard Hannon.

WADILSAFA
b.c. Frankel – Rumoush (Rahy). *"A lovely colt and a very athletic horse with a lovely stride on him, he could be anything. A very exciting colt that should be a July/August 2-y-o".* Owen Burrows.

ZOFFY
b.f. Zoffany – Saldenaera (Areion). *"A beautiful filly, I really like her and she's just starting to show the right signs. I'd be very hopeful that she'll come the right side of Ascot and she covers the ground beautifully. A filly with a lot of quality".* Jamie Osborne.

UNNAMED
b.f. Scat Daddy – Me And Miss Jones (Smarty Jones). *"She did a great breeze, looked fabulous and has a great stride on her. I thought she fitted the bill as a possible Royal Ascot 2-y-o. There's a long way to go but she looks real fast".* Jeremy Noseda.

UNNAMED
b.c. Invincible Spirit – Turama (Pivotal). *"He's not over-big but he's good-bodied and good-moving. We haven't pushed him yet but he's probably one of the more forward colts and he looks promising. One to watch out for we think".* Roger Charlton.

Ten to Follow in Ireland

BROTHER BEAR (IRE)
b.c. Kodiac – Hurricane Emma (Mr Greeley).
"He's a nice colt that should be running when the six furlong races start. He's done a good bit of work, I'm happy with him, he looks like a 2-y-o as he's built like a little tank". Jessie Harrington.

FLAVIUS (USA)
b.c. War Front – Starformer (Dynaformer).
"He's a very nice colt from a good family and he'll appear in July or August over seven furlongs. He's one I particularly like". Dermot Weld.

GOTTARDO (IRE)
b.c. Choisir – Chantarella (Royal Academy).
"He seems quite precocious and typical of the family. He's a bit plain, which is probably typical of the sire, but he'll have enough pace for five/six furlongs and he's a sharp colt". Fozzy Stack.

JEWEL MAKER (IRE)
b.c. Invincible Spirit – Sapphire (Medicean).
"A bit more forward than some, he's a nice colt and I like him. He could be running by the middle of May over six furlongs before moving up in trip. He's worth an extra star". Dermot Weld.

MOGHAMARAH
ch.f. Dawn Approach – Shimah (Storm Cat).
"One of our stars. I trained the dam who was a stakes winner and only just got beaten in the Moyglare. I like this filly just as much. She'll be a six furlong 2-y-o". Kevin Prendergast.

MOONLIGHT BAY (IRE)
b.c. Pivotal – Naadrah (Muhtathir). *"She won the first 2-y-o race of the season, at Naas on the 26th March. We like her a lot, she'll probably run in the Swordlestown Stakes next. Not a big filly, but quality and a typical Pivotal".* Kevin Prendergast.

SHAPES (IRE)
b.f. So You Think – Maskaya (Machiavellian).
"She'll be our first 2-y-o filly to run. She goes to Navan at the end of April and she's showing me plenty of speed and precocity. A tough filly, I'm looking forward to running her".
Ger Lyons.

WOULD BE KING (IRE)
b.c. Lethal Force – Smart Coco (Smarty Jones).
"A smart colt, he'll be top of the class going off what he's showing us at the moment. He shows us plenty, we won't be in any hurry to run him but he's precocious enough".
Ger Lyons

UNNAMED
b.c. Street Cry – Mahkama (Bernardini).
"A lovely, strong colt with a lovely action and he looks a real 2-y-o. He does everything well and should be running by the end of May or June over six furlongs". Michael Halford.

UNNAMED
b.f. Mastercraftsman – Red Feather (Marju).
"She's quite a sharp-looking 2-y-o type and it's a 2-y-o family as well. I haven't had her that long, but she's definitely precocious and wants to get on with it. A good-looking filly that should show what she can do at two, probably in mid-season". John Oxx.

Star Two-Year-Olds

The stars placed along the side of each two-year-old in the main section of the book give the reader an instant appraisal of the regard in which they are held. The highest rating a horse can attain is five stars.

Bear in mind that some of the 'Five Star' horses will be at their peak as three-year-olds, so you should definitely keep an eye on them next year as well.

The five-star two-year-olds of 2017 are listed below for quick reference.

SECRET GAZE
b.f. Galileo – Shastye (Danehill).

Ralph Beckett

BEST BLUE
b.c. Oasis Dream – Filia Regina (Galileo).

Michael Bell

TASNEEM
ch.c. Teofilo – Almass (Elnadim).

Saeed bin Suroor

HERCULEAN
ch.c. Frankel – African Rose (Observatory).

Roger Charlton

FORMIDABLE KITT
b.f. Invincible Spirit – Ceiling Kitty (Red Clubs).

Tom Dascombe

GLOBAL GIANT
b.c. Shamardal – Aniseed (Dalakhani).

Ed Dunlop

COSMOPOLITAN QUEEN
ch.f. Dubawi – Barshiba (Barathea).

David Elsworth

RESTIVE SPIRIT
b.c. Intello – Hooray (Invincible Spirit).

William Haggas

REWAAYAT
b.c. Pivotal – Rufoof (Zamindar).

Charlie Hills

QUARGENT
b.f. War Front – Naples Bay (Giant's Causeway).

Jeremy Noseda

THE REVENANT
ch.c. Dubawi – Hazel Lavery (Excellent Art).

Hugo Palmer

FLIRTARE
b.f. Oasis Dream – Federation (Motivator).

Amanda Perrett

UNNAMED
b.c. New Approach – Arsaadi (Dubawi).

James Tate

ORBAAN
b.c. Invincible Spirit – Contradict (Raven's Pass).

Roger Varian

CHIARA LUNA (USA)
b.br.f. War Front – Princess Highway (Street Cry).

Dermot Weld

The Bloodstock Experts Mark Your Card

Last year the Experts tipped 45 winners of 58 races in this section, so make sure you take careful note of these selections!

The Experts who selected two individual winners apiece last year were Ross Doyle, Will Edmeades, Alex Elliott, Trevor Harris, Richard Knight and Chris Richardson (who gave just three selections).

With three winners apiece were Alastair Donald (from only four selections), Harry Herbert, David Redvers and Robin Sharp.

Those canny enough to pick four winners were Malcolm Bastard, Charlie Gordon-Watson (from eight picks), Amanda Skiffington (four out of six) and Bruce Raymond (four from five).

I'm calling the result of the top tipster award a draw between Amanda and Bruce. Bruce had one less pick than Amanda but her number of wins totalled six as opposed to Bruce's five, so I think naming them joint winners is only right.

Let's hope all the experts this year have been inspired to pick a similarly successful group of two-year-olds.

Remember, most of the two-year-olds selected here can be found in the main section of the book listed under their trainers and highlighted by the symbol ♠

A few of these selections were yet to enter training when the book went to press, so you may not find them listed under their trainer.

MALCOLM BASTARD
GLENCADAM MASTER
ch.c. Mastercraftsman – Coquet (Sir Percy). He's a lovely, strong horse that travels really well on the bridle. One for September time

and as a 3-y-o, he's a very nice horse. John Gosden.

INTELLOGENT (IRE)
ch.c. Intello – Nuit Polaire (Kheleyf). An amazing horse bought by Amanda Skiffington, he's a medium-sized colt, strong and travels very well. One for September this season and he'll be a very nice 3-y-o, he's a particularly nice horse. Owned by Fiona Jennings. Nicholas Clement.

MARECHAL NEY
b.c. Frankel – Hidden Hope (Daylami). He looks a serious type of colt. A beautiful horse owned by Sir Philip Oppenheimer. John Gosden.

MR MARRAKESH
c. Scat Daddy – Morocco Moon (Rock Of Gibraltar). A beautiful colt, he's a July/August type 2-y-o and he moves particularly well. Owned by Lady Bamford. John Gosden.

ROCOCO
b.f. Dubawi – Intrigued (Darshaan). A medium-sized filly that travels very well on the bridle, she's a lovely filly". John Gosden.

SEEING STARS (USA)
ch.c. Tapit – Rainbow View (Dynaformer). A quality colt that travels nicely on the bridle. A colt for the back-end of the season, he's very nice. John Gosden.

STREAM SONG
f. Mastercraftsman – Montare (Montjeu). A gorgeous filly that moves really well and I think a lot of her. I think she's really special. Owned by George Strawbridge. John Gosden.

UNNAMED
c. Point Of Entry – Sacred Feather (Carson City). A big, strong colt for the back-end of this season and hopefully he'll be a pretty

good 3-y-o. I think he's pretty special. He's in the Tattersalls Craven breeze up sale.

UNNAMED

b.c. Sea The Stars – Sentaril (Danehill Dancer). A very nice colt, he's one for the back-end and next year but he travels really well on the bridle and does everything well". William Haggas.

MATT COLEMAN

CHILLALA

b.f. Requinto – Positive Step (Footstepsinthesand). A full sister to last year's smart two year-old Broken Stones, she's showing all the right signs on the gallops for Harry Dunlop.

TANGLED

b.c. Society Rock – Open Verse (Black Minnaloushe). Bought in conjunction with Peter Doyle and reportedly working well for Richard Hannon.

UNNAMED

b.c. Sir Prancealot – Three Knots (Chineur). Working well for Simon Crisford

UNNAMED

br.c. Farhh – Generous Diana (Generous). A more backward type, but an excellent mover and as a half-brother to Dandino is one to look forward to later in the season. Harry Dunlop.

ALASTAIR DONALD

BARTHOLOMEU DIAS

b.c. Mount Nelson – Lady Francesca (Montjeu). 60,000 guineas Tattersalls Book 2. A three-parts brother to Purr Along, this is a great looking, scopey horse. Bred for a mile, he looks like being ready in mid-summer. Charlie Hills.

CARADOC (IRE)

b.c. Camelot – Applause (Danehill Dancer). He cost 270,000 guineas and is probably the best looking horse I have bought. He oozes class, will take some time and is bred for ten furlongs, so he'll be ready September time. Ed Walker.

ELIZABETH BENNET

b.f. Acclamation – Littlepromisedland (Titus Livius). A filly that cost €140,000, she's a very attractive filly, has a great attitude and covers a lot of ground. She should be ready around June and has loads of quality. Charlie Hills.

GROVEMAN

b.c. Holy Roman Emperor – Raving Monsun (Monsun). 250,000 guineas from Tattersalls Book 2. He was my pick of this sale, he's a real man of a horse and we love the way he does everything. Charlie Hills.

ROCK OF ESTONIA (IRE)

ch.c. Society Rock – Estonia (Exceed And Excel). A 90,000 guineas yearling, he's a strong 2-y-o type that should be ready early and is looking fast. Charlie Hills.

SIMPSON (IRE)

ch.c. Dragon Pulse – Salydora (Peintre Celebre). He only cost €22,000 and I feel he was a huge bargain. He's a great looking, strong horse, should be ready around June and bred for 6 furlongs to a mile. Ed Walker.

PETER DOYLE

AUMALE

b.f. Dansili – Amber Silk (Lawman). A real nice filly, she's a half-sister to Just The Judge and cost 300,000 guineas from Book One. Trained by Nicolas Clement at Chantilly.

OCEAN SIDE

gr.c. Dark Angel – Mundus Novus (Unbridled's Song). A lovely horse by Dark Angel, he'll get better as the year progresses. Richard Hannon.

SALLAB (IRE)

b.c. Havana Gold – Waveband (Exceed And Excel). A lovely moving colt we bought from Tattersalls October Book One for 200,000 guineas. Richard Hannon.

TULLYALLEN IRE)

b.c. Arcano – Come April (Singspiel). A half-brother to Limato, who we also bought as a yearling, this colt is improving all the time. Richard Hannon.

ROSS DOYLE

AL FUJAIRAH

b.c. Showcasing – First Term (Acclamation). Purchased at the Goffs Sportsman Sale for €62,000. He was a very good looking yearling with great depth for his age and a very good mover. He's by a stallion that can get you a very good racehorse so fingers crossed he's the next. He looks like he won't take too long to come to hand and hopefully he appears in the early part of the season. In training with Richard Hannon.

EMBOUR

b.c. Acclamation – Carpet Lady (Night Shift). Purchased at the Goffs UK Premier Sale for £145,000. A very racy looking individual with a great walk and temperament by a stallion we have been very lucky with through the likes of Mehmas & Harbour Watch. He looks like he should be ready to run sooner rather than later. Richard Hannon.

LETHAL LUNCH

br.c. Lethal Force – Pin Cushion (Pivotal). Purchased at the Goffs UK Premier Sale for £62,000. He is a strong, well-made colt by a fast son of Dark Angel which hopefully will be a big plus. He always looked like he would be quite early physically and seems to have a great temperament as well. Richard Hannon.

RESHAAN

b.c. Dark Angel – Bluebell (Mastercraftsman). Purchased at the Arqana August Sale for €260,000. He was a mature, good sized & good looking colt with a nice walk. He is from a family we know well, being out of a Black Type half-sister to Lilbourne Lad. Hopefully he will be a nice horse for the middle of the season. Richard Hannon.

WILL EDMEADES

ALL OUT

b.f. Acclamation – Time Over (Mark Of Esteem). A Barnett home-bred, this filly is a typical Acclamation. Her dam won over one mile and has bred two staying winners, but this is her first produce by a precocious sire. She looks very sharp and she has been sent to Richard Hannon, who does so well with the stallion and who trained the champion two-year-old filly Best Terms for us.

BOING

b.c. Bated Breath – Lomapamar (Nashwan). A real bargain buy, he was the first horse through the ring on Day 2 of Tattersalls Book 2 - which may or may not have influenced his price. I was very surprised to get him, especially with a big catalogue update. He scored very highly as an individual in terms of conformation, action and outlook and they all seem to like him at Richard Hannon's.

KOSHI

b.f. Kyllachy – Espagnolette (Oasis Dream). A charming filly with a lot of her father about her and, importantly, with a good Juddmonte page. She was, for me, the pick of the sharper fillies early in Tattersalls Book 3 and she will seek to replicate the success of Robanne, who was also sourced in Book 3 for Bunny Roberts and trained by William Knight.

PIVOTAL MAN

b.c. Pivotal – Privacy Order (Azamour). A lovely, correct colt, who walked like a cat at Tattersalls Book 1 where he was bought for the Waney family who raced Redback. The first foal from the mare won a 2-y-o Listed race some three weeks after this purchase which was a comfort and a close cross produced dual Group 1 winner Somnus. Probably a midsummer type, he is with Roger Varian.

ALEX ELLIOTT

GENERAL SLIM

b.c. Street Cry – Force One (Dansili). Only recently purchased at Ascot's breeze up sale for £100,000. From one of the best Juddmonte families around, a colt that did an exceptional breeze the day before his sale and one who should be seen in a maiden shortly. He's owned by Sarah Spencer and trained by George Scott.

PULITZER

b.f. Kodiac – Solola (Black Sam Bellamy). Purchased for 130,000 guineas from Tattersalls Book One, this is a strong, early type of filly. By the exceptional sire of two year olds Kodiac and a half-sister to the Group 3 winning two year old Smaih. I would expect this filly to be breaking her maiden pre Royal Ascot and moving on from there. Reports from the trainer are good so far. Owned by Bill and Tim Gredley and in training with Hugo Palmer.

SLIPSTREAM (IRE)
b.c. Invincible Spirit – Kiltubber (Sadler's Wells). A stunning colt, as his price tag of €420,000 reflects, he is a half-brother to numerous stakes winners including Opinion (Group 1) and Fox Hunt (Group 3). Should be ready for an early summer six furlong maiden. Owned by Mrs Sarah Spencer and Ballylinch Stud, in training with George Scott.

TAUREAN DANCER (IRE)
b.c. Intello – Traou Mad (Barathea). From Book 2 of Tattersalls October sale, he cost 100,000 guineas. Having loved Intello as a racehorse I was keen to like his progeny and was not disappointed. This colt will take a little time and I would not expect to see him until later in the year but he has a beautiful frame and is a real athlete. Owned by Brian Goodyear and in training with Michael Bell.

TOM GOFF
AGAR'S PLOUGH
ch.c. Dutch Art – Cloud's End (Dubawi). A lovely colt bred by Manor Farm Stud, Rutland who I've always thought breed a nice horse. He was led out of the ring unsold and we did a private sale through Tattersalls for 55,000gns. I saw him at Ed Dunlop's recently and he has grown into a really impressive individual and is a smooth mover. I would have high hopes for him. Ed Dunlop.

CAPTAIN SCOTT (IRE)
b.c. Tamayuz – Capriole (Noverre). A smart bay colt that I was very keen on at Tattersalls, where he was sold by Lynn Lodge Stud to Blandford for 100,000gns. Because of what he's by, I was convinced that Shadwell would be on him but fortunately they were otherwise engaged. It's obviously very early days but they seem to be very happy with him so fingers crossed. John Gosden.

CORINTHIA KNIGHT (IRE)
ch.c. Society Rock – Victoria Lodge (Grand Lodge). A really nice, sharp colt we bought with Archie Watson at Tattersalls (Ireland) for €15,000 from Roger O'Callaghan's Tally Ho Stud. He has gone well from the word go and

Archie has always liked him. I was delighted to see him break his maiden by 3 1/2 lengths the other day to give Archie his first two-year-old winner of this campaign. I would very much hope he can go on to better things in time. Archie Watson.

UNNAMED
b.c. Kodiac – Azia (Desert Story). A smart and fairly sharp colt who cost 120,000gns at the Tattersalls December Yearling Day from Rathbarry Stud, Ireland, who are very good breeders. I saw him the other day with George Baker at Manton and he looks to have progressed very well indeed. I would hope he'd be out over six furlongs in the not too distant future. George Baker.

UNNAMED
b.f. Sir Percy – Crystal Gal (Galileo). This filly was purchased for Andrew Black's Chasemore Farm for 120,000gns at Tattersalls from Glebe Stud. We bought the elder sister the previous year and she broke her maiden well. This filly was a more robust model and they appear to be happy with her so far. Lucy Wadham.

ANGUS GOLD
JAWWAAL
ch.c. Bahamian Bounty – Avenbury (Mount Nelson). This was a very nice horse that we bought on the first day of Doncaster by a good solid stallion and everybody likes the look of him so far. John Gosden.

ITQAN (IRE)
gr.f. Dark Angel – Prodigal Daughter (Alhaarth). She was a very expensive filly from Book 1 at Newmarket who looked to have a lot of class about her and seems to have a very good attitude so far. John Gosden.

TANSEEQ
b.c. Havana Gold – Roslea Lady (Alhaarth). A Doncaster purchase who cost plenty of money by a first season sire, but he looked a very good sort – I don't expect him to be early, but hopefully he could make a nice horse for the second part of the season. William Haggas.

WAFEER (IRE)
b.c. Equiano – Star Approval (Hawk Wing).

A very nice stamp of a horse from Book 2 at Newmarket who Richard Hannon seems to like a lot at this early stage.

WAFY (IRE)
b.c. Dubawi – Ghanaati (Giant's Causeway). The apple of his trainer's eye, he will obviously not be early but he and his team like the horse very much. Hopefully he will win races towards the end of the year and make a Classic horse as a three year old. Charlie Hills.

CHARLIE GORDON-WATSON
DUKHAN
b.c. Teofilo – Vedela (Selkirk). Untypical of the sire, he looks a 2-y-o type. Hugo Palmer.

GLOBAL GIANT
b.c. Shamardal – Aniseed (Dalakhani). Showing good signs and the sire is ever reliable. Ed Dunlop.

GLOBAL SPIRIT
b.c. Invincible Spirit – Centime (Royal Applause). He's developed very well and wasn't expensive for an Invincible Spirit. Ed Dunlop.

MERWEB (IRE)
ch.c. Shamardal – Ashley Hall (Maria's Mon). A very strong, powerful son of Shamardal. John Gosden.

SHAHEEN
b.c. Society Rock – La Chicana (Invincible Spirit). Al Shaqab asked me to find a 2-y-o for John Quinn. This colt is fairly forward and the stallion has made a good start.

UNNAMED
b.c. Al Kazeem – Resort (Oasis Dream). A 75,000 guineas purchase from Tattersalls Book One, he's very neat and looks forward to me. Sir Michael Stoute.

ED HARPER
AIRSHOW
ch.g. Showcasing – Belle Des Airs (Dr Fong). The trainer has done a great job with him as he had a difficult start to life. He has blossomed since being in training and would be one to follow second or third start after gaining a bit of confidence. Rod Millman.

PRINCE AHWAHNEE
b.c. Harbour Watch – Ahwahnee. He was a lovely, strong yearling that was always very uncomplicated. The dam has bred some promising types and he would be the nicest individual she's had. Clive Cox.

THE BROGHIE MAN
ch.c. Cityscape – Suelita (Dutch Art). I was very surprised that he didn't make more at the yearling sales as he is a striking individual with an immensely powerful shoulder. He looked like a bargain to me. Brendan Duke.

TREVOR HARRIS
AWSAAF
b.c. Swiss Spirit – Atheera (Shamardal). A homebred by a homebred stallion! He was sold to Hamdan Al Maktoum for 38,000 guineas at Tattersalls Book 2 and is a lovely strong athletic mover out of a 2-y-o winning Shamardal mare. Early reports are very positive and he should be out May/June. Simon Crisford.

LETHAL LUNCH
br.c. Lethal Force – Pin Cushion (Pivotal). This colt passed through our hands as a successful pinhook and was sold to Peter & Ross Doyle for £62,000. A real 2-y-o type, he looks very sharp and will be out early, I know the Hannon team like him. From the family of Frizzante, he could be a bit special. Richard Hannon.

MISTY SPIRIT
br.f. Swiss Spirit – Irrational (Kyllachy). This filly was purchased at Tattersalls Book 3 for 30,000 guineas. The dam won first time out at two and her half-sister also won as a 2-y-o. She is extremely athletic and has been pleasing in her work. David Elsworth.

UNNAMED
gr.c. Dark Angel – Swiss Dream (Oasis Dream). A homebred out of a triple listed winning mare who is a half-sister to exciting first season sire Swiss Spirit, this colt was sold to Peter & Ross Doyle for £280,000 topping the Doncaster Premier Yearling Sale. A lovely colt from a family of smart sprinters, we have high hopes for him. Richard Hannon.

HARRY HERBERT
Harry's selections are split between the Highclere and Al Shaqab horses.

HIGHCLERE
TIMPANI
ch.f. Raven's Pass – Fanny Cerrito (Gulch). This is a very sharp, athletic daughter of Raven's Pass. She took the eye of pre-trainer Malcolm Bastard and it's not difficult to see why because she does everything very easily. She could well be ready to run around Royal Ascot time. Trained by John Gosden

WHITEHALL
b.c. Dansili – Majestic Roi (Street Cry). An athletic, easy going son of Dansili who oozes class. Obviously Sir Michael won't rush him but physically he looks the type who could be ready to run in July/August. Sir Michael Stoute.

PREDICTION
b.c. Dream Ahead – Sho Girl (Lawman). This is a strong and precocious son of Dream Ahead who is likely to be one of our first runners. He has been pleasing the trainer and on looks alone just could be a two year old to look forward to. Trained by Kevin Ryan

FLAMENCO
b.f. Showcasing – Astrantia (Dansili). A beautiful daughter of Showcasing trained by William Haggas. This filly has size and strength and really caught my eye on a recent trip to Newmarket.

AL SHAQAB
FAJJAJ
ch.c. Dawn Approach – Pleasantry (Johannesburg). This is a lovely, big, scopey son of Dawn Approach and although he won't be early he does look as though he could be one to follow for the second half of the season. Hugo Palmer

FRAIHA
b.f. Camelot – Effervesce (Galileo). This filly was one of the standouts at the Goffs Sale in Ireland. I was very taken with the Camelots in general and this was one of the best fillies I saw at the sales. Hopefully she will make up into a mid to late summer starter. On looks, movement and pedigree she's hard to beat! Trained by John Gosden

RESHAAN
b.c. Dark Angel – Bluebell (Mastercraftsman). Trained by Richard Hannon. This is another cracking son of Dark Angel bought for 260,000 Euros. He, too, is a strong, powerful colt who looks sure to make his mark early in the season and again he could make up into a Royal Ascot performer. Trained by Richard Hannon

UNNAMED
b.c. Dark Angel – Jeu De Plume (Montjeu). This is a typically strong, precocious and athletic son of Dark Angel who has already caught his trainer's eye. Hopefully he will run before Royal Ascot in the hope that he will take his place at the Royal meeting. Trained by Richard Hannon

UNNAMED
b.c. Exceed And Excel – Time Control (Sadler's Wells). This is an exceptional looking colt and one who looks as though he will make into an exciting summer two year old. It's early days but it's hard not to get a tingle of excitement looking at him in the box and out at exercise. John Gosden.

UNNAMED
b.f. More Than Ready – Whipsaw City (Elusive City). This is a strong, athletic and precocious filly who is giving all of the right signs of being an exciting two year old in the making. Richard Hannon

RICHARD KNIGHT
AREEN FAISAL (IRE)
ch.c. Bahamian Bounty – Yellow Trumpet (Petong). Cost €80,000 from Goffs Orby and had a lot of class about him. He is coming along well and should be out by early May. Richard Fahey.

MISS MUMTAZ (IRE)
f. Lope De Vega – Ispanka. Purchased as a foal for 55,000gns, she's a classy filly who will need seven furlongs and a bit of time but she could be worth waiting for. In training with Tony Carroll.

SHOBROM (IRE)
b.c. Acclamation – Strasbourg Place (Compton Place). Purchased for £70,000 as a yearling from Goffs UK Premier sale. I'm told he's sharp and goes well. In training with Richard Fahey.

WEELLAN
ch.c. Mayson – Regal Salute (Medicean). A £55,000 yearling and brother to a nice horse we bought called Worlds His Oyster. Will be seen at his best over six furlongs and I'm told he has ability. With John Quinn.

UNNAMED
br.f. Society Rock – Silk Fan (Unfuwain). A €19,000 yearling purchase from Tatts Ireland. He's well forward and liked. With William Knight.

LUKE LILLINGSTON
CUBAN HEEL
gr.c. Havana Gold – Tipping Over (Aussie Rules). Bought at Fairyhouse, his trainer was in touch early on this year wanting to discuss the big auction races later in the year. As he's already had two 2-y-o winners we have to be encouraged. Clive Cox.

GOLDEN SALUTE
b.f. Acclamation – Golden Shadow (Selkirk). Leased from Airlie Stud for the Hot To Trot Racing Club, she's a sharp type and a full sister to the 2-y-o winner of last year and promising Victory Angel. Her trainer has been very positive about her so far. Andrew Balding.

RIVENDICATO
b.f. Showcasing – Carsulae (Marju). Bought as a replacement for Madam Dancealot, she really looks the part of a good 2-y-o, but with the scope to go on. By a sire that can really get one, Oisin Murphy has ridden her and spoken positively about her. She's a half-sister to Andrew Balding's Itsakindamagic who also looks talented and promising. Joe Tuite.

UNNAMED
ch.c. Intello – Marika (Marju). I bought him as a foal and was, frankly, stunned when we failed to sell him in the ring as a yearling. Brendan Holland of Grove Stud bought him privately and has been very high on the horse approaching the sale. He knows a good one

when it comes along and while this horse is unlikely to see a racecourse until later in the year I believe he will be a horse well worth following and into next year. Due to go to the Tattersalls Craven Breeze Up sale.

UNNAMED
b.f. Cape Cross – Oatcake (Selkirk). We have leased this filly from Mount Coote Stud to trainer Ed Walker. I've always loved her since she was a young foal and determined to keep her for the stud. She comes from the very speedy Overbury family of Scarcely Blessed and while she may not necessarily be very precocious she has a powerful back end on her and a beautiful head at the other end. All these ingredients suggest plenty of promise! Ed Walker.

JOHNNY McKEEVER
ALTERED METHOD
A nice Dawn Approach colt that we bought as a foal at Goffs for €70,000. Hugo Palmer tells me he likes him.

UNNAMED
gr.f. Oasis Dream – Amarillo Starlight (Dalakhani). A filly that was co-bred by Cornerstone Stud Australia and now in training with Luca Cumani.

UNNAMED
gr.f. Cape Cross – Whatami (Daylami). A filly bought from Furnace Mill Stud in Tattersalls October Book 2 sale. In training with Brian Meehan.

KIRSTEN RAUSING
ALACRITAS
gr.f. Leroidesanimaux – Albaraka (Selkirk). A Lanwades homebred, this granddaughter of world champion 3-y-o filly Alborada has always been a physical standout. She impresses in her early work, but we don't expect to see her out until the second part of the season. David Simcock.

ALAQRAB (USA)
b.c. Speightstown – Albamara (Galileo). An imposing sort, this classically-bred colt (out of a stakes-placed, winning daughter of triple Gr 1 winner Albanova) was sold to Shadwell for 525,000 guineas at Tattersalls Oct Book One in

2016. He is bred to come into his own towards the end of his 2-y-o season. John Gosden.

CENTRIFOLIA

gr.f. Dark Angel – Araqella (Oasis Dream). Bred at Lanwades by The BBA 2010 Ltd and sold by Staffordstown for 200,000 guineas at the Tattersalls October Sales 2016, this is a filly bred to be a speedy 2-y-o. Her winning dam is an own sister to Prix du Moulin winner Aqlaam. (J. Murphy, Ireland).

WATHEER

ch.c. Leroidesanimaux – Sunset Shore (Oasis Dream). Sold as a foal to Shadwell, this colt is bred to be a speedy sort and could well figure as a 2-y-o. His dam is a winning three-parts sister to the exceptionally speedy Starlit Sands, herself a Group winner over five furlongs at 2 yrs, and also a half-sister to four individual black type winners. (Marcus Tregoning).

UNNAMED

ch.c. Leroidesanimaux – Caribana (Hernando). A very nice, well-balanced colt, he met with a minor setback as a yearling and did not make his October Sales appointment; he was sold to Mark Johnston at Tattersalls December Yearling Sale. A half-brother to dual Group winner and champion older mare in Germany, Cubanita, this promising colt is likely to be seen out in the second half of the season. (Mark Johnston).

BRUCE RAYMOND

ELEDEED

b.c. Al Kazeem – Resort (Oasis Dream). This is a good-looking horse, he looks sure to go on. Sir Michael Stoute.

UNNAMED

b.c. New Approach – Arsaadi (Dubawi). Sure to go to the top. James Tate.

UNNAMED

b.f. Acclamation – Fortune Hunter (High Chaparral). Very sharp and very forward, she looks sure to win early. Simon Crisford.

UNNAMED

ch.f. Exceed And Excel – Lady Of The Desert (Rahy). A half-sister to Queen Kindly. She's a big, strong filly and is bred to take off. Richard Fahey.

UNNAMED

b.c. Invincible Spirit – Rajeem (Diktat). Unsold at £290,000 Craven Breeze up sale last night. Will start off at six furlongs and progress to a mile. He's looks a good horse. James Tate.

DAVID REDVERS

FLYING DEMON

gr.c. Nathaniel – Gossamer Seed (Choisir). My favourite yearling and an unlikely choice as he's more of a middle-distance type. He's just a bit special and I hope he still looks that way when he goes faster. John Gosden.

NATURAL

b.f. Kodiac – Catch The Sea (Barathea). A gorgeous and extremely expensive filly who is related to a couple of good previous runners of ours. She's showing plenty and we're hopeful she'll make into an Ascot filly. Richard Hannon.

SPECIAL PURPOSE

b.f. Scat Daddy – Pussycat Lips (Holy Roman Emperor). A lovely, precocious filly from Doncaster who looks powerful and should prove quick. William Haggas.

UNNAMED

b.c. Havana Gold – Remarkable Story (Mark Of Esteem). This colt did the fastest time at Goffs UK breeze up at Doncaster. Hopefully he'll be seen on the track by the time this book is out. David Simcock.

CHRIS RICHARDSON

MAYBRIDE

b.f. Mayson – Wedding Party (Groom Dancer). A full sister to the useful Rosebride, rated 95, who was second in the Group 3 Firth of Clyde Stakes and a half-sister to two other Stakes placed fillies. Richard Fahey.

VERANDAH

b.f. Medicean – Palatial (Green Desert). A full-sister to the tough and consistent Dimension and a half sister to Spacious, who was a multiple Group 2 winner and placed in the 1000 Guineas Stakes, Matron Stakes and Falmouth Stakes. John Gosden.

TALLOW
b.f. Kodiac – Flames (Blushing Flame). A half-sister to the highly talented Lahaleeb from a long standing Cheveley Park Stud family. Purchased as a yearling for €100,000 at the Goffs Orby Sale. William Haggas.

MOON SONG
gr.f. Lethal Force – West of the Moon. A sharp-looking filly, by the exciting first-season sire who still holds the track record at Newmarket in the July Cup. From a well-established bloodline, tracing back to multiple Group 1 winners, East of The Moon, Miesque and Kingmambo. Clive Cox.

ROBIN SHARP
GODODDIN
b.c. Camelot – Spritza (Spectrum). Probably the best looking colt by the sire I saw. Bought by Amanda Skiffington, he looked like a Derby horse to me and it would be great for Denis and Clare Barry who own the mare. Hugo Palmer.

PIVOTAL MAN
b.c. Pivotal – Privacy Order (Azamour). A fine, athletic colt who moved like a tiger. Bought by a very good judge in Will Edmeades, his dam could turn out to be high-class. I was very keen on him. Roger Varian.

PROTECTED GUEST
b.c. Helmet – Reem Star (Green Tune). A fine looking colt bought by the excellent Amanda Skiffington. He's very forward going and an attractive colt. George Margarson.

UNNAMED
ch.c. Champs Elysees – Galicuix (Galileo). A half-brother to Galileo Gold, we sold him for a good friend Colin Murfitt to John Gosden. He's a big strong colt who won't be early but he's well-balanced and the dam could turn out to be a blue hen. John Gosden.

UNNAMED
ch.f. Exceed And Excel – Lady Of The Desert (Rahy). A very well-bred filly, she was small but very powerful and a good mover. I hope a few a people might rue her slipping through the net. Richard Fahey.

AMANDA SKIFFINGTON
ALBA POWER (IRE)
b.c. Fast Company – Shehila (Zamindar). A very strong 2-y-o type who looks every inch the part of what I hope might be an Ascot horse. Hugo Palmer.

GODODDIN
b.c. Camelot – Spritza (Spectrum). I can't leave him out even though he's unlikely to be early, as he's a lovely horse and a great mover. Hugo Palmer.

HEDONISM
b.f. Excelebration – Knapton Hill (Zamindar). A very racy 2-y-o type who looks to be blooming since she has come in. Should be one from June onwards. Hugo Palmer.

MIDNIGHT GUEST
b.f. Acclamation – Midnight Martini (Night Shift). A sharp, attractive sort who moves very well. I look forward to seeing her on the racecourse. George Margarson.

PEPPER STREET
b.f. Born To Sea – Mindy (Zamindar). A filly I bought privately after Doncaster sales. She is very attractive and seems to love her work. There's quite a lot of stamina in her pedigree though, so we probably won't see her before mid-season. Hugo Palmer.

SOCIETY LILLY (IRE)
b.f. Society Rock – Lilly Be (Titus Livius). She came into the yard late, which could compromise her chance of being early, but she looks every inch a 2-y-o type. Hugo Palmer.

TAOISEACH
b.c. Roderic O'Connor – Munaa's Dream (Oasis Dream). He looks a nice horse – and what a great name. Hugo Palmer.

VERVE
b.f. Epaulette – Onomatomania (Mr Greeley). Very expensive for Fairyhouse, but she looked

very like a filly I bought called Audacia, who was a stakes winner for the owner. Let's hope she will be too! Hugo Palmer.

PETER STANLEY

CHARABANC
b.c. Exceed And Excel – Ruby Rocket (Indian Rocket). A very powerful, sharp 2-y-o type, built in the mode of his mother. He's a beautiful mover with lots of quality and a great temperament. Trained by Charlie Appleby.

MISS MINDING
b.f. Kodiac – Lady Hawkfield (Hawk Wing). A mid-summer type, she's active and from a very good family. Ed Dunlop

UNNAMED
b.f. Oasis Dream – A Huge Dream (Refuse To Bend). She has a great step and was not expensive at the sales. A quality filly by a top quality stallion overlooked by the market last year. Closely related to 2-y-o stakes winners, she needs to finish growing but should be a mid-summer filly. William Jarvis.

UNNAMED
b.c. Oasis Dream – Household Name (Zamindar). Sold as a foal and goes to the breeze up sale. He should be an early sort as he's showing plenty at present.

LARRY STRATTON

HEADWAY
b.c. Havana Gold – On Her Way (Medicean). A 60,000 guineas yearling, he was bred by Whatton Manor Stud, Global Equine and me. Out of a good winning mare who got 10 furlongs, but a sharp early sort who ought to be one of the earlier runners for his first-crop sire. Trained by William Haggas.

INCA'S DAWN (IRE)
b.f. Equiano – Up At Dawn (Inchinor). All quality and one of the finest movers sold at last year's yearling sales, she made 55,000 guineas and, without denigrating the excellent Equiano, had she been by a 'sexy' sire would have brought six figures – she is, after all, a half-sister to a Grade 2 winner. Ger Lyons.

SHANGHAI ELASTIC
b.f. Swiss Spirit – Reveille (Sakhee's Secret). Out of a mare I bred, sold and bought back, breeding this first foal in partnership with my partner Louise Parry and her brother Peter Steele Mortimer. An early type to look at and reportedly physically and temperamentally mature, he's in very good hands so shouldn't be too long appearing. David Barron.

UNNAMED
ch.f. Dandy Man – Balladiene (Noverre). Her dam won five times, mostly at a mile, and comes from a talented but arguably lesser branch of the great Moller 'Urshalim' family. A smart filly who could have plenty of the family's talent and is by a sire who gets lots of winners and some with real class. David O'Meara.

UNNAMED
b.f. Power – Dayrose (Daylami). A 40,000 foal purchase who went on to be an 80,000 guineas yearling, she is half-sister to a very good horse in Dubday. This is not an early family but it is a quality one and she is a supremely athletic filly with a lot of class. Richard Hannon.

PAUL & SARA THORMAN

DEVA DANDY
ch.c. Midshipman – Yankee Belle (Yankee Gentleman). I saw him at Clive's open day and he'd grown and developed markedly since we sold him at the December sale. I doubt him being early but he looked a nice, mid-season prospect. Clive Cox.

GREAT MIDGE
b.c. Kyllachy – Super Midge (Royal Applause). Nicked off us by Henry Candy. He always buys a lovely type and his record speaks for itself, this was a good-moving correct horse. A half-brother to a very capable filly called Squash, so the mare can breed one too.

RAJASINGHE
b.c. Choisir – Bunditten (Soviet Star). A gorgeous horse, although he made 85 Grand I was slightly disappointed and thought he was well bought – he did everything right. Phil Cunningham bought him and the last horse

he bought off us was Cockney Rebel! Trained by Richard Spencer.

UNNAMED

b.f. Showcasing – Perfect Echo (Lycius). Hopefully well-bought by Joe Foley for Steve Parkin. Both Sara and I loved this filly's attitude, not buzzy, but she enjoyed and tried at everything she was asked to do. Although it's a fast family they all improve with age, so I'm delighted she's gone to Richard Fahey who will give her the time she needs. We sold the same agent/owner combo a very good filly called Beyond Desire and it would be nice if this one was as good.

CHARLIE & TRACY VIGORS

CAROUSE

b.c. Excelebration – Terre Du Vent (Kutub). Sold at Tattersalls October Book 2 for 30,000 Guineas. His stakes winning dam stayed well but he always looked like one who would come to hand reasonably early. Andrew Balding.

GARDINIA

b.f. Pivotal – Garden Row (Invincible Spirit). Sold at Tattersalls October Book 2 for 26,000 Guineas. She's out of an Invincible Spirit mare who is an own sister to a Flying Childers winner. She's bred to be quick and looked quick. Tim Easterby.

SHAWWAL

b.c. Harbour Watch – Orton Park (Moss Vale). Sold to Shadwell at Doncaster Premier Sale. He's a strong, precocious looking colt whose dam was an early and fast two year old. John Gosden.

UNNAMED

b.f. Teofilo – Lady Lahar (Fraam). Sold to Blandford Bloodstock for 280,000 guineas at Tattersalls October Book 1, she's a lovely filly who will be one for the second half of the season. Sir Michael Stoute.

UNNAMED

b.c. Bahamian Bounty – Sally Can Wait (Sakhee). To be sold at the Tattersalls Guineas Breeze Up Sale. He's from the last crop of Bahamian Bounty and he's impressed with his action, attitude and fast work at home.

Trainers' Bargain Buys

It's always interesting to find out the trainers' picks from those purchases bought with a relatively modest sum. Each spring I put the following to each trainer "Name one of your two-year-olds, bought at the yearling sales for 30,000 Guineas or less, you think will prove to be a bargain?" The horses listed below are their recommendations.

In 2016 we got 23 winners of 26 races from this section, an improvement on both the previous two years. Those with the most handsome starting prices were Fiery Character

33-1, Jackhammer 25-1, Balgair 20-1 and Party Nights 10-1. Jackhammer was actually unnamed at the time of going to press, which underlines the importance of checking on the names update from my website.

Eve Johnson Houghton is the still the boss here with seven winners in the last eight years (Orientalist, Bling King, Vestibule, Drive On, British Embassy, Cara's Muse and Diable d'Or). Other trainers to note are Tom Dascombe with an excellent six winners from seven and James Given (five winners from the last six).

FROZEN BERE	€22,000	George Baker
RECULVER	€18,000	Andrew Balding
ARABIAN JAZZ	€11,000	Michael Bell
LONDON'S BURNING	£600	Ralph Beckett
b.c. Worthadd – Capsaicin	£27,000	James Bethell
EESHA BEAUTY	€28,000	Marco Botti
SARSTEDT	£16,000	Henry Candy
DIAMOND DOUGAL	£22,000	Mick Channon
gr.f. Sir Percy – Half Moon Hotel	5,500 Gns	Robert Cowell
b.f. Acclamation – Fortune Hunter	28,000 Gns	Simon Crisford
WILSON	£25,000	Luca Cumani
ROCKET MAN DAN	£12,000	Keith Dalgleish
ADMIRAL SPICE	22,500 Gns	Tom Dascombe
b.f. Raven's Pass – Lyric Of Fife	€30,000	Harry Dunlop
ch.c. Medicean – Skara Brae	9,000 Gns	David Elsworth
HEMINGFORD	€20,000	Charlie Fellowes
DORCAS	£8,500	James Given
b.f. Kodiac – Party Appeal	6,000 Gns	Rae Guest
ONE FOR JUNE	€30,000	William Haggas
REGIMENTED	£18,000	Richard Hannon
ROBINSON CRUSOE	30,000 Gns	Richard Hannon
WHITEFOUNTAINFAIRY	€3,000	Jessica Harrington
HIGH CHANGE	€15,000	Charlie Hills
b.f. Mayson – Mrs Greeley	30,000 Gns	Richard Hughes
RED FOR DANGER	£11,000	Eve Johnson Houghton
br.f. Society Rock – Silk Fan	£19,000	William Knight
DISAPPROVAL	€15,000	Dan Kubler
LEXINGTON EMPIRE	20,000 Gns	David Lanigan
DROP THE BEAT	€11,500	Ger Lyons
LORD GUEST	€10,000	George Margarson
b.f. Footstepsinthesand – Sancai	2,000 Gns	P J McBride
ch.f.Mastercraftsman –Station House	13,000 Gns	Martyn Meade
DADDIES GIRL	£5,500	Rod Millman

ROSES IN JUNE	€1,800	**Stan Moore**
JEDHI	24,500 Gns	**Hughie Morrison**
DATA PROTECTION	12,000 Gns	**William Muir**
SICARIO	€5,000	**Jamie Osborne**
BURFORD BROWN	€22,000	**Hugo Palmer**
br.c. Kodiac – Lightwood Lady	£18,000	**Amanda Perrett**
MADAM POMFREY	5,000 Gns	**Jonathan Portman**
LORD RIDDIFORD	€27,000	**John Quinn**
HOLY TIBER	20,000 Gns	**George Scott**
ch.f. Universal – Dance For Georgie	20,000 Gns	**David Simcock**
CLUB TROPICANA	£25,000	**Richard Spencer**
b.c. Foxwedge – Chicklade	£4,000	**Henry Spiller**
GOODTHINGSTAKETIME	€2,200	**Fozzy Stack**
LAST REQUEST	£27,000	**James Tate**
LITIGATION	13,000 Gns	**James Tate**
MOTHER OF DRAGONS	€2,000	**Joseph Tuite**
ch.c. Dragon Pulse – Salydora	€22,000	**Ed Walker**
ECLAIRANTE	11,000	**Chris Wall**
WE ARE THE WORLD	€22,000	**Archie Watson**

Two-Year-Olds of 2017

CHARLIE APPLEBY
(GODOLPHIN)
1. DATHANNA (IRE) ★★★
b.f. Dubawi – Colour (More Than Ready).
March 8. Fourth foal. Half-sister to the
unraced 2016 2-y-o Dream In Colour (by
Frankel) and to the Australian dual 6f winner
and Group 3 third Chamarel (by Exceed And
Excel). The dam, a 2-y-o Group 3 6f winner in
Australia, is out of Regrowth (by Unbridled's
Song). *"This filly is a strong individual with
plenty of pace in her pedigree. Her mother
was a Group 3 winner as a 2-y-o in Australia.
She has a good action and moves well and I'm
hopeful she can develop into a nice filly over six
and seven furlongs".*

2. DUBHE ★★★
b.c. Dubawi – Great Heavens (Galileo).
March 11. Second foal. The dam won the
Group 1 Irish Oaks and the Group 2 Lancashire
Oaks and is a sister to the King George VI and
Queen Elizabeth Stakes and Eclipse winner
Nathaniel and a half-sister to 8 winners
including Playful Act (Group 1 Fillies' Mile),
Percussionist (Group 3 11.5f Lingfield Derby
Trial) and Echoes In Eternity (Group 2 1m Sun
Chariot Stakes). The second dam, Magnificent
Style (by Silver Hawk), won the Group 3 10.5f
Musidora Stakes and is a half-sister to the US
Grade 1 10f winner Siberian Summer. *"This
colt has obvious appeal on his pedigree being
out of the Irish Oaks winner Great Heavens.
He's working well and has a nice action but is
one for the second half of the season over 7
furlongs to a mile".*

3. FOUNTAIN OF TIME ★★★
b.f. Iffraaj – Key To Peace (Kheleyf). January
30. First foal. The dam, a 1m winner in France,
was listed-placed twice over 7f (all at 3yrs) and
is a half-sister to numerous winners including
the Irish dual Group 3 winner of 8 races Mkuzi.
The second dam, African Peace (by Roberto),
a French listed-placed winner, is a half-sister
to 2 winners. *"An Iffraaj filly that shows natural
speed. She has a good constitution and has
taken to her work well at this early stage. I'll
probably start her at six furlongs. Her dam*

*was listed placed over seven but there is some
stamina in her pedigree so she may get further
in time".*

4. GLORIOUS JOURNEY ★★★
b.c. Dubawi – Fallen For You (Dansili).
February 9. Second foal. 2,600,000Y. Tattersalls
October Book 1. John Ferguson. The dam, a
very smart Group 1 1m Coronation Stakes
winner, is a half-sister to 4 winners including
the smart 7f (at 2 yrs) and listed 1m winner
Fallen Idol and the useful 2-y-o 1m winner
and Group 2 12f Lancashire Oaks second
Fallen In Love. The dam, Fallen Star (by Brief
Truce), a listed 7f winner, is a half-sister to 7
winners including Fly To The Stars (Group 1 7f
Lockinge Stakes). *"A Dubawi colt with a lovely
pedigree being out of the Group 1 Coronation
Stakes winner, Fallen For You. He's doing
everything naturally and has settled into the
stable routine very well. Whatever he does as a
2-y-o will be a bonus, but I'm hopeful we'll see
him at the races in mid-Summer".*

5. GOLDSTEIN (IRE) ★★★★
b.c. Exceed And Excel – Rachelle (Mark Of
Esteem). May 2. Ninth foal. Brother to the
useful 2-y-o Group 3 6f Sirenia Stakes winner
Rouleau and half-brother to the Group 1
Middle Park Stakes, Group 2 Duke Of York
Stakes and Group 2 Gimcrack Stakes winner
Amadeus Wolf (by Mozart), the fairly useful
10f winner Benedicte (by Galileo) and the
quite useful 7f and 1m winner Always A Rock
(by Rock Of Gibraltar). The dam, a minor
winner in Italy at around 1m, is a half-sister
to one winner. The second dam, Rose Violet
(by Alleged), won a listed event in Italy and
was third in the Group 1 Italian Oaks and is
a half-sister to 4 winners including the US
Grade 3 winner Storm Creek. *"A full brother to
Rouleau and a half-brother to Amadeus Wolf,
he's a strong individual and looks like a natural
2-y-o".*

6. GOLD TOWN ★★★★
b.c. Street Cry – Pimpernel (Invincible Spirit).
March 28. Second foal. The dam, a very useful
2-y-o 5f and listed 7f winner, was second in

the Group 2 7f Rockfel Stakes. The second dam, Anna Pallida (by Sadler's Wells), a quite useful 10f winner, is a half-sister to the very smart Group 1 10f Hong Kong Cup, Group 2 1m Beresford Stakes and Group 2 10f Royal Whip Stakes winner Eagle Mountain, the smart 2-y-o Group 1 1m Prix Marcel Boussac winner and triple Group 1 placed Sulk and the smart 1m listed winner Wallace. *"This colt is a mature, fast, strong individual. He's very forward going in his work but will be better seen stepping up to six and seven furlongs. He has a fast, early pedigree being out of an Invincible Spirit mare that was a listed winner over seven furlongs".*

7. SOUND AND SILENCE ★★★★
b.c. Exceed And Excel – Veil Of Silence (Elusive Quality). March 29. Sixth foal. Brother to the fairly useful 2-y-o dual 7f winner Silver Bullet and half-brother to the fair 2-y-o 8.5f winner Stay Silent (by Cape Cross). The dam is an unraced half-sister to 6 winners including the 2-y-o Group 1 Racing Post Trophy winner Ibn Khaldun. The second dam, Gossamer (by Sadler's Wells), won the Group 1 Fillies' Mile and the Group 1 Irish 1,000 Guineas and is a sister to the Breeders' Cup Mile and Irish 2,000 Guineas winner Barathea and a half-sister to 6 winners including the Group 3 winners Zabar and Free At Last (herself dam of the US multiple Grade 2 winner Coretta). *"This colt is a natural 2-y-o with plenty of pace and he's one that will be out early in the season. He has a fast pedigree and his second dam, Gossamer, won the Irish 1,000 Guineas and the Fillies' Mile".*

8. WAY OF WISDOM ★★★
b.c. Lonhro – La Pelegrina (Redoute's Choice). March 26. Third foal. Half-brother to the quite useful 2-y-o 7f winner Albernathy (by Dubawi). The dam is an unplaced sister to the Australian filly Miss Finland, a winner of five Group 1 stakes from 6f to 12.5f out of Forest Pearl (by Woodman). *"A sharp, compact colt, he looks to have natural pace and should be seen out early. He's pleased us in his work at home and his pedigree suggests he should have every chance as a 2-y-o, being from the family of the Golden Slipper winner Miss Finland".*

9. UNNAMED ★★★
b.br.f. New Approach – Discourse (Street Cry). March 6. Second foal. The dam, a smart 2-y-o Group 3 7f Sweet Solera Stakes winner, is a sister to one winner and half-sister 8 winners including the US Grade 1 and Grade 3 winner Bandini. The second dam, Divine Dixie (by Dixieland Band), a stakes-placed winner of 2 races at 3 yrs in the USA, is a half-sister to 4 winners including the stakes winner and sire Stormy Atlantic and to the unraced dam of the Group/Grade 2 winners Incanto Dream and Atlando. *"A good looking filly with a nice attitude. She probably won't be seen until the second half of the season and I think she'll be at her best from seven furlongs to a mile this year. She's from a Group 3 winning Street Cry mare that's a half-sister to Group 1 winner Bandini".*

10. UNNAMED ★★★★
b.c. New Approach – Khawlah (Cape Cross). April 16. Second foal. The dam, a very useful 1m (at 2 yrs) and subsequent UAE 9.5f Group 2 and Group 3 winner, is a half-sister to the Group 2 10f Prix Guillaume d'Ornano winner Vancouverite. The second dam, Villarrica (by Selkirk), a fair 10f and 11f winner, is a half-sister to 5 winners including Masterstroke (Group 2 12.5f Grand Prix de Deauville. *"An athletic colt that's taken to life in a racing stable well. He should get a trip in time but he's one with a nice action and should be ready mid-season. His dam won the UAE Derby and he's from a lovely family, so I have high hopes for him".*

GEORGE BAKER
11. BARRITUS ★★★★
b.c. Exceed And Excel – Flambeau (Oasis Dream). April 28. Second foal. 58,000Y. Tattersalls October Book 1. Sackville/Donald. The dam, a very useful listed 7f winner and second in the Group 3 Chartwell Stakes, is a half-sister to 5 winners. The second dam, Flavian (by Catrail), a fairly useful 6f (at 2 yrs) and 7f winner, is a half-sister to 7 winners. (George Baker & Partners). *"A beautifully put together son of Exceed And Excel, we love the sire because we've had plenty of success with him and this colt reminds us of a nice colt I trained called Belgian Bill. He's not going to be madly precocious but I should imagine he'll*

set off over six furlongs in June or July. A lovely horse and the apple of a few people's eyes around here".

12. COLORADO DREAM ★★★

b.c. Oasis Dream – Colorado Dawn (Fantastic Light). February 7. Fourth foal. 50,000Y. Tattersalls October Book 1. John & Jake Warren. The dam is an unraced half-sister to 7 winners including Opera House (King George VI and Queen Elizabeth Stakes, Eclipse Stakes, Coronation Cup), Kayf Tara (Ascot Gold Cup and Irish St Leger) and Zee Zee Top (Prix de l'Opera and herself dam of the Group 1 winner Izzi Top). The second dam, Colorspin (by High Top), won the Irish Oaks and is a half-sister to 8 winners including the Irish Champion Stakes winner Cezanne and the Group 2 Prix de l'Opera winner Bella Colora (dam of the high class colt Stagecraft). (Highclere Thoroughbred Racing – Trinity II). *"We thought he'd be very early but I don't think he's a five furlong horse. I think he's one to start off over six in May and he's a lovely, compact, well put together horse. He has no quirks, is very straightforward and hopefully a very "cheap" Oasis Dream".*

13. FROZEN BERE (FR) ★★★

b.c. Peer Gynt – Fitness Queen (Gilded Time). April 20. Tenth foal. €22,000Y. Osarus September. ITS Bloodstock. Brother to the fair dual 7f (at 2 yrs) and 1m winner Chicago Bere and half-brother to 5 winners including the 2016 French 2-y-o 7f winner Elvis (by Della Francesca) and the French 2-y-o 7f winner and 3-y-o listed-placed Rafale Bere (by Verglas). The dam is an unplaced half-sister to the Italian Group 3 winner Dream Impact. The second dam, One Fit Cat (by Storm Cat), a minor US 2-y-o winner, is a half-sister to 8 winners. (Free French). *"He's a nice horse that looks like a seven furlong type. Strong and powerful, he's doing really well".* TRAINERS' BARGAIN BUY

14. JURISPRUDENCE (FR) ★★★

b.f. Panis – L'Aventura (Librettist). January 10. First foal. €30,000Y. Osarus September. ITS Bloodstock. The dam, a minor French 2-y-o winner, is a half-sister to 4 winners, two of them listed-placed. The second dam, Berceuse

(by Mtoto), is an unplaced half-sister to 2 winners. (Free French). *"We bought this filly from Bordeaux which is not like an English sale because the horses are raw and straight out of a field rather than looking like shiny conkers! She's nice, very sharp and if she runs well on her debut in France I should imagine we'll be running there again in April".* This filly was third on her debut over 4.5f in France in March.

15. LA MAQUINA ★★★★

b.c. Dutch Art – Miss Meltemi (Miswaki Tern). April 6. Twelfth foal. 52,000Y. Tattersalls October Book 2. George Baker. Half-brother to 7 winners including the very useful 7f (at 2 yrs) and listed 1m winner and Group 3 Dahlia Stakes third Don't Dili Dali, the useful listed-placed 7f to 8.5f winner Balducci, the fairly useful listed-placed 1m winner Ada River (all by Dansili), the quite useful 2-y-o 5f winner Haigh Hall (by Kyllachy) and the quite useful 12f winner Zafarana (by Tiger Hill). The dam, a 2-y-o winner in Italy and third in the Group 1 Italian Oaks, is a half-sister to 3 winners. The second dam, Blu Meltemi (by Star Shareef), a winner of 5 races at 2 and 3 yrs in Italy and second in the Italian Oaks, is a half-sister to 3 winners. (PJL Racing & Pittam). *"He came to hand really nicely through February but then told us that he needed a bit more time, so we've given him that. He's a lovely horse for May or June and was doing things very easily, but I think he just looked a bit stronger than he actually was. He's the apple of a few people's eyes here".*

16. LUCKY LOVER BOY ★★★

b.c. Teofilo – Mayonga (Dr Fong). March 17. Fourth foal. 105,000Y. Tattersalls October Book 1. Blandford Bloodstock. Half-brother to the quite useful Irish dual 7f winner Surreal (by Shamardal) and to the modest 1m winner Palace Dragon (by Lawman). The dam, a useful listed 1m winner, is a half-sister to 3 minor winners. The second dam, Mayara (by Ashkalani), a fairly useful 1m winner, is a half-sister to 2 winners. (PJKL Racing). *"A pretty expensive yearling for us, but he's the type we like because he's one to go on with rather than be just an early 2-y-o. He's done everything nicely and he'll be ready for when the seven* furlong races start. A very nicely put-together horse and the type you'd buy again and again".

17. WATCH TAN ★★★
gr.f. Harbour Watch – High Tan (High Chaparral). March 22. Third foal. Half-sister to the fair 7f (including at 2 yrs) and 10f winner of 4 races Boutan (by Tobougg). The dam is an unraced half-sister to one winner. The second dam, Tanda Tula (by Alhaarth), is an unplaced half-sister to 7 winners including the German Group 2 winner Stormont. (Seaton Partnership). "A nice filly, she's been doing things in a very uncomplicated, straightforward, slightly workmanlike way and she's giving herself every chance. I hope she'd be one to start off in a fillies' maiden over six furlongs – she wouldn't be disgraced in that sort of company for sure".

18. UNNAMED ★★★★ ♠
b.c. Kodiac – Azia (Desert Story). April 14. Seventh foal. 120,000Y. Tattersalls December. Blandford Bloodstock. Half-brother to the useful listed Ripon Champion 2-y-o Trophy winner Hold Your Colour, to the modest 11f to 14f and hurdles winner Taste The Wine (both by Verglas) and the quite useful 2-y-o 8.5f winner Arcano Gold (by Arcano). The dam, a 2-y-o 7f winner in Ireland, is out of the unraced Safdara (by Shahrastani), herself an unraced half-sister to 10 winners including the Group 2 Lockinge Stakes winner Safawan. "Typical of Kodiacs, he looks a proper 2-y-o. Compact, well put together, he'll be ready to go in May and he's pleasing me very much".

19. UNNAMED ★★★
b.f. Exceed And Excel – Guarantia (Selkirk). February 12. Sixth foal. 80,000Y. Tattersalls October Book 2. Blandford Bloodstock. Half-sister to the quite useful 6f (at 2 yrs) and 7f winner Certified (by Raven's Pass), to the fair 6f winner Surety and the fair 2-y-o 6f winner Daraa (both by Cape Cross). The dam, a fairly useful listed-placed 7f winner, is a half-sister to 6 winners including the very smart dual Group 3 12f winner Laaheb. The second dam, Maskunah (by Sadler's Wells), is an unraced half-sister to 6 winners including the high-class middle-distance horses and multiple Group 1 winners Warrsan and Luso, the Nell Gwyn Stakes winner Cloud Castle and

the Group 2 Gallinule Stakes winner Needle Gun and to the dams of five Group 3 winners. (PJL Racing). "She's going to take a bit more time than our colt by the same sire because she's just a bit weak. So we need to be patient with her and I see her being out by mid-season at the earliest. She'll probably start off at six furlongs and then move up in trip".

20. UNNAMED ★★★
b.c. Nathaniel – Indigo River (Kodiac). April 22. Second foal. 68,000Y. Tattersalls October Book 2. Blandford Bloodstock. The dam, an Irish 2-y-o 7f and subsequent US Grade 2 winner, is a half-sister to 3 minor winners. The second dam, Sunny Slope (by Mujtahid), a modest 1m and 9f winner, is a half-sister to 2 minor winners. (PJL Racing). "A big colt and not one for pressing buttons too soon, but he's cantering every day and doing it all nicely. A well put-together horse, he looks like one to get out in mid-summer over seven furlongs and I do like him".

21. UNNAMED ★★★
b.f. Invincible Spirit – Lady Glinka (Galileo). March 11. Second foal. 100,000Y. Tattersalls October Book 2. Blandford Bloodstock. The dam is an unraced sister to the listed 9f (at 2 yrs), UAE Group 2 City Of Gold Stakes and Group 3 2m Queen's Vase winner and Group 1 Criterium de Saint-Cloud second Mikhail Glinka. The second dam, Lady Karr (by Mark Of Esteem), a fair 12f winner, is a sister to the Dewhurst Stakes and Derby winner Sir Percy and a half-sister to 2 winners. (Baker, Bailye Partnership). "A big, backward, slightly raw filly that's just taking time to come to herself and we've given her plenty of time. She's in the paddock now until the end of April and she'll be one for July or August at the earliest".

ANDREW BALDING
22. BALLYQUIN (IRE) ★★★
b.c. Acclamation – Something Mon (Maria's Mon). March 1. Half-brother to 7 winners including the fairly useful 2016 2-y-o 8.5f winner on his only start Big Challenge (by Sea The Stars), the useful 2-y-o 7f Oh So Sharp Stakes winner Raymi Coya (by Van Nistelrooy), the US stakes-placed winner Olympia Fields (by Alydeed), the fairly useful 11.5f winner Hikari and the quite useful 12f

winner Theturnofthesun (both by Galileo). The dam is an unraced half-sister to 5 winners including the champion German 2-y-o and Group 2 winner Somethingdifferent. The second dam, Try Something New (by Hail The Pirates), won the Grade 1 Spinster Stakes in the USA and is a half-sister to 5 winners. (Palmer-Brown, Gleeson, Engel). *"A nice colt who came to us in January and he's done very well. A typical Acclamation in that he's a bit long in his back, I wouldn't have thought he'd be particularly early but he's a nice type, moves well and he's very straightforward. One for seven furlongs I would have thought. We're a little bit behind with our 2-y-o's this year and they're definitely behind in their coats although the older horses look great".*

23. BERKSHIRE BLUE (IRE) ★★★★
b.c. Champs Elysees – Lemon Rock (Green Desert). February 25. Third foal. 58,000Y. Tattersalls October Book 2. Andrew Balding. Half-brother to About Glory (by Nayef), unplaced in one start at 2 yrs in 2016. The dam, a fair 5f and 6f placed 2-y-o, is a half-sister to 4 winners including the useful listed 6f (at 2 yrs) and listed 7f winner Selinka. The second dam, Lady Links (Bahamian Bounty), a dual listed 6f winner (including at 2 yrs), is a half-sister to 5 winners. (Berkshire Parts & Panels). *"A grand horse, I'm really pleased with him. He's a very good-looking, scopey horse and obviously he's going to stay a bit of a trip in time, although there is some speed in the family and I see him as a seven furlong type 2-y-o. A really nice type".*

24. BERKSHIRE ROYAL ★★★
b.c. Sir Percy – Forest Express (Kaaptive Edition). February 27. Twelfth foal. 60,000Y. Tattersalls October Book 2. Andrew Balding. Half-brother to 3 winners including the fair 12f winner Edge Of Reason (by Acclamation) and the fair 2-y-o 7f winner Nouveau Foret (by Myboycharlie). The dam, a Grade 3 winner and Grade 2 placed in Australia, is a half-sister to 4 winners including the German listed winner Waky Na (dam of the Italian Group 1 winner Waky Nao). The second dam, Myra's Best (by Pampapaul), won the listed 5f Firth Of Clyde Stakes and is a half-sister to 6 winners including the Irish Champion Stakes winner Park Express (dam of the champion and sire

New Approach). (Berkshire Parts & Panels). *"A big, scopey horse and he should be suited by seven furlongs this year. More of a 3-y-o type, but he'll have a 2-y-o career alright".*

25. BODIE AND DOYLE ★★★★
ch.c. Raven's Pass – Queenofthenorth (Halling). February 16. First foal. 50,000Y. Tattersalls October Book 2. BBA (Ire). The dam is an unraced sister to the very useful 2-y-o listed 7f winner and Group 2 1m May Hill Stakes second Queen Of Poland and a half-sister to 8 winners including the useful 2-y-o dual 7f winner White Hawk and the fair 5f and 6f winner Grizel (herself dam of the US dual Grade 2 winner Whatsthescript). The second dam, Polska (by Danzig), a useful winner of the 2-y-o listed 6f Blue Seal Stakes and listed-placed at 3 yrs, is closely related to the Group 3 Ballyogan Stakes and Group 3 Cornwallis Stakes winner Millstream. (Chelsea Thoroughbreds). *"A really nice, forward-going type and a mid-summer type 2-y-o. A neat horse that goes well, there's plenty to look forward to with him".*

26. BOLD BRIEF (IRE) ★★★
b.c. Lilbourne Lad – Bold Assumption (Observatory). March 28. Seventh foal. €32,000Y. Goffs Orby. Andrew Balding. Half-brother to the 2-y-o listed 1m winner and Group 1 French 1,000 Guineas third Irish Rookie (by Azamour), to the fairly useful 1m and hurdles winner Altruism (by Authorized) and the modest 7f winner Alice Rose (by Manduro). The dam is an unraced half-sister to 5 winners and to the unraced dams of the German/Italian Group winners Daring Love and Exhibit One. The second dam, Bold Empress (by Diesis), a fairly useful 2-y-o 6f winner, is a half-sister to 8 winners including the champion 2-y-o and 3-y-o and sire Zafonic. (R R Hetherington & Partner). *"A racy colt who looks like an Acclamation (the sire of Lilbourne Lad), he's grand and should be a 2-y-o type. I'm looking forward to him and he's racy enough for six furlongs".*

27. CAROUSE ★★★ ♠
b.c. Excelebration – Terre Du Vent (Kutub). January 31. First foal. 30,000Y. Tattersalls October Book 2. Andrew Balding. The dam, a listed 12f and listed 15f winner in France, was

second in the Group 2 Prix de Malleret and is a half-sister to 6 minor winners abroad. The second dam, Phlizz (by Kaldoun), was placed over 1m in France and is a half-sister to 10 winners including the French Group 3 winner Latona. (Mick & Janice Mariscotti). *"A 2-y-o type without a doubt. He's the first one to work on the grass this weekend and he's a stocky, racy type and the first Excelebration I've had. Although the dam's family look like they stay this colt is actually built like a sprinter. Hopefully he'll start over a stiff five furlongs in May".*

28. CELESTIAL SECRET ★★★
ch.f. Sakhee's Secret – Lochangel (Night Shift). April 26. Sister to the fairly useful listed-placed 5f winner of 5 races Verne Castle and half-sister to the quite useful 7f winner Star Pupil (by Selkirk), to the quite useful 6f winner Strictly Dancing (by Danehill Dancer) and the fair 5f winner Celestial Dream (by Oasis Dream). The dam, a very smart winner of the Group 1 5f Nunthorpe Stakes, is a half-sister to the champion sprinter Lochsong. The second dam, Peckitts Well (by Lochnager), was a fairly useful winner of five races at 2 and 3 yrs from 5f to 6f. (Mr J C Smith). *"Jeff's horses were a bit later in than usual this year but they're all from good families and this one is no exception. She's a good type for five furlongs".*

29. CHANGE MAKER ★★
ch.c. Havana Gold – Belle Allemande (Royal Academy). April 25. Ninth foal. 95,000Y. Tattersalls October Book 2. David Redvers / Alastair Donald. Half-brother to 6 winners including the very useful Irish 10f winner of 3 races and subsequent Australian Group 2 winner Johann Zoffany, the fairly useful 10f winner Hail (both by Galileo), the fairly useful winner of 5 races from 4 to 6 yrs Crown Choice (by King's Best) and a winner in Japan by Cape Cross. The dam, a minor French 11f winner, is a half-sister to 10 winners including the German Oaks winner Que Belle. The second dam, Qui Bid (by Spectacular Bid), is an unraced sister to the US Grade 3 winner Sum and a half-sister to 9 winners including the Group 1 winner Bakharoff and the Group 2 winner Emperor Jones. (Qatar Racing Ltd, Mrs B Keller). *"A grand type that's just going through a growing spell after looking stunning as a yearling. No doubt he'll pick up again and he's by a promising first season sire".*

30. COLENSO ★★★
b.c. New Approach – Pearl Dance (Nureyev). April 10. Half-brother to the Group 3 9f Prix Chloe winner Sparkling Beam (by Nayef), to the very useful 9f winner and Group 1 Prix Marcel Boussac third Rainbow Springs, the useful 2-y-o dual 7f winner Ridge Dance (both by Selkirk) and the fairly useful dual 1m winner Born In Bombay. The dam, a useful 2-y-o 6f winner and third in the Group 1 Moyglare Stud Stakes, is a half-sister to the German listed winner and Group 1 German Derby fourth Ocean Sea and the US winner and Grade 3 third Dixie Splash. The second dam, Ocean Jewel (by Alleged), is an unraced half-sister to 6 minor winners. (George Strawbridge). *"Still in pre-training, but we've had some success with a lot of the family so I'm looking forward to seeing him".*

31. DAWN DANCER ★★★
b.c. Dawn Approach – Ballet Ballon (Rahy). March 1. Seventh foal. 48,000Y. Tattersalls October Book 1. Not sold. Half-brother to the useful French 2-y-o 6f to 1m winner of 4 races and French 2,000 Guineas second Havane Smoker (by Dubawi), to the quite useful dual 1m winner Ballet Concerto (by Dansili), the fair 7f (at 2 yrs) and 1m winner Halling Dancer (by Halling) and the fair 9.5f and 12f winner Maxie T (by Danehill Dancer). The dam, a fair 10f winner, is a half-sister to the useful listed-placed 10f winner Design Perfection. The second dam, Bella Ballerina (by Sadler's Wells), a quite useful 9f winner, is a half-sister to 6 winners including the Group 2 10f Prince of Wales's Stakes winner Stagecraft, the Group 3 Strensall Stakes winner Mullins Bay and the dual 1m listed winner Hyabella. (Castle Down Racing). *"A Meon Valley bred 2-y-o who was late to come in but he's ridden away now and doing well".*

32. DIOCLETIAN (IRE) ★★★
b.c. Camelot – Saturday Girl (Peintre Celebre). January 31. Third foal. Half-brother to the useful 6f (at 2 yrs) and 7f winner and Group 2 7f Vintage Stakes third Room Key (by Mount Nelson). The dam is an unraced half-sister to 5 winners including the 7f (at 2 yrs) and listed 10f winner Splashdown, the listed 10f winner Cosmodrome and the fairly useful stakes-placed Boogie Shoes and Tadreeb. The second

dam, Space Time (by Bering), was placed over 7f at 2 yrs in France and is a half-sister to 6 minor winners in France and Australia. (M R Wilmot-Smith). *"Pretty smart looking, it's the sire Camelot's first season and we have two by him. We like them both and this is a grand horse, very athletic and good-looking. We won't be hurrying him but he's a great mover and it's a case of 'so far so good' with him. The owner takes a lot of time and trouble doing the matings for his mares, so I'm sure there are plenty of good reasons why the mare went to Camelot. This colt ticks a lot of boxes".*

33. DREAM CATCHING (IRE) ★★★
b.c. Dream Ahead – Selfara (Oasis Dream). May 6. Second foal. €26,000Y. Tattersalls Ireland September. Andrew Balding. Half-brother to the fair 2016 6f placed 2-y-o Grand Myla (by Dark Angel). The dam, a fair dual 5f winner, is a half-sister to 3 minor winners. The second dam, Rustic (by Grand Lodge), a useful 2-y-o 6f winner and third in the Group 3 6f Princess Margaret Stakes, is a half-sister to 8 winners including the Irish Derby winner Grey Swallow and the Group 3 1m winner Moonlight Dance. (Mr M Payton). *"He was a late foal and he's going through a bit of a growth spurt at the moment, but he's straightforward and a nice type. Hopefully he'll be a mid-summer 2-y-o and I'm looking forward to him".*

34. ENSIGN EWART ★★★★
ch.c. Lope De Vega – Caerlonore (Traditionally). January 30. Fourth foal. €100,000Y. Goffs Orby. Stephen Hillen. Half-brother to the fair 4-y-o 7f winner Glorious Star (by Soviet Star). The dam is an unraced half-sister to 7 winners including the Irish 1,000 Guineas third La Nuit Rose (dam of the US Grade 2 winner Tam Lin). The second dam, Caerlina (by Caerleon), won the Group 1 Prix de Diane and the Group 3 Prix de la Nonette and is a full or half-sister to 8 winners including the dam of the dual Group 2 winner Sri Putra. (Mrs F H Hay). *"A very nice horse. He goes well, he's done bits upsides and it looks like he could be speedy enough for six furlongs. He'll develop into a really nice horse because he's a good, physical type".*

35. EXEAT ★★★
b.f. Oasis Dream – Brevity (Street Cry). May 8. Third foal. Half-sister to the quite useful 10f winner Brief Visit (by Fastnet Rock). The dam, a useful 2-y-o listed 6f winner, is a half-sister to 4 winners including the quite useful 2-y-o 1m winner and subsequent US Grade 1 third Concise. The second dam, Cut Short (by Diesis), a quite useful 1m (here) and US winner, is a sister to the dual Group 2 2-y-o winner Daggers Drawn and a half-sister to 3 winners. (Cliveden Stud). *"In pre-training with Malcolm Bastard, but we're due to get her in early April. I have the half-sister Brief Visit and she's a lovely filly but enormous. This filly is a much more manageable size, so I'm looking forward to getting her. Her dam had a lot of speed and as she's by Oasis Dream (also an influence for speed) I think she'll be busy this year".*

36. FOXTROT LADY ★★★★
ch.f. Foxwedge – Strictly Dancing (Danehill Dancer). February 6. Third foal. Half-sister to the useful 6f winner of 5 races at 2 and 3 yrs (including the Steward's Cup) Dancing Star (by Aqlaam) and to the quite useful 1m and 8.5f (both at 2 yrs) and 10f winner Dance Of Fire (by Norse Dancer). The dam, a quite useful 6f winner, is a half-sister to 3 winners here and abroad. The second dam, Lochangel (by Night Shift), a very smart winner of the Group 1 5f Nunthorpe Stakes, is a half-sister to the champion sprinter Lochsong. (J C Smith). *"A really nice type, she looks speedy and strong so I'd be disappointed if she doesn't do something this year. Certainly a five/six furlong type".*

37. GOLDEN SALUTE (IRE) ★★★ ♠
b.f. Acclamation – Golden Shadow (Selkirk). March 9. Eighth foal. 140,000Y. Tattersalls October Book 2. Andrew Sime. Half-sister to 5 winners including the fairly useful 2-y-o 5f and 1m winner and listed-placed Lord ofthe Shadows (by Kyllachy), the French 2-y-o 6f winner You're Golden (by Lawman), the modest dual 1m winner Snappy Guest (by Kodiac) and the moderate 2m 1f winner Tigerino (by Tiger Hill). The dam, a fair 2-y-o dual 1m placed maiden, is a half-sister to 7 winners including the Group 1 1m Coronation Stakes winner Balisada. The second dam,

Balnaha (by Lomond), a modest 1m winner, is a sister to the Child Stakes winner Inchmurrin (dam of the very smart and tough colt Inchinor) and a half-sister to the Mill Reef Stakes winner Welney. (Hot To Trot). *"A nice filly, she goes well and looks a lovely type that should make a 2-y-o".*

38. ICONIC GIRL ★★★
b.f. Cape Cross – Snoqualmie Star (Galileo). April 6. Third foal. Half-sister to the fair 2016 dual 6f placed 2-y-o Star Maker (by Mastercraftsman). The dam, a quite useful 1m and 10f winner, is a half-sister to numerous winners including the smart listed 10f winner and Group 2 Dante Stakes third Snoqualmie Boy and to the very useful listed 1m (at 2 yrs) and listed 10f winner Snoqualmie Girl. The second dam, Seattle Ribbon (by Seattle Dancer), placed over 9f and 10f at 3 yrs, is a sister to the 2-y-o Group 1 1m winner Seattle Dancer. (J C Smith). *"A lovely home-bred of Jeff Smith's, she's more of a middle-distance type and she'll want seven furlongs to a mile as a 2-y-o. She's a nice type and I'm very happy to have her".*

39. KABRIT ★★★★
ch.c. Mastercraftsman – Twinkling Ice (Elusive Quality). February 7. Third foal. €100,000Y. Goffs Orby. Stephen Hillen. The dam, a poor maiden, was placed fourth once at 3 yrs and is a half-sister to 3 winners including the US Grade 1 Carter Handicap winner Forest Danger. The second dam, Starry Ice (by Ice Age), won the US Grade 2 Landaluce Stakes and is a half-sister to 6 winners. (Mrs F H Hay). *"Another nice type, he'll be a seven furlong or mile type 2-y-o, goes very nicely and is straightforward. A good, scopey individual, I'm very happy with him at the moment".*

40. KING LUD ★★★
b.c. Cape Cross – Natural Flair (Giant's Causeway). April 20. Third foal. 60,000Y. Tattersalls October Book 1. Andrew Balding. Half-brother to the quite useful 2-y-o 7.5f and 1m winner Natural Charm (by City Zip) and to the fair 12f winner Shoofly (by Azamour). The dam, a quite useful dual 10f winner, subsequently won once in the USA and is a half-sister to 3 minor winners. The second dam, Forest Lady (by Woodman), is

an unraced sister to 2 winners including the triple Group 1 winner Ciro and a half-sister to 6 winners. (Mick & Janice Mariscotti). *"He'll be a seven furlong/mile type 2-y-o this year. He's done very well just recently and he's done a few bits upsides. He goes nicely but we haven't got after him yet. A grand type".*

41. LOPITO ★★★
b.c. Lope De Vega – Stellar Brilliant (Kris S). March 2. Seventh foal. £32,000Y. Goffs UK Premier (Doncaster). Andrew Balding. Half-brother to the fairly useful Irish 2-y-o 6f winner He's No Saint (by Dutch Art), to the fair 7f (at 2 yrs) and 10f winner Keepax (by Dubai Destination) and two 2-y-o winners abroad by Ishiguru and Haafhd. The dam, a fair 10f winner, is a half-sister to 6 winners including the US Grade 3 winner Stupendous Miss (herself dam of the UAE Group 2 winner Do It All). The second dam, Subeen (by Caerleon), a winner at 2 yrs and third in the Group 1 Cheveley Park Stakes, is a half-sister to 4 winners. (Thurloe Thoroughbreds XLII). *"A colt we bought at Doncaster and then Thurloe bought him from us. He goes well and is a big, tall, scopey horse with a bit of a knee action, so he may prefer a bit of cut in the ground. We're very happy with him at the moment".*

42. MASTER OF WINE ★★
b.c. Maxios – Magma (Dubai Destination). April 13. First foal. 60,000Y. Tattersalls October Book 2. Andrew Balding. The dam, placed twice at 3 yrs in Germany, is a half-sister to 6 winners. The second dam, Mahamuni (by Sadler's Wells), a minor French 3-y-o winner, is a sister to the Group 1 winners Insight and Saffron Walden and a half-sister to the Group 1 winner Dolphin Street. (Another Bottle Racing). *"He goes nicely, I'm very happy with him and although he has a middle-distance pedigree he's shown a bit already, so I'm happy with him. He's out of a Dubai Destination mare which isn't a bad thing and he'll be a seven furlong/mile 2-y-o. I like the way he goes".*

43. NORTHWEST PASSAGE ★★★
b.c. Oasis Dream – Sequence (Selkirk). February 24. First foal. The dam, a fairly useful 10f and 12f winner, is a half-sister to numerous winners including the top-class middle-distance colt Sinndar, winner of the Derby, the

Irish Derby and the Prix de l'Arc de Triomphe. The second dam, Sinntara (Lashkari), won 4 races in Ireland at up to 2m. (The Queen). *"He's done very well since he came in and I'd be hopeful that he'll be up to running over seven furlongs this year and we'll go on from there. He's been upsides a couple of times and he goes nicely but we won't be chasing him".*

44. OCALA ★★★
ch.f. Nathaniel – Night Carnation (Sleeping Indian). March 14. Second foal. Sister to the fair 2016 2-y-o 5f winner Night Law (by Lawman). The dam, a very useful winner of 5 races including the Group 3 5f Sandown Sprint Stakes, is a half-sister to 2 winners including the useful 1m winner Yeaman's Hall. The second dam, Rimba (by Dayjur), a fair 7f placed maiden, is closely related to the very useful 7f and 7.3f winner Rainald. (Mr G Strawbridge). *"Yet to come in from a pre-training yard but we had the half-sister last year who won over five furlongs, so hopefully she'll make a 2-y-o a bit later on".*

45. PAK CHOI ★★★
ch.c. Paco Boy – Spring Green (Bahamian Bounty). February 4. Third foal. £48,000Y. Goffs UK Premier (Doncaster). John & Jake Warren. Brother to the fair multiple 5f winner at 2 and 3 yrs New Road Side and half-brother to the fairly useful 2-y-o 6f winner and listed-placed Byzantium (by Dutch Art). The dam, a fair dual 5f winner, is a half-sister to 7 minor winners. The second dam, Star Tulip (by Night Shift), a useful winner of 3 races over 6f including the listed Sandy Lane Stakes, is a half-sister to 4 minor winners. (Highclere Thoroughbred Racing). *"He's not here yet but I've seen him and he looks a good, racy type. I think Paco Boy is an underrated stallion and hopefully we'll have a bit of luck with this colt".*

46. PRIVATE CASHIER ★★★
b.f. Leroidesanimaux – Vicksburg (Cape Cross). April 14. First foal. The dam, a quite useful 10.5f winner, is a half-sister to 2 winners. The second dam, Totality (by Dancing Brave), a quite useful 14f winner from just two outings, is a sister to the Epsom and Irish Derby winner Commander in Chief and a half-sister to numerous winners including the champion 2-y-o and miler Warning, the Irish Derby

second Deploy, the Great Voltigeur Stakes winner Dushyantor and the Flower Bowl Handicap and Ribblesdale Stakes winner Yashmak. (Mr R Wilmot-Smith). *"A home-bred, I trained the dam and she won a maiden impressively but unfortunately she kept having niggling problems. My feeling is that she'd have got black-type if she'd stayed sound. This is her first and only foal because unfortunately she died. This is a really nice type and it looks like she could be a 2-y-o as well".*

47. REBEL STREAK ★★★★
b.c. Dark Angel – Siren's Gift (Cadeaux Gener, eux). February 21. Third foal. Closely related to the fairly useful 2-y-o 5f winner Merdon Castle (by Acclamation). The dam, a fairly useful triple 5f winner (including at 2 yrs) was listed-placed and is a sister to the useful 2-y-o listed 5.2f winner and Group 2 Flying Childers Stakes third Speed Cop and a half-sister to 2 winners. The second dam, Blue Siren (by Bluebird), a very useful winner of three races from 5f to 7f, was disqualified from first place in two more, notably the Group 1 5f Nunthorpe Stakes (the winner on merit) and is a half-sister to several winners including the quite useful 9f winner Northern Habit. (Mr J C Smith). *"I trained the dam who was very talented but a real handful. So far this fella has been 100% straightforward and being by Dark Angel is no bad thing obviously. One to look out for".*

48. RECULVER (IRE) ★★★
b.c. Tagula – Lady Kildare (Bachelor Duke). February 16. First foal. €18,000Y. Tattersalls Ireland September. Andrew Balding. The dam, a fair 5f and 6f winner of 3 races at 3 yrs, is a half-sister to 7 minor winners. The second dam, Teodora (by Fairy King), a fairly useful 2-y-o 6f winner, was fourth in the Group 3 6f Princess Margaret Stakes and is a half-sister to 6 winners. (Martin & Valerie Slade). *"He's done very well and I'd be disappointed if we couldn't do something with him. A proper 2-y-o type for June onwards over six furlongs".* TRAINERS' BARGAIN BUY

49. SILVER SWIFT ★★
b.f. Dutch Art – Silver Kestrel (Silver Hawk). April 16. Eighth foal. £42,000Y. Goffs UK Premier (Doncaster). Bobby O'Ryan. Half-

sister to the 2-y-o Group 3 6f Albany Stakes winner and Group 2 Cherry Hinton Stakes second Habaayib and to the fair dual 5f winner (including at 2 yrs) Golden Flower (both by Royal Applause). The dam, a minor winner of 2 races at 3 and 4 yrs in the USA, is a half-sister to 5 winners. The second dam, Salty Perfume (by Salt Lake), won the Grade 2 Adirondack Stakes in the USA and is a half-sister to 6 winners including the German Group 2 winner Green Perfume. (Mr J Nedas). *"She's gone a little bit awkward and backward in her coat but she's from a good family and she's a nice type, so I'm sure she'll come back to how she was earlier".*

50. SOVRANO ★★★★

ch.c. Leroidesanimaux – Alchemilla (Dubai Destination). March 24. Fourth foal. 70,000Y. Tattersalls October Book 1. Andrew Balding. Half-brother to the listed 7f Surrey Stakes winner Smuggler's Moon (by Danehill Dancer) and to the fair 7f (at 2 yrs) to 9.5f winner Stardrifter (by Rock Of Gibraltar). The dam is an unraced half-sister to 8 winners including the smart 2-y-o dual Group 2 winner Strategic Prince and the listed winner and Group 2 placed Yorkshire. The second dam, Ausherra (by Diesis), won the listed 12f Lingfield Oaks Trial and is a full or half-sister to 9 winners including the Oaks, Irish Oaks and Yorkshire Oaks winner Ramruma. (Mick & Janice Mariscotti). *"He's not going to be early and he's a bit unfurnished at the moment, but he's a really nice type and he looks like he's got a bit about him. One for the second half of the season".*

51. UNTIL AGAIN ★★★

b.f. Iffraaj – Sara Lucille (Dansili). January 22. First foal. The dam, a French dual 5f winner at 2 and 3 yrs, was second in the Group 3 7f Prix du Calvados. The second dam, Magic America (by High Yield), a 2-y-o Group 3 7f Prix Miesque winner and second in the Group 1 6f Prix Morny, is a half-sister to the US Grade 3 placed Psychic Income. (Mr G Strawbridge). *"She's a good, strong type of filly that looks like she could have a bit of speed. A real 2-y-o type, she was an early foal and it's a speedy pedigree, so I'm looking forward to doing a bit more with her soon".*

52. WHITE TURF ★★★

gr.c. Clodovil – Holda (Docksider). February 28. Sixth foal. €58,000Y. Goffs Orby. Kern/ Lillingston. Half-brother to the useful Group 2 1m Topkapi Trophy winner Blond Me (by Tamayuz), to the fair dual 6f winner at 2 and 4 yrs Red Larkspur (by Red Clubs) and the fair 10.5f winner Antarctic (by Alhaarth). The dam, a 2-y-o 7f maiden winner at Newmarket on her only start, is a half-sister to the Group 3 10f and subsequent Australian Group 1 10f winner Glass Harmonium and to the Group 3 12f winner Arab Spring. The second dam, Spring Symphony (by Darshaan), a fairly useful 12f winner, is a sister to the very smart Group 2 Great Voltigeur Stakes winner Hard Top and a half-sister to the St Leger, King George VI and dual Breeders' Cup Turf winner Conduit. (Kennet Valley Thoroughbreds IV). *"A half-brother to Blond Me – a filly we've done well with. He's a good type, doing alright and should be one for seven furlongs in July".*

53. YOUNG BERNIE ★★★

b.c. Sixties Icon – Hot Pursuits (Pastoral Pursuits). April 30. Third foal. €15,000Y. Tattersalls Ireland September. Andrew Balding. Half-brother to the modest 2-y-o 6f winner Desirable (by Stimulation). The dam, a fair 5f (at 2 yrs) and 6f winner, is a half-sister to 3 minor winners. The second dam, Perfect Partner (by Be My Chief), is an unraced half-sister to 6 winners including the Ayr Gold Cup winner Funfair Wane and the Italian listed winner Cabcharge Striker. (Mr B McGuire). *"A fine type of horse, we'll take our time with him because he's grown a lot but we've done bits upsides with him. Hopefully we'll be able to win a race with him this year".*

54. ZATORIUS (GER) ★★★

b.c. Pastorius – Zarah Top (Big Shuffle). April 16. Second foal. €20,000Y. Baden Baden. Richard Venn. The dam, a 6.5f winner in Germany at 3 yrs, is a half-sister to the 2-y-o Group 3 1m Premio Dormello second Zaza Top and to the German listed 10f winner Zatoof. The second dam, Zorina (by Shirley Heights), is a full or half-sister to 4 winners. (Mr G Rafferty). *"He goes nicely and should be in the book I think. He could be the Bargain Buy because he wasn't expensive and he's a nice type". The sire, a son of Soldier Hollow,* won three Group 1's over middle distances including the Prix Ganay. His first crop are 2-y-o's this year.

55. UNNAMED ★★
b.c. Bahamian Bounty – Luna Forest (Holy Roman Emperor). February 10. First foal. 40,000Y. Tattersalls October Book 2. Rabbah Bloodstock. The dam, a quite useful Irish 1m winner, is a half-sister to 5 winners including the useful Irish 2-y-o 7f winner and dual Group 3 placed Kyniska. The second dam, Lunadine (by Bering), is an unplaced half-sister to 3 winners including the Group 3 winner Prix Corrida winner Luna Mareza. (Sheikh Juma Dalmook Al Maktoum). *"A nice type, he's done everything right so far but I won't be chasing him anytime soon".*

56. UNNAMED ★★★
b.c. Al Kazeem – Perfect Delight (Dubai Destination). February 17. First foal. 110,000Y. Tattersalls October Book 1. Not sold. The dam, a fair 10f winner, is a half-sister to 2 winners including the Group 3 7f Chartwell Stakes and listed 6f Pavilion Stakes winner Perfect Tribute. The second dam, Perfect Spirit (by Invincible Spirit), is an unraced half-sister to 4 winners including the listed winner Swift Tango. (Mildmay Racing / D H Caslon). *"A lovely horse, I was happy when the owner bought him back from the sales because I loved him as a yearling. He's a just a lovely type from a good family and very athletic, although I wouldn't be hurrying him. Looks encouraging so far".*

57. UNNAMED ★★★
ch.c. Harbour Watch – Princess Mood (Muhtarram). March 7. Half-brother to the very useful 6f and 7f listed winner and subsequent UAE Group 1 placed Kingsgate Prince (by Desert Sun), to the useful 2-y-o listed 7f winner of 6 races Captain Ramius (by Kheleyf), the fairly useful 6f and 7f winner Avenuesnalleyways (by Bertolini), the quite useful 6f winner of 6 races Munfallet (by Royal Applause), the fair 2-y-o 6f winner Barolo Top (by Amadeus Wolf), the fair 8.5f winner Smugglers Bay (by Celtic Swing) and the modest 7f winner Old English (by Marju). The dam, placed over 1m in Germany, is a half-sister to 6 minor winners. The second dam, Princess Nana (by Bellypha), won the Group 2

German 1,000 Guineas. (Qatar Racing Ltd). *"He goes well, he's done a lot of growing and gone tall and leggy but he does alright. We'll see how we go when we get him on the grass but I'd be disappointed if he didn't have the speed for six furlongs in June".*

58. UNNAMED ★★★★
b.f. Camelot – Saturn Girl (Danehill Dancer). February 4. Fourth foal. The dam, a fair 1m winner, is a half-sister to 8 winners including the useful listed 10f winner Livadiya. The second dam, Lilissa (by Doyoun), a French 9f and 10.5f winner, is a half-sister to 5 winners including the Group 3 12f Prix Minerve winner Linnga. (Mr M Tabor). *"I had the half-sister by Pour Moi who didn't show a lot, but this is a different story altogether. She's very athletic, goes nicely and is a lovely filly".*

59. UNNAMED ★★★
ch.f. Shamardal – Sweet Rose (New Approach). March 28. First foal. The dam is an unraced half-sister to 5 winners including the very useful listed 12f winner Elite Army (by Authorized), to the German listed 10f winner Promesse De L'Aube, the useful dual 1m (at 2 yrs) and UAE listed 7f winner Pure Diamond and the fairly useful 2-y-o 7f winner and 3-y-o listed-placed Champagnelifestyle . The second dam, White Rose (by Platini), won the 2-y-o Group 3 7f Prix Miesque, was placed in the German 1,000 Guineas and German Oaks and is a half-sister to 4 winners including the German Group 2 winners Wild Side and Win For Us. (Sheikh Juma Dalmook Al Maktoum). *"A grand filly, really nice and with a bit of character, she likes to have a play around in the morning but she'll be alright. I think she'll be a seven furlong 2-y-o".*

60. UNNAMED ★★★
b.c. Havana Gold – Tentpole (Rainbow Quest). February 4. Tenth foal. Half-brother to 6 winners including the fairly useful 8.5f (at 2 yrs) to 12f winner Shakopee (by High Chaparral), the fairly useful 1m (at 2 yrs) and 12f winner and UAE Group 3 third Too Much Trouble, the fair 11f winner Loden (both by Barathea) and the fair 1m to 14f and hurdles winner Bivouac (by Jade Robbery). The dam, an Irish 14f winner, is a half-sister to 4 winners including the Group 3 third and US Grade

2 third Philatelist. The second dam, Polent (by Polish Precedent), a minor French 13f and 15.5f winner, is a half-sister to 6 winners including the Oaks winner Snow Bride (herself dam of the Derby, King George and 'Arc' winner Lammtarra). (Qatar Racing Ltd). *"He's growing at the moment but he's a good type. A good looking horse, he might take a little bit of time but he'll be worth the wait".*

61. UNNAMED ★★★
br.f. Cape Cross – Terentia (Diktat). April 1. Third foal. 75,000Y. Tattersalls October Book 1. Rabbah Bloodstock. Half-sister to the quite useful 2-y-o 6f winner Publilia (by Makfi) and to the modest triple 6f winner Shades Of Silk (by Bahamian Bounty). The dam, a useful 5f winner of 5 races at 2 to 4 yrs, is a half-sister to 3 winners including the dual listed 6f winner and Group 3 Ballyogan Stakes third Cartimandua. The second dam, Agrippina (by Timeless Times), a useful 2-y-o listed 7f winner, is a half-sister to 2 winners. (Sheikh Juma Dalmook Al Maktoum). *"Sheikh Juma loved her at the sales and she's done nothing wrong since she's been here. She'll be a 2-y-o type for six/seven furlongs I'd hope".*

DAVID BARRON
62. GLORIOUS ECLIPSE
b.c. Pastoral Pursuits – First Eclipse (Fayruz). March 11. Fifth foal. 57,000Y. Tattersalls October Book 3. Sackville/Donald. Brother to the modest Scandinavian 6f winner Ta Ajabb and half-brother to the fairly useful 5f and 6f winner at 2 and 3 yrs and Group 3 Curragh Stakes third Blood Moon (by Equiano) and the quite useful 1m winner of 4 races Jacob Black (by Amadeus Wolf). The dam, a modest 2-y-o 5f winner, is a half-sister to 5 winners. The second dam, Naked Poser (by Night Shift), a quite useful 2-y-o 6f winner, is a half-sister to 4 winners including the useful dual listed winning sprinter Damalis. (Kangyu International Racing (HK)).

63. HOP MADDOCKS (IRE)
b.c. Roderic O'Connor – Yurituni (Bahamian Bounty). March 17. Second foal. €32,000Y. Tattersalls Ireland September. Harrowgate Bloodstock. The dam, a quite useful 6f (at 2 yrs) and 5f winner of 5 races, is a half-sister to 6 winners. The second dam, Vax Star (by

Petong), a fairly useful 2-y-o 5f listed winner, is a half-sister to 4 winners. (Dr N J Barron).

64. KODI BEACH
b.c. Kodiac – Annie Beach (Redback). March 18. Second foal. £62,000Y. Goffs UK Premier (Doncaster). Not sold. The dam, a quite useful dual 5f winner at 2 and 3 yrs, is a half-sister to 7 winners. The second dam, Kiva by Indian Ridge), is an unraced half-sister to 5 winners. (Mrs S C Barron).

65. SHANGHAI ELASTIC ♠
b.f. Swiss Spirit – Reveille (Sakhee's Secret). February 8. First foal. 5,000Y. Tattersalls October Book 3. Harrowgate Bloodstock. The dam, a modest 1m placed 2-y-o, is a half-sister to 3 winners including the useful 7f (at 2 yrs) and subsequent US 1m Grade 2 and Grade 3 stakes winner Up In Time. The second dam, Up At Dawn (by Inchinor), is an unplaced half-sister to 7 winners including the dam of the Group 3 winner Summer Fete.

66. TEMBER
b.c. Sayif – Tranquil Flight (Oasis Dream). January 30. Third foal. 16,000Y. Tattersalls October Book 3. Harrowgate Bloodstock. Half-brother to the modest 6f (including at 2 yrs) and 5f winner of 5 races Classic Flyer (by Stimulation). The dam is an unraced half-sister to one winner. The second dam, Umniya (by Bluebird), a quite useful 2-y-o 6f winner, was third in the Group 3 Premio Dormello and is a half-sister to 5 winners including the dual listed 6f winner Lady Links (herself dam of the dual listed winner Selinka). (Mr H D Atkinson).

67. UNNAMED
b.c. Arcano – Amber Heights (Kyllachy). March 1. First foal. 50,000Y. Tattersalls October Book 3. Harrowgate Bloodstock. The dam, a modest 5.5f and 6f winner, is a half-sister to 6 winners including the Group 3 7f Gladness Stakes winner Millennium Force. The second dam, Jumairah Sun (by Scenic), a fairly useful 10f winner, was listed placed over 12f and is a half-sister to 3 winners. (L G O'Kane).

RALPH BECKETT
68. AUTHENTIC ART ★★★
ch.c. Dutch Art – Tahirah (Green Desert). March 20. Ninth foal. 75,000Y. Tattersalls

October Book 1. Barberini Bloodstock. Half-brother to 6 winners including the useful dual 6f winner and Group 2 Richmond Stakes second Louie De Palma (by Pastoral Pursuits), the fairly useful 9f and 10f winner Little Rocky (by Cadeaux Genereux), the fairly useful dual 6f winner Bahamian Heights (by Bahamian Bounty) and the quite useful 6f winner Edward Lewis (by Kyllachy). The dam, a useful 7f and 1m winner, was listed-placed twice and is a sister to one winner and a half-sister to 5 winners. The second dam, Kismah (by Machiavellian), a very useful dual 1m winner, is a half-sister to 10 winners including the dam of the US dual Grade 2 winner Shakis. (Thurloe Thoroughbreds XLI). *"We had to geld him quite early on because he was as badly behaved a yearling as we can remember having – virtually unrideable! But that cured him. He's quite a leggy sort so we won't be asking him any questions just yet. An attractive horse but quite immature still, so he'll be one for seven furlongs or a mile in the second half of the year. He's a horse I like now he's gelded!"*

69. AZPEITIA ★★★
ch.f. Showcasing – Leaves You Baby (Pivotal) March 3. First foal. The dam, a fair dual 10f winner, is a half-sister to 2 winners. The second dam, Royal Devotion (by Sadler's Wells), an Irish listed 12f winner, is a closely related to the 2-y-o listed 6f Silver Flash Stakes winner April Starlight and to the dual listed winner Thady Quill and a half-sister to the US Grade 3 8.5f winner Humble Eight. (James Ortega Bloodstock). *"She's almost dip-backed but she's a very laid-back filly – like a lot by the sire – with plenty of size and bone. She's out of a mare that got ten furlongs well but I should imagine we'll start her off at six furlongs in mid-to-late summer. She's very straightforward and a nice filly to have".*

70. CAMOMILE LAWN (IRE) ★★★
b.f. Camelot – Endure (Green Desert). March 21. Eighth foal. 52,000Y. Tattersalls October Book 2. Biddestone Racing. Half-sister to 5 winners including the very useful 2-y-o listed 7f winner Bunker (by Hurricane Run), the fairly useful dual 5f winner Imtiyaaz (by Starspangledbanner), the quite useful 2-y-o 6f winner Atacama Crossing and the fair 2-y-o 5f

and 6f winner of 4 races at 2 and 3 yrs Beach Candy (both by Footstepsinthesand). The dam ran twice unplaced and is a half-sister to 7 winners including the Canadian Grade 3 winner Alexis and the Irish listed winners Miss Helga and Freshwater Pearl. The second dam, Sister Golden Hair (by Glint Of Gold), a listed-placed winner at 2 yrs in Germany, is a half-sister to 2 winners. (Biddestone Partnership). *"She's a good-moving filly that needs a bit of time. There's quite a bit of talk about Camelot, with some of his 2-y-o's appearing to be relatively early types, but ours are not. She'll be appearing in mid-to-late summer and she's quite a light framed filly, although an athletic one, so we'll be looking after her in the short term".*

71. CEILIDHS DREAM ★★
b.f. Oasis Dream – Ceilidh House (Selkirk). May 8. The dam, a useful 1m (at 2 yrs) and listed 10f winner, is a sister to two quite useful 10f winners and a half-sister to 3 winners. The second dam, Villa Carlotta (by Rainbow Quest), a smart 12f listed winner of four races, is a full or half-sister to 9 winners including the US dual Grade 2 stakes winner Battle Of Hastings. (Mr J H Richmond-Watson). *"We trained her dam who was pretty good and won her only start as a 2-y-o in October. I should think this filly will take a bit of time, she's leggy and still growing. We'll probably start her off at seven furlongs and she'll get ten next year".*

72. CITY GENT ★★★
b.c. Holy Roman Emperor – City Girl (Elusive City). March 4. First foal. The dam, a fairly useful listed-placed 6f winner of 2 races at 2 and 3 yrs, is a half-sister to 2 winners. The second dam, Lochridge (by Indian Ridge), a smart listed 6f winner of 5 races, is a half-sister to 3 winners including the useful listed 5f winner Loch Verdi. (J C Smith). *"A forward sort of horse, the dam was quick and was second in the Carnarvon Stakes for us. It's very much a speedy family and I would think we'll be getting on with him early. He's very straightforward especially considering some by the sire need a bit of managing and the dam wasn't that easy either. He'll start at five furlongs and then we'll see how we go".*

73. CONSTRUCT ★★★
b.c. Maxios – Airfield (Dansili). March 22.
First foal. The dam is an unraced sister to 3
winners including the 2-y-o Group 3 7f Prix
La Rochette winner and Group 1 Prix Jean-Luc
Lagardere second Early March and the smart
1m (at 2 yrs) and Group 3 10.4f Musidora
Stakes and subsequent US Grade 2 1m winner
Aviate and a half-sister to 3 winners. The
second dam, Emplane (by Irish River), a useful
3-y-o 1m winner, is a sister to the useful 2-y-o
1m winner Boatman and a half-sister to the
quite useful 2-y-o 7f winner Palisade. (Khalid
Abdulla). *"It's a very good pedigree and this is
a big horse but he's an athletic sort and I could
see him making a 2-y-o later in the year".*

74. CROSS MY MIND ★★★★
b.f. Cape Cross – Zaaqya (Nayef). March
26. Fourth foal. €58,000Y. Goffs Orby. Kern/
Lillingston. Sister to the quite useful 2-y-o
8.5f winner Laafiraaq. The dam, a quite useful
7f, 1m (both at 2 yrs) and 12f winner, is a
sister to 3 minor winners. The second dam,
Classical Dancer (by Dr Fong), a fairly useful
8.3f winner, was listed-placed twice and is a
half-sister to 6 winners including the Group
1 Premio Roma winner Imperial Dancer.
(Kennet Valley Thoroughbreds). *"I saw her as
a yearling and liked her very much and she's
grown into a lovely filly. She's going to need a
bit of time because she's a big, lengthy filly, but
she's a very good mover and makes good use
of herself. I would think that she'll want a mile
and it'll be mid-summer before we see her. A
forward-going filly and very attractive".*

75. DAWN DASH ★★★
ch.f. Dawn Approach – Dashiba (Dashing
Blade). May 14. Half-sister to the dual Group
2 Lancashire Oaks winner of 7 races Barshiba
(by Barathea), to the useful 2-y-o listed 1m
winner Doctor Dash, the fair 2-y-o 1m winner
Dashing Doc (both by Dr Fong), the fairly
useful 1m (at 2 yrs) and 12f winner Dashing
Star (by Teofilo) and the modest dual 10f
winner Westhaven (by Alhaarth). The dam,
a useful 9f and 10f winner, is a half-sister to
several winners including the fairly useful 10f
and 12f winner Smart Blade. The second dam,
Alsiba (by Northfields), a modest winner of
one race at 4 yrs, was a staying half-sister to
several winners and to the dam of the Irish

St Leger winner Oscar Schindler. (J C Smith).
*"A big, tall, lengthy filly that's going to need a
bit of time as you'd expect with that pedigree
and her foaling date, but there are 2-y-o's on
the page and we shouldn't be too dogmatic
about where she's going to end up. A lovely
filly with a very good way of going, she's
straightforward. The first season sire Dawn
Approach was an exceptional racehorse and
hopefully he's passed that on".*

76. DI FEDE ★★★
b.f. Shamardal – Dibiya (Caerleon). April 20.
Sister to the useful 2-y-o 7f winner and dual
listed-placed Dibayani and half-sister to 6
winners including the fairly useful Irish 7f
winning 2-y-o's Dirar (by King's Best) and
Dilinata (by Spinning World), the quite useful
Irish 9f winner Diylawa (by Mastercraftsman),
the quite useful Irish 12f winner Dibella (by
Observatory) and the fair 2-y-o 6f winner
Justice Lass (by Canford Cliffs). The dam, a
fairly useful 12f and 14f winner, was listed-
placed. The second dam, Dabtiya (by Shirley
Heights), won the listed Ballyroan Stakes. (Mr
R Ng). *"A very forward sort of filly, she wasn't
a particularly early foal but she has a very
active mind and we have to challenge her a
bit at home just to make sure she doesn't get
above herself. We like the way she goes, it's a
good family and she's by a very good stallion.
She could well be appearing in May over six
furlongs".*

77. DIOCLES OF ROME ★★★
b.c. Holy Roman Emperor – Serisia (Exit To
Nowhere). March 19. Tenth foal. €38,000Y.
Arqana Deauville October. David Redvers.
Half-brother to the Australian dual Group
1 winner (over 1m and 10f) Contributer (by
High Chaparral), to the French listed-placed
7f winner Saimaa (by Zoffany), the modest
7f to 10f winner of 5 races Greek Islands (by
Oasis Dream) and the French 7.5f and 1m
winner Pivon (by Pivotal). The dam, winner of
the Group 3 Prix de Psyche, is a half-sister to 6
winners including the French listed 7f winner
and Group 3 7f second Mayyadah. The second
dam, Seralia (by Royal Academy), a French
2-y-o listed 6f winner and third in the Group 3
Prix du Calvados, is a half-sister to the Group
1 Criterium de Saint-Cloud winner Shaka. (Mrs
P Snow & Partners). *"This is a nice horse. I*

thought he was very well-bought considering he's a full brother to a Group 1 winner. A heavy-topped horse that's just starting to fill his frame now, I'd expect him to get seven furlongs and a mile this year. He'll appear sometime in mid to-late summer and he's a good sort of horse and straightforward".

78. EDGE OF THE WORLD ★★★

b.f. Fastnet Rock – Lady Links (Bahamian Bounty). April 4. Eleventh foal. €110,000Y. Goffs Orby. David Redvers. Half-sister to the useful listed 6f (at 2 yrs) and listed 7f winner Selinka (by Selkirk), to the quite useful 2-y-o 7f winners Tidal Wave (by Canford Cliffs) and Swanky Lady (by Cape Cross) and a minor winner abroad by Oasis Dream. The dam, a dual listed 6f winner (including at 2 yrs), is a half-sister to 5 winners including the quite useful 2-y-o 6f winner and Group 3 placed Umniya. The second dam, Sparky's Song (by Electric), a moderate 10.2f and 12f winner, is a half-sister to 3 winners including the Group 1 6.5f winner Bold Edge. (Qatar Racing Ltd & Mrs B M Keller). *"A strong filly, but she's big and the sire suggests she'll need a bit of time. After all, Fastnet Rock didn't win himself at two. I would say she'll be a six/seven furlong filly later in the year, it's a fast family and one I know a bit about. She's a sweet filly with a big action".*

79. FIRST SPIRIT USA) ★★★

b.f. First Defence – Choice Spirit (Danzig). February 25. Tenth foal. Half-sister to 4 winners including the quite useful 7f winner Hachita (by Gone West) and the dam of the Group 1 Prix Jean Romanet winner Announce. The dam won the listed 1m Prix de la Calonne and is a half-sister to 8 winners including Zafonic and Zamindar. The second dam, Zaizafon (by The Minstrel), a dual 2-y-o 7f winner, was placed in the Group 1 1m Queen Elizabeth II Stakes and is a half-sister to the dam of the Eclipse Stakes and Phoenix Champion Stakes winner Elmaamul. (Khalid Abdulla). *"She's going to need a bit of time and we haven't done much with her yet. I'm working out where she's going to end up as we speak, but I would think she'll be a late summer 2-y-o. The home-bred 2-y-o's seem to change very quickly so it'll be a watching brief with her, but she's a lovely filly with an equally lovely pedigree".*

80. FORCE MAJEURE (IRE) ★★

b.f. Smart Strike – Forces Of Darkness (Lawman). April 6. First foal. €150,000Y. Arqana Deauville August. Private Sale. The dam, a 1m (at 2 yrs) and Group 3 12.5f Prix Minerve winner, was third in the Group 1 Prix Saint-Alary and is a half-sister to 4 winners including the 2-y-o Group 2 5f Norfolk Stakes winner Waterloo Bridge. The second dam, Miss Childrey (by Dr Fong), an Irish 2-y-o listed 6f winner, was third in the Group 3 Irish 1,000 Guineas Trial and is a half-sister to 6 winners. (Miss K Rausing). *"Quite a tall, leggy, very backward filly, but she's a good mover. I would think she could go away for a spring break shortly and we'll see her in the autumn, but it's a lovely pedigree. Her owner doesn't buy many yearlings so maybe we should take note!"*

81. HAN DYNASTY (USA) ★★★★

b.f. More Than Ready – Silk Route (Empire Maker). April 3. Second foal. Half-sister to the US 2016 2-y-o 6f winner South Sea (by Into Mischief). The dam is an unraced daughter of the listed 10f winner and Group 1 Fillies' Mile second Jibe (by Danzig), herself a sister to the US Grade 1 winner Yashmak and a half-sister to 7 winners including the Epsom and Irish Derby winner Commander In Chief, the champion 2-y-o and miler Warning and the Irish Derby second Deploy. (Khalid Abdulla). *"A lovely filly, she has a really good temperament and has a very good way about her. Like most of the Prince's I doubt she'd be appearing in the first wave of 2-y-o's, but she'll make a 2-y-o at some point and More Than Ready is a very good sire".*

82. JIM ROCKFORD ★★★

ch.c. Showcasing – Positivity (Monsieur Bond). March 23. Third foal. £47,000Y. Goffs UK Premier (Doncaster). R Beckett. Half-brother to the modest 2-y-o 6f winner Cumbrianna (by Hellvelyn). The dam, a modest 1m winner at 4 and 5 yrs, is a half-sister to 5 winners. The second dam, Pretty Pollyanna (by General Assembly), is an unraced half-sister to 2 minor winners. (Chelsea Thoroughbreds). *"He was bought to be a forward 2-y-o for the first part of the season and he looks like being so. A strong horse who looks like he's finished growing for the time being, I would think he'd appear over five/six furlongs in either April or May".*

83. KINAESTHESIA ★★★

b.f. Sea The Stars – Kinetica (Stormy Atlantic). February 14. Second foal. 90,000 foal. Tattersalls December. Lanwades Stud. The dam, a 2-y-o listed 7f winner, was third in the Group 3 Sweet Solera Stakes and the Prix d'Aumale and is a half-sister to 2 winners. The second dam, Kiswahili (by Selkirk), won 4 races including a listed 14f event in Germany and is a half-sister to 3 winners including the dam of the Group 1 winner Madame Chiang. (Miss K Rausing). *"By Sea The Stars which suggests she'll need a lot of time and this filly will be getting it. A very raw looking filly when she arrived, she's done very well of late and has started to fill her frame now. Her dam was a listed winner at two and she should appear this year, probably over a mile from late summer at the earliest. A sweet filly".*

84. LONDON'S BURNING ★★★

ch.g. Cityscape – Even Hotter (Desert Style). March 2. Fifth foal. £600Y. Ascot December. Half-brother to the moderate 5f winner of 5 races (including at 2 yrs) Spray Tan, to the modest 5f winner Even Hotter and the moderate dual 5f winner Warm Order (all by Assertive). The dam, a moderate 1m placed maiden, is a half-sister to 4 winners. The second dam, Level Pegging (by Common Grounds), unplaced on her only 2 starts at 2 yrs, is a sister to the listed Scarborough Stakes winner and Group 2 King's Stand Stakes second Flanders (herself dam of the US Grade 3 winner Louvain) and a half-sister to 6 winners. (Kimpton Down Racing Club). *"We bought him as a foal for 800gns and bought him back as a yearling for even less! He's very forward, should be racing in April and I expect him to pick up a little race".* TRAINERS' BARGAIN BUY

85. MALMESBURY (IRE) ★★★

b.f. Holy Roman Emperor – Maakrah (Dubai Destination). May 14. Fourth foal. Half-sister to the fair 7f and 1m winner Matravers (by Oasis Dream). The dam is an unraced sister to 2 winners including the Group 3 Winter Derby winner and Grade 1 Breeders' Cup Juvenile third Farraaj and a half-sister to 9 winners including the triple Group 2 winner and sire Iffraaj and the useful 2-y-o Group 3 7f Prix du Calvados winner Kareymah. The second dam, Pastorale (by Nureyev), a fairly useful 3-y-o 7f winner, is a half-sister to 8 winners including the Group 1 Lockinge Stakes winner and high-class sire Cape Cross. (Millennium Madness). *"She was a late foal but it's a terrific pedigree and Dubai Destination is an exceptional broodmare stallion. We've had a lot of luck with Holy Roman Emperor fillies and although this one will not be at all early I can see her being a 2-y-o in August or September. She'll start over seven furlongs or a mile but she's done very well of late. Quite a tall, leggy filly, but she'll change a good deal between now and then".*

86. MCCOOL ★★★

b.f. Giant's Causeway – Nobilis (Rock Of Gibraltar). January 22. First foal. 95,000Y. Tattersalls October Book 1. Not sold. The dam, a 3-y-o winner in France and placed in the Group 2 Prix de Malleret and Group 3 Prix Minerve, is a half-sister to 4 winners including the Group 2 Lonsdale Cup second Drill Sergeant. The second dam, Dolydille (by Dolphin Street), won 7 races including two listed events from 9f to 12f and is a half-sister to 9 winners including the Irish listed 1m winner La Meilleure (the dam of four stakes winners). (China Horse Club). *"I would say this filly was well-bought. She's strong, forward-going and hasn't been here long but she's an attractive sort and I'd expect her to make a 2-y-o. By the way she goes we'll be getting on with her quite soon I should think. I like her".*

87. MERCHANT MARINE ★★★★

b.c. Epaulette – Chantilly Beauty (Josr Algarhoud). February 12. Fourth foal. The dam, an Italian 2-y-o listed 6f winner of 3 races, was second in the Group 2 Premio Regina Elena and in the Group 3 7f Chartwell Fillies' Stakes and is a half-sister to 3 winners in France. The second dam, Lysabelle (by Lesotho), a listed-placed winner of 5 races in France, is a half-sister to 7 winners. (Mr Robert Ng). *"He's a forward sort of horse. The dam was a good 2-y-o and then a good miler at three. He looks sharp and should appear in April or May over five/six furlongs. He's got a good way of going and is forward in every way. We like him".*

88. MESQUITE ★★★★
b.f. High Chaparral – Puff (Camacho). March 23. First foal. The dam, a useful 6f (at 2 yrs) and Group 3 7f Fred Darling Stakes winner, is a half-sister to 4 winners including the Group 1 Lockinge Stakes second Sovereign Debt. The second dam, Kelsey Rose (by Most Welcome), a fairly useful 2-y-o 5f winner of 3 races, was listed-placed three times and is a half-sister to 3 winners. (Mr & Mrs David Aykroyd). *"She's a tough filly in every way including to deal with because she's hard on her riders. Her mother was the same but she was very good and won the Fred Darling for us. Although she's by High Chaparral I can see her appearing by early-to-mid summer. We'll get on with her rather than hold on and she's a filly with plenty of bone as well as plenty of attitude. Her dam went the right way so I'd expect this filly to progress with racing".*

89. NEYLAND ★★★
b.f. Oasis Dream – Milford Sound (Barathea). March 1. Sister to the quite useful 2016 2-y-o 1m winner Sound Bar and half-sister to the useful 2-y-o 1m winner and listed Derby Trial second Carntop, to the 10.5f (in France) and hurdles winner Quebec (both by Dansili) and the quite useful 9.5f winner Mitre Peak (by Shamardal). The dam, a fair French 1m winner, is a half-sister to 7 winners including the Prix de l'Arc de Triomphe and Grand Prix de Paris winner Rail Link, the French Group 2 12f and dual Group 3 10f winner Crossharbour and the smart French 1m and 10f performer Chelsea Manor. The second dam, Docklands (by Theatrical), a French 1m and 10f performer, is a half-sister to the smart performer at up to 9f Wharf. (Khalid Abdulla). *"A big filly, we trained two of her brothers Carntop and Sound Bar and both won over a mile at two. I would expect she'll go the same route, it's a staying family so she's one for the second half of the year. She has more bone and size than either of her brothers at the same stage, so that's good. There's every chance she'll turn into a lovely filly".*

90. NINE BELOW ZERO ★★★★
b.c. Showcasing – Finesse (Shamardal). March 8. First foal. The dam, a fair 5f to 7f winner of 4 races at 3 and 4 yrs, is a half-sister to the quite useful 6f winner My Delirium – herself dam of the dual Group 1 winning sprinter Quiet Reflection (by Showcasing). The second dam, Clare Hills (by Orpen), won the 2-y-o listed 5f Hilary Needler Trophy and is a half-sister to 3 winners. (Mr P K Gardner). *"He's a three-parts brother to Quiet Reflection and it's a family I know well because I trained both Finesse and My Delirium. He's done very well of late because he was a smallish yearling and he's grown from the New Year onwards. He has a good way of going, it's a good family and I would say he'll be the same. We'll run him sooner rather than later, so he might be ready in May and he's got every chance with that pedigree for sure".*

91. OCCUPY ★★★★
b.c. Declaration Of War – Circumstances (Galileo). February 17. Second foal. $80,000Y. Keeneland September. James Delahooke. The dam, a modest 11f winner, is a sister to the Group 2 Hardwicke Stakes and Group 2 Voltigeur Stakes winner and dual Group 1 placed Telescope. The second dam, Velouette (by Darshaan), is an unraced half-sister to 5 winners including the Group 2 10.5f Dante Stakes and Group 3 10f Select Stakes winner Moon Ballad. (Highclere Thoroughbred Racing). *"I can see why James Delahooke bought him because he's a very good individual. It's a staying family but we'll carry on as we are with him and let him tell us when he's ready. We shouldn't forget that the sire won the Coventry and I think this colt was well bought because he's a gorgeous individual. You would think he'd be a seven furlong colt or a miler later on, but he's a good looker with a very good action and he could be a bit earlier than that".*

92. RICHENZA ★★★
b.f. Holy Roman Emperor – Nantha (King's Best). April 22. First foal. 42,000Y. Tattersalls December. Oliver St Lawrence. The dam, an Italian 2-y-o winner and second in the Group 3 1m Premio Dormello, is a half-sister to 2 winners. The second dam, Nashatara (by Nashwan), a listed 10f winner in Italy, is a half-sister to 5 winners. (Mrs Lynn Turner & Mr Guy Brook). *"A strong filly, she was almost heavy-topped as a yearling but she's done very well since the sales. The sire has been good for us lately and King's Best has proved to be a very*

good broodmare sire. I can see her making a 2-y-o over seven furlongs in late summer. She has a good way of going and has plenty of size and strength about her, so we should have a bit of luck with her".

93. SECRET GAZE ★★★★★
b.f. Galileo – Shastye (Danehill). February 15. Eighth foal. 1,350,000Y. Tattersalls October Book 1. David Redvers. Sister to the Group 2 10.5f Middleton Stakes and dual listed winner and Group 1 Oaks second Secret Gesture and to the smart 7f winner Sir Isaac Newton and half-sister to the Australian listed winner Maurus (by Medicean) and the fair 10f winner Secret Sense (by Shamardal). The dam, a useful listed-placed 12f and 13f winner, is a half-sister to 8 winners including Sagamix (Prix de l'Arc de Triomphe), Sagacity (Group 1 Criterium de Saint-Cloud) and the Group 2 Prix de Malleret winner Sage Et Jolie (dam of the Group 1 winner Sageburg). The second dam, Saganeca (by Sagace), won the Group 3 12.5f Prix de Royallieu. (Qatar Racing Ltd & Newsells Park Stud). *"From a family I know well, this is a lovely filly that has more bone and more size than her full-sister Secret Gesture. She might be anything and let's hope she's as good as her sister because we'll be in business then. I like her obviously, I loved her as a yearling and was delighted that Sheikh Fahad bought half of her and sent her to me. A gorgeous filly".*

94. SMART DART ★★★
b.f. Mastercraftsman – Dark Missile (Night Shift). May 6. Third foal. Closely related to the fair dual 6f winner Midnight Dance (by Danehill Dancer) and half-sister to the quite useful dual 5f winner Dark Shot (by Acclamation). The dam, a very useful 6f winner of 4 races and second in the Group 2 6f Diadem Stakes, is a full or half-sister to several winners including the fairly useful dual 1m winner Breakheart. The second dam, Exorcet (by Selkirk), a fair 3-y-o 6f winner, is a half-sister to 2 winners including the useful UAE 7f and 1m winner Rock Music. (J C Smith). *"She's quite forward despite her fairly late foaling date. We had her sister Midnight Dance here and she was pretty quick and I think she will be too. I loved her as a yearling on the farm and I'm delighted they sent her to*

me because I'm a confirmed fan of the family and of her as an individual. She's more forward than Midnight Dance was at this stage".

95. SOLID MAN ★★★★
b.c. Lord Kanaloa – Maruka Sawayaka (Sunday Silence). April 17. Eighth foal. Half-brother to 6 winners in Japan. The dam was a stakes winner of 5 races in Japan and is a half-sister to champion Japanese sprinter Durandal out of Sawayaka Princess (by Northern Taste). (Acing Lead Ltd). *"This is a nice horse. He's very forward and although it isn't easy for an imported yearling because it takes a lot out of them he's handling life very well at the moment. He's a horse we think a fair bit of and I he'll make a 2-y-o. I would expect him to be winning his maiden and then going on from there. He goes very well. We haven't galloped him yet but anyone could see that he's a nice horse". The sire won the Group 1 Hong Kong Sprint twice.*

96. VICTORY CHIME (IRE) ★★
b.c. Campanologist – Patuca (Teofilo). January 21. First foal. 48,000Y. Tattersalls October Book 2. Ralph Beckett. The dam, a minor German 3-y-o winner, is a half-sister to 4 winners including the Group 1 Premio Roma and Group 2 Prix Dollar winner Potemkin and the German listed 1m winner and Group 3 placed Paraisa. The second dam, Praia (by Big Shuffle), a listed-placed 3-y-o winner in Germany, is a half-sister to 4 winners including the Group 1 Criterium de Saint-Cloud winner Paita. (Mr Andrew Nevin). *"He's done very well of late and the pedigree has improved significantly lately, particularly through Potemkin. The horse has come on too and he looks like he'll make a 2-y-o in the second half of the year. The sire has died now so it's hard to say how successful he might have been. This colt is a medium to long-term prospect, he's done really well of late and I like him".*

97. ZILARA ★★★
b.f. Big Bad Bob – Celtic Slipper (Anabaa). January 23. Half-sister to the useful listed 14f winner of 6 races Moonrise Landing (by Dalakhani) and to the fair 9f winner Are You Mine (by Nayef). The dam, a very useful 7f (at 2 yrs) and Group 3 1m Premio Dormello winner, was third in the Group 2 May Hill

Stakes and is a half-sister to 2 winners. The second dam, Celtic Silhouette (by Celtic Swing), was placed four times at 4 and 5 yrs in France and is a sister to the listed winner and Group 2 Dante Stakes second Celtic Silence and a half-sister to the dual Group 3 winner Royal And Regal. (Mr P D Savill). *"I trained the dam and this filly's half-sister Moonrise Landing who won a listed race last year. Quite a neat, round filly, she's going to need a bit of time but she's strong and not at all like Moonrise Landing. They're like chalk and cheese. This filly might end up being a summer 2-y-o and she's bullet proof, like most of the family".*

98. UNNAMED ★★★
b.c. Kodiac – Emma Dora (Medaglia d'Oro). April 8. Fourth foal. €160,000Y. Goffs Orby. The dam, a fair 2-y-o 6f winner, is a half-sister to 6 winners including the Group 3 Princess Margaret Stakes third Explosive Lady. The second dam, My Girl Lisa (by With Approval), a US stakes winner of 6 races at 2 to 4 yrs, is a half-sister to 4 winners. (Acing Lead Ltd). *"A forward sort of horse and the dam won over six furlongs for David Elsworth. We'll be getting on with him shortly, he looks tough like most of his sire's produce, so he should certainly make a 2-y-o".*

99. UNNAMED ★★★
ch.f. Kitten's Joy – Empress Of France (Storm Cat). February 25. Third foal. The dam, a minor winner of 2 races at 4 yrs in the USA, is a sister to the Group 3 Irish 1,000 Guineas Trial winner Kamarinskaya and a half-sister to 4 winners including the champion 2-y-o colt Fasliyev and to the unraced top-class broodmare Butterfly Cove (dam of the Group 1 winners Ballydoyle and Misty For Me). The second dam, Mr P's Princess (by Mr Prospector), is an unraced half-sister to the US Grade 1 winners Menifee and Desert Wine. (HH Sheikh Mohammed Bin Khalifa Al Thani). *"She's quite a hot filly, but she moves well and I suspect she'll go well. We won't have her ready for a while yet, but it's a terrific pedigree and she'll appear in the second half of the year. I haven't had a Kitten's Joy before, but he's a terrific sire and I'm told they come in all sorts of shapes and sizes".*

100. UNNAMED ★★
b.c. Sea The Stars – Ice Mint (Awesome Again). April 22. Fifth foal. €375,000Y. Goffs Orby. Little Kwok Hing Hung / Bahen Bloodstock. Brother to the Japanese winner of 3 races from 2 to 4 yrs A Shin Allonsy and closely related to the quite useful 12f winner Mazaz (by Galileo). The dam, a minor US 3-y-o winner, is a half-sister to 6 winners including the French 2,000 Guineas winner Falco and the French 2-y-o Group 3 winner Iron Lips. The second dam, Icelips (by Unbridled), a minor French 3-y-o winner, is a half-sister to 7 winners including the French Group 2 winner Legerette. (Acing Lead Ltd). *"His three-parts brother Mazaz took a lot of time to come to hand and I would think he will too, but he's a lovely horse and he's done very well since the sale. He'll be getting 'plenty of nourishment and not much punishment' for the time being".*

101. UNNAMED ★★
b.c. Orfevre (JPN) – Miss Emma (Key Of Luck). February 17. Half-brother to the French 6.5f (at 2 yrs) and listed 5f winner Kagura (by Vindication). The dam, winner of the Group 3 6f Greenlands Stakes, is a full or half-sister to 5 winners. The second dam, Disregard That (by Don't Forget Me), is an unraced half-sister to 5 winners including the 2-y-o Group 3 Killavullen Stakes winner Sedulous and the listed Tyros Stakes winner Tapolite (herself the dam of 3 listed winners). (Acing Lead Ltd). *"The sire should have won the Arc when he drifted across the track and the general feeling was that he went for home too soon. This colt is a big, scopey sort of horse, so although he comes from a fast damline I don't expect him to be doing any fast work until mid-summer at the earliest. He's a good sort and he's got a bit about him".*

102. UNNAMED ★★★
b.f. Harbour Watch – Tell The Wind (Mujadil). March 18. Third foal. Half-sister to the 2-y-o 7f winner and Group 3 Horris Hill Stakes third Return Of The Mak (by Makfi). The dam, a fairly useful listed-placed Irish 2-y-o 7f winner, is a half-sister to 3 winners including the useful 2-y-o 7f and listed 1m winner and Group 3 1m third Coupe de Ville and to the US stakes winner and dual Grade 3 placed Fantastico Roberto. The dam is an unraced

half-sister to 3 minor winners. (Qatar Racing Ltd). *"She's a strong, forward filly that will make a 2-y-o and we'll be getting on with her early. A straightforward sort with a good temperament, she should be racing before the end of May over five/six furlongs".*

103. UNNAMED ★★★
ch.f. Dutch Art – Time Honoured (Sadler's Wells). April 2. Eighth living foal. Half-sister to the fairly useful dual 10f winner Huge Future (by Shamardal), to the quite useful 12f winner Infinitum (by Dalakhani), the fair UAE 7f and 1m winner Baroot (by Dubawi), the fair 10f to 12f winner of 3 races Bona Fortuna (by Mark Of Esteem) and a hurdles winner by Daylami. The dam, a quite useful 2-y-o 1m winner, is a sister to the Group 3 12f Princess Royal Stakes winner Time Allowed and a half-sister to the Group 3 12f Jockey Club Stakes winner Zinaad and the dams of five Group winners. The second dam, Time Charter (by Saritamer), won the Oaks, the King George VI and Queen Elizabeth Diamond Stakes, the Champion Stakes and the Coronation Cup. *"She's only just arrived, but she came with a very positive report from a very good judge who had her in pre-training, so I hope he's right about her. With that pedigree you'd think it would be the second half of the year before we got going with her, but she's a bit stronger and more robust than the previous one we had out of the family".*

104. UNNAMED ★★★
b.f. Galileo – Untouched Talent (Storm Cat). March 18. Seventh foal. $1,200,000 foal. Hunter Valley Farm. Half-sister to the US 2-y-o 5f winner Finnegan (by Unbridled's Song), to the US Grade 1 9f Arkansas Derby winner Bodemeister (by Empire Maker) and the US dual Grade 1 placed Fascinating (by Smart Strike). The dam, a US 2-y-o Grade 3 6.5f winner and Grade 1 second, is a half-sister to the fairly useful 1m and 10f winner Kydd Gloves out of Parade Queen (by A P Indy). *"She's only just arrived so I'm still finding out about her, but obviously with that pedigree and her price tag she's a very attractive filly. She won't be appearing early though".*

MICHAEL BELL

105. ANY LITTLE RHYME ★★★
b.f. Shamardal – Free Verse (Danehill Dancer). March 8. Second foal. Sister to the promising 2016 2-y-o 7f winner, on his only start, Frontispiece. The dam, a fairly useful 2-y-o 6f and 7f winner, is a sister to the useful 6f, 7f (both at 2 yrs) and 1m winner and listed-placed Quadrille and a half-sister to 4 winners. The second dam, Fictitious (by Machiavellian), a useful 10f listed winner, is a sister to the smart Group 2 12f Ribblesdale Stakes and Group 2 13.3f Geoffrey Freer Stakes winner Phantom Gold (herself dam of the Oaks second Flight Of Fancy). (The Queen). *"She's not that precocious but she's a strong, well-made filly. We haven't done much with her yet and it's not a family that comes to hand particularly quickly, but she's a good mover and so far so good. Completely untried at this stage but goes promisingly".*

106. ARABIAN JAZZ (IRE) ★★★
b.f. Red Jazz – Queen Of Rap (Alhaarth). March 25. Second foal. €11,000Y. Tattersalls Ireland September. Michael Bell. Half-sister to Ancient King (by Ramonti), a winner of 6 races in Italy and Australia and third in the Group 2 Italian Derby. The dam, a fairly useful Irish dual 7.5f winner, is a half-sister to 5 winners. The second dam, Sudden Stir (by Woodman), is an unplaced half-sister to 7 winners including two Italian Group 2 winners. (Ontoawinner, K Stewart & Partner). *"A sharp, mature looking filly, her half-brother was stakes-class, we didn't have to break the bank to buy her and she should be relatively easy to place".* TRAINERS' BARGAIN BUY

107. BEST BLUE ★★★★★
b.c. Oasis Dream – Filia Regina (Galileo). February 28. First foal. 210,000Y. Tattersalls October Book 1. Bill Gredley. The dam, a fair 14f winner, is a sister to the top-class colt Australia (winner of the Derby, Irish Derby, etc) and a half-sister to the Australian Group 3 winner Voodoo Prince. The second dam, Ouija Board (by Cape Cross), was a top-class winner of 10 races from 7f (at 2 yrs) to 12f including seven Group/Grade 1 races and is a half-sister to 6 winners. (W J & TCO Gredley & Lord Derby). *"A beautiful, big horse with a proper stallion's pedigree. We really like him, he's*

going to take a bit of time but he's got a licence to be a good horse. Everything he's done so far suggests he might be just that. If anything I'd say he's more Oasis Dream than Galileo, he's done nothing but improve since the sale and seven furlongs will suit him to start with".

108. CHOICE ENCOUNTER ★★★★
ch.c. Choisir – Gimme Some Lovin (Desert Style). February 5. Second foal. £65,000Y. Goffs UK Premier (Doncaster). Not sold. Half-brother to the quite useful 2016 2-y-o 5f and 6f winner Thammin (by Dark Angel). The dam, a modest 6f winner here, later won 13 races in Greece and is a half-sister to 8 winners including the Group 1 Golden Shaheen winner Muarrab and the dual 2-y-o Group 3 winner Bungle Inthejungle. The second dam, Licence To Thrill (by Wolfhound), a quite useful dual 5f winner, is a half-sister to 4 winners. (Chris Wright & Emily Asprey). *"He's going to be ready to run sooner rather than later. It's a very precocious family, the dam was as tough as old boots and the first foal is useful. An early foal, he looks exactly what he should look like and he's going exactly as he should go".*

109. ESME KATE ★★★★
b.f. Arch – Francisca (Mizzen Mast). April 16. Second foal. 72,000Y. Tattersalls October Book 1. A C Elliott. The dam, a stakes-placed winner in the USA, is a half-sister to 3 winners including the US Grade 2 and Grade 3 winner Wilcox Inn. The second dam De Aar (by Gone West), a dual US Grade 3 winner, is a half-sister to 11 winners including US Grade 1 winners Cetewayo and Dynaforce. (Mrs B Sangster, Mr D Hanafin, Mr N Warnock). *"Not bred to be particularly early, but she's a fine, strong filly. To look at her she reminds me a bit of the nice filly we had called Red Evie. We like what we see, but she's not in the forward batch so we're letting her come to herself quietly".*

110. FIRST DRIVE ★★★
b.f. Street Cry – Dawn Glory (Oasis Dream). January 30. Second foal. The dam, a modest 6f placed maiden, is a half-sister to 5 winners including the Australian Group 1 10f winner of 7 races My Kingdom Of Fife and the useful 1m (including at 2 yrs) and 7f winner of 6 races and Group 3 1m Autumn Stakes third Four Winds. The second dam, Fairy Godmother (by

Fairy King), a listed 10f winner, is a half-sister to several winners including the Group 2 12f Jockey Club Stakes winner Blueprint. (The Queen). *"A well-made filly, she was an early foal and looks quite mature. Probably one to be getting on with around May time, so she'll be a mid-season 2-y-o".*

111. FLYING SPARKLE (IRE) ★★★
b.f. Fast Company – Titian Saga (Titus Livius). April 17. Fifth foal. 70,000Y. Tattersalls December. A C Elliott. Half-sister to the fairly useful listed 5f winner of 4 races from 2 to 5 yrs Hay Chewed (by Camacho), to the quite useful 2-y-o 5f winner Pres Rapide (by Fast Company) and the fair 5f winner of 6 races Imperial Legend (by Mujadil). The dam, a fair 2-y-o 6f winner, is a half-sister to 7 winners including Nova Tor (the dam of two stakes winners). The second dam, Nordic Living (by Nordico), is an unplaced half-sister to one winner. *"She's built like a barrel, well-related but a bit behind some of the others because she was a December sales yearling. She's catching up quickly though and so far so good".*

112. FREEBE ROCKS (IRE) ★★★
ch.c. Camacho – Shamardyh (Shamardal). March 15. First foal. £42,000Y. Goffs UK Premier (Doncaster). A C Elliott. The dam, a modest 7f winner, is a half-sister to 5 winners including the listed Masaka Stakes second Song Of Silence. The second dam, State Secret (by Green Desert), a winner over 6.5f at 2 yrs in France, is a half-sister to 8 winners including the 2-y-o Group 2 Criterium de Maisons-Laffitte winner Bitooh and the dams of the Group/Grade 1 winners Storming Home, Music Note and Musical Chimes. (Karmaa Racing Ltd). *"A very well-made colt from a good family, he's mature and very strong. Will probably be coming to hand in April, he's done bits of work and shows he's got plenty of dash".*

113. GIRLS TALK (IRE) ★★★
b.f. Shamardal – Tasha's Dream (Woodman). April 6. Eighth foal. 125,000Y. Tattersalls October Book 1. BBA (Ire). Half-sister to 5 winners including the useful 7f (at 2 yrs) and 10f winner and Group 3 Acomb Stakes third Basateen (by Teofilo), the fairly useful 2-y-o 6f winner and Group 2 1m May Hill Stakes second Al Madina (by Noverre), the

fairly useful 2-y-o 7f winner and French listed-placed winner Unquenchable Fire (by Invincible Spirit) and the fair 1m winner Truly Asia (by Acclamation). The dam, an Irish 1m placed maiden, is a sister to the Group 3 Tetrarch Stakes winner Major Force and a half-sister the Peruvian Grade 2 winner Dancing Action and the Group 3 Curragh Cup winner Quality Team. The second dam, Ready For Action (by Riverman), won at 3 yrs and is a half-sister to 4 winners. (Colin Bryce). *"She hasn't done a great deal at this stage but the dam has produced three horses rated at least 90 and the sire upgrades his mares. Hopefully she can be a stakes filly one day but we haven't done enough with her yet. A seven furlong 2-y-o".*

114. HIGHLIGHT REEL (IRE) ★★★

b.c. Big Bad Bob – Dance Hall Girl (Dansili). March 13. Fourth foal. €40,000Y. Goffs Sportsmans. R Frisby. Brother to the very useful 2-y-o listed 7f winner Tashweeq (by Big Bad Bob) and half-brother to the fairly useful Irish 5f (including at 2 yrs) and 6f winner Kasbah (by Acclamation). The dam, a quite useful Irish 7f winner, is a half-sister to 3 winners including the listed winner Solar Deity. The second dam, Dawn Raid (by Docksider), a quite useful Irish 3-y-o 7f winner, is a half-sister to 8 winners including the French and Irish 2,000 Guineas and Richmond Stakes winner Bachir. (The Deflators). *"He's a very strong, powerful horse, his full-brother was very useful and he gets up Warren Hill very nicely. I think he was well-bought, all things considered. He's one that should start off in mid-season".*

115. IMMORTAL ROMANCE ★★★★

br.c. Society Rock – Sundown (Polish Precedent). May 1. Eleventh foal. 50,000Y. Tattersalls October Book 2. A C Elliott. Half-brother to 5 winners including the fairly useful Irish 5f and 6f winner of 8 races Copper Dock (by Docksider), the fairly useful 1m to 12f winner Forgotten Hero (by High Chaparral) and the fairly useful 2-y-o 5f and 6f winner Human Nature (by Kodiac) and the fair Irish 6f to 7.5f winner Topadee (by Golan). The dam is a 6f placed half-sister to 5 winners. The second dam, Ruby Setting (by Gorytus), a fairly useful 10f winner at 3 yrs, is a half-sister to 7 winners including the high-class 2-y-o Prince

Of Dance, winner of the Dewhurst Stakes (in a dead-heat) and the Group 2 Scottish Derby winner Princely Venture. (32 Red Syndicate). *"A particularly good mover. I thought Society Rock's yearlings were rather nice and it's a real shame he's no longer with us – he really stamped them. This horse is mature looking for his age, we like him, he's quite sharp and certainly looks like he'll do himself justice at two".*

116. JOE'S SPIRIT (IRE) ★★★★

b.c. Swiss Spirit – Dimensional (Dansili). April 1. Third foal. £42,000Y. Goffs UK Premier (Doncaster). Alex Elliott. The dam is an unraced three-parts sister to the US Grade 1 winner Light Jig and a half-sister to 10 winners. The second dam, Nashmeel (by Blushing Groom), won the Group 2 1m Prix d'Astarte, was second three Group 1 events and is a half-sister to 9 winners. (Middleham Park Racing XCI & Partner). *"He may well have run before this book goes to print. He goes well, he's very speedy and every inch a 2-y-o. I think he's a good ambassador for his sire and he has a proper pedigree".*

117. MAIN DESIRE ★★★★

b.f. High Chaparral – Purple Glow (Orientate). March 18. Second foal. €40,000Y. Tattersalls Ireland September. J Foley. The dam, a useful 2-y-o 6f winner, was second in the listed 5f Marble Hill Stakes and is a half-sister to one winner. The second dam, Napping (by Danzig), a minor US 2-y-o winner, is a sister to the Grade 1 Go For Wand Stakes winner Easy Now and a half-sister to 7 winners including Easy Goer (nine Grade 1 wins in the USA) and the US Grade 1 winner Cadillacing (herself dam of the Grade 1 winner Strolling Along). (Clipper Logistics). *"The dam was a rocket. I think she ran four times before the Queen Mary and this filly looks sharp too. She's all 2-y-o, goes alright and hopefully might be one of those that can compete in the 2-y-o sprinting stakes division, like her mother did".*

118. SAILING HOME ★★★

b.f. Shamardal – Tidespring (Monsun). March 22. The dam, a French 14.5f winner, was dual Group 3 placed in Germany and is a half-sister to the quite useful 2-y-o listed-placed 1m winner Sweet Dream. The second dam, Sweet

Stream (by Shantou), won 7 races including the Group 1 Prix Vermeille and the Group 2 Park Hill Stakes and is a half-sister to 6 minor winners in Italy. (The Queen). *"Not bred to be early because the dam was a thorough stayer but this is a good-moving filly, she's light on her feet and we like her. Very athletic, we'd be hopeful that she'll be ok later in the season".*

119. SMART STEP ★★★
b.f. Nathaniel – Atiza (Singspiel). April 16. Eighth living foal. 50,000Y. Tattersalls October Book 1. Tim Gredley. Half-sister to the Grade 2 Del Mar Handicap, Grade 2 San Marcos Stakes and dual French Group 3 winner Vagabond Shoes (by Beat Hollow) and two minor winners abroad by Iceman and Sakhee. The dam, a minor French 3-y-o winner, is a half-sister to 4 winners. The second dam, Isabena (by Star Appeal), a listed winner in Spain, is a half-sister to 7 winners including Irish Memory (Group 3 Tetrarch Stakes). (W J & TCO Gredley). *"She's a backward filly, has an enormous stride and really covers the ground. So although she was a mid-April foal and we're not in a hurry with her given her pedigree and her sire, it's encouraging how she moves".*

120. TAUREAN DANCER (IRE) ★★★ ♠
b.c. Intello – Traou Mad (Barathea). April 26. Eleventh foal. 100,000Y. Tattersalls October Book 2. A C Elliott. Half-brother to 5 winners including the French 7.5f winner and listed-placed Roscoff (by Daylami and herself dam of the Italian dual Group 3 winner Hero Look), the quite useful 10f to 12f winner of 6 races Honoured (by Mark Of Esteem) and the fair 6f winner Harbour Patrol (by Acclamation). The dam, a French 2-y-o listed 5f winner, was Group 3 placed four times and is a half-sister to 7 winners including the Group 2 winners Josr Algharoud and Saint Marine. The second dam, Pont-Aven (by Try My Best), won the Group 3 Prix de Saint-Georges, was second in the French 1,000 Guineas and is a half-sister to 6 winners. (Brian Goodyear). *"We like him. A fairly late foal but a very good mover, the dam was speedy and he looks a good advertisement for his sire. The mare has produced plenty of winners but probably needs a proper one sooner rather than later and hopefully it might be him".*

121. UNNAMED ★★★
b.f. Camelot – Jewel In The Sand (Bluebird). March 24. Seventh foal. 38,000Y. Tattersalls October Book 2. A C Elliott. Closely related to the quite useful 10f winner Falkirk (by Montjeu) and half-sister to the fair 2-y-o 5f winners The Rising (by Pivotal) and Dansili Dual (by Dansili), and the moderate 5f winner Fearbuster (by Fastnet Rock). The dam, a winner of 4 races including the Group 2 6f Cherry Hinton Stakes and the Albany Stakes, is a half-sister to 4 winners including the German 3-y-o listed 6f winner Davignon. The second dam, Dancing Drop (by Green Desert), a useful dual 2-y-o 6f winner, was listed-placed and is a half-sister to 9 winners. (Mrs P Shanahan, M V Magnier, Mr C Brooks, Mr C Conroy). *"She's in the early batch of our 2-y-o's and the vibe about Camelot is good. This filly is bred to be early and we were delighted to buy a Camelot with that money, especially out of a Group 2 winner. I'm very happy to have her, she goes well and definitely has the boot for six furlongs".*

122. UNNAMED ★★★
b.c. First Defence – Seeking Ema (Seeking The Gold). April 28. Fourth foal. 38,000Y. Tattersalls December. A C Elliott. Half-brother to a winner in Peru by Arch. The dam was placed 9 times in the USA including in a minor stakes and is a half-sister to one winner. The second dam, Ema Bovary (by Edgy Diplomat), a Grade 2 and Grade 3 stakes winner in the USA, is a full or half-sister to 8 winners. *"He's a nice horse that'll take a bit of time. We haven't done a lot with him yet, but the mare's had two winners out of three because the 3-y-o has recently won and looks useful. This colt was a late April foal but he'll come to hand in the second half of the season. A fine, good-moving horse".*

123. UNNAMED ★★★
gr.f. Declaration Of War – Warling (Montjeu). February 18. Third foal. Half-sister to the fairly useful 2-y-o 7f winner Hayadh (by Oasis Dream). The dam, a fairly useful 11f winner, is closely related to the French 2-y-o 10f winner of 3 races and Group 3 Prix Exbury second War Is War and a half-sister to 3 winners. The second dam, Walkamia (by Linamix), won the Group 3 10.5f Prix Fille de l'Air and is a sister to 2 winners including the Group 2 11f Prix

Noailles winner Walk On Mix and a half-sister to 8 winners. (Mrs P Shanahan & M V Magnier). *"She hasn't arrived yet, she's in pre-training with Willie Browne but apparently she goes well and they really like her. So I wouldn't leave her out".*

JAMES BETHELL

124. FIRBY ★★
b.c. Rock Of Gibraltar – Huffoof (Dalakhani). March 31. First foal. 5,500Y. Tattersalls October Book 3. JDW Bethell. The dam, a fair 10f winner, is a half-sister to 3 winners. The second dam, Albahja (by Sinndar), a useful 12f winner, was second in the Group 3 10f Golden Daffodil Stakes and in the listed 12f Galtres Stakes and is a half-sister to 7 winners. *"Hopefully he'll make a 2-y-o by mid-season and you'd think he'd get ten furlongs next year. He's very well put-together and the reason we bought him was because he looks rather like a useful Rock Of Gibraltar horse I trained called Arlequin. He won five races".*

125. HARROGATE ★★★
br.c. Society Rock – Invincible Me (Invincible Spirit). April 18. Second foal. 60,000Y. Tattersalls October Book 2. J Bethell. Half-brother to the quite useful 2016 2-y-o 5f winner Monte Cinq (by Bushranger). The dam is an unplaced half-sister to 2 winners. The second dam, Megec Blis (by Soviet Star), a fairly useful Irish dual 7f winner, was third in the Group 3 Athasi Stakes and is a half-sister to 5 minor winners. *"The sire's started well because he's had a couple of winners already and at the breeze up sales they were selling well. This colt is nice but his knees aren't mature enough yet so we can't push him too hard, he should be out in mid-season and he'll definitely be a sprinter. He was fairly small and sharp, but he has grown a bit over the last month or so".*

126. HOWBAAR (USA) ★★★
b.c. Lonhro – Going Day (Daylami). March 23. Fifth foal. 55,000Y. Tattersalls October Book 1. J Bethell. Half-brother to the minor US stakes-placed winner Daylight Ride (by El Prado). The dam, a French listed-placed 10f winner, is a half-sister to 4 winners including the Japanese Group 2 winner and Group 1 second Albiano. The second dam,

Antics (by Unbridled), is an unraced half-sister to 6 winners including the US Grade 1 winners Arch and Acoma. (Mrs J A Tabet). *"A very nice, mid-season type, he'll be a seven furlong 2-y-o but he's shown us a bit and from what we've done I couldn't more pleased with him. He's a big horse, 16 hands and quite rangy".*

127. STRAWBERRYANDCREAM ★★★
ch.f. Cityscape – Miss Apricot (Indian Ridge). April 24. Sixth foal. 7,000Y. Tattersalls October Book 4. Not sold. Half-sister to the quite useful 5f and 6f winner of 5 races Apricot Sky (by Pastoral Pursuits), to the fair dual 5f winner at 2 and 3 yrs Fruit Salad, the modest 8.5f winner Charlcot (both by Monsieur Bond) and the moderate 1m winner Princess Peaches (by Notnowcato). The dam, placed fourth once over 6f from two starts, is a half-sister to 2 winners. The second dam, Mora (by Second Set), an Irish listed 1m winner, is a half-sister to 5 winners including the Irish listed winner Broadway Rosie. *"From a family we know well, this filly will be one for mid-season, she's a very good mover and reminds me a bit of Selkirk (the sire of Cityscape)".*

128. TOWTON (IRE) ★★★
b.c. Zebedee – Amber Tide (Pursuit Of Love). April 15. Eleventh foal. 60,000Y. Tattersalls October Book 2. J Bethell. Half-brother to the Irish Group 3 1m Amethyst Stakes and subsequent US Grade 2 1m winner Ferneley (by Ishiguru), to the fair 10f winner Brown Bee (by Camacho) and two minor 4-y-o winners in Hong Kong and the USA by Holy Roman Emperor and Encosta Del Lago. The dam, a fair 5f (at 2 yrs) to 10f placed maiden, is a half-sister to 7 winners including the French 2-y-o 1m winner and subsequent US Grade 2 San Clemente Handicap winner Uncharted Haven. The second dam, Tochar Ban (by Assert), a quite useful 10f winner, is a half-sister to 6 winners. (Towton Vickers and Clarke Partnership). *"The owner is a Yorkshireman and he wanted to name the horse after the battle of Towton where the Lancastrians were defeated! This horse is quite big, and not quite 'together' yet, but hopefully the more he does he'll strengthen. He's just a big baby at present, but I think he'll be out in mid-season, he'll probably be a sprinter and he goes quite well".*

129. ULSHAW BRIDGE ★★★★
b.c. High Chaparral – Sharaarah (Oasis Dream).
February 10. First foal. €30,000Y. Goffs Orby.
Sackville/Donald. The dam, a quite useful 6f
(at 2 yrs) and 5f winner of 4 races, is a half-
sister to 3 winners including the useful 2-y-o
5f winner and dual Group 2 placed Burwaaz.
The second dam, Nidhaal (by Observatory), a
very useful 2-y-o listed 6f winner and second
in the Group 3 6f Princess Margaret Stakes, is
a half-sister to 4 winners. *"He's quite sharp for
a High Chaparral, so perhaps he takes after
the damsire Oasis Dream. He goes nicely and
I should think he could be out in May, he's not
very big but well put-together and there's quite
a bit of speed in the family".*

130. WENSLEY ★★
b.c. Poet's Voice – Keladora (Crafty
Prospector). March 14. Sixth foal. 16,000Y.
Tattersalls October Book 3. JDW Bethell.
Half-brother to the fair 12f and 14f winner
Kelamita (by Pivotal), to the modest 12f to
14f winner of 3 races Coarse Cut (by Duke Of
Marmalade) and a minor winner at 3 and 4
yrs in Italy by Cape Cross. The dam, a French
listed-placed winner of 3 races, is a half-sister
to 4 winners including the Group 1 Prix Marcel
Boussac second On Verra. The second dam,
Karmifira (by Always Fair), winner of the listed
Prix Finlande and second in the French 1,000
Guineas, is a half-sister to 5 winners including
the listed 1m Prix Coronation winner Kart Star.
*"Fairly sharp, he had a small setback but he
seems fine now and hopefully I'll get him going
soon and he'll be out in May or June".*

131. UNNAMED ★★★
b.c. Worthadd – Capsaicin (Invincible Spirit).
March 5. First foal. £27,000Y. Goffs UK Premier
(Doncaster). Salcey Forest Stud. The dam is an
unraced half-sister to 5 winners including the
dam of the Group 2 May Hill Stakes winner
Agnes Stewart. The second dam, a quite
useful 2-y-o 6f winner, is a half-sister to 6
winners including the very smart Group 1 7f
National Stakes and Group 2 10f Tattersalls
Rogers Gold Cup winner Definite Article and
the Group winners Salford Express and Salford
City. *"He looked a really nice colt at the breeze
up, I should think he'll be out in early May
and he looks a six furlong type. A well-made
horse, he's really well put-together".* TRAINERS'
BARGAIN BUY

SAEED BIN SUROOR
(GODOLPHIN)
*Many thanks to the Godolphin Assistant
Trainer Tony Howarth for discussing these two-
year-olds with me.*

132. AL MUSTASHAR (IRE) ★★★★
b.c. Shamardal – Dresden Doll (Elusive
Quality). April 23. Fifth foal. Half-brother to
the 1m (at 2 yrs) and UAE Group 2 12f winner
Prize Money (by Authorized), to the quite
useful 2016 5f and 6f winner Dubai One and
the quite useful 6f and 7f winner Role Player
(both by Exceed And Excel). The dam, a fair
2-y-o 5f winner, is a half-sister to 9 winners
including the Irish 1,000 Guineas, Coronation
Stakes and Nassau Stakes winner Crimplene,
the Group 3 12.3f Chester Vase winner Dutch
Gold and the Group 2 12f Lancashire Oaks
second Loyal Spirit. The second dam, Crimson
Conquest (by Diesis), a quite useful 2-y-o 6f
winner, is a half-sister to the US stakes winner
Sword Blade. *"A very nice type, he's really
finding his feet, has a very good attitude and
shows some precocity to go with his size and
scope. A nice horse, he's starting to stand out
a little".*

133. BEAUTIFUL MEMORY (IRE) ★★★
b.f. Invincible Spirit – Express Way (ARG)
(Ahmad). March 16. Tenth foal. Half-sister to
the Group 1 7f Prix Jean-Luc Lagardere and
Italian dual Group 1 winner Rio De La Plata,
to the quite useful 2016 2-y-o 7f winner Voice
Of Truth (by Dubawi), the quite useful 2-y-o
7f winner Ihsas (both by Rahy), the Argentine
Grade 1 winner El Expresivo (by Candy
Stripes), the fairly useful 1m winner Expressly
(by Street Cry) and the fair 10f and 12f
winner Arabian Beauty (by Shamardal). The
dam, placed in Argentina, is a half-sister to 2
minor winners out of the unraced Escaline (by
Hawk). *"A nice, leggy individual, she won't be
particularly early but she's a good mover with
plenty of size and scope. An attractive filly".*

134. CARING TOUCH (USA) ★★★
f. Elusive Quality – Blue Petrel (Distorted
Humor). February 9. Second foal. The dam,
placed in France over 10f, is a sister to the US
2-y-o winner and Grade 1 Champagne Stakes
third Fortify and a half-sister to the US stakes
winner and Grade 3 placed Bay Of Plenty. The

second dam, Kotuku (by A P Indy), was placed in the USA a sister to the US 2-y-o 1m winner and Grade 3 placed Anasheed and a half-sister to 4 winners. *"Still a bit on the weak side so we won't be in any rush, she's one for the middle of the season and she's a good-looking, good-moving individual"*.

135. CILEOPATRA (IRE) ★★★★
b.f. Kodiac – Beatrix Potter (Cadeaux Genereux). April 16. Fifth foal. 160,000Y. Tattersalls October Book 2. John Ferguson. Half-sister to the 2016 2-y-o Group 2 6f Mill Reef Stakes winner Harry Angel (by Dark Angel) and to the fair 10f winner Golden Journey (by Nayef). The dam is a placed half-sister to 3 winners including the 2-y-o Group 2 7f Vintage Stakes and subsequent Hong Kong dual Group 1 1m winner Xtension. The second dam, Great Joy (by Grand Lodge), won at 3 yrs in Germany and was listed placed and is a half-sister to 4 winners. *"A nice, sharp-looking type, she's going well at present. She's just gone into fast work and could be one of our first 2-y-o fillies to run. Shows natural speed"*.

136. DESERT MOUNTAIN ★★★
b.c. Epaulette – Al Andalyya (Kingmambo). April 29. Third foal. 120,000Y. Tattersalls October Book 2. John Ferguson. Half-brother to the smart 2016 2-y-o Group 3 1m Autumn Stakes winner and Group 1 Criterium de Saint-Cloud second Best Solution (by Kodiac). The dam, a modest 6f (at 2 yrs) and 8.5f fourth-placed maiden, is a half-sister to 4 winners including the Group 2 Prix Hocquart second Cape Clear Island. The second dam, Kushnarenkovo (by Sadler's Wells), a fairly useful 12f winner, was second in the Group 3 12f Noblesse Stakes and is a sister to the Group 1 Racing Post Trophy and St Leger winner Brian Boru and a half-sister to the Group 2 winners Sea Moon and Moon Search and to the unraced dam of the Derby and Prix de l'Arc de Triomphe winner Workforce. *"Quite a tall, leggy, good-moving colt, he's cantering daily at present and does everything easily but isn't one to be rushed. A nice type"*.

137. ELECTRICAL STORM (IRE) ★★★★
b.br.c. Cape Cross – Theola (Kalanisi). April 28. Fourth foal. €140,000Y. Goffs November. John Ferguson. Half-brother to the French 10.5f and

12f winner Theomour (by Azamour). The dam, a quite useful winner of four races at around 2m, is a half-sister to 5 winners including the 14f winner and Group 2 Beresford Stakes second Orgilgo Bay. The second dam, Third Dimension (by Suave Dancer), a minor French 3-y-o winner, is a half-sister to 7 winners. *"A nice, slender, forward-going 2-y-o. It's looking like he could be one of the better types and the little we've asked of him he does easily. We wouldn't be in a rush with him but he's a nice type with a good action"*.

138. JALAAD (IRE) ★★★★
b.c. Kodiac – Surrey Storm (Montjeu). April 1. Second foal. 200,000Y. Tattersalls October Book 2. John Ferguson. Half-brother to the modest 2016 2-y-o 1m winner Booshbash (by Dark Angel). The dam, a minor French 3-y-o winner, is a half-sister to 2 winners including the French listed winner Andry Brusselles. The second dam, Dont Dili Dali (by Dansili), a very useful 7f (at 2 yrs) and listed 1m Masaka Stakes winner, was third in the Group 3 Dahlia Stakes and is a half-sister to 5 winners. *"Not the biggest but with a strong top line, he's showing precocity and does everything with ease at present. One to go forward with and hopefully he'll run in early May"*.

139. KASER (IRE) ★★★
b.c. Invincible Spirit – Lethal Quality (Elusive Quality). March 11. Fourth foal. €500,000Y. Goffs Orby. John Ferguson. Brother to the useful 2016 2-y-o maiden Promising, placed second in the Group 3 7f Prestige Stakes. The dam, a US stakes-placed winner of 3 races at 3 and 4 yrs, is a half-sister to 2 winners. The second dam, Lethal Temper (by Seattle Slew), a winner of 3 minor races at 3 and 4 yrs in the USA, is a half-sister to 8 winners including the very smart colt Diffident, winner of the Group 3 6f Diadem Stakes and the Group 3 6f Prix de Ris-Orangis. *"A nice moving individual, not over-big and still with some developing to do, but he's cantering daily and is one for the middle part of the season. Possibly a seven furlong type"*.

140. MAJOR PARTNERSHIP (IRE) ★★★
gr.c. Iffraaj – Roystonea (Polish Precedent). April 9. Ninth foal. 200,000 foal. Tattersalls December. John Ferguson. Half-brother to the

smart 2-y-o Group 2 1m Royal Lodge Stakes winner Foundation (by Zoffany), to the fairly useful 2-y-o 7f winner Misterioso (by Iffraaj), the fairly useful 7f (at 2 yrs) to 8.5f winner Vastonea (by Verglas), the quite useful Irish 2-y-o 7f winner Take A Chance (by Hawk Wing) and a minor 2-y-o winner abroad by Xaar. The dam, a listed-placed winner of 2 races over 7f and 1m in France, is a half-sister to 4 winners including the French listed winners Bermuda Grass and Bermuda Rye. The second dam, Alleluia Tree (by Royal Academy), a French 2-y-o winner, is a half-sister to 7 winners and to the unraced dam of the triple Group 1 winner Scorpion. *"A nice, good-topped individual with good bone, he's not to be rushed and is a mid-season prospect. A good mover but still a little backward at present".*

141. MILITARY BAND ★★★★
ch.c. New Approach – Rhadegunda (Pivotal). May 1. Fifth living foal. 80,000Y. Tattersalls December. John Ferguson. Half-brother to the promising 2016 2-y-o 1m winner on his only start Cracksman (by Frankel), to the useful 2-y-o Group 3 7f Solario Stakes winner Fantastic Moon (by Dalakhani) and the quite useful 10f winner Strong Force (by Sea The Stars). The dam, a fairly useful dual 1m winner here, won a listed 9f event in France and is a half-sister to 5 winners. The second dam, St Radegund (by Green Desert), a fairly useful 7f winner, is a half-sister to 7 winners including the very useful listed 6f Sirenia Stakes winner Art of War. *"Not over-big but he's a good moving horse who is doing everything nicely at present. Looks a nice prospect and one that could get his first run in May, probably over six furlongs. A nice horse".*

142. MO'AFFEFF ★★★★
b.c. Acclamation – Map Of Heaven (Pivotal). January 19. Third foal. 90,000Y. Tattersalls October Book 2. John Ferguson. Brother to the quite useful 2-y-o 6f winner Field Of Stars and half-brother to the quite useful 2016 2-y-o 6f winner, from one start, Pennsylvania Dutch (by Dutch Art). The dam, a fair 7f winner, is a sister to the very useful Group 3 5f Molecomb Stakes and Group 3 5f King George Stakes winner Enticing and a half-sister to 5 winners including the useful listed 1m winner and Group 3 7f Jersey Stakes second Sentaril.

The second dam, Superstar Leo (by College Chapel), a very smart 2-y-o, won the Group 2 5f Flying Childers Stakes, the Group 3 Norfolk Stakes and the Weatherbys Super Sprint and is a full or half sister to 10 winners. *"A nice moving individual, we're not in a real rush with him but we think a lot of him and he's doing everything easily so far".*

143. MOQARRAB (USA) ★★★★
b.br.c. Speightstown – Grosse Pointe Anne (Silver Deputy). May 1. Third foal. $400,000Y. Keeneland September. Shadwell Estate Co. Half-brother to the US sakes-placed winner Indian Annie (by Indian Charlie). The dam, a minor US 3-y-o winner, is a half-sister to the US Grade 1 Breeders' Cup Juvenile and Grade 1 Champagne Stakes winner Uncle Mo. The second dam, Playa Maya (by Arch), was a US stakes-placed winner of 3 races. *"Probably the most precocious and forward going of our 2-y-o's at present, he's very sharp and could be our first runner. He's not just an early type either – he looks to have a bit of quality".*

144. MOSEEB (IRE) ★★★
b.c. Invincible Spirit – Boastful (Clodovil). February 21. First foal. €190,000 foal. Goffs November. John Ferguson. The dam, a useful listed 1m winner, is a half-sister to 4 winners including the Group 3 6f Ballyogan Stakes and dual listed winner and Group 1 second Lesson In Humility and the Group 3 Oh So Sharp Stakes winner Poet's Vanity. The second dam, Vanity (by Thatching), a fair 5f and 6f placed maiden, is a half-sister to 6 winners including the listed winner Ffestiniog (herself the dam of 3 stakes winners). *"A nice, powerful, straightforward type and one that will probably come to hand quickly. We're in no rush at present though and he moves well".*

145. TASNEEM ★★★★★
ch.c. Teofilo – Almass (Elnadim). April 13. Sixth foal. Brother to the fair 1m winner Amaany. The dam, a smart listed 7f and listed 1m winner, is a half-sister to numerous winners including the very smart dual listed 10f winner and dual Group 1 placed Volochine and the listed winners Kahtan, Sakha and Ghataas. The second dam, Harmless Albatross (by Pas de Seul), won the Group 3 1m Prix des Chenes at 2 yrs and a 1m listed event at 3 yrs and is a

half-sister to the Group 2 10f Prix d'Harcourt winner Fortune's Wheel. *"A really well put together colt, he moves particularly well and finds everything easy at present. We won't be in any rush with him but with the little he's done he shows potential quality. A five-star horse in my book".*

146. TEAM DECISION (IRE) ★★★
ch.c. Teofilo – Precipitous (Indian Ridge). March 23. Eighth foal. €50,000 foal. Goffs November. John Ferguson. Brother to the Group 3 Brownstown Stakes winner Tobann and half-brother to the quite useful 2-y-o 6f winner Cardigan (by Barathea). The dam, a quite useful Irish 7f and 1m winner, is a half-sister to 6 winners. The second dam, Dathuil (by Royal Academy), a fairly useful 1m winner, was subsequently Grade 3 placed in the USA and is a half-sister to 6 winners including the 2-y-o listed 6f winner and Group 1 placed Luminata. *"A good-moving sort who is showing some speed at present, he's very forward-going with a nice attitude".*

147. ZAHEE ★★★
b.c. Iffraaj – Havin' A Good Time (Jeremy). March 22. Second foal. 200,000Y. Tattersalls October Book 1. John Ferguson. Half-brother to the modest 2016 5f placed 2-y-o Poppy Pivot (by Pivotal). The dam, a fair triple 5f winner, is a half-sister to 9 winners including the Group 1 Haydock Park Sprint winner G Force, the US Grade 3 Miesque Stakes winner Louvain (herself dam of the dual Group 1 winner Flotilla) and the useful listed 10f winner Laajooj. The second dam, Flanders (by Common Grounds), winner of the listed Scarbrough Stakes and second in the Group 2 King's Stand Stakes, is a half-sister to 8 winners. *"This colt has size, scope and a big stride. He's a bit unfurnished and may need a bit of time but he's doing everything with ease at present".*

148. UNNAMED ★★★★
b.f. Shamardal – Eastern Joy (Dubai Destination). April 16. Fifth foal. Sister to the 2-y-o Group 3 1m May Hill Stakes winner and Group 1 Fillies' Mile third Ihtimal and half-sister to the 2016 2-y-o Group 1 7f Criterium International and 2017 UAE Group 2 9.5f winner Thunder Snow (by Helmet), to the 2-y-o Group 3 7f Oh So Sharp Stakes winner First Victory (by Teofilo) and the very useful listed-placed triple 1m winner at 2 and 3 yrs Always Smile (by Cape Cross). The dam, placed fourth over 11f in France, is a half-sister to 6 winners including the Group 1 10.5f Prix de Diane winner West Wind and the very useful listed 12f winner Redbridge. The second dam, Red Slippers (by Nureyev), a Group 2 10f Sun Chariot Stakes winner, is a sister to the Derby third Romanov and closely related to the Oaks and Irish Derby winner Balanchine. *"A fantastic looking filly with plenty of bone and a good, strong top line. She's done very little so far but she's very well-related and is one for the middle-to-back-end of the season starting over seven furlongs".*

149. UNNAMED ★★★
c. Kitten's Joy – Tanaami (Elusive Quality). February 22. Second foal. The dam, a fair 1m winner, a half-sister to the US Grade 1 9f Queen Elizabeth II Challenge Cup winner Alwajeeha out of Ridaa (by Seattle Slew). *"Although in the forward group at present it wouldn't surprise me if he just started growing again. He's showing enough to suggest he's one of the nicer types. A nice moving colt with good bone".*

JIM BOLGER
150. BACK AT DAWN (IRE)
b.f. Dawn Approach – Yes Oh Yes (Gone West). March 17. Half-sister to the quite useful 2-y-o 7f winner Theodorico (by Teofilo). The dam is an unraced half-sister to 4 winners including the Group/Grade 3 placed Aaroness and Sumba Sunset. The second dam, Diamonds For Lil (by Summer Squall), a minor US 2-y-o winner, is a half-sister to 5 winners. (Mrs J S Bolger).

151. DECKED (IRE)
ch.f. Teofilo – Bedecked (Holy Roman Emperor). January 11. First foal. €75,000Y. Goffs Orby. BBA (Ire). The dam, a modest 6.5f and 7f placed 2-y-o, is a half-sister to the Group 3 Somerville Tattersall Stakes winner Sanus Per Aquam. The second dam, Fainne (by Peintre Celebre), ran once unplaced and is a half-sister to the champion 2-y-o and 2,000 Guineas winner Dawn Approach and the Group 2 Futurity Stakes winner Herald The Dawn. (Mrs J S Bolger).

152. IMPACTFUL (IRE)
b.c. Iffraaj – Take Flight (Pivotal). February 6. Third foal. €80,000Y. Goffs Orby. Bobby O'Ryan. Half-brother to the 2016 Irish 7f placed 2-y-o Tradfest (by High Chaparral) and to the 2-y-o Group 3 6f Round Tower Stakes winner and Group 2 Criterium de Maisons-Laffitte third Smash Williams (by Fracas). The dam, a fair 2-y-o 5f winner, is a half-sister to 6 winners including the Irish 1,000 Guineas winner Saoire. The second dam, Polish Descent (by Danehill), is an unraced half-sister to 4 winners. (Mrs J S Bolger).

153. LUCEITA (IRE)
ch.f. Dawn Approach – Lura (Street Cry). April 13. Half-sister to the smart 2-y-o Group 2 7f Rockfel Stakes winner and multiple Group 1 placed Lucida (by Shamardal). The dam was unplaced on her only start and is a half-sister to 3 winners including the multiple US Grade 1 winner English Channel and the US Grade 2 placed Sedgefield. The second dam, Belva (by Theatrical), is an unraced sister to the US Grade 1 winner Pharma and to the multiple US Grade 2 winner Hap and a half-sister to 5 winners. (Godolphin).

154. MEET AT DAWN (IRE)
b.f. Dawn Approach – Imeall Na Speire (Galileo). March 19. Fourth foal. Half-sister to the 2016 2-y-o 7f winner and Group 3 7f CL & MF Weld Park Stakes second Legitimus (by Lawman). The dam is an unraced sister to 2 winners including the Group 3 12f Blue Wind Stakes and 9.5f listed winner Galatee. The second dam, Altana (by Mountain Cat), is an unplaced half-sister to the top-class Grade 1 10f Breeders' Cup Classic, Group 1 9f Prix d'Ispahan and Group 2 10f Prix Eugene Adam winner Arcangues and the very useful Group 3 10f Prix de Psyche winner and French 1,000 Guineas and Prix de Diane placed Agathe. (Mrs J S Bolger).

155. NATIONAL SECURITY (IRE)
ch.c. Teofilo – Halla Siamsa (Montjeu). May 28. Brother to the very smart 2-y-o Group 1 7f Dewhurst Stakes winner Parish Hall, to the useful 2-y-o 1m winner and Group 2 Futurity Stakes third Hall Of Fame and to fairly useful listed-placed 9f (at 2 yrs) and 10f winner Siamsaiocht,. The dam, a quite useful Irish 10f winner, is a half-sister to the Group 2 Irish Derby Trial winner Light Heavy. The second dam, Siamsa (by Quest For Fame), a fair Irish 9f and 11f winner, is a half-sister to 4 winners. (Godolphin).

156. PLEISIUR (IRE)
b.f. Vocalised – Toirneach (Thunder Gulch). February 2. Fourth foal. Sister to the fair dual 10f winner Brontide and half-sister to the Group 1 Irish 1,000 Guineas and Yorkshire Oaks winner Pleascach (by Teofilo). The dam, a fairly useful Irish 7f (at 2 yrs) and 10f winner, is a half-sister to 2 minor winners in the USA. The second dam, Wandering Pine (by Country Pine), won at 3 yrs in the USA and is a half-sister to 4 winners including the listed winner and high-class broodmare Drina (the dam of 3 Group winners including the dual US Grade 1 winner Spain). (Mrs J S Bolger).

157. SCRIOBH NUA (IRE)
b.f. New Approach – Scribonia (Danehill). February 16. Tenth foal. €675,000Y. Goffs Orby. Peter & Ross Doyle. Closely related to 6 winners including the Irish 2-y-o 7f winner, Coronation Stakes second and 1,000 Guineas third Gile Na Greine, the 2-y-o dual Group 3 6f winner and 1,000 Guineas second Cuis Ghaire, the Group 3 9f Meld Stakes winner and Group 1 Moyglare Stud Stakes second Scintillula, the smart listed 12f winner The Major General and the Irish 1m winner and dual Group 3 placed Claiomh Solais (all by Galileo). The dam is an unraced half-sister to 7 winners including the 2-y-o listed 6f winner and dual Group 1 placed Luminata. The second dam, Smaoineamh (by Tap On Wood), a 2-y-o 6f winner, is a half-sister the champion sprinter Double Form. (Mrs J S Bolger).

158. VENETIAN ROCK (IRE)
b.c. Fastnet Rock – Marina Of Venice (Galileo). May 19. Half-brother to the fairly useful 2016 Irish 2-y-o 7f winner Vociferous Marina (by Vocalised) and to the useful dual 6f winner at 2 and 3 yrs and listed-placed Focus On Venice (by Intense Focus). The dam, a fairly useful 2-y-o 7f winner, is a half-sister to numerous winners including the useful listed winner Dawnus. The second dam, the French 1m winner Dame's Violet (by Groom Dancer), is a full or half-sister to 6 winners including the Group 2 Princess Of Wales's Stakes winner Wagon Master. (Mrs J S Bolger).

MARCO BOTTI

159. CHABUCA GRANDA ★★★
ch.f. Zoffany – Red Roxanne (Rock Of
Gibraltar). March 4. Second foal. £36,000Y.
Goffs UK Premier (Doncaster). Not sold.
Half-sister to the moderate 2016 5f to 7f
placed 2-y-o Black Redstart (by Big Bad Bob).
The dam is an unraced half-sister to a minor
winner abroad. The second dam, Virtuosity (by
Pivotal), a quite useful 10f winner, is a sister
to the Group 1 1m Lockinge Stakes winner
Virtual, closely related to the very smart 2-y-o
Group 2 6f Coventry Stakes winner and Group
1 6f Middle Park Stakes third Iceman and a
half-sister to 3 winners. *"A nice type, she's been
very straightforward and she goes well. She's
out of a Rock Of Gibraltar mare so she'll need
a bit of time and is one for seven furlongs in
mid-summer".*

160. CLOUD EIGHT ★★★
b.c. Dream Ahead – Night Cam (Night Shift).
March 14. Fourth foal. 42,000Y. Tattersalls
October Book 2. Barberini Bloodstock. Half-
brother to the Irish 7f (at 2 yrs) and Hong
Kong 6f winner Oriental Fantasia (by Holy
Roman Emperor) and to the modest dual 1m
winner at 2 and 3 yrs Camrock Star (by Rock
Of Gibraltar). The dam, placed fourth once
over 7f at 2 yrs in Ireland, is a half-sister to 5
winners including the 2-y-o Group 3 7f C L
Weld Park Stakes and 3-y-o 6f listed winner
and Group 1 7f Moyglare Stud Stakes second
Ugo Fire. The second dam, Quiet Mouse (by
Quiet American), is an unraced half-sister to 7
winners including the smart broodmare Witch
Of Fife (the dam of 3 stakes winners). (Classic
Racing, Night Cam). *"A strong, powerful colt.
My impression is that he might just need a bit
of give in the ground but he goes nicely and
needs a bit of time because his knees are still
open. It's hard to say what sort of trip he'll
want and we're in no hurry with him so he'll
probably be a July type, starting at six furlongs.
Going nicely, but he hasn't done any fast work".*

161. CYCLADES (IRE) ★★
b.f. Bated Breath – Parakopi (Green Desert).
March 19. Fifth foal. €31,000Y. Tattersalls
Ireland September. Jamie Lloyd. Half-sister
to the modest 7f to 8.5f winner of 5 races
Tanawar (by Elusive City). The dam, a minor
winner at 3 yrs in Germany, is a half-sister to

2 winners abroad. The second dam, Siringas
(by Barathea), won the Group 2 Nassau Stakes
and the listed Brownstown Stakes and is a
half-sister to 4 winners. (Fabfive). *"She was
very unfurnished when she came in and hasn't
done a lot so she'll take time. She's a big, fine
filly but one for the back-end of the season. I
like the stallion, we have a nice 3-y-o by him
called Unabated".*

162. EARLY DAWN ★★★
ch.f. Dawn Approach – Born Something
(Caerleon). April 22. Ninth foal. 60,000Y.
Tattersalls October Book 1. Scuderia Vittadini.
Half-sister to the quite useful 2016 2-y-o 8.5f
winner Red Label (by Dubawi), to the UAE
listed-placed 10f winner Tarbawi (by Anabaa)
and the quite useful 7f (at 2 yrs) and 1m
winner Best Example (by King's Best). The
dam, a winner of 4 races in France and the
USA and third in the Group 3 Prix de la Grotte,
is a sister to the Group 3 Prix Cleopatre winner
Gold Round and a half-sister to 10 winners
including the outstanding multiple Group
1 winner Goldikova and the Group 1 Prix
Vermeille winner Galikova. The second dam,
Born Gold (by Blushing Groom), won over 8.3f
and is a sister to the Group 1 1m Prix Marcel
Boussac and Group 1 1m Coronation Stakes
winner Gold Splash. (Scuderia Vittadini SRL).
*"Very athletic with a good temperament and
straightforward. Not a five furlong filly, but
more of a June/July type 2-y-o and so far she's
doing everything nicely. She shows ability but
it's early days yet".*

163. EESHA BEAUTY (IRE) ★★★★
b.f. Born To Sea – Eastern Glow (Cape Cross).
April 3. Third foal. €28,000Y. Tattersalls Ireland
September. Jamie Lloyd. Sister to Time To Sea,
last on her only start at 2 yrs in 2016. The
dam ran once unplaced and is a half-sister to
3 winners. The second dam, Come What May
(by Selkirk), a modest 5f winner, is a sister to
the very smart 2-y-o Group 2 7f Champagne
Stakes winner Etlaala and to the useful 7f and
1m winner and listed-placed Selective and
a half-sister to 5 winners. *"A very strong filly,
she's quite forward and showing some speed
so we're about to step her up in work with a
view to running her in late April. She's quite
sweet and everything she's doing so far is nice".*
TRAINERS' BARGAIN BUY

164. ELUSIF (IRE) ★★★
b.c. Elusive Quality – Appealing (Bertolini).
April 13. First foal. The dam, a fairly useful
dual 7f winner at 2 and 3 yrs, was third in the
Group 3 Oak Tree Stakes and second in the
Grade 2 Yellow Ribbon Handicap. She is a
half-sister to the 2-y-o Group 3 5f Cornwallis
Stakes winner Electric Waves. The second dam,
Radiant Energy (by Spectrum), a 1m winner
at 3 yrs, is a half-sister to 6 winners. (Mrs Y
M G Jacques). *"Not the biggest, he's quite
small but he's done well since we got him as a
yearling. I trained the dam who was a seven
furlong filly and I think this colt will want seven
furlongs or a mile later on. He has a very good
temperament, I like the way he moves and
he's probably one for the middle of the season
onwards".*

165. GALACTIC SPIRIT ★★★
ch.c. Dutch Art – Gino's Spirits (Perugino).
March 31. Eleventh foal. 40,000Y. Tattersalls
December. Not sold. Half-brother to 8 winners
including the 9f (at 2 yrs) and subsequent US
Grade 1 9f and Group 1 Singapore Airlines
International Cup winner Gitano Hernando,
the fairly useful 11f and 14f winner Sizzler
(both by Hernando), the useful 12f and 14f
winner Battersea (by Galileo) and the minor
Italian winner of 8 races from 2 to 5 yrs India
Spirit (by Dr Fong). The dam won 9 races here
and in the USA including the Grade 3 Noble
Damsel Handicap and was second in the
Group 2 Sun Chariot Stakes and is a half-sister
to 5 winners. The second dam, Rising Spirits
(by Cure The Blues), a fair 2-y-o 7f winner,
later won in the USA and is a half-sister to 6
winners including the dual Group 3 winner
and Group 1 placed Citidancer. (Newsells Park
Stud). *"He's a very attractive colt and we've
done well with the family through Gitano
Hernando. Knowing the family he'll take a bit
of time but he's by Dutch Art and seems more
forward at this stage than Gitano Hernando
was. So I'm very pleased with him, he canters
nicely and we'll set him off over seven furlongs
in mid-summer. He's showing ability, so we're
quite pleased with him at this early stage".*

166. HEEYAAM ★★★
b.f. Invincible Spirit – Shalwa (Galileo). March
3. First foal. The dam, a fair maiden, was
placed 6 times from 10f to 12f and is a sister

to the Group 2 Prix Vicomtesse Vigier and
triple Group 3 winner (including at 2 yrs) Kite
Wood and to the useful 9f winner and Group
2 Great Voltigeur Stakes third Odeon and
half-sister to 3 winners. The second dam, Kite
Mark (by Mark Of Esteem), ran once unplaced
and is a half-sister to the dual Group 2 winner
Madame Dubois (dam of the Group 1 winners
Indian Haven and Count Dubois) and the
dam of the Richmond Stakes winner Daggers
Drawn. *"She's done really well because when
we broke her in she was a little bit small and
weak but she's really got stronger in the past
couple of months. Out of a Galileo mare, I'm
very pleased with her and she's a good mover,
so she'll be a nice filly in time. It's a middle-
distance family and I think she'll need seven
furlongs to begin with".*

167. HOULTON ★★★
ch.c. Declaration Of War – Greek Goddess
(Galileo). March 4. First foal. 50,000Y.
Tattersalls October Book 2. Jamie Lloyd. The
dam, a quite useful 2-y-o 1m winner, is a
half-sister to 3 minor winners. The second
dam, Beauty Bright (by Danehill), an Irish 5f (at
2 yrs) and Group 3 6f winner, is a full or half-
sister to 7 winners including the listed Queen's
Vase winner and Group 1 second Aloft. *"A
huge colt, he'll take time but he's a nice mover
and we like him. He hasn't done anything
wrong but he's one for the second half of the
season over seven furlongs".*

168. JELLMOOD ★★★★
b.c. Acclamation – Emotif (Giant's Causeway).
March 3. First foal. The dam was a 2-y-o 7f
winner in South Africa and is a half-sister to
the fairly useful 10f, 2m and jumps winner
Salesin. The second dam, Elistia (by Ride The
Rails), a Grade 2 1m winner in Argentina, is a
half-sister to the champion South African filly/
mare Empress Club. *"He's one we're hoping will
be an early type. He's very strong, looks a 2-y-o
and he's taken the fast work we've given him
really well. He has speed, so if all goes well we'll
have him on the track by the end of April".*

169. LADY FARHH ★★★
b.f. Farhh – Monjouet (Montjeu). April 9.
Fifth foal. Half-sister to the useful listed 5f
(in Italy at 2 yrs) and listed 1m winner Lady
Dutch (by Dutch Art), to the Italian winner

and 2-y-o listed 1m second Wiston (by Hawk Wing) and the minor Italian winner at 2 and 3 yrs Capitan Jack (by Dubawi). The dam is an unplaced half-sister to 5 winners in Italy. The second dam, Alberelle (by Rudimentary), a 2-y-o winner in France and third in the Group 3 Prix Du Bois, is a half-sister to 3 winners. *"A half-sister to Lady Dutch who won a listed race for us, she's still very unfurnished and weak but a good mover and has ability. I don't think we'll do anything with her until later on, she has a long stride and I'd say she'll want at least a mile".*

170. LITTLE POEM ★★
b.f. Holy Roman Emperor – Gerika (Galileo). April 8. €58,000Y. SGA September (Italy). Not sold. Half-sister to the fair 2016 2-y-o 7f winner Pirate Look (by Canford Cliffs). The dam, a 10f winner in Italy, is a half-sister to 6 winners including the Italian triple listed 1m winner Donoma and the Italian dual listed 10f winner Right Connection. The second dam, Green Tern (by Miswaki Tern), won once at 2 yrs in Italy and is a full or half-sister to 8 winners including the Group 3 Italian St Leger winner Green Senor. *"Disappointing physically because she was small at the sales and she hasn't grown much, but she moves nicely and we'll step her up during April. She moves well and she's coping OK but she's probably the type that will win a race or two but not with black type".*

171. LOSINGMYRELIGION (FR) ★★★
b.c. Planteur – Marie Dar (Sinndar). March 1. Third foal. €28,000Y. Arqana Deauville August. A Botti. The dam is an unraced half-sister to 6 winners including the Group 2 Prix d'Harcourt winner and triple Group 1 placed Ana Marie. The second dam, Marie De Ken (by Kendor), won the Group 3 Prix Fille de l'Air and is a half-sister to 12 winners. *"A nice type, I like him as an individual and knowing the sire he'll need seven furlongs and a bit of time. He has a very easy action, he's light on his feet and we like him a lot. One for the second part of the season".*

172. SWEET SYMPHONY ★★★
ch.f. Helmet – Solfilia (Teofilo). February 16. Second foal. 32,000Y. Tattersalls October Book 3. Marco Botti. The dam, a quite useful 2-y-o

6f winner, is a half-sister to 2 winners. The second dam, Suntory (by Royal Applause), an Irish 6f and 7f winner, is a half-sister to 7 winners including Fracas (Group 2 Derrinstown Stud Derby Trial). (Mr C J Murfitt). *"She's a good-looking filly that didn't cost a lot and she's taking her time because she's still a bit weak, but I like her. She has a good attitude and her sire is doing well. It's difficult to assess what trip she'll want, but I think she'll come to hand from July onwards".*

173. VOLEVO LUI ★★★
b.c. Farhh – Veronica Franco (Lomitas). April 14. Sixth foal. 50,000Y. Tattersalls October Book 2. Scuderia Blueberry. Half-brother to 3 winners in Italy including the Group 3 placed Vola E Va (by Oratorio) and the dual listed-placed Valuta Pregiata (by Holy Roman Emperor). The dam, a minor 3-y-o winner in Italy, is a half-sister to 3 other minor winners. The second dam, Gravette (by Kris), a fair triple 1m winner, is a half-sister to 6 winners including the Italian dual Group 1 winner Welsh Guide. *"Quite a rangy, tall horse that has a bit of a knee action which suggests he may need a bit of juice in the ground. He definitely wants a trip and has 3-y-o written all over him. He'll be a nice 2-y-o, but for much later in the season over seven furlongs to start with".*

174. UNNAMED ★★★
b.c. Oasis Dream – Applauded (Royal Applause). March 23. Sixth foal. 90,000Y. Tattersalls October Book 1. Jamie Lloyd. Brother to the quite useful 2-y-o 7f and subsequent US stakes winner Mirage and half-brother to the fairly useful 2016 Irish 3-y-o 6f winner Alphabet (by Lawman), the quite useful 2-y-o 6f winner (here) and subsequent minor US stakes winner Amnesia (by Invincible Spirit), the modest 1m winner Reddot Express (by Iffraaj) and the French 10f and 12.5f winner Arthur The King (by Medicean). The dam, a quite useful 2-y-o 7f winner, is a half-sister to the Group 1 National Stakes winner Power, the Grade 1 E P Taylor Stakes winner Curvy and the Group 2 winner and Thakafaat. The second dam, Frappe (by Inchinor), a fairly useful 2-y-o 6f winner, is a half-sister to Footstepsinthesand (2,000 Guineas) and Pedro The Great (Phoenix Stakes). *"A nice type, he's very compact and*

looks a 2-y-o. We're not pushing him at this stage but I'm sure once we step him up he'll come to hand quickly. His pedigree suggests he'll be a six/seven furlong type".

175. UNNAMED ★★★★

br.c. Footstepsinthesand – Think Again (Dubawi). March 6. First foal. €40,000Y. Tattersalls Ireland September. Jamie Lloyd. The dam, placed fourth once over 5f at 2 yrs, is out of the quite useful Irish 2-y-o 7f winner Maziona (by Dansili), herself a half-sister to 5 winners including the Group 3 Gordon Stakes winner The Geezer. *"Not the biggest colt, but he's quite stocky and well put-together. He's going nicely and we'll probably step him up in fast work in time for six furlongs in June. Everything he's doing is pleasing and he seems very straightforward".*

DAVID BROWN

176. BIB AND TUCKER ★★★

br.c. Dandy Man – Dhuyoof (Sinndar). April 21. Sixth foal. €20,000Y. Goffs Sportsmans. David Brown. Half-brother to the Group 3 Premio Parioli winner Salford Secret (by Sakhee's Secret) and to the fair 9.5f (at 2 yrs) and hurdles winner Gioia Di Vita (Sakhee). The dam is an unraced half-sister to 3 minor winners. The second dam, Chatifa (by Titus Livius), a quite useful 1m winner, is a half-sister to 6 winners including the Group 1 winners Homecoming Queen (1,000 Guineas), Queen's Logic (Cheveley Park Stakes) and the top-class Dylan Thomas. (J C Fretwell). *"A medium-sized colt with good conformation, he's be a nice, five furlong 2-y-o".*

177. CREEL ★★

b.c. Aussie Rules – Spate Rise (Speightstown). February 11. Third foal. 3,000 foal. Tattersalls December. Not sold. The dam is an unraced half-sister to two minor winners in the USA and to the modest 2-y-o 6f winner X Raise. The second dam, Raise (by Seattle Slew), a minor US winner at 4 yrs, is a half-sister to 7 winners including the Irish Group 2 Railway Stakes winner Lizard Island and to the dams of the US Grade 1 winner Corinthian and the Group 3 Ballycorus Stakes winner Six Of Hearts. (Peter Onslow). *"One for the second half of the season, he's a big colt that'll need some time and he'll be a miler later on".*

178. HARD GRAFT ★★★

ch.c. Lethal Force – Molly Brown (Rudimentary). April 16. Twelfth foal. 50,000Y. Tattersalls October Book 3. J C Fretwell. Half-brother to 8 winners including the smart 2-y-o dual 6f winner and Group 2 Mill Reef Stakes second Doctor Brown (by Dr Fong), the fairly useful 6f (at 2 yrs) and 1m winner Insaaf (by Averti) and the quite useful 2-y-o 6f winners Brazen (by Kyllachy), Bright Moll (dam of the Group 3 winner Aeolus) and Ballyalla (both by Mind Games). The dam, a fairly useful 5f (at 2 yrs) and 6f winner, is a half-sister to 4 winners including the listed 1m Premio Nearco winner Stato King. The second dam, Sinking (by Midyan), is an unraced half-sister to 3 winners. (J C Fretwell). *"A nice, well-made, strong colt for the second half of the season over six furlongs".*

179. HEADWEAR (IRE) ★★★

ch.f. Helmet – Indian Dumaani (Indian Ridge). April 28. Third foal. 30,000Y. Tattersalls October Book 3. J C Fretwell. Half-sister to the modest 10f (at 2 yrs) to 2m winner of 3 races Masterson (by Lawman). The dam won four minor races at 2 and 3 yrs in Italy and is a half-sister to 2 other minor winners. The second dam, Mubadalah (by Dumaani), a modest 7f fourth placed 2-y-o, is a half-sister to 8 winners including the Group 1 Queen Elizabeth Stakes II winner Maroof. (J C Fretwell). *"A lovely filly, I think she'll be very nice. She's quite big and wasn't an early foal, so we won't see her out until the second half of the season".*

180. MAKE GOOD (IRE) ★★

b.c. Fast Company – Rectify (Mujadil). March 12. Seventh foal. €31,000Y. Goffs Sportsmans. John Fretwell. Half-brother to the fair 5f (at 2 yrs) to 7f winner of 7 races Transfixed (by Trans Island) and to the modest triple 6f winner Red Tide (by Tamayuz). The dam is an unraced half-sister to 6 minor winners. The second dam, Sacristy (by Godswalk), is a placed half-sister to 8 winners including the Group 1 winners Alydaress, Desirable and Park Appeal (the dam of Cape Cross). (J C Fretwell). *"A fine, big colt and more of a 3-y-o type I'd say. He's a strong horse but one for the back-end of the season as a 2-y-o".*

181. MUCH BETTER ★★★
b.f. Exceed And Excel – Mawaakeb (Diesis).
February 28. Sixth foal. 32,000Y. Tattersalls
December. J C Fretwell. Closely related to
the quite useful 2-y-o 6f winner (from two
starts) Tanfeer (by Dansili) and half-sister to
the fair 2-y-o 1m and 9f winner Daaree (by
Teofilo). The dam is an unraced half-sister
to 3 winners. The second dam, Muwakleh
(by Machiavellian), winner of the UAE 1,000
Guineas and second in the Newmarket 1,000
Guineas, is a sister to 2 winners including the
high-class Dubai World Cup and Prix Jean
Prat winner Almutawakel and a half-sister to
10 winners. (J C Fretwell). *"A nice filly for mid-
season, she's coming along lovely but we've
done no fast work with her yet. She'll want fast
ground and the sire gets speedy horses so she'll
probably be suited to six furlongs".*

182. PLUNDERED (IRE) ★★★
b.c. Camacho – Jouel (Machiavellian). April
15. Fourth foal. €60,000Y. Tattersalls Ireland
September. John Fretwell. Half-brother to
the quite useful 2016 2-y-o 5f and 6f winner
Hyperfocus (by Intense Focus), to the quite
useful 6f and 1m winner King Bertie (by
Clodovil) and the modest 7f winner Ingleby
Spring (by Zebedee). The dam, placed twice
at 3 yrs in France, is a half-sister to 3 minor
winners. The second dam, Visions On Space
(by Lure), a minor French 3-y-o winner, is
a half-sister to 10 winners including the
Group 1 winners Dolphin Street, Insight and
Saffron Walden. (J C Fretwell). *"One of our
earlier runners, he's a nice colt for five and six
furlongs".*

183. SNAFFLED (IRE) ★★★
b.c. Camacho – Little Oz (Red Ransom). April
30. Third foal. 57,000Y. Tattersalls October
Book 2. J C Fretwell. Half-brother to the
modest 8.5f (at 2 yrs) and10f winner of 3 races
Weardiditallgorong (by Fast Company). The
dam, a modest 12f placed maiden, is a half-
sister to 2 winners including the French listed
winner Mireille. The second dam, Australie
(by Sadler's Wells), winner of the Group 3 11f
Prix de Flore, is a sister to one winner and a
half-sister to 7 winners including the Group
3 Glorious Stakes winner Forgotten Voice. (J
C Fretwell). *"An early 2-y-o, he's a five furlong
type, not over-big but very strong".*

184. UNNAMED ★★
ch.c. Medicean – Crimson Cloud (Kyllachy).
March 10. Second foal. 53,000Y. Tattersalls
October Book 2. John Fretwell. The dam, a
fair dual 5f winner at 2 and 3 yrs, is a sister
to the smart listed 5f winner and Group 3
second Corrybrough and a half-sister to 4
winners and to the unplaced dam of the triple
Group 3 winning sprinter Amour Propre. The
second dam, Calamanco (by Clantime), a
fair 5f winner at 3 and 4 yrs, is a sister to the
sprint winner Cape Merino (herself dam of the
Group 1 Golden Jubilee Stakes winner Cape
Of Good Hope) and a half-sister to 3 winners.
(J C Fretwell). *"A big colt for the back-end
of the season, it's a good family but he's not
precocious and probably one for seven furlongs
or a mile".*

185. UNNAMED ★★
b.f. Epaulette – Hi Katriona (Second Empire).
March 28. Ninth foal. €32,000Y. Goffs
Sportsmans. John Fretwell. Half-sister to 7
winners including the modest 2016 2-y-o
7f winner Hi Milady (by Sir Prancealot), the
fairly useful Irish 2-y-o 7f winner and Group 3
Anglesey Stakes second Hard Yards (by Moss
Vale), the quite useful dual 6f (at 2 yrs) and
dual 7f winner Beyleyf (by Kheleyf), the quite
useful 1m winner Lehbab (by Fast Company)
and the fair 6f winner of 6 races (including at
2 yrs) Shostakovic (by Fasliyev). The dam, a
modest 6f placed 2-y-o, is a half-sister to 11
winners including the Group 2 Premio Melton
winner Fred Bongusto. The second dam, Hi
Bettina (by Henbit), a fairly useful Irish sprint
winner and Group 3 second, is a half-sister to
the Group 3 winner Marouble and the Irish
Oaks and Irish 1,000 Guineas second Kitza. (J
C Fretwell). *"Probably a 3-y-o type, she's very
backward and quite weak at present. A good-
sized filly that needs time".*

KARL BURKE
186. ASHLAR
b.c. Mayson – Jillolini (Bertolini). April 9. Fifth
foal. £35,000Y. Goffs UK Premier (Doncaster).
Salcey Forest Stud. Half-brother to the quite
useful 2016 2-y-o dual 5f winner Pretty Vacant
(by Elzaam) and to 2 minor winners abroad by
Dutch Art and Kodiac. The dam is an unplaced
half-sister to 3 winners. The second dam,
Someone's Angel (by Runaway Groom), is an
unplaced half-sister to 6 minor winners.

187. BROKEN TIME (IRE)
b.f. Iffraaj – Miranda Frost (Cape Cross). April 27. Third foal. €50,000Y. Goffs Orby. Salcey Forest Stud. Half-sister to the fairly useful 2016 2-y-o 6f winner and Group 3 7f Solario Stakes third Eqtiraan (by Helmet). The dam is an unraced half-sister to 8 winners including the triple Group 3 winning sprinter Majestic Missile and the Irish listed winner Santo Padre. The second dam, Tshusick (by Dancing Brave), a quite useful 7f winner at 3 yrs, is a half-sister to 3 winners here and abroad.

188. HAVANA GREY
b.c. Havana Gold – Blanc De Chine (Dark Angel). February 12. First foal. €70,000Y. Arqana Deauville August. BBA (Ire). The dam, a quite useful 5f winner of 6 races at 2 and 4 yrs, is a half-sister to 7 winners including the Group 3 Molecomb Stakes second Fast Act. The second dam, Nullarbor (by Green Desert), a minor French 2-y-o winner, is a half-sister to 5 winners including Radevore (Group 2 10f Prix Eugene Adam).

189. HUMBLE GRATITUDE
ch.c. Foxwedge – Gilt Linked (Compton Place). May 3. Seventh foal. 58,000Y. Tattersalls October Book 2. BBA (Ire). Half-brother to the fairly useful 5f to 7f winner of 5 races from 2 to 5 yrs and Group 3 7f Criterion Stakes third Lincoln (by Clodovil) and to the quite useful 6f winner Operative (by Pastoral Pursuits). The dam, a quite useful 2-y-o 5f winner, is a half-sister to 5 winners including the Group 3 John Of Gaunt Stakes winner and dual Group 2 placed Pastoral Player. The second dam, Copy-Cat (by Lion Cavern), is an unplaced half-sister to 7 winners including the very useful Group 3 5f King George Stakes winner Averti.

190. LAURENS (FR)
b.f. Siyouni – Recambe (Cape Cross). April 12. Fourth foal. £220,000Y. Goffs UK Premier (Doncaster). Salcey Forest. Half-sister to a jumps winner in France by Solon. The dam, a minor dual winner in France, is a half-sister to 6 winners including the multiple listed winner Salford Mill. The second dam, Razana (by Kahyasi), a fair 10f winner here, later won at up to 12f in France and is a half-sister to 5 winners and to the unplaced dam of the Group 1 Prix de l'Opera winner Kinnaird.

191. LUMI (IRE)
b.f. Canford Cliffs – Ravish (Efisio). March 23. Seventh foal. €80,000Y. Goffs Orby. Salcey Forest. Half-sister to the useful 1m (at 2 yrs) and listed 8.5f winner Off Limits (by Mastercraftsman), to the Italian winner and listed placed 2-y-o Seinellanima (by Oratorio), the fair 7f to 10.5f winner Swift Cedar and the minor Italian winner of 7 races Eccellente Idea (both by Excellent Art). The dam, a moderate 1m placed maiden, is a half-sister to 5 winners including the French listed 7f winner Special Discount. The second dam, Looks Sensational (by Majestic Light), is an unplaced half-sister to the dual US Grade 1 winner Awe Inspiring and the US Grade 2 winner Recognizable.

192. RECKS (IRE)
ch.c. Reckless Abandon – Welsh Diva (Selkirk). January 28. Tenth foal. €45,000Y. Goffs Orby. Not sold. Half-brother to 6 winners including the useful dual 7f and UAE Group 3 5f winner Fityaan (by Haafhd), the modest 6f and 7f winner of 4 races Swansea Jack (by Singspiel) and the modest 5f and 6f winner of 3 races Welsh Opera (by Noverre). The dam, an Italian Group 3 1m and Ascot listed 1m winner, is a sister to 2 winners including the Group 2 1m Prix du Rond-Point and Group 3 8.5f Diomed Stakes winner Trans Island and a half-sister to 7 winners. The second dam, Khubza (by Green Desert), a quite useful 7f winner, is a half-sister to 7 winners including the Group 2 winners Barrow Creek and Last Resort.

193. ROCKIN FELLA (IRE)
b.c. Society Rock – Dearest Daisy (Forzando). April 9. Eighth foal. £56,000Y. Goffs UK Premier (Doncaster). Salcey Forest. Half-brother to the useful 2-y-o dual 5f winner and Group 2 Norfolk Stakes third Excel Bolt (by Exceed And Excel), to the winner Clive Clifton (by Wootton Basset) and two minor winners abroad by Monsieur Bond and Amadeus Wolf. The dam, a quite useful 2-y-o 5f winner, is a sister to 2 winners including the useful 2-y-o dual 6f winner and listed-placed Crimson Silk and a half-sister to 2 minor winners. The second dam, Sylhall (by Sharpo), is an unraced half-sister to 6 minor winners.

194. WUNDERBAR
ch.f. Havana Gold – Wunders Dream (Averti). March 24. Ninth foal. €50,000Y. Goffs Orby.

BBA (Ire). Half-sister to 6 winners including the useful listed 6f winner of 3 races at 2 and 3 yrs Inyordreams (by Teofilo), the useful 2-y-o 5f winner and listed-placed Fire Eyes (by Exceed And Excel), the fairly useful dual 1m winner Strong Steps (by Aqlaam) and the modest 1m to 12f winner Spartilla. The dam, a winner of 5 races at 2 yrs including the Group 2 5f Flying Childers Stakes and the Group 3 5f Molecomb Stakes, is a half-sister to 7 winners including the Irish Group 3 winner Grecian Dancer. The second dam, Pizzicato (by Statoblest), a modest 5f and 5.3f winner, is a half-sister to the high-class Hong Kong horses Mensa and Firebolt.

195. UNNAMED

gr.f. Dark Angel – Cover Girl (Common Grounds). April 10. Fifth foal. £210,000Y. Goffs UK Premier (Doncaster). BBA Ire. Sister the fair Irish 2-y-o 7f winner Angel Bright, closely related to the fair Irish 7f and 1m winner Luxie (by Acclamation) and half-sister to 3 winners including the 2-y-o 5f and 5.7f winner, Group 3 Cornwallis Stakes third and subsequent US Grade 3 placed Shermeen (dam of the Group 1 Phoenix Stakes winner Sudirman) and the very useful listed 5f and listed 6f winner Mister Manannan (both by Desert Style). The second dam, Peace Carrier (by Doulab), a fair 2-y-o 6f and 7f and subsequent Scandinavian listed winner, is a half-sister to 5 winners.

OWEN BURROWS

196. ALFARQAD (USA) ★★★

b.br.c. War Front – Love And Pride (A P Indy). May 6. Second foal. $1,300,000Y. Keeneland September. Shadwell Estate Co. The dam won 7 races in the USA at 3 and 4 yrs including the Grade 1 Personal Ensign Stakes and the Grade 1 Zenyatta Stakes and is a half-sister to 2 winners. The second dam, Ile de France (by Storm Cat), a US winner at 2 and 3 yrs, was third in the Grade 1 Santa Anita Oaks and is a half-sister to the US triple Grade 1 winner and sire Bernardini. (Hamdan Al Maktoum). *"He's not in at the moment, I saw him back at the stud in November and they like him there and he's cantering away but a minor hiccup has kept him from coming here up to now. Hopefully he'll arrive here soon".*

197. ALYAMAAMA (USA) ★★

ch.f. Kitten's Joy – Sarayir (Mr Prospector). January 31. Half-sister to 7 winners including the 1,000 Guineas and Coronation Stakes winner Ghanaati (by Giant's Causeway), the Group 3 12f Cumberland Lodge Stakes winner and Group 1 Champion Stakes second Mawatheeq, the quite useful 1m winner Itqaan (both by Danzig) and the useful 1m (at 2 yrs) and listed 9f winner Rumoush (by Rahy). The dam, a listed 1m winner, is closely related to the Champion Stakes winner Nayef and a half-sister to Nashwan and Unfuwain. The second dam, Height Of Fashion (by Bustino), won the Group 2 Princess of Wales's Stakes. (Hamdan Al Maktoum). *"A well-bred filly, she's quite big and a bit backward so you won't be seeing too much from her until later in the season. She has a good temperament but as she's quite big and tall we'll have to be patient with her ".*

198. BAWAASIL ★★★

b.c. Oasis Dream – Hedaaya (Indian Ridge). March 15. Half-brother to the useful listed-placed dual 7f winner Tamadhor (by Arcano) and to the quite useful 1m winner Madroos (by Teofilo). The dam, a quite useful Irish 9f winner, is a half-sister to 5 winners including the 2-y-o Group 3 Tyros Stakes winner Remember Alexander and the 2-y-o Group 2 Cherry Hinton Stakes and Group 3 Albany Stakes winner Memory. The second dam, Nausicaa (by Diesis), won 3 races at 2 and 3 yrs in France and the USA over 7f and 1m, was third in the Grade 3 Miesque Stakes and is a half-sister to 3 winners. (Hamdan Al Maktoum). *"A nice model, he's cantering away and he moves nicely. A good-looking colt, he should make a 2-y-o because he's not over-big".*

199. ELWAZIR ★★★

ch.c. Frankel – Dash To The Front (Diktat). April 3. Sixth foal. 500,000Y. Tattersalls October Book 1. Shadwell Estate Co. Half-brother to the Group 1 10f Prix Jean Romanet and Group 1 10f Prix de l'Opera winner Speedy Boarding (by Shamardal), to the quite useful 9f and 12f winner of 4 races Miss Dashwood (by Dylan Thomas) and the quite useful 2-y-o 1m winner Next Stage (by Dubawi). The dam, a useful listed 10.8f winner, is a half-sister to 3 winners including Dash To The Top, a 2-y-o listed 1m winner and placed in the Group 1 Fillies' Mile and the Group 1 Yorkshire Oaks. The second dam, Millennium Dash (by Nashwan), a fairly useful 10.2f winner, is a half-sister to 4 winners. (Hamdan Al Maktoum). *"A lovely, big, tall colt, he's cantering away but he's one for the second half of the season. From what he's done so far you can't do anything but like him. Quite leggy and tall, but he's filled out a bit in the last few weeks and his temperament is good".*

200. ENJAZAAT ★★★★

b.c. Acclamation – Miliika (Green Desert). February 18. First foal. 115,000 foal. Tattersalls December. Shadwell Estate Co. The dam, a quite useful 6f winner, is a sister to the quite useful triple 7f winner Emkanaat and a half-sister to one winner. The second dam, Miss Anabaa (by Anabaa), a winner of 3 races including the Group 3 5f Ballyogan Stakes, is a half-sister to 5 winners including Out After Dark, a smart 5f and 6f winner of 6 races including the Portland Handicap. (Hamdan Al Maktoum). *"A nice, neat colt, he's only been cantering but on looks you'd say he could be out sooner rather than later. A good-moving colt and out of a Green Desert mare, he could be pretty sharp. A nice model with the scope to go on".*

201. GANAYEM (IRE) ★★★★

gr.f. Frankel – Rose Of Summer (El Prado). February 20. Ninth foal. $900,000Y. Keeneland September. Shadwell Estate Co. Half-sister to 5 winners including the US Grade 1 Hollywood Starlet Stakes winner Laragh (by Tapit) and the US Grade 2 and triple Grade 3 winner Summer Front (by War Front). The dam is an unraced half-sister to 7 winners including the Grade 1 Hollywood Futurity winner Siphonic. The second dam, Cherokee Crossing (by Cherokee Colony), was placed in the USA and is a half-sister to the US Grade 2 winner Dixie Dot Com. (Hamdan Al Maktoum). *"Not the biggest horse in the world but she's cantering away, she moves nicely and just looking at her you'd have to say that when we start to step her up she could be out in the first half of the season. She has a good temperament too, maybe a bit "jig-joggy" but not like one of those very keen Frankels that you have to keep the lid on".*

202. JAALBOOT ★★★

b.c. Invincible Spirit – Selinka (Selkirk). February 3. Fifth living foal. Half-brother to the 2016 2-y-o Group 3 5f Curragh Stakes winner Hit The Bid (by Exceed And Excel), to the fair 6f (at 2 yrs) and 7f winner Pivotal Movement (by Pivotal) and a minor winner abroad by Green Desert. The dam, a useful listed 6f (at 2 yrs) and listed 7f winner, is a half-sister to 2 winners. The second dam, Lady Links (by Bahamian Bounty), a dual listed 6f winner (including at 2 yrs), is a half-sister to 5 winners. (Hamdan Al Maktoum). *"He could be out relatively early, he's a neat model with plenty of muscle about him and he has a good temperament".*

203. KASAYID (IRE) ★★★

ch.f. Pivotal – Serious Dowth (Iffraaj). February 7. First foal. €250,000Y. Goffs Orby. Shadwell Estate Co. The dam is an unraced half-sister to 8 winners including the Group 2 5.5f Prix Robert Papin winner Zipping and the Group 3 5f Prix du Bois winner Zelding. The second dam, Zelda (by Caerleon), a French 6.5f winner, is closely related to the dam of the French 1,000 Guineas winner Valentine Waltz and a half-sister to the dual Group 1 winner Last Tycoon and the Group winners Astronef and The Perfect Life. (Hamdan Al Maktoum). *"She's one that needs a bit of time and maybe some sun on her back but she has a good action, she's very athletic and I don't mind her at all. She's a nice filly and I do like her".*

204. KASBAAN ★★★

b.c. Dansili – Aghareed (Kingmambo). February 17. Second foal. The dam, a listed 10f winner in France, is a half-sister to one winner. The second dam, Lahudood (by Singspiel), a listed 9f winner, is a half-sister to several winners including the listed winner Kareemah. (Hamdan Al Maktoum). *"A nice type of horse that needs a bit of time, he's got a good temperament, he moves well and he's probably a 2-y-o for the second half of the season".*

205. KATLEEN ★★★

b.f. Lonhro – Nasmatt (Danehill). February 12. Half-sister to the useful 2-y-o 1m and subsequent UAE listed 10f winner Emmrooz (by Red Ransom), to the quite useful UAE 6f and 7f winner of 4 races Latkhaf (by Pivotal), the fair 7f winner Owaseyf (by Medaglia d'Oro) and the fair 1m winners Jaahiez (by More Than Ready) and Towbaat (by Halling). The dam, a fairly useful listed-placed 2-y-o 6f winner, is closely related to the Group 2 6f Lowther Stakes and Group 3 5f Queen Mary Stakes winner Bint Allayl and to the Group 3 7f Jersey Stakes winner Kheleyf. The second dam, Society Lady (by Mr Prospector), a fair 6f and 7f placed 2-y-o, is a full or half-sister to numerous winners including the useful French 2-y-o 5.5f winner Kentucky Slew. (Sheikh Ahmed Al Maktoum). *"She looks as if she could be out relatively early. A nice model, not over big but with a bit of scope and she moves nicely".*

206. LAUBALI ★★★

ch.c. Kyllachy　Different (Bahamian Bounty). February 22. First foal. 125,000Y. Tattersalls October Book 2. Shadwell Estate Co. The dam, a modest 5f winner, is a sister to the useful dual winner and 2-y-o Group 3 Molecomb Stakes second Mary Read and a half-sister to 7 winners. The second dam, Hill Welcome (by Most Welcome), was placed twice at 2 yrs and is a half-sister to 5 winners including the Group 1 6f Middle Park Stakes winner Stalker. (Hamdan Al Maktoum). *"He was one of my picks from Book Two, there's plenty of speed in the family and he looks a 2-y-o. He'll be stepped up in his work soon and he has a good mind on him. Barring problems he should be one of the first to run".*

207. MANTHOOR ★★★

gr.c. Swiss Spirit – Enchanting Way (Linamix). February 6. Sixth foal. £110,000Y. Goffs UK Premier (Doncaster). Shadwell Estate Co. Half-brother to the useful listed 5f winner Silver Rainbow (by Starspangledbanner), to the fair 7f winner Jun Huo (by Excellent Art) and a winner in Italy by Holy Roman Emperor. The dam is an unraced half-sister to 2 winners including the US Grade 1 Citation Handicap winner Ashkal Way and the US Grade 2 winner Sentiero Italia. The second dam, Golden Way (by Cadeaux Genereux), a fairly useful 10f and 10.5f winner, is a half-sister to 8 winners including the French and US listed winners Go Boldly and Polish Spring. (Hamdan Al Maktoum). *"There's plenty of speed in the*

family but actually he doesn't look an early type. He's neat but he still looks like he needs to strengthen up".

208. MODHAFARAH ★★★

ch.f. Dubawi – Kareemah (Peintre Celebre). April 15. Fifth foal. Half-sister Alfawaris (by Frankel), placed third on both his starts at 2 yrs in 2016, to the quite useful 1m winner Ehtiraas (by Oasis Dream) and the fair 12f winner Saraha (by Dansili). The dam, a French listed 10f winner, is a half-sister to 4 winners including the French listed 9f and subsequent US Grade 1 10f and Grade 1 11f winner Lahudood. The second dam, Rahayeb (by Arazi), a fair 12.3f winner, is a full or half-sister to 4 winners. (Hamdan Al Maktoum). *"A similar model to the 2-y-o Pivotal filly we have but with a bit more substance about her. She has a good action and a good temperament and just needs the sun on her back for a few weeks and she could change inside out. I have the 3-y-o and 4-y-o out of the mare and although neither of them won at two the Frankel colt was third on both his starts and I think a fair bit of him".*

209. MOKAATIL ★★★

br.c. Lethal Force – Moonlit Garden (Exceed And Excel). March 30. Second foal. 100,000 foal. Tattersalls December. Shadwell Estate Co. Half-brother to the quite useful 2-y-o 5f winner Dream Dreamer (by Dream Ahead). The dam, a fairly useful 2-y-o 6f winner, was listed-placed three times and is a half-sister to one winner. The second dam, Fingal Nights (by Night Shift), was a fair 6f and 7f winner at 2 and 3 yrs. (Hamdan Al Maktoum). *"He looked pretty early but he's had a touch of sore shins so we had to back off him. He's a neat model and a good mover but we'll just have to wait a bit. I've got a few by Lethal Force and they're all nice types".*

210. MONTSHI ★★★

b.c. Dubawi – Tantshi (Invincible Spirit). March 21. First foal. The dam, fairly useful 6f (at 2 yrs) and listed 7f winner of 4 races, is a full or half-sister to 6 winners including the very useful 2-y-o listed 7f winner Toolain. The second dam, Qasirah (by Machiavellian), a useful 2-y-o 6f winner, was third in the Group 3 8.5f Princess Margaret Stakes. (Sheikh Ahmed Al

Maktoum). *"The first foal of a listed winner, he was very wary of everything when we first broke him in and he took a lot of time to gain any confidence, but he got over it and now he's actually quite bullish! He goes out in a hood every morning and although he's a first foal and isn't over-big he's changing every week. He's only cantering away at the moment, but he certainly looks as if he'd make a mid-season 2-y-o".*

211. MOTAJAASID (IRE) ★★
b.br.c. Harbour Watch – Cape Joy (Cape Cross). February 25. First foal. €125,000 foal. Goffs November. Shadwell Estate Co. The dam, a modest 10f winner, is a half-sister to 6 winners including the Irish listed 1m winner Hymn Of Love. The second dam, Perils Of Joy (by Rainbow Quest), a 1m winner in Ireland, is a half-sister to 5 winners including the Italian Group 3 winner Sweetened Offer. (Hamdan Al Maktoum). *"This colt looks a 2-y-o type although he is out of a middle-distance mare. He moves nicely, he's cantering away and as soon as the gallops have dried up we'll give him a spin".*

212. MUKTASHIF (IRE) ★★★
gr.c. Shamardal – Silent Secret (Dubai Destination). February 18. Fifth foal. Half-brother to the modest dual 6f winner at 2 and 3 yrs Boolass (by Bushranger) and to the modest Irish 2-y-o 5f winner Gwen Lady Byron (by Dandy Man). The dam, a fair 2-y-o 5f winner, is a half-sister to 4 winners including the smart Irish Group 3 7f and Group 3 1m winner Cheyenne Star and to the dam of the triple Group 1 winner Gordon Lord Byron. The second dam, Charita (by Lycius), a listed 1m winner in Ireland, is a half-sister to 4 winners including the Italian Group 2 winner Stanott. (Hamdan Al Maktoum). *"A big colt that's cantering away, he only came in from Ireland a few weeks ago and he looks like he wants a bit of time. He's got a good mind on him and moves easily enough, so we'll see how we go".*

213. MURAAHIN ★★★
ch.c. Teofilo – Fatanah (Green Desert). April 21. Third foal. Half-brother to the quite useful 2016 2-y-o 1m winner Baashiq (by New Approach). The dam, a useful listed-placed 10f winner, is a half-sister to 5 winners including

the Group 2 1m Premio Ribot winner Oriental Fashion, the very useful listed 7f and subsequent US Grade 2 10f winner Makderah and the useful 1m and 10f winner Ezdiyaad. The second dam, Wijdan (by Mr Prospector), a useful 1m and 10.4f winner, is a sister to the 7f (at 2 yrs) and listed 1m winner Sarayir and a half-sister to Nashwan, Nayef and Unfuwain. (Hamdan Al Maktoum). *"A neat colt that moves nice and has a very good temperament. Out of a Green Desert mare, he should be a mid-season 2-y-o, all being well".*

214. MUTAAQEB ★★★
b.c. Invincible Spirit – Mejala (Red Ransom). March 26. Third foal. The dam, a fair 10f winner, is a half-sister to the very useful 2-y-o listed 7f Star Stakes winner and Group 3 7f Prestige Stakes second Mudaaraah, to the useful listed 6f winner Ethaara and the useful 2-y-o listed 7f winner Sudoor. The second dam, Wissal (Woodman), is an unraced sister to the high-class 2-y-o Group 2 7f Laurent Perrier Champagne Stakes Bahhare and a half-sister to the Group 1 1m St James's Palace Stakes and Group 1 1m Queen Elizabeth II Stakes winner Bahri. (Hamdan Al Maktoum). *"Quite tall and leggy, but he moves really well. He's a very athletic horse and we just have to watch he doesn't get too buzzed up. Looks a nice horse".*

215. MUTAFARRID (IRE) ★★★
gr.c. Dark Angel – Margarita (Marju). February 18. Fourth foal. 250,000 foal. Tattersalls December. Shadwell Estate Co. Half-brother to the fair 2016 2-y-o 6f winner Meetyouatthemoon (by Excelebration). The dam, a modest 8.5f placed maiden, is a sister to 2 winners including the Group 1 Fillies Mile, Falmouth Stakes, Sussex Stakes and Matron Stakes winner Soviet Song and a half-sister to 3 winners including the useful 5f (at 2 yrs) and triple 6f winner Baralinka and the dam of the Group 1 winner Ribbons. The second dam, Kalinka (by Soviet Star), a quite useful 2-y-o 7f winner, is a half-sister to 2 winners. (Hamdan Al Maktoum). *"He's one that looks as if he should be out sooner rather than later, but he's got a bit of size about him as well so he's not just going to be a 2-y-o. He has a good temperament and he moves nicely".*

216. MUTANAQEL ★★★
b.c. Havana Gold – Audaz (Oasis Dream).
February 11. Fourth foal. 40,000 foal.
Tattersalls December. Shadwell Estate Co.
Half-brother to the fair 11.5f and hurdles
winner Authorized Too (by Authorized). The
dam won four races in France including over
9f at Chantilly at 4 yrs and is a half-sister to
3 winners including the Group 3 Prix Eclipse
winner Bonaire. The second dam, Albahaca
(by Green Dancer), a minor French 3-y-o
winner, is a half-sister to 6 winners. (Hamdan
Al Maktoum). *"He was very quirky to break in
and he's certainly a bit of a boy – you have to
keep on top of him with his work. Everything I
throw at him he shrugs off, he's got a big, long
stride on him and he takes a bit of handling.
You wouldn't like to see your name down as
his rider in the morning! He surprises me, he
moves well and he's doing everything good.
Not an obvious one for the first half of the
season, but we'll see".*

217. NAQAAWA ★★
b.f. Shamardal – Hammiya (Darshaan). April
8. Half-sister to the useful 7f winner Masaalek
(by Green Desert), to the German listed 10f
winner Shaqira (by Redoute's Choice) and the
fairly useful 7f (at 2 yrs) and 1m winner and
listed second Adhwaa (by Oasis Dream). The
dam, a useful listed Cheshire Oaks winner, is
a half-sister to 3 winners including the useful
2-y-o 1m winner Achill Bay. The second
dam, Albacora (by Fairy King), winner of the
listed 1m Prix Herod, is closely related to the
Prix de Saint-Georges winner and French
1,000 Guineas second Pont-Aven (dam of
the Gimcrack Stakes winner Josr Algharoud
and the dual Group winner Saint Marine).
(Hamdan Al Maktoum). *"She's a right madam!
Nevertheless she's a nice filly that moves well
but will want plenty of time. She takes a bit of
riding and the Head Lad rides her all the time.
A back-end type 2-y-o".*

218. ORIENTAL SONG (IRE) ★★★
ch.f. Shamardal – Oriental Melody (Sakhee).
March 25. Fifth foal. The dam, an Irish 2-y-o 7f
winner, is a half-sister to 7 winners including
the useful dual 1m winner (including at 2 yrs)
and Group 3 Irish 2,000 Guineas third Famous
Warrior and the useful 7f and UAE 1m winner
and UAE Group 2 second Green Coast. The

second dam, Oriental Fashion (by Marju), won
3 races including the Group 2 1m Premio
Ribot and is a half-sister to 5 winners including
the US Grade 2 winner Makderah. (Hadi Al
Tajir). *"A neat filly, she'll be one we'll take a
look at early on and she's a good model that
moves well and has a good mind. She should
make a 2-y-o, perhaps over six furlongs".*

219. RUMORS OF WAR (USA) ★★
b.br.c. War Front – Sweet Lulu (Mr Greeley).
January 31. First foal. $700,000Y. Keeneland
September. Shadwell Estate Co. The dam
won 4 races in the USA at 3 yrs including the
Grade 1 Test Stakes and is a half-sister to the
US Grade 3 winner Anchor Down. The second
dam, Successful Outlook (by Orientate), won
the Grade 3 Tempted Stakes in the USA and
was Grade 2 placed. (Hamdan Al Maktoum).
*"He's back at the stud and I haven't seen him
since January, so I can't say too much about
him to be truthful".*

220. SUNOOF (IRE) ★★★
b.f. Raven's Pass – Arwaah (Dalakhani).
February 21. Half-sister to the quite useful
7f and 1m winner Almuheet (by Dansili). The
dam, a very useful 10f winner, is a half-sister
to one winner. The second dam, Sahool (by
Unfuwain), a 1m (at 2 yrs) and listed 12f
winner, was second in the Group 2 Lancashire
Oaks and is a half-sister to 2 winners.
(Hamdan Al Maktoum). *"A good-moving filly
that doesn't look like she'll be early, but she's
not big and backward so she should make a
mid-season 2-y-o".*

221. WADILSAFA ★★★★
b.c. Frankel – Rumoush (Rahy). February 28.
Fourth foal. Half-brother to the fairly useful
2016 2-y-o 7f winner, on her only start,
Talaayeb (by Dansili) and to the useful 2-y-o 7f
winner and Group 2 Royal Lodge Stakes third
Muntazah (by Dubawi). The dam, a very useful
1m (at 2 yrs) and listed 9f winner, was third
in the Oaks and is a half-sister to numerous
winners including the 1,000 Guineas and
Coronation Stakes winner Ghanaati and
the Group 3 12f Cumberland Lodge Stakes
winner and Group 1 Champion Stakes second
Mawatheeq. The second dam, Sarayir (by Mr
Prospector), winner of a listed 1m event, is
closely related to the Champion Stakes winner

Nayef and a half-sister to Nashwan and Unfuwain. (Hamdan Al Maktoum). *"A lovely colt, he came in a bit later than most of them but he's been here a while now. A very athletic horse with a lovely stride on him, he could be anything. A very exciting colt that should be a July/August 2-y-o".*

222. UNNAMED ★★★
ch.f. Dubawi – Daymooma (Pivotal). February 20. First foal. The dam, a fairly useful listed-placed 9f and 10f winner, is a half-sister to 5 winners including the useful 2-y-o 6f winner and Group 3 7f Killavullan Stakes third Aaraas and the useful Irish 2-y-o 6f winner and Group 3 7f Silver Flash Stakes third Alshahbaa. The second dam, Adaala (by Sahm), an Irish 7f (at 2 yrs) and listed 9f winner, is a half-sister to 2 winners. (Hamdan Al Maktoum). *"Quite a tall, leggy filly. She's had a small problem but she'll be fine and she's back cantering now. A nice mover with a good temperament".*

223. UNNAMED ★★★★
gr.f. Frankel – Hathrah (Linamix). April 11. Ninth foal. Half-sister to the smart listed 10f winner and Group 1 Prix de l'Opera third Hadaatha (by Sea The Stars), to the quite useful 10f to 2m winner of 8 races Itlaak (by Alhaarth), the quite useful 1m winner Aghaany (by Dubawi) and the fair 8.5f winner Raddeh (by Shamardal). The dam, winner of the listed 1m Masaka Stakes and third in the 1,000 Guineas, is a half-sister to 5 winners including the smart Group 2 12f Premio Ellington winner Ivan Luis and the French/German listed winners Amathia and Zero Problemo. The second dam, Zivania (by Shernazar), a useful Irish winner of 4 races from 1m to 9.5f, is a half-sister to the Group 3 Prix Gontaut Biron winner Muroto. (Hamdan Al Maktoum). *"She's a lovely filly. A big girl that's going to want a bit of time but she floats along and she's very athletic. An exciting filly, we'll have to be patient for now because of her size and she'll be a big 3-y-o next year".*

224. UNNAMED ★★★
b.f. War Front – Lahudood (Singspiel). March 13. Sicth foal. Half-sister to the French listed 10f winner Aghareed (by Kingmambo) and to the US 7f and 1m winner Munasara (by

Bernardini). The dam, a French listed 9f and subsequent US Grade 1 10f and Grade 1 11f winner, is a half-sister to 4 winners including the French listed 10f winner Kareemah. The second dam, Rahayeb (by Arazi), a fair 12.3f winner, is a full or half-sister to 4 winners. (Hamdan Al Maktoum). *"A lovely, big filly that covers a lot of ground, she wants some time but she could be anything. Very nice".*

225. UNNAMED ★★★
b.c. New Approach – Mudaaraah (Cape Cross). March 1. Fourth foal. The dam, a very useful 2-y-o listed 7f Star Stakes winner and second in the Group 3 7f Prestige Stakes, is closely related to the listed 6f winner Ethaara and a half-sister to 3 winners. The second dam, Wissal (by Woodman), is an unraced sister to the high-class 2-y-o Group 2 7f Laurent Perrier Champagne Stakes Bahhare and a half-sister to the Group 1 1m St James's Palace Stakes and Group 1 1m Queen Elizabeth II Stakes winner Bahri. (Hamdan Al Maktoum). *"He's a real nice colt, he moves very well and has a good mind on him. He doesn't look like he'll be early but he should certainly be one for the late summer. You can't help but like him".*

226. UNNAMED ★★★
gr.f. Dubawi – Natagora (Divine Light). April 13. Sixth foal. Sister to the fairly useful 2-y-o listed-placed 6.5f winner Raaqy and half-sister to the 2016 French 2-y-o 1m winner Mankib and the quite useful 2-y-o 6f winner Rayaheen (by Nayef). The dam, a champion 2-y-o filly and winner of the Group 1 Cheveley Park Stakes and the 1,000 Guineas, is a half-sister to 3 winners in France (including one over jumps). The second dam, Reinamixa (by Linamix), a minor French 11f winner, is a half-sister to 6 winners including the French listed winner Reinstate. (Hamdan Al Maktoum). *"Quite a big, backward filly that wants a bit of time. She's got a bit more substance, bone and scope than her sister Raaqy who didn't really train on as a 3-y-o. Certainly won't be seen out until the second half of the season".*

227. UNNAMED ★★★★
b.c. Kyllachy – On The Brink (Mind Games). February 7. Eighth foal. 270,000Y. Tattersalls October Book 2. Shadwell Estate Co. Half-brother to the listed winner Aetna (by

Indesatchel), to the quite useful 2-y-o dual 5f winner Boundaries (by Kyllachy), the quite useful 1m (at 2 yrs) to 11f and hurdles winner Dubai Crest (by Dubai Destination), the quite useful dual 7f winner Hot Spark and the fair 2-y-o 1m winner Emef Diamond (both by Firebreak). The dam, a quite useful 2-y-o listed 5f winner, is a sister to the listed-placed winner Silaah and a half-sister to 5 winners including the listed winner and dual Group 3 second Eastern Romance. The second dam, Ocean Grove (by Fairy King), a quite useful 2-y-o 6f winner, is a half-sister to 5 winners here and abroad. (Hamdan Al Maktoum). *"Another I picked from Book Two, he's a very athletic colt. He's had sore shins but they won't hold us up too much. He moves very nicely and he should certainly be a 2-y-o".*

228. UNNAMED ★★★★
b.c. War Front – Prize Catch (A P Indy). February 3. Second foal. $1,900,000Y. Keeneland September. Shadwell Estate Co. The dam won three minor races at 3 and 4 yrs in the USA and is a half-sister to 8 winners including the US triple Grade 2 winner Lead Story and the Grade 2 placed Strike Midnight. The second dam, Gwenjinsky (by Seattle Dancer), is a half-sister to the Grade 1 Breeders' Cup Distaff winner Unbridled Elaine. (Hamdan Al Maktoum). *"A lovely looking colt, he's very exciting and obviously cost a lot of money. He's doing everything right, moves well and he's got a good mind on him. A very nice horse with plenty of scope, so he won't just be a 2-y-o".*

229. UNNAMED ★★★
ch.c. Havana Gold – Puzzled (Peintre Celebre). January 26. Second foal. 42,000 foal. Tattersalls December. Shadwell Estate Co. The dam, a quite useful 10f and 12f placed maiden, is a half-sister to 6 winners including the Derby second Walk In The Park and the listed winner Soon. The second dam, Classic Park (by Robellino), won 3 races including the Irish 1,000 Guineas and is a half-sister to 10 winners including the US Grade 2 winner Rumpipumpy. (Hamdan Al Maktoum). *"A nice colt, he's had a touch of sore shins but he was a January foal so once we get him through this stage he'll be ready to do a bit more. I think he'll be a mid-season 2-y-o".*

230. UNNAMED ★★★
ch.c. Kyllachy – Regatta (Giant's Causeway). March 31. Fifth foal. £58,000Y. Goffs UK Premier (Doncaster). Shadwell Estate Co. The dam is an unraced half-sister to 3 winners including the US Grade 2 winner and Grade 1 second Sightseeing. The second dam, Resort (by Pleasant Colony), a winner of four races in the USA at 2 and 3 yrs, was second in the Grade 1 CCA Oaks and is a half-sister to 6 winners including the Graded stakes winners Living Vicariously and With Distinction. (Hamdan Al Maktoum). *"He's grown a lot and he's a very powerful looking colt now so he looks as if he'll be sharp, but not early. I wouldn't be in any rush with him but he moves nice and he won't half be a big horse next year".*

231. UNNAMED ★★★
br.c. Lethal Force – Rush (Compton Place). February 20. First foal. 120,000 foal. Goffs November. Shadwell Estate Co. The dam, a fair 6f placed 2-y-o, is a half-sister to the Group 3 Fred Darling Stakes winner and Group 1 Cheveley Park Stakes second Rimth. The second dam, Dorelia (by Efisio), a fair 1m winner, is a half-sister to 3 winners including the smart Group 2 5f King's Stand Stakes and Group 3 5f Cornwallis Stakes winner Dominica. (Hamdan Al Maktoum). *"He looks as if he'll make a 2-y-o in the first half of the season. It's a quick family and he moves nice, so he's on the list to step him up in April. A neat colt and my Lethal Force 2-y-o's look as if they can run a bit".*

232. UNNAMED ★★★
b.c. Helmet – Sakhya (Barathea). March 2. Ninth foal. £60,000Y. Goffs UK Premier (Doncaster). Shadwell Estate Co. Closely related to the quite useful 7f (at 2 yrs) and 1m winner Al Mukhdam (by Exceed And Excel) and half-brother to 4 winners including the quite useful dual 7f winner at 2 and 3 yrs Dagher (by New Approach), the fair 1m winner Andalieb (by Zamindar) and the fair 7f winner Falakee (by Sakhee). The dam, unplaced in one start, is a half-sister to 4 winners. The second dam, Um Lardaff (by Mill Reef), a winner over 11f and 12f at 3 yrs in France, is a sister to the Derby winner and high-class sire Shirley Heights and a half-sister

to the good broodmare Bempton. (Hamdan Al Maktoum). *"When I bought him I thought he'd be quite sharp but he's done a lot of growing and he still is doing. He's a very good-actioned horse and now that he has grown he's got plenty of scope and he's going to make a nice horse next year. He'll make a 2-y-o from the end of the summer onwards, he has a good mind on him and he moves nicely".*

233. UNNAMED ★★★
b.c. Oasis Dream – Tanfidh (Marju). April 16. Fifth foal. Brother to the fair 7f winner Kestrel Dot Com. The dam, a quite useful dual 10f winner, is a sister to the Group 2 1m Premio Ribot winner Oriental Fashion and a half-sister to numerous winners including the very useful listed 7f and subsequent US Grade 2 10f winner Makderah and the useful 10f winners Ezdiyaad and Fatanah. The second dam, Wijdan (by Mr Prospector), a useful 1m and 10.4f winner, is a sister to the 7f (at 2 yrs) and 1m listed winner Sarayir and a half-sister to the brilliant 2,000 Guineas, Derby, Eclipse and King George winner Nashwan and to the high-class middle distance colt Unfuwain. (Hamdan Al Maktoum). *"A neat type, he covers a lot of ground and if he hadn't popped a splint he wouldn't be too far off going on a stride now. He's fine now and just needs to get a bit of belly fat off him. He covers a lot of ground, likes to get on with it and you wouldn't want to mess him about too much".*

234. UNNAMED ★★★★
b.c. Shamardal – Zahoo (Nayef). March 13. Fourth foal. Half-brother to the listed 7.5f (at 2 yrs) and Group 3 7f Ballycorus Stakes winner Convergence (by Cape Cross) and to the quite useful 2-y-o 1m winner Zaakhir (by Raven's Pass). The dam, a fairly useful 1m (at 2 yrs) and 10f winner and listed 10f second, is a full or half-sister to 5 winners including the smart Group 3 14f winner Tactic and the listed 12f winner Yaazy. The second dam, Tanaghum (by Darshaan), a useful listed-placed 10f winner, is a half-sister to 7 winners including the smart Group 2 10f Premio Lydia Tesio winner Najah. (Hamdan Al Maktoum). *"He's a lovely colt. He's just getting over some sore shins but we wouldn't be in any rush with him anyway. A good sized colt with a really good, athletic action and I do like him. He's very nice".*

HENRY CANDY

235. ALIZETI (IRE) ★★★
b.f. Dutch Art – Ushindi (Montjeu). March 25. Seventh living foal. 32,000Y. Tattersalls December. Form Bloodstock. Half-sister to the useful 2-y-o dual 6f winner and triple listed-placed Mon Cadeaux (by Cadeaux Genereux), to the Irish 2-y-o 7f winner, on his only start, Territory (by Acclamation), the fair 11f winner King Muro (by Halling) and the fair Irish 1m and 12f winner Mont Blanc (by Singspiel) and the modest 1m winner Scots Fern (by Selkirk). The dam, a modest 12f winner, is a half-sister to 8 winners including the smart broodmares Frond and Frangy. The second dam, Fern (by Shirley Heights), a fairly useful 12f winner and third in the listed 10f Lupe Stakes, is a half-sister to 6 winners including the Group 1 Fillies Mile winner Shamshir. (First Of Many & Turner). *"She's going to take a bit of time because she's grown a lot, but she's very active and I like her. She just needs to improve mentally as well as physically, she's a cracking mover and it looks as if she'll live up to her good pedigree. She looks nice".*

236. BE MY ANGEL ★★★★
b.br.f. Dark Angel – Mullein (Oasis Dream). April 30. Fifth foal. Half-sister to the useful 6f (at 2 yrs) to 1m winner Carry On Deryck (by Halling), to the fair 7f winner Tarboosh (by Bahamian Bounty) and the fair 2-y-o 6f winner Got To Dance (by Selkirk). The dam, a useful listed 6f winner of 5 races, is a half-sister to 5 winners including the Group 2 Goodwood Cup and dual Group 3 winner of 10 races Illustrious Blue. The second dam, Gipsy Moth (by Efisio), a quite useful dual 5f winner at 2 yrs here, won a listed event in Germany and is a half-sister to 4 winners including the useful listed 1m winner and Group 2 Falmouth Stakes second Heavenly Whisper. (Landmark Racing Ltd). *"She looks really nice. Growing at a tremendous rate at the moment but she's a lovely mover and I should imagine she'll be ready to run in June or July. She'll be a six furlong filly and I like her for sure".*

237. BIRD OF WONDER ★★★
b.c. Hellvelyn – Phoenix Rising (Dr Fong). April 27. Fifth foal. 20,000Y. Tattersalls October Book 4. H Candy. Half-brother to

the modest 7f winner Arizona Sunrise (by Sakhee's Secret). The dam is an unplaced half-sister to 9 winners including the very useful 2-y-o 5f and 6f winner and Group 3 Cornwallis Stakes second Deadly Nightshade. The second dam, Dead Certain (by Absalom), a very smart winner of the Group 1 6f Cheveley Park Stakes and the Group 2 6.5f Prix Maurice de Gheest, is a half-sister to 7 winners and to the placed dam of the Group 2 Gimcrack Stakes winner Bannister. (H Candy & D Altham). *"He's gone very backward at the moment. He was quite a neat little horse when we bought him but he's grown a full hand over the winter. He's going to take a bit of time to come together but he's a lovely moving horse and he has a good pedigree. We have hopes for him and he'll make a 2-y-o in the second half of the year".*

238. CHOOSEY ★★★★
ch.c. Choisir – Petit Chou (Captain Rio) April 1. Third foal. 14,000Y. Tattersalls December. H Candy. The dam, a modest 1m winner, is a half-sister to 3 other minor winners. The second dam, Incense (by Unfuwain), a modest dual 1m placed maiden, is a half-sister to 6 winners including the useful Group 3 7f Prestige Stakes winner Icicle. (Thomas Frost). *"A very strong, mature colt – he looks like a 3-y-o already. He'll be working in April and I can see him being out around June time".*

239. CLAUDINE (IRE) ★★★
b.br.f. Zoffany – Hamalka (Alhaarth). March 4. Second foal. £7,000Y. Goffs UK Autumn. H Candy. The dam, a fair 10f and hurdles winner, is a half-sister to 6 winners including the fairly useful 7f and 1m winner Distant Connection. The second dam, Night Owl (by Night Shift), a modest 6f placed maiden, is a half-sister to 5 winners including Audacieuse (Group 3 10.5f Prix de Flore) and Waiter's Dream (Group 3 Acomb Stakes). (H Candy & Partners III). *"She looks quite sharp. Small and strong, she's going quite nicely at the moment and should be able to run in June".*

240. CLEVERLEY (IRE) ★★★
br.f. Mastercraftsman – Turning Point (Dalakhani). April 4. First foal. The dam is an unraced half-sister to several winners including the French listed 9f winner and Group 3 placed Rainbow Dancing, the fairly useful 1m (at 2 yrs) to 14f winner and listed-placed Handsome Man and the fairly useful 2-y-o 6f winner Zaffaan. The second dam, Danceabout (by Shareef Dancer), won the Group 2 Sun Chariot Stakes and is a half-sister to the dual Group 3 winner Pole Position. (Bloomsbury Stud). *"She looks very nice, she's big and strong but being by Mastercraftsman she wouldn't want to be doing much until the second part of the year".*

241. CONSTANCEA (IRE) ★★★
b.f. High Chaparral – Starfly (Invincible Spirit). March 24. Third foal. 19,000Y. Tattersalls October Book 3. H Candy. Half-sister to the fair 2-y-o 6f winner Harry Speed (by Dark Angel). The dam, a fair 2-y-o 5f winner, is a half-sister to 7 winners including the French listed 2-y-o 6f winner Mytographie and the dam of the Group 3 Nell Gwyn Stakes winner Esentepe. The second dam, Mythologie (by Bering), won once at 2 yrs and once over 1m at 3 yrs in France and is a half-sister to 7 winners including Malaspina (Group 3 Prix Perth). (M Hughes / A Frost). *"Another filly that's grown a lot over the last couple of months and she's just gone a bit backward. She's a lovely looking filly, very athletic but very much one for the second half of the year which isn't surprising given that she's by High Chaparral. She'll still have enough speed for a 2-y-o career though".*

242. CUBAN SPIRIT ★★★★
b.g. Harbour Watch – Madam Mojito (Smart Strike). March 16. Second foal. £16,000Y. Goffs UK Autumn. H Candy. Half-brother to Cuban Isabella (by Harbour Watch), placed fourth once over 7f from two starts at 2 yrs in 2016. The dam, a quite useful dual 5f winner at 2 yrs, is a half-sister to 2 minor winners. The second dam, Asuncion (by Powerscourt), is an unraced half-sister to 9 winners including the 2-y-o Group 2 and Group 3 winner Enthused. (Candy, Pritchard & Thomas). *"Another sharp 2-y-o, he's strong and knows his job. Going along nicely at the moment, he'll be one of the earlier ones and I can see him being out in late May or June".*

243. GOSCOTE ★★★
ch.f. Pivotal – Gosbeck (Dubawi). March 20.
Second foal. Half-sister to Beck And Call (by
Holy Roman Emperor), placed third twice
over 6f on both her starts at 2 yrs in 2016.
The dam, a quite useful 10f and 14f winner, is
a half-sister to one winner. The second dam,
Goslar (by In The Wings), a fairly useful 12f
winner, is a half-sister to 7 winners. (Major M
G Wyatt). *"She's very tall and fairly typical of
the sire. It's a lovely pedigree, she's very strong
and active but because of her size we'll have
to leave her until September time. A really
likeable filly and very classy".*

244. GREAT MIDGE ★★★★ ♣
b.c. Kyllachy – Super Midge (Royal Applause).
March 11. Fourth foal. £38,000Y. Goffs UK
Premier (Doncaster). Henry Candy. Half-
brother to the useful 2-y-o listed-placed 6f
winner Squash (by Pastoral Pursuits) and to
the modest 2-y-o 5f winner Frozen Princess
(by Showcasing). The dam ran twice unplaced
and is a sister to the 2-y-o Group 3 6f Prix
Eclipse Stakes winner Tremar and a half-sister
to 5 winners. The second dam, Sabina (by
Prince Sabo), a quite useful 2-y-o 5.7f winner,
is a half-sister to 8 winners including the
Group 2 Sun Chariot Stakes winner Lady In
Waiting, the US dual Grade 2 winner Grassy
and the Group 3 winner Savannah Bay. (Mr E
Penser). *"He's done well over the winter and
looks nice. He's very like his sire in many ways,
so I'd have high hopes for him. Hopefully he'll
be running in June".*

245. JUPITER ★★★
b.g. Finjaan – Medicea Sidera (Medicean).
February 21. Fourth foal. 35,000Y. Tattersalls
October Book 2. H Candy. Half-brother to
the quite useful 1m winner of 5 races winner
Hidden Rebel (by Cockney Rebel) and to the
fair dual 7f winner Brick Lane (by Bahamian
Bounty). The dam, a fairly useful triple 7f
winner, was listed-placed twice and is a
half-sister to 3 winners. The second dam,
Broughtons Motto (by Mtoto), a modest 5f
(at 2 yrs) to 10f winner, is a half-sister to 4
winners. (Girsonfield Ltd). *"I'm very pleased
with the way he's going now. He was very
coltish so we gelded him earlier on and he's
really settling in to his work now. He goes
nicely and I see him as a six furlong 2-y-o".*

The sire Finjaan, a son of Royal Applause, won
the Group 3 5f Molecomb Stakes at 2 and the
Group 2 7f Lennox Stakes at 3.

246. MARBLE BAR ★★★
b.c. Makfi – Presbyterian Nun (Daylami).
April 3. The dam, a fairly useful 2-y-o 7f
winner, was listed-placed and is a half-sister
to 5 winners including the Group 3 7f Minstrel
Stakes winner Jedburgh. The second dam,
Conspiracy (by Rudimentary), a useful 2-y-o
listed 5f winner, is a half-sister to 7 winners
including the Group 2 10f Sun Chariot Stakes
winner Ristna and the dual listed winner
Gayane. (The Earl Cadogan). *"He's remarkably
well up-together, well balanced and seems
very straight forward. By the look of him I
would think that even though he's out of a
Daylami mare he'll cope with six furlongs. He
should be out in June or July".*

247. ORD RIVER ★★★
b.f. Intello – Free Offer (Generous). March
24. Half-sister to the smart listed 1m winner
Cape Peron (by Beat Hollow), to the fair 8.5f
winners Tunnel Creek (by Tobougg) and Faure
Island (by Myboycharlie) and the modest
11.5f winner Free Passage (by Medicean). The
dam was a quite useful 7f (at 2 yrs) and dual
10f winner. The second dam, Proserpine (by
Robellino), a fairly useful 2-y-o 1m winner,
is a half-sister to the 1m and 10f winner and
subsequent US Grade 1 14f placed Chelsea
Barracks. (The Earl Cadogan). *"Backward at
the moment, but she's making giant strides
and she's a very strong, robust little filly. I
would think that once she starts work she'll
come to hand pretty quickly. I like her a lot
actually but she's just going through a bit of
a baby stage at the moment. It's a staying
pedigree, so she'll get a trip".*

248. ROSE HIP ★★★
b.f. Acclamation – Poppy Seed (Bold Edge).
February 20. Half-sister to the quite useful
2-y-o 5f winner Nisser (by Dream Ahead). The
dam won 3 races over 6f at 3 and 4 yrs and
was listed-placed and is a full or half-sister
to 5 winners. The second dam, Opopmil (by
Pips Pride), was placed twice at 2 yrs and is a
sister to the Group 1 6f Haydock Park Sprint
Cup winner Pipalong and a half-sister to 12
winners including the 2-y-o 6f listed winner

Out Of Africa. (Lady Whent). *"A filly with a lovely pedigree, she's big and has slightly outgrown her strength at the moment. It's going to take a fair while and she's not ready to do anything much at the moment, but she's a lovely, big, scopey filly and a typical Acclamation. We like her but it's a matter of time"*.

249. SARSTEDT ★★★★

b.c. Sixties Icon – Saluem (Salse). March 6. Third foal. £16,000Y. Goffs UK Silver Sale (Doncaster). Henry Candy. Half-brother to the minor Italian winner of 7 races from 3 to 5 yrs Monserat (by Dr Fong). The dam, a 4-y-o winner, is a half-sister to 5 winners including Triskel (listed Silver Flash Stakes). The second dam, Pat Or Else (by Alzao), placed three times over 14f, is a half-sister to 7 winners including the Group 1 12f Prix Vermeille winner My Emma and the Group 1 St Leger and Group 1 Ascot Gold Cup winner Classic Cliché. *"He's very sharp, although he's not really bred to be so. He loves his work and he'll be one of the earlier 2-y-o's the way things are looking at the moment, so he may well start at five furlongs"*. TRAINERS' BARGAIN BUY

250. SOVEREIGN DUKE ★★★

b.c. Jukebox Jury – Shadow Queen (Lando). March 30. Fifth foal. 50,000Y. Tattersalls October Book 2. H Candy. Half-brother to the German Group 3 winners Survey (by Big Shuffle) and Shadow Sadness (by Soldier Hollow). The dam, a minor German 3-y-o winner, is a half-sister to 5 winners. The second dam, Simply Red (by Dashing Blade), a minor German 3-y-o winner, is a half-sister to 8 winners. (One Too Many). *"A big horse, he's one for the second half of the year. A strong colt and a good mover, he looks quite classy and we're hopeful for him"*.

251. THRAVE ★★★

b.c. Sir Percy – Feis Ceoil (Key Of Luck). March 28. Third foal. £88,000Y. Goffs UK Premier (Doncaster). Henry Candy. The dam, a fair 7f winner, is a half-sister to 7 winners including the French Group winners Stretarez and Street Shaana. The second dam, Street Opera (by Sadler's Wells), a minor Irish 14f winner, is a half-sister to 10 winners including the Group winners Grape Tree Road, Red Route and Windsor Castle. (T Barr). *"A nice, big horse that looks quite classy, I haven't done much with him and he's just cantered upsides. I like the way he goes and I think he'll come to hand around July time. A lovely, big, scopey horse"*.

252. TWILIGHT THYME ★★★

b.f. Bahamian Bounty – Twilight Mistress (Bin Ajwaad). March 27. Half-sister to the Group 1 Diamond Jubilee Stakes and Group 1 6f Haydock Park Sprint Cup winner Twilight Son (by Kyllachy), to the Group 3 6f Hackwood Stakes winner Music Master, the fairly useful 6f and 7f winner The Confessor (both by Piccolo), the fairly useful dual 6f winner Spring Fling (by Assertive), the fair 6f (including at 2 yrs) and 5f winner Night Affair and the modest 6f and 7f winner of 6 races Shaded Edge (both by Bold Edge). The dam, a quite useful 5f to 7f winner of 3 races, is a half-sister to 3 winners including the useful 2-y-o 6f winner and listed 7f placed Romantic Evening. The second dam, By Candlelight (by Roi Danzig), was a quite useful 6f winner at 3 yrs. (G Wilson). *"The dam has been a fantastic broodmare, with Twilight Son (now a stallion) being the best of them. He certainly did us proud. This filly was tiny when she came in and very naughty, but she's growing rapidly at the moment and looks lovely. I think she'll be nice and I can see her starting off at six furlongs"*.

253. WEAR IT WELL ★★★

b.f. Kodiac – Choosey Girl (Choisir). February 19. Fifth foal. £32,000Y. Goffs UK Premier (Doncaster). Henry Candy. Half-sister to the fair 6f winner Bay Mirage (by Kheleyf). The dam is an unplaced half-sister to 9 winners including the Group 2 Superlative Stakes and Group 2 Bosphorus Cup winner Halicarnassus. The second dam, Launch Time (by Relaunch), is a US placed half-sister to 4 winners including the US Grade 2 winner Palace March. (Andrew Whitlock Racing Ltd). *"A small, strong, sharp filly that should come to hand early. She's just starting to do a bit now and the combination of Kodiac and Choisir should be reasonably sharp I think!"*

MICK CHANNON

254. AQUADABRA ★★★
b.f. Born To Sea – Amazing Win (Marju). May 10. Third foal. 18,000Y. Tattersalls October Book 4. Gill Richardson. Half-sister to the moderate 2016 dual 5f placed 2-y-o Zaatar (by Fast Company). The dam, a modest 5.5f and 6f winner of 4 races at 4 yrs, is a half-sister to one minor winner. The second dam, Aqaba (by Lake Coniston), a modest 6f placed 2-y-o, is a half-sister to 4 winners including Alcazar (Group 1 Prix Royal-Oak) and Lady Of Chad (Group 1 Prix Marcel Boussac). (Insignia Racing, Flag). *"She's quite sharp and looks like a 2-y-o. She'll be one of our earlier ones, she'll be OK and despite being by Born To Sea she's got plenty of speed".*

255. BEER WITH THE BOYS ★★★
b.c. Nathaniel – Bathilde (Generous). April 18. Eighth living foal. 120,000Y. Tattersalls October Book 1. Gill Richardson. Half-brother to the Group 1 Dubai Duty Free and Group 2 Dante Stakes third Al Shemali (by Medicean), to the Group 2 Henry II Stakes winner Tungsten Strike (by Smart Strike), the useful 10f to 15f winner and listed-placed Hammerfest (by Fantastic Light), the fairly useful 7f (at 2 yrs) and 6f winner and listed-placed Arabian Mirage (by Oasis Dream) and the quite useful 2-y-o 7f winner Baillieston (by Indian Ridge). The dam, a useful listed-placed 10.4f winner, is a half-sister to 10 winners including Crimson Quest (Group 2 Prix du Conseil de Paris) and four listed winners. The second dam, Bex (by Explodent), won the Group 3 10.5f Prix de Flore and is a half-sister to 12 winners. (G D P Materna). *"If he's not a nice horse I'll be very disappointed. He's a lovely colt but his pedigree is all about next year. So we haven't done anything with him yet and I couldn't say anything more than he'll probably have a run or two later in the season".*

256. BILLY RAY ★★★
b.c. Sixties Icon – Fiumicino (Danehill Dancer). April 17. Brother to the fairly useful 6f (at 2 yrs), French listed 1m and 2017 Group 3 1m Park Express Stakes winner Czabo. The dam, a fairly useful 2-y-o 1m winner, was listed-placed and is a half-sister to the German

2-y-o 7f winner Bagutta Sun. The second dam, Valhalla (by Sadler's Wells), ran twice unplaced and is a half-sister to the winners and Group 3 placed Sugar Ray and Gaspar Van Wittel. (Mr P Trant). *"A smashing horse, he's one for the end of the season and he's a full-brother to Czabo. He's a big horse, so he'll need time and seven furlongs plus".*

257. BREXITMEANSBREXIT ★★★
b.f. Helmet – Lady Scarlett (Woodman). February 16. Tenth foal. Half-sister to 7 winners including the Group 3 7f Prix du Palais Royal winner Rossa Corsa (by Footstepsinthesand), the quite useful 2-y-o 1m winner Whistleinthewind (by Oratorio), the quite useful 5f and 6f winner of 7 races and listed-placed Sunrise Safari (by Mozart), the quite useful 10f winner Val O'Hara (by Ad Valorem) and the fair 7f winner Lady Estella (by Equiano). The dam is an unraced half-sister to 5 winners including the Hong Kong listed winner and Irish Derby third Desert Fox and the US Grade 3 winners Poolesta and Home Of The Free. The second dam, Radiant (by Foolish Pleasure), won once at 3 yrs and is a half-sister to the triple Grade 1 winner Gold And Ivory. (Mr M Stewksbury). *"Going nicely, she's probably a six furlong 2-y-o rather than five and she does everything real well. A lovely filly".*

258. CHARMING GUEST ★★★★
b.f. Kodiac – Na Zdorovie (Cockney Rebel). March 16. Second foal. 120,000Y. Tattersalls October Book 1. Gill Richardson. The dam, a quite useful 2-y-o 7f winner, is a sister to the winner and Group 2 Park Hill Stakes second Groovejet and a half-sister to 7 winners including the useful 2-y-o 7f winner and US triple Grade 2 10f winner Slim Shadey. The second dam, Vino Veritas (by Chief's Crown), placed fourth once over 7f at 2 yrs, is a half-sister to the multiple Hong Kong and Japanese Group 1 winner Bullish Luck. (John Guest Racing Ltd). *"She goes well. She's a nice filly and I can see her being out in May or June. When she's sharpened up we think she'll be pretty good, so we'll see how we go. She is just a bit hairy in her coat, that's why I haven't done a lot with her yet".*

259. DARK BLUE ★★★
b.f. Dark Angel – Lapis Blue (Invincible Spirit).
February 18. First foal. €75,000Y. Goffs Orby.
Gill Richardson. The dam, a fair 6f winner at 4
yrs, is a half-sister to 5 winners including the
Irish listed winner Go For Goal. The second
dam, Triple Try (by Sadler's Wells), a quite
useful Irish dual 10f winner, is a sister to the
Irish Oaks and Tattersalls Gold Cup winner
Dance Design and a half-sister to 4 winners.
(Mrs A C Black). *"A nice filly, just doing good
canters at the moment. Once they start to
come in their coats we'll do a bit more. She'd
be in the main bunch I think and I'm very
happy with her"*.

260. DIAMOND DOUGAL ★★★
b.c. Zebedee – Blue Saphire (Acclamation).
April 7. First foal. £22,000Y. Goffs UK Premier
(Doncaster). Gill Richardson. The dam is an
unraced half-sister to 4 winners including the
Irish listed 6f winner of 5 races Minalisa. The
second dam, Mina (by Selkirk), a modest 6f
winner at 4 yrs, is a half-sister to 5 winners
including the Group 3 5f Ballyogan Stakes
winner Miss Anabaa and the smart 5f and 6f
winner of 6 races Out After Dark. (Insignia
Racing, Flag). *"A definite 2-y-o that shows all
the right signs. He might need six furlongs I
suppose because he's got a bit of scope, but
he'll be quick enough to start over five and
he'll be ready soon"*. TRAINERS' BARGAIN BUY

261. DUSTY ★★★
ch.f. Paco Boy – Hairspray (by Bahamian
Bounty). April 25. Third foal. Half-sister to
the useful listed 7f (at 2 yrs) and Group 3
8.5f Princess Elizabeth Stakes winner Epsom
Icon (by Sixties Icon). The dam, a fairly useful
6f winner of 4 races (including at 2 yrs), is
a sister to 2 winners and a half-sister to 5
winners including the useful listed-placed
2-y-o Medieval. The second dam, Quickstyx
(by Night Shift), a fair 1m winner, is a half-
sister to 5 winners including the smart 12f
listed winner and US dual Grade 1 placed
Red Fort and the useful 12f listed winner Red
Carnation. (Norman Court Stud). *"A little,
busy, half-sister to Epsom Icon. She looks real
sharp, has had a little setback otherwise she'd
have been one of the early ones. Built to be a
2-y-o and a five/six furlong one"*.

262. EDEN ROSE ★★★
b.f. Dansili – Gallic Star (Galileo). May 3. Third
foal. Half-sister to the quite useful 1m winner
Star Blaze (by Shamardal). The dam, a fairly
useful 2-y-o 6f and listed 1m winner, was
third in the Group 2 Ribblesdale Stakes and is
a half-sister to one winner. The second dam,
Oman Sea (by Rahy), a quite useful 2-y-o 6f
winner, is a sister to the Group 3 Criterion
Stakes winner Racer Forever. (Jon & Julia
Aisbitt). *"A big filly, I trained the mare and this
is a nice looking filly but one for much later
on"*.

263. ERASTUS ★★★★
b.c. Swiss Spirit – Blakeshall Rose (Tobougg).
April 29. Eighth foal. Half-brother to the
quite useful listed-placed 5f and 6f winner
of four races at 2 and 3 yrs Effie B, to the fair
6f (at 2 yrs) to 7f winner Willsy (by Sakhee's
Secret) and the modest 2-y-o dual 6f winner
Miss Muga (by Imperial Dancer). The dam, a
modest 6f placed maiden, is a half-sister to
2 winners. The second dam, Giggleswick Girl
(by Full Extent), was a modest 6f (at 2 yrs) and
5f winner of 4 races. (Bastian Family). *"A nice
horse and one of the earlier 2-y-o's. He shows
all the right signs, he's sharp and we have two
nice ones by Swiss Spirit"*.

264. FAYROUZ ROSE ★★★
b.f. Epaulette – Very Nice (Daylami). April
28. Eighth foal. 26,000Y. Tattersalls October
Book 2. Gill Richardson. Half-sister to the
2-y-o 1m listed-placed (from only two starts)
Teofilo's Princess (by Teofilo), to the fairly
useful triple 7f winner Seek N' Destroy (by
Exceed And Excel), the quite useful Irish 2-y-o
6f winner Very Elusive (by Elusive City) and
the modest 7f (at 2 yrs) and dual 6f winner
Dream Number (by Fath). The dam is an
unraced half-sister to 5 winners. The second
dam, All Time Great (by Night Shift), a fairly
useful 2-y-o 6f winner, is closely related to the
Dante Stakes and Craven Stakes winner Alnasr
Alwasheek and a half-sister to 7 winners
including the One So Wonderful (Juddmonte
International Stakes) and Relatively Special
(Rockfel Stakes). (Mr Jaber Abdullah). *"She's
grown on us but she's quite a nice filly and
a good goer. I don't think she'll be real early
simply because of her size"*.

265. HELVETIAN ★★★
b.c. Swiss Spirit – Lucky Dip (Tirol). April 14. Fifteenth foal. €33,000Y. Tattersalls Ireland September. Gill Richardson. Half-brother to 8 winners including the useful 2-y-o listed 5f and subsequent US stakes winner Fortunately (by Forzando), the quite useful 2-y-o 5f winner Everyday Lettuce (by Showcasing), the fair 5f to 1m winner of 9 races Halsion Chancer (by Atraf), the fair 2-y-o 5f winner Wittily (by Whittingham), the modest 6f winner Diamond Surprise (by Mark Of Esteem) and the modest 7f winner Kinky (by Kingsinger). The dam, a modest 3-y-o 5f winner, is a half-sister to 8 winners. The second dam, Miss Loving (by Northfields), a fairly useful 2-y-o 5f and 7f winner, is a half-sister to 6 winners including the useful 5f to 1m winner Cremation and the dam of the Australian Group 1 winner Sapieha. (Box 41). *"He goes well, he did his first bit of work yesterday and went nicely. A very nice colt, he'll be a 2-y-o when the six furlong races come along".*

266. JAZEEL (IRE) **★★★**
b.c. Roderic O'Connor – Simla Bibi (Indian Ridge). April 25. Ninth foal. 40,000Y. Tattersalls October Book 2. Hugo Merry. Half-brother to 5 winners including the useful 1m to 11f winner of 12 races Emerald Wilderness (by Green Desert), the fairly useful dual 5f (at 2 yrs) and 6f winner and listed-placed Ooh Aah Camara (by Danehill Dancer), the quite useful 9f (at 2 yrs) to 12f winner Swift Alhaarth (by Alhaarth) and the quite useful 7f and 1m winner Simla Sunset (by One Cool Cat). The dam, placed over 1m at 2 yrs, is a half-sister to 10 winners including the German Group 1 winner Lady Jane Digby. The second dam, Scandalette (by Niniski), is an unraced half-sister to the Group 1 July Cup winner Polish Patriot. (Mr A Al-Abdulrazzaq). *"He's probably going to need seven furlongs or a mile, he moves well and does everything right but he just needs time".*

267. JEAN PAGET ★★★
b.f. Choisir – Betty Fontaine (Mujadil). February 24. Second foal. Half-sister to the modest 2016 6f placed 2-y-o Smiley Riley (by Fast Company). The dam, a fairly useful 2-y-o 5f winner of 3 races, is out of the Irish 7f placed Dance Fontaine (by Danehill Dancer), herself a half-sister to 7 winners. (Mrs T Burns). *"A nice filly out of a mare I trained, she does everything right and she's one that could come relatively early. She's still a bit hairy and backward but doing nice canters and we're happy with her".*

268. MIDSUMMER KNIGHT ★★★★
b.c. Dream Ahead – High Spice (Songandaprayer). May 10. Fourth foal. Brother to the modest 2016 2-y-o 5f winner Fiery Spice and half-brother to the modest dual 5f winner More Spice (by Exceed And Excel). The dam, a quite useful triple 5f winner at 2 and 3 yrs, is a half-sister to 2 minor winners in the USA. The second dam, Erin Moor (by Holy Bull), a US 2-y-o 7f and 1m winner, is out of a half-sister to the US Grade 1 winners Will On The Move and Will's Way. (K A Dasmal). *"A lovely, big horse that goes well. He'll make a 2-y-o when the six furlong races start. Come May time when he gets a bit of sun on his back he could be a very nice colt".*

269. NEOLA ★★★★
b.f. Foxwedge – Effie B (Sixties Icon). February 6. First foal. The dam, a quite useful listed-placed 5f and 6f winner of four races at 2 and 3 yrs Effie B, is a half-sister to 2 winners including the fair 6f (at 2 yrs) to 7f winner Willsy. The second dam, Blakeshall Rose (by Tobougg), a modest 6f placed maiden, is a half-sister to 2 winners. (Bastian Family). *"She's very sharp and goes really well. It's a family we know well, she'll be a nice 2-y-o filly and one of our earliest"*

270. ROYAL GOLDIE (IRE) ★★★
b.f. Havana Gold – Dream Maker (Bahamian Bounty). January 24. First foal. £20,000Y. Goffs UK Premier (Doncaster). The dam, a quite useful 2-y-o dual 6f winner, is a half-sister to 2 winners including the fairly useful 8.5f (at 2 yrs) to 12f winner Farquhar. The second dam, Pointed Arch (Rock Of Gibraltar), a modest 12f winner, is closely related to the listed 12f winner Chartres and a half-sister to 7 winners including the dual listed winner Pugin and the dam of the 2-y-o Group 2 Railway Stakes winner Lilbourne Lad. (Mr Jaber Abdullah). *"A seven furlong type 2-y-o, she's a nice big filly with size and scope".*

271. SHORT CALL (IRE) ★★★

b.f. Kodiac – Wiwilia (Konigstiger). March 6. First foal. €45,000Y. Goffs Orby. Gill Richardson. The dam won 2 minor races at 2 yrs in Switzerland and is a half-sister to 7 winners including the US Grade 1 Man O'War Stakes winner Wake Forest. The second dam, Wurfspiel (by Lomitas), a listed-placed 3-y-o winner in Germany, is a half-sister to 8 winners including the dual Group 2 winner Wurftaube. (Mr Jaber Abdullah). *"This is a nice filly. She's just a bit backward in her coat but a few of ours are like that at the moment. She goes well and she'll be a 2-y-o".*

272. SILCA MISTRESS ★★★

ch.f. Dutch Art – Strictly Silca (Danehill Dancer). March 2. First foal. The dam, a quite useful listed-placed 2-y-o, won over 6f and 1m at 3 yrs. The second dam, Silca Chiave (by Pivotal), a smart 2-y-o 6f winner, was placed in the Group 1 Moyglare Stud Stakes and the Group 1 Cheveley Park Stakes and is a half-sister to 8 winners including the Group 1 6f Prix Morny winner Silca's Sister and the Group 2 6f Mill Reef Stakes and German Group 2 winner Golden Silca. (Aldridge Racing Partnership). *"I'm delighted with her – she's a real 'Silca' horse. We'll just let her come to herself, she's very laid-back and when the weather changes she'll change too. I think she's a 2-y-o alright".*

273. SIXTIES SECRET ★★★★

b.f. Sixties Icon – Jollyhockeysticks (Fantastic Light). May 9. Fourth foal. Sister to the modest 7f and 1m placed 2-y-o Barefoot Sandy. The dam, placed over 1m from four runs as a 2-y-o and a modest 3-y-o 1m winner, was also disqualified from first place in another 1m event. She is a half-sister to 5 winners including Pic Up Sticks (a fairly useful listed-placed winner of 9 races at up to 7f). The second dam, Between The Sticks (by Pharly), a listed-placed dual 5f winner at 2 yrs, is a half-sister to 4 winners. (J P Coggan). *"She's a very nice filly and very like another good Sixties Icon filly of ours, Epsom Icon. Tall and leggy, she needs time but she holds her own with the early ones. We won't be seeing her until the six/seven furlong races".*

274. SO NEAR SO FARHH ★★★

ch.f. Farhh – Protectress (Hector Protector). February 24. Tenth foal. 10,000Y. Tattersalls October Book 1. Oliver St Lawrence. Half-sister to the quite useful multiple all-weather winner from 9f to 14f Stand Guard (by Danehill), to the fair dual 12f winner Omnipresent and the fair 1m winner Wafeira (by Dansili). The dam, a useful 2-y-o listed 7f winner, is a half-sister to 5 winners including the useful 12f to 14f winner and listed-placed Market Forces (by Lomitas). The second dam, Quota (Rainbow Quest), a useful 10f winner, is a sister to 4 winners including the Group 1 1m Racing Post Trophy winner and St Leger second Armiger. *"She goes nicely and will probably be a seven furlong 2-y-o. Quite a nice filly that just needs a bit of time".*

275. STILL GOT IT ★★★

b.f. Captain Gerrard – Petaluma (Teofilo). March 28. First foal. The dam, a fair 2m 1f winner, is a half-sister to 3 winners including the French 7.5f (at 2 yrs) to 9.5f winner of 3 races and listed-placed Nabbaash. The second dam, Poppo's Song (by Polish Navy), a Canadian stakes winner of 2 races at 3 and 4 yrs, is a half-sister to 3 winners. *"She goes alright and she's probably a six furlong filly because she's got a bit of size about her. Quite a good-looking filly".*

276. TROGON (IRE) ★★★

ch.c. Leroidesanimaux – Savanna Days (Danehill Dancer). February 11. First foal. The dam, a fair 1m winner, is a half-sister to a 2-y-o winner. The second dam, Dominante (by Monsun), a German listed 10f winner, was second in the Group 1 German Oaks. (Jon & Julia Aisbitt). *"A lovely, big horse that's doing everything right but I think he's going to need at least seven furlongs".*

277. WHY WE DREAM (IRE) ★★★★

b.f. Al Kazeem – Sandreamer (Oasis Dream). February 5. First foal. The dam, a useful 2-y-o, won twice over 6f including a listed event in Italy and was second in the Group 3 6f Princess Margaret Stakes. She is a half-sister to four winners including the French listed-placed Assume. The second dam, Alsharq (by Machiavellian), a modest 7f winner, is a full or half-sister to 6 winners including Sayedah (Group 2 7f Rockfel Stakes). (Jon & Julia Aisbitt). *"She's very nice, goes really well and I think she'll be a May/June type 2-y-o. A good-looking filly with a bit of size and scope to her, she's much bigger than her dam who was small and sharp".*

278. UNNAMED ★★
b.c. Sepoy – Bold Bidder (Indesatchel). March 8. Third foal. 68,000Y. Tattersalls October Book 2. Gill Richardson. Half-brother to the quite useful triple 5f winner at 2 and 3 yrs Celebration (by Equiano). The dam, a quite useful 2-y-o dual 5f winner, is a half-sister to 4 winners. The second dam, Quiz Show (by Primo Dominie), a quite useful 7f winner, is a half-sister to 4 winners including the high-class sprinter Mind Games, winner of the Group 2 Temple Stakes (twice), the Norfolk Stakes and the Palace House Stakes. *"A nice but backward colt that had a bit of a setback so we haven't done a lot with him. We'll have to get on with him soon".*

279. UNNAMED ★★★
b.c. Red Jazz – Clodilla (Clodovil). March 1. Third foal. £45,000Y. Goffs UK Premier (Doncaster). Gill Richardson. The dam, a minor Italian 3-y-o winner, is a full or half-sister to 4 winners including the fairly useful 2-y-o 7f winner and listed-placed One More Road and the fairly useful 5f winner of 4 races and Group 3 Molecomb Stakes third Archers Road. The second dam, Somoushe (by Black Minnaloushe), is an unraced half-sister to 9 winners including the German Group 1 10f winner Ransom O'War. *"He goes well and looks quite sharp. A bit of a playboy, but he's a nice horse and just starting to go the right way. He'll be a 2-y-o over six furlongs".*

280. UNNAMED ★★★
b.f. Fast Company – Common Cause (Polish Patriot). February 18. €20,000Y. Goffs Sportsmans. John Walsh. Half-sister to 5 winners including the Irish listed 9f winner of 9 races Wovoka, the moderate 7f winner Banjo Bandit (both by Mujadil), the fair 1m and hurdles winner Letham Island and the moderate 10f and 11f winner Litenup (both by Trans Island) and to the placed dam of

the Italian 2-y-o Group 2 second Singapore Lilly. The dam, a quite useful 11.5f and 11.8f winner, is a half-sister to 4 minor winners. The second dam, Alongside, (by Slip Anchor), an Irish 4-y-o 9f winner, is a half-sister to 3 winners including the Group 2 Prix Eugene Adam winner Kirkwall. (Mrs T Burns). *"A very nice filly, she's quite big and just prone to overreaching which has held us up. But I think she's a 2-y-o alright".*

281. UNNAMED ★★★
b.c. Sixties Icon – Evanesce (Lujain). February 21. Brother to the fair 2-y-o dual 7f winner Yorkshire Icon and to the fair 2-y-o 5f winner Amahoro and half-brother to the fair 6f winner (including at 2 yrs) to 2m and jumps winner Alfraamsay (by Fraam) and the modest 2-y-o dual 5f seller winner Selinda (by Piccolo). The dam, a fair 2-y-o 6f winner, is a half-sister to 4 winners and to the unraced dam of the Group 3 Supreme Stakes and UAE Group 2 winner Opal Tiara. The second dam, Search Party (Rainbow Quest), a fair 8.3f and 10f placed maiden, is a half-sister to 5 winners including the 6f (at 2 yrs) and US Grade 1 10f winner Bequest. (Gill & Dave Hedley). *"He's one of the Sixties Icon's that'll be better next year and possibly be classic types. A seven furlong/mile type for later in the season, he's a nice, big horse with loads of scope".*

282. UNNAMED ★★★
b.c. Camacho – Fanciful Dancer (Groom Dancer). April 25. Fifth foal. 50,000Y. Tattersalls October Book 2. Gill Richardson. Half-brother to the useful 6f (at 2 yrs) and listed 1m winner and Group 2 German 2,000 Guineas second Fanciful Angel (by Dark Angel) and to the minor French 2-y-o winner Naloudia (by Piccolo). The dam is an unraced half-sister to 3 winners including the dam of the dual listed winners Distinctly Dancer and Evening Time. The second dam, Fanciful (by Gay Mecene), a minor French 3-y-o winner, is a half-sister to 8 winners including the Group 2 6f Lowther Stakes winner and Group 1 second and smart broodmare Kingscote. (Box 41 Racing). *"He's a lovely, big colt and we paid a fair amount for him. I couldn't say he'll be a five furlong 2-y-o, he's more than likely one for the middle of the season".*

283. UNNAMED ★★
b.f. Kodiac – Jeritza (Rainbow Quest). May 14. Seventh foal. 20,000Y. Tattersalls October Book 3. Gill Richardson. Half-sister to a minor 4-y-o winner in Germany by Tiger Hill. The dam, a minor French 12f winner, is a sister to the useful listed-placed 9f to 13f winner Jade Quest and a half-sister to 6 winners. The second dam, Jade Jewel (by Mr Prospector), is an unplaced sister to the US dual Grade 1 winner Jade Hunter. *"She's just had a hold-up but she was going really nicely. I was hoping to get on with her but we'll have to be a bit more patient. Quite nice though".*

284. UNNAMED ★★★
b.c. Canford Cliffs – Josphiel (Okawango). February 9. Fourth foal. 42,000Y. Tattersalls October Book 2. Gill Richardson. Half-brother to the minor Italian 2-y-o winner Incantevole Maggie (by Intense Focus). The dam, a moderate dual 6f placed maiden, is a half-sister to 7 winners including the listed winner and Group 1 Cheveley Park Stakes third Good Girl. The second dam, Indian Honey (by Indian King), is an unraced half-sister to 7 winners. *"A lovely, big colt that could be anything. He does everything really well, he's pretty mature and has a good mental outlook".*

285. UNNAMED ★★★
b.c. Sixties Icon – Selinda (Piccolo). March 5. Second foal. The dam, a modest 2-y-o dual 5f seller winner, is a half-sister to 3 winners including the 2-y-o dual 7f winner Yorkshire Icon, the 2-y-o 5f winner Amahoro and the 6f . winner (including at 2 yrs) to 2m and jumps winner Alfraamsay – all fair winners and to the unraced dam of the Group 3 Supreme Stakes and UAE Group 2 winner Opal Tiara. The second dam, Evanesce (by Lujain), a fair 2-y-o 6f winner, is a half-sister to 4 winners. (Dave & Gill Hedley). *"A good-looking horse, he's quite mature so he'll probably make a 2-y-o but not until later in the year".*

286. UNNAMED ★★★
b.c. Arcano – Semplicita (In The Wings). February 2. Fifth foal. 28,000Y. Tattersalls October Book 3. Gill Richardson. Half-brother to the minor Italian winner at 2 and 3 yrs Real Acclamation (by Acclamation). The dam, a

winner of 10 races from 3 to 6 yrs in Italy, is a half-sister to 3 other minor winners and to the placed dam of the dual Group 1 King's Stand Stakes winner Equiano. The second dam, Mirmande (by Kris), is an unplaced half-sister to 5 winners including the listed winner Sir Simon and the Group 2 placed Dartrey. *"He's done a fair bit of growing so we haven't pressed any buttons with him yet. He'll be alright for six or seven furlongs in mid-season".*

287. UNNAMED ★★★
b.f. Lethal Force – Spritzeria (Bigstone). March 3. Seventh foal. 24,000Y. Tattersalls October Book 2. Gill Richardson. Half-sister to the quite useful 6f and 7f winner of 8 races Esprit De Midas (by Namid), to the fair 5f and 6f winner of 4 races Be Lucky (by Kyllachy) and a 4-y-o winner in Hong Kong by Green Desert. The dam, a quite useful 2-y-o 6f winner, is a half-sister to 8 winners including the smart 2-y-o 6f winner and Group 1 1m Racing Post Trophy third Henrik , the useful 2-y-o 6f winner and Group 2 6f Gimcrack Stakes third Sir Reginald and the fairly useful listed 7f winner Intense Pink. The second dam, Clincher Club (by Polish Patriot), a fair 5f (at 2 yrs) and 7.5f winner, is a half-sister to 9 winners. *"She goes well, she's a big filly and should be alright over six or seven furlongs".*

288. UNNAMED ★★★
b.f. Dandy Man – The Last Laugh (Kyllachy). March 7. Third foal. €22,000Y. Tattersalls Ireland September. Gill Richardson. Half-sister to the modest 7f seller (at 2 yrs) and 4-y-o 6f winner Laughing Rock (by Rock Of Gibraltar). The dam, a fair Irish 2-y-o 5f winner, is a half-sister to 6 winners including the Irish Group 3 third Turnkey. The second dam, Persian Air (by Persian Bold), is an unplaced half-sister to 3 minor winners. *"She goes well and she'll be a 2-y-o alright. She's nice, but a couple of minor issues set us back a bit".*

289. UNNAMED ★★★
b.c. Invincible Spirit – Three Days In May (Cadeaux Genereux). May 12. Seventh living foal. Half-brother to the quite useful 2016 2-y-o 7f winner Naval Warfare (by Born To Sea), to the Group 2 Hungerford Stakes and Group 3 Diomed Stakes winner Gregorian, the useful listed-placed 8.5f winner Manderley

and the fairly useful 2-y-o 6f winner Kalam Daleel (all by Clodovil). The dam, a fair 3-y-o 6f winner, is a half-sister to 8 winners including the very useful Group 1 Cheveley Park Stakes second Crazcc Mental - herself dam of the multiple Group 2 winner Premio Loco. The second dam, Corn Futures (by Nomination), a fair 2-y-o 6f winner, is a half-sister to 7 winners. (Irish National Stud & Mrs T Burns). *"A nice colt but he was a May foal and I don't think he'll be real early. A good mover that's doing everything right, he'll make a 2-y-o in mid-season".*

PETER CHAPPLE-HYAM
290. GIOVANNA ★★
b.c. So You Think – Golden Wave (Green Desert). February 22. Fourth foal. €15,000Y. Goffs Sportsmans. Troy Steve. The dam, a modest 10f and 12f placed maiden, is a half-sister to 4 winners and to the placed dam of the Group winners Turret Rocks and Beyond Thankful. The second dam, Gold Bust (by Nashwan), a minor winner at 3 yrs in France, is a half-sister to the dual Group 1 winner Gold Splash and the dam of the top-class filly Goldikova. *"He hasn't been here that long and he obviously didn't cost a lot, but he goes well. To me his action suggests he's going to want a trip and he could be a seven furlong/ miler when he starts. The sire's done well in Australia but so far not here. This horse will win races though".*

291. LUBINKA ★★★★
gr.f. Mastercraftsman – Petite Nymphe (Golan). February 19. Fourth foal. 55,000Y. Tattersalls October Book 2. Not sold. Half-sister to the quite useful 2016 2-y-o 7f winner Paulownia (by Nathaniel). The dam, a minor 3-y-o winner in France, is a half-sister to 11 winners including the French 1,000 Guineas and Prix de la Foret winner Danseuse Du Soir (herself dam of the Group 1 Gran Criterium winner Scintillo and the listed winners Dana Springs and Don Corleone and the dam of the Group 3 winners Audacieuse and Waiter's Dream. The second dam, Dance By Night (by Northfields), won twice over 7f at 2 yrs and is a half-sister to 3 winners. *"A very nice filly, she goes really nicely and does everything right. A quality filly for seven furlongs to a mile, she'll probably prefer a bit of ease in the ground and she's one I like a lot. She could be very good".*

292. MIRROR MIRROR ★★★
ch.f. Intello – Nouvelle Lune (Fantastic Light). February 10. Fifth foal. 30,000Y. Tattersalls October Book 2. Not sold. Half-sister to the quite useful 7f to 10f winner of 10 races from 3 to 8 yrs Maverik (by Iceman), to the quite useful 14f winner of 3 races Pleasure Dome (by Makfi), the fair 7f (including at 2 yrs), 6f and Qatar 9f winner Glassy Posse (by Dubawi) and the fair 8.5f winner Valley Of Destiny (by Three Valleys). The dam is an unraced half-sister to 6 winners including Audacieuse (Group 3 Prix de Flore winner and dam of the St Leger winner Kingston Hill) and Waiter's Dream (Group 3 Acomb Stakes). The second dam, Sarah Georgina (by Persian Bold), a quite useful 2-y-o 6f winner, is a half-sister to 11 winners including the French 1,000 Guineas winner Danseuse du Soir (dam of the Group 1 Gran Criterium winner Scintillo). *"I had the half-sister Pleasure Dome last year and they're totally different apart from their temperaments. She can be a madam in the box, she's sharper than Pleasure Dome and a nice filly that could run over six furlongs around June/July time. Andre Fabre brought Intello here to win at Newmarket and when I saw him I thought he was one of the most beautiful horses I've ever seen".*

293. UNNAMED ★★★
ch.c. Helmet – Countermarch (Selkirk). February 3. Second foal. 16,000Y. Tattersalls October Book 3. Not sold. The dam was a fair 8.5f winner at 3 yrs. The second dam, Day Of Reckoning (by Daylami), a fair 10f winner from two starts, is a half-sister to 5 winners including the Group 2 12f Ribblesdale Stakes and Group 2 13.3f Geoffrey Freer Stakes winner Phantom Gold. *"I like this horse. He wasn't sold but he goes along really well. Quite a big horse, he's possibly not as early as the owner would like him to be. I could see him running six or seven furlongs in June time. I like him, he's got a good engine and goes really well".*

294. UNNAMED ★★★
b.c. Clodovil – Lally Mut (Muhtathir). February 23. Third foal. Half-brother to the 2016 French 2-y-o 7f and 7.5f winner of 3 races Barbarigo (by Canford Cliffs) and to the minor Italian dual winner at 3 yrs Mersi (by

Kodiac). The dam, a minor winner in Italy 3 yrs, is a half-sister to 6 other minor winners. The second dam, Hadra (by Dayjur), placed at 2 yrs, is a half-sister to 4 winners. *"Quite sharp, she's not a big filly, wants to get on with things and is very active, so I'll give her until mid-April then see if she can take some work and if she can we'll kick on. She wouldn't be quick enough for five furlongs but she'll be a six furlong 2-y-o and could be racing in May".*

295. UNNAMED ★★★

b.c. Lope De Vega – Mauresmo (Marju). February 27. Third foal. 150,000Y. Tattersalls October Book 1. MakinStallions.com. Half-brother to the 2-y-o Group 1 1m Racing Post Trophy winner Marcel (by Lawman). The dam is an unraced sister to the winner of 6 races and Group 2 Diadem Stakes second Munjiz and a half-sister to 3 winners. The second dam, Absaar (by Alleged), a fair 11f winner, is a half-sister to 10 winners including Group/Grade 1 winners Annoconnor and At Talaq. The Great. *"A very nice horse, he's Marcel's half-brother but he doesn't look anything like him. Just going through a growing phase at the moment, he's got the Lope De Vega head which is quite ugly and he needs to fill into his frame but he goes up the canter so easy. He does everything perfectly well, but if I said July that would be early enough. All the sire's runners seem to like a bit of dig in the ground so I don't think this one will be any different. He'd be my nicest colt I think and he'll want seven furlongs".*

296. UNNAMED ★★★

b.c. Holy Roman Emperor – Peaceful Kingdom (King Of Kings). May 6. Sixth foal. 31,000Y. Tattersalls October Book 2. C McCormack. Half-brother to the fair 7f (at 2 yrs) and 10f winner Asgardella (by Duke Of Marmalade) and to the quite useful Irish 2-y-o 1m winner Righteous Man (by Mr Greeley). The dam is an unraced half-sister to 4 winners including the US Grade 1 Man O'War Stakes winner Magistretti. The second dam, Ms Strike Zone (by Deputy Minister), won once in the USA and is a half-sister to 6 other minor winners. *"A late foal, but having said that he's sharp and when it's his birthday he'll work. He'll be running at the end of May over six furlongs, he*

has a good engine and goes really well. I like him, I've had loads by this sire and I love them, but they're all buggers! I've worked it out that if they're quiet they're no good."*

297. UNNAMED ★★★

b.c. Kodiac – Quantum (Alhaarth). May 3. Seventh foal. 45,000Y. Tattersalls October Book 2. C McCormack. Half-brother to the fair 11f winner Captain Navarre (by Excellent Art) and to the fair 10f winner Sinaadi (by Kyllachy). The dam, a fairly useful 10f winner, is a half-sister to the 2-y-o Group 1 7f National Stakes winner Power, the Grade 1 EP Taylor Stakes winner Curvy and the Group 2 12f Ribblesdale Stakes winner Thakafaat. The second dam, Frappe (by Inchinor), a fairly useful 2-y-o 6f winner, is a half-sister to the Group 1 winners Footstepsinthesand and Pedro The Great. *"Another May foal, but that's the reason I got to buy him really, considering how expensive Kodiacs can be. He'd be my sharpest despite his foaling date and he'll definitely be running in May over six furlongs. He goes really well, he's strong and if I've got a Royal Ascot 2-y-o it's him".*

ROGER CHARLTON

298. AL KHERB ★★★

b.c. Al Kazeem – Perfect Spirit (Invincible Spirit). February 13. Sixth living foal. 180,000Y. Tattersalls October Book 1. Charlie Gordon-Watson / Al Shaqab. Closely related to the Group 3 7f Chartwell Stakes and listed 6f Pavilion Stakes winner Perfect Tribute (by Dubawi) and to the quite useful 2-y-o 7f winner Tadqeeq (by Makfi) and half-brother to the fair 10f winner Perfect Delight (by Dubai Destination). The dam is an unraced half-sister to 4 winners including the listed winner Swift Tango and the Group 3 Chester Vase third First Row. The second dam, Ballet Society (by Sadler's Wells), ran once unplaced and is a sister to the listed winner Synergetic and a half-sister to the 2,000 Guineas second Enrique. (Al Shaqab). *"A nice horse, he was very highly strung when he came here but he's settled down really well. Forward-going and a good mover, he's never going to be an over-heavy horse and he doesn't look backward. One for seven furlongs in mid-summer and we like him".*

299. ANTAGONIST ★★★
b.c. Dansili – Melodramatic (Sadler's Wells).
March 26. Third living foal. 150,000Y.
Tattersalls October Book 1. Not sold.
Half-brother to the very useful 10f and 11f
winner and Group 2 Hardwicke Stakes third
Almodovar (by Sea The Stars). The dam, a
useful 1m winner and second in the listed
Ballymacoll Stud Stakes, is closely related to
the Group 1 6f Haydock Sprint Cup winner
Tante Rose and a half-sister to 5 winners
including the dam of the Group 1 winners
Make Believe and Dubawi Heights. The
second dam, My Branch (by Distant Relative),
winner of the listed 6f Firth Of Clyde Stakes
(at 2 yrs) and the listed 7f Sceptre Stakes,
was second in the Group 1 Cheveley Park
Stakes and is a half-sister to 7 winners. (Mr
B Nielsen). *"He hasn't been here very long,
I trained the dam and grandam and we like
him. He's a good mover and a half-brother to
a good horse in Almodovar and although he'll
never be as big as that horse we like him".*

300. BLUE MIST ★★★
ch.c. Makfi – Namaskar (Dansili).
February 19. First foal. Half-brother to the
2016 French 2-y-o 7f winner and listed-
placed Obedient (by Motivator) and to the
smart 10f winner and Group 2 10.3f York
Stakes third Countermeasure (by American
Post). The dam was a quite useful 2-y-o 1m
winner. The second dam, Namaste (by Alzao),
is a modest 12f placed half-sister to the Irish
Oaks winner Wemyss Bight (dam of the
Group 1 winner Beat Hollow) and the dams of
three other Group 1 winners including Oasis
Dream. (Khalid Abdulla). *"A strong horse from
a good Juddmonte family, but he won't be
early. One for the second half of the year, like
most of mine".*

301. BUFFER ZONE ★★★
br.c. Bated Breath – Buffering (Beat Hollow).
April 17. Half-brother to the fair 1m winner
Roller (by Rail Link). The dam, a French
listed-placed 10f winner, is a half-sister to
one winner. The second dam, Mooring (by
Zafonic), a French 3-y-o listed 1m winner,
is a sister to 2 winners and a half-sister to 5
winners including the very useful 2-y-o Group
3 6f July Stakes and listed 3-y-o 9f winner
Wharf. (Khalid Abdulla). *"He's a good-looking,*

powerful horse with quite a lot of stamina on
the dam's side of his pedigree. Again, he's one
for the second half of the year".*

302. CANTERBURY ★★
b.f. Invincible Spirit – Mince (Medicean).
February 2. First foal. The dam, a Group 3 6f
Bengough Stakes and triple listed 6f winner,
is a half-sister to 3 winners. The second dam,
Strut (by Danehill Dancer), a 2-y-o listed
5.2f winner, was Group 3 placed twice and
is a half-sister to 3 winners including the US
Grade 3 6.5f third Vaunt. (Lady Rothschild).
*"The first foal of a good sprinter, she's quite
small but probably like the rest of the family in
that she won't be that early".*

303. CHIPPIE HILL ★★★
b.f. Camacho – With Colour (Rainbow Quest).
April 8. Sixth foal. 25,000Y. Tattersalls
December. Amanda Skiffington. Half-sister
to the useful 2-y-o 5f and 6f winner Pearl
Acclaim (by Acclamation), to the fair 1m to
10f and hurdles winner Our Phylli Vera (by
Motivator) and the modest 9f and 10f winner
Quest Of Colour (by Iffraaj). The dam is an
unplaced half-sister to 8 winners including the
smart 7f (at 2 yrs) and listed 10f winner With
Interest. The second dam, With Fascination
(by Dayjur), won the Group 3 6f Prix de
Cabourg and was Group 1 placed twice at 2
yrs and is a half-sister to 5 winners including
the US multiple Grade 1 winner With
Anticipation. (Michael Pescod). *"A powerful,
strong filly but out of a Rainbow Quest dam,
so there's a bit of stamina combined. But she
looks quite early so hopefully she'll be a 2-y-o
for June/July. I don't think she'll be out much
before that, but she's strong".*

304. CRAFTINESS ★★★★
b.f. Al Kazeem – Artful (Green Desert). January
19. Fifth foal. Half-sister to the 2-y-o listed 6f
winner Duplicity (by Cadeaux Genereux). The
dam, a minor 3-y-o winner in France, is a half-
sister to 4 winners including the Irish Group
3 C L Weld Park Stakes winner Chintz (dam
of the dual Group 1 winner The Gurkha). The
second dam, Gold Dodger (by Slew O'Gold),
a listed 10f winner of 2 races in France, is a
half-sister to 11 winners including the Prix
de l'Arc de Triomphe winner Solemia and the
Group winners Prospect Wells and Prospect

Park. (The Queen). *"She's pleased us and she's attractive and stronger than you might expect for a daughter of Al Kazeem. Probably more Green Desert to look at than him, but she looks quite forward and is certainly a positive for her sire".*

305. DIVINE ACT (IRE) ★★★

ch.f. Frankel – Ramruma (Diesis). April 19. Twelfth foal. €225,000Y. Goffs Orby. Joe Foley. Half-sister to 2 winners including the smart 1m and 12f winner and Group 1 Irish St Leger third Flying Cross (by Sadler's Wells). The dam won the Oaks, the Irish Oaks and the Yorkshire Oaks and is a half-sister to 9 winners including the Lingfield Oaks Trial winner and good broodmare Ausherra. The second dam, Princess Of Man (by Green God), won three races including the Group 3 Musidora Stakes and is a half-sister to 6 winners. (Clipper Logistics). *"Not here yet, but I saw her at the sales and thought she looked nice".*

306. FLEETING VIEW ★★

b.f Sixties Icon – Flash Of Gold (Darshaan). April 8. Seventh foal. Half-sister to the fairly useful 1m (at 2 yrs) and dual 12f winner Mustard, to the quite useful 10f winner Audacious (both by Motivator), the fairly useful 7f (including at 2 yrs) and 6f winner of four races Firestreak (by Green Desert), the quite useful 1m (at 2 yrs) to 13f winner Moidore (by Galileo) and the fair 12f winner Going For Gold (by Barathea). The dam, a fair 12f placed maiden, is a half-sister to 6 winners including the smart Group 2 12f Ribblesdale Stakes and Group 2 13.3f Geoffrey Freer Stakes winner Phantom Gold. The second dam, Trying For Gold (by Northern Baby), was a useful 12f and 12.5f winner at 3 yrs. (The Queen). *"Not yet in training, but the sire has certainly done alright from relatively limited opportunities".*

307. GAVOTA ★★★

b.f. Bated Breath – Ombre (Galileo). February 13. Second foal. The dam is an unraced half-sister to 4 winners including the useful French 7f (at 2 yrs) and 1m winner and listed placed World Ruler and the useful French 2-y-o dual 6f winner and Group 3 1m third Grand Vista. The second dam, Revealing (by Halling), a very useful 2-y-o 1m winner, is a half-sister

to the useful 12f winner and dual Group 3 placed Singleton and the useful 6f winner Brevity. (Khalid Abdulla). *"She moves well and looks quite forward, so despite being out of a Galileo mare by the middle of the year she should be running fast".*

308. GIOVANNI ACUTO (FR) ★★★

ch.c. Kendargent – Maybe (GER) (Dashing Blade). March 6. Fourth foal. 75,000Y. Tattersalls October Book 2. Amanda Skiffington. Brother to the minor French 3-y-o 1m winner of 3 races Kenbest and half-sister to 2 minor winners in France by Gentlewave and Stormy River. The dam, a minor French winner and listed-placed in Germany, is a half-sister to 3 other minor winners abroad. The second dam, Mamourina (by Barathea), won once at 3 yrs in Germany and is a half-sister to 7 winners including the French Group 2 winner and smart broodmare Mouramara. (Michael Pescod). *"He's a strong, powerful looking horse that I thought would be quite early, but he's going to need a bit more time. The stallion is doing well".*

309. HERCULEAN ★★★★★

ch.c. Frankel – African Rose (Observatory). April 21. Fifth foal. Brother to the smart 2016 2-y-o Group 3 6f Princess Margaret Stakes winner and dual Group 2 placed Fair Eva and half-brother to the fairly useful dual 1m winner Hakka (by Dansili). The dam, winner of the Group 1 6f Sprint Cup and a listed 7f event in France, is a sister to the 2-y-o Group 3 1m Prix d'Aumale winner Helleborine and a half-sister to one winner. The second dam, New Orchid (by Quest For Fame), a useful 10f winner and third in the Group 3 Lancashire Oaks, is a half-sister to 3 winners including the champion 2-y-o and Group 1 7f Dewhurst Stakes winner Distant Music. (Khalid Abdulla). *"A full-brother to Fair Eva, he's another nice Frankel. A good mover, a nice natured horse and bigger than her, he'll take more time than she did. But from what we've seen of him he looks very promising".*

310. KASSAR (IRE) ★★★

b.c. Exceed And Excel – Inchiri (Sadler's Wells). March 2. Twelfth foal. 100,000Y. Tattersalls October Book 2. Charlie Gordon-Watson / Al Shaqab. Half-sister to 6 winners including the very useful 10f winner and Epsom Oaks fourth Inchila (by Dylan Thomas), the quite useful dual 10f and subsequent South African Grade 3 winner Hawk's Eye (by Hawk Wing), the fairly useful 12f and 13f winner Inchwood (by Dubai Destination), the quite useful dual 7f (at 2 yrs) and 1m winner Celtic Step (by Selkirk) and the fair 7f (at 2 yrs) to 8.5f winner of 10 races Saharia (by Oratorio). The dam, a very useful listed 12f winner, is a half-sister to 4 winners. The second dam, Inchyre (by Shirley Heights), a useful 1m winner, is a half-sister to 7 winners including the triple Group 3 7f winner and sire Inchinor. (Al Shaqab). *"This colt has done well and I know the family well enough too. He's a good moving horse for seven furlongs from the mid-summer onwards".*

311. KLOSTERS ★★★

b.f. Kodiac – Seminova (Cape Cross). February 19. Fourth foal. 45,000Y. Tattersalls October Book 1. Bradley/Kelly. The dam ran once unplaced and is a half-sister to 2 minor winners abroad. The second dam, Snow Polina (by Trempolino), won 10 races including the Grade 1 Beverly D Stakes and is a half-sister to 2 winners. (Nick Bradley Racing). *"She looks quite forward and I should think she needs to press on and be a 2-y-o if possible".*

312. LOW PROFILE ★★

ch.c. Galileo – Dynaforce (Dynaformer). March 16. Fourth foal. €100,000Y. Goffs Orby. Badgers Bloodstock. Half-brother to promising 2016 2-y-o 1m winner Aljezeera (by Frankel) and to the minor US 3-y-o winner Lady Dyna (by Tapit). The dam won 5 races including the Grade 1 Flower Bowl Invitational and the Grade 1 Beverly D Stakes and is a half-sister to 11 winners including the US dual Grade 1 winner Cetewayo and the US Grade 2 winner Bowman Mill. The second dam, Aletta Maria (by Diesis), won 3 races in the USA at 3 and 4 yrs and is a sister to the Group 3 Lancashire Oaks winner Pharian and a half-sister to the Group 2 winner Raah Algharb. (Brook Farm Bloodstock). *"Very immature and backward at present, but he's a good mover and light framed. I should imagine he'd need a bit of time, but he has a good pedigree".*

313. PERPETRATOR (IRE) ★★★

b.c. Shamardal – Palmeraie (Lear Fan). May 17. Half-brother to 10 winners including the multiple French Group 2 middle-distance winner Policy Maker (by Sadler's Wells), the very useful listed 11f winner Place Rouge (by Desert King), the useful 1m (at 2 yrs) and listed 2m winner Pushkin (by Caerleon) and the fairly useful 1m to 10f winner Tinghir (by Dansili). The dam is a placed half-sister to the US Grade 2 12f winner Peinture Bleue (dam of the Arc winner Peintre Celebre) and to the Group/ Grade 3 winners Provins and Parme. The second dam, Petroleuse (by Habitat), won the Group 3 8.5f Princess Elizabeth Stakes and is a half-sister to the King George VI and Queen Elizabeth Stakes, Oaks and Prix de Diane winner Pawneese. (Mr B Nielsen). *"The dam breeds nothing but winners it seems and good horses at that. I worked out that her ten winners have an average rating of over 100. I think he's nearly the last foal of the mare and he hasn't been here long but he's a deep, good-moving, potentially nice horse. Hopefully he's one to win a maiden race in the autumn".*

314. PERSIAN RHAPSODY ★★★★

b.c. Camelot – Hector's Girl (Hector Protector). March 30. Eighth foal. 80,000Y. Tattersalls October Book 2. Roger Charlton. Closely related to the Group 3 10f Rose Of Lancaster Stakes and dual listed 10f winner Class Is Class (by Montjeu) and half-brother to the quite useful 10f winners Ascot Lime (by Pivotal) and Always The Lady (by Halling), the fair dual 6f winner Jubilant Queen (by Kyllachy) and the modest 1m winner Lysander The Greek (by Exceed And Excel). The dam, a useful 2-y-o 6f winner, was third in the Group 3 7f Nell Gwyn Stakes. The second dam, Present Imperfect (by Cadeaux Genereux), a modest 5f placed 3-y-o, is a half-sister to 5 winners including the high-class sprinter College Chapel. (Dr Jamal Ahmadzadeh). *"We have his 3-y-o half-brother Magellan and we like him. This is an active, deep, good-moving colt and quite forward. The dam raced for Sir Michael Stoute and she was out quite early as a 2-y-o. She's one to start in June or July I should think and the vibes are quite good for Camelot. We like him".*

315. PILOT WINGS ★★★
b.c. Epaulette – Intaglia (Lomitas).
April 1. Sixth foal. 70,000Y. Tattersalls October
Book 2. Amanda Skiffington. Half-brother
to 5 winners including the useful Group 3
7f Irish 1,000 Guineas Trial winner Stormfly
(by Dark Angel), to the quite useful 6f (at 2
yrs) to 1m winner of 5 races Fred Willetts (by
Noverre), the quite useful 5f (including at 2
yrs) to 7f winner of 9 races Whozthecat (by
One Cool Cat) and the fair 2-y-o 6f winner Zal
Zilhom (by Verglas). The dam is an unraced
half-sister to 6 winners including two listed
winners in Germany. The second dam, Indian
Jewel (by Local Suitor), won twice 2 and 3 yrs
in Germany and is a half-sister to 5 winners.
(P Inglett & Partners). *"By a first season sire in
Epaulette who was talked up at the sales, this
is a half-brother to several very tough horses
that ran a huge number of times. A very big
horse, we won't be seeing him until later in
the year".*

316. SCOOTER (IRE) ★★★★
gr.c. Iffraaj – Cassandra Go (Indian Ridge).
March 11. Eleventh foal. 70,000Y. Tattersalls
October Book 1. Not sold. Half-brother to
6 winners including the Irish 1,000 Guineas,
Nassau Stakes and Sun Chariot Stakes winner
Halfway To Heaven (by Pivotal), the very
useful Group 3 5f and Group 3 6f winner
Tickled Pink (by Invincible Spirit), the Group
3 6f Summer Stakes winner Theann (by
Rock Of Gibraltar), the fairly useful triple
1m winner Jayed Jidan (by Teofilo) and the
fairly useful dual 5f winner Neverletme Go
(by Green Desert). The dam won the Group
2 5f King's Stand Stakes and is a half-sister
to 8 winners including Verglas (Group 3 6f
Coventry Stakes). The second dam, Rahaam
(by Secreto), a fairly useful 7f winner, is a
half-sister to 8 winners. (Trevor Stewart). *"He's
got a very nice pedigree and we like him. He's
strong and ought to be a 2-y-o at around six
furlongs".*

317. TIADARGENT (FR) ★★★
b.f. Kendargent – Restia (Montjeu). February
28. Sixth foal. 525,000Y. Tattersalls October
Book 1. Juddmonte Farms. Sister to 3 winners
including Restiadargent (Group 2 6f Criterium
de Maisons-Laffitte) and the listed 10f winner
Restiana. The dam is an unraced half-sister to

2 minor winners in France including the dam
of the Grade 2 winner Restiadargent. The
second dam, Restifia (by Night Shift), a listed
winner in France, is a half-sister to 3 winners.
(Khalid Abdulla). *"A very attractive filly and
a full sister to the filly Restiadargent who was
third to Black Caviar at Ascot. A very nice filly
but one that will need time and much more of
a trip than her sister did. I don't see her as a
sprinter".*

318. TINSMITH ★★★
ch.c. Mastercraftsman – Catopuma (Elusive
Quality). March 24. Third foal. Half-brother
to the modest 12f winner Kip (by Rip Van
Winkle). The dam is an unraced half-sister
to 5 winners including the US Grade 2 1m
Breeders' Cup Juvenile (Turf) winner and
Group 1 Prix Jean-Luc Lagardere second
Pounced, the useful dual 10f winner and
Group 3 placed Big Bound, the useful dual 10f
winner and Group 3 placed Pampas Cat and
the useful Irish 5f winner and listed 7f Acomb
Stakes second Celtic Cat. The second dam,
Golden Cat (Storm Cat), a listed placed 1m
winner, is a half-sister to 7 winners including
the very useful Irish listed 1m and 10f winner
and subsequent US winner Eurostorm. (Lady
Rothschild). *"I've seen him but he's not here
yet. One for the second half of the year, he's a
good-moving, attractive horse. A nice colt".*

319. UNIVERSAL COMMAND ★★★
b.c. Delegator – Telescopic (Galileo). April 6.
Second foal. Half-brother to the fairly useful
dual 10f winner Imperial Aviator (by Paco
Boy). The dam is an unplaced half-sister to 6
winners. The second dam, Orlena (by Gone
West), a minor 2-y-o 7f winner in France, is
a half-sister to 8 winners including the listed
winner and 1,000 Guineas third Vista Bella. (D
Hunt & E Markham). *"An attractive horse that
moves well, we like him and his half-brother
surprised us last year".*

320. USHER ★★★
b.c. Oasis Dream – Nimble Thimble (Mizzen
Mast). March 3. Second foal. The dam, a fair
9.5f winner, is a sister to one winner and a
half-sister to 6 winners including the 2-y-o
Group 3 Coventry Stakes and subsequent US
Grade 2 winner Three Valleys. The second
dam, Skiable (by Niniski), won four times at

up to 9f in France and the USA and is a half-sister to several winners including the listed winner Arrive and the outstanding broodmare Hasili (the dam of Dansili and of the Group 1 winners Heat Haze, Intercontinental, Banks Hill, Cacique and Champs Elysees). (Khalid Abdulla). *"I trained the dam and her half-brother Three Valleys. This colt has the make and shape to be a 2-y-o but he's not done much yet. A strong horse that should be a 2-y-o".*

321. UNNAMED ★★★
b.c. Henrythenavigator – Could It Be (Galileo). February 5. First foal. The dam is an unraced sister to the Group 1 Moyglare Stud Stakes, Prix Marcel Boussac (both at 2 yrs), Irish 1,000 Guineas and Pretty Polly Stakes winner Misty For Me, to the 2-y-o Group 1 1m Prix Marcel Boussac winner Ballydoyle and the useful listed 9f winner and dual Group 3 placed Twirl. The second dam, Butterfly Cove (by Storm Cat), is an unraced sister to the Irish 1,000 Guineas Trial winner Kamarinskaya and a half-sister to the champion 2-y-o colt Fasliyev. *"He had a bit of a setback earlier but he has a very nice pedigree and he's a good-looking individual".*

322. UNNAMED ★★★★
b.f. Oasis Dream – Island Dreams (Giant's Causeway). February 14. Fourth foal. Half-sister to the quite useful 2-y-o 8.5f winner Mr Khalid and to the quite useful 2-y-o 1m winner Who'sthedude (by Duke Of Marmalade). The dam, placed fourth over 10f on her only start, is a half-sister to 3 winners including the Group 2 Betfred Mile winner and Group 1 Champion Stakes second Rob Roy. The second dam, Camanoe (by Gone West), ran unplaced twice and is a half-sister to 8 winners including the US Grade 1 winner Super Staff. (Saleh Al Homaizi & Imad Al Sagar). *"A nice filly that should be quite forward, looking at her. She could be out over six furlongs in June or July, she's attractive and goes well".*

323. UNNAMED ★★★
b.c. Oasis Dream – Loulwa (Montjeu). April 5. Seventh foal. Brother to the useful listed winner of 5 races over 5f and 6f and Group 2 third Justineo and half-brother to the fair 7f

winner Bella Lulu (by Iffraaj) and the modest 6f winner Elhaam (by Shamardal). The dam, a fairly useful 11f and listed 13f winner, is a half-sister to 5 winners including the Group 2 6f Mill Reef Stakes winner and Group 1 placed Galeota and the fairly useful 2-y-o 5f Weatherbys Supersprint winner Lady Livius. The second dam, Refined (by Statoblest), a fairly useful dual 5f winner, is a half-sister to 6 winners including the very smart Group 3 7f Criterion Stakes winner Pipe Major. (Saleh Al Homaizi & Imad Al Sagar). *"A nice horse with plenty of size and scope, he's a full-brother to a good horse in Justineo and we like him. There are mixed messages in the pedigree and although the Oasis Dream/Montjeu cross hasn't been tried much the stats say that seven out of eight have won. He's a nice horse but more of a 3-y-o than 2-y-o".*

324. UNNAMED ★★★
b.f. Kodiac – Pitrizza (Machiavellian). March 27. Twelfth foal. 80,000Y. Tattersalls October Book 2. Rabbah Bloodstock. Half-sister to 7 winners including the fair 2016 2-y-o 7f winner Winston C (by Rip Van Winkle), the useful Irish 2-y-o 6f winner and Group 3 Tyros Stakes third Vilasol, the 2-y-o listed 7.5f winner Snow Watch (both by Verglas), the quite useful 1m to 12f winner of 15 races The Lock Master (by Key Of Luck) and the fair 6f and 7f winner of 4 races Perfect Treasure (by Night Shift). The dam, a minor French 12f winner, is a half-sister to 4 other minor winners. The second dam, Unopposed (by Sadler's Wells), is an unraced half-sister to 11 winners including the dam of the dual Group 2 winner and sire Titus Livius. (Sheikh Rashid Dalmook Al Maktoum). *"She's not that forward considering she's by Kodiac and I'd say she's a mid-term type of 2-y-o for six/seven furlongs. Quite attractive".*

325. UNNAMED ★★★★
b.c. Invincible Spirit – Turama (Pivotal). March 2. Second foal. Half-brother to the quite useful 2016 7f placed 2-y-o Zefferino (by Frankel). The dam, unplaced on her only start, is a half-sister to 6 winners including the Group 1 1m Sun Chariot Stakes winner Spinning Queen and the listed-placed 10f and 12f winner Shannon Springs. The second dam, Our Queen Of Kings (by Arazi), is an

unraced half-sister to 7 winners including the Grade 1 9f Hollywood Derby winner Labeeb and the Group/Grade 2 winners Alrassaam and Fanmore. (Saleh Al Homaizi & Imad Al Sagar). *"A half-brother to a horse we have here called Zefferino, he's not over-big but he's good-bodied and good-moving. We haven't pushed him yet but he's probably one of the more forward colts and he looks promising. One to watch out for we think".*

TOM CLOVER

326. DECLARATIONOFLOVE (IRE) ★★★

b.c. Declaration Of War – Mary's Daughter (Royal Applause). March 23. €28,000Y. Goffs Orby. Badgers Bloodstock. The dam, a fairly useful 2-y-o 6f winner, was second in the Group 3 Firth Of Clyde Stakes and is a half-sister to 5 winners. The second dam, Aunty Mary (by Common Grounds), a quite useful 2-y-o 5f winner, is a half-sister to 4 winners including the multiple Group 1 winner Attraction. (Ian Barratt, Stephen Short & Adam Signy). *"He'll start his career at Windsor in early April and he was bought to try and win an early season maiden with the dream of going to Royal Ascot. He's not the biggest but he has a lovely way of going, he's ready to go, he's athletic and has a lovely action so I think he'll want decent ground. The lad who rides him, Dean, used to ride Belardo and he's done a lovely job with him. On pedigree he'd get six furlongs later on but that remains to be seen".*

327. GO FOX ★★★

ch.g. Foxwedge – Bling Bling (Indian Ridge). February 19. Eighth foal. £11,000Y. Goffs UK Premier (Doncaster). Tom Clover (private sale). Half-brother to the fairly useful dual 6f (at 2 yrs) to 10f winner Bling King (by Haafhd), to the quite useful 2-y-o 7f winner Male Model (by Iffraaj), the fair triple 10f winner Go Sakhee (by Sakhee) and the modest 6f winner of 6 races New Rich (by Bahamian Bounty). The dam, a fair fourth over 1m and 10f, is a sister to the very smart dual listed 5f winner Watching and a half-sister to 4 winners. The second dam, Sweeping (by Indian King), a useful 2-y-o 6f winner, was listed placed and is a half-sister to 10 winners. (R & S Marchant, J Allen, G Jarvis). *"When we saw him at the sale he looked like he was going*

to have a bit of scope and I think that put a few people off, because they go to Doncaster looking for an early 2-y-o. He finds his work very straightforward, he should be out in mid-summer and he has a good way of going. I'm a big fan of the sire and there are loads of options with this colt because of his low auction price and the sire's low median. We should have some fun with him this summer".

328. LE MAHARAJAH (FR) ★★★

b.c. Cacique – Sign Of Life (Haafhd). March 4. Fourth foal. 36,000Y. Tattersalls December. Anglia Bloodstock. The dam placed fourth twice over 7f at 2 and 3 yrs and is a half-sister to 6 winners including the French 2,000 Guineas winner Victory Note. The second dam, Three Piece (by Jaazeiro), an Irish placed 2-y-o, is a half-sister to 8 winners including Orchestration (Group 2 Coronation Stakes) and Welsh Term (Group 2 Prix d'Harcourt). (Egerton House Racing). *"He'll make a 2-y-o, I think he'll want decent ground and I'm a fan of the sire who has good stats. I think we did well to get this horse for what he cost, he's just getting going now and hopefully he'll be on the racecourse by mid-summer, probably over six/seven furlongs".*

329. OBRIGADA ★★★

b.f. Worthadd – Oblige (Robellino). March 4. Half-sister to the useful 10f and 12f winner of 5 races Barye (by Archipenko) and to the French 2-y-o 10f winner Herrbuga (by Hernando). The dam, a useful 2-y-o dual 7f winner, was listed-placed twice and is a half-sister to 4 winners. The second dam, Acquiesce (by Generous), is an unraced half-sister to 4 winners including the Group 1 Prix Morny second Endless Summer. (Miss K Rausing). *"This filly should be running in high summer, probably over seven furlongs. In the last month she seems to have come a long way. She'd been prepped nicely in Ireland but when she arrived she hadn't seen cars or the road before and had to learn everything. She's done all the ground work and now she's just extending and getting a bit more 'Go' about her. She's getting stronger every day and has the 'Dubawi' constitution – quite robust with a huge girth. It's really nice to have the owner Miss Rausing's support of course".*

330. PHEIDIPPIDES ★★★
ch.c. Sepoy – Bounty Box (Bahamian Bounty).
March 3. Third foal. £53,000Y. Goffs UK
Premier (Doncaster). Omie Rangabashyam.
The dam, a useful dual listed 6f winner of 6
races from 2 to 5 yrs, is a sister to the French
2-y-o winner and listed-placed Bahamian
Box and a half-sister to 3 winners. The second
dam, Bible Box (by Bin Ajwaad), was a quite
useful 7f to 9f winner of 3 races from 3 to 5
yrs. (Dr O Rangabashyam). *"A lovely Sepoy
we picked up for a new owner who has owned
racehorses all over the world but is new to this
country. This colt will be out in the summer, he
hits the ground quite hard so will want a bit of
cut and I'd say six furlongs will be his starting
point with a view to stepping up to seven later
on. He has a high cruising speed and is getting
stronger every day. We saw Sepoy at the stud
recently and this colt looks the spitting image
of him".*

331. VIENTO DE CONDOR (IRE) ★★
b.c. Dragon Pulse – Polska (Danzig).
March 13. Tenth foal. £75,000Y. Goffs UK
Premier (Doncaster). Omie Rangabashyam.
Half-brother to 9 winners including the very
useful 2-y-o listed 7f winner and Group
2 1m May Hill Stakes second Queen Of
Poland (by Halling), the useful 2-y-o dual
7f winner White Hawk (by Silver Hawk), the
fairly useful 6f and 7f winner Persian Sea (by
Dubai Destination), the quite useful dual 1m
and hurdles winner Curzon Line (by Dubai)
and the fair 5f and 6f winner Grizel (by Lion
Cavern and herself dam of the US dual Grade
2 winner Whatshescript). The dam, a useful
winner of the 2-y-o listed 6f Blue Seal Stakes
and listed-placed at 3 yrs, is closely related
to the dual Group 3 winner Millstream. The
second dam, Aquaba (by Damascus), a US
Grade 3 stakes winner, is a half-sister to 8
winners. (Dr O Rangabashyam). *"He's very
innocuous at the moment and is one for
the back-end of the season. A big, scopey
looking horse, he looks lovely but has a lot of
strengthening up to do and needs time".*

332. UNNAMED ★★
b.c. Acclamation – Galistic (Galileo). March
21. Sixth foal. 27,000Y. Tattersalls December.
Tom Clover. Brother to the quite useful 7f

winner Aldayha and half-brother to the fair
2016 2-y-o 5f winner Trick Of The Light (by
Dragon Pulse), the German listed 7f winner
Guinnevre (by Duke Of Marmalade) and the
fair 2-y-o 7f and 1m winner Hala Hala (by
Invincible Spirit). The dam, a useful 10f, 12f
and listed 14f winner in Ireland at 3 and 4 yrs,
is a half-sister to one winner. The second dam,
Mockery (by Nashwan), won 2 minor races at
3 yrs in France and is a half-sister to 3 other
minor winners. (Rinus Roofing Ltd & F H Lee).
*"A long-striding horse with a lovely walk on
him, he's a big colt and I hope we'll see him
out at the back-end. Ultimately I'd like to think
he'll be a good miler, but he looks great and
just needs time. On looks he takes after the
damsire Galileo rather than Acclamation".*

333. UNNAMED ★★★
ch.c. Bahamian Bounty – Oceana Blue (Reel
Buddy). March 15. Fourth foal. £7,500 2-y-o.
Goffs UK January. Tom Clover. Half-brother to
the fair 6f and 7f winner of 3 races Gold Club
(by Multiplex) and to the moderate 7f winner
Moi Aussie (by Aussie Rules). The dam, a quite
useful 6f and 7f winner of 4 races, is a half-
sister to 4 winners. The second dam, Silken
Dalliance (Rambo Dancer), was a fairly useful
6f and 1m winner of 4 races at 3 yrs. (The CHF
Partnership). *"He only came to us a couple of
months ago but since then he's really gone
from strength to strength. He'll step up a bit in
mid-April with a view to getting him onto the
racecourse in high summer. He has a nice way
of going and just needs to strengthen up a bit
but he's doing well".*

DENIS COAKLEY
334. GIVEPEACEACHANCE ★★★
b.f. Declaration Of War – Mount Crystal
(Montjeu). February 12. Second foal.
100,000Y. Tattersalls October Book 2. Norris/
Huntingdon. Half-sister to the quite useful
1m to 10.5f winner Al Neksh (by Zoffany).
The dam, a modest 12f winner, is a half-sister
to 8 winners including the fairly useful 2-y-o
7f winner and 3-y-o listed placed Crystal
Curling. The second dam, State Crystal (by
High Estate), winner of the Group 3 12f
Lancashire Oaks and placed in the Yorkshire
Oaks and the Prix Vermeille, is a half-sister to
6 winners including the Group 1 Fillies' Mile

winner Crystal Music, the Group 3 winners Dubai Success and Solar Crystal and the Irish Derby third Tchaikovsky. (Chris Van Hoorn Racing). *"She's cantering nicely and hopefully when the six furlong races are out she'll be running. A good-looking filly and quite precocious, she shouldn't take too long".*

335. LILY OF YEAR (FR) ★★★
b.f. Siyouni – Arpagone (Victory Note). May 6. Fourth foal. 130,000Y. Arqana Deauville October. Powerstown Stud. The dam, placed once at 4 yrs, is a half-sister to 5 winners. The second dam, Mille Miglia (by Exit To Nowhere), a French listed-placed winner of 6 races from 2 to 4 yrs, is a half-sister to 6 winners including the US Grade 2 winner Miatuschka. *"A lovely, big filly and a great walker, she won't be out until the seven furlong races".*

336. UNNAMED ★★
b.f. Red Jazz – Margie (Marju). March 8. First foal. Tattersalls December. 7,000Y. Tattersalls December. D Coakley. The dam was unraced. The second dam, Anyuta (by Singspiel), a modest maiden, was fourth twice over 1m and 12f and is a half-sister to 3 minor winners. *"She should be sharp enough to race early, not over five furlongs but maybe over six in May. She didn't cost much but she goes well".*

PAUL COLE

337. ABANDON SHIP (IRE)
b.c. Mastercraftsman – No Explaining (Azamour). January 31. First foal. 80,000Y. Tattersalls October Book 1. P Cole. The dam, a 2-y-o 6f winner here, subsequently won a Grade 3 8.5f stakes in the USA, was Grade 2 placed twice over 9f and is a half-sister to 5 winners. The second dam, Claustra (by Green Desert), an Irish 4-y-o 9f winner, is a half-sister to 7 winners including the US Grade 2 winner Bayamo and the German Group 3 7f winner Wessam Prince. (Denford Stud, Arbib, Robinson & Tabet).

338. CAPITAL FLIGHT (IRE)
ch.c. Zoffany – Mackenzie's Friend (Selkirk). February 4. Ninth foal. €115,000Y. Goffs Orby. Hugo Merry. Half-brother to 6 winners including the French 2-y-o 10f winner and listed-placed Sallen, the modest 7f winner

Represent Yourself (both by Oratorio), the quite useful 2-y-o 1m winner Ballard Down (by Canford Cliffs), the fair 12f winner Juno The Muffinman (by Holy Roman Emperor) and the fair 12f and hurdles winner Know The Law (by Danehill Dancer). The dam is an unraced half-sister to 6 winners including the Group 2 winners Allied Powers and Dane Friendly. The second dam, Always Friendly (by High Line), winner of the Group 3 12f Princess Royal Stakes, was second in the Group 1 Prix Royal-Oak. (Mrs F H Hay).

339. DOCTOR KNOX (IRE)
b.c. Dawn Approach – Queen Of Carthage (Cape Cross). February 19. Third foal. €175,000Y. Goffs Orby. Hugo Merry. Half-sister to the unplaced 2016 2-y-o Mezyan (by Acclamation) and to the fairly useful triple 5f winner at 2 and 3 yrs Lady Clair (by Canford Cliffs). The dam is an unraced half-sister to a 4-y-o listed winner in Germany. The second dam, Satwa Queen (by Muhtathir), a Group 1 Prix de l'Opera and dual Group 2 winner, is a half-sister to 8 winners including the Group 1 Criterium de Saint-Cloud winner Spadoun. (Mrs F H Hay).

340. MAY REMAIN
b.c. Mayson – Ultimate Best (King's Best). March 12. Third foal. £26,000Y. Goffs UK Premier (Doncaster). Paul Cole. Half-brother to the quite useful 8.5f winner Ultimate Star (by Starspangledbanner). The dam, a moderate 12f placed maiden, is a half-sister to 6 winners including the useful 10f and 12f listed winner Film Script (herself dam of the listed winner Free Agent), the Group 3 Chipchase Stakes winner Barney McGrew and the fairly useful 6f and 7f and subsequent US stakes winner National Park. The second dam, Success Story (by Sharrood), a modest dual 10f winner, is a half-sister to 7 winners including the Group 2 13.5f Prix de Pomone winner Interlude. (PJL Racing, Wright, Asprey, Meyrick & Wilcock).

341. MUSICAL ART (IRE)
ch.f. Dutch Art – Musical Bar (Barathea). April 18. Fifth foal. €115,000Y. Goffs Orby. Stephen Hillen. Half-sister to the quite useful 2-y-o 6f winner Chord Chart (by Acclamation). The dam, a fairly useful 7f winner and second in

a listed event over 1m (both her starts), is a half-sister to 4 winners including the Prix Marcel Boussac, 1,000 Guineas and Irish 1,000 Guineas winner Finsceal Beo and the Group 2 German 2,000 Guineas winner Frozen Power. The second dam, Musical Treat (by Royal Academy), a useful 7f winner and listed-placed twice, won at 4 yrs in Canada and the USA and is a half-sister to 6 winners. (Mrs F H Hay).

342. PLUNGER
ch.c. Helmet – Percolator (Kheleyf). March 31. Fourth foal. Half-brother to the fair 2016 2-y-o 5f winner Cajmere (by Kyllachy). The dam, a 2-y-o winner of the Group 3 Prix du Bois and second in the Group 2 Prix Robert Papin, is a half-sister to 4 minor winners. The second dam, Coffee Cream (by Common Grounds), was a quite useful 7f (at 2 yrs) and 1m winner. (A H Robinson).

343. PINK PHANTOM
b.f. Oasis Dream – Pink Symphony (Montjeu). March 11. Second foal. Half-sister to African (by Dubawi), unplaced in two starts at 2 yrs in 2016. The dam, a useful Group 3 12f Give Thanks Stakes winner, is closely related to 2 winners including the Group 3 7f Prestige Stakes (at 2 yrs), Group 3 Nell Gwyn Stakes and US Grade 3 winner and Group/Grade 1 placed Fantasia. The second dam, Blue Symphony (by Darshaan), a fair 10f winner, is a half-sister to one winner. (Mrs F H Hay).

344. SECRET EYE (IRE)
ch.f. Street Cry – What A Treasure (Cadeaux Genereux). March 27. Fifth foal. 90,000Y. Tattersalls October Book 1. Paul Cole. Sister to the fair 7f winner Strada Facendo and half-sister to the fairly useful 7f, 1m (both at 2 yrs) and listed 10f winner Hoarding (by Elusive Quality). The dam, a fair dual 7f winner, is a sister to the Group 1 Prix de la Foret winner Toylsome and a half-sister to 6 winners including Coral Mist (Group 3 Firth of Clyde Stakes). The second dam, Treasure Trove (by The Minstrel), is a placed half-sister to the US Graded stakes winners Dance Parade and Ocean Queen. (Mr A H Lootah).

345. SUMMER THUNDER (USA)
b.f. Street Cry – Satulagi (Officer). May 5. Sixth foal. Sister to Many Waters, placed second over 10f from two starts at 3 yrs in 2017 and half-sister to the quite useful 1m (at 2 yrs) to 11f winner Teolagi (by Teofilo) and to the modest 6f and 7f winner of 4 races at 2 and 3 yrs One More Roman (by Holy Roman Emperor). The dam, a useful listed 7f winner at 2 yrs, is a half-sister to 8 winners including the Grade 3 Iroquois Stakes winner Motor City. The second dam, Shawgatny (by Danzig Connection), won over 9f in Ireland and is a sister to the dual Group 3 winner Star Of Gdansk. (Mrs F H Hay).

346. UNITED KINGDOM
b.c. Equiano – Lucky Legs (Danehill Dancer) January 31. Third foal. €50,000Y. Arqana Deauville October. Paul Cole. Brother to the US 3-y-o Grade 3 8.5f winner Baciami Piccola. The dam, a fair 1m and 10f winner, is a sister to 3 winners including the fairly useful Irish 2-y-o 6f winner Choir. The second dam, Singing Diva (by Royal Academy), is an unraced half-sister to 8 winners including Amfortas (Group 2 12f King Edward VII Stakes) and the dam of the 1,000 Guineas winner Virginia Waters. (P F I Cole Ltd)

ROBERT COWELL
347. CALEDONIA EARL ★★★
b.c. Rip Van Winkle – Granuaile O'Malley (Mark Of Esteem). March 18. Eighth foal. 32,000Y. Tattersalls October Book 3. Not sold. Half-brother to the very useful 5f (at 2 yrs) and Group 3 5f winner Caledonia Lady, to the modest 7f and 1m winner Caledonia Laird (both by Firebreak), the fair 5f and 6f winner of 6 races from 2 to 5 yrs Caledonia Princess, the fair 5f and 6f winner Coursing (by Kyllachy) and the fair 1m winner of 5 races Caledonia Prince (by Needwood Blade). The dam, a moderate 6f placed maiden, is a half-sister to 6 winners. The second dam, Dame Laura (by Royal Academy), a useful 5f (at 2 yrs) and 6f winner, was second in the Group 3 May Hill Stakes and the Group 3 Queen Mary Stakes and is a half-sister to 7 winners. (Isla & Colin Cage). *"He's a big, rangy horse and I quite like him, he's forward enough but we won't be in a hurry. He's by Rip Van Winkle but there's a lot of speed in the pedigree too. He's likeable and an interesting horse for later in the season, over six furlongs to start with".*

348. COWBOY SOLDIER ★★★★
b.c. Kodiac – Urgele (Zafonic). March 26.
Tenth foal. 105,000Y. Tattersalls October Book
1. Hugo Merry. Half-brother to the very useful
2-y-o listed 6f winner Al Aasifh, to the quite
useful 2-y-o 6f and 7f winner Invincible Gold
(both by Invincible Spirit), the fairly useful 1m
winner of 3 races Cordell (by Fasliyev) and
the fair 1m winner Zora Seas (by Marju). The
dam, a French listed 1m winner and third in
the Group 3 Prix Miesque, is a half-sister to 7
winners. The second dam, Urmia (by Persian
Bold), a listed-placed winner of 3 races in
France, is a half-sister to 10 winners including
Gunboat Diplomacy (Group 2 Prix Noailles).
(Mrs F H Hay). *"A very nice horse, he's an early
2-y-o and will probably be running in April.
He looks sharp, has a lot of speed and is very
straightforward. An out and out 2-y-o type".*

349. DOLLAR VALUE ★★
gr.c. Exchange Rate – Makoma (Malibu
Moon). April 17. Third foal. $95,000Y.
Keeneland September. R Cowell. Half-brother
to the US 3-y-o 8.5f winner American Pioneer
(by Awesome Again), the dam, a minor US
winner at 3 and 4 yrs, is a half-sister to a
minor winner. The second dam, Rhapsodic (by
Dixieland Band), won the Grade 2 Landaluce
Stakes and is a half-sister to 8 winners.
(Khalifa Dasmal). *"A good-looking horse, he
comes into the bracket of a late maturing
type. He's a great moving horse, he won't be a
sprinter and will be a seven furlong/mile type.
He'll appear towards at the back-end of the
season".*

350. DUBAI SILK ★★★
ch.f. Helmet – Silken Express (Speightstown).
March 22. First foal. The dam was a fairly
useful triple 5f winner from 3 to 5 yrs. The
second dam, Laureldean Express (by Inchinor),
a fairly useful 7f and 9f placed maiden here,
was listed-placed over 1m in France and
is a half-sister to 3 winners including the
Group 2 third Ellmau. (Malih L Al Basti). *"We
trained the dam who was above average and
won a couple of races on the grass and on
the all-weather. This filly was actually foaled
here, she's in pre-training at the moment and
the last time I saw her she looked stocky, not
particularly big and a 2-y-o type".*

351. NO MORE CALLS (IRE) ★★★★
b.c. Dawn Approach – Semayyel (Green
Desert). February 25. First foal. 26,000Y.
Tattersalls October Book 3. Rabbah
Bloodstock. The dam, a fairly useful 7f (at
2 yrs) and listed 10f winner, is a half-sister
to 3 minor winners. The second dam, Lil
Najma (by Medicean), a modest 7f and 1m
winner of 4 races, is a half-sister to 3 winners.
(Mohammed Jaber). *"A stocky colt that looks
an out-and-out 2-y-o, he's one of those that'll
do all his winning at two. He's set, he knows
his job and he's a bit like the Kodiac 2-y-o
we have – they've both worked their way up
together. One to keep on your side in the early
weeks of the season".*

352. UNNAMED ★★★
b.f. Henrythenavigator – Azenzar (Danehill
Dancer). February 11. First foal. The dam,
a fair 7f winner, is a half-sister to the quite
useful middle-distance winner Baadi. The
second dam, Dashing (by Sadler's Wells), is an
unraced half-sister to 6 winners including the
top-class multiple Group 1 winner Alexander
Goldrun and the Group 3 Prix de la Jonchere
winner and Group 1 placed Medicis. (Saleh Al
Homaizi & Imad Al Sagar). *"A good-moving,
good-bodied filly, she's very likeable but not
an early sort. One for six/seven furlongs from
the mid-season onwards".*

353. UNNAMED ★★★
b.f. Dutch Art – Bouyrin (Invincible Spirit).
February 3. First foal. 35,000Y. Tattersalls
October Book 1. Not sold. The dam, a fair 6f
winner, is a half-sister to 4 winners including
the useful 2-y-o Group 3 7f Oh So Sharp
Stakes winner and UAE Group 3 10f third
Alsindi. The second dam, Needles And
Pins (by Fasliyev), a useful 2-y-o listed 5.2f
winner and second in the Group 3 5.5f Prix
d'Arenburg, is a half-sister to 3 winners. (Saleh
Al Homaizi & Imad Al Sagar). *"Quite a nice
filly and one of the earlier 2-y-o's we have, she
looks quite set and she's done a few pieces of
work. I'd keep her on your side".*

354. UNNAMED ★★
gr.f. Sir Percy – Half Moon Hotel (With
Approval). April 9. Third foal. 5,500Y.
Tattersalls October Book 3. R Cowell. Half-

sister to the unplaced 2016 2-y-o Buena Luna (by Bahamian Bounty). The dam is an unraced half-sister to 3 minor winners. The second dam, Slew The Moon (by Kitwood), won five Graded stakes in Argentina including a Grade 1 and is a sister to the Argentine Grade 2 winner Spice Girl and a half-sister to the Argentine triple Grade 1 winner Slew Of Reality. *"She didn't cost very much but she's a fairly good-looking filly. She's got a great walk to her and there's a lot of attractive attributes about her".* TRAINERS' BARGAIN BUY

355. UNNAMED ★★★
b.f. Mayson – Instructress (Diktat). March 25. Third foal. Half-sister to the moderate 2015 5f placed 2-y-o Miss Uppity (by Notnowcato. The dam, a fair dual 5f winner (including at 2 yrs), is a half-sister to 5 winners including the quite useful 2-y-o listed-placed dual 5f winner Smooch. The second dam, Two Step (by Mujtahid), a modest 5f and 7f winner at 4 and 5 yrs, is a half-sister to 3 winners. (Bottisham Heath Stud). *"A small, set filly she hasn't done enough for me to be able to evaluate her yet. I don't think she'll be particularly early but if she does any winning it'll be this year".*

356. UNNAMED ★★★★
b.c. Poet's Voice – Lilli Marlane (Sri Pekan). February 5. Eighth foal. Tattersalls October Book 3. Robert Cowell. Half-brother to the quite useful 6f to 8.5f winner of 4 races at 2 and 3 yrs Dubai's Secret (by Paco Boy), to the fair 6f (at 2 yrs) and 7f winner Pearl Rebel (by Cockney Rebel), the Hong Kong 6f winner Treadstone (by Myboycharlie) and the moderate 7f winner Philmack Dot Com (by Traditionally). The dam, a fair and 1m and 10f winner, is a half-sister to 5 winners including the US Grade 2 Del Mar Derby winner Medici Code. The second dam, Fiveofive (by Fairy King), a modest 5f (at 2 yrs) and 1m winner, is a half-sister to 4 winners. (Heart Of The South Racing). *"A really nice, good-looking colt and a strong individual. He looks like a Kodiac rather than a Poet's Voice because he's got that type of bulky look to him and I like him a lot. He had a break but he's back cantering now and should be racing in May I would have thought".*

357. UNNAMED ★★★
ch.c. Bahamian Bounty – Welanga (Dansili). April 10. Sixth foal. 7,000 foal. Tattersalls December. Troy Steve. Half-brother to the fairly useful 2-y-o 5f and 6f winner of 3 races Receding Waves (by Dick Turpin), to the fair 10f to 13f winner of 5 races Udogo (by Lucky Story) and the fair 2-y-o 5f winner Chasing Dreams (by Pastoral Pursuits). The dam is an unraced half-sister to 8 winners including the listed 1m and subsequent US Grade 3 8.5f winner Out Of Reach and the 2-y-o 6f winner and Group 3 Cherry Hinton Stakes third Well Warned (herself the dam of three listed winners) and a half-sister to 4 winners. The second dam, Well Beyond (by Don't Forget Me), a 2-y-o 5f and 3-y-o listed 1m October Stakes winner, is a half-sister to 3 winners. (Mrs D Swinburn, Mr F Read, Mr R Gough & Partner). *"A lovely horse we bought privately. A good mover, I like the sire and the dam (although she's not really done herself justice yet) and he's a really fluent mover. One for the middle of the season onwards".*

SIMON CRISFORD
358. AL AMIR ★★★
b.c. Frankel – Emirates Queen (Street Cry). February 27. The dam, a Group 2 12f Lancashire Oaks winner, is a half-sister to the Group 1 National Stakes (at 2 yrs), Irish 2,000 Guineas and Prix Jacques le Marois winner and top-class sire Dubawi and to the listed 10f winner Princess Nada. The second dam, Zomaradah (by Deploy), a winner of 6 races including the Group 1 Italian Oaks, the Group 2 Royal Whip Stakes and the Group 2 Premio Lydia Tesio, is a half-sister to several winners. *"A Frankel colt out of a half-sister to Dubawi, he's a nice colt to look forward to in the second half of the season and should be a ten furlong type for next year".*

359. AWSAAF ★★★ ♠
b.c. Swiss Spirit – Atheera (Shamardal). January 29. First foal. 38,000Y. Tattersalls October Book 2. Shadwell Estate Co. The dam, a modest 2-y-o 5f winner, is a half-sister to 3 winners. The second dam, Alshamatry (by Seeking The Gold), is an unraced half-sister to 9 winners including the smart Group 2 10f Premio Lydia Tesio winner Najah and to the useful listed-placed 10f winner Tanaghum.

"He was bought specifically because he looks an early type, so as soon as the six furlong races start we'll be thinking about getting him going. He'll get seven later on and I suspect that'll be his trip next year as well".

360. BOBBY K ★★★
br. g. Dabirsim – Shanjia (Soldier Hollow). May 7. First foal. 27,000Y. Tattersalls December. Crisford Racing. The dam, a listed 9f winner at 4 yrs in France, is a half-sister to 3 winners including the German Group 3 winner Shivajia. The second dam, Shivara (by Monsun), a minor German 3-y-o winner, is a half-sister to 9 winners. *"When the seven furlong races start he should be ready to go and he may even have the speed for six. He's making progress".*

361. DARK ROSE ANGEL (IRE) ★★★★
b.f. Dark Angel – Roseraie (Lawman). January 24. First foal. 60,000Y. Tattersalls October Book 1. Stephen Hillen. The dam, a 2-y-o 6f winner, was third in the Group 3 7f Silver Flash Stakes and is a half-sister to the very useful listed 6f and listed 7f winner and dual Group 3 placed Rose Bonheur. The second dam, Red Feather (by Marju), a Group 3 1m winner in Ireland, was second in the Group 1 Moyglare Stud Stakes and is a half-sister to 3 winners including the smart dual 10f winner and dual Group 3 placed Frankies Dream. *"I'd like to get her started as soon as we can although she's not quite as forward as we first thought. A very nice filly that's doing everything right, but I don't think we'll see her coming into her own until the seven furlong races start".*

362. GLOBAL CONQUEROR ★★★
b.c. Dubawi – Nargys (Lawman). February 9. First foal. The dam, a useful 6f (at 2 yrs) and Group 3 7f Sceptre Stakes winner, was second in the Group 2 7f Rockfel Stakes, is a full or half-sister to 3 winners. The second dam, Spesialta (by Indian Ridge), a quite useful Irish 7f winner, is a half-sister to 5 winners including the Group 3 Prix du Pin winner Best Dating. *"He'll start as a seven furlong 2-y-o and build up to be a mile and a quarter horse next year. He's a very straightforward colt".*

363. MAKANAH ★★★★
b.c. Mayson – Diane's Choice (Komaite). March 8. Fourth foal. £58,000Y. Goffs UK Premier (Doncaster). Shadwell Estate Co. Half-brother to the modest 6f winner Minister Of Fun (by Pastoral Pursuits). The dam, a quite useful 5f and 6f winner of 9 races, is a half-sister to 3 winners. The second dam, Ramajana (by Shadeed), won 2 races at 2 and 4 yrs in Germany and is a half-sister to 6 winners here and abroad. *"He's all speed and should be racing over six furlongs in May or June. A nice sort and one of those we can move forward with".*

364. OSTILIO ★★★★
ch.c. New Approach – Reem Three (Mark Of Esteem). April 11. Half-brother to the fairly useful 2016 2-y-o 7f winner from two starts Cape Byron (by Shamardal), to the useful 7f (at 2 yrs) to 12f winner Naqshabban and a hurdles winner (both by Street Cry). The dam, a useful 8.5f to 10.5f winner of 3 races, was listed placed and is a half-sister to 3 winners including the very smart Group 2 Celebration Mile winner Afsare. The second dam, Jumaireyah (by Fairy King), a fairly useful 8.3f (at 2 yrs) and 10.3f winner, is a half-sister to numerous winners including the useful 10f to 14f winner Lost Soldier Three and the useful 10.5f and 12f winner Altaweelah. *"He's quite a sharp type and should come to hand by mid-summer. Seems to have plenty of speed and should be a seven furlong 2-y-o".*

365. RED MIST ★★★★
b.c. Frankel – Red Dune (Red Ransom). February 8. Half-brother to the fairly useful 2-y-o 7f and 1m winner and 3-y-o UAE Group 3 9.5f third Feedyah (by Street Cry). The dam, a useful 7f and 1m winner, was listed-placed and is a full or half-sister to 4 winners. The second dam, Desert Beauty (Green Desert), a useful 7f and 1m winner, is a half-sister to the Yorkshire Oaks and Nassau Stakes winner Islington, to the smart stayer Election Day and the smart 10f performer Greek Dance. *"He'll be a seven furlong type 2-y-o in mid-summer. He's a very nice, straightforward horse and will be a miler next year".*

366. REVOLUTIONARY MAN (IRE) ★★★
b.c. Exceed And Excel – Bint Almukhtar (Halling). February 19. Second foal. The dam

is an unraced half-sister to one winner. The second dam, Dabawiyah (by Intikhab), placed once over 10f from two starts, is a half-sister to 7 winners including the very smart 7f (at 2 yrs) and Group 3 12f Gordon Stakes winner Rabah and the useful 2-y-o 6f winner and Group 1 Cheveley Park Stakes third Najiya and to the placed dam of the Irish Oaks second Ice Queen. *"A nice sort, he'll make a 2-y-o by the mid-summer and he'll want seven furlongs".*

367. UNNAMED ★★★
b.f. Kodiac – Epistoliere (Alzao). May 5. Ninth foal. 70,000Y. Tattersalls October Book 2. Stroud/Coleman. Half-sister to 6 winners including the smart 7f (at 2 yrs) to 2m 5f winner and Group 1 Ascot Gold Cup second Simenon (by Marju), the useful listed-placed 10f to 13f winner of 5 races and Vivacious Vivienne (by Dubai Destination) and the French 2-y-o 1m winner and listed-placed Kyurem (by Verglas). The dam is a placed sister to the Group 2 Grand Prix de Deauville winner Epistolaire and a half-sister to the Group 2 Prix Hubert de Chaudenay winner Epitre. The second dam, Epistolienne (by Law Society), is a listed-placed half-sister to 10 winners including Acclimatise (Group 2 Nassau Stakes). *"She's moving forward and I guess she'll be ready to run over six furlongs in mid-summer".*

368. UNNAMED ★★★
gr.f. Dark Angel – Extricate (Exceed And Excel). February 24. First foal. 88,000Y. Tattersalls October Book 2. Stroud/Coleman. The dam, a minor winner of 2 races at 3 and 4 yrs in Norway, is a half-sister to 5 winners including the Scandinavian Group 3 winner Entangle. The second dam, Entwine (by Primo Dominie), a quite useful 2-y-o dual 5f winner, is a half-sister to 6 winners including the Group 2 Lowther Stakes winner Soar. *"A nice filly from Tattersalls Book 2, she's going forward and we'd like to get her out relatively early".*

369. UNNAMED ★★★
b.f. Kodiac – Fearn Royal (Ali-Royal). April 14. Seventh foal. €80,000Y. Goffs Orby. D Cantillon. Half-sister to the 2-y-o 7f winner Our Way Only (by Oratorio), to the 7f to 10.5f winner Shabra Emperor (by Holy Roman Emperor), the 1m to 13f winner Rosie Royale

(by Verglas) and the Irish 1m winner Oasis Fire (by Oasis Dream) – all fair winners – and the modest dual 1m winner Princess Tamay (by Tamayuz). The dam won 3 races over 7f and 1m from 3 to 5 yrs including the listed Knockaire Stakes and was second in the Group 3 Concorde Stakes. She is a half-sister to one winner out of the fair 12f winner Sparrowhawk (by Doyoun). *"She's in one of the early groups, moving forward and should be given a mention. She'll probably start at six furlongs in the summer and a mile will be her maximum trip next year".*

370. UNNAMED ★★★
b.f. Acclamation – Fortune Hunter (High Chaparral). February 3. First foal. 28,000Y. Tattersalls October Book 3. Stroud/Coleman & Crisford Racing. The dam won 3 races over 6f at 3 and 4 yrs in France at 3 and 4 yrs and is a half-sister to one winner. The second dam, King's Folly (by King's Best), was placed once at 3 yrs in France and is a half-sister to 6 winners including the Group 1 second Dansuse d'Etoile. *"She wasn't overly expensive but she'll be one to move forward with quickly. Six furlongs is going to be her trip to start with and despite being out of a High Chaparral mare her maximum trip next year will be a mile".* TRAINERS' BARGAIN BUY

371. UNNAMED ★★★
b.f. Poet's Voice – Loveable (Oasis Dream). March 5. Second foal. The dam is an unraced half-sister to the Group 2 6f Duke Of York Stakes and Group 3 1m Craven Stakes winner and triple Group 1 placed Delegator and to the useful 7f (including at 2 yrs) and 1m winner of 4 races Correspondent. The second dam, Indian Love Bird (by Efisio), is an unraced sister to the smart Group 1 7f Prix de la Foret winner Tomba and the French Derby winner Holding Court. *"She should come to hand soon enough and she's pleasing in what she does so far. One to start at six furlongs I'd say".*

372. UNNAMED ★★★
b.f. Invincible Spirit – Nidhaal (Observatory). May 18. Half-sister to the useful 2-y-o 5f winner and dual Group 2 placed Burwaaz (by Exceed And Excel), to the quite useful 6f (at 2 yrs) and 5f winner of 4 races Sharaarah, the quite useful 2-y-o 5f and 6f winner Sadafiya

(both by Oasis Dream) and the modest 7f winner Kafoo (by Dansili). The dam, a very useful 2-y-o listed 6f winner and second in the Group 3 6f Princess Margaret Stakes, is a half-sister to 2 winners. The second dam, Jeed (by Mujtahid), a quite useful 2-y-o 6f winner, is a half-sister to 2 winners. *"I would expect this filly will come to hand quickly and we can move forward with her. A mid-May foal, it would be nice to think she could be running around the time of her birthday".*

373. UNNAMED ★★★★
b.f. Exceed And Excel – Phoenix City (El Prado). January 25. First foal. The dam, a quite useful 7f winner, is a half-sister to 2 winners. The second dam, Warsaw Girl (by Polish Precedent), won once at 4 yrs in the USA and is a half-sister to 3 stakes winners including the Derby and Racing Post Trophy winner Motivator and the Group 2 Hardwicke Stakes winner Macarthur. *"A speedy type that may even have enough toe for five furlongs, so we'll see how she shapes up. She's in the forward batch of our 2-y-o's anyway"*

LUCA CUMANI

374. ASHINGTON ★★★
b.c. Canford Cliffs – Kadoma (Danehill Dancer). February 13. First foal. 55,000Y. Tattersalls October Book 2. Charlie Gordon-Watson. The dam, a minor 2-y-o winner in Germany, is a half-sister to 2 winners including the Group 2 German 2,000 Guineas winner Karpino. The second dam, Kahara (by Habitat), a French listed-placed 2-y-o winner, is a sister to the St Leger winner Milan and a half-sister to 8 winners. (Bengough, Boorer, Booth, Stilvi). *"A good-looking son of Canford Cliffs, he cost quite a bit of money given his pedigree, but he's a real looker. He seems to be going well at this stage, I think he's going to be a miler but he'll be mature enough to run sometime in July".*

375. BESSIE WARFIELD ★★★
b.f. Oasis Dream – Wallis (King's Best). April 24. Third foal. Half-sister to the fair 2016 6f and 7f placed 2-y-o Atteq (by Invincible Spirit). The dam, a quite useful 6f and 1m winner here, subsequently won and was stakes-placed in the USA. She is a half-sister to 5 winners including the Grade 1 Northern Dancer Turf and dual Grade 2 Sky Classic winner Forte Dei Marmi (by Selkirk) and the very useful 12f and listed 14f winner Savarain. The second dam, Frangy (by Sadler's Wells), a fair dual 12f winner, is a full or half-sister to 8 winners including the German 1m to 9.5f winner of 7 races and listed-placed Flying Heights. (Fittocks Stud). *"A good-looking daughter of Oasis Dream out of a good mare from a good family, she's going well, looks quite precocious and should be one of more forward 2-y-o's. Perhaps she'll be out in June or July from six furlongs to start with. Bessie Warfield was the maiden name of Wallis Simpson".*

376. CONSOLIDA ★★★
b.f. Sir Percy – Red Larkspur (Red Clubs). March 19. First foal. The dam, a fair dual 6f winner at 2 and 4 yrs, is a half-sister to the useful Group 2 1m Topkapi Trophy winner Blond Me. The second dam, Holda (by Docksider), a 2-y-o 7f maiden winner at Newmarket on her only start, is a half-sister to the Group 3 10f and subsequent Australian Group 1 10f winner Glass Harmonium and to the Group 3 12f winner Arab Spring. (Shack, Castle Down Racing, Scuderia Archi Romani & Mrs L Cumani). *"She wasn't expensive and she's well put-together, not very big and could be the type to do well as a 2-y-o. Not a sprinter, but maybe a six/seven furlong filly to start in July".*

377. CROQUE MONSIEUR ★★
b.c. Intello – Soft Centre (Zafonic). March 14. Sixth foal. Closely related to the Group 1 10f Nassau Stakes and Group 3 12f Pinnacle Stakes winner Sultanina (by New Approach). The dam, a very useful 7f (at 2 yrs) and listed 10f winner, is a half-sister to the smart 7f (at 2 yrs), listed 10f and subsequent US Grade 3 12f winner Dalvina. The second dam, Foodbroker Fancy (by Halling), a smart 6f (at 2 yrs) and dual listed 10f winner, is a half-sister to the useful listed 2-y-o 6f winner Femme Fatale. (Normandie Stud). *"He's only just arrived here after having been in pre-training. Obviously I can't tell you a lot, other than the fact he's a very good-looking colt. It's the sire's first season, but everyone seemed to like his yearlings at the sales and he was a very good-looking horse and a very good racehorse".*

378. FOUR WHITE SOCKS ★★★★

ch.f. Lope De Vega – Peppermint Green (Green Desert). February 24. Fourth foal. 110,000Y. Tattersalls October Book 2. Stuart Shuckey. Half-sister to a minor winner in Germany at 4 and 5 yrs by Medicean. The dam is an unplaced half-sister to 4 winners including the US Grade 2 winner Sun Boat. The second dam, One So Wonderful (by Nashwan), won the Group 1 Juddmonte International and the Group 2 Sun Chariot Stakes and is a half-sister to 8 winners including the Group 2 Dante Stakes winner Alnasr Alwasheek. (Mr S A Stuckey). *"A very attractive filly, she's from a good family and appears to be going well. I don't think she's particularly precocious but I can see her starting in mid-summer over seven furlongs".*

379. MERSEYBEAT ★★★

b.f. New Approach – Hippy Hippy Shake (Danehill Dancer). March 25. First foal. 100,000Y. Tattersalls October Book 1. Not sold. The dam, a listed 10.5f winner of 3 races at 3 and 4 yrs, is a half-sister to 8 winners including the Group 3 7f Tetrarch Stakes winner and Irish 2,000 Guineas second France. The second dam, Hyperspectra (by Rainbow Quest), a fairly useful 10.2f winner, is a half-sister to 6 winners including the dual Group 3 winner Poet. *"The dam was quite smart, we trained her and she was a listed winner. This filly has only just come in so it's hard to form an opinion at this stage other than she's a correct, attractive filly".*

380. OUTLANE ★★★

b.f. Camelot – Batik (Peintre Celebre). April 8. Sixth foal. Half-sister to the Italian dual listed 1m winner at 2 and 3 yrs Bezique (by Cape Cross), to the fair 10f winner Buffett (by Bertolini) and the Italian 10f to 1m 7f winner Barkis (by Selkirk). The dam, a fairly useful 10.2f to 12f winner, is a half-sister to 3 winners including the 10f to 14f and subsequent Australian Group 3 winner and Melbourne Cup second Bauer. The second dam, Dali's Grey (by Linamix), a French 11f winner, is a sister to the French Group winners Diamilina and Diamonixa and a half-sister to 6 winners including the Group 3 winner and sire Diamond Green. (Aston House Stud). *"A filly from a good family that includes horses*

we've been successful with. I'm happy to have her, she's very attractive and full of spirit, but the family isn't precocious. She'll be out in summertime over seven furlongs though".

381. RECOLLECT ★★★

b.c. Invincible Spirit – Forgotten Dreams (Olden Times). April 15. Fifth foal. Half-brother to the fairly useful listed-placed 6f and 7f winner at 2 and 3 yrs Remember (by Selkirk), to the 2-y-o 7f winner (on his only start) Roundsman (by Pivotal) and the fair 10f winner Fiesole (by Montjeu). The dam ran unplaced twice and is a half-sister to 4 winners including the Group 1 Italian Oaks and dual Group 2 winner Zomaradah (herself the dam of three stakes winners including Dubawi). The second dam, Jawaher (by Dancing Brave), was placed over 1m and 9f and is a half-sister to 9 winners including the Derby winner High-Rise. (Fittocks Stud). *"He's a likeable horse, well put-together and attractive. It's a middle-distance family but he seems a nice horse that should be ready for July time, probably over seven furlongs".*

382. WILSON (IRE) ★★★★

b.c. Born To Sea – Alkhawarah (Intidab). April 4. Second foal. £25,000Y. Goffs UK Premier (Doncaster). Kevin Ross. The dam, a modest7.5f placed maiden, is a half-sister to 9 winners including the smart 2-y-o Group 1 6f Middle Park Stakes winner Hayil, the US Grade 2 second Tamhid and the dam of the dual Group 1 winning 2-y-o Shalaa. The second dam, Futuh (by Diesis), a fairly useful 2-y-o 6f winner, is a half-sister to 7 winners including the Canadian stakes winner Rose Park (dam of the dual US Grade 1 winner Wild Rush). (Stilvi, Boorer, Booth, Bengough). *"He's named after the ball that was named 'Wilson' by Tom Hanks in the film Castaway! This colt is very good-looking, perhaps a bit on the small side, but he's a very nice character, very enthusiastic about his work and he'll be one of the earlier 2-y-o's, perhaps in June over six furlongs".* TRAINERS' BARGAIN BUY

383. UNNAMED ★★★ ♠

gr.f. Oasis Dream – Amarillo Starlight (Dalakhani). February 26. First foal. 70,000Y. Tattersalls December. Not sold. The dam is an unraced half-sister to 3 winners. The second dam, Briolette (by Sadler's Wells), won the listed 10f Trigo Stakes, was second in the Group 3 12f Princess Royal Stakes and is a sister to the Irish listed winner Peach Out Of Reach and a half-sister to 6 winners including the multiple Grade 1 winner Pilsudski and the champion Japanese filly Fine Motion. (O.T.I Racing). *"She's slightly backward despite her sire being Oasis Dream, so she won't appear until mid-summer. A good-looking filly but just not very forward".*

384. UNNAMED ★★

b.f. Cape Cross – Brigitta (Sadler's Wells). April 6. Tenth foal. 180,000Y. Tattersalls October Book 1. Amanda Skiffington. Half-sister to the listed 1m (at 2 yrs), German Group 2 1m and Group 3 9.5f Prix Daphnis winner Emerald Commander, to the fair 11f winner Past Forgetting (both by Pivotal), the quite useful 2-y-o 5f winner Gold Lace (by Invincible Spirit) and the fair 2-y-o 7f winner Albaraari (by Green Desert). The dam won over 1m and 10f and is a sister to the 2-y-o Group 1 1m Racing Post Trophy winner Commander Collins, closely related to the Grade 1 Breeders' Cup Sprint winner Lit de Justice and the 2,000 Guineas and Derby placed Colonel Collins and a half-sister to the Group 2 Royal Lodge Stakes winner City Leader. The second dam, Kanmary (by Kenmare), won the 2-y-o Group 3 5f Prix du Bois. (Coolmore). *"She's a big filly that hasn't been in that long. Probably one for the autumn because she's not a precocious type".*

385. UNNAMED ★★

b.c. Invincible Spirit – Cascata (Montjeu). April 6. Fourth foal. Half-brother to the 2015 unplaced 2-y-o Pacaharana and to the fairly useful 10f and 12f winner Richard Of Yorke (both by Oasis Dream). The dam, a fair 2-y-o 1m winner, is a sister to the high-class multiple Group 1 winning middle-distance colt St Nicholas Abbey and a half-sister to the US dual Grade 2 winner and Grade 1 placed Grammarian. The second dam, Leaping Water (by Sure Blade), is an unraced half-sister to the dual Group 1 winners Starborough and Ballingarry and the Racing Post Trophy winner Aristotle. (Mr S A Stuckey). *"A nice horse, he's quite big and it's one of those strange crosses because it's a staying family with a sprinter on*

top. *He seems to take more from the female line because he's a scopey horse and probably won't be out until the autumn".*

386. UNNAMED ★★★★

b.c. Lope De Vega – Flaming Song (Darshaan). April 1. Fourteenth foal. 70,000Y. Tattersalls October Book 2. Charlie Gordon-Watson. Half-brother to 8 winners including the very smart German 10f Group winners Fight Club (by Laverco) and Flambo (by Platini), the fairly useful dual 7f winner Bullwhip (by Whipper), the quite useful 2-y-o 7f winner Adelasia (by Iffraaj) and the fair Irish 10f winners Legal Lyric (by Lawman) and Slan Abhaile (by Montjeu). The dam, a 2-y-o winner in France, is a half-sister to 2 other minor winners. The second dam, Pale Blue (by Kris), was listed-placed and is a half-sister to 7 winners. (O.T.I Racing). *"A big, strong horse and he's actually quite a bruiser and looks like a rugby player! He goes well, we quite like him and he's probably a horse for mid-summer starting over seven furlongs. I think he'll do well as a 2-y-o".*

387. UNNAMED ★★★

b.c. Equiano – London Welsh (Cape Cross). February 9. Second foal. 80,000Y. Tattersalls October Book 2. Charlie Gordon-Watson. Half-brother to the quite useful 2016 2-y-o listed 6f winner Wick Powell (by Sakhee's Secret). The dam ran once unplaced and is a half-sister to 4 minor winners. The second dam, Croeso Cariad (by Most Welcome), a very useful 2-y-o 5f and 7f Italian listed winner, was second in the Group 2 1m Falmouth Stakes and is a half-sister to 6 winners including the Irish listed winner and multiple Group 1 placed Mona Lisa. (Buxted Partnership). *"A big, strong and very attractive horse. The sire was a sprinter and perceived to be one that would produce precocious stock, but actually it seems they tend to improve with age. I like this horse, I think he should be a nice horse one day and perhaps he'll start his career this summer. He could be a sprinter, but not a precocious one".*

388. UNNAMED ★★

b.c. Dansili – Pongee (Barathea). April 15. Eighth foal. Half-brother to 5 winners including the listed 10f winner Pinzolo (by

Monsun), the fairly useful listed-placed 2-y-o 1m winner Poplin (by Medicean), the fairly useful 7f (at 2 yrs) and 8.5f winner Materialistic (by Oasis Dream) and the fair 10f winner Paisley (by Pivotal). The dam, a Group 2 12f Lancashire Oaks winner, is closely related to the listed 12f and listed 14f winner Lion Sands and to the listed-placed 11f winner Pukka and a half-sister to 5 winners. The second dam, Puce (by Darshaan), a listed 12f winner, is a half-sister to 10 winners including the dam of the dual Oaks winner Alexandrova and the Cheveley Park Stakes winner Magical Romance. (Fittocks Stud). *"A slightly backward horse, he's attractive and good-looking. Probably one for late summer onwards over seven furlongs and a mile".*

389. UNNAMED ★★★
b.c. Dansili – Victoire Finale (Peintre Celebre). May 5. Seventh foal. Half-brother to 5 winners including the 2016 2-y-o 8.5f winner Vanity Queen (by Fastnet Rock), the useful 1m, 9f (both at 2 yrs) and listed 10f winner and Group 1 Epsom and Irish Oaks third Volume (by Mount Nelson), to the useful dual 1m winner (including at 2 yrs) Validus and the fairly useful dual 1m winner Velox (both by Zamindar). The dam, a useful French 1m winner, was fourth in a listed event and is a half-sister to numerous winners including the French Group 2 winner Vertical Speed. The second dam, Victoire Bleue (by Legend Of France), won the Group 1 Prix du Cadran. (Mr S A Stuckey). *"I've trained quite a few out of this family but she seems to be the most backward we've had. However, they're all very useful and there's every chance that this one will turn into a useful horse one day".*

KEITH DALGLEISH
390. CHE BELLA (IRE) ★★★★
gr.f. Holy Roman Emperor – Satwa Ruby (Verglas). March 23. First foal. £90,000Y. Goffs UK Premier (Doncaster). Bobby O'Ryan / Keith Dalgleish. The dam, a 10.5f and 11.5f winner in France, is a half-sister to 3 winners including the Group 1 Criterium de Saint-Cloud winner Morandi. The second dam, Vezina (by Bering), is a French placed full or half-sister to 13 winners. (Weldspec Glasgow Ltd). *"This filly looks a real 2-y-o, she has a good attitude and she's been working well. I'd*

like to think she'd be capable of going close in her first two starts. A nice filly, I should imagine she'll stick to five furlongs this year, she's not over-big but a good size for a 2-y-o filly".*

391. CHEESEANDPICKLE ★★★★
ch.f. Helmet – Branston Gem (So Factual). February 11. Eleventh living foal. £26,000Y. Goffs UK Premier (Doncaster). Bobby O'Ryan / Keith Dalgleish. Half-brother to 7 winners including the quite useful 2016 2-y-o 5f winner Plata O Plomo (by Paco Boy), the fair 2-y-o 5f winner The Terrier (by Foxhound and herself dam of the Group 3 winner Dutch Masterpiece), the fair 7f winner Wear 'Em Out Wolf and the modest 5f winner Braille (both by Bahamian Bounty). The dam, placed over 5f at 2 yrs, is a half-sister to the dual listed winner Falcon Hill. The second dam, Branston Jewel (by Prince Sabo), a fairly useful 2-y-o dual 5f winner, is a half-sister to 11 winners including the very useful and tough mare Branston Abby (a winner of 24 races at up to 7f including numerous listed events) and the Group 2 winner Desert Deer. (Equus I). *"A winner already, she's a big, scopey filly and she's pleased us from day one because her work has always been good. She's always had a fantastic, sleepy attitude and she brought that to the race because she was switched off but quickened when it mattered. Hopefully she's got a bit of quality and I think she'll get six furlongs in the summer. Next step could be the Hilary Needler at Beverley and if she does well there we could think of Royal Ascot".*

392. CHOOKIE DUNEDIN ★★★★
b.c. Epaulette – Lady Of Windsor (Woods Of Windsor). April 8. Half-brother to 6 winners including the very useful listed winner of 15 races from 6f to 9.5f Chookie Royale (by Monsieur Bond), the fair 1m (at 2 yrs) to 14f winner of 18 races Chookie Hamilton, the modest 2-y-o 6f winner Chookie's Lass (both by Compton Place) and the modest 2-y-o 6f winner Ninety Years Young (by Paco Boy). The dam, a modest 3-y-o 7f and 1m winner, is a half-sister to 5 other minor winners. The second dam, North Lady (by Northfields), is an unplaced half-sister to the 2-y-o Group 2 Lowther Stakes winner Miss Demure. (Raeburn Brick Ltd). *"A big, strong colt, he's*

working really well at home at the minute. I like his attitude because his half-brother Chookie Royale was a bit temperamental but he's a lot more straightforward. I'll wait for a six furlong race for him, so hopefully he'll be out in mid-May. A strong-topped colt with good bone".

393. DROVER ★★★
ch.c. Foxwedge – Brooksby (Diktat). March 17. Third foal. €65,000Y. Goffs Sportsmans. Bobby O'Ryan/Keith Dalgleish. The dam, a fair 2-y-o 1m winner, is a half-sister to 7 winners. The second dam, Lovely Lyca (by Night Shift), a fair 1m and 11.8f winner, is a sister to the listed 1m winner Barboukh (herself dam of the Group 3 10f Prix Exbury winner Barbola) and a half-sister to 6 winners. (Weldspec Glasgow Ltd). *"We like him, he's a strong fella with a lot of bone to him. He's been working well enough but he's another I'm going to keep to six furlongs, or maybe a stiff five. He's maybe he's one of those that shows a bit but it's because he has ability, rather than because he's sharp. He's doing everything well".*

394. GERMAN BIGHT (IRE) ★★★
br.f. Makfi – Saint Lucia (Whipper). March 1. Second foal. £13,000Y. Goffs UK Premier (Doncaster). Bobby O'Ryan / Keith Dalgleish. Half-sister to the unplaced 2016 2-y-o Hawridge Glory (by Royal Applause). The dam ran once unplaced and is a half-sister to 4 winners including the useful 2-y-o listed 6f winner and Group 2 6f Mill Reef Stakes second Sir Xaar and the fairly useful Irish 1m to 9.5f winner and listed-placed Fuerta Ventura. The second dam, Cradle Brief (by Brief Truce), ran once unplaced in a bumper and is a half-sister to the Group 3 6f Greenlands Stakes winner Tiger Royal. (Mr M Beaumont). *"She was a bit slow getting going and was a touch behind the others, mentally and a bit physically too. In the last couple of weeks she's clicked, done a couple of pieces of work and now we like what we're seeing. She should be ready to start over five furlongs from late April onwards, but I think she'll get six later".*

395. MISS BAR BEACH ★★★
b.f. Choisir – Whitegate Way (Greensmith). April 3. Eleventh foal. €9,000Y. Tattersalls

Ireland September. F Barberini. Half-sister to 5 winners including the fairly useful 1m, 9f and hurdles winner Brog Deas (by Arakan), the quite useful 9f and 10f winner Oneofapair (by Pyrus) and the moderate Irish 6f winner Withnail (by Rossini). The dam, placed fourth once over 7f, is a sister to the US Grade 2 and Grade 3 winner Lord Smith and a half-sister to the listed winner The Lord. The second dam, Lady Longmead (by Crimson Beau), won over hurdles and is a half-sister to 2 minor winners. (Middleham Park Racing). *"A couple of months ago she was looking like she'd need time, but all of a sudden the penny's dropped and her work's been good. She's an athletic filly, quite light on her feet and she'll be racing by the end of April".*

396. MOVE IT MOVE IT ★★★
gr.c. Lethal Force – Madam Valentine (Primo Valentino). March 7. Third foal. £41,000Y. Goffs UK Silver Sale (Doncaster). Bobby O'Ryan / Keith Dalgleish. Half-brother to the useful 5f and 6f winner of 8 races from 2 to 6 yrs Piper's Note (by Piccolo). The dam is an unraced half-sister to 5 minor winners. The second dam, Madam Bold (by Never So Bold), is an unraced half-sister to 3 minor winners. (Paul & Clare Rooney). *"A nice, strong 2-y-o type, he was a bit backward early doors but the penny's dropping now. I'll start him off at five furlongs in late April/early May and he's one that'll definitely benefit for a run".*

397. ROCKET MAN DAN (IRE) ★★★
b.c. Dandy Man – Manalisa (Manduro). March 28. First foal. £12,000Y. Goffs UK Premier (Doncaster). Bobby O'Ryan / Keith Dalgleish. The dam ran once at 4 yrs unplaced and is a half-sister to 5 winners including the US Grade 2 and dual Grade 3 winner and dual Grade 1 second Valbenny. The second dam, Dark Indian (by Indian Ridge), an Italian listed-placed winner, is a half-sister to 4 winners. (Equus I). *"He was showing us a lot early doors, very sharp and went to the Brocklesby but they went far too hard, he didn't last out and we just have to draw a line through it. He needs a little break now to get over it then we'll bring him out over a sharp five furlongs somewhere".* TRAINERS' BARGAIN BUY

398. SPARK OF WAR (IRE) ★★★
b.c. Declaration Of War – Acts Of Grace
(Bahri). February 13. Third foal. 65,000Y.
Tattersalls October Book 2. Bobby O'Ryan /
Frank Brady / Johayro Investments. Half-
brother to the fair 10f winner Contradict (by
Raven's Pass), to the fair 9f winner Damascene
(by Oasis Dream) and the minor 6f winner
(from two starts) Blaugrana (by Exceed
And Excel). The dam won the Group 3 12f
Princess Royal Stakes and is a half-sister to
10 winners including the Group 1 Sprint Cup
winner and good sire Invincible Spirit. The
second dam, Rafha (by Kris), won the Group
1 10.5f Prix de Diane and is a half-sister to
9 winners including the Group 2 Blandford
Stakes winner Chiang Mai (dam of the Group
1 winner Chinese White). (Mr F Brady). *"A
beautiful colt – a real looker with good bone,
he's nice topped and I'll wait for six furlongs
with him, possibly at Ayr in mid-May. He's
been working ok, his attitude's fine and he's a
real good-looking horse that'll get further later
in the year. After his debut we may even give
him a break until later in the season because I
think his best year will as a 3-y-o".*

399. UNNAMED ★★★
b.c. Most Improved – Beautiful Dreamer
(Red Ransom). May 9. Third foal. 65,000Y.
Tattersalls October Book 3. Bobby O'Ryan/
Keith Dalgleish. The dam ran once unplaced
and is a half-sister to 5 minor winners. The
second dam, Flight Of Fancy (by Sadler's
Wells), a smart 2-y-o 6f winner and second
in the Oaks, is a sister to the listed winner
Golden Stream and a half-sister to 7 winners.
(Weldspec Glasgow Ltd). *"A big 2-y-o, he's
nicely topped and with good bone. He's been
working quite well but I'm waiting for six
furlongs with him. I won't be in a mad rush
but I like his attitude and everything I've asked
him to do he's done it. He's one of those that
tempts you to race him soon, but your head
tells you to wait a bit because you'll get more
out of him that way".*

400. UNNAMED ★★
ch.f. Dandy Man – La Rochelle (Salse). April
23. Eighth foal. €6,500Y. Goffs Sportsmans.
Bobby O'Ryan/Keith Dalgleish. Half-sister to
the modest 2-y-o 6f winner Doctor Kananga
(by Dr Fong), to the modest 2-y-o 7f winner

Citelle (by City On A Hill) and two minor
winners in Italy by Majestic Missile and Iron
Mask. The dam, a fair 1m winner, is a half-
sister to 5 winners. The second dam, Lagta
(by Kris), won twice at 3 yrs and is a half-sister
to 3 other minor winners. *"She's a small,
2-y-o type and almost went unnoticed for the
first couple of months, but lately she's done
a couple of pieces of work and shown speed.
We'll get her out in the next two or three
weeks over five furlongs, although I wouldn't
be surprised if she got a bit further as she's by
Dandy Man".*

401. UNNAMED ★★
b.c. Worthadd – Let Your Love Flow (Iffraaj).
March 29. Second foal. €45,000Y. Goffs
Sportsmans. Bobby O'Ryan / K Dalgleish. The
dam, a modest 2-y-o 9f winner, is a half-sister
to 5 minor winners. The second dam, Miss
Odlum (by Mtoto), a fair 10f winner in Ireland,
is a half-sister to one winner. (Weldspec
Glasgow Ltd). *"He's a big, tall, athletic colt
and more of a 3-y-o type. We'll take our
time with him and if he's ok we'll think about
giving him a run over a mile around the end of
September, if not I'll be happy to keep him and
run him in maidens as a 3-y-o".*

402. UNNAMED ★★
b.c. Sir Percy – Mookhlesa (Marju). April
1. Sixth foal. £65,000Y. Goffs UK Premier
(Doncaster). Bobby O'Ryan / Keith Dalgleish.
Half-brother to the fair 6f winner Najd
(by Dick Turpin), to the modest 5f winner
Traditionelle (by Indesatchel) and the
moderate 6f winner Wiggle (by Dutch Art).
The dam, a quite useful 2-y-o 5f winner, is
a half-sister to 3 winners. The second dam,
Ikhlas (by Lahib), is an unraced sister to the
2-y-o Group 3 Horris Hill Stakes winner La-
Faah and a half-sister to 6 winners. (Weldspec
Glasgow Ltd). *"A tall, athletic colt and very like
our Worthadd 2-y-o, he's been doing quite
well but we'll only run him in September if he's
ready. If not we'll wait for next year, but he's a
quality horse that just needs patience".*

TOM DASCOMBE
403. ADMIRAL SPICE ★★★★
b.c. Lethal Force – Rustam (Dansili). April
28. Fourth foal. €32,000Y. Tattersalls Ireland
September. Sackville/Donald. Half-brother

to the fair 2016 2-y-o 6f winner Many A Tale (by Poet's Voice), to the fair triple 5f winner Foxtrot Knight (by Kyllachy) and the fair dual 6f winner at 2 and 3 yrs Dodgy Bob (by Royal Applause). The dam, a minor winner at 3 yrs in Italy, is a half-sister to 5 winners including the Italian Group 2 and multiple Group 3 winner Cornelius. The second dam, Rainbow Mountain (by Rainbow Quest), a fair 11f winner, is a half-sister to 4 winners. (Passant & Wallace). *"We have two by Lethal Force and we like them both very much. I think he could be a good first season sire. This colt is pencilled in for a race at Newbury on the 21st of April which tells you we like him – going to a track like that. He's probably more of a six furlong colt than five but he's ready now so he may as well run. He's a little bit leggy and narrow, so he's going to develop as he goes through the season".* TRAINERS' BARGAIN BUY

404. A LITTLE ACTION (IRE) ★★★

b.f. Mastercraftsman – Lace (Sadler's Wells). April 15. Sixth foal. 14,000Y. Tattersalls December. Sackville/Donald. Closely related to two minor winners in the USA by Danehill Dancer including the 2-y-o winner Solan. The dam is an unraced half-sister to 4 winners including Zarani Sidi Anna (third in both the Group 1 Coronation Stakes and the Grade 1 Milady Handicap). The second dam, Emmaline (by Affirmed), won twice at up to 9f in the USA including a stakes event and is a half-sister to 8 winners including the Grade 1 winners Bates Motel and Hatim. *"She's a backward type for the mid-season onwards. A nice filly, she probably needs seven furlongs and was bought at the December sale which usually means they need a bit of time. She's alright".*

405. ALLNITE ★★★

b.c. Arcano – Paint The Town (Sadler's Wells). February 16. Fifth foal. €5,000Y. Tattersalls Ireland September. D Huggins. Half-brother to the minor French dual 2-y-o winner Olympian Gold (by Holy Roam Emperor) and to the moderate 12f winner Great Ormond (by Zamindar). The dam, placed once over 7f at 2 yrs in Ireland, is a sister to the Irish listed winners In The Limelight and On The Nile, closely related to the Group 1 Gran Premio

del Jockey Club and dual German Group 1 winner Kutub and a half-sister to 4 winners. The second dam, Minnie Habit (by Habitat), an Irish 4-y-o winner, is closely related to the dual sprint Group 3 winner Bermuda Classic (dam of the Coronation Stakes winner Shake The Yoke). (Laurence Bellman & David Ward). *"A cheap buy, but we've had a bit of success with Arcano, they're not popular but I see nothing wrong with this one. He definitely wants six and probably seven as the season goes on. He's a big, strong colt that's just going to want a bit more time and he's just cantering away at the moment".*

406. AUNTIE PAM (IRE) ★★★

b.f. Sir Prancealot – Sans Reserve (Foxhound). March 31. Fifth foal. €30,000Y. Tattersalls Ireland September. Sackville/Donald. Half-sister to the listed-placed 2-y-o 6f winner En Un Clin D'Oeil (by Chineur). The dam, a fair Irish 1m winner, is a half-sister to 2 minor winners. The second dam, Brandish (by Warning), was placed once in France and is a half-sister to 5 winners. (PAM Ties Ltd). *"A Sir Prancealot filly, so you'd say she's probably an out-and-out five furlong 2-y-o. She's sharp, knows her job and will have raced a couple of times before your book is out".* This filly was a close second first time out at Wolverhampton on the 8th April.

407. BIG TIME MAYBE (IRE) ★★★★

b.c. Dandy Man – Divine Design (Barathea). April 30. Fifth foal. £44,000Y. Goffs UK Premier (Doncaster). Sackville/Donald. Half-brother to the very useful 2-y-o 5f and 6f winner and listed-placed Angelic Lord (by Dark Angel). The dam is an unplaced half-sister to the useful 2-y-o listed 5f winner and Group 1 Nunthorpe Stakes third Piccadilly Filly. The second dam, Tortue (by Turtle Island), a quite useful Irish 1m and 9f winner, is a half-sister to 5 winners including Tiraaz (Group 1 Prix Royal-Oak). (Jones, Langford & Owen). *"We still have his 3-y-o half-brother Angelic Lord who was rated 107 as a 2-y-o. We like Dandy Man because they tend to be 2-y-o's and this colt looks just the same. He'll be out in the middle of April and he's a racy sort, a nice individual that looks sharp".*

408. BILLYCOCK HILL ★★★

b.c. Kyllachy – Red Kyte (Hawk Wing). April 8. Fifth foal. 45,000Y. Tattersalls October Book 2. Sackville/Donald. Half-brother to the quite useful 2016 2-y-o 8.5f winner Auberge Du Lac (by Lope De Vega) and to the modest 6f (at 2 yrs) and 7f winner Scarlet Bounty (by Bahamian Bounty). The dam, a quite useful dual winner (including at 2 yrs), is a half-sister to 7 winners including the useful 2-y-o 6f and UAE listed 5f winner Hammadi. The second dam, Ruby Affair (by Night Shift), a modest 7f placed 3-y-o, is a half-sister to 5 winners including the 2,000 Guineas winner Island Sands. (Famous Five Partnership). *"A backward type, he's very big and he's going to take time, as a lot of Kyllachy's do. Probably a six furlong horse, but we'll see how we go because we're just trying to get some condition off him at the moment and get him going forward".*

409. BOOZIE ★★

b.c. Dragon Pulse – Extreme Pleasure (High Chaparral). February 10. Fourth foal. The dam, a modest 8.5f placed maiden, is a half-sister to numerous winners including the listed 12f winner and Group 2 placed Treble Heights (dam of the Group 1 Irish St Leger winner Brown Panther), the Group 1 Ascot Gold Cup third Warm Feeling and the Group 1 Italian Derby third Precede. The second dam, Height Of Passion (by Shirley Heights), is an unplaced half-sister to 8 winners. (Owen Promotions Ltd). *"He was terribly small when he arrived but he's done a hell of a lot of growing. He's had sore shins and he's needed time, but now he looks like a racehorse so we'll start training him. He's out of a half-sister to Brown Panther's dam, so it's hard to say on pedigree what his trip's going to be".*

410. CAPOMENTO ★★

b.f. Casamento – Satin Cape (Cape Cross). February 10. €13,000Y. Goffs February. Deva Racing. Half-sister to the fairly useful 6f to 8.5f winner of 8 races Capo Rosso (by Red Clubs), to the fair triple 10.5f winner Caponova (by Bushranger), the quite useful Irish 2-y-o 5f winner Jolly Snake, the fair 2-y-o 5f winner Molamento and the moderate Irish 7f winner Elusive Gent (all by Elusive City). The dam, placed once over 5f at 2 yrs from 2 starts, is a half-sister to 6 winners abroad. The

second dam, Marylou Whitney (by Fappiano), was placed in the USA and is a half-sister to 3 winners. (Deva Racing Casamento Partnership). *"She's just been growing and is very similar to both her half-brothers in that she's short-backed and terribly round, so she's just going steady away. I think those two both needed five runs before the penny dropped and she's probably similar, so we'll see how we go but I think she's more one for next year".*

411. CELESTIAL FORCE ★★

b.c. Sea The Stars – Aquarelle Bleue (Sadler's Wells). March 24. Sixth foal. €75,000Y. Goffs Orby. Sackville/Donald. Brother to the fair 13.5f winner Taqdees and closely related to the useful 7f to 9f winner of 5 races Baraweez (by Cape Cross). The dam, placed over 13f in France, is a half-sister to 4 winners in France including the listed winner Ame Bleue and the Group 3 13f second Artiste Divine. The second dam, Aquarelliste (by Danehill), won the Prix de Diane, the Prix Vermeille and the Prix Ganay (all Group 1 events) and is a sister to the US dual Grade 1 winner Artiste Royale and the Australian listed winner and Group 1 placed Annenkov and a half-sister to 3 winners. (Mr John Dance). *"He's very leggy, quite backward and been in pre-training more than training. He'll be given all the time he needs and one would hope that he'd run in the second half of the season".*

412. CUDDINGTON ★★★

gr.c. Dark Angel – Pindrop (Exceed And Excel). January 23. First foal. €115,000Y. Goffs Orby. Sackville/Donald. The dam, a moderate unplaced maiden, is a half-sister to 10 winners including the Group 3 Select Stakes winner Leporello and the listed winners Calypso Grant and Poppy Carew. The second dam, Why So Silent (by Mill Reef), is an unraced half-sister to 5 winners. (Mr D W Armstrong & Manor House Stables). *"A very boisterous colt. He's very sure of his own ability and a free-going sort that just needs nurturing at the moment, not revving up. I see him as a six furlong horse and he's a good individual".*

413. DANCE ON THE DAY IRE) ★★★

b.f. Epaulette – Skeleton (Tobougg). March 3. Fourth foal. 55,000Y. Tattersalls October Book 1. Sackville/Donald. Half-sister to the minor Italian winner of 3 races at 2 and 3 yrs My Sister Genny (by Dark Angel). The dam, a modest 2-y-o 1m and 9f winner, is a half-sister to 6 winners including the Group 3 10.5f Rose Of Lancaster Stakes winner of 8 races Mulaqat. The second dam, Atamana (by Lahib), a quite useful 1m winner, is a half-sister to 7 winners. (Mr Gerry Lowe). *"Yes, she's a nice filly. We have three by this sire and they're all big, quite backward thinking and yet they've all got a bit of quality about them. This filly is just cantering away but she's not bred to be an early type. She has plenty of scope so I'd say he'd be one for the second half of the season over sprinting trips".*

414. DEECIDER ★★★
b.c. Captain Gerrard – Plead (Bering). February 21. Tenth foal. €26,000Y. Tattersalls Ireland September. Sackville/Donald. Half-brother to 5 winners including the fairly useful 2-y-o 9f winner and listed-placed Play Gal (by Multiplex), the quite useful 2-y-o 6f winner Adele Blanc Sec (by Marchand De Sable) and 2 minor winners in France by Hernando. The dam, a minor winner at 3 yrs in France, is a half-sister to 6 winners including the French listed winners Playact and Play Around. The second dam, Play Or Pay (by Play Fellow), a listed-placed winner of 2 races at 2 and 3 yrs in France, is a half-sister to 9 winners. (Silversheen Partnership). *"A very sharp colt, I trained the half-sister Adele Blanc Sec who was very good but had terrible knees and after winning easily on her second start she never ran again. He's very robust, takes lots of training and is pencilled in to possibly run at Beverley at the end of April. The lads who own him would love to run him in the maiden at Chester in May if possible. He'll be a five/six furlong horse".*

415. DEMONS ROCK (IRE) ★★★
b.c. Requinto – Afnoon (Street Cry). April 30. Second foal. €45,000Y. Tattersalls Ireland September. Sackville/Donald. The dam, a fair 2-y-o 7f winner, is a half-sister to 4 winners. The second dam, Tashawak (by Night Shift), a smart 6f (at 2 yrs) and Group 2 1m Falmouth Stakes winner, is a sister to one winner and a half-sister to 4 winners including the Group 2 12f Ribblesdale Stakes and Group 2 12.5f Prix de la Royallieu winner Fairy Queen and the Group 1 1m Criterium International

third Acropolis. (Famous Five Partnership). *"A sharp type, he's ready to run and he's a good-looking colt that probably wants six furlongs but will start over five. Not a star but we like him, he has a good attitude and is very honest".*

416. DEVIATE ★★
b.f. Acclamation – Divert (Averti). April 18. Sixth foal. £25,000Y. Goffs UK Premier (Doncaster). Not sold. Sister to the fairly useful 2-y-o 5f winner and 3-y-o dual listed 5f placed Reroute and to the fair 5.5f (at 2 yrs) and 6f winner The Art Of Racing and half-sister to the fair 5f and 6f winner Available (by Moss Vale) and the moderate 5f winner Frangarry (by Lawman). The dam, a quite useful Irish 5f winner at 3 yrs, is a half-sister to 8 winners including the Irish 7f (at 2 yrs) to 10f and subsequent Hong Kong stakes winner Solid Approach and the useful Irish 7f winner and listed-placed Dangle. The second dam, Dawn Chorus (by Mukaddamah), is an unraced half-sister to 6 winners. (Hot To Trot Racing). *"She came in late after an injury in Ireland, so I couldn't really tell you a lot about her. She's been coughing a bit so we're going easy with her until she can be trained. She looks a sharp type but we'll have to be patient".*

417. DIAMOND SET ★★★
b.c. Dutch Art – Asaawir (Royal Applause). April 29. Fifth living foal. 85,000Y. Tattersalls October Book 1. Sackville/Donald. Half-brother to the fairly useful 2-y-o dual 5f winner and Group 2 5f Queen Mary Stakes third Hairy Rocket (by Pivotal), to the useful 2-y-o dual 7f winner and Group 3 7f second Marsh Hawk (by Invincible Spirit) and the modest 6f winner Awjila (by Oasis Dream). The dam, a fairly useful 2-y-o dual 6f winner, was listed-placed and is a half-sister to 8 winners including the listed 10.5f winner Trinity Joy. The second dam, Triple Joy (by Most Welcome), a useful 6f and 7f winner and second in the listed Abernant Stakes, is a half-sister to 7 winners including the Sun Chariot Stakes winner and useful broodmare Talented. (Russell Jones & David Lowe). *"A tall, angular colt, he'll be given plenty of time. He's cantering away and he looks a nice 2-y-o type for the middle of the season onwards. It's a 2-y-o family but Dutch Art doesn't get many early ones".*

418. DRAGONS TAIL (IRE) ★★★
b.c. Dragon Pulse – Mastoora (Acclamation).
April 29. Fourth foal. €30,000Y. Tattersalls
Ireland September. Sackville/Donald. Half-
brother to the fair Irish 5f winner Knoxville
Bullet (by Clodovil). The dam, a quite useful
7f winner, is a half-sister to 3 winners. The
second dam, Sacred Love (by Barathea),
placed fourth once over 1m, is a half-sister
to 5 winners. (Goss, Hyden, Jones & Owen).
*"He's just run up a little bit light. He was just
looking average in March but he's suddenly
come good and we're thinking about running
him at the end of April. I quite like these
Dragon Pulses' because they're honest types, I
think he's probably a six furlong 2-y-o but he's
showing me he's ready to run".*

419. ENDLESS TANGENT ★★★
br.f. Lawman – Passion Planet (Medicean).
March 21. First foal. €26,000Y. Goffs Orby.
Sackville/Donald. The dam, a modest 14f
winner, is a half-sister to 5 winners including
the Group 2 Lonsdale Cup and listed Galtres
Stakes winner Pale Mimosa. The second dam,
Katch Me Katie (by Danehill), a fair 9f winner,
is a half-sister to 4 winners including the
Grade 2 E P Taylor Stakes winner and Grade
1 Gamely Handicap and Group 2 Sun Chariot
Stakes second Kool Kat Katie and the Group
3 10.4f Musidora Stakes winner, Epsom Oaks
second and Grade 1 Beverly Hills Handicap
third Kalypso Katie. (Mr John Dance). *"A six
furlong filly, she's a nice individual who'll be
ready in May. She's a good mover so I think
she'll want good ground".*

420. EPAULEMENT (IRE) ★★
b.c. Epaulette – Little Whisper (Be My Guest).
March 10. Sixth foal. 12,000Y. Tattersalls
October Book 2. Viola Arthur. Half-brother to
the quite useful 10f to 12f winner of 3 races
Ex Oriente, to the moderate 2m winner of 4
races Par Three (both by Azamour), the fair
2-y-o 7f winner If You Whisper (by Iffraaj)
and the moderate 9f winner Lilli Palmer (by
Bertolini). The dam, an Irish 2-y-o 6f and 7f
winner and listed-placed, is a half-sister to 5
winners including the dual Group 3 winner
Confuchias. The second dam, Schust Madame
(by Second Set), won over 11f in Ireland and
is a half-sister to 4 winners including the dual
US Grade 2 winner Sweet Ludy. (Deva Racing

Partnership). *"He's enormous. He was bought
by some very good, patient owners Deva
Racing and he's just had a couple of niggles
with his foot which has stopped us from
getting on with him, but that's ok because he'll
come when he's ready. I think he was cheap
and if you were buying him by the pound
you'd certainly have to pay more because he's
massive!"*

421. FANCIFUL MISS ★★★
b.f. New Approach – Fann (Diesis). March 8.
Sixth foal. 32,000Y. Tattersalls October Book
1. Sackville/Donald. Sister to the useful 2-y-o
7f winner and triple Group 3 placed Future
Empire and closely related to the German
listed 1m winner and dual Group 3 second
Black Arrow and the fair 1m (at 2 yrs), 10f and
hurdles winner Muhtaris (both by Teofilo). The
dam, a useful 9f winner, was listed-placed and
is a half-sister to 5 winners. The second dam,
Forest Storm (by Woodman), is an unraced
half-sister to 4 winners including the Group
1 Hollywood Turf Cup Handicap winner
Storm Trooper and the dual Group 3 winner
Marillette. (The Forty Three Partnership).
*"She's a lovely filly that I thought we bought
really cheaply. We gave her plenty of time
through the winter – just lots of trotting. She's
cantering away now but she's not an early
type and is one for the future. I guess she'll
come good around June time around seven
furlongs".*

422. FINNISTON FARM ★★★★
b.c. Helmet – Logic (Slip Anchor). March 18.
Twelfth foal. 65,000Y. Tattersalls October
Book 2. Sackville/Donald. Half-brother to
9 winners including the useful 7f (at 2 yrs)
and Canadian stakes winner and US Grade 2
second Crowley's Law (by Dubawi), the 1m
and 10f winner Everybody Knows (by King's
Best), the 1m to 14f winner Rationale (by
Singspiel) and the 6f (at 2 yrs) to 9f winner
of 7 races Logsdail (by Polish Precedent) – all
quite useful. The dam, a useful 1m placed
2-y-o, is a half-sister to 4 winners including
the listed Oaks Trial winner and Group 2 Park
Hill Stakes third Port Helene. The second
dam, Docklands (by On Your Mark), a listed-
placed winner of 3 races, is a half-sister to the
1,000 Guineas winner Night Off. (Famous Five
Partnership). *"I think he could be one of the*

nicer ones we've got. He hasn't worked yet but he looks a lovely horse. He moves beautifully, he's aggressive and we're probably thinking of setting him off in the second half of May over six furlongs. We trained his half-sister Crowley's Law who was second for us in a Grade 1 in America. He looks a really lovely 2-y-o and a bigger, stronger type than she was".

423. FIRE TO THE REIGN ★★★
br.f. Showcasing – Adele Blanc Sec (Marchand De Sable). April 24. Fourth foal. €60,000Y. Tattersalls Ireland September. Sackville/Donald. The dam, a quite useful 2-y-o 6f winner from two starts, is a half-sister to 4 winners. The second dam, Plead (by Bering), a minor winner at 3 yrs in France, is a half-sister to 6 winners including the French listed winners Playact and Play Around. (Lowe, McHale, Jackson, Singh, Kavanagh & Co). "I trained the dam who was a decent 2-y-o but lightly raced. This filly is 'up behind' at the moment and a little bit weak, but she's a nice type, probably a six furlong horse, but not ready yet. Hopefully she'll come good in May and then we'll start galloping her".

424. FLOREAT FLOREAT (IRE) ★★★
b.c. Epaulette – Flying Flag (Entrepreneur). March 26. Ninth foal. 68,000Y. Tattersalls October Book 2. Sackville/Donald. Half-brother to 7 winners including the fairly useful 7f (at 2 yrs) and 10f winner of 4 races and listed-placed Montsarrat (by Poet's Voice), the Italian 2-y-o listed 7.5f and 3-y-o listed 9f winner Laguna Salada (by Invincible Spirit) and the Italian listed-placed 10f winner Ladiesandgentleman (by Celtic Swing). The dam is an unplaced half-sister to the winner and US Grade 2 placed Azillion. The second dam, Olivia (by Ela-Mana-Mou), won once at 3 yrs and is a half-sister to 4 winners. (Kangyu International Racing, HK, Ltd). "He's a big colt but the most forward of the Epaulette's we've got. He looks a really nice individual. He's got a good attitude, he's straightforward and he'll be working soon with a view to running him towards the end of May/June time".

425. FORMIDABLE KITT ★★★★★
b.f. Invincible Spirit – Ceiling Kitty (Red Clubs). February 16. Second foal. Half-sister to the

quite useful 2016 2-y-o 6f winner, from two starts, Eartha Kitt (by Pivotal). The dam, winner of the Group 2 5f Queen Mary Stakes, is a half-sister to the fair 2-y-o triple 5f winner Van Go Go. The second dam, Baldovina (by Tale Of The Cat), is a placed half-sister to 4 winners including the Japanese dual Group 3 winner One Carat. (Chasemore Farm). "The apple of my eye. She's out of Ceiling Kitty who won the Queen Mary for us but has unfortunately died so we have to find a replacement broodmare for her owner. Hopefully this is the one. All being well she'll run at Newmarket's Craven meeting and she's really nice. She a little bit quirky, but her dam was the same so you can't blame her! She's honest, a five furlong type and she's done well because she's grown and is only going to get stronger and better. Going nicely, I think she's pretty smart".

426. FOUR CHAMPS ★★
gr.c. Champs Elysees – Lana Jolie (Whipper). April 15. Second foal. 9,000Y. Tattersalls October Book 3. Manor House Stables. The dam won twice at 3 yrs and was listed placed four times in Germany from 9f to 12f and is a half-sister to 4 winners. The second dam, the unraced Linamox (by Linamix), is a half-sister to 7 winners including Lune D'Or (Group 1 Premio Lydia Tesio). (Dodd, O'Halloran, Satchell & Towns). "He's a very backward horse that was bought with his 3-y-o career in mind, so there's no rush with him".

427. FROZEN ANGEL (IRE) ★★★
gr.c. Dark Angel – Cut No Ice (Verglas). January 27. First foal. £165,000Y. Goffs UK Premier (Doncaster). Sackville/Donald. The dam, a fair 2-y-o 5f winner, is a half-sister to 12 winners including the Group 1 6f Haydock Park Sprint Cup and Group 3 5f Palace House Stakes winner Pipalong, the listed winner Out Of Africa and the useful 2-y-o 5f winner and Group 2 5f Flying Childers Stakes second China Eyes. The second dam, Limpopo (by Green Desert), a poor 5f placed 2-y-o, is a half-sister to 8 winners here and abroad. (Cleverley, Dance, Mound, Owen). "A beautiful colt. For a time he looked really average, I don't think he understood what we wanted him to do, but over the last month he's really begun to impress. We'll probably go to Newmarket with him because rather than

having electric speed he just keeps going, so we want a track where he can get rolling early enough. He looks like a proper 2-y-o, so I hope he is. He cost a lot of money and we don't normally get to invest that amount so I hope he rewards his owners. I'm sure he will, he certainly looks the part anyway".

428. GLORIOUS PLAYER (IRE) ★★★
b.c. Kyllachy – Playwithmyheart (Diktat). February 21. Third foal. 90,000Y. Tattersalls October Book 2. Sackville/Donald. Half-brother to the moderate 2-y-o 10f winner Silas R (by Pour Moi). The dam, a 2-y-o 1m winner in France, is a half-sister to 7 winners including the Group 1 7f Prix de la Foret winner of 16 races Toylsome and the 2-y-o Group 3 winner Coral Mist. The second dam, Treasure Trove (by The Minstrel), a modest 5f to 7f placed 2-y-o, is a half-sister to 4 winners including the US Grade 3 winner Ocean Queen and the Queen Mary Stakes and Fred Darling Stakes winner Dance Parade – subsequently a Grade 2 winner in the USA. (Kangyu International Racing, HK, Ltd). *"A lovely, big, strong Kyllachy colt, because of his size we won't do anything with him until May comes. He looks like a second half of the season colt".*

429. HARRY CALLAHAN (IRE) ★★★
b.c. Dutch Art – Sovana (Desert King). February 22. Tenth foal. 54,000Y. Tattersalls October Book 1. Sackville/Donald. Half-brother to 7 winners including the Group 2 Kilboy Estate Stakes and Group 2 Dance Design Stakes winner Bocca Baciata (by Big Bad Bob), the Group 3 Prix Miesque winner and French 1,000 Guineas third Topeka and the Group 3 Prix Edmund Blanc winner Kalsa (both by Whipper). The dam, a 3-y-o winner in France and third in the Group 3 Prix Minerve, is a half-sister to 4 winners including the Group 3 Prix Eclipse Stakes winner Perugia. The second dam, Piacenza (by Darshaan), a minor French 3-y-o winner, is a half-sister to 5 winners. (Dirty Harry Syndicate). *"A nice colt with plenty of size, he's run up a little light and he's a six furlong colt so he just needs a bit of time. I guess he'll be ready for June time and we're going nice and easy with him for now. He's had no problems but he's just not quite ready".*

430. HOPE AND GLORY (IRE) ★★★
ch.f. Dandy Man – Tashyra (Tagula). April 5. Eighth foal. 10,000Y. Tattersalls December. Manor House Stables. Half-sister to the fair 2 y o 6f winner I'malwaysright (by Namid), to the modest dual 5f winner Simply Black (by Kheleyf) and a winner in Greece by Acclamation. The dam was placed fourth once and is a sister to 2 winners including the German 2-y-o Group 2 winner Tagshira and a half-sister to one winner. The second dam, Shiyra (by Darshaan), a minor Irish 1m and 10f winner, is a half-sister to 3 winners. (British Racing Club). *"A sharp, racy filly, we should know our fate pretty quickly with her. She'll be racing in April, she's as tough as nails and quite small but my word she's aggressive! She'll be alright I'm sure"*

431. HOT JAZZ ★★
b.c. Red Jazz – Pelican Waters (Key Of Luck). May 30. Sixth foal. €5,000Y. Tattersalls Ireland September. Dennis Huggins. Half-brother to the fair Irish 7f winner Crafted Mastery (by Mastercraftsman), to the modest 1m to 10f winner of 6 races Exclusive Waters (by Elusive City) and a minor 3-y-o winner in Italy by Excellent Art. The dam, a fairly useful 9.5f winner, is a half-sister to 5 winners. The second dam, Orlena (by Gone West), a minor 2-y-o 7f winner in France, is a half-sister to 8 winners including the listed winner and 1,000 Guineas third Vista Bella. (Laurence Bellman & David Ward). *"By the first season sire Red Jazz, he hasn't done an awful lot yet but he was a very late foal. He doesn't look it though, he's quite strong, cantering away and hasn't worked yet so we'll see how we go".*

432. KENDERGARTEN KOP (IRE) ★★★★
ch.c. Kendargent – Elsa T (Duke Of Marmalade). March 25. First foal. €48,000Y. Goffs Orby. Not sold. The dam, placed twice at 3 yrs in France, is a half-sister to 3 winners including the dual Group 3 winner Russian Soul. The second dam, Russian Hill (by Indian Ridge), a French listed 10f winner and placed in two Group 2 events, is a half-sister to 10 winners including the Group 2 Sun Chariot Stakes winner Esoterique and the Group 2 winners Russian Hope, Russian Cross and Archange D'Or. (Jones, Nolan, O'Halloran, Satchell). *"Our jockey Richard Kingscote gave*

this a gallop in late March and thought he was a really nice 2-y-o, but he got a touch of sore shins and we had to back off him. He hasn't galloped for three weeks but people seem to like these Kendargents and this colt has done nothing wrong, we'll give him another gallop and hopefully he'll be out in May. At the moment he looks like a five furlong horse".

433. KRAKA (IRE) ★★★
b.c. Dark Angel – Manuelita Rose (Desert Style). February 2. Third foal. €140,000Y. Tattersalls Ireland September. Sackville/Donald. Half-brother to the fair dual 1m winner Ubla (by Arcano). The dam is an unraced half-sister to 5 winners including the Irish listed winner and dual Group 3 third Rose Hip. The second dam, Rose Tint (by Salse), is an unplaced half-sister to 8 winners. (Jones, Lowe, Mound, Trowbridge). *"A nice, big, strong Dark Angel colt, he's been cantering, got a touch of sore shins, we've left him alone and we're just building him back up now. He's probably a six furlong horse and one that you'd be thinking about running in mid-May just to see if he's good enough for Royal Ascot".*

434. LEVANTE PLAYER (IRE) ★★★★
b.c. Kodiac – Isolde's Return (Avonbridge). March 15. Second foal. £100,000Y. Goffs UK Premier (Doncaster). Sackville/Donald. The dam is an unplaced half-sister to 7 winners including the dams of the Group winners Up In Time and Summer Fete. The second dam, Up And About (by Barathea), a fair 14.8f winner, is a half-sister to 9 winners including the listed Atalanta Stakes winner and Group 1 placed Musicanna and to the unplaced dam of the champion European 3-y-o sprinter Overdose. (Scott, Fletcher, Owen). *"A lovely colt, I've got him pencilled in to run in late April, he's been going really nicely and I like him. A little bit narrow I suppose, if you were to be critical, because you'd like to see more bulk, but he does remind me a lot of Roudee who was a decent 2-y-o and got better with age. I'm sure this horse will be the same".*

435. MAGNUS (IRE) ★★★
b.c. Makfi – Royale Danehill (Danehill). April 7. Fifth living foal. 10,000Y. Tattersalls October Book 3. Woodbine Bloodstock. Closely

related to the quite useful 2-y-o 6f winner Bircham (by Dubawi) and half-brother to the quite useful triple 6f winner from 2 to 4 yrs Souville (by Dalakhani) and the fair 2017 3-y-o 8.5f winner Commodity (by Dutch Art). The dam won two minor races at 4 yrs in France including over 7.5f at Deauville and is a half-sister to 6 winners including the Group 3 placed Juliet Capulet and the listed-placed Fly To The Moon. The second dam, Royal Ballerina (by Sadler's Wells), won the Group 2 12f Blandford Stakes, was second in the Oaks and is a half-sister to 7 winners including the dual Group 2 10f Sun Chariot Stakes winner Free Guest (dam of the Group 1 Fillies Mile winner and Oaks second Shamshir). (Living Legend Racing Partnership). *"He's surprised me because I didn't think he'd be anywhere near as forward as he is, but he is forward. He should want more than five furlongs, but he's raring to go, he's straightforward and has a good attitude. It always bothers me a little bit if you're seeing what you shouldn't, but hopefully in this case it's a good thing. He's doing everything right and should be suited by six furlongs".*

436. MAKE IT SIMPLE ★★
ch.c. Compton Place – It's Complicated (Cape Cross). April 17. First foal. £5,000Y. Goffs UK Premier (Doncaster). The dam is an unraced half-sister to 4 minor winners here and abroad. The second dam, Only Alone (by Rahy), is an unraced half-sister to 9 winners including the French dual Group 1 winner and good broodmare Occupandiste. (Laurence Bellman & David Ward). *"He's had a bit of a stop-start campaign so far, he's quite leggy with long cannon bones and he hasn't really grown into himself yet. I thought he was going to be really sharp and early but now he's grown a bit so we haven't done too much with him. I'd like to think he'll be out May and getting on with it".*

437. MISS DD (IRE) ★★★
b.f. Dandy Man – Dynaperformer (Dynaformer). March 28. First foal. 16,000Y. Tattersalls December. Manor House Stables. The dam, an Irish 4-y-o 1m 6f winner, is a half-sister to 4 winners including the useful Irish 5f to 7f winner and Group 3 Flying Five Stakes third Roicead. The second dam,

Coachella (by Danehill), is an unraced half-sister to 5 winners including the Group 1 1m Coronation Stakes winner and 1,000 Guineas second Maids Causeway. (First Capital Cashflow & Partner). *"She's just a bit light but she's had a couple of gallops and is doing everything right. She'll be out pretty soon and she's straightforward, so I don't mind her at all".*

438. NEW DAY DAWN (IRE) ★★★

ch.f. Dawn Approach – Roo (Rudimentary). April 3. Eleventh living foal. 82,000Y. Tattersalls October Book 1. Sackville/Donald. Half-sister to 7 winners including the very smart 6f (at 2 yrs) and 7f winner and Group 2 Prix Morny second Gallagher (by Bahamian Bounty), the very useful 7f (including at 2 yrs) to 10f winner and listed-placed Quick Wit (by Oasis Dream), the useful 5f (at 2 yrs) and 7f winner and listed-placed Roodeye (by Inchinor and dam of the dual Grade 2 winner Prize Exhibit) and the quite useful 2-y-o winners Cockney Dancer (by Cockney Rebel) and Roodolph (by Primo Valentino). The dam, a listed-placed 2-y-o 5f and 6f winner, is a half-sister to Bannister (Group 2 6f Gimcrack Stakes). The second dam, Shall We Run (by Hotfoot), a 5f placed 2-y-o, is a half-sister to the Group 1 6f Cheveley Park Stakes winner Dead Certain. (Laurence Bellman & David Ward). *"Everyone I've spoken to about these Dawn Approach 2-y-o's have been raving about them. We've only got this one and she's just running up a bit light, finding life a bit hard, so I've just eased off the gallop a bit. I see her as a six/seven furlong horse so there's no rush obviously and I'm just minding her for a bit until she strengthens up".*

439. NOBRASSNOLASS (IRE) ★★★

b.f. Kodiac – Hams (Dixie Union). April 26. Sixth foal. €38,000Y. Tattersalls Ireland September. Sackville/Donald. Half-sister to the quite useful 6f (at 2 yrs) to 1m winner of 4 races Dixie's Dream (by Hawk Wing) and to a 2-y-o winner in Italy by Refuse To Bend. The dam, a fair 7f placed maiden, is a half-sister to the US Grade 2 winner Desert Digger. The second dam, Desert Victress (by Desert Wine), placed fourth twice here and a winner in the USA, is a half-sister to 6 winners including the US Graded stakes winners Explicit and Flying

Victor. (Mr Peter Birbeck). *"She runs shortly and looks like a proper, sharp 2-y-o filly. We like her, she's ready to go and I'd like to think she might win before your book comes out".*

440. OUR MAN IN HAVANA ★★★

b.c. Havana Gold – Auntie Kathryn (Acclamation). April 6. Second foal. €16,000Y. Tattersalls Ireland September. Sackville/ Donald. Half-brother to the moderate 2016 2-y-o 5f winner Royal Celebration (by Excelebration). The dam, a moderate 5f winner, is closely related to the Irish 7f (at 2 yrs) and listed 10f winner Royal Intrigue and a half-sister to 6 winners. The second dam, Congress (by Dancing Brave), a quite useful 2-y-o 1m winner, is a sister to the Group 1 6f Haydock Park Sprint Cup and Group 1 Prix Maurice de Gheest winner Cherokee Rose and a half-sister to 3 winners. (John Abbey & Mike Nolan). *"He's entered to run in mid-April at Lingfield, he's very sharp, very honest and hasn't done anything wrong, so hopefully we'll get these new owners off to a good start".*

441. POPPY LOVE ★★

br.f. Harbour Watch – Don't Tell Mary (Starcraft). February 13. Third foal. The dam, a fairly useful 2-y-o listed 5f winner, is a half-sister to the very useful 2-y-o 5f and 6f winner and Group 2 July Stakes second Cape Fear and to the useful 6f (at 2 yrs) and listed 5f winner Exceptional Art. The second dam, Only In Dreams (by Polar Falcon), a fair 2-y-o 7f winner, is a full or half-sister to 4 other minor winners. (Keith & Mary Trowbridge). *"A home-bred, I trained the dam but we haven't had much luck from her. This filly was going really well until she got a bug which knocked her for six, so she's had a month off and we'll have to build her back up slowly. She'll be a five furlong filly but not until June".*

442. PORCHY PARTY (IRE) ★★★

ch.c. Dragon Pulse – Shawaaty (Monsun). March 15. Third foal. 18,000Y. Tattersalls December. Manor House Stables. Half-brother to Intisha (by Intikhab), placed fourth once over 6f at 2 yrs in 2016 and to a 2-y-o winner in the Czech Republic by Lilbourne Lad. The dam, placed once at 3 yrs in France, is a half-sister to 5 winners including the French listed winner Mahaatheer. The second dam,

Al Ihtithar (by Barathea), a very useful 10f and 10.3f listed winner, is a full or half-sister to 9 winners including the Group 3 Prix Berteux winner and dual Group 2 second Samsaam. (RFH Partnership One). *"He's a nice shape, seems to have a good attitude and he's done nothing wrong. He's ready for a gallop next week and we like him. He's straightforward and a five/six furlong 2-y-o".*

443. PROSCHEMA (IRE) ★★
ch.c. Declaration Of War – Notable (Zafonic). April 2. Seventh foal. 65,000Y. Tattersalls December. Sackville/Donald. Half-brother to the Group 2 13f Prix de Royallieu winner Maria Royal and to the useful 11.5f and 12f winner and German Group 1 second Red Cardinal (both by Montjeu). The dam is an unraced half-sister to 3 winners including the Group 3 Prix de Sandringham winner and smart broodmare Orford Ness. The second dam, Nesaah (by Topsider), a fairly useful listed-placed 10f and 10.5f winner, is a half-sister to 8 winners including the Group winners Privity and Zindari. (Empire State Racing Partnership). *"A big, backward horse and a nice type. I sold him to an existing owner who's always had sprinters and he wanted something that wanted more time and a trip. He's just cantering and swimming for now, taking life pretty easy. A big, rangy horse with a good, wide chest on him. He'll be out at the end of the season".*

444. QUANTATMENTAL (IRE) ★★★
ch.c. New Approach – Anayid (A P Indy). March 10. Ninth foal. €60,000Y. Goffs Orby. Sackville/Donald. Half-brother to the very useful 2-y-o listed 7f winner Titus Mills, the fairly useful Irish 2-y-o 7f winner Sniper (both by Dubawi), the quite useful 2-y-o 7f winner Mirabella (by Motivator), the quite useful 7f (at 2 yrs in France) and 9f winner Sand Tiger (by Indian Ridge) and the fair French 10f winner of 4 races Ana Lichious (by Makfi). The dam is an unraced half-sister to 3 winners. The second dam, Aqaarid (by Nashwan), winner of the Group 1 Fillies Mile and the Group 3 7.3f Fred Darling Stakes, was second in the 1,000 Guineas and is a half-sister to 2 winners. (Mr John Dance). *"He was given plenty of time in the winter, he's cantering now and he's physically he's done well because he*

was a bit weak. His shoulders have exploded outwards, his quarters have grown and he looks like a racehorse now".

445. QUEEN OF SALSA ★★
b.f. Havana Gold – Royal Whisper (Royal Applause). February 1. Second foal. £6,000Y. Goffs UK Silver. Hawthorn Bloodstock. Half-sister to the fair 7f (including at 2 yrs in 2016) and 6f placed Circulate (by Dutch Art). The dam is an unraced sister to the useful 5f, 7f (both at 2 yrs) and listed 7f winner and Group 2 7f Rockfel Stakes third Royal Confidence and to the quite useful 2-y-o 6f winner and US stakes-placed Imperious One and a half-sister to 2 winners. The second dam, Never A Doubt (by Night Shift), a very useful 2-y-o winner of the Group 2 5.5f Prix Robert Papin, is a half-sister to 4 winners. (Living Legend Racing Partnership). *"She's had a few little problems, mainly because I think she's growing. She's just doing light exercise for now, but she'll come good soon. I think five furlongs would be too sharp for her so she needs a further trip and a month or two to mature".*

446. RED FORCE ONE ★★★
ch.c. Lethal Force – Dusty Red (Teofilo). April 25. Second foal. 52,000Y. Tattersalls October Book 2. Sackville/Donald. The dam is an unplaced half-sister to 6 winners including the listed 1m and subsequent US Grade 2 Lake Placid Handicap winner Spotlight and the dam of the Group 1 Phoenix Stakes winner Zoffany. The second dam, Dust Dancer (by Suave Dancer), won 4 races including the Group 3 10f Prix de la Nonette and is a half-sister to 6 winners including the Group 3 7.3f Fred Darling Stakes winner Bulaxie (herself dam of the Group 2 winner Claxon). (Ferguson, Done, Mason). *"We like the sire and we like this horse. He was very forward and galloping in early March but just went a little bit sore so I gave him a break and he's back cantering now. A nice, big individual that looks like a five/six furlong horse and one we could have around here for a few years because he's just going to keep getting bigger. Showing all the right signs at the moment".*

447. REDTEDD ★★
ch.c. Mazameer – Mermaid Melody (Machiavellian). April 1. Seventh foal. Half-

brother to the moderate 2-y-o 1m winner Adam Eterno (by Spartacus). The dam is an unraced half-sister to 2 minor winners. The second dam, Jet Ski Lady (by Vaguely Noble), won the Oaks. (Sleeve It Ltd). *"A home-bred who has just found life a bit tricky and he's been suffering from growing pains. He was pretty small when he arrived but now he fits in with everything else. He probably hasn't had the sales prep that a lot of them have had, so he's just finding it tough at the moment".* The sire, a son of Green Desert, won three sprints including the Group 3 Prix de Cabourg.

448. ROCK FORCE ★★

b.c. Fastnet Rock – Sweepstake (Acclamation). January 27. Fifth foal. 150,000Y. Tattersalls October Book 1. Not sold. Half-brother to the fairly useful 12f winner Horseshoe Bay (by Arch). The dam, a 2-y-o listed 5f winner, was third in the Group 3 6f Princess Margaret Stakes and second in a US Grade 3 stakes and is a full or half-sister to 5 winners. The second dam, Dust Flicker (by Suave Dancer), placed fourth once over 10f, is a half-sister to 5 winners including the Group 3 winners Dust Dancer (dam of the US Grade 2 winner Spotlight) and Bulaxie (dam of the Group 2 winner Claxon). (Laurence Bellman & David Ward). *"When we bought the yearlings I must admit he was my favourite and I like Fastnet Rock as a stallion – I don't know why everyone's off him. He's a really good-looking colt and is a beautiful shape, but he's had a pretty moderate winter. He'll come good though, he's cantering and I still think highly of him even though he's struggling a bit. He looks like a sprinter, but we haven't done enough with him to tell yet".*

449. SAUSAGE FINGERS ★★

b.c. Red Jazz – Italian Affair (Fumo di Londra). March 6. Eighth foal. 4,000Y. Tattersalls October Book 4. Champagne Bloodstock. Half-brother to the poor 2016 5f fourth placed 2-y-o Neigh Kid (by Dandy Man) and to the fair 6f and subsequent Norwegian Group 3 7f winner Chicken Momo (by Pyrus). The dam, a moderate dual 6f winner, including at 2 yrs, is out of the placed Sergentti (by Common Grounds), herself a half-sister to 2 minor winners. (MHS Racing Club). *"I had a half-sister to him that never*

won but was very honest. As soon as he's ready he'll be running regularly for our Racing Club. He looks the type that can cope with that. We don't really know what we've got yet, particularly as Red Jazz is a first season sire. He was working but he's just gone a bit weak. He'll be out in May and once he starts he won't stop".*

450. SHA LA LA LA LEE ★★★

b.c. Helmet – Shamara (Spectrum). April 14. Sixth foal. 52,000Y. Tattersalls October Book 2. Sackville/Donald. Half-brother to the quite useful 2-y-o 6f and 1m winner Rafiqa (by Mujahid). The dam, a fairly useful 10f and 12f winner, was listed-placed and is a half-sister to one winner in Germany. The second dam, Hamara (by Akarad), is an unraced half-sister to a French listed winner. (Nigel & Sharon Mather and Charles Ledigo). *"I don't think these Helmets are that early and this one is definitely very leggy. He's a little bit 'stressy' at times but he's a good-looking horse that's not doing much more than cantering at the moment. He'll step up in May and then we'll know more about him. I like the sire but on the whole they take a bit more time than some people think".*

451. SHOOTINGTHE BREEZE ★★★

b.c. Dutch Art – Clinet (Docksider). April 13. Sixth foal. £75,000Y. Goffs UK Premier (Doncaster). Sackville/Donald. Half-brother to the fairly useful French 2-y-o 5.5f and 6f winner Exceed The Limit (by Exceed And Excel) and to a minor winner abroad by Kyllachy. The dam won 5 races at 2 to 4 yrs and from 7f to 9f, including a listed event in the UAE, was Grade 2 placed in the USA and is a half-sister to 3 winners. The second dam, Oiche Mhaith (by Night Shift), won once at 3 yrs and is a half-sister to 7 winners. (Done, Ferguson, Mason, Morris). *"Out of a good mare that John Hills trained called Clinet, he's done nothing wrong but I wouldn't think there are many early Dutch Arts, so we'll just continue cantering him until May. A good-moving horse with a good attitude".*

452. SILVER BULLET (IRE) ★★★

gr.f. Camacho – Sixfields Flyer (Desert Style). April 28. Sixth foal. €55,000Y. Tattersalls Ireland September. Sackville/Donald. Sister to the fair 6f winner Rich Forever and the Singapore winner Flambard House and half-sister to the quite useful 2-y-o 6f and 7f winner Malachim Mist and the fair 2-y-o 5f winner Jersey Breeze (both by Dark Angel). The dam, a moderate 1m placed maiden, is a half-sister to 6 winners including Rich Ground (Group 3 July Stakes). The second dam, Gratclo (by Belfort), a modest winner of 5 races from 2 to 4 yrs, is a half-sister to 3 winners. (Laurence Bellman & Caroline Ingram). *"A five furlong filly, she's very sharp and was due to run next week but unfortunately she had a dirty scope. She'll be out soon, I love her and she's very honest. She's reasonably small but when we get her to the track she won't look so small against the other 2-y-o's and she'll be winning shortly".*

453. SILVER CHARACTER (IRE) ★★

gr.c. Camelot – Convocate (Exchange Rate). January 25. First foal. 65,000Y. Tattersalls October Book 2. Sackville/Donald. The dam, a quite useful 10f winner, is a half-sister to 6 winners including the Group 3 10.5f Prix Fille de'Air winner Dance Dress (herself dam of the US dual Grade 2 winner Costume). The second dam, Private Line (by Private Account), a useful 7f (at 2 yrs) and listed 1m winner, is a half-sister to the French 2-y-o listed 1m winner and Group 1 placed Most Precious. (Aykroyd & Sons Ltd). *"A nice, big, imposing individual. He falls into the category of second half of the season 2-y-o's. He's just doing easy canters and we haven't got stuck into him at all because he's one we're treating with his 3-y-o career in mind".*

454. SIREN SONG ★★

b.f. Poet's Voice – Present Danger (Cadeaux Genereux). February 18. Third foal. The dam, a fair 6f (at 2 yrs) and 1m winner, is a half-sister to 5 winners including the fairly useful 2-y-o 5f winner and listed placed All For Laura (herself dam of the Group 2 Cherry Hinton Stakes winner Misheer). The second dam, Lighthouse (by Warning), a fairly useful 3-y-o 8.3f winner, is a half-sister to 4 winners including the Group 1 Middle Park Stakes, Group 3 July Stakes and Group 3 Richmond Stakes winner First Trump. (Chasemore Farm & Owen Promotions). *"Poet's Voice has been a disappointing stallion, the dam was good*

(although quirky) and well-bred, but she hasn't bred anything of note yet. This is a tall, angular, leggy filly that needs time, so I hope she's worth that time".

455. SMUGGLERS TOP ★★★

ch.c. Kendargent – Penny's Gift (Tobougg). January 31. Third foal. 55,000Y. Tattersalls October Book 2. Sackville/Donald. Half-brother to the quite useful 2-y-o 5f winner Dittander (by Exceed And Excel). The dam, a 2-y-o listed 6f and Group 2 1m German 1,000 Guineas winner, is a sister to one winner and a half-sister to 3 winners. The second dam, Happy Lady (by Cadeaux Genereux), a fair 1m placed maiden, is a half-sister to 4 winners including the smart middle-distance stayer and Group 2 Yorkshire Cup second Rainbow Ways. (Famous Five Partnership). *"He was going really well through the winter but had a setback and we had to give him a month off. He's back cantering now and I see no reason why he shouldn't be anything but a nice horse. The dam was good and the sire is quite well thought of, but I couldn't tell you any more than that at the moment".*

456. SOCIETY SECRET (IRE) ★★★

ch.c. Society Rock – Bond Deal (Pivotal). April 16. Sixth foal. €36,000Y. Goffs Sportsmans. Sackville/Donald. Half-brother to the useful 7f (including at 2 yrs) and 1m winner of 4 races Arcanada (by Arcano). The dam, a winner of 6 races in Italy and the USA including a minor stakes, was third in the Group 3 1m Premio Carlo Chiesa and is a half-sister to 3 winners including the fairly useful triple 6f winner and listed-placed Dawn Eclipse. The second dam, Prima (by Primo Dominie), a fair 5f and 6f placed 2-y-o, is a half-sister to 4 minor winners. (Wilmshurst, Cronshaw & Attenborough). *"A half-brother to a winner of ours, Arcanada, he's done a lot of growing, so although when we bought him he was small he's now a big horse with a good, strong neck and quarters on him. He's one for May/June and we're not in a big rush with him".*

457. SPUD (IRE) ★★★

b.c. Fast Company – Nightswimmer (Noverre). May 2. Fourth foal. 75,000Y. Tattersalls October Book 2. Sackville/Donald. Brother to the fairly useful 7f and 1m winner (including at 2 yrs) Mutarakez and half-brother to the fair 2016 1m placed 2-y-o Casina Di Notte (by Casamento) and the quite useful 5f winner of 8 races Bashiba (by Iffraaj). The dam is an unplaced half-sister to 4 winners including the 2-y-o listed 5f winner and Group 3 placed Waterways. The second dam, Buckle (by Common Grounds), a fair dual 1m winner at 3 yrs, subsequently won in France and is a half-sister to 8 winners. (Stuart Banks & Owen Promotions). *"Fast Company is a stallion I like. This colt just grew and grew throughout February and March, so as a result we had to back off him a bit. He's level now and he's put on weight so we'll get stuck into him and see what we've got".*

458. STORY MINISTER (IRE) ★★★
ch.c. Camacho – Hartstown House (Primo Dominie). March 9. Ninth foal. £45,000Y. Goffs UK Premier (Doncaster). Salcey Forest Stud. Half-brother to the 2-y-o listed 5f winners Promised Money (by Dark Angel) and Beldale Memory (by Camacho), to the 7f and 1m winner Hacienda (by Kheleyf), the Irish 2-y-o 6f winner Sheltingham (by Intikhab) – all fairly useful – and the fair dual 7f winner Little Wing (by Hawk Wing). The dam, a fairly useful Irish 2-y-o dual 5f winner, is a half-sister to 6 winners including the Irish 2,000 Guineas second Fa-Eq and the smart listed 7.3f and 1m winner Corinium. The second dam, Searching Star (by Rainbow Quest), a modest 6f (at 2 yrs) to 11.3f placed maiden, is a half-sister to 8 winners, two of them listed. (Mr John Dance). *"We really liked him and he was doing everything nicely, but he met with an accident and had to have a month off. He's back cantering now and he's a fine looking horse with a good, strong neck on him and I think he's quite nice".*

459. SUPERSYMMETRY (IRE) ★★★
br.f. Kyllachy – Duniatty (Green Desert). March 22. Second foal. 60,000Y. Tattersalls October Book 1. Sackville/Donald. Half-sister to the modest 2016 5f to 1m placed 2-y-o Book Of Poetry (by Poet's Voice). The dam, a minor French 2-y-o winner, is a half-sister to 3 winners including the Group 2 Lennox Stakes and Group 3 Jersey Stakes winner Tariq, and to the dams of the Group winners Mobsta and Ross Castle. The second dam, Tatora (by

Selkirk), is an unraced half-sister to 3 winners and to the placed dam of the Group 2 Flying Childers Stakes winner Wi Dud. (David Lowe). *"A leggy filly who was doing some work but we backed off her because she's definitely going to want six furlongs. Nevertheless she's the sharpest of our Kyllachy's and she'll be out in mid-May in a fillies' maiden and I like her. You'd like to think she's one that could run in May and maybe go for something like the Albany if she's good enough. She looks like a nice filly".*

460. THIS GIRL ★★
b.f. Nathaniel – Fibou (Seeking The Gold). April 18. Eighth foal. 12,000Y. Tattersalls December. Sackville/Donald. Half-sister to the fair 2016 2-y-o 5f winner Kachess (by Kyllachy), to the useful UAE 6f to 9.5f winner from 4 to 6 yrs and Group 1 10f third Faulkner, the modest 2-y-o 6f winner Finoon (both by Pivotal) and to two winners abroad by Oasis Dream and Cape Cross. The dam ran once unplaced and is a half-sister to 4 winners. The second dam, Lilium (by Nashwan), a listed 7f (at 2 yrs) and listed 12f winner, was third in the Group 3 Princess Royal Stakes and is a half-sister to 6 winners including the 2-y-o Group 1 6f Middle Park Stakes winner Lujain. (David Lowe & Russell Jones). *"A half-sister to Kachess who won first time out at Goodwood for us last year and then just disappointed. This filly is by Nathaniel, which is a lot different to Kyllachy. She's growing, a bit weak and is going to take some time. She's quite similar to her half-sister in that she's quite a free-going sort so we need to manage her mind and I think she'll be alright over seven from mid-summer".*

461. UNCOVERED ★★
b.c. Helmet – Caritas (Generous). March 3. First foal. 9,000Y. Tattersalls October Book 3. Not sold. The dam is an unraced half-sister to 4 minor winners. The second dam, Celia Brady (by Last Tycoon), a modest 1m winner at 3 and 5 yrs, is a half-sister to 5 winners including the multiple Group 1 winners Warrsan and Luso. (Laurence Bellman & David Ward). *"A well-named Helmet colt! He's a nice horse, wants a bit of time and you'd think he'd be out in June. He's not galloped yet but he's cantering away".*

462. VODKA PIGEON ★★
ch.f. Sepoy – Hanging On (Spinning World). March 2. Fourth foal. 60,000Y. Tattersalls October Book 1. Sackville/Donald. Half-sister to 2 minor winners abroad by Barathea and Leporello. The dam, a fairly useful 2-y-o 7f winner, is a half-sister to 9 winners including the Irish listed winner Barolo. The second dam, Lydia Maria (by Dancing Brave), a moderate 1m and 10f placed maiden, is a half-sister to 7 winners. (Kathy Fletcher & Michael Owen). *"She was cantering away all through the winter but she's gone a bit weak, she's quite tubby and went through a difficult stage like a lot of them do. So she's had a relatively easy month and we'll start stepping her up in May".*

463. ZOFFALEE (FR) ★★★★
ch.c. Zoffany – Senderlea (Giant's Causeway). March 1. Seventh foal. €110,000Y. Arqana Deauville August. Sackville/Donald. Half-winners in France. The dam is an unplaced half-sister to 4 winners including the Group 2 10f Prix Greffulhe winner Quest For Honor and the listed 11f and 12f winner Astrologie. The second dam, Quest For Ladies (by Rainbow Quest), a US listed stakes winner, is a half-sister to 4 winners including the dam of the French Derby winner Blue Canari. (Mr D R Passant). *"He's a cracker – a lovely horse that keeps dropping his rider so we put a different one on and he drops that one too! He's mentally sharp but physically he's going to want six furlongs and he'll be out in the middle of May. We like him, he's aggressive and if he's good enough we might take him to Deauville in August because he's French-bred and we might be able to pick up some prize money and premiums".*

464. UNNAMED ★★
ch.f. Excelebration – Boast (Most Welcome). May 4. Half-sister to the useful 2-y-o listed 5.2f winner and dual Group 3 placed Strut (by Danehill Dancer), to the 2-y-o dual 5f winner and subsequent US Grade 3 placed Vaunt (by Averti), the 9.5f winner Toast Of The Town, the 12f winner Snobbery (both by Duke Of Marmalade), the 1m winner of 5 races No Dominion (by Dylan Thomas) and the 2-y-o 5f and subsequent US winner Brag (by

Mujadil) – all quite useful. The dam, a useful 5f and 6f winner, is a half-sister to 6 winners including the fairly useful 2-y-o 5f and 4-y-o 1m winner Great Bear. The second dam, Bay Bay (by Bay Express), a useful 7.6f winner, was listed-placed twice and is a half-sister to 7 winners. (Mr M Smith). *"A filly that was sent to us, she's a little bit weak. She was going nicely and has done some work but she just went a little bit backward. I think the sire has been a bit disappointing and he needs his 3-y-o's to do better this year. We won't rush this filly even though she looks like an early 2-y-o because she's just not quite strong enough for it yet".*

465. UNNAMED ★★
ch.f. Declaration Of War – Emily Blake (Lend A Hand). March 23. Third foal. 30,000Y. Tattersalls October Book 2. Not sold. Half-sister to the modest Irish 5.5f (at 2 yrs) and 6f winner Gallena (by Invincible Spirit). The dam won the Group 3 7f Athasi Stakes and the Group 3 1m Equestrian Stakes (both at the Curragh). The second dam, Kirri (by Lycius), was unplaced in one start and is a half-sister to 2 minor winners. (Bob & Pauline Scott and Partner). *"A nice, big filly with a big white face, she's cantering but that's all and you'd think she'd want seven furlongs. She's done nothing wrong, her coat looks good and I'm happy with her".*

466. UNNAMED ★★
b.f. Harbour Watch – Epernay (Tiger Hill). March 16. Second foal. 5,000Y. Tattersalls December. Manor House Stables. The dam, a fair 1m and 9f winner of 3 races, is a half-sister to 8 winners including the very useful 9f (at 2 yrs), Turkish Group 10f, Group 3 11.5f Lingfield Derby Trial and listed 9f winner Dordogne. The second dam, Riberac (by Efisio), a smart winner of 10 races from 5f to 1m including three listed events, was third in the Group 2 Sun Chariot Stakes and is a full or half-sister to 5 winners. *"A nice type of horse, we're not in a rush with her because she had a quiet winter but she's cantering now. She was pretty weak and a cheap purchase and I'd say she probably wants seven furlongs. I don't know why, but we're still looking for an owner for her".*

467. UNNAMED ★★
ch.f. Harbour Watch – Lisa's Strong (Kalanisi). April 3. Second foal. €40,000 foal. Goffs November. Peter & Ross Doyle. Half-sister to Safwah (by Dark Angel), unplaced in one start at 2 yrs in 2016. The dam, a winner of 6 races at 3 and 4 yrs in Italy, was listed placed over 10f and 12f and is a half-sister to the 2-y-o listed 5f winner Faithfilly. The second dam, Bauci (by Desert King), is an unraced half-sister to 7 winners. (Denis Barry & Manor House Stables). *"She was doing everything right through the winter but she's gone a bit weak and we've just had to back off her. It got to that stage where she was finding life tough but she'll come back and she'll be fine".*

468. UNNAMED ★★
b.f. Vision D'Etat– Monster Munchie (JPN) (Deep Impact). February 5. The dam, a modest dual 9.5f winner, is a half-sister to the Japanese Grade 1 placed Stratagem. The second dam, the smart Group 1 10f Prix Saint-Alary winner Muncie (by Sadler's Wells), is a half-sister to the smart Group 1 15.5f Prix Royal-Oak winner Mersey and to the dam of the US Grade 1 winner Subtle Power. (Chasemore Farm). *"We had the dam and she's a well-bred Japanese mare, so somewhere along the way there's got to be some good to come out. I guess this filly is bred for a mile but she looks a bit sharper than that. She had a setback so we haven't done as much with her as we might have done. Come back in a month's time and I might know a bit more about her!"*

469. UNNAMED ★★
b.c. Animal Kingdom – Ocicat (Storm Cat). April 3. Fifth foal. 1,500Y. Tattersalls December. Manor House Stables. Half-brother to 3 minor winners in North America and Japan by Street Sense (2) and Medaglia d'Oro. The dam is an unraced sister to two Group-placed winners. The second dam, Blissful (by Mr Prospector), is an unplaced sister to the Kentucky Derby winner Fusaichi Pegasus. (Mr D R Passant). *"He was so cheap I couldn't leave him at the sale for that. He's very leggy and turned out in a field at the moment. I've sold half of him to a good owner and I've kept the other half. If he doesn't run this season it doesn't matter, he's by an amazing racehorse*

in Animal Kingdom and I just thought that for what he cost you can't do much damage, let's see what happens". The sire, a son of Leroidesanimaux, won the Kentucky Derby and the Dubai World Cup. His first 2-y-o's appear this year.

470. UNNAMED ★★★
b.c. Sepoy – Snow Dust (First Defence). February 28. First foal. 50,000Y. Tattersalls October Book 2. Sackville/Donald. The dam is an unraced half-sister to 2 winners including the US Grade 2 10f and triple Grade 3 winner Starformer. The second dam, Etoile Montante (by Miswaki), won 7 races including the Group 1 7f Prix de la Foret and is a half-sister to 5 winners. (Laurence Bellman & David Ward). *"A nice horse, he's strong and racy but it doesn't look like these Sepoys are early. It looks like he'll want six or seven furlongs and I guess he'll be out in June, maybe before. He seems to have a good attitude and he's very honest so we like him".*

ANN DUFFIELD
471. CANFORD'S JOY
b.c. Canford Cliffs – Joyful (Green Desert). March 9. Fourteenth foal. £14,000Y. Goffs UK Premier (Doncaster). Ann Duffield. Half-sister to 5 winners including the fairly useful 2-y-o 9f and subsequent Hong Kong winner Enabling (by High Chaparral), the fairly useful listed-placed 5f and 6f winner Roker Park (by Choisir), the quite useful 5f (at 2 yrs) and 6f winner Springinmystep (by Footstepsinthesand) and the dams of Shaweel (Gimcrack Stakes), Samitar (Irish 1,000 Guineas) and Nijoom Dubai (Albany Stakes). The dam, a fair 7f winner, is a half-sister to 7 winners including Golden Opinion (Group 1 1m Coronation Stakes). The second dam, Optimistic Lass (by Mr Prospector), won the Group 2 10f Nassau Stakes and is a half-sister to 9 winners. (John Dwyer).

472. COTTON SOCKS (IRE)
b.c. Dream Ahead – Kartella (Whipper). May 11. Third foal. 9,000Y. Tattersalls October Book 3. Ann Duffield. The dam is an unraced half-sister to 2 winners. The second dam, Kart Star (by Soviet Star), won the listed Prix Coronation and is a half-sister to 5 winners including the listed winner and Group 1

French 1,000 Guineas second Karmifira. (Mrs Ann Starkey & Partner).

473. CUPPACOCO
b.f. Stimulation – Glen Molly (Danetime). March 26. Fourth living foal. 14,000Y. Tattersalls October Book 4. Ann Duffield. Half-sister to the modest 2016 French 2-y-o 6.5f winner If I Say So (by Sayif). The dam, a fairly useful 6f (at 2 yrs) and 7f winner, is a half-sister to one winner. The second dam, Sonorous (by Ashkalani), an Irish 1m and 10f winner, was listed-placed and is a half-sister to 5 winners.

474. FASCINATOR
ch.f. Helmet – Mary Read (Bahamian Bounty). March 23. Fifth foal. £28,000Y. Goffs UK Premier (Doncaster). Ann Duffield. Half-sister to the quite useful 6f (including at 2 yrs) and 7f winner Jacquotte Delahaye (by Kyllachy) and to the quite useful 8.5f (at 2 yrs) to 12.5f winner by Dubai Bounty (by Dubai Destination and herself dam of the Molecomb Stakes winner and Group 1 second Kachy). The dam, a useful 2-y-o dual 5f winner, was second in the Group 3 Molecomb Stakes and is a full or half-sister to 8 winners. The second dam, Hill Welcome (by Most Welcome), placed twice at 2 yrs, is a half-sister to 5 winners including the Group 1 6f Middle Park Stakes winner Stalker. (E & R Stott).

475. GORSE (IRE)
b.c. Zebedee – Golden Flower (Royal Applause). March 22. Second foal. £16,000Y. Goffs UK Premier (Doncaster). Ann Duffield. The dam, a fair dual 5f winner (including at 2 yrs), is a sister to the 2-y-o Group 3 6f Albany Stakes winner and Group 2 Cherry Hinton Stakes second Habaayib. The second dam, Silver Kestrel (by Silver Hawk), a minor winner of 2 races at 3 and 4 yrs in the USA, is a half-sister to 5 winners. (Duchess Of Sutherland).

476. HEAVENLY PULSE
ch.c. Dragon Pulse – Bogini (Holy Roman Emperor). March 23. Third foal. €34,000Y. Tattersalls Ireland September. Middleham Park. Half-brother to the quite useful 2016 Irish 2-y-o 5f winner Imagine If (by Dream Ahead). The dam, a quite useful 5f (including at 2 yrs) and 6f winner of 4 races, is a half-

brother to 3 winners including the listed Tetrarch Stakes winner Alkasser. The second dam, Alexander Queen (by King's Best), a fairly useful 2-y-o 5f winner, is a half-sister to 5 winners including the Group 2 Queen Mary Stakes winner Anthem Alexander and the Group 3 Palace House Stakes winner and sire Dandy Man. (Middleham Park Racing CII & Partner).

477. LILYTHEFILLY
b.f. Mount Nelson – Ziefhd (Haafhd). March 22. First foal. 12,000Y. Tattersalls October Book 4. Ann Duffield. The dam, a quite useful 7f (including at 2 yrs) and 6f winner of 3 races, is a half-sister to 4 winners and to the placed dam of the Group 2 Coventry Stakes third Psychedelic Funk. The second dam, Zietory (by Zieten), a 2-y-o 6f and 3-y-o dual 1m listed winner, is a half-sister to 4 winners. (The Gathering Partnership).

478. LORETTA (IRE)
b.f. Henrythenavigator – Laurentina (Cadeaux Genereux), April 9. Fifth foal. Half-sister to the quite useful 1m winner Justice Smart (by Kyllachy) and to the fair Irish 7f and 1m winner Best Not Argue (by Acclamation). The dam, a quite useful 2-y-o 6f and 7f winner, was listed placed over 1m and is a half-sister to 6 winners. The second dam, Trois Heures Apres (by Soviet Star), is an unraced half-sister to 4 winners including the very useful 7f (at 2 yrs) and 10f listed winner and Oaks third Mezzogiorno (herself dam of the Group 2 Blandford Stakes winner Monturani). (Mr & Mrs Shewring and Partner).

479. TROOP
ch.c. Lethal Force – Bendis (Danehill). March 14. Tenth foal. £15,000Y. Goffs UK Premier (Doncaster). Ann Duffield. Half-brother to four winners including the fairly useful 2-y-o 5f winner and dual listed-placed Walkingonthemoon (by Footstepsinthesand), the quite useful dual 6f (including at 2 yrs) and 7f winner Rubirosa and the modest 2m and hurdles winner Goldan Jess (by Golan). The dam, a 7f winner at 3 yrs in Germany, is a half-sister to 6 winners. The second dam, Berenice (by Groom Dancer), a fair 10f winner, was listed-placed and is a half-sister to 3 winners. (Mr & Mrs Shewring, Mr B Craig).

480. WATCHING SPIRITS

br.c. Harbour Watch – Naayla (Invincible Spirit). February 24. Fifth foal. £14,000Y. Goffs UK Premier (Doncaster). Craig Buckingham. Half-brother to the fair 5f winner of 4 races at 2 and 3 yrs La Sylphe (by Refuse To Bend). The dam, a quite useful 2-y-o 6f winner, is a half-sister to 7 winners including the useful 2-y-o 5f winner and Group 3 6f second Broken Applause, the German 2-y-o 6f winner and Group 3 placed Medina and the useful 2-y-o dual 5f winner Pike Bishop. The second dam, Pink Cashmere (by Polar Falcon), is an unraced three-parts sister to the Group 1 6f July Cup winner Owington and a half-sister to 8 winners. (Mr C Buckingham).

ED DUNLOP

481. AGAR'S PLOUGH ★★★★ ♠

ch.c. Dutch Art – Cloud's End (Dubawi). April 24. Third foal. 55,000Y. Tattersalls October Book 1. Blandford Bloodstock. Half-brother to the fair 2016 2-y-o 6f winner Zamjar (by Exceed And Excel). The dam, a quite useful 6f (at 2 yrs) and 7f winner, is a half-sister to 7 winners including the champion 2-y-o filly and Group 1 6f Cheveley Park Stakes winner Airwave (herself the dam of three stakes winners) and the Group 1 5f Nunthorpe Stakes winner Jwala. The second dam, Kangra Valley (by Indian Ridge), a moderate 2-y-o 5f winner, is a half-sister to 7 minor winners. (Old Etonian Racing Syndicate II). *"An attractive horse, I trained his brother who won twice as a 2-y-o but this horse won't be quite so early. He will be a 2-y-o but is probably more of a seven furlong horse and we like him".*

482. BELLE DE NEIGE (IRE) ★★★

b.br.f. Elusive Pimpernel – Snow Fairy (Intikhab). February 4. First foal. The dam won eight races including six Group 1's from 10f to 12f in England, Ireland, Japan and Hong Kong. The second dam, Woodland Dream (by Charnwood Forest), a quite useful 7f winner, is a half-sister to 5 winners including the smart Group 3 10f and dual listed winner and sire Big Bad Bob. (Anamoine). *"Snow Fairy's first foal. She hasn't arrived here yet, she's a big, scopey filly and has been broken in Ireland. She's due to come to me in April, so I haven't seen her yet but they like her".*

483. CANIMAR ★★★

b.f. Havana Gold – Acquifer (Oasis Dream). March 20. Fourth foal. £40,000Y. Goffs UK Premier (Doncaster). Stroud/Coleman & Ed Dunlop. Half-sister to the fair 2016 2-y-o 5.5f winner Santaflora (by Poet's Voice) and to the quite useful 2-y-o dual 7f winner Arethusa (by Rip Van Winkle). The dam, a fair dual 6f placed maiden at 2 and 3 yrs, is a half-sister to 6 winners including the Italian Group 3 winner Guest Connections, the listed winner Lady Of the Lake and the smart broodmare Llia (dam of the Group 1 Irish St Leger winner Sans Frontieres). The second dam, Llyn Gwynant (by Persian Bold), won the Group 3 1m Desmond Stakes and the Group 3 1m Matron Stakes and is a half-sister to 2 winners. (Serendipity Partnership). *"I like her, she has a good attitude and tries. A six furlong filly, her half-sister won two as a 2-y-o for us and this filly looks racy so I wouldn't be surprised if she was relatively capable".*

484. GLOBAL ANGEL ★★★

br.c. Dark Angel – Authoritarian (Authorized). February 15. First foal. 70,000Y. Tattersalls October Book 2. Charlie Gordon-Watson. The dam, a modest triple 1m winner, is a half-sister to 2 minor winners. The second dam, Favourita (by Diktat), a useful 2-y-o 7f winner, Group 2 7f Rockfel Stakes second and Group 3 7f Nell Gwyn Stakes third, is a half-sister to 4 winners including the very useful 12f winner and Group 3 12f Gordon Stakes second Time Zone. (Dr J Hon). *"A strong colt, he's a little bit up behind and looks more of a seven furlong type but he has a good attitude, moves well and goes ok so far. He's not done anything fast yet and is probably one for the mid-season onwards".*

485. GLOBAL ART ★★★

b.c. Dutch Art – Constant Dream (Kheleyf). April 9. First foal. 110,000Y. Tattersalls October Book 1. Charlie Gordon-Watson. The dam, a moderate 2-y-o 5f winner, is a half-sister to 7 winners including the 2-y-o Group 2 5f Flying Childers Stakes and Group 3 5f Molecomb Stakes winner Wunders Dream and the Group 3 1m Ridgewood Pearl Stakes winner Grecian Dancer. The second dam, Pizzicato (by Statoblest), a modest 5f and 5.3f winner at 3 yrs, is a half-sister to 5 winners including the high-class Hong Kong horses Mensa and Firebolt. (Dr J Hon). *"He's grown quite a lot which suggests he's a mid-season 2-y-o. He's very athletic, has a good temperament so far for a Dutch Art, moves well and I like him but he won't be early".*

486. GLOBAL EXCEED ★★★
b.c. Exceed And Excel – Blue Maiden (Medicean). January 21. Second foal. 200,000Y. Tattersalls October Book 1. Charlie Gordon-Watson. Half-brother to the fair 2016 2-y-o 7f winner Red Gunner (by Oasis Dream). The dam, a winner of four races here and in the USA including a listed stakes, was second in the Nell Gwyn Stakes and the Sweet Solera Stakes (both Group 3) and is a half-sister to 4 minor winners. The second dam, Bluebelle (by Generous), a quite useful 12.5f winner, is a half-sister to 6 winners including the German Group 2 winner Centaine. (Dr J Hon). *"A six furlong horse for the middle of the season. He's done well since we purchased him and will have some speed obviously being by Exceed And Excel. He's had no problems whatsoever and he's going ok".*

487. GLOBAL GIANT ★★★★★ ♠
b.c. Shamardal – Aniseed (Dalakhani). April 11. First foal. 185,000Y. Tattersalls October Book 1. Charlie Gordon-Watson. The dam, a fairly useful 12f winner, was listed-placed twice and is a half-sister to 3 winners including the useful Irish listed 7.5f winner Anna's Rock (dam of the Group 2 and Group 3 winner Breton Rock). The second dam, Anna Karenina (by Atticus), is an unraced half-sister to 10 winners including the French Group 3 winner and dual Group 1 placed Agathe (dam of the Grade/Group 1 winners Artiste Royale and Aquarelliste), the Breeders' Cup Classic winner Arcangues and the dams of the Group/Grade 1 winners Cape Verdi and Angara. (Dr J Hon). *"He's a horse we like very much. Probably a six/seven furlong 2-y-o, he moves well, he's very athletic and he's quite a tall, scopey horse, but he goes well".*

488. GLOBAL JEWEL (IRE) ★★
br.c. Society Rock – Furnival (Street Cry). March 23. First foal. 175,000Y. Tattersalls October Book 1. Charlie Gordon-Watson. The dam is an unraced half-sister to 2 minor

winners. The second dam, Wild Queen (by Loup Sauvage), a dual Group 3 winner in Australia, is a half-sister to 6 winners including the dual Group 2 winner and smart broodmare So Gorgeous. (Dr J Hon). *"He needs a bit of time, I thought he'd be earlyish but he had a minor setback. It's nothing very serious but he's probably one for the future. He cost plenty of money and he's a good-looking horse, but not for the moment".*

489. GLOBAL SPIRIT ★★★★ ♠
b.c. Invincible Spirit – Centime (Royal Applause). February 23. Third foal. 120,000Y. Tattersalls October Book 1. Charlie Gordon-Watson. Half-brother to the fairly useful 2-y-o 1m winner and 3-y-o 10f listed-placed Encore d'Amour (by Azamour). The dam, a modest 10f winner, is a half-sister to 6 winners including the US Grade 1 9f and 10f winner Ticker Tape, the Group 3 winning sprinter Brando and the dam of the dual Group 1 winner Reckless Abandon. The second dam, Argent Du Bois (by Silver Hawk), placed five times at 2 and 3 yrs in France, stayed 1m and is a half-sister to 8 winners including the 2-y-o Group 1 Racing Post Trophy winner Crowded House. (Dr J Hon). *"Another horse we like but he came in late, he's a scopey individual and is more of a mid-season type. The team like him, he's very athletic and moves well".*

490. GLOBAL STYLE ★★★
b.c. Nathaniel – Danaskaya (Danehill). April 6. Ninth foal. €250,000Y. Arqana Deauville August. Charlie Gordon-Watson. Closely related to the minor 15f winner Smoky Hill (by Galileo) and half-brother to the 2-y-o Group 1 7f Dewhurst Stakes winner Belardo (by Lope De Vega), to the fairly useful listed 13f winner Berling, the Irish Group 2 Debutante Stakes second Diamond Sky (both by Montjeu) and the fair Irish 2-y-o 7f and subsequent US winner Kayd Kodaun (by Traditionally). The dam, a useful Irish 2-y-o 6f winner and third in the Group 1 6f Cheveley Park Stakes, is a half-sister to 7 winners including the triple listed 7f winner Modeeroch and the Group 1 1m Gran Criterium third Chinese Whisper (by Montjeu). The second dam, Majinskaya (by Marignan), was a listed 12f winner. (Dr J Hon). *"He's Belardo's half-brother, but Nathaniel's look*

like they need time. This colt is a racy horse though, he's not big and backward, he's a very good moving horse. As you'd expect from his pedigree he goes well, but he's very much one for the latter part of the year and as a 3-y-o".

491. GLOBAL WEALTH ★★★

b.c. Havana Gold – Inner Sea (Henrythenavigator). March 13. First foal. 60,000Y. Tattersalls October Book 3. Charlie Gordon-Watson. The dam, a minor French placed 3-y-o, is a half-sister to 4 winners including the Group 1 12f Grand Prix de Paris winner Erupt and the listed 10f winner Marie De Medici. The second dam, Mare Nostrum (by Caerleon), won the Group 3 Prix Vanteaux and was placed in the Prix Vermeille and Prix Saint-Alary and is a half-sister to 7 winners including the US Grade 1 winner Aube Indienne. (Dr J Hon). *"I'm not sure about him. I thought he was going to be a nice horse, he looked precocious but got a sore shin recently and we had to back off him. He's cantering again now, he's very mature looking and looks quite fast, but the jury is out a little".*

492. INDIAN WARRIOR ★★★★

b.c. Sepoy – Night Gypsy (Mind Games). February 18. Tenth foal. 45,000Y. Tattersalls October Book 2. Charlie Gordon-Watson. Half-brother to 6 winners including the useful 2-y-o 6f and listed 7f winner and Group 3 Oh So Sharp Stakes second Electric Feel (by Firebreak), the fairly useful 2-y-o 6f winner and listed placed Aunt Nicola, the 5f and 6f winner Mymumsaysimthebest (both by Reel Buddy), dual 7f winner Discression (by Indesatchel) and the 5f winner of 6 races from 3 to 5 yrs Safari Mischief (by Primo Valentino) – all quite useful. The dam, a fair 2-y-o 5f winner, is a sister to the listed 2-y-o winner On The Brink and a half-sister to 4 winners including the listed winner and Group 2 placed Eastern Romance. The second dam, Ocean Grove (by Fairy King), a quite useful 2-y-o 6f winner, is a half-sister to 5 winners here and abroad. (The Hope Partnership). *"I like this colt. There's a lot of speed on the dam's side, he has a very good temperament, goes well and will be one of the earliest 2-y-o's. The previous Sepoys I've had have all been seven furlong/mile horses, but this one is much more precocious. He'll definitely start over five or six furlongs".*

493. MAGHROOM (IRE) ★★★★

b.c. Iffraaj – French Fern (Royal Applause). March 23. Sixth foal. 140,000Y. Tattersalls October Book 2. Shadwell Estate Co. Half-brother to the useful 6f to 1m winner of 6 races from 3 to 6 yrs and 2-y-o Group 3 7f Acomb Stakes second Fort Bastion (by Lawman), to the moderate 2-y-o 6f winner Piping Dream (by Approve) and a minor winner abroad by Librettist. The dam, placed at 2 yrs in Ireland and a minor US dual 4-y-o winner, is a half-sister to 3 winners including the Group 2 Criterium de Maisons-Laffitte winner Captain Marvelous. The second dam, Shesasmartlady (by Dolphin Lady), is an unplaced half-sister to 8 winners including the Irish listed winners Dashing Colours and Dash Of Red. (Hamdan Al Maktoum). *"A nice horse, I like him and he'd be one of the more athletic individuals. A scopey sort, he goes well up Warren Hill and wouldn't be far off going a little bit faster, but he's an Iffraaj so he won't be a five furlong horse I wouldn't have thought. Looks racy".*

494. MISS MINDING ★★★★ ♠

b.f. Kodiac – Lady Hawkfield (Hawk Wing). April 25. Fourth foal. Half-sister to the useful 8.5f (at 2 yrs) and Group 3 Classic Trial winner Master Apprentice (by Mastercraftsman) and to the quite useful 7f (at 2 yrs) and 1m winner Royal Reserve (by Duke Of Marmalade). The dam ran once unplaced and is a half-sister to the Group 1 1m Coronation Stakes and Group 1 1m Matron Stakes winner Lillie Langtry (dam of the top-class filly Minding) and to the listed 7f winner and Group 3 third Count Of Limonade (by Duke Of Marmalade). The second dam, Hoity Toity (by Darshaan), is an unraced half-sister to 5 winners. *"A very well-bred filly, she's very athletic, very racy and goes nicely. She's not going to be early, she's very much a mid-season filly and one that we like so far".*

495. MURAADEF ★★★

b.c. Kodiac – Dominatrix (Whipper). January 24. Fourth foal. £130,000Y. Goffs UK Premier (Doncaster). Shadwell Estate Co. The dam, placed at 3 yrs over 7f in France, is a half-sister to 3 minor winners. The second dam, Gaelic Swan (by Nashwan), is a placed half-sister to 5 winners including Bonny Scot

(Group 2 Great Voltigeur Stakes). (Hamdan Al Maktoum). *"A tallish Kodiac, not one of the normal little squat ones but he moves well. He needs to furnish a little, but he seems to be coping alright. He's ok, but he's not a really fast Kodiac".*

496. MUTABAAHY (IRE) ★★★★
b.c. Oasis Dream – Habaayib (Royal Applause). April 6. Brother to the fair 1m and subsequent UAE 5f winner Ejbaar. The dam, a useful 2-y-o Group 3 6f Albany Stakes winner, was second in the Group 2 Cherry Hinton Stakes and is a sister to a winner. The second dam, Silver Kestrel (by Silver Hawk), a minor winner of 2 races at 3 and 4 yrs in the USA, is a half-sister to 5 winners. (Hamdan Al Maktoum). *"I trained the dam to win the Albany and she's bred a half decent horse. This is a very strong, powerful, neat horse. He looks quite quick, probably one for six furlongs and he's very mature looking. One of the earlier types I would have thought".*

497. STORM JAZZ ★★★
b.f. Red Jazz – Singitta (Singspiel). April 9. Ninth foal. 28,000Y. Tattersalls October Book 3. Amanda Skiffington. Half-brother to 6 winners including the useful 5f winner of 10 races (including four times at 2 yrs) and listed placed Singeur (by Chineur), the quite useful 1m winner Sighora (by Royal Applause), the fair 9.5f winner Pamushana (by Teofilo) and the modest 7f and 1m winner Samasana (by Redback). The dam is an unplaced half-sister to 3 winners including the dam of the Group 2 July Stakes winner Nevisian Lad. The second dam, Ferber's Follies (by Saratoga Six), a US 2-y-o winner and third in the Grade 2 Adirondack Stakes, is a half-sister to 11 winners including Blue Jean Baby (Grade 2 Sorority Stakes). (J Strauss & Sir A Page Wood). *"I quite like her, she's quite precocious, strong and powerful, won't be that early but looks to go ok so far".*

498. TEENAGE GAL (IRE) ★★
b.f. Acclamation – Bobbie Soxer (Pivotal). January 29. Sister to the Irish 3-y-o 1m winner and US Grade 2 1m second Mittersill. The dam, a fair 7f (at 2 yrs) and 6f winner, is a half-sister to 5 winners including the 2-y-o Autumn Stakes and German Group 3 winner and useful

sire Big Bad Bob. The second dam, Fantasy Girl (by Marju), is an unplaced half-sister to 4 winners very useful listed 11.5f winner of 6 races Persian Lightning. (Windflower Overseas Holdings). *"She's backward at present. Nice and racy, but needs time".*

499. UNNAMED ★★★
b.f. Dutch Art – Convention (Encosta De Lago). April 22. Third foal. Half-sister to the unplaced 2016 2-y-o Prosecution (by Lawman). The dam, a fair 9.5f winner, is a half-sister to 6 winners including the Group 1 6f Haydock Park Sprint Cup winner Regal Parade and the Group 3 Acomb Stakes winner Entifaadha. The second dam, Model Queen (by Kingmambo), a fair 3-y-o 7f winner, is a half-sister to 5 winners including the French listed 1m winner Arabride. (St Albans Bloodstock). *"A strong, powerful filly, she looks racy and is more than likely a six/seven furlong 2-y-o. I trained the mother who was no great shakes but she did win. This filly is ok so far".*

500. UNNAMED ★★★
b.c. Frankel – Debonnaire (Anabaa). February 3. Fourth foal. 250,000Y. Tattersalls December. Charlie Gordon-Watson. Half-brother to 3 winners including the Australian dual Group 1 winner Hartnell (by Authorized) and to the 2-y-o listed 7f Star Stakes winner and Group 1 Fillies' Mile second Roz (by Teofilo). The dam, a fair 7f (at 2 yrs) and 1m winner, is a half-sister to 6 winners including the useful listed-placed winners Proceed With Care and Dramatic Quest. The second dam, Ultra Finesse (by Rahy), a useful French 8.5f and 10f winner, was second in the Group 2 12f Prix de Malleret and is a half-sister to 6 winners including Suave Dancer (winner of the Prix de l'Arc de Triomphe, the Prix du Jockey Club and the Phoenix Champion Stakes). (Mohammed Jaber). *"A half-brother to Hartnell, he's not an early horse and he'll want seven furlongs later in the year and will probably stay a mile and a half next year. A good-looking horse, he hasn't done as much as some because he came in late".*

501. UNNAMED ★★★★
gr.f. Dark Angel – Folga (Atraf). April 19. Fourth foal. 400,000Y. Tattersalls October

Book 1. Charlie Gordon-Watson. Sister to the dual Group 1 5f Nunthorpe Stakes winner of 10 races Mecca's Angel and to the Group 3 7f Criterion Stakes and Group 3 6f Chipchase Stakes winner Markaz. The dam, a quite useful 5f (including at 2 yrs) and 6f winner of 6 races, was listed-placed and is a half-sister to 9 winners. The second dam, Desert Dawn (by Belfort), won the Group 3 Prix d'Arenburg and the listed Trafalgar House Sprint and is a half-sister to 2 winners. (Mr A S Al Naboodah). *"A full-sister to Mecca's Angel, I think the family all need a little bit of time. She's not bred to be an early 2-y-o but she's athletic, racy and good-looking, so she's very similar to her siblings".*

502. UNNAMED ★★
b.c. Exceed And Excel – Jabhaat (Hard Spun). February 13. First foal. The dam, a quite useful dual 7f winner (including at 2 yrs), was listed-placed over 10f and is a half-sister to 2 winners. The second dam, Ishraak (by Sahm), is an unraced half-sister to 6 winners including the US Grade 2 7f winner Kayrawan. (Hamdan Al Maktoum). *"A tall, scopey horse, I trained the dam who was stakes-placed as a 3-y-o. A nice, athletic-looking horse but he is big and I don't expect him to be early. A back-end type I would have thought".*

503. UNNAMED ★★★★
b.c. Acclamation – Ladyship (Oasis Dream). February 20. First foal. 200,000Y. Tattersalls October Book 2. Shadwell Estate Co. The dam, a useful listed 7f winner of 3 races at 3 and 4 yrs, is a half-sister to one winner. The second dam, Peeress (by Pivotal), a very smart winner of 7 races including the Group 1 1m Lockinge Stakes and the Group 1 1m Sun Chariot Stakes, is a full or half-sister to 6 winners. (Hamdan Al Maktoum). *"He's nice. Bought at the sales, he's strong, mature-looking and should be a six furlong 2-y-o. He goes well and he's a neat, powerful horse with a good temperament so far".*

504. UNNAMED ★★★
b.c. Dark Angel – Quelle Affaire (Bahamian Bounty). February 13. First foal. £130,000Y. Goffs UK Premier (Doncaster). Shadwell Estate Co. The dam, a poor 5f and 6f placed maiden, is a half-sister to one winner. The second dam, Qui Moi (by Swain), a quite useful 10f

winner, is a half-sister to 10 winners including the Group 2 German Oaks winner Que Belle and the dams of the Group 2 winners Quelle Amore, Johann Zoffany and Know More. (Hamdan Al Maktoum). *"He's done well, had a bit of a hiccup but he's over it and is back cantering now. Although Dark Angel's run as 2-y-o's I haven't had any that are really precocious and they seem to improve with age. He's done nothing wrong, he's a good shaped horse and a nice horse to look at".*

505. UNNAMED ★★★
b.c. Sixties Icon – Strictly Lambada (Red Ransom). March 2. Fourth foal. 140,000Y. Tattersalls October Book 1. Charlie Gordon-Watson. Half-brother to the useful listed-placed 2-y-o 1m winner Last Tango Inparis (by Aqlaam) and to the fair dual 12f and hurdles winner Sleep Easy (by Rip Van Winkle). The dam, a fair 10f and 12f placed maiden, is a half-sister to 6 winners including the listed 10f winner Marsh Daisy. The second dam, Bella Lambada (by Lammtarra), a quite useful 10.4f winner, is a half-sister to 6 winners including the Group 2 10f Prince of Wales's Stakes and dual US Grade 2 winner Stagecraft, the Group 3 winner Mullins Bay and the listed winners Hyabella and Balalaika and to the unraced dam of the triple Group 2 winner Caspar Netscher. (Mohammed Jaber). *"Cost a lot of money for a Sixties Icon, bred by Meon Valley Stud, he's not slow but he's bred to want a mile or more. A beautiful looking horse, he goes well but is very much one for later on".*

HARRY DUNLOP
506. ARACHINA ★★★
ch.f. Arakan – Tibouchina (Daylami). April 4. Seventh foal. €11,000Y. Goffs Sportsmans. Stroud/Coleman & H Dunlop. Half-sister to the fair 2016 2-y-o 1m winner Viking Hoard (by Vale Of York) and to the Italian and Australian winner of 4 races and Group 2 Italian Derby second Wish Come True (by Aussie Rules). The dam, a modest 4-y-o 11.5f and 12f winner, is a half-sister to 3 other minor winners. The second dam, Kalimar (by Bigstone), is an unplaced half-sister to 5 winners including Karliyka (the dam of three Group winners). (Be Hopeful 2). *"She's a sister to Viking Hoard who won his maiden for us*

last year. We think quite a bit about him and I'm hoping this filly will follow suit. She'll take some time but I think she'll be a bit earlier than he was and she's straightforward, so I'm happy with her".

507. BILLIE FLYNN ★★
b.f. Lawman – Lyric Art (Red Ransom). March 16. €13,000Y. Baden-Baden. Blandford Bloodstock. Half-sister to the quite useful 12f winner of 5 races Knight Music and to the quite useful 1m (at 2 yrs) and 10f winner Mirsaalah (both by Sir Percy). The dam, a moderate 7f winner, is a half-sister to 5 winners including the Group 2 Park Hill Stakes and Group 3 Lillie Langtry Stakes winner Meeznah and the smart Group 2 12f Princess Of Wales's Stakes second Shahin. The second dam, String Quartet (by Sadler's Wells), a 12.5f listed winner in France and third in the Group 3 Lancashire Oaks, is a sister to the Irish listed 10f winner Casey Tibbs and a half-sister to 4 winners. (Crimbourne Stud). *"Quite a backward filly, she came from Germany and qualifies for some of those sales races. She's been in pre-training and hasn't been here that long but I like what I see".*

508. CHILLALA (IRE) ★★★★ ♠
b.f. Requinto – Positive Step (Footstepsinthesand). February 1. Third foal. 125,000Y. Tattersalls October Book 1. Stroud/ Coleman & H Dunlop. Sister to the useful 2016 2-y-o dual 6f winner and Group 2 July Stakes third Broken Stones. The dam, a fair 11.5f placed Irish maiden, is a half-sister to 5 winners including the fairly useful Irish listed-placed Derivative and Harrington. The second dam, Our Hope (by Dancing Brave), is an unraced half-sister to 5 winners including the Irish listed winner Golden Temple. (Daniel MacAuliffe & Anoj Don). *"A nice filly that cost quite a lot of money from October Book One, I like her a lot. She's quite rangy but she shows plenty of speed and I see her starting over six furlongs in May. I like her".*

509. DUTCH STRANGER ★★★
b.f. Dutch Art – Passing Stranger (Dixie Union). May 13. Third foal. The dam, a fair 6f winner, is a half-sister to one winner. The second dam, Square Pants (King Of Kings),

a minor US 4-y-o winner, is a half-sister to 4 winners including the Group 2 Cherry Hinton Stakes and Group 3 Albany Stakes winner Sander Camillo. (Mrs S M Roy). *"A butty little filly and hopefully one that we're going to get out early, around May time. She goes alright and I think the sire has added some sharpness. A mid-May foal but he looks OK and seems a sharp type".*

510. FIGHTING IRISH (IRE) ★★★
b.c. Camelot – Quixotic (Pivotal). March 19. Fourth foal. £70,000Y. Goffs UK Premier (Doncaster). Stroud/Coleman. Half-brother to the quite useful 2016 2-y-o 5f winner Well Done (by Lawman). The dam is an unraced sister to the Group 1 Lockinge Stakes winner Virtual and a half-sister to 6 winners including the Group 2 Coventry Stakes winner Iceman. The second dam, Virtuous (by Exit To Nowhere), a fairly useful 2-y-o 1m winner, was third in the listed 11.5f Oaks Trial and is a half-sister to 3 winners. (Daniel MacAuliffe & Anoj Don). *"A strong, butty colt and one of those we should get out reasonably early. He's done a fair bit of work and he's quietly going the right way. Hopefully an early runner for the sire".*

511. INVINCIBLE PEACE ★★
b.f. Declaration Of War – Invincible Cara (Invincible Spirit). February 26. First foal. The dam, a fair 10f winner, is a half-sister to 6 winners including the Group 3 7f Acomb Stakes and Group 3 1m Craven Stakes winner and Group 1 Racing Post Trophy second Elusive Pimpernel, the Group 3 10f Strensall Stakes winner Palavicini and the listed 1m winner Prince Gagarin. The second dam, Cara Fantasy (by Sadler's Wells), a quite useful dual 12f winner, is a half-sister to the Group 2 Topkapi Trophy winner Lucky Guest. (Windflower Overseas Holdings). *"A home-bred filly that came in last month, she has a nice temperament and it looks like the Declaration Of War's are going quite well. From what we've done with her so far we like her and I would imagine she'll be a seven furlong 2-y-o to begin with".*

512. JACKFINBAR (FR) ★★★
b.c. Whipper – Anna Simona (Slip Anchor). March 1. €41,000Y. Arqana Deauville October.

Stroud/Coleman. Brother to the useful 2-y-o listed 1m winner and Group 1 10f Criterium de Saint-Cloud second Willie The Whipper and half-brother to 3 winners. The dam, a French/German 9.5f to 14f winner, is a half-sister to the German Group 2 11f and Group 3 1m winner Aspectus. *"A big, rangy colt, I like him a lot and he's a good mover but he needs time. He could be interesting later on".*

513. KNIGHT TO BEHOLD (IRE) ★★★★
b.c. Sea The Stars – Angel Of The Gwaun (Sadler's Wells). March 16. Eighth foal. Half-brother to the 7f (at 2 yrs) and Group 3 10f Blue Wind Stakes winner Beauty O'Gwaun (by Rainbow Quest), to the Japanese Grade 3 2m winner Cosmo Meadow, the fairly useful 2-y-o 7f winner Angelonmyshoulder, the fair Irish 12f winner Missy O'Gwaun (all by King's Best) and the quite useful 12f winner Whitey O'Gwaun (by Dalakhani). The dam is an unraced sister to 3 winners including the Derby third Let The Lion Roar and a half-sister to the St Leger winner Millenary and the Group 3 Princess Royal Stakes winner Head In The Clouds. The second dam, Ballerina (by Dancing Brave), a quite useful 2-y-o 7f winner, is a half-sister to the Group 3 12f Princess Royal Stakes winner Dancing Bloom and to the 1,000 Guineas third River Dancer (dam of the Champion Stakes winner Spectrum). (Mr L Neil Jones). *"A nice, home-bred colt, he walks well and I like him a lot. He should be a seven furlong type, although he could well start him over six in mid-summer and I think he could be interesting. A good-moving horse, he's improving all the time".*

514. LOOKING FOR CARL ★★★
b.c. Lope De Vega – Dam Beautiful (Sleeping Indian). May 9. Second foal. €23,000Y. Arqana Deauville October. Stroud/Coleman & H Dunlop. The dam, a fairly useful listed-placed 5f winner at 2 and 3 yrs, is a half-sister to 2 winners. The second dam, Nellie Melba (by Hurricane Sky), a fair 7f and 1m winner of 3 races, is a half-sister to 4 other minor winners. (Kevin & Maureen Freeman). *"A backward colt, he was bought to try and run in the new Criterium race for 2-y-o's at the Arc meeting. I don't know a huge about him at the moment but I'm happy with him".*

515. MAFEKING ★★★★
b.c. Makfi – Save Me The Waltz (Halling). March 17. €52,000Y. Arqana Deauville October. Stroud/Coleman & H Dunlop. Half-brother to 4 winners including the French listed 10f winner and US Grade 3 third Dealbata (by Dubawi), the fairly useful 10f winner King's Warrior (by King's Best) and the quite useful dual 5f (at 2 yrs) and 1m winner Furiant (by Invincible Spirit). The dam, a minor 3-y-o winner, is a half-sister to 6 winners including the Group 3 Prix Penelope winner Ombre Legere. The second dam, Flawlessly (by Rainbow Quest), is a placed half-sister to 9 winners. (Hearson, Pascall, Thornely-Taylor). *"I like him, he's looking relatively forward and he's done a fair amount of fast work. He's another one that's entered for the Criterium race on Arc weekend. Some of these Makfi's can be a bit over-excitable but he's well-behaved and we'll look to start him off in May over six furlongs".*

516. MAYAMOUR ★★★
b.f. Mayson – Amour Fou (Piccolo). March 10. Second foal. £18,000Y. Goffs UK Premier (Doncaster). Stroud/Coleman (private sale). Half-sister to the quite useful 2016 2-y-o dual 6f winner Groupie (by Requinto). The dam, a modest dual 5f winner, is out of the quite useful 2-y-o 7f winner Elm Dust (by Elmaamul), herself a half-sister to numerous winners including Dust Dancer (Group 3 10f Prix de la Nonette) and Bulaxie (Group 3 7.3f Fred Darling Stakes). (Mr John Troy & Mrs Carolyn Elwes). *"She's shaping up nicely and looks a sharp filly that should be racing in May or June. I'm very pleased with her at the moment and I'd say she'll be a six furlong 2-y-o".*

517. RAVEN'S SONG (IRE) ★★★
b.f. Raven's Pass – Lyric Of Fife (Strategic Prince). March 3. First foal. €30,000Y. Goffs Orby. Anthony Stroud / H Dunlop (private sale). The dam is an unraced half-sister to 7 winners including Witch Of Fife (dam of the stakes winners Cabaret, Drumfire and Ho Choi). The second dam, Fife (by Lomond), a fairly useful listed-placed 1m winner, is a half-sister to the dam of the Group/Grade 1 winners Frenchpark and Pearly Shells. (Mrs Sonia Rogers & Foxtrot Racing). *"A filly that I*

like, she's likely to be a six/seven furlong 2-y-o from June/July time onwards. She has a nice pedigree and she should give us some fun". TRAINERS' BARGAIN BUY

518. SHEHASSPENTTHELOT ★★★
b.f. Kodiac – Jenlen (Lemon Drop Kid). January 19. First foal. 55,000Y. Tattersalls October Book 1. Stroud/Coleman & Harry Dunlop. The dam is an unraced half-sister to 4 winners including the Group 3 Round Tower Stakes winner Great White Eagle and the Group 2 Mill Reef Stakes third Quarrel. The second dam, Gender Dance (by Miesque's Son), a minor US dual winner at 3 yrs, is a half-sister to 5 winners including a stakes winner in Japan. (Kevin & Graham Freeman, Frank McAffrey). *"A filly that's quite long, so she's not one of those 'butty' Kodiac's. She's done a little bit of faster work and seems to be enjoying it and she'll probably be a seven furlong 2-y-o".*

519. STAR OF VENDOME (FR) ★★★
b.f. Style Vendome – Celestina Agostino (Street Cry). March 13. Fifth foal. €70,000Y. Arqana Deauville August. Stroud/Coleman. Half-sister to 3 winners including the French dual 10.5f winner and Group 2 Prix Eugene Adam third Toruk (by Arcano), The dam won once at 3 yrs in France and is a half-sister to 6 winners including the US Grade 1 Flower Bowl Invitational Handicap winner Chelsey Flower (herself dam of the French Group 3 winner Kentucky Dynamite). The second dam, Chelsey Dancer (by Affirmed), is an unplaced half-sister to 10 winners. (Mr Richard Foden). *"By a first season sire in Style Vendome and I like her a lot. She's a big-bodied, strong filly and I hope she'll be running in Deauville in August to take advantage of the French prize money and premiums".*

520 WHISPERING SANDS (IRE) ★★★
ch.f. Dubawi – Roses For The Lady (Sadler's Wells). February 5. The dam, a smart Irish listed 13f winner, was second in the Group 1 Irish Oaks, is a half-sister to 2 winners. The second dam, Head In The Clouds (by Rainbow Quest), won the Group 3 12f Princess Royal Stakes and is a sister to the high-class St Leger, Chester Vase and Jockey Club Stakes winner Millenary and a half-sister to the very

smart 1m (at 2 yrs) and 10f winner and Derby third Let The Lion Roar. (Mr L Neil Jones). *"It's very exciting to have a Dubawi in the yard. This is a big filly that'll take some time but I very much like what I see and she's one for later in the season I think. Very pleased with her for the moment".*

521 UNNAMED ★★★
ch.c. Casamento – Emreliya (Danehill Dancer). April 16. Third foal. 28,000Y. Tattersalls October Book 3. Stroud/Coleman & H Dunlop. Half-brother to the quite useful 2016 2-y-o listed-placed 6f winner Just An Idea (by Lilbourne Lad) and to the Italian listed-placed winner of 3 races at 2 and 3 yrs Staisenzapenziei (by Royal Applause). The dam is an unraced half-sister to 4 winners, two of them listed-placed. The second dam, Fhatana (by Rainbow Quest), an Irish middle distance placed maiden, is a half-sister to 10 winners. (Best Of Both Worlds Partnership). *"A half-brother to Just An Idea who did well for us last year. This is a nice colt that'll take some time and I don't think he'll be out much before August. I like him at this stage but he hasn't done very much yet".*

TIM EASTERBY
522. ALASKAN BEAUTY
b.f. Kodiac – My American Beauty (Wolfhound). April 29. Ninth foal. €31,000Y. Tattersalls Ireland September. Tim Easterby. Half-sister to 6 winners including the quite useful 7f and 1m winner Outback Ruler (by Aussie Rules), the quite useful 5f and 6f winner of 5 races Beauty Pageant (by Bahamian Bounty), the modest triple 1m winner Miller Beach (by Sakhee's Secret) and the moderate 5f winner Marie's Fantasy (by Whipper). The dam, a fairly useful 5f and 6f winner of 7 races, is a half-sister to the US dual Grade 3 winner Desert Lady. The second dam, Hooray Lady (by Ahonoora), a fairly useful listed-placed winner of 6 races at around 1m, is a half-sister to 7 winners. (Ryedale Partners No.1).*

523. GARDINIA ♣
b.f. Pivotal – Garden Row (Invincible Spirit). February 4. First foal. 26,000Y. Tattersalls October Book 2. Tim Easterby. The dam is an unraced sister to the 2-y-o Group 2 6f Flying

Childers Stakes and listed St Hugh's Stakes winner Madame Trop Vite and a half-sister to 8 winners. The second dam, Gladstone Street (by Waajib), a winner over 1m at 2 yrs in Germany, is a half-sister to 7 winners. (Reality Partnerships X).

524. GRAPHITE GIRL (IRE)
gr.f. Kodiac – My Girl Lisa (With Approval). February 3. Ninth foal. £42,000Y. Goffs UK Premier (Doncaster). Tim Easterby. Half-sister to 7 winners including the fairly useful 2-y-o 5f winner and Group 3 third Explosive Lady, the quite useful 6f (at 2 yrs) and 7f winner Explosive Power (both by Alfred Nobel), the fair 2-y-o 6f winner Emma Dora (by Medaglia d'Oro) and the fair Irish 1m winner Giving Orders (by Encosta de Lago). The dam, a US stakes winner of 6 races at 2 to 4 yrs, is a half-sister to 4 winners. The second dam, Amynteon (by Rahy), is an unraced half-sister to 5 winners including the Canadian Grade 2 winner Benburb. (CDM Developments North West).

525. SILVER STARLIGHT
gr.f. Showcasing – Pendulum (Pursuit Of Love). March 19. Ninth foal. £19,000Y. Goffs UK Premier (Doncaster). Tim Easterby. Half-sister to the quite useful 2-y-o 5f winner Every Second , to the moderate 6f winner Abraham Monro (both by Kyllachy), the quite useful 5f and 6f winner of 8 races Medici Time (by Medicean), the quite useful 5f to 7.5f winner of 8 races My Son Max (by Avonbridge), the quite useful dual 5f winner Ticking Away (by Monsieur Bond) and the fair 1m winner Pendulum Star (by Observatory). The dam, a quite useful 7f winner, is a half-sister to 6 winners. The second dam, Brilliant Timing (by The Minstrel), is a placed half-sister to the US Grade 1 winners Timely Writer and Timely Assertion. (Reality Partnerships I).

526. SIR DERRICK (IRE)
ch.g. Sir Prancealot – Alexander Confranc (Magical Wonder). May 2. Eleventh foal. £10,000Y. Goffs UK Premier (Doncaster). Not sold. Half-brother to 7 winners including the smart 7f (at 2 yrs) to 12f winner of 6 races and Group 2 6f Coventry Stakes third Capable Guest (by Cape Cross), the fairly useful 2-y-o 6f winners Pleasant Bay (by Bushranger) and

Petardia's Magic (by Petardia), the quite useful 2-y-o 6f winner Idiom (by Iffraaj) and the modest 2-y-o winners Alexander Monarchy (by Royal Applause) and Heidi's Delight (by Red Clubs). The dam, a fair 2-y-o 7f winner, is out of Fair Song (by Pitskelly), herself an unraced half-sister to 9 winners.

527. UNNAMED
gr.f. Mastercraftsman – Back In The Frame (Dutch Art). February 17. First foal. £24,000Y. Goffs UK Premier (Doncaster). Tim Easterby. The dam, placed second over 5f on her first two outings at 2 yrs, is a half-sister to 3 winners including the very useful 2-y-o 6f winner and Group 2 6f Coventry Stakes third St Barths. The second dam, Ile Deserte (by Green Desert), is an unraced half-sister to the dual Group 1 winner (Racing Post Trophy and St Leger) Kingston Hill. (Middleham Park Racing XV & Partners).

528. UNNAMED
b.f. Gio Ponti – Brocatelle (Green Desert). February 21. Thirteenth foal. €60,000Y. Goffs Orby. Elwick Stud/Peter Nolan. Half-sister to 6 winners including the fairly useful listed-placed 7f winner Ahlaain, the minor US 2-y-o winner Julie Bugs (both by Bernstein), the moderate 6f to 10f winner Penbryn (by Pivotal) and a stakes-placed winner in Japan by Machiavellian. The dam, a modest 7f placed maiden, is a half-sister to the top-class milers Barathea and Gossamer (dam of the 2-y-o Group 1 winner Ibn Khaldun) and the Group 3 winner Free At Last (dam of the multiple Grade 2 winner Coretta). The second dam, Brocade (by Habitat), won the Group 1 Prix de la Foret. (Mr & Mrs G Turnbull).

DAVID ELSWORTH
529. AMANDINE ★★★
b.f. Shamardal – Kissable (Danehill Dancer). January 20. First foal. The dam, a smart Irish 2-y-o 7f winner, was third in the Group 1 Moyglare Stud Stakes and subsequently won a listed 12f race in the USA. She is a sister to 2 winners including the quite useful 2-y-o 7f winner and listed placed Kingdom Of Munster and a half-sister to 3 winners. The second dam, Kitty O'Shea (by Sadler's Wells) ran twice winning won both races over 1m (including at 2 yrs and a listed event at 3 yrs). She is a

sister to the Group 1 Racing Post Trophy and Group 1 St Leger winner Brian Boru and a half-sister to the Group 2 winners Sea Moon and Moon Search and to the dam of the Derby winner Workforce. (Lordship Stud). *"A well-related filly by a much sought-after sire, she's on the small side and was an early foal, but nevertheless I'd expect her to want a bit of time and seven furlongs".*

530. CLOONEY ★★

b.c. Dansili – Love Divine (Diesis). March 21. Half-brother to 7 winners including the Group 1 St Leger and Group 2 Jockey Club Cup winner and sire Sixties Icon (by Galileo), the useful 10f winner and Group 2 12f Jockey Club Stakes second Native Ruler, the fairly useful dual 12f winner Hamelin (both by Cape Cross) and the fair 9.5f winner Kissing (by Grand Lodge). The dam won the Oaks and the listed Lupe Stakes and is a half-sister to 6 winners including the listed winners Floreeda and Dark Promise. The second dam, La Sky (by Law Society), a useful 10f winner and second in the Lancashire Oaks, is closely related to the Champion Stakes winner Legal Case and a half-sister to 4 winners. (Lordship Stud). *"A half-brother to Sixties Icon, you won't see him out until the autumn and he's much more of a 3-y-o type".*

531. COSMOPOLITAN QUEEN ★★★★★

ch.f. Dubawi – Barshiba (Barathea). February 10. Sister to the Group 1 10.5f Juddmonte International and Group 2 6f Duchess Of Cambridge Stakes winner Arabian Queen and half-sister to the fairly useful 1m winner Australian Queen (by Fastnet Rock). The dam, a dual Group 2 Lancashire Oaks winner of 7 races, is a half-sister to several winners including the useful 2-y-o listed 1m winner Doctor Dash and the fairly useful 1m (at 2 yrs) and 10f winner Dashing Star. The second dam, Dashiba (by Dashing Blade), a useful 9f and 10f winner, is a half-sister to several winners including the fairly useful 10f and 12f winner Smart Blade. (J C Smith). *"A very attractive filly and obviously her pedigree speaks volumes for her because she's a full-sister to Arabian Queen and at this stage she seems to be the most precocious we've had out of the mare. She has a very sound temperament and is perhaps an improved specimen on her sister*

if only because she's a bit bigger, but whether she's as good is unlikely. Having said that, at this stage we've no reason to think she won't be a star. Arabian Queen was an early 2-y-o and won the Cherry Hinton (now called the Duchess Of Cambridge) and she was a versatile filly from five furlongs to a mile and a quarter. This two-year-old is good and she could be an Ascot 2-y-o, but she should also improve further with a bit of time and perhaps the Cheveley Park Stakes will fit the bill".

532. ENSEMBLE (IRE) ★★★

b.c. Zoffany – Fifer (Soviet Star). March 17. Second living foal. 110,000Y. Tattersalls October Book 2. Suzanne Roberts. Half-brother to the useful 7f and 1m winner Udododontu (by Lope De Vega). The dam is an unplaced half-sister to 7 winners including the fairly useful 2-y-o 6f and 7f winner Witch Of Fife (the dam of three stakes winners). The second dam, Fife (by Lomond), a fairly useful listed-placed 1m winner, is a half-sister to 5 winners including Piffle (dam of the Group 1 winners Frenchpark and Pearly Shells). (Mr Ben C M Wong). *"He was bought for a Hong Kong client and he's bred to be a middle-distance horse but he ought to be a second half of the season 2-y-o. It's more than likely he'll be in Hong Kong next year. A nice, quality colt who will probably show his best form next year, but if he's good we'd hope to see some evidence of that later on as a 2-y-o".*

533. ICONIC BOY ★★★

b.c. Cape Cross – Snoqualmie Girl (Montjeu). March 20. Half-brother to the fair 2016 dual 7f placed 2-y-o Snow Squaw (by Excelebration). The dam, a very useful listed 1m (at 2 yrs) and listed 10f winner, is a sister to the smart listed 10f winner and Group 2 Dante Stakes third Snoqualmie Boy and a half-sister to 6 winners including the fairly useful 2-y-o 7f winner Seattle Drive. The second dam, Seattle Ribbon (Seattle Dancer), placed over 9f and 10f at 3 yrs, is a sister to the 2-y-o Group 1 1m winner Seattle Dancer. (J C Smith). *"We trained the dam for owner-breeder Jeff Smith. He's my type of horse because he'll be a middle-distance sort next year but if he's going to be good we'd hope to reap some sort of reward later on this season. A lovely horse and his 3-y-o half-sister is definitely a winner waiting to happen".*

SHADWELL STALLIONS

Muhaarar
Oasis Dream - Tahrir

£30,000 (1st JAN, SLF)

Mukhadram
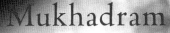
Shamardal - Magic Tree

£7,000 (1st JAN, SLF)

Nayef

Gulch - Height Of Fashion

£5,000 (1st JAN, SLF)

WORTHADD

Fee: €5,000 1st October terms

» The Champion by The Champion Dubawi
» Won Derby Italiano **(Gr.2)**, Premio Parioli (2000 Guineas) **(Gr.3)**, 2nd JLT Lockinge Stakes **(Gr.1)** to Canford Cliffs
» Timeform Rated 124
» Horses in training with N. Clement, Tom Clover, Keith Dalgleish, P.J. McBride, J. Santos
» First runners 2017

IRISH NATIONAL STUD

Contact: John Osborne, Sinéad Hyland, Gary Swift, Patrick Diamond or Helen Boyce
Tel: +353 (0)45 521251 / +353 (0)86 6031979 (Gary Swift) www.irishnationalstud.ie

TWILIGHT SON
BY KYLLACHY

DUAL GR.1 SPRINTER

Winner of the **Gr.1** Sprint Cup, 2015 and the
Gr.1 Diamond Jubilee Stakes, 2016

He defeated **Gr.1** winners including
**BELARDO, HOLLER, GORDON LORD BYRON,
SIGNS OF BLESSING** and **UNDRAFTED**.

By a sprint sire from a
proven sprinters family.

LETHAL FORCE
BY DARK ANGEL

GR.1 JULY CUP WINNER

Fastest horse ever over 6f at Newmarket.

Beat **Gr.1** winners including
SLADE POWER and **SOLE POWER**.

Also won the
Gr.1 Diamond Jubilee Stakes.

First crop 2yos in 2017

Cheveley Park Stud
Duchess Drive, Newmarket, Suffolk CB8 9DD
Tel: (01638) 730316 enquiries@cheveleypark.co.uk

SWISS SPIRIT (GB)
INVINCIBLE SPIRIT EX SWISS LAKE (INDIAN RIDGE)

First 2yo's in 2017

534. MERLIN MAGIC ★★★

b.c. Camelot – Seattle Ribbon (Seattle Dancer). March 2. Closely related to the smart listed 10f winner and Group 2 Dante Stakes third Snoqualmie Boy, the very useful listed 1m (at 2 yrs) and listed 10f winner Snoqualmie Girl (both by Montjeu) and the fairly useful 2-y-o 7f winner Seattle Drive (by Motivator) and half-brother to the quite useful 1m and 10f winner Snoqualmie Star (by Galileo), the quite useful 2-y-o 6f winner Robocop and the fair 10f winner Seattle Storm. The dam, placed over 9f and 10f at 3 yrs, is a sister to the 2-y-o Group 1 1m winner Seattle Dancer. The second dam, Golden Rhyme (by Dom Racine), was a quite useful 7f winner. (J C Smith). *"From the first crop of a well-touted stallion, this is an attractive, quality colt and although he's quite well-grown I would expect him to show us some ability as a 2-y-o. I think he'll be relatively early but I don't tend to ask my 2-y-o's too many questions early on. I like to let them tell me if they're precocious and if they are I'll carry on".*

535. MISTY SPIRIT ★★★ ♠

br.f. Swiss Spirit – Irrational (Kyllachy). February 8. Second foal. 30,000Y. Tattersalls October Book 3. One Agency. Half-sister to the fair 2016 2-y-o 5f winner Whiteandgold (by Major Cadeaux). The dam, a modest 2-y-o 5f winner, is a half-sister to 6 winners, two of them listed-placed. The second dam, Belladera (by Alzao), won over 6f at 2 yrs and is a half-sister to 7 winners including the listed 6f winner Silca Blanka. (Lordship Stud). *"From the first crop of Swiss Spirit who was trained here, his yearlings sold very well and this is an attractive filly who certainly looks like she'll be a 2-y-o. A precocious type, her pedigree suggests she'll be a 2-y-o too and we bought her with that in mind".*

536. POLAR LIGHT ★★★

b.f. Norse Dancer – Dimelight (Fantastic Light). March 4. Sister to the quite useful 7f to 14f and hurdles winner Odin and to the fair 11.5f and hurdles winner Norse Light and half-sister to the quite useful 6f and 7f winner of 4 races (including at 2 yrs) Elusive Flame (by Elusive City) and the modest 7f (at 2 yrs) to 1m winner of 5 races Secret Lightning (by

Sakhee's Secret). The dam, a fair 9f and 10f placed maiden, is a half-sister to numerous winners including the smart Group 3 Prix La Rochette winner Guys And Dolls, the smart 1m (including at 2 yrs) to 11f listed winner Pawn Broker and the useful dual 7f 2-y-o winner and Group 3 placed Blushing Bride. The second dam, Dime Bag (by High Line), a quite useful winner of 4 races at up to 2m, is a half-sister to 7 minor winners. (J C Smith). *"This is a quality filly out of a mare I trained who was slightly disappointing. A good moving filly, I'm a big supporter of the sire so you might not get a balanced opinion about her because of my prejudice! One for the second half of the season, I'd like to think she'll train on too because it's a lovely family I've had a lot to do with".*

537. ROSEAU CITY ★★

ch.f. Cityscape – Dominica (Alhaarth). May 1. Half-sister to the quite useful 6f and 7f winner of 6 races Jungle Bay, to the quite useful 5f winner Lulla (both by Oasis Dream), the quite useful 2-y-o 5f winner Percy Alleline (by Sir Percy) and the modest 5f and 6f winner of 3 races Todber (by Cape Cross). The dam, winner of the Group 2 5f King's Stand Stakes and the Group 3 Cornwallis Stakes, is a half-sister to 3 winners. The second dam, Dominio (by Dominion), a 2-y-o listed 5f winner, was second in the Group 2 5f Temple Stakes and is a half-sister to 6 winners including the Group 1 5f Nunthorpe Stakes winner Ya Malak. (Hot to Trot & Stowell Hill Stud). *"I've only had her for a couple of weeks, she's a small filly, a May foal from a fast family and a contender for the smallest I've trained. You'd think she'd be an early 2-y-o for that reason alone, but it's a bit early for me to say".*

538. UNNAMED ★★★

b.c. Kyllachy – Bonnie Brae (Mujahid). February 16. Second foal. 95,000Y. Tattersalls October Book 2. Suzanne Roberts. Half-brother to Davinci Dawn (by Poet's Voice), unplaced in one start at 2 yrs in 2016. The dam, a useful 6f and 7f winner of 5 races, is a half-sister to 4 winners. The second dam, Skara Brae (by Inchinor), is an unraced half-sister to 5 minor winners. (David Elsworth). *"I trained the dam and although she didn't get black type she was a good filly and won the Bunbury Cup. This colt looks a 2-y-o, he should be early and I'd be disappointed if he doesn't get into the winner's enclosure by the summer".*

539. UNNAMED ★★★
ch.c. Paco Boy – Decorative (Danehill Dancer). February 9. Third foal. 40,000Y. Tattersalls October Book 2. Gordon Li. Half-brother to the fair 2016 2-y-o 5f winner Fabric (by Acclamation) and to the fair 2-y-o 7f winner Aneesah (by Canford Cliffs). The dam, a fairly useful 6f (at 2 yrs) and 1m winner, is a full or half-sister to 4 minor winners. The second dam, Source Of Life (by Fasliyev), is an unraced half-sister to 9 winners including the Group 3 winners Australie and Forgotten Voice. (Mr G W Y Li). *"I'm quite a supporter of Paco Boy and this is a big, well-grown colt but nevertheless I'd expect him to be quite precocious. I haven't got after him properly yet but he's a very attractive colt, a bit flashy and he goes well. The pedigree certainly suggests he'll be a 2-y-o and he's a nice horse".*

540. UNNAMED ★★★
b.f. Declaration Of War – Turning Top (Pivotal). March 22. Second foal. The dam, a fair 7f and 8.5f winner here, later won a Grade 3 over 10f in the USA and is a half-sister to 3 winners. The second dam, Pietra Dura (by Cadeaux Genereux), an Irish 2-y-o 7f winner, was listed-placed and is a half-sister to 3 winners. (Mrs D A Tabor). *"Simon Callaghan trained the mare and she was a good filly. This is a delightful little filly that's turned herself inside out since I've had her and she's done nothing but improve. Whilst initially I might have been a bit disappointed, now I'm looking forward to her. She's a nice filly".*

541. UNNAMED ★★★
ch.c. Medicean – Skara Brae (Inchinor). February 5. Seventh foal. 9,000Y. Tattersalls October Book 2. Suzanne Roberts. Half-brother to the useful 6f and 7f winner of 5 races Bonnie Brae (by Mujahid), to the moderate 7f and 1m winner Vogarth (by Arkadian Hero), the fair 7f winner Mustajjid (by Byron) and a minor 2-y-o winner abroad by Josr Algarhoud. The dam is an unplaced half-sister to 5 minor winners. The second dam, Tahilla (by Moorestyle), won 7 races at

2 and 3 yrs including two listed events and is a half-sister to 8 winners including the Group 1 Nunthorpe Stakes winner Piccolo. (Mr D Elsworth). *"A delightful little colt and whilst he came in late I think he's very nice. He was cheap as well".* TRAINERS' BARGAIN BUY

542. UNNAMED ★★★
ch.f. Dawn Approach – Romie's Kastett (Halling). April 10. Fourth foal. 32,000Y. Tattersalls October Book 2. Suzanne Roberts. Half-sister to 3 winners including the quite useful 2016 Irish 2-y-o 1m winner Eagle Spirit (by Holy Roman Emperor) and the minor French 3-y-o winner Al Dweha (by Invincible Spirit). The dam, a quite useful Irish 9f winner, is a sister to the Group 3 Earl Of Sefton Stakes and Group 3 Sovereign Stakes winner and multiple Group 1 placed Norse Dancer and a half-sister to 8 winners. The second dam, River Patrol (by Rousillon), a fairly useful 10.2f winner, is a half-sister to 3 winners including the smart middle-distance stayer Dry Dock and to the dams of the Group/Grade 1 winners Mail The Desert, Good Faith and Band Gipsy. *"By Dawn Approach, who was a proper horse, she's out of a full-sister to Norse Dancer and I began as a spectator as she went through the ring, but I ended up being pleased to buy her for 32,000 Guineas. An attractive filly that'll take a bit of time and I haven't asked her any questions yet, but I like her".*

JAMES EUSTACE
543. ALL ROUND ★★★★
b.f. Champs Elysees – Alice Alleyne (Oasis Dream). April 26. Fourth foal. Half-sister to the quite useful 2016 2-y-o 5f and 6f winner Looting (by Bahamian Bounty) and to the quite useful Irish 1m winner Araqeel (by Dutch Art). The dam, a quite useful 7f (at 2 yrs) and 6f winner, is a half-sister to 2 winners including the Irish listed winner and Group 2 third Avenue Gabriel. The second dam, Vas Y Carla (by Gone West), a quite useful 7f placed 2-y-o, is a half-sister to 5 winners including the Group 2 Great Voltigeur Stakes third Avalon. (Major M G Wyatt). *"She's been in since the end of October and has been cantering for a while. Very straightforward, she has a very good temperament and is a three-parts sister to Avenue Gabriel (also by Champs Elysees) who won over 7f and a 1m*

listed event as a 2-y-o. I think this filly will take after her and be more of a 2-y-o than most by the sire. One for seven furlongs to a mile, but precocious enough to do some good this year".

544. BLUE WHISPER ★★★
ch.c. Bated Breath – Vivid Blue (Haafhd). March 25. Second foal. 22,000foal. Tattersalls December. Hursley Bloodstock. Half-brother to Ejaaby (by Helmet), placed second over 7f from two starts at 2 yrs in 2016. The dam, a fair 7f winner, is a half-sister to 5 winners including the 6f, 7f and subsequent US Grade 2 1m and Grade 3 1m winner Diamond Diva. The second dam, Vivianna (by Indian Ridge), won at 3 yrs in France and is a half-sister to one winner. (J C Smith). *"Stood still he looks a real 2-y-o type but I'm very conscious of the fact that the sire's first crop last year needed time. Not a very tall colt, but very strong, butty and well put-together, so I'm pretty sure he'll make a 2-y-o at some point. Probably a mid-season type".*

545. MEDIAN ★★
b.f. Medicean – Gale Green (Galileo). January 24. Second foal. Half-sister to the quite useful 10f winner (previously placed over 6f and 7f at 2 yrs) Skeaping (by Excellent Art). The dam, a fair 10f winner, is a half-sister to 7 winners including the dam of the French 2-y-o Group 2 winner Smooth Operator. The second dam, Anna Of Brunswick (by Rainbow Quest), a fair 3-y-o 10f winner, is a half-sister to 5 winners including the German Group 3 winner Anno Luce to the dams of the Group winners Annus Mirabilis, Anna of Saxony, Annaba, Piping Rock and Pozarica. (Major M G Wyatt). *"He came in late because of a hind leg issue and she's only being broken in now. She's a good-looking filly, I think her hind leg problem is literally behind her and she's very straightforward and has a good temperament. A home-bred of Major Wyatt's, I like this filly and I don't think the delay will do her any harm".*

546. KILLER PUNCH ★★★
gr.f. Lethal Force – La Gessa (Largesse). March 22. Sixth foal. Half-sister to Envoy (by Delegator), unplaced in 2 starts at 2 yrs in 2016, to the fairly useful 2-y-o 5f and 6f winner Poet's Prize (by Compton Place), the

quite useful 5f, 6f (both at 2 yrs) to 1m winner Tommy's Secret (by Sakhee's Secret), the ill-fated Irish 2-y-o 7f winner Case Statement (by Showcasing) and the fair 7f (at 2 yrs) to 9f winner of 8 races Wordismybond (by Monsieur Bond). The dam, a moderate 10f and 13f winner at 3 and 4 yrs, is a half-sister to one winner. The second dam, En Grisaille (by Mystiko), a moderate 6f (at 2 yrs) and 10f winner, is a half-sister to 5 winners including the multiple listed winner Angus Newz. (H R Moszkowicz & Upperwood Farm). *"She's from a family I know quite well, I like her but she's particularly tall and will need a bit of time. I quite like the 3-y-o out of the dam, Envoy, who ran a couple of promising races for us last year and Lethal Force should add a bit more speed to the pedigree I think".*

547. NORDIC FLIGHT ★★★★
b.c. Norse Dancer – Winged Diva (Hawk Wing). February 18. Second foal. Brother to the modest 1m winner Winged Dancer. The dam, unplaced in two starts, is a half-sister to 3 winners including the very useful listed 10f and listed 12f winner Opera Gal. The second dam, Opera Glass (by Barathea), a quite useful 8.5f winner, is a sister to the very smart 2-y-o Group 3 7f Solario Stakes winner and Group 1 Dewhurst Stakes third Opera Cape and a half-sister to the high-class stayer Grey Shot and the smart sprint winner of 4 races Night Shot. (J C Smith). *"Last but not least – and I do mean that. Although he's by Norse Dancer and he's a big horse he's just cruised through everything so far. He moves very well, he doesn't find anything difficult – not that's he's ever been asked a question – and he's a racehorse I think. He'll most likely want seven furlongs or a mile this year".*

548. SPEED CRAFT ★★★
ch.f. Mastercraftsman – Exorcet (Selkirk). April 27. Ninth foal. Half-sister to the very useful 6f winner of 4 races and Group 2 6f Diadem Stakes second Dark Missile, to the fair 2-y-o 6f winner Guided Missile, the fair dual 6f winner Night Rocket (all by Night Shift) and the fairly useful dual 1m winner Breakheart (by Sakhee). The dam, a fair 3-y-o 6f winner, is a half-sister to 2 winners including the useful UAE 7f and 1m winner Rock Music. The second dam, Stack Rock (by

Ballad Rock), a very useful winner of 9 races from 5f to 1m including the listed Hopeful Stakes, was second in the Group 1 Prix de l'Abbaye. (J C Smith). *"A nice filly and a very good mover, I do like her. I haven't had a Mastercraftsman before but I suspect that unlike a lot of them this filly will make a 2-y-o. She's quite 'together' even though she's a nice-sized filly and she does look physically quite mature. I'm quite hopeful of her and she's a particularly good mover".*

RICHARD FAHEY

549. A BIT OF A TOUCH (IRE)

b.c. Arcano – La Vita E Bella (Definite Article). April 14. Ninth foal. €72,000Y. Goffs Orby. Robin O'Ryan. Half-brother to the US stakes-placed winner Wittgenstein, to the fair 9f to 14f winner Lifetime (both by Shamardal), a hurdles winner by Tiger Hill and to the unraced dam of the Group 2 Lennox Stakes winner Dutch Connection. The dam, a 2-y-o listed 1m winner and second in the Group 3 Prix Saint-Roman, is a half-sister to 4 winners including the useful 2-y-o dual listed 5f winner and Group 2 third Bella Tusa. The second dam, Coolrain Lady (by Common Grounds), was placed 12 times in Ireland from 1m to 10f and is a half-sister to 4 winners.

550. ALMANE (IRE)

ch.c. Sir Prancealot – Red Rosanna (Bertolini). February 6. Third foal. €18,000Y. Goffs Sportsmans. Robin O'Ryan. Half-brother to the moderate triple 5f winner Frank The Barber. The dam, a quite useful triple 5f winner including at 2 yrs, is a half-sister to the Group 3 Summer Stakes winner Rose Blossom. The second dam, Lamarita (by Emarati), a quite useful dual 5f winner, is a half-sister to 12 winners. A winner at Beverley in id-April.

551. AREEN FAISAL (IRE) ♠

ch.c. Bahamian Bounty – Yellow Trumpet (Petong). March 26. Eighth foal. €80,000Y. Goffs Orby. Richard Knight. Half-brother to the useful dual 5f (including at 2 yrs) and subsequent Hong Kong winner and triple listed-placed City Of Tribes (by Invincible Spirit), to the fairly useful 2-y-o 5f winner of 4 races Viva Verglas, the quite useful 2-y-o 7f winner Right Divine, the fair 10f winner

Silverglas (all by Verglas) the quite useful 2-y-o 5f winner Canary Island (by Groom Dancer) and the fair 1m (at 2 yrs) and 10f winner Golden Aria (by Rakti). The dam, a fair 2-y-o 5f winner, is a full or half-sister to 7 winners including the listed 5.2f St Hugh's Stakes winner Petula and the Group 3 Ballycorus Stakes winner Naahy. The second dam, Daffodil Fields (by Try My Best), placed 6 times in Ireland, is a half-sister to 3 winners.

552. DELPH CRESCENT (IRE)

b.c. Dark Angel – Zut Alors (Pivotal). April 20. Sixth foal. 100,000Y. Tattersalls October Book 1. Robin O'Ryan. Half-brother to the 2016 French listed-placed 2-y-o Precieuse (by Tamayuz), to the useful listed-placed 7f (including at 2 yrs) and 6f winner of 6 races Baccarat (by Dutch Art), the French 10f winner and Group 3 Prix Fille de l'Air second Peut Etre (by Whipper) and the quite useful 8.5f (at 2 yrs) and 12f winner Grey Blue (by Verglas). The dam won once at 2 yrs in France and was third in the Group 3 Prix Miesque and is a half-sister to 7 winners including Royal Empire (Group 3 Geoffrey Freer Stakes). The second dam, Zeiting (by Zieten), won four listed events in France and is a half-sister to the Group 3 Prix du Bois winner Dolled Up.

553. DUBAI ACCLAIM (IRE)

b.c. Acclamation – Bahati (Intikhab). February 27. Third foal. 50,000Y. Tattersalls December. Robin O'Ryan. Brother to the useful dual 7f winner at 2 and 3 yrs Tabarrak and to the quite useful 2-y-o listed-placed 5f and 6f winner The Wagon Wheel. The dam, a quite useful listed-placed 2-y-o 6f winner, is a half-sister to 9 winners including the Irish 7f (at 2 yrs) to 10f and subsequent Hong Kong stakes winner Solid Approach. The second dam, Dawn Chorus (by Mukaddamah), is an unraced half-sister to 7 winners.

554. EL CHAPO

b.c. Lethal Force – Never Lose (Diktat). May 2. Fifth foal. 40,000Y. Tattersalls October Book 2. Robin O'Ryan. Half-brother to Eternal Endeavour (by Mayson), placed second over 7f on her first start at 3 yrs in 2017) and to the fair 7f (at 2 yrs) to 10f winner of 4 races Miss Lillie (by Exceed And Excel). The dam, a fairly useful 6f and 7f winner, was third in the listed Cecil Frail Stakes and is a half-sister to 3 winners including the fairly useful 6f winner of 4 races (including at 2 yrs) and Group 3 placed Morache Music. The second dam, Enchanted Princess (by Royal Applause), a fair 3-y-o 8.3f winner, is a half-sister to 5 winners.

555. EXHORT
ch.f. Dutch Art – Entreat (Pivotal). April 16. Fourth foal. Sister to the fair 2016 2-y-o 10f winner Plead and to the fair 10f winner Suitor. The dam, a fair 10f winner, is a half-sister to 4 winners including the Group 3 Supreme Stakes and Group 3 Criterion Stakes winner Producer (by Dutch Art). The second dam, River Saint (by Irish River), is a placed half-sister to 5 winners including the multiple US Grade 1 winner Serena's Song (herself the dam of four Group winners including Group 1 Coronation Stakes winner Sophisticat). (Cheveley Park Stud).

556. GANGLAND
gr.c. Lethal Force – Miss Dutee (Dubawi). March 29. Second foal. €42,000Y. Tattersalls Ireland September. Robin O'Ryan. Half-brother to the modest 6f and 7f winner False Id (by Aqlaam). The dam, a modest 6f (at 2 yrs) and 7f winner, is a half-sister to 6 winners. The second dam, Tee Cee (by Lion Cavern), a fair 3-y-o 7f winner, is a half-sister to 5 winners.

557. GREAT PROSPECTOR (IRE)
b.c. Elzaam – Guana (Dark Angel). April 19. Second foal. £95,000Y. Goffs UK Premier (Doncaster). The dam is an unraced half-sister to 3 winners including the dam of the Group 2 Superlative Stakes winner Birchwood. The second dam, Guana Bay (by Cadeaux Genereux), is an unraced full or half-sister to 6 winners including the Group 2 winners Prince Sabo and Millyant, and the listed winner Bold Jessie (dam of the Group 2 Gimcrack Stakes winner Abou Zouz).

558. INDOMENEO
b.c. Piccolo – Cherrycombe-Row (Classic Cliche). February 7. Seventh living foal. £62,000Y. Goffs UK Premier (Doncaster). Middleham Park. Half-brother to the US Grade 2 Santa Maria Handicap winner and Grade 1 Vanity Handicap second St Trinians

and to the fair 7f and 8.5f winner Beat Goes On (both by Piccolo). The dam, a fair 2-y-o 7f winner, is s half-sister to 5 winners abroad. The second dam, Key To The Ring (by Pyjama Hunt), is an unraced half-sister to 7 winners. (Middleham Park Racing).

559. INTERNATIONAL MAN
b.c. Epaulette – Right Answer (Lujain). April 27. Fifth foal. 72,000Y. Tattersalls October Book 2. Robin O'Ryan. Half-brother to the very useful 2-y-o 5f and 6f winner and dual listed-placed Galtymore Lad (by Indesatchel), to the fair 6f and 7f winner Cadeaux Power (by Major Cadeaux) and a winner in Greece by Exceed And Excel. The dam, a fairly useful listed-placed 2-y-o 5f winner, is a half-sister to 4 winners. The second dam, Quiz Show (by Primo Dominie), a quite useful 7f winner, is a half-sister to 4 winners including the high-class sprinter Mind Games, winner of the Group 2 Temple Stakes (twice), the Norfolk Stakes and the Palace House Stakes.

560. INVIOLABLE SPIRIT (IRE)
b.c. Zebedee – Mediska (Medicean). March 28. First foal. £20,000Y. Goffs UK Premier (Doncaster). Aidan O'Ryan & R Fahey. The dam, unplaced in two starts, is a half-sister to 5 winners including the listed winner Lightscameraaction. The second dam, Silca Boo (by Efisio), a useful 2-y-o 5f and 6f winner and listed-placed twice, is a half-sister to the very useful dual 6f winner and Group 2 6f Gimcrack Stakes second Zilch. This colt won over 5f at Redcar on the 10th April on his debut.

561. IT DON'T COME EASY (IRE)
b.c. Kyllachy – Eleganza (Balmont). February 19. First foal. £60,000Y. Goffs UK Premier (Doncaster). Aidan O'Ryan / R Fahey. The dam is an unraced half-sister to 9 winners including the smart Irish 5f and listed 6f winner Rolo Tomasi and the German Group 2 1,000 Guineas second Elegant Ridge. The second dam, Elegant Bloom (by Be My Guest), a quite useful Irish 2-y-o 6f winner, stayed 7f and is a full or half-sister to 12 winners.

562. I WAS ONLY JOKING (IRE)
b.f. Helmet – Lady Angele (Ski Chief). April 15. Seventh foal. €55,000Y. Arqana Deauville

August V2. F Barberini / Middleham Park. Half-sister to the minor French 2-y-o 5f and 6.5f winner Lady Jak (by American Post). The dam, a 2-y-o listed 5f winner, is a half-sister to 2 winners. The second dam, Ladygoon (by Rangoon), a French 2-y-o 5f winner, is a half-sister to 3 winners.

563. JASI
b.c. Kodiac – Late Night Movie (Holy Roman Emperor). April 15. Second foal. £50,000Y. Goffs UK Premier (Doncaster). Sheikh Abdullah Al Malek Al Sabah. The dam is an unraced half-sister to 7 winners including the useful 2-y-o 7f winner and Group 2 Beresford Stakes third Going Public. The second dam, Gifts Galore (by Danehill Dancer), is a placed full or half-sister to 7 winners. A winner at Southwell in a four runner event.

564. JAVELIN
ch.f. Lethal Force – Amitola (Choisir). March 2. Third foal. £40,000Y. Goffs UK Premier (Doncaster). Cheveley Park Stud. The dam, a quite useful 6f (including at 2 yrs) and 7f winner, was listed-placed and is a half-sister to 5 winners. The second dam, Emily Express (by High Estate), won once over 11f at 4 yrs in France and is a half-sister to 7 winners including the Irish Group 3 winner Rainbows For All. (Cheveley Park Stud).

565. LUCKY LUCKY MAN (IRE)
b.c. Raven's Pass – Regrette Rien (Unbridled's Song). April 23. Ninth foal. 30,000Y. Tattersalls October Book 2. John Ryan. Half-brother to the quite useful 2016 2-y-o 1m winner Walter Raleigh (by Nathaniel), to the smart 2-y-o Group 2 7f Superlative Stakes winner Silver Grecian, the fair Irish 12f and hurdles winner Chebona Bula (both by Haafhd), the quite useful 1m and 11f winner Cloud Seven (by New Approach) and the fair 13f winner Lettre De Cachet (by Authorized). The dam, unplaced in France at 2 yrs, is a half-sister to 8 winners including the US stakes winner Salty Sea. The second dam, Rose Indien (by Crystal Glitters), a winner of 5 races including the listed 6f Hopeful Stakes, is a half-sister to 8 winners including the French Group 2 12f winners America and Majorien.

566. LULU STAR (IRE)
b.f. Oasis Dream – Jeanie Johnston (One Cool Cat). February 16. First foal. £100,000Y. Goffs UK Premier (Doncaster). Aidan O'Ryan / R Fahey. The dam, a fairly useful 2-y-o 6f winner, was listed placed and is a half-sister to 3 winners including the Group 3 placed Switcher. The second dam, Bahamamia (by Vettori), won over 1m at 2 yrs in France and is a half-sister to 4 winners including the German Group 2 winner Accento.

567. MAGGIES ANGEL (IRE)
b.f. Dark Angel – Last Bid (Vital Equine). January 26. First foal. €36,000Y. Goffs Orby. Robin O'Ryan. The dam, a fairly useful listed-placed 2-y-o triple 5f winner, is a half-sister to 4 minor winners. The second dam, Manderina (by Mind Games), is an unplaced half-sister to 4 winners.

568. MAYBRIDE ♣
b.f. Mayson – Wedding Party (Groom Dancer). April 7. Ninth foal. Sister to the fairly useful 2016 2-y-o 5f and 6f winner and Group 3 Firth Of Clyde Stakes second Rosebride and half-sister to the very useful 7f winner and triple listed-placed Party Doctor (by Dr Fong), to the German listed-placed Dream Wedding (by Medicean), the fair 5f to 7f winner First Knight (by Kyllachy) and the modest 2-y-o 5f winner Wedlock (by Pivotal). The dam, a quite useful 6f and 7f winner, was listed-placed and is a half-sister to 4 winners including the Group 2 May Hill Stakes winner Pollenator. The second dam, Ceanothus (by Bluebird), was placed over 7f and 12f and is a half-sister to 4 winners including the US Grade 2 12f Orchid Handicap and Grade 3 8.5f Suwannee River Handicap winner Golden Pond. (Cheveley Park Stud).

569. NARCOS (IRE)
bl.c. Lethal Force – Western Eyes (Rock Of Gibraltar). March 20. Fourth foal. 45,000Y. Tattersalls December. Robin O'Ryan. Half-brother to the quite useful dual 12f winner Hubertas (by Lord Of England) and to a listed placed winner in Switzerland by Cockney Rebel. The dam is an unplaced half-sister to 7 winners including the Australian Group winners Newquay and Civil List. The second

dam, Duchy Of Cornwall (by The Minstrel), a quite useful 7f winner, is a half-sister to 5 winners.

570. PANOPHOBIA
b.c. Bated Breath – Methayel (Araafa). April 14. Second foal. 38,000Y. Tattersalls October Book 2. Robin O'Ryan. Half-brother to the quite useful 2016 2-y-o 5f winner Prince Of Cool (by Royal Applause). The dam, a fair 1m and 9f winner at 3 and 4 yrs, is a half-sister to 5 winners. The second dam, First Breeze (by Woodman), a minor Irish 7f winner, is closely related to the winner Market Slide (dam of the 2,000 Guineas winner Refuse To Bend and the Melbourne Cup winner Media Puzzle) and a half-sister to the Breeders' Cup Classic second Twilight Agenda and the dam of the Belmont Stakes winner Go And Go.

571. PETER LEONARD
b.c. Kyllachy – Nardin (Royal Applause). February 25. First foal. 70,000Y. Tattersalls October Book 2. Robin O'Ryan. The dam, a modest 2-y-o 6f winner, is a half-sister to 5 winners including the very useful listed 7f and listed 1m winner Party Boss. The second dam, Third Party (by Terimon), a modest 3-y-o 6f winner, is a half-sister to 6 winners including the German Group 3 winning sprinter Passion For Life.

572. PUSH N'PULL
b.c. Epaulette – Zoudie (Ezzoud). April 10. Twelfth foal. €85,000Y. Goffs Orby. Robin O'Ryan. Half-brother to 5 winners including the useful Irish 5f (at 2 yrs) and listed 6f winner and Group 3 placed Croisultan, the quite useful dual 1m winner Diesel Ten (both by Refuse To Bend), the quite useful dual 1m winner Bromyard (by Dark Angel) and the fair 7f and 1m winner Lily Of Kenmare (by Exceed And Excel). The dam, a fair 10f winner, is a half-sister to 7 winners including the dual Group 3 winner Redback. The second dam, Patsy Western (by Precocious), a quite useful 6f winner, is a half-sister to 7 winners including Mr Fluorocarbon (Queen Anne Stakes) and Western Jewel (Cornwallis Stakes).

573. QUAYSIDE
ch.c. Harbour Watch – Fantacise (Pivotal). February 17. First foal. £85,000Y. Goffs UK

Premier (Doncaster). Kevin Ross. The dam, a quite useful 2-y-o 6f winner, is a half-sister to 12 winners including the Group 3 Queen Mary Stakes winners Romantic Myth and Romantic Liason. The second dam, My First Romance (by Danehill), ran twice unplaced and is a half-sister to 6 minor winners here and abroad.

574. QUEEN PENN
gr.f. Dark Angel – The Manx Touch (Petardia). March 29. Ninth foal. 67,000Y. Tattersalls October Book 2. Bradley/Kelly. Half-sister to 7 winners including the very useful 7f and 1m winner of 6 races and US Grade 3 placed Moone's My Name, the fairly useful 2-y-o dual 7f winner Frog Hollow, the fair 7f winner Daring Dragon (all by Intikhab) and the fairly useful 5f (at 2 yrs) and listed 6f winner of 10 races and Group 2 Criterium de Maisons-Laffitte second Baby Strange (by Superior Premium). The dam, a moderate 7f and 1m winner at 3 yrs, is a half-sister to 2 winners. The second dam, Chapter And Verse (by Dancer's Image), is an unraced half-sister to 4 winners out of the 1,000 Guineas and Oaks winner Altesse Royale.

575. REQUINTO DAWN (IRE)
br.c. Requinto – Till Dawn (Kheleyf). April 19. First foal. €24,000Y. Goffs Sportsmans. Robin O'Ryan /R Fahey. The dam, a moderate 5f and 6f placed maiden, is a half-sister to 6 winners including the Group 3 placed 2-y-o Rosabee. The second dam, Tilbrook (by Don't Forget Me), won over 1m at 3 yrs in Ireland and is a half-sister to 8 winners including the listed winner and Group 1 Phoenix Stakes second Maledetto. Winner of one division of the Brocklesby.

576. SABELLUM (IRE)
b.f. Iffraaj – Startarette (Dixieland Band). April 25. Eighth foal. €58,000Y. Goffs Orby. Norman Steel. Half-sister to the fair 7f (at 2 yrs) to 10f winner of 13 races Star Links (by Bernstein), to the fair 2-y-o 6f winner Angels Wings (by Dark Angel), the moderate dual 7f winner at 2 and 3 yrs Ada Misobel (by Alfred Nobel) and the minor US winner of 6 races Star Over Malibu (by Malibu Moon). The dam, placed once at 2 yrs in the USA, is a half-sister to 5 winners including the dual sprint listed

winner and Group 3 placed Elrafa Ah (herself dam of the Group 1 Dewhurst Stakes winner Mujahid). The second dam, Bubbles Darlene (by Fappiano), won twice at up to 1m and is a half-sister to 6 winners.

577. SHOBROM (IRE) ♠
b.c. Acclamation – Strasbourg Place (Compton Place). March 10. Second foal. £70,000Y. Goffs UK Premier (Doncaster). Sheikh Abdullah Al Malek Al Sabah. The dam, a moderate 7f placed 2-y-o, is a sister to the Group 2 6f Richmond Stakes winner Prolific and a half-sister to 7 winners. The second dam, Photo Flash (by Bahamian Bounty), a fair 1m winner, is a half-sister to 8 winners including the smart 2-y-o Group 2 1m Royal Lodge Stakes winner Atlantis Prince.

578. SIMMY'S COPSHOP
ch.c. Bahamian Bounty – Conversational (Thousand Words). March 28. First foal. €45,000Y. Goffs Orby. Robin O'Ryan. The dam, a fair 7f and 1m winner, is a half-sister to 5 winners including the listed Free Handicap winner Kamakiri. The second dam, Alpine Flair (by Tirol), is an unraced half sister to two listed winners in the France and Italy.

579. SINALOA
ch.c. Camacho – Rose Of Battle (Averti). March 22. Seventh foal. €40,000Y. Goffs Orby. R O'Ryan. Half-brother to the quite useful 2-y-o 7f winner Winter Rose, to the fair 6f to 8.5f winner He's My Boy (both by Dark Angel), the modest 2-y-o 6f winner Pendle Lady (by Chineur) and the moderate 2-y-o 6f winner Windsor Rose (by Windsor Knot). The dam, a quite useful Irish 2-y-o 5f winner, is a half-sister to 6 winners including the Group 2 second Orpen Grey. The second dam, Sky Red (by Night Shift), a fair 5f winner of 3 races, is a full or half-sister to 3 winners including the French listed winner Shoalhaven.

580. SUGAR COATING
b.f. Dutch Art – Muscovado (Mr Greeley). March 18. Fifth foal. 90,000Y. Tattersalls October Book 1. Cheveley Park Stud. Half-sister to the fairly useful triple 10f winner and dual listed-placed Maybelater (by Mount Nelson) and to the fair dual 1m winner

Monsieur Rieussec (by Halling). The dam ran twice unplaced and is a half-sister to 4 minor winners here and abroad and to the dam of the Australian Group 1 winner Prince Of Penzance. The second dam, Only Royale (by Caerleon), won 9 races including the Group 1 Yorkshire Oaks (twice) and the Group 2 Jockey Club Stakes and is a half-sister to 5 winners. (Cheveley Park Stud).

581. THE RIGHT CHOICE (IRE)
ch.c. Choisir – Expedience (With Approval). March 24. Seventh foal. €32,000Y. Goffs Orby. Robin O'Ryan / R Fahey. Half-brother to the minor Italian 2-y-o winner Azamourday (by Azamour) and a 4-y-o winner in Qatar by Bahamian Bounty. The dam, a fair 1m winner, is a half-sister to 8 winners including the 2-y-o Group 3 Autumn Stakes winner and Group 1 Racing Post Trophy second Fantastic View. The second dam, Promptly (by Lead On Time), a quite useful 6f winner here, also won a minor 1m stakes in the USA and is a half-sister to 7 winners.

582. VENTURA DRAGON (IRE)
b.c. Dragon Pulse – Dancing Duchess (Danehill Dancer). January 1. Sixth foal. £60,000Y. Goffs UK Premier (Doncaster). Middleham Park. Half-brother to the quite useful dual 2-y-o 6f winner Ailsa Carmel, to the fair 2-y-o 5f winner Roman Dancer and the minor Italian winner at 2 to 4 yrs Volami Nei Cuore (all by Antonius Pius). The second dam, Lady Karam (by Baba Karam), a quite useful Irish listed-placed 2-y-o 5f winner, is a half-sister to one winner abroad. (Middleham Park Racing).

583. VENTURA GOLD
b.c. Red Jazz – Desert Shine (Green Desert). March 27. First foal. €36,000Y. Tattersalls Ireland September. F Barberini / Middleham Park. The dam, a fair 7f winner, is a half-sister to 3 winners. The second dam, Star Express (by Sadler's Wells), a minor 12f winner, is a sister to the Group 3 Greenham Stakes winner Yalaietanee and a half-sister to 6 winners including the Group 3 Molecomb Stakes winner Sahara Star (dam of the Group 2 winner Land Of Dreams). (Middleham Park Racing).

584. ZAP
b.c. Mayson – Moonglow (Nayef). February 10. Second foal. 70,000Y. Tattersalls October Book 1. Robin O'Ryan. The dam, a modest 11f fourth placed 3-y-o, is a half-sister to 5 winners including the Group 1 Eclipse Stakes and Group 1 Lockinge Stakes winner and sire Medicean. The second dam, Mystic Goddess (by Storm Bird), a fairly useful 2-y-o listed 7f Sweet Solera Stakes winner, was placed in the Queen Mary Stakes, the Cherry Hinton Stakes and the Rockfel Stakes and is a half-sister to 4 winners including the Group 1 Gran Criterium winner Sanam and the South African Grade 2 winner Shaybani.

585. ZOFFINIA (IRE)
b.f. Zoffany – Princess Nala (In The Wings). April 1. Fifth foal. €130,000Y. Goffs Orby. Norman Steel. Half-brother to two minor winners abroad by Sir Percy and Tamayuz. The dam, an Irish 10f and listed 12f winner, is a half-sister to 2 winners. The second dam, Adjala (by Doyoun), is an unraced half-sister to 5 winners including the Irish 2,000 Guineas second Adjareli.

586. UNNAMED ♠♠
ch.f. Exceed And Excel – Lady Of The Desert (Rahy). January 28. Second foal. 110,000Y. Tattersalls October Book 1. Not sold. Half-sister to the smart 2016 2-y-o Group 2 6f Lowther Stakes winner Queen Kindly (by Frankel). The dam, a Group 2 6f Lowther Stakes, Group 3 6f Princess Margaret Stakes and Group 2 6f Diadem Stakes winner, is a half-sister to 6 winners including the fairly useful dual 10f winner Prince Of Stars. The second dam, Queen's Logic (by Grand Lodge), a champion 2-y-o filly and winner of the Group 1 6f Cheveley Park Stakes and the Group 2 6f Lowther Stakes, is a half-sister to 6 winners including the top-class multiple Group 1 winner Dylan Thomas.

587. UNNAMED ♠
b.f. Showcasing – Perfect Echo (Lycius). May 10. Sixth foal. £27,000Y. Goffs UK Premier (Doncaster). Joe Foley. Half-sister to the quite useful 6f and 7f winner of 6 races Perfect Silence (by Dansili) and to the quite useful triple 5f winner Perfect Muse (by Oasis

Dream). The dam, a fair 1m winner at 4 yrs, is a sister to the winner and listed-placed Perfect Peach and a half-sister to 2 winners. The second dam, Perfect Timing (by Comedy Star), won 6 races including the listed 5f Scarborough Stakes and is a half-sister to 3 winners.

CHARLIE FELLOWES

588. BUCKLAND BOY ★★★★
b.c. Bated Breath – Rancho Montoya (High Chaparral). April 7. First foal. 48,000Y. Tattersalls October Book 2. Charlie Fellowes. The dam, a moderate 12f and 14f placed maiden, is a half-sister to 8 winners including the Irish 7f (at 2 yrs) and listed 10f winner Royal Intrigue and the dam of the South African Group 1 winner Noordhoek Flyer. The second dam, Congress (by Dancing Brave), a quite useful 2-y-o 1m winner, is a sister to the Group 1 6f Haydock Park Sprint Cup and Group 1 Prix Maurice de Gheest winner Cherokee Rose and a half-sister to 3 winners. (Mr P S McNally). *"A beauty, he's a really nice horse and one of my fav's. He finds everything easier than he should do because being by Bated Breath he's not going to be forward and yet he's with the most forward group. I've just backed off him because I don't want to do too much with him too early. I'm hoping he'll be an August type, he's a beautiful mover and finds everything easy. I'm very positive about my 2-y-o's this year, they're the best bunch I've had".*

589. BURGAM ★★★
b.br.c. Footstepsinthesand – Movie Queen (Danehill). April 24. Ninth foal. €20,000Y. Tattersalls Ireland September. Charlie Gordon-Watson. Half-brother to the modest 9f winner Arte Del Calcio (by Manduro). The dam is an unraced half-sister to 6 winners including the Irish 2-y-o listed 6f winner Desert Ease and the dual Group 3 7f winner Two-Twenty-Two and to the unraced dam of the US Grade 2 winner Dixieland Gold. The second dam, Easy To Copy (by Affirmed), won 5 races from 1m to 12f including the Group 2 Premio Legnano and is a sister to the Irish 1,000 Guineas winner Trusted Partner (dam of the Grade 1 winner Dress To Thrill). (J Bin Ali Al Attiyah). *"A very sharp 2-y-o, he'll probably be my first 2-y-o runner. He's not*

the most straightforward mentally because he's a real character, but he's a good-looking, very agile horse. I have a good record with Footstepsinthesand, I find them quite easy to train because they're very willing. This fella has also got his quirks, but I do like him and he finds everything easy. I'll be starting him at five furlongs but then looking to move him up to six pretty soon".

590. CALSHOT ★★★

b.f. Shamardal – Tullynally (Dansili). March 30. Fourth foal. Sister to the quite useful triple 7f winner at 2 and 3 yrs Ashamaly and half-sister to the fairly useful 2-y-o 5f winner Zeb Un Nisa (by Iffraaj). The dam is an unraced half-sister to the Group 1 winners Footstepsinthesand and Pedro The Great and the dam of the dual Group 1 winner Power and the Group 2 winner Thakafaat. The second dam, Glatisant (by Rainbow Quest), winner of the Group 3 7f Prestige Stakes, is a half-sister to 8 winners and to the placed dam of the very smart 2-y-o Superstar Leo. (Sir Anthony Oppenheimer). "A strong, good-sized filly, currently in pre-training and she looks like a very nice type. She's by a top stallion, her sister was pretty sharp but she hasn't arrived here yet".

591. HAVERLAND ★★★

b.c. Big Bad Bob – Pivotal's Princess (Pivotal). February 15. €20,000Y. Tattersalls Ireland September. Charlie Gordon-Watson. Half-brother to the useful 5f and 6f winner of 7 races Robot Boy (by Shamardal), to the fairly useful 6f (including at 2 yrs) and 7f winner of 5 races Accession (by Acclamation), the quite useful 6f (at 2 yrs) and 1m winner Yorkee Mo Sabee (by Teofilo) and the quite useful 6f winner Three D Alexander (by Aqlaam). The dam, a useful 5f winner of 6 races, was listed placed five times and is a half-sister to one winner. The second dam, Art Princess (by Fairy King), is an unplaced half-sister to 10 winners. (Lady De Ramsey). "He's a half-brother to one of my best horses, Accession. We bought him because we thought he was good value, he's small but Accession is too, so that didn't bother us. He's got plenty of strength and in the last two months he's turned himself inside out. He's about to start some faster work, he's very straightforward and a really nice little horse".

592. HEMINGFORD ★★★

ch.c. Famous Name – Fantastic Anna (Fantastic Light). February 11. Fourth foal. €20,000Y. Tattersalls Ireland September. Charlie Gordon-Watson. Half-brother to the quite useful 4-y-o 1m and 12f winner Sharalam (by Alamshar). The dam, a minor 3-y-o winner in Italy, is a half-sister to 5 other minor winners. The second dam, Vlaanderen (by In The Wings), a minor French 3-y-o winner, is a half-sister to 10 winners including the multiple Group 3 winning stayer Solo Mio. (Never So Bold Partnership). "He certainly doesn't have the pedigree of a 2-y-o, but he's galloping already and he's so far forward it's ridiculous. A really nice, flashy chestnut with a lovely attitude, he's not very big which is why he's quite forward but he has a beautiful action and finds everything easy. He could be a really fun horse, starting at six furlongs". TRAINERS' BARGAIN BUY

593. LADY OF ARAN ★★★

b.f. Sir Prancealot – Tipperary Boutique (Danehill Dancer). March 13. Fourth foal. €24,000Y. Tattersalls Ireland September. Charlie Gordon-Watson. Half-sister to the Italian 2-y-o winner and Group 3 1m Premio Dormello second Identity Run Fast (by Footstepsinthesand). The dam, a quite useful 2-y-o 7f winner, is a half-sister to 4 winners here and abroad. The second dam, Moselle (by Mtoto), won the listed Virginia Stakes and the listed Middleton Stakes and is a half-sister to 5 winners. (O'Callaghan, Bengough, Horsford & Capon). "She's a good-looking filly but she's just growing now and gone a bit weak. She's got a very nice mind, she's good-looking, strong and will be a very good-looking filly come August".

594. TREASURE ME ★★★

b.f. Poet's Voice – Treasured Dream (Oasis Dream). January 30. Second foal. The dam is an unplaced half-sister to 3 winners including the listed Esher Stakes winner King Of Wands. The second dam, Maid To Treasure (by Rainbow Quest), a fair 7f (at 2 yrs) and 10f placed maiden, is a half-sister to 8 winners. (Normandie Stud). "A lovely, big, powerful filly. She's quite typical of her sire and although she hasn't been with me long she's very relaxed and straightforward. Looks like a very nice *type but it's early days, she's a powerful filly and I'm very happy with her".*

595. VICE MARSHAL ★★★★
b.c. Wootton Bassett – Celsius Degre (Verglas). January 12. First foal. £38,000Y. Goffs UK Premier (Doncaster). Charlie Gordon-Watson. The dam won two minor races in France and is a half-sister to 3 winners. The second dam, Celebre Fragrance (by Peintre Celebre), is an unplaced half-sister to 7 winners including Fragrant Mix (Group 1 Grand Prix de Saint-Cloud) and Alpine Rose (Prix Jean Romanet). (Frost, Gouthier & Hughes). *"A gorgeous horse, probably the best looking of mine. He's very laid back, very straightforward and doesn't know he's a racehorse yet but he's about to go into fast work. Just a nice looking 2-y-o and I hope he's as good as he looks".*

596. UNNAMED ★★★★
b.c. Frankel – Funny Girl (Darshaan). April 9. Twelfth foal. €300,000Y. Arqana Deauville August. Al Attiyah Khalifa Bin Hamad. Half-brother to 7 winners including the Group 2 1m Prix de Sandringham winner of 4 races Laugh Out Loud (by Clodovil), the useful 6f (at 2 yrs), 10f and listed 12f winner of 6 races Suzi's Decision (by Act One), the fairly useful 10f and 12f winner of 4 races Pippa Greene (by Galileo) and the fair 5f winner of 3 races Brynfa Boy (by Namid). The dam was placed from 7f to 9f and is a half-sister to 2 winners out of the minor German winner Just For Fun (by Lead On Time), herself a sister to listed winner Judge Decision. (Mohammed Bin Hamad Al Attiyah). *"He's only just come to me and he's an average sized colt, very good-looking with a deep girth. It's a bit early to judge him on his character but I think he's just one of those that wants to get on with it, but I think that's just typical of the sire. He'll definitely be a 2-y-o, I won't be hanging around with him and looking at him now I'd say he'll be a mid-season type. It's great to have a horse with such a nice pedigree in the yard".*

597. UNNAMED ★★★
b.c. Redoute's Choice – Navajo Queen (Monsun). January 1. Third foal. 55,000Y. Tattersalls October Book 1. Charlie Gordon-Watson. Half-brother to a minor German

3-y-o winner by Dashing Blade. The dam, a minor German 3-y-o winner, is a sister to Novellist (four Group 1 wins including the King George VI and Queen Elizabeth Stakes) and a half-sister to 5 winners. The second dam, Night Lagoon (by Lagunas), a champion German 2-y-o filly and Group 3 winner, is a half-sister to the Group 1 German Derby second Night Tango. (Mr K F V Kong). *"He has a good pedigree and I thought he was cheap for a Book One yearling. He's a nice type, he's going well, switched off at the moment but he'll be going into faster work soon. He's quite long bodied, which may have put a few people off at the sales, but he's strong and well-made. I'd say he'll be ready for a run by the end of May".*

598. UNNAMED ★★
ch.c. Exceed And Excel – Overturned (Cape Cross). February 22. Third foal. The dam, a minor 3-y-o winner in France, is a sister to the listed 1m winner and Group 1 Falmouth Stakes and Group 1 Sun Chariot Stakes third Musicanna and a half-sister to 8 winners. The second dam, Upend (by Main Reef), winner of the Group 3 St Simon Stakes and second in the Group 3 Princess Royal Stakes, is a half-sister to 6 winners including the dam of the high-class stayer and champion hurdler Royal Gait. (Three Of A Kind). *"A lovely, big, scopey individual, but he's a 3-y-o in the making. I'd still put him in the book because he's very athletic, has a lovely mind and he'll have a run or two at the back-end. He's just ticking over for now but he's a lovely individual".*

599. UNNAMED ★★
b.c. Cape Cross – Sayyedati Symphony (Gone West). April 5. Fifth foal. Half-brother to the fair UAE dual 6f winner Dear Rashid (by Exceed And Excel). The dam was placed at 2 and 3 yrs and is a half-sister to 5 winners including the Group 2 Champagne Stakes winner Almushahar. The second dam, Sayyedati (by Shadeed), was a high-class winner of five Group 1's at 2 and 3 yrs. (Mohammed Obaida). *"Another one for the second part of the season, but he's a nice horse, really good-looking and he's a nice size. He can be a bit buzzy now and again but he's pretty straightforward and I'd say he'd be one for August at the earliest".*

600. UNNAMED ★★★
b.f. Galileo – Secrete (Cape Cross).
March 18. Second foal. €380,000Y. Arqana
Deauville August. Al Attiyah Mohammed bin
Hamad bin Khalifa. The dam, unplaced in one
start, is a half-sister to 7 winners including
Plumania (Group 1 Grand Prix de Saint-Cloud)
and Balladeuse (Group 2 Prix de Royallieu).
The second dam, Featherquest (by Rainbow
Quest), a minor winner in France, is a half-
sister to the Group 1 Prix Lupin winner and
sire Groom Dancer. (Mohammed Bin Hamad
Al Attiyah). *"She hasn't been here very long
but she's a good-looking, straightforward filly,
not over big but just a nice size and she should
make into a 2-y-o for the second half of the
year".*

601. UNNAMED ★★★
b.c. Cacique – Slieve (Selkirk). February 2.
Seventh foal. 62,000Y. Tattersalls October
Book 2. Charlie Gordon-Watson. Brother to
the very smart 1m (at 2 yrs) and Group 3
13f Geoffrey Freer Stakes winner Census and
half-brother to the fairly useful 7f (including
at 2 yrs) and 6f winner of 11 races Amadeus
Wolfe Tone (by Amadeus Wolf). The dam is
an unraced sister to the Group 1 Gran Premio
di Milano winner Leadership and a half-sister
to 6 winners including Havant (Group 3 Oh
So Sharp Stakes). The second dam, Louella
(by El Gran Senor), is a placed half-sister to
7 minor winners in Europe and the USA. (Mr
K F V Kong). *"A good-looking horse and I'm
perplexed as to why there wasn't more interest
in him at the sales. He's a big boy and needs
time but he's a lovely looking type. I hope he'll
make into a nice 2-y-o at the back-end of the
year. A strong, powerful colt and we've got
time on our side with him".*

602. UNNAMED ★★★★
b.f. Mastercraftsman – Souter's Sister (Desert
Style). February 11. Third foal. Half-sister to
the fair 1m and 10.5f winner of 4 races Mia
Tesoro (by Danehill Dancer). The dam, a
useful 2-y-o Group 3 7f Oh So Sharp Stakes
winner, is a half-sister to several winners
including the fairly useful 5f (at 2 yrs) to 7f
winner of 3 races Premier Fantasy. The second
dam, Hemaca (Distinctly North), was unraced.
(Mr Deron Pearson). *"I think she's got a bit
more substance and quality that her older*
*sister Mia Tesoro. I won four on the bounce
with her last year. This is a lovely filly, a good
size, one for the second half of the season but
she's strong and I really like her".*

JAMES GIVEN

603. BAILEYS ROCKSTAR ★★
b.f. Rock Of Gibraltar – Biased (Haafhd).
March 20. Fourth foal. 22,000Y. Tattersalls
October Book 3. James Given. The dam, a
French 10f winner of 3 races, was listed-
placed twice and is a half-sister to 6 winners
including the French Group 3 Prix Exbury
winner and dual Group 2 second Court
Canibal. The second dam, Pas d'Heure (by
Arazi), a minor French 3-y-o winner, is a
half-sister to 8 minor winners. (Baileys Horse
Feed). *"Just going through a growing phase at
the moment, she's lengthened quite a bit and
she's a nice-moving horse for a bit later in the
season. So she's a work in progress".*

604. BLYTON LASS ★★
ch.f. Havana Gold – Cesseras (Cape Cross).
March 8. Third foal. 6,000Y. Tattersalls
October Book 3. James Given Racing. Half-
sister to the moderate 2016 6f to 1m placed
2-y-o Amy Gardner (by Bated Breath). The
dam, a minor French 3-y-o winner, is a sister
to the smart 6f, 7f (both at 2 yrs) and Group
3 9f Darley Stakes winner and Group 1 1m
Racing Post Trophy second Charlie Farnsbarns
and a half-sister to 2 minor winners. The
second dam, Lafleur (by Grand Lodge), is an
unplaced half-sister to 10 winners including
the listed winners and Group 1 placed Crown
Of Light and Alboostan. (Mr A Clarke). *"We
had her half-sister Amy Gardner last year,
she started off in early July over five furlongs
and progressed gradually to a mile. This filly
won't be particularly early either, although
everything she does she does well and I see
her starting at six furlongs and then going
seven. We have three Havana Gold 2-y-o's
and they all take everything in their stride,
they just get on with it. I trained Havana
Gold's dam, Jessica's Dream, and she was just
the same – an absolute sweetie and there was
never an argument".*

605. DORCAS ★★★
b.f. Havana Gold – Mortitia (Dansili).
February 27. Second foal. £8,500Y. Goffs UK
Autumn. James Given. The dam was a fairly

useful 2-y-o 6f winner. The second dam, Simianna (by Bluegrass Prince), a fairly useful listed 6f winner of 5 races from 2 to 5 yrs and second in the Group 3 Ballyogan Stakes, is a half-sister to 2 winners. (Mrs S Oliver). *"She's working now, she's quite forward, precocious and willing to please. She could easily be running in mid-May and although she's not a big filly she's strong. Hopefully she'll follow her mother and win as a 2-y-o".* TRAINERS' BARGAIN BUY

606. MISS MOLLIE ★★★
b.f. Havana Gold – Erebis (Green Desert). March 28. First foal. The dam is an unraced half-sister to the smart dual Group 3 5f winner Moorhouse Lad and to the useful 5f (including at 2 yrs) and 6f winner of 5 races Off The Record. The second dam, Record Time (by Clantime), a fair 5f winner at 3 and 4 yrs, is a sister to the listed winning sprinter Lago Di Varano and a half-sister to 3 winners. (Ingram Racing). *"We trained the dam's half-brother Off The Record as well as Havana Gold's dam Jessica's Dream, so we have a strong connection with this filly. The dam met with an accident in the paddock due to the owner's neighbour setting off fireworks and frightening her, so as a result she wasn't able to race. This filly is a bit small, looks like a sprinter but because she's still growing she won't be that precocious. Once she's ready I don't think she'll take long to come to hand and she'll be speedy".*

607. MISTRESS OF VENICE ★★★
b.f. Bated Breath – Rohlindi (Red Ransom). February 24. Second foal. £27,500Y. Goffs UK Premier (Doncaster). J Portman & Stroud/ Coleman (private sale). Half-sister to the quite useful 2016 dual 7f placed 2-y-o War Of Succession (by Casamento). The dam, a modest 5.5f placed maiden, is a half-sister to 8 winners including the listed 7f winner Kalindi (herself the dam of 3 stakes winners) and the useful 6f and 7f winners Mahmoom and Tayseer. The second dam, Rohita (by Waajib), a fairly useful 2-y-o 5f and 6f winner, was third in the Group 3 6f Cherry Hinton Stakes and is a half-sister to 5 winners. (Cool Silk Partnership). *"She was very nervy at the sales and I think that's why she slipped through the gaps a bit and we bought her*

privately afterwards. The boys did a great job with her during the winter, gaining her trust and getting her used to people. She'll be racing in April, she's sharp has done a few bits of work now and shows a good bit of speed, so I'm very happy with her".*

608. MOUNT VICTORIA (IRE) ★★★
b.f. Arakan – Salingers Star (Catcher In The Rye). January 21. Second foal. The dam, a fair 2-y-o 6f winner, is a sister to one winner and a half-sister to 4 winners. The second dam, Head For The Stars (by Head For Heights), is an unplaced half-sister to 2 minor winners. (T Gibbons & T Gaunt Partnership). *"She's sharp and she'll be racing in April. Five furlongs will be fine for her but her dam won over six and she might well go six a bit later on too. She's very forward and ready to go".*

609. REACTIVE ★★
ch.c. Cityscape – Hollowina (Beat Hollow). March 6. First foal. The dam, a quite useful 2-y-o 1m winner, is a half-sister to 3 winners including the listed 11f winner and dual Group 3 placed Medrano. The second dam, Trick Or Treat (by Lomitas), a winner of 7 races including the Group 3 12f Princess Royal Stakes and the listed Pinnacle Stakes, was third in the Group 1 Yorkshire Oaks and is a half-sister to 3 winners. (Peter Onslow). *"A very nice horse but he's big and very much a work in progress. He's one of those that looks so much better from the side because from behind he looks a bit narrow and weak, but that's just because he's developing. Since the turn of the year we've been pleased with the way he's come on, he has a lovely big stride on him and a good attitude. I trained his grandam Trick Or Treat who was very smart. I should think this colt will be seen to better effect next season, but we'll hopefully get him out in the autumn over seven furlongs or a mile".*

610. UNNAMED ★★★★
b.c. Shamardal – Airline Hostess (Sadler's Wells). March 4. Fourth foal. 50,000Y. Tattersalls October Book 1. Not sold. Brother to the modest 2016 Irish 7f placed 2-y-o Cloudy Miss and half-brother to the minor French 12f winner Amami (by Peintre Celebre). The dam is an unplaced sister to the

French listed 11f winner and multiple Group 1 placed Argentina. The second dam, Airline (by Woodman), won the listed Prix de la Cochere and is a full or half-sister to four stakes winners including the Group 3 winners Article Rare and Android. (Mr A Owen). *"A lovely horse, it's very nice to have a Shamardal and particularly one out of a Sadler's Wells mare as I believe that's the best nick. He was bought privately after the sale because he had slack pasterns, but they have improved somewhat since then and he's had no issues with them throughout the winter. A mighty fine, good-topped, athletic horse, he's not one to rush obviously but he canters well, does everything asked of him easily and he has a level head on him. A 3-y-o in the making, but I'd expect him to be out in the second half of the season over seven furlongs or a mile".*

611. UNNAMED ★★★
b.c. Society Rock – Gift Time (Cadeaux Genereux). April 29. Fourth foal. £75,000 2-y-o. Goffs UK Breeze Up (Doncaster). Cool Silk & Stroud/Coleman. The dam is an unraced half-sister to 6 minor winners. The second dam, Watchkeeper (by Rudimentary), a modest triple 10f winner, is a half-sister to 5 winners including Savannah Belle (the dam of three stakes winners including the Group 2 Celebration Mile winner Dubawi Gold). (Cool Silk Partnership). *"A sharp horse, he did a fast breeze and I'd expect him to be racing in May. When they come here from the breeze up sale you have to give them a little break and watch them for a week or so. The sales prep can be quite intense and you need to check they're eating well, that sort of thing. Some vendors will drill their 2-y-o's much more than others, so you'd prefer one that leaves plenty left in the tank".*

612. UNNAMED ★★★★
b.c. Swiss Spirit – Marmot Bay (Kodiac). February 25. First foal. £78,000 2-y-o. Goffs UK Breeze Up (Doncaster). Cool Silk & Stroud/Coleman. The dam, a modest 2-y-o triple 6f winner, is a half-sister to 4 winners (three of them at 2 yrs). The second dam, Tides (by Bahamian Bounty), is an unplaced half-sister to 5 winners including the listed winner Amazing Bay. (Cool Silk Partnership). *"A first foal but a decent-sized horse, he breezed*

nicely and for a breeze-up horse seems very level headed. There's a lot of speed in the pedigree and he's likely to be out in May".

613. UNNAMED ★★
b.c. Delegator – Mosa Mine (Exceed And Excel). April 11. Second foal. 8,000 foal. Tattersalls December. Gill Bostwick. Half-brother to the modest 2-y-o 5f winner Lady Kheleyf (by Kheleyf). The dam, a moderate 5f placed maiden, half-sister to 5 winners including the very useful 7f winner of 4 races here and in the UAE Sirocco Breeze. The second dam, Baldemosa (by Lead On Time), won over 1m in France at 3 yrs and is a half-sister to 4 winners including the Group 1 5.5f Prix Robert Papin winner Balbonella (herself dam of the top-class sprinter and sire Anabaa, the French 1,000 Guineas winner Always Loyal and the sire Key Of Luck). (Tim Bostwick). *"A strong-looking horse, he had a setback which made him miss the yearling sale and we didn't get him until February. I like him a lot and he's an athletic sort but obviously we haven't done much with him. I think he's likely to make a 2-y-o although we haven't been able to see any real evidence yet".*

JOHN GOSDEN

614. ALAQRAB ★★★ ♠
b.c. Speightstown – Albamara (Galileo). March 16. First foal. 525,000Y. Tattersalls October Book 1. Shadwell Estate Co. The dam, a quite useful 2-y-o 9f winner, was listed-placed three times and is a half-sister to 5 winners including the listed winners All At Sea, Algometer and Alwilda. The second dam, Albanova (by Alzao), a triple Group 1 12f winner in Germany, is a sister to the dual Champion Stakes winner Alborada and a half-sister to 7 winners. (Hamdan Al Maktoum). *"The type for seven furlongs and a mile in the autumn. He won't be a sprinter, there's a lot of the dam's side in him".*

615. ALMOGHARED (IRE) ★★★
b.c. Dansili – Ezima (Sadler's Wells). February 7. Half-brother to the 1m (at 2 yrs), Group 1 12f Epsom Oaks and Group 1 12f King George VI winner Taghrooda and to the fairly useful 12f winner Taqaareed (both by Sea The Stars). The dam, a smart 1m, listed 10f and listed 12f winner, is a full or half-sister to 3 winners

including the listed placed Ezalli. The second dam, Ezilla (by Darshaan), is an unraced sister to the top-class broodmare Ebaziya, a triple listed winner from winner from 7f (at 2 yrs) to 12f in Ireland (herself dam of the Group 1 winners Edabiya, Ebadiyla and Enzeli) and a half-sister to 7 winners. (Hamdan Al Maktoum). *"He'd be a horse for the autumn, particularly as he's out of that mare and I can see him going straight to a mile".*

616. ATYAAF ★★★★
b.c. Invincible Spirit – Eshaadeh (Storm Cat). April 11. Half-brother to Loujain (by Dubawi), placed third over 7f on her only starts at 2 yrs in 2016 and to the very useful 2-y-o Group 2 5f Queen Mary Stakes winner and Group 1 6f Cheveley Park Stakes third Maqaasid (by Green Desert). The dam, unplaced in two starts, is a half-sister to 7 winners including the 1,000 Guineas and Coronation Stakes winner Ghanaati and the Group 3 12f Cumberland Lodge Stakes winner Mawatheeq. The second dam, Sarayir (by Mr Prospector), a listed 1m winner, is closely related to the top-class Champion Stakes winner Nayef and a half-sister to the 2,000 Guineas, Eclipse, Derby and King George winner Nashwan. (Hamdan Al Maktoum). *"He did a little half-speed this morning so he's a forward type – as the pedigree would suggest. He goes fine and I'm perfectly happy with him, so I'd be hoping to run him in May".*

617. BEN VRACKIE ★★★
b.c. Frankel – Kinnaird (Dr Devious). March 14. Eighth foal. 450,000Y. Tattersalls October Book 1. Blandford Bloodstock. Half-brother to the Group 2 Royal Lodge Stakes and Group 3 Darley Stakes winner Berkshire (by Mount Nelson), to the very useful 1m (at 2 yrs) and 10.5f winner and dual listed-placed Abdon (by Cacique), the quite useful dual 1m winner Keene Dancer (by Danehill Dancer) and the fair 10f and 12f winner Keenes Royale (by Red Ransom and herself dam of the 2-y-o dual Group 2 winner Ivawood). The dam won the Group 1 Prix de l'Opera and the Group 3 May Hill Stakes and is a half-sister to the Group 3 Chester Vase winner Mickdaam. The second dam, Ribot's Guest (by Be My Guest), is an unplaced half-sister to 6 winners. *"A big, rangy horse, I'm very happy with him but he's*

going to be one for the end of the season and next year".

618. BURLINGTON (IRE) ★★★
b.c. Zoffany – Peig (Refuse To Bend). January 18. First foal. €130,000Y. Goffs Orby. John & Jake Warren. The dam is an unraced half-sister to 8 winners including the US Grade 1 Gulfstream Park Breeders' Cup Handicap and Group 2 King Edward VII Stakes winner Subtle Power and the UAE dual Grade 1 placed Mutahadee. The second dam, Mosaique Bleue (by Shirley Heights), is an unraced half-sister to the Prix Royal-Oak winner Mersey and to the 10f Prix Saint-Alary winner Muncie. *"He's grown and is weak at the moment, but he's doing his canters and he's a January foal so I'll be thinking about him in mid-season".*

619. CASSINI (IRE) ★★★★
b.c. Galileo – Chrysanthemum (Danehill Dancer). January 12. Second foal. Closely related to the useful 2016 2-y-o 6f winner and triple listed-placed Cunco (by Frankel). The dam, a winner of 5 races including the 2-y-o Group 3 7f C L Weld Park Stakes and the Group 3 Park Express Stakes, was third in the Group1 Pretty Polly Stakes and is a half-sister to 2 winners. The second dam, Well Spoken (by Sadler's Wells), a jumps winner in France, is a half-sister to 6 winners. *"A good-looking horse and a brother to Cunco. He's attractive, a good mover and a nice type, but we're talking about a horse that will want middle-distances next year".*

620. CULPABILITY (IRE) ★★★★
b.c. Blame – Princess Consort (Dixieland Band). April 1. Seventh foal. $350,000Y. Keeneland September. Blandford Bloodstock. Closely related to the 2-y-o Group 3 Oh So Sharp Stakes and US Grade 3 Beaugay Stakes winner Waterway Run (by Arch) and half-brother to 4 winners including the US stakes-placed King Of New York (by Street Boss). The dam is an unplaced half-sister to one winner. The second dam, Camella (by Housebuster), a US stakes winner of 7 races from 2 to 5 yrs, is a half-sister to 4 winners. *"A nice type of colt, he's well-balanced and a good mover. He should be running over six/seven furlongs and he's a nice type".*

621. DICHATO (USA) ★★★
b.c. Scat Daddy – Dolce Lemone (Lemon Drop Kid). February 11. Second foal. The dam, a minor winner at 3 yrs in Canada, is a half-sister to 8 winners including the stakes winner Noble Strike (dam of Canadian stakes winners Inglorious and Dixie Strike). The second dam, Green Noble (by Green Dancer), a stakes winner of 8 races in North America, is a half-sister to 10 winners including the US Grade 2 winner Abigailthewife. *"A nice colt, he's neat and well-balanced and will make a 2-y-o over six furlongs".*

622. DOSWELL (USA) ★★★
br.c. Giant's Causeway – Ballet Pacifica (Minardi). May 26. Sixth foal. Brother to the US Grade 3 9f third Entrechat. The dam, a 7f (at 2 yrs) and French listed 10f winner, is a half-sister to the Group 1 Santa Anita Oaks winner Ariege. The second dam, Kostroma (by Caerleon), won three Grade 1 events in the USA and is a half-sister to Grise Mine (Group 1 Prix Saint-Alary). *"A good-moving, well-balanced horse, he's likeable and one for mid-season over seven furlongs".*

623. EMARAATY ★★★
b.c. Dubawi – Zee Zee Top (Zafonic). April 2. Ninth foal. 2,600,000Y. Tattersalls October Book 1. Shadwell Estate Co. Half-brother to the 2014 7f placed 2-y-o Jazzy Top (by Danehill Dancer), to the Group 1 10f Pretty Polly Stakes and Group 1 10f Prix Jean Romanet winner Izzi Top (by Pivotal) and the fairly useful 1m to 11f winner of 4 races Rock N Roll Ransom (by Red Ransom). The dam won the Group 1 10f Prix de l'Opera and is a half-sister to the Group 1 winners Opera House and Kayf Tara and to the unraced dam of the Group 1 winner Necklace. The second dam, Colorspin (by High Top), won the Irish Oaks and is a half-sister to the Irish Champion Stakes winner Cezanne. *"He's athletic, light on his feet and moves well. Whether one would have him out in a six furlong maiden, or wait for seven which would be more logical, we'll have to wait and see. A nice, athletic colt".*

624. ENBIHAAR (IRE) ★★★
b.f. Redoute's Choice – Chanterelle (Trempolino). March 22. Fourth foal. €500,000Y. Arqana Deauville August. Shadwell

France. Half-sister to the fairly useful 1m winner and Group 2 Topkapi Trophy second Silent Attack and to the quite useful 8.5f (at 2 yrs) and 11f winner King Bolete (by Cape Cross). The dam ran once unplaced and is a sister to the multiple Grade 3 winner Cox Orange (dam of the 1,000 Guineas third Vista Bella) and a half-sister to 9 winners including the 2-y-o Group 1 Prix Marcel Boussac winner Amonita. The second dam, Spectacular Joke (by Spectacular Bid), won the Group 2 Prix Maurice de Gheest and the Group 3 Prix Maurice de Gheest. (Hamdan Al Maktoum). *"A big, powerful girl, she's showing signs of immaturity at the minute but she does everything very easily. Very much a filly for the second half of the year".*

625. FIRST ELEVEN ★★★
b.c. Frankel – Zenda (Zamindar). February 9. Eighth foal. Half-brother to the high-class Group 1 1m Irish 2,000 Guineas, St James's Palace Stakes, Sussex Stakes and Prix Jacques le Marois winner Kingman (by Invincible Spirit), to the smart Group 3 10f winner of 3 races Remote and the quite useful 7f winner Panzanella (both by Dansili). The dam won the French 1,000 Guineas, was second in the Coronation Stakes and the Grade 1 Queen Elizabeth II Challenge Cup at Keeneland and is a half-sister to the July Cup and Nunthorpe Stakes winner Oasis Dream and the dual listed 1m winner Hopeful Light. The second dam, Hope (by Dancing Brave), is an unraced sister to the Group 1 Irish Oaks winner Wemyss Bight. (Khalid Abdulla). *"He's fine, he's settled in well, I know the family well and he's a strong colt that's going along nicely at present. I don't want to rush him and I'd like to get him out in mid-season over six or seven furlongs".*

626. FLYING DEMON ★★★ ♠
gr.c. Nathaniel – Gossamer Seed (Choisir). February 9. Second foal. 140,000Y. Tattersalls October Book 1. David Redvers. The dam, winner of the Group 3 7f Athasi Stakes and third in the Group 3 Ballyogan Stakes, is a half-sister to 3 minor winners. The second dam, Light And Airy (by Linamix), is an unraced half-sister to 3 minor winners. *"A nice colt, he's well-balanced, he moves well and I see him starting in a seven furlong/mile maiden".*

627. GEORGE VILLIERS (IRE) ★★★★
b.c. Dubawi – Comic (Be My Chief). February
17. Eleventh foal. 750,000Y. Tattersalls
October Book 1. Blandford Bloodstock.
Brother to the fair 2-y-o 8.5f winner Nice
Future and half-brother to 6 winners
including the US dual Grade 1 winner
Laughing (by Dansili), the listed winner of
5 races here and Hong Kong dual Grade 1
winner Viva Pataca (by Marju) and the quite
useful 10f to 14f and hurdles winner Comedy
Act (by Motivator). The dam, a quite useful
10f and 11.5f winner, is a half-sister to 4
winners including the 2-y-o Group 3 Solario
Stakes and multiple US Grade 2 winner Brave
Act. The second dam, Circus Act (by Shirley
Heights), is an unraced sister to the listed
winner Lady Shipley and a half-sister to the
listed winner Ellie Ardensky. *"He moves very
well and he's fined down nicely because he
was quite a heavy colt. He's gone the right
way, he's an athletic chap and pleasing me in
everything he does. One for seven furlongs
plus".*

628. GLENCADAM MASTER ★★★★ ♠
ch.c. Mastercraftsman – Coquet (Sir Percy).
February 11. First foal. Tattersalls October
Book 1. Blandford Bloodstock. The dam,
a useful listed 1m (at 2 yrs) and listed 10f
winner, was third in the Group 3 Newbury
Arc Trial and is a half-sister to 2 winners.
The second dam, One So Marvellous (by
Nashwan), a fair 10f winner, is a sister to the
Juddmonte International winner One So
Wonderful (dam of the US Grade 2 winner
Sun Boat) and a half-sister to 7 winners
including Alnasr Alwasheek (Group 2 Dante
Stakes) and Relatively Special (Group 3
Rockfel Stakes). *"An attractive, well-balanced
colt that moves well. One for mid-season over
seven furlongs and he's likeable".*

629. GRATOT (FR) ★★
b.c. Le Havre – Absolute Lady (Galileo). April
27. Fifth foal. €520,000Y. Arqana Deauville
August. Blandford Bloodstock. Brother to the
Group 1 Prix de Diane and Group 1 French
1,000 Guineas winner La Cressonniere. The
dam is a placed sister to the useful 1m (here)
and US stakes winner and third in the Group
2 10f Blandford Stakes and is a half-sister to
4 winners. The second dam, Lil's Jessy (by

Kris), won 4 races at 2 and 3 yrs including
the Group 3 7f Nell Gwyn Stakes and is a
half-sister to 9 winners including the smart
French 1m listed winner Lone Bid. *"A big,
rangy colt that's immature at present as you
would expect from his pedigree. He's all about
middle-distances at three and he'll hopefully
have a couple of runs in the autumn".*

630. ITQAN (IRE) ★★★★ ♠
gr.f. Dark Angel – Prodigal Daughter
(Alhaarth). March 25. Sixth foal. 400,000Y.
Tattersalls October Book 1. Shadwell Estate
Co. Half-sister to the very useful 2-y-o Group
3 7f Horris Hill Stakes winner Carnaby Street
(by Le Vie Dei Colori) and to the Swedish
winner at 2 and 3 yrs Kodiac King (by Kodiac)
and another minor winner abroad by Poet's
Voice. The dam is an unraced half-sister to
2 minor winners. The second dam, Shallow
Ground (by Common Grounds), a listed-
placed 6f winner in Ireland, is a half-sister to
5 winners including the US Grade 2 winner
Shanawi and the dam of the Australian
Group 1 winner Brazilian Pulse. (Hamdan Al
Maktoum). *"An attractive, well-balanced filly,
she moves well and is a nice type of filly. I'm
not going to rush her forward but I'd hope to
have her on the track in mid-season".*

631. JAWWAAL ★★★★ ♠
ch.c. Bahamian Bounty – Avenbury (Mount
Nelson). January 26. First foal. £140,000Y.
Goffs UK Premier (Doncaster). Shadwell Estate
Co. The dam is an unraced half-sister to 5
winners including Ouqba (Group 3 Jersey
Stakes). The second dam, Dancing Mirage (by
Machiavellian), a quite useful 2-y-o 7f winner,
is a half-sister to 4 winners including the dam
of the good Hong Kong horse Housemaster.
(Hamdan Al Maktoum). *"He's a big, powerful
horse that goes well. I'll probably wait for
the six furlong maidens but hopefully he'll be
ready for those".*

632. JULIET CAPULET ★★★★
b.f. Dark Angel – Capulet Monteque
(Camacho). March 13. Third foal. €235,000Y.
Goffs Orby. Cheveley Park Stud. Sister to the
modest 2016 7f placed maiden Teqany and
to the fairly useful Irish listed-placed 2-y-o 6f
winner Juliette Fair. The dam, a quite useful
5f and 6f placed maiden in Ireland, won at 3

yrs in Qatar and is a half-sister to 8 winners including the listed Scarbrough Stakes winner and Group 2 King's Stand Stakes second Flanders (dam of the Group 1 Haydock Park Sprint Cup winner G Force) and to the dam of the dam of the dual Group 1 winning sprinter Lethal Force. The second dam, Family at War (by Explodent), a fair 2-y-o 5f winner, is a half-sister to 4 minor winners in the USA. (Cheveley Park Stud). *"She's an active filly, she moves nicely and there's no reason not to be running her over six furlongs in May. She's going the right way".*

633. LAH TI DAR ★★★

b.f. Dubawi – Dar Re Mi (Singspiel). March 22. Fourth foal. Sister to the very smart 1m (at 2 yrs) and Group 3 10.5f Musidora Stakes winner So Mi Dar (by Dubawi) and half-sister to the 7f (at 2 yrs) and 10f winner and multiple Group 3 placed De Treville (by Oasis Dream). The dam won the Pretty Polly Stakes, Dubai Sheema Classic and Yorkshire Oaks (all Group 1 events) and is a half-sister to 9 winners including the Group 1 winners Rewilding, Diaghilev and Darazari. The second dam, Darara (by Top Ville), won the Group 1 Prix Vermeille and is a half-sister to 11 winners including the French Derby winner and high-class sire Darshaan. *"She's a big, rangy filly and about to have a break for six weeks. A filly for the back-end, she's all about what happens as a 3-y-o".*

634. LAST PEARL ★★★

ch.f. Sepoy – Swain's Gold (Swain). May 4. Eighth foal. 200,000Y. Tattersalls October Book 1. Blandford Bloodstock. Half-sister to the Group 1 Irish Derby and Group 3 September Stakes winner and Derby second Jack Hobbs (by Halling), to the useful 9f to 11f winner and Group 3 Brigadier Gerard Stakes third Niceofyoutotell me (by Hernando), the fairly useful 7f (at 2 yrs) and 1m winner Manson (by Equiano) and the fair 6f and 7f winner Mrs Greeley (by Mr Greeley). The dam won 3 minor races at 3 yrs in the USA and is a half-sister to a US stakes winner. The second dam, Golden Pond (by Don't Forget Me), won the Grade 2 12f Orchid Handicap and the Grade 3 8.5f Suwannee River Handicap and is a half-sister to 3 winners. *"She's done well, going the right*

way and I'm very happy with her. A nice type of filly, she won't be making her debut in December like her brother did, but she should be running in the autumn".

635. MAGNETIC BOUNDARY (USA) ★★★

ch.c. Union Rags – Enthused (Seeking The Gold). February 17. Half-brother to the very useful 2-y-o Group 3 6f Round Tower Stakes winner and Group 2 6f Criterium de Maisons-Laffitte second Norman Invasion (by War Chant), to the useful 1m winner and subsequent US Grade 3 turf 8.5f second Ea (by Dynaformer), the fairly useful 1m (at 2 yrs) and 10f winner Flow, the quite useful dual 1m winner Galvanise (both by Medaglia D'Oro) and the quite useful 2-y-o dual 6f winner Erytheis (by Theatrical). The dam won the Group 2 6f Lowther Stakes and the Group 3 6f Princess Margaret Stakes and is a half-sister to the listed 12f Prix Vulcain winner From Beyond. The second dam, Magic Of Life (by Seattle Slew), won the Group 1 1m Coronation Stakes and the Group 2 Mill Reef Stakes and is a half-sister to 4 winners. (Niarchos Family). *"He's grown a lot and has gone through a weak stage. There's no harm in that because they can do that at this time of year. I'll just let him do easy canters now and wait for him to come. Probably an August time horse".* The sire, a son of Dixie Union, won the Grade 1 Champagne Stakes and Belmont Stakes. Sire of two Grade 1 winners in his first crop in 2016.

637. MARECHAL NEY ★★★ ♣

b.c. Frankel – Hidden Hope (Daylami). March 16. Half-brother to the useful 1m (at 2 yrs), 10f and listed 12f winner Our Obsession (by Shamardal), to the fairly useful dual 1m winner Westwiththenight (by Cape Cross), the quite useful dual 12f winner Dawn Horizons (by New Approach) and the modest 11f winner Fine Style (by Pivotal). The dam, a useful listed 11.4f Cheshire Oaks winner, is a half-sister to 9 winners including Rebecca Sharp (Group 1 1m Coronation Stakes) and the Group 3 Lingfield Derby Trial winner Mystic Knight. The second dam, Nuryana (by Nureyev), a useful winner of the listed 1m Grand Metropolitan Stakes, is a half-sister to 5 winners. (Mr A E Oppenheimer). *"A nice colt for the middle of the season. We need to patient with him and wait for seven furlongs".*

638. MIQYAAS ★★★★
b.c. Oasis Dream – Fawaayed (Singspiel). February 2. Second foal. The dam is an unraced half-sister to the Group 2 5f Queen Mary Stakes winner Maqaasid. The second dam, Eshaadeh (by Storm Cat), unplaced in 2 starts, is a half-sister to 7 winners including the 1,000 Guineas winner Ghanaati and the Group 1 placed Mawatheeq and Rumoush. (Hamdan Al Maktoum). *"A nice type and a forward colt, he did a little half speed this morning, I like him and I'd hope to have him out in late April/early May".*

639. NAWAASI ★★★★
b.f. Dubawi – Maqaasid (Green Desert). January 26. Third foal. Half-sister to Luqyaa (by Smart Strike), placed third over 7f on her only start at 2 yrs in 2016. The dam, a very useful 2-y-o Group 2 5f Queen Mary Stakes winner, was third in the Group 1 6f Cheveley Park Stakes. The second dam, Eshaadeh (by Storm Cat), unplaced in 2 starts, is a half-sister to 7 winners including the 1,000 Guineas and Coronation Stakes winner Ghanaati and the Group 3 12f Cumberland Lodge Stakes winner Mawatheeq. (Hamdan Al Maktoum). *"A nice, strong type which is just what you'd expect out of the mare and I'm happy with her at this stage, but we're probably heading for seven furlongs with her in mid-season".*

640. ODE TO AUTUMN ★★★
br.c. Showcasing – Turning Leaf (Last Tycoon). March 23. Thirteenth foal. 220,000Y. Tattersalls October Book 2. Blandford Bloodstock. Half-brother to 5 winners including the German 3-y-o Group 3 1m and listed 11f winner Turning Light (by Fantastic Light and herself dam of the US stakes winner Surrey Star), the fairly useful 2-y-o 7f winner and listed-placed Oxsana (by Dubawi) and the quite useful 2-y-o 6f winner Exceptionelle (by Exceed And Excel). The dam, a German 2-y-o winner and third in the Group 2 German 1,000 Guineas, is a half-sister to 6 winners. The second dam, Tamacana (by Windwurf), a German listed winner of 3 races at 2 and 3 yrs, is a half-sister to 4 winners. *"He's done a lot of growing and it's a staying family. I don't want to run away with the idea that because he's by Showcasing I've got to go early. I'll probably set him off over six furlongs and then go seven".*

641. PERFECTION ★★★
ch.f. Dutch Art – Cantal (Pivotal). February 21. Second foal. Sister to the fair 2016 2-y-o 8.5f winner, from two starts, Munawer. The dam, a fair 2-y-o 7f winner, is a half-sister to 3 winners including the 2-y-o Group 3 7f winner Horris Hill Stakes winner Evasive. The second dam, Canda (by Storm Cat), is an unraced half-sister to 3 winners including the 2-y-o Group 3 5.5f Prix d'Arenburg winner Moon Driver and the Grade 2 Californian Stakes second Mojave Moon. (Cheveley Park Stud). *"She's a grand sort of filly but she's not going to be precocious. A back-end of the season type of 2-y-o".*

642. PETIT PALAIS ★★★ ♠
ch.c. Champs Elysees – Galicuix (Galileo). March 10. Third foal. 220,000Y. Tattersalls October Book 1. Blandford Bloodstock. Half-brother to the Group 1 2,000 Guineas and Group 1 St James's Palace Stakes winner Galileo Gold (by Paco Boy). The dam ran twice unplaced and is a half-sister to the Group 1 Prix de l'Abbaye and Group 1 King's Stand Stakes winner Goldream. The second dam, Clizia (by Machiavellian), is an unraced half-sister to 3 winners including the multiple listed winner and Group 2 placed Mont Rocher. *"He's done well this horse, he's taken a good shape since the sale, he moves well and I'm happy with him. Nevertheless with his pedigree I still think he's all about next year".*

643. PLAYFULL SPIRIT ★★★
b.f. Invincible Spirit – Annabelle's Charm (Indian Ridge). March 12. Fourth foal. Closely related to the 2-y-o Group 1 6f Middle Park Stakes winner of 4 races Charming Thought (by Oasis Dream) and half-sister to the quite useful 5f and 6f winner Spanish City (by Exceed And Excel). The dam, a very useful listed 1m winner, was Group 3 placed twice over 1m and is a half-sister to 5 winners including the fairly useful 2-y-o 7f winner and listed UAE 1,000 Guineas third Purple Sage. The second dam, Kylemore (by Sadler's Wells), ran twice unplaced and is a sister to the dual Group 1 winner Ballingarry and to the Racing Post Trophy winner Aristotle and a half-sister to the St James's Palace Stakes and Prix Jean Prat winner Starborough. *"She's very well-named because she has plenty of energy*

and she'll come to hand from the middle of the season onwards. A very lively filly".

644. SALTY SUGAR ★★★
b.f. Oasis Dream – Shamandar (Exceed And Excel). March 6. Second foal. 120,000Y. Tattersalls October Book 1. S Hillen. The dam, a fairly useful listed 6f winner of 3 races, is a half-sister to the listed winner and Group 3 second Hung Parliament. The second dam, Sensational Mover (by Theatrical), a moderate 12f placed maiden, is a half-sister to 5 winners. *"A forward going filly, I'd hope to be running her in May and she's going the right way".*

645. SEEING STARS (USA) ★★★ ♠
ch.c. Tapit – Rainbow View (Dynaformer). February 19. Second foal. The dam won the Group 1 Fillies' Mile and the Group 1 1m Matron Stakes and is a half-sister to the Canadian Grade 1 winner Just As Well, the 7f (at 2 yrs) and US Grade 2 8.5f winner Utley and the US Grade 3 9f and Grade 3 12f winner Winter View. The second dam, No Matter What (by Nureyev), winner of the Grade 1 Del Mar Oaks, is a half-sister to the Grade 2 Suburban Handicap and Grade 2 Dwyer Stakes winner E Dubai. *"A nice colt, he's a good mover and I know the sire isn't an obvious one for the UK but his mother was. A nice, active colt with plenty of white about him".*

646. SENSORY (IRE) ★★★
gr.f. Dream Ahead – Dookus (Linamix). April 23. Sixth foal. 170,000Y. Tattersalls October Book 2. Cheveley Park Stud. Half-sister to the 2016 listed-placed 2-y-o Frankuus (by Frankel), to the 2-y-o Group 3 Prix Thomas Bryon winner and Group 1 Criterium International third US Law (by Lawman) and two minor winners in France by Lawman and Rip Van Winkle. The dam ran once unplaced and is a half-sister to 7 winners including the Irish 2-y-o listed 6f winner Pharmacist (herself the dam of four stakes winners including the Breeders' Cup Turf winner Red Rocks). The second dam, Pharaoh's Delight (by Fairy King), won the Group 1 5f Phoenix Stakes, was Group 1 placed four times and is a half-sister to 8 winners. *"She's quite a character – she has an opinion on everything, but she's active and moves well. She'll make a 2-y-o by mid-season".*

647. SHAKOUR ★★★
b.c. Declaration Of War – Another Storm (Gone West). May 9. Tenth foal. 250,000Y. Tattersalls October Book 1. Emirates Park. Half-brother to 6 winners including the 1m (at 2 yrs), Group 1 Ascot Gold Cup and Group 1 Irish St Leger winner Order Of St George (by Galileo), the 2-y-o 1m and subsequent French Group 3 1m winner Asperity (by War Chant), the US Grade 3 9f winner Angel Terrace (by Ghostzapper) and the Scandinavian listed 12f winner Sehoy (by Menifee). The dam, a minor US 2-y-o winner, is a half-sister to 3 winners including the Grade 1 second Trojan Nation. The second dam, Storm Song (by Summer Squall), was a dual Grade 1 winner and champion 2-y-o filly. *"A mid-season type, June/July, he's scopey and moves well".*

648. SHAWWAL ★★★ ♠
b.c. Harbour Watch – Orton Park (Moss Vale). January 27. First foal. £60,000Y. Goffs UK Premier (Doncaster). Shadwell Estate Co. The dam, a fair 2-y-o 5f winner, is a half-sister to 7 winners including the Group 3 Chipchase Stakes winner Knot In Wood. The second dam, Notley Park (by Wolfhound), placed three times over 7f at 3yrs, is a half-sister to 5 winners including the US Grade 3 winner Prince Bobby B and the listed 5f Scarborough Stakes winner Notley. *"He's the dam's first foal and he'll either be an early type or nothing, but we'll try our best with him".*

649. SUPPORTER ★★★
b.f. Dubawi – Very Good News (Empire Maker). February 19. Third foal. Half-sister to Weekender (by Frankel), placed fourth over 1m on his only start at 2 yrs in 2016. The dam is an unraced half-sister to the Grade 1 Matriarch Stakes and Grade 1 Beverly D Stakes winner Heat Haze, to the Coronation Stakes, Prix Jacques Le Marois and Breeders' Cup Filly & Mare Turf winner Banks Hill, the US Grade 1 winners Intercontinental, Champs Elysees and Cacique, and the Group 2 1m winner and top-class sire Dansili. The second dam, Hasili (by Kahyasi), won over 5f at 2 yrs and stayed a mile. (Khalid Abdulla). *"A nicely balanced filly, she's doing her canters and I'm happy with her. One for later in the season".*

650. THE MUMS ★★★
b.f. Holy Roman Emperor – Ballyalla (Mind Games). April 23. Fourth foal. 65,000Y. Tattersalls October Book 2. Blandford Bloodstock. Half-sister to the fair 2016 7f placed 2-y-o Heavenly Angel (by Dark Angel) and to the fair 5f and 6f winner of 3 races at 2 and 3 yrs Pixeleen (by Pastoral Pursuits). The dam, a quite useful 2-y-o 6f winner, is a half-sister to 7 winners including the smart 2-y-o dual 6f winner and Group 2 Mill Reef Stakes second Doctor Brown. The second dam, Molly Brown (by Rudimentary), a fairly useful 5f (at 2 yrs) and 6f winner, is a half-sister to 4 winners including the listed 1m Premio Nearco winner Stato King. *"She goes well and has done quite a bit of growing through the winter but she has a good action and I'd hope to be running her over six furlongs in late May/June".*

651. TIMPANI ★★★ ♣
ch.f. Raven's Pass – Fanny Cerrito (Gulch). February 20. Eleventh foal. 170,000Y. Tattersalls October Book 1. John & Jake Warren. Half-sister to 6 winners including the Irish 1m (at 2 yrs), 12f and German listed 14f winner and French dual Group 2 placed Poseidon Adventure, the Irish 2-y-o 1m winner and listed-placed Kisses For Me and the fairly useful Irish 11f winner Chirkova (all by Sadler's Wells). The dam is an unraced half-sister to 7 winners including the US stakes winners Al Sabin and Sabina. The second dam, Sabin (by Lyphard), won two Grade 1 events in the USA. *"She's an attractive, easy-moving filly and we'll be waiting for the seven furlong maidens, but she's light on her feet".*

652. TIVOLI (IRE) ★★★★
b.f. Dark Angel – Fluvial (Exceed And Excel). January 22. Second foal. 180,000Y. Tattersalls October Book 1. Juddmonte Farms. The dam, a fair 2-y-o 7f winner, is a half-sister to 5 winners including the 2-y-o Group 2 5f Queen Mary Stakes winner and Group 1 6f Phoenix Stakes third Elletelle (dam of the US and Australian Grade 1 winner Adelaide), the useful Irish 7f winner and Group 3 third Mizzava and the German listed 10f winner Freedom. The second dam, Flamanda (by Niniski), was placed over 9.5f here prior to

winning 5 races at 4 yrs in Germany from 1m to 9f and is a half-sister to 8 winners. (Khalid Abdulla). *"A strong filly that moves well, she's a mid-season type but she was a January foal so we could get to run her over six furlongs to begin with. She moves fine".*

653. TRES QUEEN ★★★
br.f. Teofilo – Tres Ravi (Monsun). February 10. Thirteenth foal. €500,000Y. Arqana Deauville August. Shadwell France. Half-sister to 8 winners including the Group 2 Grand Prix de Deauville winner Tres Blue, the multiple Group 2 placed Tres Rapide (both by Anabaa Blue), the German Group 3 winner Tres Rock Danon (by Rock Of Gibraltar) and the French listed winner Tres Rock Glory (by Fastnet Rock). The dam, a winner and second in the Group 3 Prix de la Nonette, is a half-sister to the German dual Group winner Tres Heureux. The second dam, Tres Magnifique (by Gay Fandango), was second in the Group 3 German 1,000 Guineas. *"A lovely filly but she's all about next year. I think I'll be looking for one run late on and then ten furlongs in the spring. Out of a Monsun mare, she's a lovely mover and has a great shape to her. Attractive".*

654. VERANDAH ★★★★ ♣
b.f. Medicean – Palatial (Green Desert). March 28. Sister to the Canadian Grade 2 7f winner Dimension and to the useful 7f (at 2 yrs) and 1m winner Artimino and half-sister to 6 winners including the Group 2 1m May Hill Stakes (at 2 yrs) and Group 2 1m Windsor Forest Stakes winner and 1,000 Guineas second Spacious (by Nayef), the fair 11.5f winner Ye Hade Ye Dalil (by Raven's Pass), the fair 6f winner Spice Run (by Zafonic). The dam, a useful 7f winner of 4 races at 2 and 3 yrs, is a half-sister to 7 winners including the listed 10f winners Portal and Ice Palace. The second dam, White Palace (by Shirley Heights), was a quite useful 3-y-o 8.2f winner. *"She goes well and she's a nice type of filly for July/August time. Very likeable".*

655. WELL YES (IRE) ★★★
ch.f. Galileo – Faraday Light (Rainbow Quest). May 9. Seventh foal. 525,000Y. Tattersalls October Book 1. Blandford Bloodstock. Half-sister to the Group 1 Irish 1,000 Guineas and Grade 1 E P Taylor Stakes winner Just The

Judge, to the fair 1m winner Amber Silk (both by Lawman) and the useful 2-y-o 1m winner and 3-y-o listed 9f second Obliterator (by Oratorio). The dam ran twice unplaced and is a half-sister to 3 winners including the Group 3 St Simon Stakes winner and dual Group 1 placed High Heeled. The second dam, Uncharted Haven (by Turtle Island), won two Grade 2 events in the USA and is a half-sister to 6 winners. *"She's a neat type, she goes well and we're happy with her. Given her pedigree her 3-y-o career should be more important than this year".*

656. WESTERLAND ★★★★
b.c. Frankel – Arabesque (Zafonic). April 17. Thirteenth foal. Half-brother to 8 winners including the very smart listed 6f winner Camacho (by Danehill), the Group 2 6f Gimcrack Stakes winner and smart sire Showcasing, the useful 2-y-o 6f winner Tendu, the fairly useful triple 6f winner (including at 2 yrs) and listed-placed Bouvardia (all by Oasis Dream) and the quite useful 2-y-o 1m winner Bluebeard (by Dansili). The dam, a listed 6f winner, is a sister to 2 winners including the useful 5f and 6f winner Threat and a half-sister to 5 winners including the Australian triple Group 1 winner Foreteller and the Group 2 1m Prix de Sandringham winner Modern Look. The second dam, Prophecy (by Warning), won the Group 1 6f Cheveley Park Stakes. (Khalid Abdulla). *"He's cantering away and he's a nice type of horse. Probably a mid-season type, I'm not going to push him but I like the way he goes. I think he'll be running over six or seven furlongs this year".*

657. WHITLOCK ★★★
ch.c. Dutch Art – Barynya (Pivotal). February 26. Fourth foal. 300,000Y. Tattersalls October Book 1. Will Edmeades. Brother to the smart Group 3 1m Sovereign Stakes and listed 1m Heron Stakes winner Zonderland and half-brother to the quite useful dual 12f winner Osipova (by Makfi). The dam, a fair 7f and 8.5f placed maiden, is a half-sister to 2 winners including the dam of the Group 3 Fred Darling Stakes winner Marenko. The second dam, Russian Rhythm (by Kingmambo), won the 1,000 Guineas, Coronation Stakes, Nassau Stakes and Lockinge Stakes and is a half-sister to 9 winners including Perfectperformance (2-

y-o Group 2 1m Royal Lodge Stakes). *"A big, powerful colt, I like him and the way he goes. Very much one for the middle of the season onwards".*

658. YIMOU (IRE) ★★★★
b.c. Kodiac – Heroine Chic (Big Bad Bob). March 20. Second foal. 170,000Y. Tattersalls October Book 2. Blandford Bloodstock. Brother to the useful 2-y-o 5f and listed 6f Doncaster Stakes winner Dhahmaan. The dam, a moderate 7f and 8.5f placed maiden, is a sister to two winners including the useful Irish listed 11f winner Backbench Blues and a half-sister to 3 winners. The second dam, Heroine (by Sadler's Wells), was unraced. *"An active little colt, he was bought to be early and he did a little breeze this morning. He did it in business-like fashion and he might run over five furlongs. We'll see, but he's one of our forward ones".*

659. UNNAMED ★★★
ch.c. Exchange Rate – Bella Jolie (Broken Vow). April 25. Fourth foal. $475,000Y. Keeneland September. Shadwell Estate Co. Half-brother to the US Grade 1 Breeders' Cup Sprint, King's Bishop Stakes and Malibu Stakes winner Runhappy (by Super Saver). The dam won 2 minor races at 3 yrs in the USA and is a half-sister to 7 winners including the listed winner Millennium Storm. The second dam, Jolie Boutique (by Northern Jove), is an unraced half-sister to the US Grade 2 winner Mindy Gayle. (Hamdan Al Maktoum). *"A big, rangy horse and an elegant mover with plenty of scope. One for seven furlongs in July/August".*

660. UNNAMED ★★★★
b.c. Invincible Spirit – Bufera (King's Best). April 24. Fifth foal. 420,000Y. Tattersalls October Book 1. Blandford Bloodstock. Half-brother to the French 1m (at 2 yrs) and listed 1m winner and Group 3 Prix Chloe and Prix Des Reservoirs placed Chartreuse (by Lawman) and to a minor winner abroad by Acclamation. The dam, a French 1m winner, was third in the Group 3 Prix des Reservoirs and is a half-sister to 7 winners including the Group 3 winners Albisola and Johnny Barnes and to the dam of the Group 1 winners Most Improved and Ectot. The second dam,

Mahalia (by Danehill), won the listed Prix Imprudence and is a half-sister to 7 winners including the Group 3 winner Muroto and the smart broodmare Zivania (the dam of five stakes winners). *"A rangy colt that does everything right, I'm very happy with him and he's a grand sort of horse but he's a big boy, so I wouldn't want to be in a hurry with him. One for the second half of the season".*

661. UNNAMED ★★★
b.f. Dubawi – Gemstone (Galileo). March 27. Third foal. 525,000Y. Tattersalls October Book 1. Blandford Bloodstock. Half-sister to the fair 2016 7f placed 2-y-o Sparkle (by Oasis Dream) and to the quite useful 6.5f (at 2 yrs) and 1m winner Bedrock (by Fastnet Rock). The dam, a useful 2-y-o listed 1m Silken Glider Stakes winner, was second in the Group 3 Park Express Stakes and is a half-sister to 4 winners. The second dam, Kincob (by Kingmambo), a modest 1m placed 3-y-o, is a half-sister to 7 winners including the Irish 2,000 Guineas winner Bachelor Duke. *"She moves fine, but I'm in no rush with her at all and she'll make a 2-y-o in the second half of the year".*

662. UNNAMED ★★
ch.f. Dubawi – Hit The Sky (Cozzene). February 8. 720,000 foal. Tattersalls December. Mayfair Speculators/ Peter & Ross Doyle. Half-sister to the Group 2 1m Prix Daniel Wildenstein winner Royal Bench, to the Group 3 10f Prix Allez France winner Mayhem (both by Whipper), the Group 3 Ormonde Stakes winner Memphis Tennessee (by Hurricane Run) and the minor French 10f winner Hidden Flame (by Barathea). The dam is an unraced half-sister to 3 winners including the Group 2 Doncaster Cup winner Honolulu. The second dam, Cerulean Sky (by Darshaan), a 1m (at 2 yrs) and Group 1 10f Prix Saint-Alary winner, is a sister to the listed 12f winner and US Grade 1 second L'Ancresse and a half-sister to the Irish Oaks winner Moonstone. *"She was a foal purchase and looks a nice filly at this stage but will be an autumn 2-y-o".*

663. UNNAMED ★★★★
b.c. Dubawi – Marine Bleue (Desert Prince). April 4. Seventh foal. 900,000Y. Tattersalls

October Book 1. Not sold. Brother to the quite useful 2-y-o 6f winner and UAE Group 3 1m third Wednaan and half-brother to the French listed 12f winner Marina Piccola (by Halling) and two minor winners in France by Beat Hollow and Medicean. The dam, a German Group 3 and listed 1m winner at 3 yrs, is a half-sister to 5 winners including the French listed winner Mystic Spirit. The second dam, Mirina (by Pursuit Of Love), a minor French 3-y-o winner, is a half-sister to 6 winners including the dam of the Group 1 Grand Prix de Paris winner Mirio. *"A nice colt, he's done a lot of growing recently and I'm just going quietly and sensibly with him. He's a tall boy with a good action and will be a 2-y-o in the second half of the year".*

664. UNNAMED ★★★
gr.c. Giant's Causeway – Marylebone (Unbridled's Song). April 12. Brother to the US Grade 3 placed winner Sloane Square and half-brother to the minor US stakes winner Bow Bells. The dam won the US Grade 1 Matron Stakes and is a half-sister to 6 winners out of Desert Queen (by Wavering Monarch). *"A nice type of horse for seven furlongs or a mile later in the year. He moves well but just needs to fill his frame out".*

665. UNNAMED ★★★
b.c. War Front – Moon Safari (Mr Prospector). May 2. Half-brother to the very smart Group 3 1m 1,000 Guineas Trial winner and dual Group 1 placed Just Pretending (by Giant's Causeway) and to the US 2-y-o Grade 3 1m winner The Leopard (by Storm Cat). The dam, a useful Irish 2-y-o 7f winner and third in the Group 3 Irish 1,000 Guineas Trial, is out of Video (by Nijinsky). *"A solid, heavy-topped colt, he's just doing his canters and I haven't asked any questions yet. He'll be a miler later on".*

666. UNNAMED ★★★
ch.c. Galileo – Native Force (Indian Ridge). May 9. Tenth foal. Half-brother to the Group 1 Golden Jubilee Stakes and Group 1 Nunthorpe Stakes winner Kingsgate Native (by Mujadil), to the quite useful 2-y-o 5f and subsequent US winner Vanishing Grey (by Verglas), the fair dual 6f winner (including at yrs) Native Picture (by Kodiac) and the 7f

seller winner Assumption (by Beckett). The dam, a quite useful 1m winner, is a half-sister to 2 winners. The second dam, La Pellegrina (by Be My Guest), is a 10f placed half-sister to 5 winners including the 1,000 Guineas winner Las Meninas. *"He's a strong, well-made colt, so he's not typical of the sire and there's a lot of Indian Ridge in there. I'm very happy with him and he's a seven furlong/mile colt".*

667. UNNAMED ★★★
b.c. Dabirsim – Nordic Spruce (Dynaformer). March 19. Second foal. The dam, a quite useful 2-y-o 6f winner, is a half-sister to 2 winners including the US Grade 3 winner Nordic Truce. The second dam, Nyramba (by Night Shift), was a very useful 2-y-o 5f, 6f listed and 6.5f Watership Down Stud Sales Race winner and was Group 3 placed. *"I rather hoped he'd be early but he's gone very weak on me. He'll be a 2-y-o, but not until the second half of the season".*

668. UNNAMED ★★★
ch.f. Iffraaj – Serena's Storm (Statue Of Liberty). March 31. Fifth foal. €410,000Y. Goffs Orby. Blandford Bloodstock. Sister to the Group 1 7f Moyglare Stud Stakes, Group 1 1m Coronation Stakes and Group 2 5f Queen Mary Stakes winner Rizeena and half-sister to the quite useful triple 12f and bumper winner by Rock Of Gibraltar. The dam, a quite useful 2-y-o 7f winner, is a half-sister to 4 winners including the Australian Group 2 winner and multiple Group 1 placed Puissance de Lune. The second dam, Princess Serena (by Unbridled's Song), a minor US 4-y-o winner, is a half-sister to 5 winners including the US Grade 2 American Turf Stakes winner Doubles Partner. *"She's grown and is a very tall filly now, so although her sister Rizeena was quick and early she'll need to be shown some patience. A nice type though".*

669. UNNAMED ★★★★
br.f. Scat Daddy – Shelley Beach (Danehill Dancer). January 26. Second foal. 260,000Y. Tattersalls October Book 1. Demi O'Byrne. The dam, a fair 6f and 7f placed 2-y-o, is a half-sister to the Australian dual listed winner Skiddaw Peak. The second dam, River Flow (by Affirmed), is an unraced half-sister to 5 winners including the Group 1 placed

King Sound and to the unraced dam of the French 2,000 Guineas and US Grade 1 winner Landseer. *"A racy filly and a January foal, I'd be hoping she could come onto the track in May time. She does everything fine at the moment but I think six furlongs would be the preference for her rather than five".*

670. UNNAMED ★★★★
b.f. Dansili – Take The Ribbon (Chester House). February 3. Half-sister to the French 1m and 9.5f winner and Italian Group 1 1m second Bookrunner (by Tiznow) and to the US 8.5f winner Take These Chains (by Fastnet Rock). The dam, a US Grade 3 1m winner and Grade 1 second, is a half-sister to three other US stakes performers out of Magical Flash (by Miswaki). *"A nice filly, she's attractive and well-balanced, she moves well and is a medium-sized filly I could see running in the summer on the July course".*

671. UNNAMED ★★★★
b.c. Camelot – Teddy Bears Picnic (Oasis Dream). April 24. Sixth foal. 260,000Y. Tattersalls October Book 1. Amanda Skiffington. Half-brother to the fairly useful 2-y-o 6f and 7f winner and Group 3 Somerville Tattersall Stakes third Nezar (by Mastercraftsman), to the quite useful Irish 1m winner Ottilie and a minor 10f winner abroad (both by Hurricane Run). The dam is an unraced half-sister to 3 winners. The second dam, Jackie's Opera (by Indian Ridge), is an unraced half-sister to 5 winners including the dual French listed winner Arabian King. *"He goes well, he's a forward going sort and looks quite a lot like the damsire Oasis Dream. He's quite 'together' and he could well be out in a 2-y-o maiden in May".*

672. UNNAMED ★★★★ ♠
b.c. Exceed And Excel – Time Control (Sadler's Wells). March 20. Sixth foal. 400,000Y. Tattersalls October Book 1. John & Jake Warren. Half-brother to the 2-y-o Group 1 7f Moyglare Stud Stakes and Group 3 6f Albany Stakes winner Cursory Glance (by Distorted Humor). The dam, a quite useful 10f winner, is a sister to the Group 2 Prix de Malleret and listed Cheshire Oaks winner Time On. The second dam, Time Away (by Darshaan), won the Group 3 10.4f Musidora Stakes, was third

in the Group 1 Prix de Diane and the Group 1 Nassau Stakes and is a half-sister to 6 winners including the Prix de Diane second Time Ahead. *"A nice colt, he's a good mover with a good mind on him. I like him and six furlongs in May should be his starting point".*

673. UNNAMED ★★★

gr.f. Style Vendome – Twyla Tharp (Sadler's Wells). March 22. Seventh foal. Half-sister to the high-class filly The Fugue, winner of the Group 1 Prince Of Wales's Stakes, Nassau Stakes, Yorkshire Oaks and Irish Champion Stakes, to the quite useful 9.5f and 10.5f winner Ducab (both by Dansili) the fair 14f and 2m winner Susan Stroman (by Monsun). The dam, a useful 9f winner and second in the Group 2 12f Ribblesdale Stakes, is a half-sister to 7 winners including the Group 1 winners Compton Admiral and Summoner. The second dam, Sumoto (by Mtoto), a useful 6f (at 2 yrs) and 7f winner, is a half-sister to 5 winners. *"She's a little unfurnished at this stage and we'll take our time, but she's a sweet filly. Seven furlongs to start with, definitely".*

674. UNNAMED ★★★

b.c. Frankel – Without You Babe (Lemon Drop Kid). March 20. Half-brother to Tamarkuz (by Speightstown), winner of the Grade 1 Breeders' Cup Dirt Mile and three Group 3 events in the UAE. The dam is an unraced half-sister to 7 winners including the stakes winners and Grade 1 placed Andromeda's Hero, Stay Thirsty and Superfly. The second dam, Morozia (by Storm Bird), a fair 12f winner, is a half-sister to 4 winners. *"He's grown a lot recently. A nice type of horse and a good mover, but I see him as being one for August time".*

675. UNNAMED ★★★

b.f. Shamardal – Yummy Mummy (Montjeu). March 11. Fifth foal. 870,000Y. Tattersalls October Book 1. Blandford Bloodstock. Half-sister to the 1,000 Guineas, Nassau Stakes and Matron Stakes winner Legatissimo (by Danehill Dancer), to the fairly useful 12f winner Another Cocktail (by Dalakhani) and a hurdles winner by Sea The Stars. The dam, a fair Irish 10f winner, is a sister to the multiple Group 1 winner Fame And Glory (Ascot

Gold Cup, Irish Derby, Coronation Cup etc) and a half-sister to 7 winners. The second dam, Gryada (by Shirley Heights), a fairly useful 2-y-o 7f and 8.3f winner and third in the Group 3 1m Premio Dormello, is a full or half-sister to 4 middle-distance winners. *"She's done well, she's had a good winter and obviously her sister was brilliant, but I see her as being more of a 2-y-o for seven furlongs or a mile in the early autumn".*

RAE GUEST

676. DAME NELLIE ★★★

b.f. Aussie Rules – Eminencia (Sadler's Wells). February 2. Eighth foal. Half-sister to the Italian winner and 10f listed-placed Edya (by Makfi), to the fair 10f winner Archduchess (by Archipenko). The dam is an unraced half-sister to 6 winners including the listed 14f winner Moments Of Joy. The second dam, My Emma (by Marju), a smart winner of the Group 1 Prix Vermeille and the Group 1 Yorkshire Oaks, is a half-sister to 5 winners including the Group 1 St Leger and Group 1 Ascot Gold Cup winner Classic Cliché. *"She's very close to our hearts because she's a granddaughter of My Emma who was our first Group 1 winner. We had her sister Archduchess who was just OK, but this one seems very nice. She'll just have a couple of runs towards the end of the season but she's a nice, big, strong filly. More of a 3-y-o type, but she has a nice way of going and Aussie Rules does get plenty of 2-y-o winners. We're looking forward to this one".*

677. DASH OF ORANGE ★★★★

br.f. Lethal Force – Princess Of Orange (Dutch Art). January 24. First foal. The dam, a quite useful 6f (at 2 yrs) and 1m winner, is a full sister to one winner and a half-sister to another. The second dam, Radiate (by Sadler's Wells), is an unraced half-sister to 4 winners including the Group 1 Phoenix Stakes third Polar Force. *"She's a big filly just like her mother who we trained – she was just below listed class. We're quite excited about this one, she's one for the late summer but she is a big filly, especially for a first foal, but the sire was big too. Her mother was fast but she got a mile, so I'd say we'll start her at six furlongs and then think about moving her up in trip".*

678. ETERNAL DESTINY ★★

b.f. Poet's Voice – Mrs Mogg (Green Desert). March 6. Second foal. 16,000 foal. Tattersalls December. Trickledown Stud. The dam, a modest 7f winner, is a half-sister to 2 winners in Japan. The second dam, Maybe Forever (by Zafonic), won the Group 3 Prix de Saint-Georges and is a half-sister to the dual Group 1 winner Court Masterpiece. *"A backward filly that'll take time. Big and strong, but we won't see her out until the back-end".*

679. INCH PINCHER ★★

b.f. Captain Gerrard – Elfine (Invincible Spirit). April 23. Third foal. The dam, a fair 1m (at 2 yrs) and 10f placed maiden, is a half-sister to 3 winners. The second dam, Donnelly's Hollow (by Docksider), a modest 1m placed Irish maiden, is a half-sister to 5 winners including the Group 1 12f Italian Derby winner and King George VI and Queen Elizabeth Stakes second White Muzzle and the Group 2 German St Leger winner Fair Question and the listed 10f winner Elfaslah (dam of the Dubai World Cup winner Almutawakel). *"She looks like she'll take time but although the sire suggests precocity I think she probably takes after her dam. So I see her being a six/seven furlong filly in the second half of the season".*

680. KACHUMBA ★★★

b.f. Mayson – Native Nickel (Be My Native). May 7. Tenth foal. Half-sister to the fair 7f (at 2 yrs) and useful UAE 7f to 9f winner Five Cents (by Exceed And Excel) and two winners in Australia and Singapore by Key Of Luck and Agnes World. The dam is an unraced half-sister to several winners including the Irish listed winner Porto Marmay. The second dam, Nordicolini (by Nordico), won once at 3 yrs and is a half-sister to 8 winners including River Verdon (champion in Hong Kong). *"She was a May foal and she's still a bit weak, but I think she'll still be a 2-y-o type because she's not big but well-made. She's bred to be fast and the dam's horses have done well abroad. She's sharp, so we'll just have to wait for her to strengthen up".*

681. UNNAMED ★★

ch.f. Poet's Voice – Dress Code (Barathea). March 25. Ninth living foal. Half-sister to 5 winners including the smart 6f Goffs Million Sprint winner Lucky General (by Hawk Wing), the quite useful Irish 2-y-o 7f winner Slaney Rock (by Rock Of Gibraltar) and the fair listed-placed dual 5f winner (including at 2 yrs) Dress To Impress (by Fasliyev). The dam, a quite useful 2-y-o 5f winner, is a sister to the useful 2-y-o Group 3 7f C L Weld Park Stakes winner Rag Top and a half-sister to 8 winners. The second dam, Petite Epaulette (by Night Shift), a fair 5f winner at 2 yrs, is a half-sister to 3 winners including the Group 1 1m Gran Criterium second Line Dancer. *"A big, backward filly and typical of the sire in that respect. A nice, big, strong filly from a good family but we're just taking our time with her as she's more of a 3-y-o type. All being well we'll get her out later in the year over seven furlongs".*

682. UNNAMED ★★

b.f. Acclamation – Million Faces (Exceed And Excel). March 1. First foal. 50,000foal. Tattersalls December. Howson & Houldsworth. The dam, a fair 5f winner, is a half-sister to 5 winners including the Group 3 Prix du Petit Couvert winner Mirza and the triple listed placed Millybaa. The second dam, Millyant (by Primo Dominie), winner of the Group 2 5f Prix du Gros-Chene, is a half-sister to 5 winners including the Group 2 5f Flying Childers winner and very useful sire Prince Sabo and the Irish listed winner Bold Jessie (herself dam of the Gimcrack Stakes winner Abou Zouz). *"A very nice filly, the family is fast but they usually take time to come to hand and they're usually better at three and four. A lengthy filly, she's typical of the sire in that respect and we won't see her until later in the season".*

683. UNNAMED ★★

ch.f. Harbour Watch – Mina (Selkirk). February 24. Sixth foal. Closely related to the quite useful 2-y-o 5f winner Miss Diva (by Acclamation) and half-sister to the listed 6f winner of 5 races Minalisa, to the quite useful 5f and 6f winner of 8 races Peace Seeker (both by Oasis Dream) and the fair 6f winner Khameela (by Equiano). The dam, a modest 6f winner at 4 yrs, is a half-sister to 7 winners including the Group 3 5f Ballyogan Stakes winner Miss Anabaa and the smart 5f and 6f winner of 6 races Out After Dark. The second dam, Midnight Shift (by Night Shift), a fair dual 6f winner at 3 yrs, is a half-sister to 8 winners including the Group 1 6f July Cup winner Owington. *"She's very backward at the moment, so she's going to take time and so she's typical of the family. We'll wait and see what she looks like later in the summer and I'm not sure what to think of the sire after his first season last year. The dam was a very tall and slim filly and she was alright but placed a lot more times than she won"*.

684. UNNAMED ★★

ch.f. Havana Gold – Miss Anabaa (Anabaa). February 18. Eighth foal. Half-sister to the quite useful 7f winner of four races Emkanaat, to the quite useful 6f winner Miliika (both by Green Desert) and the fair 7f winner Passing By (by Raven's Pass). The dam, a winner of 3 races including the Group 3 5f Ballyogan Stakes, is a half-sister to 7 winners including Out After Dark, a smart 5f and 6f winner of 6 races including the Portland Handicap. The second dam, Midnight Shift (by Night Shift), a fair dual 6f winner at 3 yrs, is a half-sister to 8 winners including the high-class Group 1 6f July Cup winner Owington. *"Not yet in the yard but I've seen her and she's nice. We trained the dam and a lot of the family, but we take our time with them. She won't race until the autumn, but next year I think she'll be a bit better than the average"*.

685. UNNAMED ★★★

b.f. Kodiac – Party Appeal (Mr Greeley). May 14. Third foal. 6,000Y. Tattersalls October Book 3. Rae Guest. The dam, placed at 3 and 4 yrs in France, is a half-sister to 11 winners including the dam of the 2-y-o Group 2 winner and sire Zebedee. The second dam, Mariamme (by Verbatim), won twice at 3 yrs in the USA and is a half-sister to 7 winners including the Grade 1 Breeders' Cup Turf winner Miss Alleged. *"A typical Kodiac, she's small and probably not quite as strong as you'd want her to be just yet. She was very small at the sales and she was a late foal but she's done very well since she came in and doing as much as the other horses. As soon as she gets past her birthday we'll press on with her. Her dam is a half-sister to Zebedee, so it's all speed and a really nice family and if things*

work out she could prove to be a bargain". TRAINERS' BARGAIN BUY

686. UNNAMED ★★★

ch.f. Intikhab – Pompeia (Singspiel). February 23. First foal. 7,500Y. Tattersalls October Book 4. Rae Guest. The dam, a fair 2-y-o 7f winner, is a full or half-sister to 9 winners including the useful 10f and 12f winner and German Group 2 and Group 3 placed Corriolanus. The second dam, Caesarea (by Generous), won 3 races at 3 yrs in Germany and is a half-sister to the German Group 1 12f winner Catella and a half-sister to 4 winners. *"We're hoping this will be a 2-y-o type. A typical sprinter in looks, she's small, stocky, square and goes well. Hopefully we'll get her out in May or June"*.

WILLIAM HAGGAS

687. ALGAFFAAL ★★★★

ch.c. Speightstown – Rockcide (Personal Flag). January 30. Seventh foal. $450,000Y. Keeneland September. Shadwell Estate Co. Half-brother to 5 winners including the US Grade 2 and Grade 3 winner and Grade 1 placed Rule (by Roman Ruler), the quite useful 1m (at 2 yrs) and subsequent US Grade 3 7f winner Matrooh and the minor US 3-y-o winners Afaaf and Satirical (both by Distorted Humor). The dam, placed at 3 and 4 yrs in the USA, is a half-sister to the Kentucky Derby and Preakness Stakes winner and champion 3-y-o colt Funny Cide. The second dam, Belle's Good Cide (by Slewacide), a minor US winner of 2 races at 3 yrs, is a half-sister to 3 stakes winners including the Grade 3 winner Belle Of Cozzene. (Hamdan Al Maktoum). *"A lovely horse. He cost a lot of money but he's got a lot of quality. If he's good he'll be out in August, he's got something about him and he's a really nice looking horse. I like him"*.

688. ALLIEYF ★★★

b.c. New Approach – Sajjhaa (King's Best). February 12. First foal. The dam, a UAE dual Group 1 9f winner, won 8 races in total from 3 to 6 yrs and is a sister to one winner and a half-sister to another. The second dam, Anaamil (by Darshaan), a quite useful 11f winner, is a half-sister to 3 winners. (Sheikh Ahmed Al Maktoum). *"One for the back-end of the season but he's a nice horse and very typical of the sire. He's got a very deep girth and he just falls away a bit behind but he's a nice mover and has a good attitude. I think he'll do well and he could be a good horse".*

689. BAHLWAN ★★★
b.c. Bahamian Bounty – Vive Les Rouges (Acclamation). March 31. Fourth foal. 100,000Y. Tattersalls October Book 2. Shadwell Estate Co. Brother to the useful 6f winner Speedfiend and half-brother to the useful 6f and 7f winner Dougan (by Dutch Art). The dam, a fairly useful 2-y-o 6f winner, was second in the listed Dick Poole Stakes and is a half-sister to 4 winners including the useful dual listed 6f winner of 6 races (including at 2 yrs) Bounty Box. The second dam, Bible Box (by Bin Ajwaad), was a quite useful 7f to 9f winner of 3 races from 3 to 5 yrs. (Sheikh Ahmed Al Maktoum). *"He's done very well since the sale and we're very pleased with him. He's grown well and got stronger, he's a fluent mover and will be a summer 2-y-o".*

690. CAVATINA ★★★
b.f. Lethal Force – Piano (Azamour). April 16. Fourth foal. The dam, a fairly useful listed-placed 10f and 11f winner, is a half-brother to 4 winners. The second dam, Humouresque (by Pivotal), a smart Group 3 10.5f Prix Penelope winner, is a sister to 2 winners including Group 2 placed Mighty and a half-sister to the very smart sprinter Danehurst, winner of the Cornwallis Stakes (at 2 yrs), the Curragh Flying Five, the Prix de Seine-et-Oise and the Premio Umbria (all Group 3 events). (Cheveley Park Stud). *"A nice filly, not particularly early but she'll be fine in mid-summer, I like her and she moves well. I've got two by this sire and I like them both. They're not particularly sharp but very uncomplicated".*

691. CONSULTANT ★★★
b.c. Kodiac – Mary Goodnight (King's Best). March 11. Third foal. 140,000Y. Tattersalls October Book 1. John & Jake Warren. Half-brother to the fair 7f winner Marydale (by Aqlaam). The dam, a quite useful 10f winner, is a half-sister to 4 winners including Namibian (Group 3 Gordon Stakes and Group 3 Queens Vase). The second dam, Disco Volante (by Sadler's Wells), a useful 1m winner, was listed-placed twice and is a

half-sister to 3 winners including the Group 1 St James's Palace Stakes second Valentino. (Highclere Thoroughbred Racing). *"A big, backward, good-looking horse, I don't think he's that early but he's a good-looking boy. He hasn't shown much yet and is possibly more for later on. I'm not sure if the bigger Kodiacs are the ones you want, but he's an attractive colt".*

692. DELFT BLUE ★★★
gr.f. Lethal Force – Delft (Dutch Art). February 25. Second foal. Half-sister to the fair 2017 3-y-o 1m winner Faience (by Holy Roman Emperor). The dam, a quite useful 7f (including at 2 yrs) and 6f winner of 3 races, is a half-sister to one winner. The second dam, Plucky (by Kyllachy), a quite useful 7f winner, is a half-sister to 7 winners including the 2-y-o Group 2 5f Flying Childers Stakes and Group 3 5f Molecomb Stakes winner Wunders Dream and the Group 3 Ridgewood Pearl Stakes winner Grecian Dancer. (Cheveley Park Stud). *"I like her attitude, she'll be a 2-y-o by July time, moves well and just gets on with it".*

693. DUTCH DESIRE ★★★
b.f. Dutch Art – Danehill Destiny (Danehill Dancer). March 2. Fifth foal. Sister to the quite useful 2-y-o 7f winner Dutch Destiny and half-sister to the fairly useful 6f winner Danehill Revival (by Pivotal) and the modest 2016 3-y-o 1m winner Daily Trader (by Medicean). The dam, a useful dual 5f (at 2 yrs) and listed 6f winner, was third in two Group 3 events over 6f and 7f and is a half-sister to 3 winners. The second dam, Comeraincomeshine (by Night Shift), a modest 5.5f winner, is a half-sister to 5 winners including the Group 1 1m Queen Elizabeth II Stakes winner Where Or When. (Cheveley Park Stud). *"Not as early as I'd hoped, she's been a bit green but I think she'll come together soon. She's well-made and quite strong, should be a June 2-y-o and probably over six furlongs".*

694. ERTIYAD ★★★★
b.f. Dark Angel – Lily Again (American Post). March 8. Second foal. £90,000Y. Goffs UK Premier (Doncaster). Blandford Bloodstock. The dam, 2-y-o listed 7f winner, is a half-sister to 4 winners including the fairly useful listed

placed 2-y-o winner Genari. The second dam, Sari (by Faustus), a quite useful 7f winner of 2 races (including at 2 yrs), is a half-sister to one winner. (Sheikh Juma Dalmook Al Maktoum). *"A really nice filly and she'll be early too. I can see her being out in May and she might be an Ascot 2-y-o. She's got a bit of scope, a bit of size and a bit of ability too. She wants six furlongs, but she should have the speed for five so she might start at Sandown over the stiff five furlongs there. A quality filly".*

695. FLAMENCO ★★★★ ♠

b.f. Showcasing – Astrantia (Dansili). February 8. Second foal. 150,000Y. Tattersalls October Book 1. John & Jake Warren. The dam is an unplaced half-sister to 8 winners including the smart 2-y-o dual Group 2 winner Strategic Prince and the listed winner and Group 2 placed Yorkshire. The second dam, Ausherra (by Diesis), won the listed 12f Lingfield Oaks Trial and is a full or half-sister to 9 winners including the Oaks, Irish Oaks and Yorkshire Oaks winner Ramruma. (Highclere Thoroughbred Racing). *"A nice filly, she moves really well. Big and scopey, I think she's got a chance to be a classy filly this year".*

696. GHANIMAH ★★★

b.f. Invincible Spirit – Gile Na Greine (Galileo). April 13. Third foal. Half-sister to Alwahsh, unplaced on his only start at 2 yrs in 2016 and to the quite useful 9f winner Mawjood (both by Dubawi). The dam, an Irish 2-y-o 7f winner, was second in the Group 1 Coronation Stakes and third in the 1,000 Guineas and is a sister to the smart 2-y-o dual Group 3 6f winner and 1,000 Guineas second Cuis Ghaire, the Group 3 9f Meld Stakes winner Scintillula and the 1m winner and dual Group 3 placed Claiomh Solais. The second dam, Scribonia (by Danehill), is an unraced half-sister to 6 winners including the very useful 2-y-o listed 6f winner and dual Group 1 placed Luminata and the very useful dual 6f winner (including at 2 yrs) and Group 3 placed Aretha. (Hamdan Al Maktoum). *"I'm not sure about her, she's small and should be more of a 2-y-o than the dam's first two foals by Dubawi. I hope she is. The dam was very smart and hopefully this is a better mating".*

697. GIVE AND TAKE ★★★

b.f. Cityscape – Grace And Glory (Montjeu). February 4. First foal. The dam is an unraced sister to 3 winners including the Irish Derby winner Fame And Glory and a half-sister to 6 winners. The second dam, Gryada (by Shirley Heights), a fairly useful 2-y-o 7f and 8.3f winner, was third in the Group 3 1m Premio Dormello and is a full or half-sister to 4 winners. (Mr N Jones). *"I like her. She's gone out for a break for a bit, has a lot of stamina and quality on the dam's side and I think she's a nice filly. She's a good advertisement for her sire and one that'll make a 2-y-o later on".*

698. HEADWAY ★★★ ♠

b.c. Havana Gold – On Her Way (Medicean). March 14. Third foal. 60,000Y. Tattersalls October Book 2. John & Jake Warren. The dam, a quite useful 10f and 11f winner of 3 races, is a half-sister to 3 winners including the useful 2-y-o dual 1m winner and Group 2 1m Royal Lodge Stakes third On Our Way. The second dam, Singed (by Zamindar), won once at around 1m in France and is a half-sister to the French listed winner and Group 3 placed Inhabitant. (Royal Ascot Racing Club). *"He's one of the sharper ones. A nice horse that goes well and I need to try and get him to Ascot for the Royal Ascot Racing Club. I don't know if it'll make the Royal meeting though. He's a nice horse, he's got speed and will be a six furlong 2-y-o".*

699. HUMBOLT CURRENT ★★★

b.c. Fastnet Rock – Humdrum (Dr Fong). February 23. Third foal. Half-brother to the fair 2016 2-y-o 1m winner Elementary (by Exceed And Excel) and to the quite useful 2-y-o 6f winner Husbandry (by Paco Boy). The dam, a fairly useful 7f and 1m winner of 4 races (including at 2 yrs), is a half-sister to 6 winners including the useful listed 6f winner of 4 races Musical Comedy. The second dam, Spinning Top (by Alzao), a useful 10f winner, is a half-sister to numerous winners including the fairly useful 3-y-o 7f and subsequent US dual 9f winner Daytime. (The Queen). *"I really like him but I think this Fastnet Rock will be better next year, although I may have thought the same about Rivet at this point last year! He's a nice horse but he doesn't need to do any more at this stage. He could come together a bit later in the season".*

700. IMPROVE ★★★
b.f. Iffraaj – Choose Me (Choisir). April 15. Fourth foal. €150,000Y. Goffs Orby. Brian Grassick Bloodstock. Half-sister to the smart Group 3 1m Atalanta Stakes winner of 5 races at 2 and 3 yrs Persuasive (by Dark Angel) and to the fairly useful 6f and 7f winner Amazour (by Azamour). The dam, a very useful 6f (at 2 yrs) to 10f winner of 4 races including a listed 7f event in Ireland, was third in the Group 2 Blandford Stakes and is a half-sister to 5 minor winners. The second dam, Hecuba (by Hector Protector), a fairly useful 10f winner, is a half-sister to 7 winners including the German Group 2 winner Bad Bertrich Again and the Group 3 Scottish Classic winner Prolix. (Yvonne Jacques). *"She's very well-bred, cost a lot of money and looks a 2-y-o. A nice filly, a bit long maybe, but she goes well and I can't see her being that backward either. I had her half-sister Persuasive who was a late developer, but I think this filly will be much sharper. If she's good she'll start at six furlongs".*

701. INTANGIBLE STAR ★★★
b.c. Sea The Stars – Wosaita (Generous). February 16. Fifteenth foal. 125,000Y. Tattersalls October Book 1. Not sold. Half-brother to 7 winners including the useful 7f (at 2 yrs), listed 1m and Italian Group 3 1m winner Whazzis (by Desert Prince), the useful 2-y-o listed 7f Chesham Stakes winner Whazzat (by Daylami), the 2-y-o 8.6f winner Whatizzit (by Galileo), the 2-y-o 7f and 1m winner Special Envoy (by Barathea) and the 10f winner High Admiral (by New Approach) – all three quite useful. The dam, a fair 12.3f placed maiden, is a half-sister to 10 winners including the Group 1 10.5f Prix de Diane winner Rafha (the dam of Invincible Spirit). The second dam, Eljazzi (by Artaius), a fairly useful 2-y-o 7f winner, is a half-sister to 8 winners including the high-class miler Pitcairn. (Sunderland Holdings Ltd). *"A nice, backward horse, we had Whazzis out of the mare and she was pretty useful. The damline adds a bit of speed to the sire and I don't think that does any harm. He's a nice looking horse and he goes well".*

702. ISTANBUL PASHA (IRE) ★★★
b.c. Fast Company – Red Red Rose (Piccolo). February 19. Third foal. €65,000Y. Goffs Orby. Highflyer Bloodstock. Brother to the fair 2-y-o 5f winner Fashionata and half-brother to the quite useful 2-y-o 5f winner Pillar Box (by Sakhee's Secret. The dam is an unraced half-sister to 6 winners including Temple Meads (2-y-o Group 2 Mill Reef Stakes) and the useful 2-y-o 6f winner and Group 3 Firth of Clyde Stakes second Sneak Preview. The second dam, Harryana (by Efisio), was a fair 2-y-o dual 5f winner. (Simon Munir & Isaac Souede). *"He's a strong, quite well-made 2-y-o. I see him being out in June and he'll do a lot of work this year I think. We've had two out of the mare that promised a bit more than they delivered".*

703. ISTANBUL SULTAN (IRE) ★★★
gr.c. Zoffany – Far Away Eyes (High Chaparral). February 8. First foal. 100,000Y. Tattersalls October Book 1. Highflyer Bloodstock. The dam is an unplaced half-sister to 8 winners. The second dam, La Luna (by Lyphard), a winner over 9f at 3 yrs in France, is a sister to the Group 3 Prix Daphnis and Group 3 Prix Thomas Bryon winner Bellypha and a half-sister to 6 winners including the Prix Eugene Adam winner Bellman. (Simon Munir & Isaac Souede). *"A scopey horse, not an early type and I don't know much about him yet, but he's nice, he's leggy and he should be a second half of the season 2-y-o with the scope to go on at three".*

704. JURRAN ★★★★
b.c. Bated Breath – Bahamian Music (Bahamian Bounty). March 14. Second foal. £60,000Y. Goffs UK Premier (Doncaster). Shadwell Estate Co. The dam, a fair 7f to 10f winner of 4 races from 2 to 4 yrs, is a half-sister to 3 winners. The second dam, Strings (by Unfuwain), is an unraced half-sister to 6 winners including the French 2,000 Guineas winner Victory Note. (Hamdan Al Maktoum). *"A really nice horse. We bought him relatively cheaply at Doncaster and he'll run in June. He's strong and although so far the Bated Breath runners haven't been precocious this doesn't look a backward horse. He's out of a Bahamian Bounty mare, so I think he'll be fine".*

705. LEARN BY HEART ★★★
b.c. Frankel – Memory (Danehill Dancer).
February 12. Third foal. Closely related to the
smart 2-y-o Group 3 7f winner Recorder (by
Galileo). The dam won the Group 2 6f Cherry
Hinton Stakes and is a sister to one winner
and a half-sister to 5 winners including the
2-y-o Group 3 Tyros Stakes winner Remember
Alexander. The second dam, Nausicaa (by
Diesis), won 3 races at 2 and 3 yrs in France
and the USA over 7f and 1m, was third in the
Grade 3 Miesque Stakes and is a half-sister to
3 winners. (The Queen). *"He's not very big and
he might even be out before this book. We're
having a look at him now but he's strange
because he's not like either of the dam's first
two foals. He's tough and hardy, so I think he
may well be out sooner rather than later. The
dam was very fast but she was difficult too
and a colt by Frankel out of Memory is bound
to have a bit of temperament! So he may have
to run a bit earlier than he should because he
needs to keep going forward".*

706. MASHAHEER ★★★
b.c. Dutch Art – Faustinatheyounger (Antonius
Pius). January 27. First foal. 110,000Y.
Tattersalls October Book 2. Shadwell Estate
Co. The dam, a moderate 12f placed maiden,
is a half-sister to 7 winners including the
French 2-y-o 1m winner and subsequent US
dual Grade 2 winner Uncharted Haven. The
second dam, Tochar Ban (by Assert), a quite
useful 10f winner, is a half-sister to 6 winners.
(Hamdan Al Maktoum). *"A nice, strong, well-
made horse. Sheikh Hamdan hasn't had a lot
of luck with the sire but I hope this will change
his fortunes. He should be a 2-y-o".*

707. MOSALIM (IRE) ★★★
b.c. Arcano – Vision Of Peace (Invincible
Spirit). April 16. Third foal. 100,000Y.
Tattersalls October Book 2. Shadwell Estate
Co. Half-brother to the fairly useful 5f and
6f winner of 5 races at 2 and 3 yrs Aguerooo
(by Monsieur Bond). The dam is an unraced
half-sister to the Group 3 Premio Tudini
winner Victory Laurel. The second dam,
Special Cause (by Fasliyev), won once over
7f at 3 yrs in France and is a half-sister to 6
winners including the dam of Zafeen (Group
1 St James's Palace Stakes). (Sheikh Ahmed Al
Maktoum). *"A nice horse, he's a bit backward

and needs a bit of time but he'll pull together.
A strong colt that's done very well since we
bought him".*

708. MOSSEYB ★★★★
b.c. Epaulette – Allegrissimo (Redback). March
29. Third foal. €95,000Y. Goffs Orby. Shadwell
Estate Co. Half-brother to the modest 10f,
11.5f and hurdles winner Skylark Lady (by
Tamayuz). The dam, a minor French 2-y-o
winner, is a half-sister to 3 winners including
the Group 3 second Silver Grey. The second
dam, Operissimo (by Singspiel), is an unraced
sister to the 2-y-o Group 3 1m Prix Thomas
Bryon winner Songlark and a half-sister
to 5 winners including the Dubai Group 3
winner Blatant and the dam of the multiple
Group 1 winner Sky Lantern. (Sheikh Ahmed
Al Maktoum). *"I loved him as a yearling, I
thought he was gorgeous. A grand horse, he
was a bit disappointing in the winter but he's
had a break and he's come back looking just
as he did as a yearling. I think he'll be a 2-y-o,
very much so".*

709. MY LORD AND MASTER (IRE) ★★★
ch.c. Mastercraftsman – Affability (Dalakhani).
March 28. Second foal. 65,000Y. Tattersalls
October Book 2. Jill Lamb. Half-brother to
Whisper A Word (by Bated Breath), unplaced
in two starts at 2 yrs in 2016. The dam is an
unraced half-sister to 8 winners including
the Group 3 Gallinule Stakes winner Grand
Ducal. The second dam, Mood Swings (by
Shirley Heights), a fair 2-y-o 6f winner, is a
sister to the listed 2-y-o Sweet Solera Stakes
winner Catwalk and a half-sister to 5 winners.
(Tim Bridge). *"A nice horse for the second half
of the season, but he's not backward and I'd
expect him to do something this year. He's a
nice size, a good sort, a good walker and a
good mover".*

710. NOMOATHAJ ★★★
b.f. Dubawi – Jadhwah (Nayef). April 26.
Second foal. Sister to the quite useful 10f
winner Mubajal. The dam, unplaced in one
start, is a half-sister to the 2,000 Guineas
and Prix Jacques le Marois winner Makfi (by
Dubawi). The second dam, Dhelaal (by Green
Desert), is an unraced half-sister to 7 winners
including the champion 2-y-o Alhaarth
(Dewhurst Stakes, Laurent Perrier Champagne

Stakes etc.,) and the very useful 2-y-o Group 3 7f Prix du Calvados winner Green Pola. (Hamdan Al Maktoum). *"Quite a late foal, but she's a nice filly. She goes well but will take a bit of time and Sheikh Hamdan gets cross if you train Dubawi's too soon because he insists they should be treated with patience".*

711. ONE FOR JUNE ★★★
b.f. Arcano – Worthington (Kodiac). February 25. First foal. €30,000Y. Goffs Sportsmans. Amanda Skiffington. The dam, a quite useful 2-y-o 5f winner, is a half-sister to 6 winners. The second dam, Idle Fancy (by Mujtahid), a fair Irish 3-y-o 1m winner, is a half-sister to 7 winners including the French listed 1m winner Danish Field and the dam of the Lancashire Oaks winner Ela Athena. (Scotney, Symonds, Fisher Partnership). *"A strong, well-made filly, she'll be heading for the Supersprint, or at least that's what we'll be trying for. She's all Kodiac, not really Arcano and she goes nicely".* TRAINERS' BARGAIN BUY

712. PERFECT THOUGHT ★★★★
ch.f. Dawn Approach – Masaya (Dansili). March 23. Third foal. 70,000Y. Tattersalls October Book 1. Jill Lamb. Half-sister to the quite useful 2-y-o 5f and 6f winner Shamsaya (by Shamardal) and to a minor winner abroad by Halling. The dam, a useful 2-y-o 5f and 7f winner, was listed-placed twice and is a half-sister to 4 minor winners. The second dam, Anbella (by Common Grounds), a French 2-y-o listed 7f winner, is a half-sister to 8 winners including Spadoun (Group 1 Criterium de Saint-Cloud) and Satwa Queen (Group 1 Prix de l'Opera). (Liam Sheridan). *"I think she's quite sharp and quite racy. A nice, solid, uncomplicated filly and I think she goes well. She'll be out in May or June".*

713. RED CYMBAL ★★
b.c. Pivotal – Red Baton (Exceed And Excel). April 24. First foal. 110,000Y. Tattersalls October Book 2. Not sold. The dam is an unraced half-sister to 3 winners including the Group 1 5f Prix de l'Abbaye and multiple Group 2/3 winner Maarek. The second dam, Ruby Rocket (by Indian Rocket), a listed 5f and listed 6f winner, was Group 3 placed twice and is a half-sister to 8 winners including the listed winners Alexander

Alliance and Inzar's Best. (Cheveley Park Stud). *"I've turned him out for a break because he's gone right up behind. So I think he'll be a later 2-y-o than we thought he'd be. I would think it's likely to be August/September for him now, but he's grown which is a good thing".*

714. REGINA NOSTRA ★★★
b.f. Pivotal – Regina (Green Desert). March 27. Eighth foal. Sister to the modest 6f winner Houdini and to the fair dual 6f winner King Of Spin, closely related to the fair 2016 dual 6f placed 2-y-o Nibras Again and the fairly useful 2-y-o 5f winner and 6f listed-placed Survived (both by Kyllachy) and half-sister to the quite useful 5f and 6f winner of 10 races from 2 to 7 yrs Six Wives (by Kingsalsa). The dam, a fairly useful dual 2-y-o dual 5f winner, is a half-sister to 5 winners. The second dam, Dazzle (by Gone West), winner of the Group 3 6f Cherry Hinton Stakes and third in the 1,000 Guineas, is a half-sister to 3 listed winners including Hypnotize (dam of the Group 1 Cheveley Park Stakes winner Hooray) and to the placed dam of the Group 2 winner Danehurst. (Cheveley Park Stud). *"She's a Pivotal out of a very fast mare and I would think this will be a 2-y-o, very much so, and she'll be out in good time".*

715. RESTIVE SPIRIT ★★★★★
b.c. Intello – Hooray (Invincible Spirit). April 7. Third foal. 200,000Y. Tattersalls October Book 1. Stroud/Coleman & Mayfair Speculators. Half-brother to the Boost (by Pivotal), placed third twice over 6f on her only starts at 2 yrs in 2016. The dam, a smart winner of 5 races including the Group 1 6f Cheveley Park Stakes and the Group 2 6f Lowther Stakes, is a half-sister to 4 winners including the 2-y-o listed 8.3f winner Hypnotic. The second dam, Hypnotize (by Machiavellian), a useful 2-y-o dual 7f winner, is a full or half-sister to 8 winners including Dazzle (Group 3 6f Cherry Hinton Stakes) and to the placed dam of the Group 2 winning sprinter Danehurst. (B Kantor & M J Jooste). *"I like him a lot, I think he's got something about him and he's always been quite a sharp horse for an Intello. There's a lot of speed on the dam's side obviously and this colt has done well. So I'd be hopeful he'd be one of the more forward ones".*

716. SPECIAL PURPOSE ★★★★ ♠
b.f. Scat Daddy – Pussycat Lips (Holy Roman Emperor). March 29. Second foal. £90,000Y. Goffs UK Premier (Doncaster). David Redvers. The dam, a quite useful 2-y-o 6f winner, was Grade 3 placed in the USA and is a half-sister to 3 winners. The second dam, On The Nile (by Sadler's Wells), an Irish 2-y-o listed 9f winner, is a sister to the Irish listed 1m winner In The Limelight and closely related to the Singapore Gold Cup and Gran Premio del Jockey Club winner Kutub. (Qatar Racing). *"She's a small, strong, fast filly and she'll love fast ground. She's not there yet but she'll be a May 2-y-o and obviously we'd love to get to Royal Ascot. We've got a bit to go yet before we get there but I suspect that when she comes to hand she'll come quickly. A small, quite racy filly with a good attitude".*

717. STRATEGIST (IRE) ★★★
b.c. Shamardal – Snow Powder (Raven's Pass) January 31. First foal. The dam, a quite useful 1m and 10f placed maiden, is a half-sister to 6 winners including the Group 1 French 1,000 Guineas and 2-y-o Group 3 7f Prix du Calvados winner Elusive Wave. The second dam, Multicolour Wave (by Rainbow Quest), is a placed half-sister to 4 winners. (The Queen). *"I like him, he's quite a strong, well-made horse and he'll be a summer 2-y-o. He's got a bit of a quirk to him but I like these Shamardals, they're hard, solid, tough horses and I think he'll be fine once we get into him".*

718. TALLOW (IRE) ★★★ ♠
b.f. Kodiac – Flames (Blushing Flame). April 19. Eleventh foal. €100,000Y. Goffs Orby. Cheveley Park Stud. Half-sister to the Group 2 6f Rockfel Stakes (at 2 yrs) and Group 1 10f E P Taylor Stakes winner Lahaleeb (by Redback), to the fairly useful dual 6f (at 2 yrs) and listed 1m Masaka Stakes winner Precocious Star (by Bold Fact) and two minor winners abroad by Red Clubs and Redback. The dam is an unraced half-sister to 8 winners including the listed winner Dance Partner. The second dam, Dancing Debut (by Polar Falcon), is a placed half-sister to the dam of the Lockinge Stakes winner Virtual and the Coventry Stakes winner Iceman. (Cheveley Park Stud). *"I like her, she coughed a lot in the winter and got a bit behind but she's quite strong and well-*

made. A typical Kodiac and I think she'll be useful".

719. TANSEEQ ★★★★ ♠
b.c. Havana Gold – Roslea Lady (Alhaarth). February 2. Seventh foal. £160,000Y. Goffs UK Premier (Doncaster). Shadwell Estate Co. Half-brother to 2 winners including the quite useful 2-y-o 6f winner Hoot (by Invincible Spirit) and the modest 10f and 12f winner Royal Roslea (by Royal Applause). The dam, placed fourth once over 1m, is a half-sister to 3 winners including the Group 2 Gimcrack Stakes winner Conquest. The second dam, Aguinaga (by Machiavellian), won over 12.5f in Ireland and is a half-sister to 7 winners including the Group 1 Haydock Park Sprint Cup winner Iktamal and the Group 2 winners First Magnitude and Rockamundo. (Hamdan Al Maktoum). *"I like him; he's a charming horse, a nice mover and a strong, well-made colt. I think he's got a bit to offer and he'll be a summer 2-y-o too".*

720. TULIP FEVER ★★★
ch.f. Dutch Art – Cara Gina (Bahamian Bounty). March 8. First foal. The dam, a fair triple 6f winner, is a half-sister to three 5f winners including Royal Birth, a fairly useful winner of 6 races over 5f from 2 to 5 yrs. The second dam, Princess Georgina (by Royal Applause), a fair 2-y-o 5.2f winner, is a sister to the Group 2 6f Richmond Stakes winner Mister Cosmi and to the smart 2-y-o listed 6f winner Auditorium. (Mrs D James). *"She's alright but she had an accident in the box and she's been off for a bit. The mother was a useful sprint handicapper and this is her first foal. She's quite tall, likes to get on with it and I think she'll be a 2-y-o. I'm not sure she's a star, but she'll be ok".*

721. UMM AL NAR ★★★★
ch.f. Shamardal – Royal Secrets (Highest Honor). March 8. Half-sister to Sheikhzayedroad (by Dubawi), a winner of 11 races including the Group 1 12f Northern Dancer Turf Stakes and three Group 2's. The dam, a fair 1m winner, is a half-sister to the French listed winner and Group 3 placed Vernoy. The second dam, Marble Maiden (by Lead On Time), won the Grade 2 All Along Stakes and the Group 3 Prix de Sandringham

and is a half-sister to 5 winners. (Mohammed Jaber). *"I like her – I think she's a nice filly. Big and scopey and by a good sire, she's got a chance to be a good filly. She'll want seven furlongs minimum".*

722. VALIDATOR ★★★
b.f. Kodiac – Enact (Kyllachy). April 11. Half-sister to the 2017 3-y-o 7f winner, from two starts, Dubai Art (by Dubawi) and to the fair 7f (at 2 yrs) and 1m winner Star Of The Stage (by Invincible Spirit). The dam, a fairly useful dual 6f winner (including at 2 yrs), was listed-placed twice and is a full or half-sister to 5 winners. The second dam, Constitute (by Gone West), a quite useful 1m winner, is a half-sister to 8 winners including the smart Group 3 10f Select Stakes second Battle Chant. (Cheveley Park Stud). *"She'll be our first 2-y-o runner I think. A home-bred of Cheveley Park's, she's quite light framed but she goes well. She knows how to go and she wants to go, a typical Kodiac. He's a sire we've had a bit of luck with, they're tough, hardy and they run a lot. I think you need to get on and run them instead of waiting".*

723. WITH A START ★★
b.c. Sea The Stars – Sudden Blaze (Soviet Star). April 14. Fourth foal. 150,000Y. Tattersalls October Book 1. Not sold. Half-brother to the French 6.5f winner Soupcon (by Footstepsinthesand). The dam is an unraced sister to the US Grade 3 11f winner and Grade 1 placed Rosinka and a half-sister to 6 winners including the US Grade 1 winner King's Drama. The second dam, Last Drama (by Last Tycoon), won and was listed placed twice over 10f in France and is a sister to the listed winner and smart broodmare Tycoon's Drama and to the dam of the Group 1 Irish 1,000 Guineas winner Nightime. (Sunderland Holdings Ltd). *"He's quite colty but he's a really nice model and as with all these Sea The Stars he could be anything. They might be backward and a bit slow at this stage but they might be good too. We've got a fair sprinkling of them this year, so let's hope one of them can be good".*

724. YAJOOLL ★★★
b.c. Invincible Spirit – Tafiya (Bahri). May 3. Fifth foal. 100,000Y. Tattersalls October

Book 1. Shadwell Estate Co. Half-brother to the fairly useful 2-y-o 6f and 7f winner Overpowered (by Choisir) and to the modest 10f winner Sovereign Power (by Royal Applause). The dam, a fair 7f (at 2 yrs) to 11f placed maiden, is a half-sister to 5 winners including the useful Group 3 Dahlia Stakes winner Tarfah (dam of the 2,000 Guineas and Derby winner Camelot). The second dam, Fickle (by Danehill), a fairly useful 1m and listed 10f winner, is a half-sister to 7 winners including the listed winners Birdie and Faru. (Hamdan Al Maktoum). *"I like him, he's a late foal but he goes really well. He won't make Royal Ascot but he'll be a July 2-y-o and he's a nice horse. I like the way he goes and I see him starting at a seven furlongs".*

725. YOUNG RASCAL ★★★
b.c. Intello – Rock My Soul (Clodovil). February 14. Second foal. €215,000Y. Arqana Deauville August. Stroud/Coleman. The dam won three 1m listed events in Germany and is a half-sister to 6 winners. The second dam, Rondinay (by Cadeaux Genereux), a quite useful 2-y-o 6f winner, is a half-sister to 8 winners. (Mr B Kantor). *"I like him too, he's a nice, solid horse with quite a high knee action so may need some cut in the ground. He needs some time and is a back-end 2-y-o".*

726. UNNAMED ★★★★
b.f. Iffraaj – Bahia Breeze (Mister Baileys). March 4. Fifth foal. 120,000Y. Tattersalls October Book 2. Blandford Bloodstock. Sister to the quite useful 7f winner Khalaas and half-sister to the quite useful 2-y-o 6f winner Alsaaden (by Acclamation) and the minor winner and French listed 9f second Brioniya (by Pivotal). The dam, a very useful 6f (at 2 yrs) and 1m dual listed winner, was second in the Group 2 Betfred Mile and the Group 2 Prix Jean Romanet and is a half-sister to 3 winners. The second dam, Ring Of Love (by Magic Ring), a fair 5f winner of 4 races (including at 2 yrs), is a half-sister to 7 winners. (Sheikh Rashid Dalmook Al Maktoum). *"I like her a lot. She's a little open of her knees so I backed off her, but she's a strong, well-made filly. I had the brother Khalaas who was alright but this is much classier looking".*

727. UNNAMED ★★★
b.c. Iffraaj – Balladonia (Primo Dominie).
February 4. Eleventh foal. 95,000Y. Tattersalls
October Book 1. Not sold. Brother to the
very smart 2-y-o Group 1 7f Prix Jean-
Luc Lagardere winner of 5 races and sire
Wootton Bassett and to the fair 2-y-o 6f
winner Glenalmond and half-brother to 7
winners including the fairly useful 5f (at 2
yrs) to 1m winner of 7 races Mister Hardy
(by Kyllachy), the fairly useful 2-y-o 6f to 1m
and subsequent Hong Kong winner Zaal (by
Alhaarth) and the quite useful 2-y-o winners
Mister Laurel (by Diktat) and Related (by
Kheleyf). The dam, a useful 9f winner, was
listed-placed twice over 10f and is a half-sister
to 5 winners. The second dam, Susquehanna
Days (by Chief's Crown), a fair 1m and 8.2f
winner, is a half-sister to the Group 3 winner
and good broodmare Clare Bridge. (Abdulla
Al Mansoori). *"A full-brother to Wootton
Bassett, he's a nice, solid horse, has quite a bit
of temperament but he goes well".*

728. UNNAMED ★★★
b.f. Camacho – Bordighera (Alysheba). May
3. Sister to the useful 12f winner and Group
3 12f Pinnacle Stakes second Wonderstruck,
closely related to the Phoenix Stakes, National
Stakes, 2,000 Guineas and Queen Elizabeth
II Stakes winner George Washington (by
Danehill) and the quite useful 12f to 2m
and hurdles winner Lord Of The House (by
Danehill Dancer) and half-sister to numerous
winners including the Irish Champion Stakes,
Prince Of Wales's Stakes and Singapore
Airlines International Cup winner Grandera
(by Grand Lodge), the very useful listed 13.5f
winner Sun Central (by Galileo). The dam won
once over 13f in France, was second in the
listed 12f Prix des Tuileries and is a half-sister
to 7 winners. The second dam, Blue Tip (by
Tip Moss), won 4 races including the Group
3 10.5f Prix Penelope, was Group 2 placed
and is a half-sister to 7 winners. (Lael Stable).
*"She's the last filly out of the mare and we
also had the full sister Wonderstruck. I think
they used Camacho because he was so fertile
– the dam is very old now. She hasn't come
in yet but all the reports say she'll be a nice
second half of the season horse, with a bit of
scope".*

729. UNNAMED ★★
b.c. Dubawi – Check The Label (Stormin Fever).
April 19. Second foal. Brother to the 2016 7f
placed 2-y-o, from two starts, Isabel's On It.
The dam won 6 races at 2 and 3 yrs in the USA
including the Grade 1 9f Garden City Stakes
and the Grade 2 Sands Point Stakes and is a
half-sister to the US Grade 1 8.5f winner Include
Me Out and the minor US stakes winner On
The Menu. The second dam, Don't Trick Her (by
Mazel Trick), is an unraced half-sister to a US
stakes winner. (Lael Stable). *"He'll need some
time and will be a back-end 2-y-o if at all, but
the dam was a Grade 1 winner and I think the
3-y-o is quite useful. So he'll be a racehorse but
maybe not until next year".*

730. UNNAMED ★★★
b.f. Mayson – Golden Dirham (Kheleyf). March
11. Second foal. £50,000Y. Goffs UK Premier
(Doncaster). Blandford Bloodstock. The dam is
an unraced half-sister to 2 winners including
the listed sprint winner of 11 races in Italy
and Germany, Gamgoom. The second dam,
Danidh Dubai (by Noverre), a fairly useful
2-y-o 6f winner, was third in the Group 3
Albany Stakes and is a half-sister to 7 winners
including the Group 1 King's Stand Stakes
winner in Profitable. (Sheikh Juma Dalmook
Al Maktoum). *"I like her, she's a little bit open
of her knees so she needs a bit of time, but I
think she's a 2-y-o".*

731. UNNAMED ★★★
b.f. Farhh – Hurricane Harriet (Bertolini).
March 24. Second foal. 70,000Y. Tattersalls
October Book 2. Rabbah Bloodstock. Half-
sister to Kyllarney (by Kyllachy), a modest
French winner of 7 races at 3 and 4 yrs
including over 7.5f. The dam, a modest
triple 6f winner at 3 yrs, is a half-sister to 3
winners including the useful listed 10f winner
Katy Nowaitee (the dam of two Graded
stakes winners in the USA and Australia).
The second dam, Cold Blow (by Posse), a
modest 7f placed 2-y-o, is a half-sister to 3
minor winners. (Sheikh Rashid Dalmook Al
Maktoum). *"She's fine, she'll need some time
and I'm not sure she's a 2-y-o although there's
speed on the dam's side. I think she's alright,
she's a nice mover and has a good attitude, so
I quite like her".*

732. UNNAMED ★★
b.c. Dansili – Izzi Top (Pivotal). February 13. Second foal. 325,000Y. Tattersalls October Book 1. China Horse Club/Mayfair Speculators / Peter & Ross Doyle. The dam, a winner of 6 races including the Group 1 Prix Jean Romanet and the Group 1 Pretty Polly Stakes, is a half-sister to 2 winners including Jazzi Top (Group 2 Prix de la Nonette). The second dam, Zee Zee Top (by Zafonic), won the Group 1 10f Prix de l'Opera and is a half-sister to the Group 1 winners Opera House and Kayf Tara and to the unraced dam of the Group 1 winner Necklace. (M J Jooste & China Horse Club). *"I saw him at the sale but I haven't seen him since. He's backward and being broken in France. He cost a lot of money but it's a wonderful pedigree and he won't be arriving for another couple of months".*

733. UNNAMED ★★★
b.f. Zoffany – Just Joey (Averti). January 14. Second foal. £160,000Y. Goffs UK Premier (Doncaster). Amanda Skiffington. The dam, a quite useful triple 5f winner (including twice at 2 yrs), was listed-placed and is a half-sister to 2 minor winners. The second dam, Fly South (by Polar Falcon), is an unraced half-sister to 5 minor winners. (Lael Stable). *"A lovely filly that was bought at Doncaster, she's having a break at the moment but she's a nice filly. A little bit long maybe, she'll be an August 2-y-o I should think".*

734. UNNAMED ★★
b.f. Kodiac – Lady Avenger (Namid). April 18. Third foal. 260,000Y. Tattersalls October Book 1. Al Shaqab Racing/Mandore. Sister to the useful Group 3 6f Firth Of Clyde Stakes winner Shaden and half-sister to the quite useful triple 10f winner I'll Be Your Clown (by Aqlaam). The dam, a fairly useful 2-y-o 5f winner, was second in the listed National Stakes. The second dam, Shioda (by Bahri), is an unplaced half-sister to 8 winners. (Al Shaqab Racing). *"It's a proper 2-y-o pedigree but she hasn't arrived here yet and I haven't even seen her, so I can't make any comment".*

735. UNNAMED ★★★
ch.f. Kitten's Joy – Midnight Music (Dubawi). March 27. Second foal. $150,000Y. Keeneland September. Blandford Bloodstock. The dam

was a quite useful listed-placed 1m (at 2 yrs) to 2m winner. The second dam, Midnight Mist (by Green Desert), a fair Irish 7f and 1m winner, is a half-sister to 11 winners including the Canadian Grade 3 winner Madeira Mist (dam of the dual Grade 1 winner Joshua Tree) and the South African Group 1 winner Inara. (Sheikh Juma Dalmook Al Maktoum). *"She's nice. A big, fine, strong filly that'll need a bit of time. I like her, she's not early but not backward either and could be a proper filly in time".*

736. UNNAMED ★★★★
b.f. Invincible Spirit – Miss Delila (Malibu Moon). May 3. Seventh foal. 280,000Y. Tattersalls October Book 1. Blandford Bloodstock. Half-sister to 5 winners including the useful 6f (at 2 yrs) and Group 3 7f Chartwell Fillies' Stakes winner Lady Of The House (by Holy Roman Emperor) and the quite useful dual 10f winner Mythical Madness (by Dubawi). The dam is an unplaced half-sister to 5 winners including Sander Camillo (Group 2 Cherry Hinton Stakes and Group 3 Albany Stakes). The second dam, Staraway (by Star de Naskra), won 20 races in North America including three listed stakes. (Sheikh Juma Dalmook Al Maktoum). *"A lovely filly, she goes well too and she'll be a 2-y-o. She's got a bit of class, she's well-made, moves well and has a bit of quality".*

737. UNNAMED ★★★
ch.c. Exceed And Excel – Nianga (GER) (Lomitas). March 28. Fourth foal. 180,000Y. Baden Baden. Mayfair Speculators. Half-brother to Nossa (by Areion), second in a listed event in Italy over 6f at 2 yrs. The dam won three listed events in Germany over middle-distances. The second dam, Nobilissima (by Bluebird), was second in a listed event in Germany over 1m. (Mr M J Jooste). *"I like him, he's done very well and I think he's a 2-y-o. A strong horse, he's got a bit of quality, he's grown and done really well".*

738. UNNAMED ★★★★
b.c. Invincible Spirit – Rain Flower (Indian Ridge). April 10. Twelfth foal. 500,000Y. Tattersalls October Book 1. Charlie Gordon-Watson / Al Shaqab. Half-brother to 5

winners including the Group 1 Oaks and Group 1 German Oaks winner Dancing Rain, the fair 7f (at 2 yrs) and 1m winner Captain Dancer (both by Danehill Dancer), the 2-y-o listed 5f winner Sumora (dam of the Group 1 Moyglare Stud Stakes winner Maybe) and the useful Irish 2-y-o 7f winner Fleeting Shadow (both by Danehill). The dam is an unraced three-parts sister to the Epsom Derby, Irish Champion Stakes and Dewhurst Stakes winner Dr Devious and a half-sister to 5 winners including the Group 3 winners Royal Court and Archway. The second dam, Rose Of Jericho (by Alleged), is an unraced half-sister to 5 winners. (Al Shaqab Racing). *"Dancing Rain's brother. He was very awkward, difficult to break and very nervous but he's coming round now. He's having a break at the moment but he's doing really well, he's a nice model and I think he'll be a 2-y-o too".*

739. UNNAMED ★★★
b.f. Camelot – Rouge Noir (Saint Ballado). April 18. Tenth foal. 95,000Y. Tattersalls October Book 2. John & Jake Warren. Half-sister to 5 winners including the useful 2-y-o listed 5f winner Light The Fire (by Invincible Spirit), the useful 2-y-o 7f winner and listed-placed Cadley Road (by Elusive City), the fair 2-y-o 7f winner Joohaina (by New Approach) and the Italian winner of 7 races from 2 to 4 yrs Crazy Duck (by Kheleyf). The dam, a minor winner at 3 yrs in the USA, is a half-sister to 6 winners in Japan. The second dam, Ardana (by Danehill), won the Group 3 Premio Bagutta and is a half-sister to 5 winners. (Magnier & Tabor). *"She's a lovely filly, looks like a colt and is very strong. She's got a bit of a temperament, but she's very well-made, moves well and does everything right. She won't be early but I like the look of her".*

740. UNNAMED ★★★ ♠
b.c. Sea The Stars – Sentaril (Danehill Dancer). January 18. First foal. The dam, a useful dual 7f and listed 1m winner, was second in the Group 3 7f Jersey Stakes and is a sister to one winner and a half-sister 6 winners including the very smart Group 3 5f Molecomb Stakes and Group 3 5f King George Stakes winner Enticing. The second dam, Superstar Leo (by College Chapel), won 5 races the Group 2 5f Flying Childers Stakes and the Weatherbys

Super Sprint and is a full or half-sister to numerous winners. (Lael Stable). *"Quite an early foal, he's not quite as nice as one or two others I have by the sire, but she was a very useful mare and it's a very useful family. So there's a bit more speed there and he's alright".*

741. UNNAMED ★★★★
b.c. Sayif – Shyrl (Acclamation). February 14. Third living foal. Half-brother to the useful 2-y-o dual 6f winner, Group 2 Gimcrack Stakes third and Group 2 6f Mill Reef Stakes third Raucous (by Dream Ahead). The dam, a useful 2-y-o 5f winner, was second in the Group 2 5f Queen Mary Stakes and is a half-sister to 4 winners. The second dam, Finicia (by Miswaki), was placed four times at 2 yrs in France. (Saleh Al Homaizi & Imad I Sagar). *"He's a sharp colt and a half-brother to Raucous who we had. He's one of those that won't be early but he'll be fast. A well-made horse that goes well, he's not quite ready yet to step up so I would think he'll be a June/July 2-y-o, but he's a nice horse".*

MICHAEL HALFORD

742. ANDESH (IRE) ★★★
ch.c. Medicean – Adelfia (Sinndar). February 8. Seventh foal. Half-brother to the quite useful 2-y-o 1m winner Adelana (by Manduro),to the fairly useful 1m (at 2 yrs) and 9f winner Adilapour (by Azamour) and a hurdles winner by Nayef. The dam, a quite useful 12f winner, is a half-sister to several winners including the smart dual Group 3 winner Adilabad. The second dam, Adaiyka (by Doyoun), was a smart winner of the Group 3 9f Prix Chloe. (H H Aga Khan). *"A lovely, big, scopey colt and a good mover that's going to want seven or eight furlongs in the second half of the season. He looks up to winning as a 2-y-o".*

743. BLACKGOLD FAIRY (USA) ★★★
b.f. More Than Ready – London Bid (Rainbow Quest). March 17. Sixth foal. €62,000Y. Goffs Orby. BBA (Ire) & Yulong Investments. The dam, placed fourth once over 10f from 2 starts, is a half-sister to 4 minor winners. The second dam, Islington (by Sadler's Wells), was a high-class winner of 6 races including the Group 1 Yorkshire Oaks (twice), the Grade 1

Filly and Mare Turf and the Group 1 Nassau Stakes. She is a half-sister to the smart stayer Election Day and the smart 10f performer Greek Dance. (Y Zhang). *"A smart filly, she shows plenty of pace in her work and would want decent ground I'd say. She goes well, we like her and she should be up and running by the end of May. For a family with a lot of stamina this filly shows plenty of pace, so the sire may have helped there".*

744. CASINOMASTER (IRE) ★★★
ch.c. Arcano – Himiko (Aussie Rules). March 29. Second foal. Half-brother to the fair Irish 1m winner Yamato (by Big Bad Bob). The dam is an unraced half-sister to 5 winners including the useful dual listed 1m winner of 5 races and Group placed Deauville Vision. The second dam, Alexia Reveuse (by Dr Devious), is an unraced half-sister to 3 minor winners (T Kimura). *"He's a heavy-set, laid-back colt that shows pace so he might be able to start off at six furlongs. A good mover, he's a straightforward horse to start off in mid-season".*

745. PLATINUM WARRIOR (IRE) ★★★★
gr.c. Galileo – Laugh Out Loud (Clodovil). April 1. First foal. €200,000Y. Goffs Orby. BBA (Ire) / Yulong Investments. The dam, a winner of 4 races including the Group 2 1m Prix de Sandringham, is a half-sister to 7 winners including the dual listed winner Suzi's Decision. The second dam, Funny Girl (by Darshaan), was placed from 7f to 9f and is a half-sister to 3 winners. (Y Zhang). *"A lovely colt, he's well-balanced and has a terrific temperament. He's going to want seven furlongs but he goes well and we like him. If anything he looks more of a Clodovil than a Galileo".*

746. PORT LIONS (IRE) ★★★★
b.c. Kodiac – Cold Cold Woman (Machiavellian). February 1. Seventh foal. €220,000Y. Goffs Orby. John Ferguson. Half-brother to the minor US winner of 3 races First Settler (by War Chant), to the fair 10f winner Nosey Barker (by Rip Van Winkle) and a minor winner in Argentina by Giant's Causeway. The dam, a fairly useful dual 9f and subsequent US listed stakes winner, is a half-sister to 8 winners including the Group 1 Tattersalls Gold

Cup third Robin Hood and the dam of the Group 2 Summer Mile winner Aljamaaheer. The second dam, Banquise (by Last Tycoon), a French 2m winner, is a half-sister to the Group winners Modhish, Russian Snows and Truly Special. (Godolphin). *"He's a colt we like; he goes well and is a lovely mover. He's not one of those Kodiacs that are like little bullets, he's got a bit of size and scope to him. He's only started fast work recently, has a great temperament and he'll be running by mid-season".*

747. TERZETTO (IRE) ★★★
ch.f. Iffraaj – Calando (Storm Cat). February 27. Ninth foal. Half-sister to the useful 2016 2-y-o listed 1m winner Calare (by Dubawi), to the useful 2-y-o listed 7f Chesham Stakes winner Champlain (by Seeking The Gold), the quite useful 10f winner Ustura (by Nayef), the modest 5f to 1m winner of 10 races Sovereignty (by King's Best) and a minor winner abroad by Echo Of Light. The dam won the Group 3 1m May Hill Stakes, was second in the Group 1 Fillies Mile and third in the French 1,00 Guineas and is a half-sister to 2 winners, Diminuendo (by Diesis), won the Hoover Fillies Mile, Cherry Hinton Stakes (both at 2 yrs), Epsom Oaks, Irish Oaks (in a dead-heat), Yorkshire Oaks and Musidora Stakes. (Godolphin). *"She's a nice filly, very straightforward and with a good attitude. She's recently started fast work and is doing well, so she'll probably start over seven furlongs in the summer".*

748. UNNAMED ★★★
b.f. Footstepsinthesand – Adjaliya (Sinndar) February 10. Fourth foal. Half-sister to the lightly raced 1m winner Arif by Nayef). The dam, a fairly useful Irish 7f (at 2 yrs) and 12f winner, is a half-sister to 6 winners including the useful Irish 7f, 1m and jumps winner Adajal. The second dam, Adalya (Darshaan), is an unplaced sister to the high-class Group 3 12f Lingfield Oaks Trial winner and disqualified Epsom Oaks winner Aliysa and a half-sister to the minor French 9f winner Aleema (herself dam of the high-class middle-distance colt Altayan). (H H Aga Khan). *"We like her, she shows us plenty of pace for an Aga Khan filly and could be running in May over six furlongs. She's got plenty of size and scope".*

749. UNNAMED ★★★
b.f. Teofilo – Bright Morning (GB) (Dubai Millennium). April 12. Ninth foal. Half-sister to the fairly useful 2-y-o 6f winner Risen Sun (by Shamardal), to the quite useful 2-y-o 6f winner Rosy Morning (by Exceed And Excel) and the French dual 7.5f winner Incorruptible (by Cape Cross). The dam, a French 2-y-o 6.5f winner, is a half-sister to numerous winners including the top-class National Stakes, Irish 2,000 Guineas and Irish Derby winner Desert King and the useful 2-y-o 6f and 7f winner and Group 2 7f Champagne Stakes third Chianti. The second dam, Sabaah (by Nureyev), a modest 8.2f placed maiden, is a full or half-sister to 8 winners including the Group 1 1m Queen Elizabeth II Stakes winner Maroof and to the placed dam of the Canadian Grade 2 winner Callwood Dancer. (Godolphin). *"She's a filly we like. A lovely, big filly, well-balanced, a good attitude and with plenty of size and scope. I can see her making a 2-y-o in the second half of the year over seven furlongs. She goes well".*

750. UNNAMED ★★★
b.f. Rock Of Gibraltar – Kaladena (Daylami). April 10. Third foal. The dam, quite useful winner over 13f, is a half-sister to numerous winners including the Champion Stakes and Breeders' Cup Turf winner Kalanisi and the Group 2 10f Scottish Derby winner and Group 1 St James's Palace Stakes second Kalaman. The second dam, Kalamba (by Green Dancer), was placed over 9f and 10f. (H H Aga Khan). *"A beautiful looking filly, she's well-balanced and a good mover. We've recently started to increase her work, she shows us pace and has an attitude to match her action. Goes really well".*

751. UNNAMED ★★★★
b.c. Street Cry – Mahkama (Bernardini). February 4. Second foal. $180,000Y. Keeneland September. BBA (Ire) & Yulong Investments. The dam, a quite useful 2-y-o 6f winner, is a half-sister to 4 winners including the US Grade 3 Tempted Stakes winner Summer Raven (herself the dam of three US Graded stakes winners). The second dam, Rahy Rose (by Rahy), won 2 minor races at 4 yrs in the USA and is a half-sister to 5 winners including the dual Grade 1 winner Wild Rush.

(Y Zhang). *"A lovely, strong colt with a lovely action and he looks a real 2-y-o. He does everything well and should be running by the end of May or June over six furlongs".*

RICHARD HANNON

I must thank Richard once again for my visit in late March to discuss his lovely two-year-olds. His assistants Tony Gorman and Tom Ward were particularly helpful.

752. ALBISHR ★★★
b.c. Clodovil – Casual Remark (Trans Island). March 3. Fifth living foal. €38,000Y. Goffs Orby. Peter & Ross Doyle. Half-brother to the fair Irish 12f winner Remarkable Lady (by Zoffany), to the modest 7f and 8.5f winner Big Sylv (by Clodovil) and the moderate 6f (including at 2 yrs) and 7f winner Dandys Perier (by Dandy Man). The dam, a modest 2-y-o 1m fourth placed maiden, is a half-sister to 4 winners including the Italian listed 1m winner Carioca and the Group 2 6f Mill Reef Stakes second Irony. The second dam, Cidaris (by Persian Bold), ran once unplaced and is a half-sister to 3 winners including the dam of the South African Grade 1 winners Rabiya and Bela-Bela. *"He's quite tall and leggy at the moment so he'll take a bit of time, but once he fills out he should be a nice horse. One for the middle-to-end of the season probably. He looks like a nice buy for the price and he's showing all the right signs so far".*

753. AL FUJAIRAH ★★★ ♠
b.c. Showcasing – First Term (Acclamation). April 30. Third foal. €62,000Y. Goffs Sportsmans. Peter & Ross Doyle. The dam, a modest maiden, was fourth twice over 6f at 2 and 3 yrs and is a half-sister to 5 minor winners. The second dam, School Days (by Slip Anchor), a fair dual 1m winner, is a half-sister to 4 minor winners. *"A lovely, straightforward horse, he's a nice colt that'll start off at six furlongs".*

754. ALL OUT ★★★★ ♠
b.f. Acclamation – Time Over (Mark Of Esteem). March 30. Fifth living foal. Half-sister to the useful 2-y-o 7f and 1m winner and Group 2 Doncaster Cup third Repeater (by Montjeu) and the quite useful 12f and 13f winner Late Shipment (by Authorized). The

dam, a fair 1m winner, is closely related to the Group 3 10.4f Musidora Stakes winner and dual Group 1 placed Time Away (dam of the Group 2 winner Time On) and a half-sister to 5 winners including the Group 1 French Oaks second Time Ahead. The second dam, Not Before Time (by Polish Precedent), is an unraced half-sister to 7 winners including the Group 2 12f winners Zinaad and Time Allowed. *"She looks sharp, she's been showing all the right signs at home and has plenty of speed on the gallops. We've haven't done a huge amount with her but from what she's done so far you can see she's got ability and you'll see her out fairly early I'd say. Not overly big, but she looks sharp".*

755. ANCHISES ★★★
b.c. Choisir – Afrodita (Montjeu). April 1. Third foal. £75,000Y. Goffs UK Premier (Doncaster). Peter & Ross Doyle. The dam ran once unplaced and is a half-sister to 8 winners including the Group 1 placed and smart broodmare Dance To The Top and the listed winner and Australian Group 1 placed Polar Bear. The second dam, Aim For The Top (by Irish River), won the Group 3 7f Premio Chiusura and is a half-sister to 6 winners including the Gimcrack Stakes winner Splendent. *"A horse that's grown a lot, so he won't be too early. He's a six/seven furlong 2-y-o and he's making up into a nice colt".*

756. ANNA NERIUM ★★★★
ch.f. Dubawi – Anna Oleanda (Old Vic). April 17. Tenth living foal. 300,000Y. Tattersalls October Book 1. Not sold. Sister to the smart 2-y-o Group 3 7f Horris Hill Stakes winner Piping Rock and to the quite useful dual 1m winner Alkawn and half-sister to 5 winners including the Group 3 Prix d'Astarte winner and Group 2 Oaks d'Italia second Middle Club (by Fantastic Light), the French dual 10.5f winner and Group 3 Prix de Royaumont third Anna Mona (by Monsun) and the German listed-placed Anna Royal (by Royal Dragon). The dam won twice at 3 yrs in Germany and is a sister to the German Group 3 winner Anno Luce and a half-sister to the dams of four Group winners. The second dam, Anna Paola (by Prince Ippi), won the Group 2 German Oaks. *"A filly from a good family and we've had plenty of them. She's not over-big but she*

shows plenty of speed and she's a lovely filly with a great temperament. Even though she's by Dubawi you'll probably see her out over six furlongs".

757. BATHSHEBA BAY (IRE) ★★★
b.c. Footstepsinthesand – Valamareha (Val Royal). April 3. Fourth foal. €85,000Y. Tattersalls Ireland September. Peter & Ross Doyle. The dam, a fair 7.5f and 8.5f winner, is a half-sister to 6 winners. The second dam, Mareha (by Cadeaux Genereux), a fairly useful listed-placed 7f and 1m winner, is a half-sister to 2 winners. *"A lovely, big colt that's going to take time but he's cantering away beautifully and he's a good mover. He has a good attitude and looks like one for the middle of the season. We're really happy with him".*

758. BEZOS ★★★
b.c. Famous Name – Midnight Oasis (Oasis Dream). March 7. Fourth foal. £85,000Y. Goffs UK Premier (Doncaster). F Barberini / Middleham Park. Half-brother to the quite useful 2016 2-y-o 6f and 7f winner Mutahaady (by Elzaam), to the useful 6f winner of 5 races at 3 and 4 yrs Mr Win (by Intikhab) and the fairly useful 6f winner of 4 races at 2 and 3 yrs George Bowen (by Dark Angel). The dam is an unplaced half-sister to 7 winners including Miss Anabaa (Group 3 Ballyogan Stakes). The second dam, Midnight Shift (by Night Shift), a fair dual 6f winner at 3 yrs, is a half-sister to 8 winners including the Group 1 6f July Cup winner Owington. *"He's done very well and looks like he'll be fairly early. Not overly tall, but there's plenty of him and he's a good-moving horse that really sticks his head down. I think you'll see him in the early part of the season and he looks like he's got a bit of ability".*

759. BODYBUILDER ★★★
b.c. Power – Looks All Right (Danehill Dancer). February 1. Second foal. £42,000Y. Goffs UK Premier (Doncaster). Peter & Ross Doyle. Half-brother to the 2016 Italian 2-y-o winner Oakville (by Arcano). The dam is an unplaced sister to the Group 3 7f C L Weld Park Stakes winner Venturi and the French listed winner and Group 1 third Feels All Right and a half-sister to 2 winners. The second dam, Zagreb Flyer (by Old Vic), is an unraced half-sister to

8 winners. *"Not overly big, but stocky enough and he's a nice colt that'll be fairly early I'd say. Showing all the right signs, it looks like he could be a nice horse and is probably one for six furlongs to start with".*

760. BOING ★★★ ♠
b.c. Bated Breath – Lomapamar (Nashwan). February 25. Eighth foal. 48,000Y. Tattersalls October Book 2. Will Edmeades. Half-brother to 5 winners including the useful 2016 2-y-o 6f and 7f winner and Group 1 Fillies' Mile third Urban Fox (by Foxwedge), the fair 1m (at 2 yrs) to 14f winner Getaway Car (by Medicean), the fair 2-y-o 6f winner Ghost Cat (by Equiano) and the moderate 1m and hurdles winner Mister Fantastic (by Green Tune). The dam, a fair 10f winner, is a half-sister to 8 winners including the 2-y-o Group 2 1m Royal Lodge Stakes winner Mons and the Irish Oaks third Inforapenny. The second dam, Morina (by Lyphard), won over 11f in France and is a half-sister to 10 winners. *"A good type of horse for the middle of the season. He's nicely made and one for the six/ seven furlong races".*

761. BOMBSHELL BAY ★★★
b.c. Foxwedge – Cumana Bay (Dansili). March 10. Half-brother to the fair 2016 2-y-o 7f winner Sans Souci Bay (by Medicean), to the fair 2-y-o 5f and 6f winner La Tinta Bay (by Compton Place) and the moderate 7f winner Guapo Bay (by Showcasing). The dam, a quite useful 5f (at 2 yrs), 7f and 1m winner, is a half-sister to one winner. The second dam, Mayaro Bay (by Robellino), a very useful 6f (at 2 yrs) to 1m winner, is a half-sister to 4 winners including the Group 2 7f Rockfel Stakes winner Distant Valley. *"He's one of the biggest from the family we've had. A nice horse that's doing everything right, he'll be a six/seven furlong type 2-y-o. We've had all the family and they've all done well for us".*

762. BON SCOTTE ★★★
b.c. Kodiac – Bonne (Namid). April 15. Fourth foal. £50,000Y. Goffs UK Premier (Doncaster). Peter & Ross Doyle. The dam, a modest 6f winner, is a half-sister to 5 winners including the South African dual Grade 2 winner Espumanti and the dual listed winner Rising Shadow. The second dam, Jouet (by

Reprimand), is a placed sister to the dual Group 3 winning sprinter Deep Finesse and a half-sister to the dam of the dual Group 1 winner Dick Turpin. *"He's quite a tall, leggy horse that's going to take some time just to strengthen up. A good mover with a good attitude, he'll be a nice horse from the middle of the season onwards but for a Kodiac he's taking a bit of time. Doing everything OK at the moment".*

763. BULLINGDON ★★★
b.c. Dansili – Rimth (Oasis Dream). March 18. Third foal. Half-brother to the 2017 3-y-o 1m debutant winner Garrick (by Galileo). The dam, a winner over 5f (at 2 yrs) and the Group 3 7f Fred Darling Stakes, was second in the Group 1 Cheveley Park Stakes. The second dam, Dorelia (by Efisio), a fair 1m winner, is a half-sister to 3 winners including the smart Group 2 5f King's Stand Stakes and Group 3 5f Cornwallis Stakes winner Dominica. *"A thick-set horse, we won't be in any hurry with him and I see him being a six/seven furlong 2-y-o".*

764. CAMPION ★★★
b.f. Exceed And Excel – Princess Janie (Elusive Quality). April 10. Sixth foal. Closely related to the modest 6f winner Wishsong (by Dansili) and half-sister to the fairly useful 2016 2-y-o listed-placed 6f winner Lundy (by Fastnet Rock), the quite useful dual 5f winner, at 2 and 4 yrs, Wild Tobacco (by More Than Ready) and the minor US 3-y-o winner Lazulite (by Harlan's Holiday). The dam, a US stakes winner of 4 races at 3 and 4 yrs, is a half-sister to 8 winners including the dual Grade 3 winner Raylene. The second dam, Petite Princess (by Dayjur), a dual 2-y-o winner in Ireland and Group 3 placed, is a half-sister to 5 winners including the dual Group 1 winner Ad Valorem. *"She's done very well because she was small and she's grown up a bit now. A nice filly for when the six furlong races start".*

765. CARP KID ★★★
b.c. Lope De Vega – Homegrown (Mujadil). March 23. Sixth foal. 55,000Y. Tattersalls October Book 2. Peter & Ross Doyle. Half-brother to the fair dual 7f and subsequent minor Italian winner Avatar Star (by Peintre

Celebre). The dam, a fairly useful 5f to 1m winner in Ireland, was listed placed and is a half-sister to 2 minor winners. The second dam, Don't Wary (by Lomond), won 7 minor races in France from 3 to 5 yrs is a half-sister to 5 winners including New Target (Group 3 Prix Exbury). *"A good, strong horse for the middle of the season over seven furlongs".*

766. CHEEKY RASCAL ★★★

b.c. Most Improved – Bessie Lou (Montjeu). March 15. Second foal. €32,000Y. Tattersalls Ireland September. Peter & Ross Doyle. The dam, placed three times from 1m to 11.5f on the Flat and a winner over hurdles, is a half-sister to 3 winners. The second dam, Almond Mousse (by Exit To Nowhere), a French listed winner of 3 races from 1m to 10f and third in the Group 2 Sun Chariot Stakes, is a half-sister to 7 winners. *"A nice horse and a great mover, he's not overly tall but has plenty of substance about him. There are a few people raving about his first season sire so he might be OK hopefully. He's doing everything nicely and is probably a six/seven furlong 2-y-o".*

767. CLEW BAY BOY ★★★★

b.c. Arakan – Gassal (Oasis Dream). February 8. Fourth foal. €40,000Y. Tattersalls Ireland September. Peter & Ross Doyle. The dam, a modest 2-y-o 7f winner, is a half-sister to 7 winners. The second dam, Hasten (by Lear Fan), was placed twice in the USA and is a half-sister to 9 winners including the 2-y-o Group 3 Autumn Stakes winner and Group 1 Racing Post Trophy second Fantastic View. *"A lovely horse, he's a really nice mover and will probably be a mid-season 2-y-o. One for six/seven furlongs, he's doing everything really well and he's got a great attitude. He looks like he could be a nice horse and the sire's been very lucky for us".*

768. COASTAL DRIVE ★★

gr.c. Harbour Watch – Added Attraction (Kendor). April 19. Fifth foal. £52,000Y. Goffs UK Premier (Doncaster). Peter & Ross Doyle. The dam, a French winner of 3 races including once at 2 yrs over 1m, is a half-sister to 5 winners including the Group 1 Criterium International winner French Fifteen. The second dam, Spring Morning (by Ashkalani), won two minor races in France at 4 yrs and is

a half-sister to 6 winners. *"A nice horse that's going to take time like most 2-y-o's by the sire last year. He's got all the substance there for you, he looks like a decent animal but we'll bide our time with him. A middle-to-late season 2-y-o for six/seven furlongs and we'll find out a lot more over the coming months".*

769. DANDIESQUE (IRE) ★★★

b.f. Dandy Man – Marigold (Marju). April 24. Seventh foal. €46,000Y. Tattersalls Ireland September. Peter & Ross Doyle. Half-sister to the quite useful 6f (at 2 yrs) to 12f winner of 10 races Art Scholar (by Pyrus) and to the fair 6f winner Jaeger Train (by Captain Rio). The dam, a quite useful 12f and 13f winner, is a half-sister to 9 winners including Imperial Monarch (Group 1 Grand Prix de Paris), the dual Group 3 winner Mount Athos and the Group 1 placed The Great Gatsby, Roman Empress and Magritte. The second dam, Ionian Sea (by Slip Anchor), a listed 12f winner in France, is a half-sister to 4 winners including the Derby second Blue Stag. *"She looks sharp. Not big but with a massive hind-end on her, she should be one of our earlier runners. Coming along nicely, she'll definitely have the speed for five furlongs, so we'll kick on and try and get a couple under our belt".*

770. DE BRUYNE HORSE ★★★

b.c. Showcasing – Right Rave (Soviet Star). February 26. Third foal. £50,000Y. Goffs UK Premier (Doncaster). Peter & Ross Doyle. The dam, a fair 5f (at 2 yrs) to 9f winner of 3 races, is a half-sister to 5 winners. The second dam, Genuinely (by Entrepreneur), is a placed half-sister to 2 winners. *"A lovely horse actually and very similar to our Famous Name 2-y-o in stature – he's very stocky and looks fairly early as well. I'd expect him to be out in the first part of the season, he sticks his head down and gallops and so hopefully he'll be a nice horse".*

771. DOCTOR JAZZ (IRE) ★★★

b.c. Most Improved – Daliyana (Cadeaux Genereux). February 27. Tenth foal. £90,000Y. Goffs UK Premier (Doncaster). Peter & Ross Doyle. The dam, a fair 10f and 12f placed maiden, is a half-sister to the Group 1 Coronation Cup and Group 1 Hong Kong Vase winner Daliapour and to the smart 2m Queens Vase winner Dalampour. The second dam, Dalara (by Doyoun), winner of the Group 2 12.5f Prix de Royallieu, was third in the Group 1 Prix Royal-Oak and is a half-sister the French Derby winner and high-class sire Darshaan and the Prix Vermeille winner Darara (dam of the Group 1 winners Dar Re Mi, Rewilding, Diaghilev and Darazari). *"A big horse by a first season sire that we don't know a lot about. A seven furlong type 2-y-o, he won't be early but he's a nice colt".*

772. DOTTED SWISS (IRE) ★★★★
b.f. Swiss Spirit – Luxuria (Kheleyf). March 3. Fifth foal. £80,000Y. Goffs UK Premier (Doncaster). Peter & Ross Doyle. Half-sister to the fair 5f and 6f winner Crisis Averted and to the fair dual 6f winner In My Place (both by Compton Place) and the fair 2-y-o 5f winner on her only start Moving Melody (by Equiano). The dam, a modest 2-y-o 6f winner, is a half-sister to 4 winners including the 2-y-o listed 5f winner and Group 3 6f Princess Margaret Stakes third Sweepstake. The second dam, Dust Flicker (by Suave Dancer), placed fourth once over 10f, is a sister to the Group 3 winner Dust Dancer (herself dam of the US Grade 2 winner Spotlight) and a half-sister to 6 winners including Bulaxie (dam of the Group 2 winner Claxon). *"A very nice filly that goes really well. We've had a few out of the family and this one will be a middle-to-back-end of the season type for six/seven furlongs".*

773. DRAKEFELL ★★★★
b.c. Canford Cliffs – Cake (Acclamation). February 10. Fourth foal. Brother to the fairly useful 2016 listed-placed 5f and 5.5f 2-y-o winner Tomily and half-brother to the useful 2-y-o 5f and listed 6f winner Fig Roll (by Bahamian Bounty). The dam, a useful 2-y-o listed 5f winner of 4 races, is a full or half-sister to 6 winners. The second dam, Carpet Lady (by Night Shift), a fair dual 6f placed 2-y-o, is a half-sister to 5 winners including the Hong Kong stakes winner Classic Fountain. *"He'll be an early type just like the rest of the family. A good, strong horse, he'll be a five/six furlong 2-y-o. He's quite like his year older brother Tomily except he's the biggest member of the family we've had. A grand horse that'll be ready to go soon".*

774. EASTERN SUNRISE ★★★
b.f. Dawn Approach – Desert Sunrise (Green Desert). March 20. Second foal. 60,000Y. Tattersalls October Book 2. Not sold. Half-sister to the quite useful 2016 2-y-o 1m winner Desert Water (by Sepoy). The dam, a fair 6f and 7f placed maiden, is a half-sister to 3 winners including the Group1 Middle Park Stakes winner Primo Valentino and the Group 2 Cherry Hinton Stakes winner Dora Carrington. The second dam, Dorothea Brooke (by Dancing Brave), a fair 9f winner, is a half-sister to 6 winners. *"A thick-set filly, we wouldn't be in a hurry with her but I see her as one to set off at six furlongs".*

775. EMBOUR ★★★★ ♠
b.c. Acclamation – Carpet Lady (Night Shift). April 28. Eleventh foal. £145,000Y. Goffs UK Premier (Doncaster). Peter & Ross Doyle. Brother to the useful 2-y-o listed 5f winner of 4 races and Group 3 Cornwallis Stakes third Cake, the quite useful 5f (at 2 yrs) and 6f winner Young John and the fair 2-y-o 7f winner Heskin and half-brother to 5 winners including the 5f and 6f winner of 7 races Tagula Night, the 7f and 1m winner Suited And Booted (both by Tagula) – both quite useful. The dam, a fair dual 6f placed 2-y-o, is a half-sister to 5 winners. The second dam, Lucky Fountain (by Lafontaine), is an unraced sister to the Group 2 Geoffrey Freer Stakes winner Shambo. *"We've had a lot of this family before and this is a good, strong colt. Hopefully we'll get into him early and he'll be racing over five/six furlongs. A very nice colt".*

776. GALACTIC ★★★
b.c. Roderic O'Connor – Star Cluster (Observatory). March 23. Eighth foal. €50,000Y. Goffs Orby. Peter & Ross Doyle. Half-brother to the fair 1m winner Executor (by Cacique), to the modest 12f winner Asterism (by Motivator) and the moderate 5.5f and 6f winner Encapsulated (by Zamindar). The dam, a useful 7f (at 2 yrs) and listed 1m winner, is a half-sister to 7 winners including the 6f (at 2 yrs here) and US Grade 2 8.5f winner Didina (herself dam of the high-class broodmare Tantina) and the smart French listed 10f winner Espionage. The second dam, Didicoy (by Danzig), a listed-placed winner of 3 races over 6f, is closely

related to the Group 3 1m Prix Quincey winner Masterclass and a half-sister to 12 winners including the champion 2-y-o Xaar. *"A lovely, big horse, he's very nice but we won't be in any hurry with him. He'll be a six/seven furlong horse from the middle of the season onwards".*

777. GENDARME ★★★
b.c. Lawman – Gravitation (Galileo). March 4. Fifth foal. Half-brother to the quite useful 2016 2-y-o listed-placed7f winner Gemina (by Holy Roman Emperor), to the useful listed-placed 7f (at 2 yrs) and 10f winner Gibeon (by Cape Cross) and the quite useful 11.5f winner Girling (by Rock Of Gibraltar). The dam won the Group 3 14f Lillie Langtry Stakes. The second dam, Guaranda (by Acatenango), a fairly useful 10f and 12.3f, was listed-placed and is a half-sister to 7 winners including the multiple Group 1 winner Fame And Glory. *"A nice horse, we've had a few from the family and he's not one we'll be in a hurry with. A seven furlong type 2-y-o".*

778. GLACEON ★★★
b.f. Zoffany – Ihtiraam (Teofilo). April 14. Second foal. €70,000Y. Goffs Sportsmans. Peter & Ross Doyle. The dam, a fair 2-y-o 6f winner, is a half-sister to one winner. The second dam, Park Romance (by Dr Fong), a fairly useful 2-y-o 6f winner, was third in the Group 3 Sweet Solera Stakes and is a half-sister to 6 winners including the 6f (at 2 yrs) and Group 3 7f Ballycorus Stakes winner Rum Charger (herself dam of the US multiple Grade 1 winner Winchester). *"A sharp filly that knows her job, she's one we'll be looking for early on and hopefully she'll be sharp enough for five furlongs".*

779. GLACIER ★★★
b.c. Canford Cliffs – Ice Pie (Mount Nelson). April 18. First foal. 65,000Y. Tattersalls October Book 2. Peter & Ross Doyle. The dam, a fair 2-y-o 1m winner, is a half-sister to 5 winners including the dual listed winner and Group 3 Diomed Stakes second St Moritz. The second dam, Statua (by Statoblest), third in the Group 3 Rockfel Stakes, later won 3 races in the USA and is a half-sister to 8 winners including the Group 3/Grade 3 winner Bluegrass Prince. *"The sire really has to pick*

his game up because he hasn't had a lot of luck, but this colt looks nice. He's showing all the right signs and I'd expect him to be racing by mid-season. He's a good mover with a good attitude, does everything nicely and I'd say he'll be sharper than his dam was".

780. HIGHLAND MARY ★★★★
b.f. Dark Angel – Albertine Rose (Namid). March 22. Fourth living foal. £36,000Y. Goffs UK Premier (Doncaster). Peter & Ross Doyle. Half-sister to the fair 2-y-o 5f winner Paytheprice (by Lawman) and to the modest 8.5f winner Mandria (by Duke Of Marmalade). The dam, a quite useful 2-y-o 6f winner, was listed placed over 6f and is a half-sister to 5 winners. The second dam, Barathiki (by Barathea), a quite useful 2-y-o dual 6f winner, is a half-sister to 3 winners including the useful Peacock Alley, a winner of 3 races at around 7f and listed-placed. *"A lovely filly, she's still growing and is quite narrow in the middle at the moment but once she fills out she should make a nice filly. A bloody good mover, she has a good attitude and could be anything really. One for the middle of the season onwards, we're happy with her. A nice filly".*

781. LADY GODIVA (IRE) ★★★★
b.f. Camelot – For Evva Silca (Piccolo). February 8. Ninth foal. €80,000Y. Goffs Orby. Peter & Ross Doyle. Half-sister to the fair 2016 2-y-o winner Joyce Compton, to the Japanese 2-y-o Group 3 6f winner Meiner Eternel (both by Tamayuz), the very useful Irish listed 5f (at 2 yrs), 6f and UAE 7f winner of 6 races Warsaw (by Danehill Dancer) and the fair 2-y-o 7f winner Ripinto (by Rip Van Winkle). The dam, placed once at 2 yrs, is a half-sister to 9 winners including the 2-y-o Group 1 6f Prix Morny winner Silca's Sister and the Group 2 6f Mill Reef Stakes and German Group 2 winner Golden Silca. The second dam, Silca-Cisa (by Hallgate), a fairly useful dual 5f winner, was listed placed over 5f at 4 yrs and is a half-sister to the Group 3 placed sprinter Azizzi. *"A lovely filly, she's very strong and has done really well. Hopefully she'll be early and I see her as is a five/six furlong type 2-y-o. A few of these Camelot's are looking sharper than you might think".*

782. LETHAL LUNCH ★★★★ ♠♠
br.c. Lethal Force – Pin Cushion (Pivotal).
April 14. Third foal. £62,000Y. Goffs UK
Premier (Doncaster). Peter & Ross Doyle.
Half-brother to the fair 2016 2-y-o 5f winner
Tadkirah (by Acclamation) and to the modest
2-y-o 7f winner Pinch A Kiss (by Sakhee's
Secret). The dam, a fair 6f winner, is a half-
sister to 3 winners. The second dam, Frizzante
(by Efisio), won 7 races including the Group
1 July Cup and is a half-sister to 4 winners
including the Stewards Cup winner Zidane
and the dual 6f listed winner Firenze. *"He
looks sharp and should be running early over
five furlongs. A nice horse, we're really happy
with him, he's not overly big but he looks
sharp and is doing everything well at the
moment".*

783. LETSBE AVENUE (IRE) ★★★
b.c. Lawman – Aguilas Perla (Indian Ridge).
May 4. Ninth foal. 36,000Y. Tattersalls
October Book 2. Peter & Ross Doyle. Half-
brother to 5 winners including the fairly
useful Irish listed-placed 2-y-o 5f and 7f
winner Spirit Of Pearl (by Invincible Spirit),
the fair 6f (at 2 yrs) to 1m winner of 8 races
Annes Rocket (by Fasliyev), the fair 2-y-o 6f
winner Al Mahmeyah (by Teofilo) and the
modest Irish dual 6f winner Hazelwood Ridge
(by Mozart). The dam is an unraced sister
to the Irish listed 7f winner Cool Clarity and
a half-sister to the listed winners Artistic
Blue and Queen Of Palms. The second dam,
Tapolite (by Tap On Wood), a listed 7f winner,
is a sister to Sedulous (2-y-o Group 3 1m
Killavullen Stakes). *"A big horse, all he's done
is grow and he won't be out until the seven
furlong or mile races in the second half of the
season".*

784. LEXINGTON GRACE ★★★★
b.f. Sir Prancealot – Bronze Baby (Silver
Charm). May 1. Fifth foal. €36,000Y.
Tattersalls Ireland September. Peter & Ross
Doyle. Half-sister to the fair 2-y-o 7f winner
Scutum, to the modest 7f winner Sunbaked
(both by Kodiac) and the poor 10f winner
Redlorryyellowlorry (by Bushranger). The
dam is an unplaced half-sister 4 winners
including the dual Group 3 winner and triple
Group 1 placed Arch Swing. The second dam,
Gold Pattern (by Slew O'Gold), a minor US

winner of 4 races, is a half-sister to 7 winners.
*"She could be sharp and we'll be looking to get
her out quite early in the season. One for five
or six furlongs, she looks like she's got plenty
of speed and may well be one to follow".*

785. MAAWARD (IRE) ★★★★
b.c. Kodiac – Caterina Di Cesi (Cape Town).
March 31. Fifth foal. £78,000Y. Goffs UK
Premier (Doncaster). Peter & Ross Doyle.
Half-sister to the quite useful dual 5f winner,
including at 2 yrs, Mignolino (by Kodiac). The
dam, a minor Italian 6f winner, is a half-sister
to 2 winners including the 2-y-o Group 3
Queen Mary Stakes and Group 3 Molecomb
Stakes winner and Group 1 Cheveley Park
Stakes winner Risky. The second dam, Dona
Krista (by King Of Spain), a 2-y-o 6f winner, is
a half-sister to 2 winners. *"A lovely, strong colt
that goes very well. We'll be waiting for the six
furlong races so we're not rushing him. A nice
colt, a good 'doer' and a good mover".*

786. MAGHAWEER (IRE) ★★★
ch.c. Dubawi – Indian Ink (Indian Ridge).
April 27. Third foal. Half-brother to the fairly
useful triple 6f winner (including at 2 yrs)
Wahaab (by Tamayuz) and to the fair 2-y-o
6f winner Abaq (by Oasis Dream). The dam
won the Group 1 6f Cheveley Park Stakes and
the Group 1 1m Coronation Stakes and is a
full or half-sister to 4 winners. The second
dam, Maid Of Killeen (by Darshaan), a fairly
useful 2-y-o 9f winner, was listed-placed
and is a half-sister to 6 winners. (Hamdan Al
Maktoum). *"He'd done well, there's not a lot to
him at the moment but he'll start to progress
as the season goes on. He was a fairly late
foal and I wouldn't be in a rush with him so
he's going to take plenty of time. He looks like
he has ability but he's definitely growing and
filling out as we speak".*

787. MAGNIFICENT ★★★★
b.c. Zebedee – Barathea Dancer (Barathea).
April 6. First foal. 12,000 foal. Tattersalls
December. Woodstock. The dam, a fair
10f winner, is a half-sister to one winner.
The second dam, Showering (by Danehill),
unplaced in one start, is a half-sister to 3
winners including the Group 3 Horris Hill
Stakes and listed Free Handicap winner and
French 2,000 Guineas second Clearing. *"A*

lovely colt, he'll take a bit of time but you'll see him out by mid-season over six furlongs and he's a smasher. Could be anything really".

788. MAYYASAH (USA) ★★★ ♠
b.f. More Than Ready – Whipsaw City (Elusive City). April 21. Second foal. €160,000Y. Arqana Deauville August. Peter & Ross Doyle. The dam, a listed-placed dual winner in the USA, is a half-sister to 2 winners including the French listed winner My Year Is A Day. The second dam, Aliyeska (by Fasliyev), won over 4.5f at 2 yrs in France and is a half-sister to 6 winners. *"She's a bit like the Dark Angel filly in that she's narrow in the middle at the moment but looks like a really nice filly in the making. A lovely mover that looks really nice, she'll just take a bit of time and I couldn't be happier with her".*

789. MISS MO BROWN BEAR ★★★
b.f. Kodiac – Currentis (Dylan Thomas). April 28. Second foal. £60,000Y. Goffs UK Premier (Doncaster). Peter & Ross Doyle. The dam is an unplaced half-sister to 3 winners including the Swedish Group 3 winner Hurricane Red and the French listed winner Bernieres. The second dam, Bounce (by Trempolino), won two minor races at 3 yrs in France and is a half-sister to 3 winners including the 2-y-o Group 1 second Simplex. *"She could be quite sharp and I see her as a six furlong filly, maybe even five. A nice filly that goes very well".*

790. MOTOWN MICK ★★★
ch.c. Intikhab – Top Row (Observatory). March 13. Sixth foal. 52,000Y. Tattersalls December. Peter & Ross Doyle. Half-brother to the useful 2-y-o 6f winner and Group 2 5f Norfolk Stakes third Crown Dependency (by Acclamation) and to the quite useful 2-y-o 7f winner Gold Top (by Teofilo). The dam is an unplaced half-sister to 10 winners including the useful 2-y-o Group 3 7f C L Weld Park Stakes winner Rag Top. The second dam, Petite Epaulette (by Night Shift), a fair 5f winner at 2 yrs, is a full or half-sister to 3 winners including the Group 1 1m Gran Criterium second Line Dancer. *"We'll be having a closer look at him soon because he could be sharp. One for the six furlong races".*

791. MOVE OVER ★★★
b.c. Acclamation – Framed (Elnadim). March 9. Second foal. 110,000Y. Tattersalls December. Peter & Ross Doyle. Closely related to the modest 2016 dual 6f placed 2-y-o Darkroom Angel (by Dark Angel). The dam is an unplaced half-sister to 3 winners including the Group 2 6f Richmond Stakes winner Prolific and the fairly useful 2-y-o 5f winner and subsequent US stakes winner Deal Breaker. The second dam, Photo Flash (by Bahamian Bounty), a fair 1m winner, is a half-sister to 8 winners including the Group 2 Royal Lodge Stakes winner Atlantis Prince. *"A good, straightforward horse, one to start off when the six furlong races come".*

792. MUSHTAQ (IRE) ★★★
b.c. Zoffany – Iamfine (Whipper). March 20. Third foal. 210,000Y. Tattersalls October Book 1. Al Shaqab / Peter & Ross Doyle. The dam is an unraced half-sister to 4 winners including the useful 2-y-o dual 6f winner and subsequent US stakes winner Alinga. The second dam, Cheyenne Spirit (by Indian Ridge), a useful winner of 7 races including a listed event over 6f, is a half-sister to 5 winners including the dam of the Group winner Ashdown Express and Hoh Buzzard. *"A thick-set horse, he's nice but we wouldn't be in any hurry with him. One for the six or seven furlong races".*

793. MUTANAASEQ (IRE) ★★★
ch.c. Red Jazz – Indaba (Indian Ridge). March 26. Ninth foal. 125,000Y. Tattersalls October Book 2. Shadwell Estate Co. Half-brother to the very useful 2-y-o 5f winner and Group 2 Railway Stakes, Gimcrack Stakes and Norfolk Stakes second Ahlan Emarati (by Holy Roman Emperor), to a winner in South Africa by Cape Cross and to a hurdles winner by Daylami. The dam, a useful 6f and 7f winner, is a half-sister to 8 winners including the useful dual 1m winner So Sedulous (dam of the German Derby and Breeders' Cup Turf winner Shirocco). The second dam, Sedulous (by Tap On Wood), a very useful 2-y-o Group 3 1m Killavullen Stakes winner of 4 races, subsequently won in the USA and is a sister to the listed Tyros Stakes winner Tapolite. *"A good, strong colt, we won't be in a hurry with*

him. Out of an Indian Ridge mare, he'll want six or seven furlongs and he's a well-built colt. Everything's nice about him".

794. NAHHAM (IRE) ★★★
b.c. Dawn Approach – Anna's Rock (Rock Of Gibraltar). March 22. Fifth foal. 275,000Y. Tattersalls October Book 1. Al Shaqab / Peter & Ross Doyle. Half-brother to the Group 2 Hungerford Stakes and Group 3 Criterion Stakes winner Breton Rock (by Bahamian Bounty), to the quite useful 10f and 12f winner of 4 races Yaakooum (by Cape Cross) and the class 4 1m winner, on his only start, Kharbetation (by Dream Ahead). The dam, a useful Irish 7f (at 2 yrs) and listed 7.5f winner, is a half-sister to 3 winners. The second dam, Anna Karenina (by Atticus), is an unraced half-sister to 10 winners including Agathe (Group 3 Prix de Psyche winner and dam of the Grade/Group 1 winners Artiste Royale and Aquarelliste), the Breeders' Cup Classic winner Arcangues and the dams of the Group/Grade 1 winners Cape Verdi and Angara. *"A lovely horse that's going to take time, he was bought for plenty of money but he's lovely to look at and has plenty of size and substance. I wouldn't be in a huge rush with him but I'm really happy with him, he has a good attitude and is probably a mid to late season type".*

795. NATURAL ★★★★ ♠
b.f. Kodiac – Catch The Sea (Barathea). February 16. Fifth foal. €305,000Y. Goffs Orby. David Redvers. Half-sister to 4 winners including the useful 2-y-o Group 3 6f Prix de Cabourg winner My Catch (by Camacho), the French 2-y-o listed 6f winner and Group 1 Prix Morny third Vladimir (by Kheleyf) and the fairly useful 2-y-o 6f winner and listed-placed Pearl Sea (by Elusive City). The dam, a modest 10f placed maiden, is a half-sister to 6 winners. The second dam, Catch The Blues (by Bluebird), a smart 5f to 7f winner of 3 races including the Group 3 5f Ballyogan Stakes, was third in the Group 1 Haydock Park Sprint Cup and is a half-sister to 6 winners. *"She cost a bit of money but she's a lovely filly. One for the middle of the season, she's showing all the right signs at the moment and we couldn't be more happy with her".*

796. NO MORE THRILLS ★★★
ch.f. Dutch Art – The Thrill Is Gone (Bahamian Bounty). February 15. Second foal. 160,000Y. Tattersalls October Book 1. Peter & Ross Doyle. Half-sister to the fair 2016 5f placed 2-y-o Speed Freak (by Fastnet Rock). The dam, a fairly useful 2-y-o 5f winner, was listed-placed three times and is a half-sister to 8 winners including the UAE Group 1 Golden Shaheen winner Muarrab, the very useful 2-y-o dual Group 3 5f winner Bungleinthejungle, the listed winner Waveband and the Group-placed Group Therapy and Classic Encounter. The second dam, Licence To Thrill (Wolfhound), a quite useful dual 5f winner, is a half-sister to 4 winners. *"A nice filly for the second half of the season over six furlongs. A very strong, well-made filly".*

797. OCEAN SIDE ★★★ ♠
gr.c. Dark Angel – Mundus Novus (Unbridled's Song). April 13. Seventh foal. 77,000Y. Tattersalls October Book 1. Peter & Ross Doyle. Half-brother to the listed Heron Stakes winner and Group 1 St James's Palace Stakes third Consort (by Lope De Vega), to the quite useful 1m (at 2 yrs) to 14f winner Castle Combe (by Dylan Thomas), the quite useful 2-y-o 6f and 7f winner Steer By The Stars (by Pivotal) and the fair 9f winner Grey Seal (by Cape Cross). The dam, a French 1m winner, is closely related to the US Grade 2 Dahlia Handicap winner Surya (herself dam of the US Grade 2 winner Aruna) and a half-sister to 7 winners. The second dam, Wild Planet (by Nureyev), won at 2 yrs here and the listed Prix Coronation in France, was third in the Group 3 Prestige Stakes and is a half-sister to 6 winners. *"A leggy colt, he's one for seven furlongs much later in the season".*

798. OLIVER REED (IRE) ★★★
b.c. Footstepsinthesand – Montbretia (Montjeu). February 20. Third foal. £100,000Y. Goffs UK Premier (Doncaster). Peter & Ross Doyle. Half-brother to the fair 6f to 8.5f winner Specialv (by Big Bad Bob). The dam, a fairly useful 10f winner, is a half-sister to 6 winners. The second dam, Bayswater (by Caerleon), a fair 12.3f winner, is a sister to the high-class Group 1 1m Ciga Grand Criterium and Group 2 10.4f Dante Stakes winner

Tenby, to the very useful 1m (at 2 yrs) and 10f winner Bright Water and a half-sister to the listed winner Bristol Channel. *"A really nice, solid horse that we'll be hoping to run over six furlongs. Hopefully he'll make up into a nice horse but we'll have another look at him in mid-April".*

799. ORANGE SUIT ★★
b.c. Declaration Of War – Guantanamera (Sadler's Wells). February 16. Sixth foal. 90,000Y. Tattersalls October Book 1. Peter & Ross Doyle. Half-brother to the Group 1 Champions Fillies' & Mares Stakes and Group 1 St Leger winner Simple Verse (by Duke Of Marmalade), to the Group 2 Ribblesdale Stakes winner Even Song (by Mastercraftsman), the useful 2-y-o 6f and 7f winner and Group 2 Superlative Stakes third Maxentius and to the fair 1m winner Lord Jim (both by Holy Roman Emperor). The dam is an unraced half-sister to 6 winners. The second dam, Bluffing (by Darshaan), a 2-y-o 1m winner at the Curragh, was listed-placed over 9f (at 2 yrs) and 12f and is a half-sister to 6 winners. *"A big horse, we won't be rushing him and he'll be a seven furlong 2-y-o for the latter part of the season".*

800. PAINT ★★★
b.f. Dutch Art – Love Magic (Dansili). April 17. First foal. The dam, a quite useful 2-y-o 7f winner, is a sister to one winner and a half-sister to 5 winners including the 11f and 12f winner here and subsequent Australian Group 2 12f second Tall Ship. The second dam, Magical Romance (by Barathea), a 2-y-o Group 1 6f Cheveley Park Stakes winner, is a sister to the fairly useful 2-y-o 7f winner and subsequent Canadian Grade 3 placed Saree and closely related to the Oaks, Irish Oaks and Yorkshire Oaks winner Alexandrova and the listed 2-y-o 1m winner Masterofthehorse. *"She looks quite sharp but we'll be waiting for six furlongs for her. She shows a bit of speed".*

801. POINT HOPE (IRE) ★★★
b.f. Kodiac – Frosted (Dr Fong). April 10. Fourth foal. €125,000Y. Goffs Orby. Peter & Ross Doyle. The dam ran unplaced twice and is a sister to the triple listed winner and Group 2 6f Gimcrack Stakes second Andronikos and a half-sister to 3 winners.

The second dam, Arctic Air (by Polar Falcon), a quite useful 2-y-o 7f winner, is a sister to the useful listed 7f winner Arctic Char and a half-sister to 6 winners including the Group 2 winners Barrow Creek and Last Resort and the dam of the Group 2 winner Trans Island. *"She's showing a bit of speed and when we get some better weather we'll be having a look at her. Five or six furlongs should suit her nicely".*

802. POPSICLE (IRE) ★★★
b.f. Acclamation – Katchy Lady (Kyllachy). January 17. First foal. 60,000Y. Tattersalls December. Peter & Ross Doyle. The dam, a quite useful dual 5f winner at 2 and 3 yrs, is a half-sister to the Italian winner and Group 3 third Kocna. The second dam, Star Approval (by Hawk Wing), is an unraced half-sister to 3 winners including the Group 1 7f Moyglare Stud Stakes winner Mail The Desert. *"A sharp filly, we'll be having a look at her soon. Hopefully she'll be racing over five furlongs but if not she'll be ready for when the six furlong races start".*

803. PUCHITA (IRE) ★★★★
b.f. Acclamation – Violet Ballerina (Namid). March 19. Sixth foal. €68,000Y. Tattersalls Ireland September. Peter & Ross Doyle. Half-sister to the fair 7f winner of 4 races Fab Lolly (by Rock Of Gibraltar), to the fair 7f and 8.5f winner Wolfie (by Duke Of Marmalade) and 2 minor winners in Germany by Cape Cross and Cadeaux Genereux. The dam, a fair 7f (at 2 yrs) and 6f winner, is a half-sister to 3 winners including the very useful 2-y-o Group 2 6f Richmond Stakes winner Carizzo Creek. The second dam, Violet Spring (by Exactly Sharp), a 5-y-o 2m winner in Ireland, is a half-sister to 3 other minor winners. *"A lovely filly and another Acclamation that looks sharp. She knows her job, moves great and should be one for five furlongs. We could have quite a bit of fun with her early on and she's not that small either, so she may have a bit of scope for later in the season. We're really happy with her and she's showing all the right signs".*

804. QUEEN OF ROME (GER) ★★★★
b.f. Holy Roman Emperor – Quilita (Lomitas). February 4. First foal. €160,000Y. Baden Baden. Mayfair Thoroughbreds. The dam, placed in a Group 3 over 10f in Germany, is

out of Quirigua (by Lomitas). *"A fairly sharp filly, we could have plenty of fun with her from May or June time. She shows plenty of speed"*.

805. RED STARLIGHT ★★★
br.f. Invincible Spirit – Star Chart (Dubawi). January 26. First foal. The dam, unplaced on her only start, is a full or half-sister to 4 winners. The second dam, Star Express (by Sadler's Wells), a minor 12f winner in France, is a sister to the Group 3 7f Greenham Stakes winner and Irish 2,000 Guineas fourth Yalaietanee and a half-sister to 5 winners including the Group 3 5f Molecomb Stakes winner Sahara Star (herself dam of the Group 2 5f Flying Childers Stakes winner Land Of Dreams). (Cheveley Park Stud). *"Quite a weak filly, we won't be asking her any questions until a bit later. A six/seven furlong type 2-y-o, she's done very well recently and is improving a lot. A very nice filly"*.

806. REGIMENTED (IRE) ★★★★
b.c. Epaulette – Colour Coordinated (Spectrum). March 13. Seventh foal. £18,000Y. Goffs UK Premier (Doncaster). Half-brother to the fair 10.5f winner Empress Of Tara (by Holy Roman Emperor) and to a minor winner abroad by Dylan Thomas. The dam, a modest 1m to 10.5f placed maiden, is a half-sister to 5 winners including the Group 2 Great Voltigeur and Group 3 Gordon Stakes winner Bonny Scot. The second dam, Scots Lass (by Shirley Heights), won over 13f and is a half-sister to Sought Out (Group 1 Prix de Cadran). *"A lovely horse by Epaulette – he could be very nice. A lovely mover that finds it all very easy, there's plenty of size about him"*. TRAINERS' BARGAIN BUY

807. RESHAAN (IRE) ★★★★ ♠♠
b.c. Dark Angel – Bluebell (Mastercraftsman). January 16. First foal. €260,000Y. Arqana Deauville August. Peter & Ross Doyle. The dam, a quite useful 2-y-o 7f winner, is a half-sister to 3 winners including the smart 2-y-o Group 3 6f Railway Stakes winner and Group 1 6f Middle Park Stakes second Lilbourne Lad and the very useful 2-y-o 7f winner and Group 3 10f Gallinule Stakes second Bobbyscot. The second dam, Sogno Verde (Green Desert), a fair Irish 9f winner,

is a half-sister to 8 winners including the dual listed winner and Group 1 Irish St Leger second Pugin. *"A lovely horse, he's quite leggy and is still filling out but he's going to be a lovely animal. He's got all the right bits in all the right places and looks like he could be very nice, so we're happy with him"*.

808. ROBINSON CRUSOE ★★★
b.c. Footstepsinthesand – Corrozal (Cape Cross). April 7. Sixth foal. 30,000Y. Tattersalls December. Peter & Ross Doyle. Half-brother to the modest 2016 2-y-o 7f winner Let's Be Happy (by Mastercraftsman), to the fair 2-y-o 6f winner Marshal Dan Troop (by Lawman) and a winner over jumps in France by Rock Of Gibraltar. The dam, a minor German 3-y-o winner, is a half-sister to 2 winners there. The second dam, Casanga (by Rainbow Quest), a German Group 3 11f winner, is a half-sister to 11 winners. *"Not one we'd be in a hurry with, he's a strong colt but with that pedigree he's one for seven furlongs"*. TRAINERS' BARGAIN BUY

809. ROGUE ★★★
b.c. Epaulette – Miskin Diamond (Diamond Green). February 25. Second foal. 45,000Y. Tattersalls December. Peter & Ross Doyle. Half-brother to a minor 3-y-o winner abroad by Intikhab. The dam, a poor 10f winner, is a half-sister to 10 winners including the Group 1 Phoenix Staked third Catch A Glimpse. The second dam, Spring To Light (by Blushing Groom), a winner over 6f and 7f and second in the Group 3 C L Weld Park Stakes, is a half-sister to 7 winners. *"A nice horse, I like the stallion and this is one that could be ready for the six furlong races. A lovely, well-made horse"*.

810. RUM RUNNER ★★★
b.c. Havana Gold – Thermopylae (Tenby). March 12. Twelfth foal. €50,000Y. Tattersalls Ireland September. Peter & Ross Doyle. Half-brother to the Group 3 Give Thanks Stakes winner and St Leger second Unsung Heroine (by High Chaparral), to the quite useful triple 7f and subsequent Australian winner Ghostmilk (by Golan), the quite useful 10.5f winner Galactic Heroine (by Galileo) and the modest 10f winners Laconicos (by Foxhound)

and Spartan King (by King's Best). The dam, a fair 7f (at 2 yrs) and 10f placed maiden, is full or half-sister to 9 winners including Posidonas (Group 1 Gran Premio d'Italia). The second dam, Tamassos (by Dance In Time), won at 3 yrs and is a half-sister to Ile de Chypre (Group 1 Juddmonte International). *"He's a lovely little horse, still filling out and once he's done that he'll make a nice horse in the end. A great mover, with a good attitude and one for the middle of the season, so we should have some fun with him. I'm really happy with Havana Gold as a stallion because we've got some nice 2-y-o's by him here".*

811. SALLAB (IRE) ★★★ ♠

b.c. Havana Gold – Waveband (Exceed And Excel). April 16. Fourth foal. 200,000Y. Tattersalls October Book 1. Al Shaqab / Peter & Ross Doyle. Half-brother to the fair 2-y-o 5f winner Archimedes (by Invincible Spirit). The dam, a fairly useful listed 6f winner of 4 races, is a sister to the smart 2-y-o dual Group 3 5f winner Bungle Inthejungle and a half-sister to 7 winners including the Group 1 Golden Shaheen winner Muarrab and the Group 2 5f King George Stakes second Group Therapy. The second dam, Licence To Thrill (by Wolfhound), a quite useful dual 5f winner, is a half-sister to 4 winners. *"A back-end of the season type, he's a lovely, big horse and a good mover. He'll be a seven furlong / mile 2-y-o".*

812. SCIMITAR (IRE) ★★★

b.c. Fast Company – Zahr Alyasmeen (Iffraaj). March 24. First foal. £26,000Y. Goffs UK Premier (Doncaster). Peter & Ross Doyle. The dam, a modest 7f winner, is a half-sister to 3 winners including the useful 2-y-o 5f and subsequent Turkish 2-y-o listed 6f winner Orvar. The second dam, Roskeen (by Grand Lodge), is an unraced half-sister to 5 winners including the dam of the Group 2 Gimcrack Stakes winner Shaweel and to the unraced dam of the dual Group 1 winner Samitar and the Group 3 Albany Stakes winner Nijoom Dubai. *"Not overly big, but he looks quite sharp and he shows plenty of speed so he should be one of our earlier runners. Five furlongs would be no problem to him, he's doing everything nicely and at the moment we're happy with him".*

813. SERGIO LEONE ★★★

b.c. Acclamation – Elizabelle (Westerner). April 27. Fourth foal. 125,000Y. Tattersalls October Book 2. Peter & Ross Doyle. Half-brother to the modest 2016 2-y-o 6f winner Benidiction, to the fairly useful 2-y-o 6f, 7f and 1m winner Power Play (both by Zebedee) and the fairly useful 6f, 9f (both at 2 yrs) and 12f winner Southdown Lad (by Lilbourne Lad). The dam, a modest 7f placed 2-y-o, is a half-sister to 3 winners including the smart 2-y-o Group 2 7f Vintage Stakes winner Orizaba. The second dam, Jus'chillin' (by Efisio), was placed twice over 6f at 2 yrs and is a half-sister to 11 winners including Bay Empress (Group 3 Brownstown Stakes). *"A nice sort that's just starting to grow again, so we'll take our time with him. One for the six/ seven furlong races, he's a good make of a horse and typical of the sire".*

814. SHUHOOD ★★★

b.c. Tamayuz – Walayef (Danzig). May 17. Half-brother to 5 winners including the modest 2016 Irish 2-y-o 7f winner Twist Of Magic (by Arcano), the fairly useful Irish 2-y-o 6f and 7f winner and 3-y-o listed-placed Jamaayel (by Shamardal), to the quite useful Irish 1m winner Estithmaar (by Pivotal) and the quite useful Irish 2-y-o 7f winner Reyaada (by Daylami). The dam, a listed 6f (at 2 yrs) and Group 3 7f Athasi Stakes winner, is a sister to the smart 2-y-o 6f winner Haatef, to the listed 6f winner and Group 1 Moyglare Stud Stakes second Shimah and the Irish dual listed 6f winner Ulfah. The second dam, Sayedat Alhadh (by Mr Prospector), a US 7f winner, is a sister to the US Grade 2 7f winner Kayrawan and a half-sister to the useful winners Amaniy, Elsaamri and Mathkurh. *"He's not over-big and if it wasn't for his late foaling date you might think he'd be sharp. He certainly looks a sharp colt and he's a good type for six furlongs plus. He's not slow".*

815. SOAR ABOVE ★★★

b.c. Lethal Force – Soar (Danzero). March 20. Seventh foal. 125,000Y. Tattersalls October Book 2. Peter & Ross Doyle. Half-brother to the fairly useful 6f (at 2 yrs), 5f and subsequent US winner Racy, to the modest 7f winner Hornboy (both by Medicean), the fairly useful 6f to 1m winner of 7 races Levitate and the fair dual 6f winner Uprise (both by Pivotal). The dam, 2-y-o winner of the Group 2 6f Lowther Stakes and the Group 3 Princess Margaret Stakes, is a half-sister to 6 winners including the very smart 6f and 7f winner of 7 races Feet So Fast. The second dam, Splice (by Sharpo), winner of the listed 6f Abernant Stakes, is a full or half-sister to 7 winners. *"He's bigger than the other Lethal Force we've got and will take more time. He's still filling out, growing and learning his trade so we've just been cantering him. He's just a bit gangly at the moment but he should make up into a nice horse once he gets the chance".*

816. SOPRANOS ROCK ★★★★

b.c. Society Rock – Honeymead (Pivotal). March 22. Second foal. 87,000Y. Tattersalls October Book 2. Peter & Ross Doyle. Half-brother to the fair 2016 2-y-o dual 5f winner Broadhaven Honey (by Harbour Watch). The dam, a quite useful 5f and 7f winner, is a half-sister to 4 winners including the useful listed placed La Conquistadora. The second dam, Camaret (Danehill), a fairly useful 7f winner, is a full or half-sister to 4 winners. *"A lovely horse, he could be sharp and we might take a good look at him over five and six furlongs. He could be one to look out for".*

817. SOTOMAYOR ★★

b.c. Havana Gold – No Frills (Darshaan). March 8. Eleventh foal. 40,000Y. Tattersalls October Book 2. Peter & Ross Doyle. Half-brother to 5 winners including the quite useful 11f winner Prairie Ranger (by Montjeu), the fair 12f and hurdles winner Ephorus (by Galileo), the US 4-y-o winner and dual Grade 2 placed (over 1m and 9f) Singalong and the fair 9f to 1f winner Potentiale (both by Singspiel). The dam, a modest 9f placed maiden, is a half-sister to 6 winners including the dams of the North American Graded stakes winners J'Ray and Millennium Dragon. The second dam, Bubbling Danseuse (by Arctic Tern), a 10f winner and second in the Group 3 1m Prix de Sandringham, is a half-sister to 6 winners. *"He's a big, leggy horse and we wouldn't be in a hurry with him. Definitely a seven furlong type for the latter part of the season".*

818. STORMER ★★★

b.c. Kodiac – Easee On (Hawk Wing). April 24. Third foal. €64,000Y. Goffs Orby. Peter & Ross Doyle. Half-brother to the modest 2016 dual 5f placed 2-y-o Quiet Moment (by Dandy Man). The dam is an unraced half-sister to 5 winners including a listed winner in Italy. The second dam, Fairy Lore (by Fairy King), won once at 3 yrs and is a half-sister to 4 winners. *"A lovely, big horse that goes very well. There's a lot to like about him but he's not one we'll be rushing. Definitely a seven furlong type 2-y-o, but a nice horse".*

819. STRAIGHT ASH ★★★

gr.c. Zebedee – Blackangelheart (Danehill Dancer). May 5. Third foal. £36,000Y. Goffs UK Premier (Doncaster). Peter & Ross Doyle. The dam is an unraced half-sister to 4 winners. The second dam, Magical Cliché (by Affirmed), was placed in the listed Irish 1,000 Guineas Trial and is a sister to four stakes winners including the Irish 1,000 Guineas winner Trusted Partner (herself dam of the US Grade 1 winner Dress To Thrill). *"Not big but he looks sharp and he'll probably be one of our earlier runners. I'm not sure about the amount of ability he's got because we haven't worked him along yet, but he's done everything nicely so far. Should be sharp enough for five furlongs and we'll get on with him soon".*

820. STRATEGIC ★★★

b.c. Kodiac – Run To Jane (Doyoun). February 12. Twelfth living foal. €70,000Y. Goffs Orby. John & Jake Warren. Half-brother to 7 winners including the quite useful 10f to 14f and hurdles winner Beyond (by Galileo), the quite useful 9f winner Tarzan (by Spinning World), the fair 2-y-o 6f winner Taro Tywod (by Footstepsinthesand) and the fair 2-y-o 7f winner Emerald Penang. The dam is an unplaced half-sister to 6 winners including the Irish listed winners Mora and Broadway Rosie (dam of the dual Group 3 winner Eastern Purple). The second dam, Broadway Royal (by Royal Match), is an unraced half-sister to the King's Stand Stakes winner African Song. *"A good type, I think all our Kodiacs look nice this year, but this colt is definitely one for six/seven furlongs later on".*

821. STRONGARM CHASER (IRE) ★★★
b.c. Footstepsinthesand – Sarawati (Haafhd).
March 19. Third foal. €200,000Y. Goffs Orby.
Peter & Ross Doyle. Half-brother to the
Group 1 Italian Derby winner Ventura Storm
(by Zoffany) and to the modest 10f winner
Bella Varenna (by Lawman). The dam, placed
fourth once over 9f in Ireland from four
starts, is a half-sister to 5 winners including
the listed winner and Group 2 Lancashire
Oaks second Sahool and the dams of the dual
Group 2 Hardwicke Stakes winner Maraahel
and the Group 2 Flying Childers winner
Gutaifan. The second dam, Mathaayl (by
Shadeed), a quite useful 6f and 10f winner, is
a half-sister to 3 winners including Muhbubh
(Group 3 Princess Margaret Stakes). *"A lovely
horse with a hell of a good pedigree, he's
doing everything very well. Possibly a six
furlong horse, but we won't know that until we
step up his work. He'll tell us when he's ready".*

822. TAJAANUS (IRE) ★★★
b.f. Arcano – Rayaheen (Nayef). March 3.
Second foal. The dam, a quite useful 2-y-o
6f winner, is a half-sister to the fairly useful
listed-placed 6.5f winner Raaqy. The second
dam, Natagora (by Divine Light), a champion
2-y-o and winner of the Group 1 Cheveley
Park Stakes and the 1,000 Guineas, is a half-
sister to 2 winners in France (including one
over jumps). (Hamdan Al Maktoum). *"A thick-
set filly that could be early enough for the six
furlong maidens. A nice sort".*

823. TANGLED ★★★★ ♠
b.c. Society Rock – Open Verse (Black
Minnaloushe). February 5. Seventh foal.
£67,000Y. Goffs UK Premier (Doncaster).
Peter & Ross Doyle. Half-brother to the useful
2-y-o 7f winner and Group 3 1m third Faithful
Creek (by Bushranger) and to the fairly useful
2-y-o dual 5f winner Peter Mac (by Kodiac).
The dam, a fair 7f placed 2-y-o, is a half-sister
to 3 winners including the Group 1 Criterium
de Saint-Cloud winner Polaris Flight. The
second dam, Anytimeatall (by It's Freezing), is
an unraced half-sister to 4 winners. *"A lovely
horse, he's a great mover that should have the
speed for five furlongs but six would be right
up his alley. A smashing horse, the sire could
have quite a good season and this colt is all
there for us at the moment. He should be one*

*of our earlier runners and hopefully we should
have a bit of fun with him because he looks a
decent colt".*

824. TATHMEEN (IRE) ★★★
b.c. Exceed And Excel – Deyaar (Storm Cat).
February 2. Half-brother to the quite useful
2-y-o 7f winner Jufn (by Nayef) and to the
fair 2-y-o 6f winner Khobaraa (by Invincible
Spirit). The dam is an unraced sister to
the US Grade 3 winner Habaya and to the
Grade 3 placed winner Hatheer. The second
dam, Golden Apples (by Loon), won the Del
Mar Oaks, the Yellow Ribbon Stakes and
the Beverly D Stakes (all Grade 1) and is a
half-sister to 6 winners including Alexander
Three D (Group 3 Park Hill Stakes). (Hamdan
Al Maktoum). *"A lovely, big, strong colt. We'll
have a look at him when the six furlongs races
come. You wouldn't be going five with him,
definitely six"*

825. THAT'S MY GIRL ★★★
b.f. Mastercraftsman – Caribbean Ace (Red
Clubs). February 11. First foal. £50,000Y.
Goffs UK Premier (Doncaster). Peter & Ross
Doyle. The dam is an unraced half-sister to
5 winners including the fairly useful 2-y-o
listed 5f winner Knavesmire. The second dam,
Caribbean Escape (by Pivotal), is an unraced
half-sister to 8 winners including the smart
listed 6f Abernant Stakes winner and good
broodmare Splice. *"She's not overly-big but
there's plenty of her, she has a massive hind
end and a good shoulder. She could be one for
May time and she's doing everything really
nicely at the moment although we haven't
done a huge amount with the 2-y-o's yet, so
we won't know where she's at for another few
weeks. She's got everything in the right places,
so that's the main thing".*

826. TIG TOG ★★★
b.f. Dark Angel – Deira Dubai (Green Desert).
March 20. Fifth foal. 90,000Y. Tattersalls
October Book 2. Peter & Ross Doyle. Half-
sister to the fair dual 6f winner at 2 and 3 yrs
Centre Haafhd (by Haafhd) and to a minor
4-y-o winner in the USA by Iffraaj. The dam, a
fair 7f winner, is a half-sister to 5 winners. The
second dam, Aspen Leaves (by Woodman),
a fairly useful Irish 7f winner at 3 yrs, is a
sister to the US triple Grade 1 winner Timber

Country and a half-sister to the Group/Grade 1 winners Hamas, Fort Wood and Northern Aspen and the dams of the Group 1 winners Dubai Millennium, Elnadim and Mehthaaf. *"A lovely, big filly and a really good goer. You wouldn't go five furlongs with her. She'll be a six or possibly seven furlong 2-y-o".*

827. TOOMER ★★★

ch.f. Iffraaj – Harlem Dancer (Dr Devious). February 27. Fifth foal. 85,000Y. Tattersalls October Book 1. Peter & Ross Doyle. Half-sister to the listed 5f Windsor Castle Stakes winner of 4 races Hototo (by Sleeping Indian). The dam, a French listed-placed 10f and 11f winner, is a half-sister to 3 winners. The second dam, Hymenee (by Chief's Crown), a minor French 3-y-o winner, is a half-sister to 7 winners including the US Grade 2 winner Globe and the dam of the Group 2 Prix Niel winner Housamix. *"She's definitely a six furlong filly and probably in the first half of the season, despite Dr Devious being the broodmare sire".*

828. TULLYALLEN IRE) ★★★★ ♠

b.c. Arcano – Come April (Singspiel). March 18. Fourth living foal. €80,000Y. Goffs Orby. Peter & Ross Doyle. Half-brother to the high-class Group 1 July Cup, Group 1 Prix de la Foret, Group 2 Park Stakes and Group 3 Pavilion Stakes winner Limato (by Tagula). The dam, a fair 10f winner, is a half-sister to 4 minor winners. The second dam, So Admirable (by Suave Dancer), is an unraced sister to the Group 1 10f Coral Eclipse Stakes winner Compton Admiral and a half-sister to 7 winners including the Group 1 1m Queen Elizabeth II Stakes winner Summoner and the dam of the multiple Group 1 winner The Fugue. *"A lovely, big horse that goes very well. He's still a bit weak but we'll be waiting for the six/seven furlong races for him. A nice horse".*

829. TURKMEN ★★★

b.c. Intello – La Gandilie (Highest Honor). February 16. Eleventh foal. €140,000Y. Arqana Deauville August. Peter & Ross Doyle. Half-brother to 5 winners including the useful 2-y-o 6f listed winner Fashion Rocks (by Rock Of Gibraltar), the quite useful 9f to 12f winner Aktia (by Danehill Dancer) and the quite useful 9.5f winner Always Annie

(by Mount Nelson). The dam, a dual 2-y-o winner in France including a listed event, was third in the Group 3 Prix Chloe and is a half-sister to 4 winners including the Italian listed winner Totostar and to the placed dams of the French Group 3 winners Linda Regina and Star Of Akkar. The second dam, Prospector's Star (by Mr Prospector), a minor winner at 3 yrs in Ireland, is a half-sister to 2 winners. *"He's really sharpened up and hopefully he can be quite a nice horse. He's doing everything right, he's been 'upsides' a couple of times and shown a little bit of ability. So we're looking forward to getting going with him and he'll be one for the middle of the season onwards. He's the only Intello we've got but we like him".*

830. UNRELENTING ★★★

b.c. Kodiac – Zara's Girl (Tillerman). March 18. Third foal. €60,000Y. Tattersalls Ireland September. Peter & Ross Doyle. The dam is an unplaced half-sister to 10 winners including the smart listed 7f winner of 8 races and multiple Group 3 placed Dohasa. The second dam, Zara's Birthday (by Waajib), placed from 7f (at 2 yrs) to 2m, is a half-sister to 4 winners. *"A lovely horse, you won't be seeing him for a while I don't think but he's doing everything nicely and looks like a really nice horse. Fingers crossed he'll turn into one but he'll take time so we're not in a rush with him".*

831. VITAMIN (IRE) ★★★★

b.f. Camelot – True Verdict (Danehill Dancer). January 15. First foal. €95,000Y. Goffs Orby. Hillen & Hughes. The dam, a fairly useful 6f winner and second in the Group 3 6f Balanchine Stakes, is a full or half-sister to 3 winners. The second dam, Foolish Act (by Sadler's Wells), is an unraced full or half-sister to 6 winners including Circle Of Gold (Group 3 Prestige Stakes) and the listed winner Crystal Crossing (dam of the St Leger winner Rule Of Law). *"A lovely filly, she as a great attitude, she's a hell of a mover and has plenty of substance and size to her. She looks like she could be very nice but we'll keep her under wraps until she's ready to run. It looks like she's got ability and we're really happy with her. She should be running by May or June".*

832. WAFEER (IRE) ★★★ ♠
b.c. Equiano – Star Approval (Hawk Wing). February 10. Fifth foal. 180,000Y. Tattersalls October Book 2. Shadwell Estate Co. Half-brother to the quite useful dual 5f winner at 2 and 3 yrs Katchy Lady (by Kyllachy) and to the Italian 2-y-o winner and Group 3 third Kocna (by Aussie Rules). The dam is an unraced half-sister to 3 winners including the Group 1 7f Moyglare Stud Stakes winner and Coronation Stakes third Mail The Desert. The second dam, Mail Boat (by Formidable), is an unraced half-sister to 4 winners including the Group 3 Chester Vase winner and St Leger third Dry Dock and the dam of the dual Group 3 winner and multiple Group 1 placed Norse Dancer. *"A lovely, big horse, he's well-made but we won't be in a hurry with him. One for seven furlongs from the mid-season onwards".*

833. YAFTA ★★★ ♠
gr.c. Dark Angel – Swiss Dream (Oasis Dream). February 5. First foal. £280,000Y. Goffs UK Premier (Doncaster). Peter & Ross Doyle. The dam, a useful listed triple 6f winner, is a half sister to 6 winners including the Group 3 winning sprinters Swiss Diva and Swiss Spirit and the triple Group 2 placed Swiss Franc. The second dam, Swiss Lake (by Indian Ridge), a dual listed 5f winner (including at 2 yrs), and second in the Group 2 Flying Childers Stakes, is a half-sister to 4 winners. *"A tidy horse that topped the sale at Doncaster, he does show a bit of speed but we won't be in a hurry with him and he's one for six/seven furlongs".*

834. ZADAR (GER) ★★★
b.c. Maxios – Zavaala (Rock Of Gibraltar). February 18. Fourth foal. €38,000Y. Baden Baden. Peter & Ross Doyle / MPR. The dam is an unraced half-sister to 10 winners including the Group 3 12f Noblesse Stakes winner Danelissima and the dam of the Group 1 Dewhurst Stakes winner and sire Intense Focus. The second dam, Zavaleta (by Kahyasi), a dual listed 7f winner, is a half-sister to 9 winners including Sholokov (2-y-o Group 1 1m Gran Criterium). *"A nice colt that looks earlier than you might expect from the sire, so he's definitely worth mentioning".*

835. ZALSHAH ★★★
ch.c. Mayson – Regal Velvet (Halling). February 8. Seventh foal. £40,000Y. Goffs UK Premier (Doncaster). Peter & Ross Doyle. Half-brother to 3 winners including the quite useful 10f winner Regal Silk (by Pivotal) and to the quite useful 1m winner Robemaker (by Oasis Dream). The dam, a quite useful 10f winner, is a half-sister to 9 winners including the Group 1 6f Cheveley Park Stakes winner Regal Rose and the Japanese dual listed winner Generalist. The second dam, Ruthless Rose (by Conquistador Cielo), ran twice unplaced and is a half-sister to 9 winners including the high-class miler Shaadi. *"Not big but sharp, there's plenty of substance to him, there's a lot behind the saddle and he has a good shoulder. Ready to rock n roll, he looks like a nice horse for early on and if he has enough speed we should have a bit of fun with him. So I'm looking forward to getting going with him".*

836. UNNAMED ★★★
b.f. Epaulette – Angel Nights (Night Shift). January 20. Fifth foal. £35,000Y. Goffs UK Premier (Doncaster). Peter & Ross Doyle. Half-sister to the fair 2-y-o 5f winner Monkey Bar Flies (by Elusive City) and to the modest 6f winner Hepworth Marble (Lilbourne Lad). The dam is an unraced half-sister to 6 winners including Sacred Nuts, a winner of two stakes events in Hong Kong. The second dam, Sagrada (by Primo Dominie), a minor German 3-y-o winner, is a full or half-sister to 10 winners. *"She looks a nice filly. A good mover, she's quite sharp although she'll probably be better over six furlongs. Not overly big but with plenty of substance about her, we should have a bit of fun with her. So we're happy with her and we've got some nice Epaulette's here".*

837. UNNAMED ★★★★
ch.c. Declaration Of War – Danetime Out (Danetime). February 25. Eighth foal. 290,000Y. Tattersalls October Book 1. M V Magnier/ Mayfair/ Peter & Ross Doyle. Half-brother to the 2-y-o Group 1 7f National Stakes and multiple Group 2 winner Toormore (by Arakan), to the 2-y-o Group 2 7f Superlative Stakes and Group 2 7f Champagne Stakes winner Estidhkaar (by Dark Angel) and the quite useful 5.5f (at 2 yrs)

and 7f winner Try The Chance (by Majestic Missile). The dam is an unraced half-sister to 7 winners including the Group 3 second Easaar. The second dam, Matila (by Persian Bold), a fairly useful 3-y-o 6f winner, is a half-sister to 6 winners. *"A lovely horse, we love the family and this is a very correct horse that does everything well. He might be quick enough for the six furlong races and he'll be one of the nicer ones".*

838. UNNAMED ★★★
b.c. Kodiac – Evangeline (Sadler's Wells). March 30. Tenth foal. 200,000Y. Tattersalls October Book 1. Al Shaqab Racing / Peter & Ross Doyle. Closely related to the modest 2-y-o 8.5f winner East Texas Red (by Danehill Dancer) and half-brother to the 2-y-o Group 2 6f Lowther Stakes winner Infamous Angel (by Exceed And Excel) and the moderate dual 7f winner No Refund (by Invincible Spirit). The dam is an unraced half-sister to four winners including the listed winner Sgt Pepper. The second dam, Amandine (by Darshaan), won once at 3 yrs in France and is a half-sister to 3 winners. *"A very nice horse, he's sharp and a six furlong 2-y-o. A good type".*

839. UNNAMED ★★★
br.f. Kodiac – Fonseca (Red Clubs). January 15. First foal. 150,000Y. Tattersalls October Book 1. Peter & Ross Doyle. The dam is an unplaced half-sister to 4 winners including the very useful dual listed winner and Group 1 Sussex Stakes third Gabrial. The second dam, Guajira (by Mtoto), a minor French 11f winner of 3 races, is a half-sister to 9 winners including the US Grade 2 winners Jaunatxo and Iron Deputy and the dam of the Italian Group 1 winner Shamalgan. *"She could be sharp because she's not over-big and has shown a bit of speed already. Could be an early five furlong type 2-y-o".*

840. UNNAMED ★★★
b.c. Iffraaj – Martagon Lily (Manduro). February 18. First foal. 100,000Y. Tattersalls October Book 2. Peter & Ross Doyle. The dam, a fair 10f placed maiden, is a half-sister to 9 winners including Monturani (Group 2 Blandford Stakes) and the listed winners Monnavanna and Mill Spring. The second dam, Mezzogiorno (by Unfuwain), a very

useful 7f (at 2 yrs) and 10f listed winner, was third in the Oaks and is a half-sister to 3 winners. *"He's a lovely, big horse and a well-made 2-y-o for six/seven furlongs. We won't be in any hurry with him but he's a very good mover".*

841. UNNAMED ★★★
b.f. Acclamation – Miss Champagne (Bering). March 9. Eighth foal. 100,000Y. Tattersalls October Book 2. Peter & Ross Doyle. Half-sister to the Irish 2-y-o 6f winner (on her only start) Play Misty For Me (by Danehill Dancer and herself dam of the dual Group 3 winner Quest For Peace), to the fairly useful 2-y-o 7f winner and Group 3 7f Sweet Solera Stakes third Minor Vamp (by Hawk Wing) and the quite useful listed-placed 1m to 10.5f and hurdles winner Beaumont's Party (by High Chaparral) and the fair 5f winner Way Of Light (by Dylan Thomas). The dam is an unraced sister to the Group 3 Prix Eclipse winner Stella Berine and a half-sister to 4 winners. The second dam, Beaujolaise (by Thatching), won the Group 3 Prix Eclipse and is a half-sister to 6 winners. *"Not overly big but she looks like she's got some ability, which is good. She seems to be doing everything right, I'd expect her to be racing in May, she'd have the speed for five furlongs but will probably be better over six. I'm really happy with her".*

842. UNNAMED ★★★
b.f. Nathaniel – Sweet Cecily (Kodiac). March 13. Third foal. 62,000Y. Tattersalls October Book 1. Peter & Ross Doyle. Half-sister to the quite useful 5.5f and 6f winner Sweet Dragon Fly (by Oasis Dream). The dam won the 2-y-o listed 6f Bosra Sham Stakes. The second dam, Yaqootah (by Gone West), a fair 5f winner at 3 yrs, is a half-sister to 6 winners including the dam of the US dual Grade 1 winner Brody's Cause. *"She's still a little bit weak so we won't be doing anything with her for a while. Definitely a seven furlong/mile filly, but she's well-made".*

843. UNNAMED ★★★
b.f. Kodiac – Switcher (Whipper). April 7. First foal. 75,000Y. Tattersalls October Book 2. Peter & Ross Doyle. The dam, a fairly useful 2-y-o 6f winner, was second in two Group

3's and three listed events and is a half-sister to 3 winners. The second dam, Bahamamia (by Vettori), won over 1m at 2 yrs in France and is a half-sister to 4 winners including the German Group 2 winner Accento. *"She shows speed already so she may be one we'll be kicking on with early. Not over-big but a compact filly".*

844. UNNAMED ★★★★
br.c. Poet's Voice – Whatizzit (Galileo). February 28. Fourth foal. 42,000Y. Tattersalls October Book 3. Charlie Gordon-Watson. Half-brother to the fair 9f winner Dream Scape (by Oasis Dream). The dam, a fair 2-y-o 9f winner, is a half-sister to 6 winners including the useful 7f (at 2 yrs), listed 1m and Italian Group 3 1m winner Whazzis and the listed Chesham Stakes winner Whazzat. The second dam, Wosaita (by Generous), a fair 12.3f placed maiden, is a half-sister to 10 winners including the very smart Group 1 10.5f Prix de Diane winner Rafha (herself the dam of four stakes winners including the Haydock Sprint Cup winner Invincible Spirit) and the Group 3 12f Blandford Stakes winner Chiang Mai (dam of the Group 1 winner Chinese White). *"A lovely horse, I really like him. He has a good attitude; he's a good mover and should be a mid-season type 2-y-o, starting over six furlongs. Doing everything really well, he has plenty of scope and size".*

JESSICA HARRINGTON
845. ALPHA CENTAURI (IRE) ★★★
gr.f. Mastercraftsman – Alpha Lupi (Rahy). February 28. Sixth foal. Closely related to the French 7f winner Elitist (by Danehill Dancer) and half-sister to the useful 2-y-o listed 7f winner and Group 2 Royal Lodge Stakes second Tenth Star (by Dansili). The dam is an unraced half-sister to 3 winners including the 2-y-o Group 3 5.5f Prix d'Arenburg winner Moon Driver and the US winner and Grade 2 Californian Stakes third Mojave Moon and to the placed dam of the Group 3 winner Evasive. The second dam, East Of The Moon (by Private Account), was a high-class winner of the French 1,000 Guineas, the Prix de Diane and the Prix Jacques le Marois and is a half-sister to the top class miler and sire Kingmambo and to the smart Miesque's Son. (Course Investment Corporation).

"She's a big, heavy filly but she goes very nicely and seems to be remarkably forward for a Mastercraftsman and the size she is. I can see her running over six furlongs in May, she's a lovely filly that that hasn't done anything wrong. You'd have to like her".

846. BALLOT BOX ★★★
br.f. Big Bad Bob – Represent (Exceed And Excel). February 7. Second foal. €18,000Y. Tattersalls Ireland September. BBA (IRE). The dam, a fair 6f and 7f winner, is a half-sister to 11 winners including the Group 2 Bosphorus Cup winner Connecticut, the smart 1m winner and listed-placed Castleton and the German listed winner and Group 3 placed Fleurie Domaine. The second dam, Craigmill (by Slip Anchor), a fair 2-y-o 7f winner, is a half-sister to 6 winners including the Group 3 Park Hill Stakes winner Coigach and the Park Hill Stakes second and smart broodmare Applecross. (Mrs P K Cooper). *"I like her, she looks sharp and should be racing over five or six furlongs. She's pretty compact, not over-big and straightforward".*

847. BELLA FIGURA (IRE) ★★★
b.f. Mastercraftsman – Ebony Street (Street Cry). February 18. Second foal. €35,000Y. Goffs Orby. BBA (Ire). The dam is an unplaced half-sister to one winner. The second dam, Menhoubah (by Dixieland Band), won the Group 1 Italian Oaks, was third in the 2-y-o Group 1 Moyglare Stud Stakes and is a half-sister to 2 winners. (Robcour, John Hennessy, Mrs J Harrington). *"Another Mastercraftsman that seems quite forward and strong, she's very nice and a good mover. I like her a lot and she could easily be running in early May over six furlongs".*

848. BRICK BY BRICK (IRE) ★★★★
b.g. Big Bad Bob – Pivka (Pivotal). March 16. Fourth foal. 34,000 foal. Tattersalls December. BBA (Ire). Half-brother to the fair dual 7f winner (including at 2 yrs) Westminster (by Exceed And Excel) and to the French 9f winner Izola (by Beat Hollow). The dam, a quite useful 7f and 1m winner, is a half-sister to 7 winners including the quite useful 6f winner and subsequent US 1m stakes winner Promptly (herself dam of the Group 3 winner Fantastic View) and the Group 3 placed Lord

Darnley and Reinaldo. The second dam, Ghariba (by Final Straw), won the Nell Gwyn Stakes, was fourth in the 1,000 Guineas and is a half-sister to the smart Yorkshire Cup winner Braashee. *"He'll be our first runner, he's very sharp should be out in April over five furlongs. He's got a good temperament, does everything easily and I'm very happy with him".*

849. BROTHER BEAR (IRE) ★★★★
b.c. Kodiac – Hurricane Emma (Mr Greeley). February 6. First foal. 125,000Y. Tattersalls October Book 2. BBA (Ire). The dam is an unraced half-sister to 5 winners including the Irish 2-y-o listed 6f Rochestown Stakes winner and Group 3 Superlative Stakes third King Hesperus. The second dam, Victorica (by Exbourne), a stakes winner of 5 races in the USA, was third in the Grade 3 Dogwood Stakes and is a half-sister to 5 winners including the French 2,000 Guineas second and Hollywood Derby third Noble Minstrel. (Mill House LLC). *"He's a nice colt that should be running when the six furlong races start. He's done a good bit of work, I'm happy with him, he looks like a 2-y-o as he's built like a little tank".*

850. BYE BYE BRUSSELS (IRE) ★★★
b.br.f. Big Bad Bob – Miss Topsy Turvy (Mr Greeley). April 6. Second foal. Half-sister to the fair 2016 1m placed 2-y-o Carol (by Acclamation). The dam, a fair 10f and 12f winner, is a half-sister to 5 winners including the very smart 2-y-o Group 3 7f Acomb Stakes and Group 3 1m Craven Stakes winner and Group 1 Racing Post Trophy second Elusive Pimpernel, the smart Group 3 10f Strensall Stakes and listed 9f winner Palavicini and the listed 1m winner Prince Gagarin. The second dam, Cara Fantasy (Sadler's Wells), a quite useful dual 12f winner, is a half-sister to the Group 2 Topkapi Trophy winner Lucky Guest. (Anamoine Ltd). *"She looks sharp and is showing me plenty of speed at the moment. I'll wait for six furlongs with her and she's a good-moving filly".*

851. CRISTALE (IRE) ★★★
ch.f. Dandy Man – Radiant Energy (Spectrum). April 8. Seventh foal. €135,000Y. Goffs Orby. BBA (Ire). Half sister to the 2-y-o Group 3 5f Cornwallis Stakes and listed 5f winner Electric

Waves (by Exceed And Excel), to the fairly useful dual 7f winner Appealing (by Bertolini) and the fair 2-y-o 7f winner Tut (by Intikhab). The dam, a 1m winner at 3 yrs, is a half-sister to 6 winners. The second dam, Blaine (by Lyphard's Wish), is a placed half-sister to 7 winners including the dam of the dual Group 1 winner Croco Rouge. (David Reid Scott, Lim Reidy, Richmond Bloodstock). *"She's a nice filly that looked like she was going to take some time because she did a bit of growing in February, but she's suddenly got herself together. I like her a lot and she's an easy moving filly for five or six furlongs".*

852. DAWN TRAVELLER (IRE) ★★★
gr.g. Dragon Pulse – Karlinha (Desert Style). April 2. Third foal. €20,000Y. Goffs Sportsmans. BBA (Ire). Half-brother to the minor French 2-y-o 5f winner Fast Kar (by Fast Company). The dam won 3 minor races at 3 and 4 yrs in France including over 9.5f at Deauville and is a half-sister to 6 winners. The second dam, Karlinaxa (by Linamix), is a placed half-sister to 6 winners including the French 1,000 Guineas second Karmifira. (Mrs John Harrington). *"A filly that's very forward, she'll be racing in late April. A compact filly but with enough size about her".*

853. IT'S MY TURN (IRE) ★★★
b.f. Dream Ahead – Majestic Dancer (Danehill Dancer). February 26. Fourth foal. €80,000Y. Goffs Orby. Amanda Skiffington. Half-sister to the quite useful 1m winner Law Major (by Lawman). The dam, a quite useful Irish 7f winner, is closely related to the useful Irish 2-y-o 6f winner and Group 1 6f Cheveley Park Stakes third Danaskaya (herself dam of the Group 1 Dewhurst Stakes winner Belardo) and a half-sister to 6 winners including the triple listed 7f winner Modeeroch and the Group 1 1m Gran Criterium third Chinese Whisper. The second dam, Majinskaya (by Marignan), a French listed 12f winner and second in the Group 3 Prix de Psyche, is a half-sister to 6 winners including the dam of the Group 1 5f Prix de l'Abbaye winner Kistena. (Westward Bloodstock). *"Very nice, straightforward and one for the middle of the season. She's a lengthy, good-moving filly and a six/seven furlong type".*

854. JOUST (IRE) ★★★★
b.c. Iffraaj – Thawrah (Green Desert). March 14. Seventh foal. 100,000Y. Tattersalls October Book 1. BBA (Ire). Half-brother to the Group 3 6f Hackwood Stakes winner Heeraat (by Dark Angel), to the useful 2-y-o listed 5f winner and Group 3 5f Molecomb Stakes third Ambiance (by Camacho) and a minor winner in Germany by Chineur. The dam is an unraced half-sister to 6 winners including Malhub (Group 1 Golden Jubilee Stakes) and the US Grade 3 winner Dhaamer. The second dam, Arjuzah (by Ahonoora), winner of the listed 7f Sceptre Stakes and third in the Group 2 7f Challenge Stakes, is a half-sister to 2 winners. (Mill House LLC). *"A lovely, big colt, he's very laid back and a great mover. He won't be running until June at the earliest because he's a big, well-developed 2-y-o".*

855. NIKU (IRE) ★★★
b.f. High Chaparral – Strawberry Fledge (Kingmambo). April 15. Fifth foal. Sister to the fairly useful 1m (at 2 yrs) and 12f winner Warrior Of Light and half-sister to the smart Group 3 1m Prix des Chenes (at 2 yrs), Group 2 Prix Greffulhe and Group 2 10f Prix d'Harcourt winner Cloth Of Stars (by Sea The Stars). The dam, placed once at 2 yrs in France, is a sister to 2 winners including the Group 1 12f Oaks winner Light Shift and a half-sister to 8 winners including the Group 2 10.5f Tattersalls Gold Cup and Group 3 10f Brigadier Gerard Stakes winner Shiva and the Group 2 12f Prix Jean de Chaudenay and Group 3 12f Prix Foy winner Limnos. The second dam, Lingerie (by Shirley Heights), placed 6 times in France, is a half-sister to 7 winners and to the placed dam of two Grade 1 winners in Brazil. (Flaxman Stables Ireland Ltd). *"She was very nervous when she came to me but she's settled in well and doing everything right. Being by High Chaparral she won't be out until mid-season over seven furlongs. Quite a big filly, she's lovely and I like her a lot".*

856. WHITEFOUNTAINFAIRY (IRE) ★★★
ch.f. Casamento – Groupetime (Gilded Time). April 13. Ninth foal. €3,000Y. Goffs Sportsmans. BBA (Ire). Half-sister to the fairly useful 8.5f (at 2 yrs) and triple 10f winner

Swing Alone (by Celtic Swing) and to 3 minor winners in Italy including 2-y-o winners by Art Connoisseur and Indian Haven. The dam, a modest 6f to 10f placed maiden, is a half-sister to 5 minor winners. The second dam, La Groupie (by Groom Dancer), a French listed 1m winner, is a half-sister to 11 winners including the French and US Group 2 winner Spring Star. (Yulong Investments Australia). *"A solid filly, not over-big and a good mover, I'd expect her to be running in April and I think she was well-bought".* TRAINERS' BARGAIN BUY

857. WRITTEN WORD ★★★
ch.f. Mount Nelson – Darmiana (Lemon Drop Kid). February 3. Third foal. €31,000Y. Goffs Sportsmans. BBA (Ire). Half-sister to the fairly useful 1m winner Dazzling Rose (by Raven's Pass). The dam, a minor French 3-y-o winner, is out of the listed 12f Prix Des Tourelles winner Darkara (by Halling), herself a half-sister to 4 winners including the dam of the triple Group 1 winner Darjina. (Mrs P K Cooper, Russell Jones). *"She's doing everything right and looks early, but being by Mount Nelson you'd think she shouldn't be. She's showing all the right signs but I'll give her a bit of time and probably bring her out in June or July. She'll want a mile later on".*

858. UNNAMED ★★★
gr.f. Lawman – Diamond Sky (Montjeu). March 3. First foal. 130,000Y. Tattersalls October Book 1. BBA (Ire). The dam was second in the 2-y-o Group 2 Debutante Stakes in Ireland and is a sister to the fairly useful Scandinavian dual Group 3 and Chester listed 13f winner Berling and a half-sister to 3 winners including the Group 1 Dewhurst Stakes and Group 1 Lockinge Stakes winner Belardo. The second dam, Danaskaya (by Danehill), a useful Irish 2-y-o 6f winner and third in the Group 1 6f Cheveley Park Stakes, is a half-sister to 7 winners including the triple listed 7f winner Modeeroch and the Group 1 1m Gran Criterium third Chinese Whisper. (Stonethorn Stud Farms Ltd). *"She's surprised me a bit, a nice filly that's not over-big but stands over a lot of ground. She has a good temperament, goes nicely and should be out in late May or June over six furlongs".*

CHARLIE HILLS

As normal Charlie's yard is full of beautifully-bred two-year-olds and it's always a privilege for me to sit down and chat about them to him and his assistant Kevin Mooney.

859. ARTHENIA (IRE) ★★★

b.f. Camelot – Miss Intimate (War Chant). March 6. Seventh foal. 50,000Y. Tattersalls October Book 1. BBA (Ire). Half-sister to the fairly useful 7f and 1m winner Life Partner (by Cape Cross), to the quite useful 2-y-o 7f winner Flirt (by Duke Of Marmalade), the fair 10f winner Honour And Obey (by Hurricane Run) and a winner in Australia by Invincible Spirit. The dam is an unraced half-sister to 7 winners including the Irish 2,000 Guineas winner Bachelor Duke and the German listed 12f winner Translucid. The second dam, Gossamer (by Seattle Slew), a winner of two races in the USA at up to 9f, is a half-sister to 5 winners. *"Quite a nice filly, she's just developing at the minute and she's quite 'hot', but she's lovely model and one for the second half of the year. A real nice filly".*

860. AUTUMN WAR (IRE) ★★★

ch.c. Declaration Of War – Autumn Leaves (Muhtathir). March 13. Second foal. 70,000Y. Tattersalls October Book 2. Sackville/Donald. The dam, placed third once at 2 yrs in France (only 3 runners), is a half-sister to 12 winners including Capal Garmon (Group 3 Jockey Club Cup). The second dam, Elevate (by Ela-Mana-Mou), a listed-placed dual 12f winner, is a half-sister to 4 winners including the Group 1 winners Sun Princess and Saddlers' Hall. *"He's a big horse, a good mover and has a good temperament. He's not doing anything serious yet but everything's fine with him so far. A nice horse for the second half of the year".*

861. BARTHOLOMEU DIAS ★★★ ♠

b.c. Mount Nelson – Lady Francesca (Montjeu). May 11. Second living foal. 60,000Y. Tattersalls October Book 2. Sackville/Donald. The dam, a fairly useful 9f and subsequent US winner, was listed-placed twice and is a half-sister to 5 winners including the dual Group 3 winner Purr Along. The second dam, Purring (by Mountain Cat), a quite useful 7f winner, is a half-sister to the Group 2 1m Falmouth Stakes

and Group 3 1m Prix de Sandringham winner Ronda. *"A nice horse, he needs time but he's a good mover, he's done well and put weight on and done everything right. One for the second half of the year".*

862. BIN DAAHIR ★★★

b.c. Exceed And Excel – Beach Frolic (Nayef). February 15. First foal. £100,000Y. Goffs UK Premier (Doncaster). Shadwell Estate Co. The dam is an unraced half-sister to 4 winners including Bonfire (Group 2 Dante Stakes) and Joviality (Group 2 Windsor Forest Stakes). The second dam, Night Frolic (by Night Shift), a modest 1m winner, is a half-sister to 5 winners including the US Grade 3 Cardinal Handicap winner Miss Caerleona (herself dam of the Group winners Karen's Caper and Miss Coronado). *"He came in looking like he'd go forward, but just lately he'd done the opposite. He's just started to grow, he's done nothing wrong, he has a good temperament and he's a good mover but he just needs a bit more time".*

863. CHAPARRAL PRINCE (IRE) ★★★

b.c. High Chaparral – Snow Gretel (Green Desert). April 26. Seventh foal. 105,000Y. Tattersalls October Book 2. Sackville/Donald. Half-brother to the quite useful 1m winner Rapid Advance (by Medicean), to the minor French 9f and 10f winner La Noe (by Nayef) and a 2-y-o 7f winner in Norway by Poet's Voice. The dam, a German listed 1m winner, is a half-sister to 6 winners including the 2-y-o Group 2 1m Royal Lodge Stakes winner and 2,000 Guineas second Snow Ridge. The second dam, Snow Princess (by Ela-Mana-Mou), a smart winner of 6 races at up to 2m including the November Handicap and an Italian listed event, was second in the Group 1 Prix Royal-Oak and is a half-sister to 7 winners. *"A lovely, big horse that's done really well. Being by High Chaparral he's not going to be early but he's nice, he's a good mover and he's got a good temperament for one by that sire. He'll be fine later on over seven furlongs".*

864. CHERUBIC ★★★

b.f. Dark Angel – Doula (Gone West). March 3. Twelfth foal. €85,000Y. Goffs Orby. BBA (Ire). Half-sister to 5 winners including the listed-placed dual 7f (at 2 yrs) to 10f winner

Humungous (by Giant's Causeway), the useful Irish 11f winner and dual Group 3 placed Amazing Beauty (by Galileo), the 2-y-o 7f winner (on his only start here) Better Announce (by Invincible Spirit) and the minor US winner of 3 races Dixie King (by Dixie Union). The dam, a minor US 3-y-o turf winner, is a half-sister to the US Grade 2 winner Cat Chat (dam of the US Grade 1 winner In Lingerie) and to the dam of the US Grade 1 winner Dixie Chatter. The second dam, Phone Chatter (by Phone Trick), was a dual US Grade 1 winner. *"She's had one swinging canter, Simon Whitworth rode her and he liked her. Barry thinks we should get on with her (he deals with this filly's owners) and he thinks she'll progress. There's a little bit of a temper in her, but Dark Angels can be like that sometimes. She's a nice filly and she'll be racing in April or May".*

865. CLASSIC RED (IRE) ★★★
b.c. Red Jazz – Ceol Loch Aoidh (Medicis). February 28. Third foal. £50,000Y. Goffs UK Premier (Doncaster). Sackville/Donald. Half-brother to the quite useful 7f and 1m winner of 5 races Bint Dandy (by Dandy Man). The dam was placed once over 6f at 2 yrs in Ireland and is a half-sister to 2 winners including Stevie Gee (listed Ripon Champion 2-y-o Trophy). The second dam, Margaree Mary (by Seeking The Gold), a stakes-placed winner in the USA, is a half-sister to 2 winners. *"He's done extremely well and we would have got on with him, but he's got a sore throat at the moment. He goes well, he's a nice horse and once he's recovered I can still see him being out in April. After all, his sire Red Jazz won first time out at Windsor in April".*

866. CONSTITUENT ★★
b.c. High Chaparral – Arum Lily (Woodman). April 22. Closely related to the very smart Canadian Grade 1 12f and Group 3 12f Glorious Stakes winner Redwood and half-brother to the very useful 2-y-o 1m winner and Group 3 1m Autumn Stakes second Perennial (by Motivator) and the quite useful 9.5f winner Premium (by Danehill). The dam, a minor French 1m and 9f winner, is a half-sister to several winners. The second dam, Jolypha (by Lyphard), won the Group 1 Prix Vermeille and the Group 1 Prix de Diane.

(Khalid Abdulla). *"He's only just come in, so all I can say is that he's a fine, big horse and he's got a good temperament. I'd say he's one for much later in the season".*

867. DARK FREEDOM (IRE) ★★★
b.c. Canford Cliffs – Arctic Freedom (War Chant). January 29. Third foal. £85,000Y. Goffs UK Premier (Doncaster). Sackville/Donald. The dam, a modest dual 6f placed 2-y-o, is a half-sister to 7 winners including the Group 2 6f Prix Robert Papin winner and Group 1 1m Coronation Stakes second Ocean Ridge, the smart 2-y-o listed 7f winner and Group 2 6f Gimcrack Stakes second Fokine and the useful 2-y-o listed 6f winner Polar Circle. The second dam, Polar Bird (by Thatching), a very useful winner of 6 races here and in the USA including the 2-y-o Group 3 5f Debutante Stakes, is a half-sister to 6 winners. *"This colt goes alright. He's done a few bits of half-speed work and to be fair to him he hasn't come in his coat yet. We'll have to consider now whether to go forward with him or just sit tight for a bit. He's a nice horse and he's tough".*

868. DEVILS COWBOY (IRE) ★★★
b.c. Helmet – Naseem Sea (Bahri). April 5. Second foal. 60,000Y. Tattersalls October Book 1. Stephen Hillen. The dam, a fairly useful 2-y-o 5f winner and third in the Group 3 6f Balanchine Stakes, is a half-sister to 3 winners. The second dam, Laqataat (by Alhaarth), placed once over 7f at 2 yrs, is a half-sister to 3 winners including the very useful 2-y-o 6f winner and Group 2 6f Lowther Stakes second Khulan. *"He goes really nicely and he's taking his work well. I can see him being a player, he's well-made and should be fine".*

869. ELIZABETH BENNET (IRE) ★★★ ♠
b.f. Acclamation – Littlepromisedland (Titus Livius). March 14. Third foal. €140,000Y. Goffs Orby. Sackville/Donald. The dam, a poor 1m placed maiden, is a half-sister to 2 winners including the Group 1 July Cup and Group 1 Diamond Jubilee Stakes winner Lethal Force. The second dam, Land Army (by Desert Style), ran once unplaced and is a sister to a French listed winner and a half-sister to 8 winners including the listed winner Flanders

(dam of the Group 1 winning sprinter G Force). *"She's a little bit backward in her coat and hasn't been on the work list yet, but she does everything nicely, she's grown and lengthened, so I think she'll be alright. Not a bad model at all".*

870. ERAAD (IRE) ★★★
b.c. Dark Angel – Tickled Pink (Invincible Spirit). February 3. First foal. 500,000Y. Tattersalls October Book 1. Shadwell Estate Co. The dam, a very useful Group 3 5f and Group 3 6f winner, is a half-sister to 5 winners including the Irish 1,000 Guineas, Nassau Stakes and Sun Chariot Stakes winner Halfway To Heaven and the Group 3 6f Summer Stakes winner Theann (dam of the US Grade 1 winner Photo Call). The second dam, Cassandra Go (by Indian Ridge), won the Group 2 5f King's Stand Stakes and is a full or half-sister to 8 winners including the Group 3 6f Coventry Stakes winner and sire Verglas. (Hamdan Al Maktoum). *"He only came to us a few weeks ago and wasn't broken in much earlier than that because of a problem he'd had, so he's only hacking around at the minute. He looks quite nice but we don't know much more than the fact he's a good looker, as his price tag tells you".*

871. ESTIJMAAM ★★★
b.f. Raven's Pass – Merayaat (Darshaan). January 31. Eighth foal. Half-sister to the smart 1m (at 2 yrs) and Group 3 12f Cumberland Lodge Stakes winner Hawaafez (by Nayef), to the quite useful 2-y-o 1m winner Midhmaar (by Iffraaj) and the fair 14f and 15f winner Nateeja (by Shamardal). The dam was a quite useful 14f winner. The second dam, Maddelina (by Sadler's Wells) an unplaced half-sister to 2 winners. (Hamdan Al Maktoum). *"This filly has had a bit of a setback so she's going back home tomorrow for a break. She's a lovely, big filly but she needs time and is one for seven furlongs in the second half of the season. A nice filly though".*

872. EXPECTING ★★★
br.c. Bated Breath – Oasis Jade (Oasis Dream). February 16. Fourth foal. 90,000Y. Tattersalls October Book 2. Sackville/Donald. Half-brother to the fair 2016 5f and 6f placed 2-y-o Kiribati (by Poet's Voice) and to the minor Italian 2-y-o winner Hot Sun (by

Equiano). The dam, a modest 5f placed 2-y-o, is a half-sister to 9 winners including the fairly useful 6f winner of 11 races and listed-placed Million Percent. The second dam, Royal Jade (by Last Tycoon), a fairly useful 7f winner, is a half-sister to 6 winners including the Group 3 5f King George Stakes winner Averti. *"He's done two or three bits of work and we're trying to get him out reasonably early. He's quite nice, well-forward in his coat and he's shown up in the few bits of work he's done. So he's got every chance".*

873. FARAWAY FIELDS (USA) ★★★
b.c. First Defence – Faraway Flower (Distant View). February 22. Half-brother to the fair 2-y-o 8.5f winner Sepal (by Afleet Alex). The dam, a useful 2-y-o 6f winner, is a half-sister to 2 winners. The second dam, Silver Star (by Zafonic), won over 1m at 2 yrs in France, was listed-placed over 1m at 3 yrs and is a sister to the champion European 2-y-o Xaar (winner of the Group 1 Dewhurst Stakes and the Group 1 Prix de la Salamandre) and a half-sister to the Group 3 10.5f Prix Corrida winner Diese and the Group 3 1m Prix Quincey winner Masterclass. (Khalid Abdulla). *"A great big horse, he must be 16.2 now, but I don't think he'll be a very late 2-y-o because he does show a bit. He's a good mover with a good temperament, but we won't be pushing any buttons too early. A nice horse for the mid-season onwards".*

874. GIGI (IRE) ★★★
b.f. Iffraaj – Dubai Flower (Manduro). April 3. Third foal. £50,000Y. Goffs UK Premier (Doncaster). Highflyer Bloodstock. Half-sister to the fair 12f winner Epsom Day (by Teofilo). The dam is an unraced half-sister to 5 winners including the smart Group 3 7f Solario Stakes (at 2 yrs) and Group 1 Prix Jean Prat winner Best Of The Bests and the smart Group 2 Dante Stakes third Dunhill Star. The second dam, Sueboog (by Darshaan), winner of the Group 3 7.3f Fred Darling Stakes, was third in the Musidora Stakes and the Nassau Stakes and is a half-sister to 8 winners. *"A big filly, she's a good mover but we tried to get on with her because she came from a breaker's yard who said she was really forward. She wasn't. So we dropped her back, got her into a rhythm and she's doing really well. A good mover and one for later on".*

875. GLOBAL TANGO (IRE) ★★★★
gr.c. Zebedee – Beautiful Dancer (Danehill Dancer). March 22. Sixth foal. €42,000Y. Goffs Orby. Sackville/Donald. Half-brother to the quite useful 2-y-o 6f winner Our Cool Cat (by One Cool Cat) and the modest 9.5f and hurdles winner The Way You Dance (by Thewayyouare). The dam ran twice unplaced and is a half-sister to 8 winners including the Irish Group 3 placed Beautiful Fire. The second dam, Beautiful France (by Sadler's Wells), an Irish 9f winner, is a half-sister to 7 winners including the Irish listed 9f winner Rimpa and to the unraced dam of the St Leger winner Scorpion. *"On the forward march, he's starting to please us. He's got a good attitude and he loves his work. He might need six furlongs rather than five but he's certainly a 2-y-o and one to follow I'd say".*

876. GROVEMAN ★★★ ♠
b.c. Holy Roman Emperor – Raving Monsun (Monsun). March 24. Second foal. 250,000Y. Tattersalls October Book 2. Sackville/Donald. The dam, a modest 12f winner, is a half-sister to another minor winner. The second dam, Rave Reviews (by Sadler's Wells), a very useful listed 10f winner and second in the Group 1 Premio Lydia Tesio, is closely related to the listed winners Fermion and Sail and to the 1,000 Guineas third Moth, and a half-sister to the Group 3 winner Hearthstead Maison. *"He's very backward in his coat for some reason, as if he's hated the cold weather. Otherwise he's done well, everyone who rides him likes him, but we won't be getting on with him just yet. He has a good way of going, he has a good temperament and I like him".*

877. HERE'S ALICE (IRE) ★★★★
b.f. Galileo – Baraka (Danehill). May 4. Ninth foal. Sister to the quite useful 2016 2-y-o 7.5f winner Sir Edwin Landseer, to the fairly useful 12f winner Min Alemarat, the fairly useful 10f and 12f winner Beyond Conceit and the quite useful 12f and 14f winner Novalina. The dam, a listed 11f winner, is a sister to the Japanese stakes winner Fine Motion and a half-sister to 6 winners including the multiple Group 1 winner Pilsudski and the Irish 2-y-o Group 3 1m winner Glowing Ardour. The second dam, Cocotte (by Troy), a very useful 10.2f winner, was second in the Group 3 Prix de

Psyche and is a half-sister to the listed winner Gay Captain. *"A nice, late-maturing filly, but a good model. She hasn't done anything wrong, I can see her making a 2-y-o in the second half of the season and she could be anything. A nice filly".*

878. HIGH CHANGE (IRE) ★★★
b.c. High Chaparral – Small Change (Danzig). January 12. Eighth foal. €15,000Y. Goffs Orby. Barry Hills (private sale). Half-brother to the modest 6f winner Common Cents (by Pivotal). The dam, a fairly useful 2-y-o 7f winner, is a sister to the smart Group 1 6f Middle Park Stakes winner Zieten and to the Group 1 6f Cheveley Park Stakes winner Blue Duster and half-sister to 8 winners including the French listed 1m winner Slow Jazz. The second dam, Blue Note (by Habitat), won 5 races from 5f to 7f in France including the Group 2 Prix Maurice de Gheest and the Group 3 Prix de le Porte Maillot and is a half-sister to 5 winners. *"He's grown and all his riders like him, he won't be an early one but for what he cost I think we'll have some fun with him".* TRAINERS' BARGAIN BUY

879. INDICIA ★★★★
b.f. Bated Breath – Indication (Sadler's Wells). March 19. Closely related to the fair 2016 2-y-o 7f winner Syndicate and to the very useful listed 9f winner and Group 2 placed Stipulate (both by Dansili). The dam, a fair 9.5f winner, is a half-sister to 5 winners including the Group 3 7f Supreme Stakes winner Stronghold and the listed winners Convey and Take The Hint. The second dam, Insinuate (by Mr Prospector), a useful listed 1m winner, is a half-sister to numerous winners including the useful 6f and 7f winner and listed-placed Imroz. (Khalid Abdulla). *"Everyone likes this filly. She's grown, has a lovely temperament and a good action. She looks a quality filly and I think this is the best of the Abdulla 2-y-o's we have".*

880. JULIET FOXTROT ★★★
b.f. Dansili – Kilo Alpha (King's Best). March 21. Fourth foal. Sister to the quite useful 2-y-o 1m and 8.5f winner Cartago and half-sister to the French 2-y-o 1m winner and Group 3 1m Prix Thomas Bryon second Alpha Bravo (by Oasis Dream). The dam, a French listed

1m winner, is a sister to the very smart triple listed 10f winner Runaway and a half-sister to 3 winners. The second dam, Anasazi (Sadler's Wells), was placed over 9f and 10f in France and is a half-sister to the outstanding colt Dancing Brave and the Prix Vermeille and Prix de Diane winner Jolypha. (Khalid Abdulla). *"Quite a nice filly but just a bit backward and she needs some time. She needs to furnish and we're just ticking away with her for now, but there's nothing wrong with her and she's very correct".*

881. KHAWAATEM (USA) ★★★

ch.c. Smart Strike – Charmed Gift (A P Indy). April 30. Eleventh foal. $550,000Y. Keeneland September. Shadwell Estate Co. Half-brother to 5 winners including the US dual Grade 3 winner Endorsement (by Distorted Humor). The dam, a US stakes winner and second in two Grade 3 events, is a half-sister to the dam of a Grade 1 winner in Argentina. The second dam, Potridee (by Potrillazo), was a Grade 1 winner in the USA and Argentina. (Hamdan Al Maktoum). *"A very good-moving horse, but he hasn't filled his frame yet and I think he's going to go weak. A very 'giving' horse, he loves to get on with things and do it. A lovely actioned horse, he floats along and he'll be a nice horse later on when he's matured a bit".*

882. KODINA ★★★

b.f. Kodiac – Quan Am (Invincible Spirit). January 16. First foal. £65,000Y. Goffs UK Premier (Doncaster). Sackville/Donald. The dam is an unplaced half-sister to one minor winner. The second am, Quan Yin (by Sadler's Wells), is an unraced half-sister to 3 winners including Moon Driver (Group 3 Prix d'Arenburg). *"She's just started to do some faster work, she's small and if she's not going to be an early 2-y-o she won't be anything. She went alright in her first piece of work".*

883. LIVVYS DREAM (IRE) ★★★★

b.f. Declaration Of War – Briolette (Sadler's Wells). April 10. Half-sister to the fairly useful Irish 2-y-o 1m winner Thomasgainsborough (by Dansili), to the quite useful 5f to 8.5f winner of 9 races Point North (by Danehill Dancer) and the fair 2-y-o 6f winner Melabi (by Oasis Dream). The dam won the listed 10f Trigo Stakes, was second in the Group 3

12f Princess Royal Stakes and is a sister to the Irish listed winner Peach Out Of Reach and a half-sister to 6 winners including the multiple Grade 1 winner Pilsudski and the champion Japanese filly Fine Motion. The second dam, Cocotte (by Troy), a very useful 10.2f winner, was second in the Group 3 Prix de Psyche. *"Owned by the same people who own the Galileo – Baraka 2-y-o and they're two lovely fillies. They're both for later on this season but they're two lovely models".*

884. MAKAMBE (IRE) ★★★

gr.c. Dark Angel – Pink Diva (Giant's Causeway). March 3. Second foal. The dam, a fair 2-y-o 1m winner, is a half-sister to 3 winners including the useful 1m (at 2 yrs) and listed 7f winner Requisition. The second dam, Saoire (by Pivotal), winner of the Irish 1,000 Guineas and third in the Group 1 Moyglare Stud Stakes, is a half-sister to 6 winners. *"He looked forward when he came in but he's grown and just seems to have gone back a bit, although he has settled a bit better than I thought he might. Maybe it's just that he's going through a growing stage because he's a nice horse that carries himself well and he goes well".*

885. MAPPED (USA) ★★★

b.c. Mizzen Mast – Geographic (Empire Maker). April 14. Fifth foal. Brother to the 7f, 9f (in Germany) and Hong Kong listed 9f winner Harbour Master and to the quite useful Irish 2-y-o 1m winner Lanyard and half-brother to the fair 2017 3-y-o 10f winner Earthly (by Spring At Last). The dam is an unraced half-sister to the Grade 1 9f Hollywood Oaks winner Sleep Easy and to the dual US Grade 1 winner Aptitude. The second dam, Dokki (by Northern Dancer), is an unraced half-sister to the champion US colt Slew O'Gold and the Belmont Stakes winner Coastal. (Khalid Abdulla). *"A great big horse, he's a good mover with a great temperament but he's not going to be out until the late summer onwards".*

886. MIRBAT ★★★

ch.c. Dutch Art – Davie's Lure (Lure). April 2. Sixth foal. €110,000Y. Goffs Orby. Sackville/ Donald. Half-brother to the Italian 2-y-o 6f and 7f winner and Group 1 Lean-Luc

Lagardere third Salure (by Sakhee), to the Italian listed-placed winner Davie's Story (by Observatory) and two other minor winners in Italy by Authorized and Zamindar. The dam won 6 minor races at 2 and 3 yrs in Italy and is a half-sister to 4 winners. The second dam, Davie's Lamb (by Unpredictable), won five stakes events in the USA and is a half-sister to 8 winners. *"He's got a few issues with his joints for now so he'll take a bit of time just to mature. But he's a nice horse with a good action and he's grown. One for a bit later on".*

887. MOON OF BARODA ★★★

gr.c. Dubawi – Millennium Star (High Chaparral). March 31. Third foal. 500,000Y. Tattersalls October Book 1. Howson & Houldsworth. Half-brother to the fairly useful 2016 2-y-o 7.5f and 1m winner Total Star (by Pivotal). The dam is an unplaced half-sister to 9 winners including the Group winners Diamond Green, Diamilina and Diamonixa and the dam of the Melbourne Cup winner Bauer. The second dam, Diamonaka (by Akarad), a French 10.5f winner, was Group 2 placed and is a half-sister to 8 winners including the Group 2 10.5f Prix Greffulhe winner Diamond Mix and the Group 3 winners Diamond Dance and Diasilixa. *"He cost a lot of money, he's lovely and has a good temperament. A nice mover, he's just a bit babyish at present because we haven't been able to get on with him like we wanted to".*

888. MUKHAATER ★★★

ch.c. Bahamian Bounty – Dame Shirley (Haafhd). May 3. Second foal. 115,000Y. Tattersalls October Book 2. Shadwell Estate Co. The dam, unplaced in two starts, is a sister to the useful 7f winner (here) and UAE Group 3 5f winner Fityaan and half-sister to 5 minor winners. The second dam, Welsh Diva (by Selkirk), an Italian Group 3 1m and Ascot listed 1m winner, is a sister to 2 winners including the Group 2 1m Prix du Rond-Point and Group 3 8.5f Diomed Stakes winner Trans Island and a half-sister to 7 winners. (Hamdan Al Maktoum). *"A late foal but a good-looking horse, he has plenty of substance and all his riders liked him but we've had to back-off him. He had sore shins and maybe he was too generous for his own good. I'm sure he'll be alright".*

889. MUTAJAWEL (USA) ★★★

b.c. Lonhro – How Cheeky (Mr Greeley). April 14. Second foal. 62,000Y. Tattersalls October Book 2. Shadwell Estate Co. The dam is an unplaced daughter of the minor US stakes winner of 5 races Barbette (by High Yield), herself a half-sister to 7 winners including the US Grade 2 winner Diamond On The Run. (Hamdan Al Maktoum). *"He's altered a lot this horse. He wasn't very big when he came in but he's done very well. Angus Gold liked him, he's just a bit immature of his joints at the minute so we'll have to sit on him for a bit and keep him ticking over. A nice horse with a lovely temperament and I loved him when he came in. He'll be alright".*

890. MUTAKATIF (IRE) ★★★★

b.c. Acclamation – Gorband (Woodman). April 29. Ninth foal. €600,000Y. Goffs Orby. Shadwell Estate Co. Brother to the 2-y-o Group 2 6f Richmond Stakes winner Harbour Watch and half-brother to the South African Grade 1 10f winner Europe Point (by Rock Of Gibraltar), the quite useful triple 6f winner Ghalib (by Lope De Vega) and the quite useful UAE dual 7f winner Cross Grain (by Cape Cross). The dam, placed in the UAE, is a half-sister to 7 winners including the dual Group 2 winner Kabool. The second dam, Sheroog (by Shareef Dancer), a fair 1m winner, is a sister to the dam of Dubai Millennium, closely related to the Group/Grade 1 winners Hamas, Northern Aspen and Fort Wood and a half-sister to the Grade 1 winner Timber Country. (Hamdan Al Maktoum). *"He's done really well, hasn't done any fast work yet because he's a bit behind the others but he could be a nice horse. He does everything well, he's a good mover and he's grown and matured. A lovely horse that could be anything".*

891. NEWBOROUGH ★★★

b.c. Farhh – Comeraincomeshine (Night Shift). March 27. Seventh foal. £170,000Y. Goffs UK Premier (Doncaster). Jill Lamb. Half-brother to the 2016 7f placed 2-y-o, from two starts, Cosimo Medici (by Medicean), to the useful dual 5f (at 2 yrs) and listed 6f winner and dual Group 3 third Danehill Destiny (by Danehill Dancer), the fair dual 7f winner Moma Lee (by Duke Of Marmalade) and the fair 1m winner Protractor (by Galileo). The dam, a modest

5.5f winner, is a half-sister to 5 winners including the Group 1 1m Queen Elizabeth II Stakes winner Where Or When and the Group 1 St Leger fourth All The Way. The second dam, Future Past (by Super Concorde), a winner of 4 races at up to 9f in the USA, is a half-sister to 8 winners. *"He's done really well physically but he's had a few niggly problems and as a result we haven't done much with him. He's quite keen and looking at just him now I can see he's changed - he's put on a lot of beef. Not the best mover in the world but he deserves a mention".*

892. ORDER OF THISTLE (IRE) ★★★
b.c. High Chaparral – Law Of The Jungle (Catcher In The Rye). January 18. Third foal. €200,000Y. Goffs Orby. Stephen Hillen. The dam, a modest 9.5f placed maiden, is a half-sister to 5 winners including the dual Group 3 7f winner Eastern Appeal. The second dam, Haut Volee (by Top Ville), a German 2-y-o 6f and 1m winner, is a half-sister to 9 winners. *"A nice horse and a good mover, he's a bit fussy and he won't be ready until the seven furlong races. He's quite a nice horse though and I can see him turning himself inside out".*

893. PORTH SWTAN (IRE) ★★★
b.c. Invincible Spirit – Propaganda (Sadler's Wells). March 20. Seventh foal. €110,000Y. Goffs Orby. BBA (Ire). Brother to the useful 2-y-o 7f winner and Group 2 May Hill Stakes third Shagah and half-brother to the quite useful 12f and hurdles winner Swnymor (by Dylan Thomas). The dam, a fair Irish 11f winner at 4 yrs, is a half-sister to 5 winners including the German Group 3 winner Pearl Banks. The second dam, Pearly Shells (by Efisio), won the Group 1 Prix Vermeille and the Group 2 Prix de Malleret and is a half-sister to 4 winners including the US Grade 1 Hollywood Turf Handicap winner Frenchpark. *"He's done well, but he won't be early and he's changed a lot. A bit backward, but he has a good temperament and everyone who rides him likes him. I think he'll be alright later on".*

894. QUEEN OF KALAHARI ★★★★
b.f. Lethal Force – Aromatherapy (Oasis Dream). February 25. Fourth foal. £15,000Y. Goffs UK Premier (Doncaster). BBA (Ire). Half-sister to the modest 5f winner Pieman's Girl

(by Henrythenavigator) and to the moderate 10f winner Scent Of Power (by Authorized). The dam, a quite useful dual 1m winner at 3 yrs, is a half-sister to one winner. The second dam, Fragrant View (by Distant View), a useful 10.3f winner, is a sister to the champion 2-y-o Distant Music, winner of the Group 1 7f Dewhurst Stakes, the Group 2 7f Champagne Stakes and the Group 2 9f Goffs International Stakes and a half-sister to the useful 10f winner and Group 3 Lancashire Oaks third New Orchid (herself dam of the Group 1 Sprint Cup winner African Rose). *"An early foal, she came to hand pretty quick and she's got plenty of boot so she'll be fine over five furlongs and the riders all seem to like her".*

895. RASAN ★★
b.f. Dansili – Misdaqeya (Red Ransom). February 23. Fifth foal. Half-sister to the quite useful 2-y-o 7f winner Taqneyya (by Raven's Pass) and to the useful 2-y-o 6f winner and Group 3 7f Prestige Stakes second Qawaasem (by Shamardal). The dam, a useful 2-y-o 7f winner, was second in the Group 3 Sweet Solera Stakes and is a half-sister to one winner. The second dam, Crystal Power (by Pleasant Colony), won once at 3 yrs in the USA and is a half-sister to 5 winners including the US Grade 1 Flower Bowl Invitational Handicap winner Chelsey Flower (herself dam of the French Group 3 winner Kentucky Dynamite). (Hamdan Al Maktoum). *"A great big filly, she's going to want loads of time and she's only just come in from a field in Ireland. She'll need all the time we can give her despite the fact it's a 2-y-o family".*

896. RED ROMAN ★★★
b.c. Holy Roman Emperor – Domitia (Pivotal). March 8. Second foal. 30,000Y. Tattersalls October Book 2. BBA (Ire). The dam is an unraced half-sister to the 2-y-o winner and Group 2 July Stakes third Elronaq. The second dam, Cartimandua (by Medicean), a dual listed 6f winner and third in the Group 3 Ballyogan Stakes, is a half-sister to 3 winners. *"He's a butty little horse, not very big and he's going to want time. A late-maturing horse, but all his riders like him and he has a good temperament. He's one of those horses you have to keep going because they'll get too heavy otherwise".*

897. REWAAYAT ★★★★★
b.c. Pivotal – Rufoof (Zamindar). February 23.
First foal. The dam, a fair dual 7f winner, is a
half-sister to the multiple Group 1 winning
sprinter Muhaarar, the very useful 2-y-o 7f
winner and subsequent UAE Group 3 1m
second Tamaathul and the useful 2-y-o listed
6f winner Sajwah. The second dam, Tahrir (by
Linamix), a useful dual 7f winner, is a sister to
the listed winners Mister Charm and Green
Channel and a half-sister to the Group 3 Prix
de Guiche winner Mister Sacha. (Hamdan Al
Maktoum). *"A lovely horse. He's big and hasn't
done anything yet, just cantering, but he's got
great presence about him and his coat looks
really good. His riders all like him, he won't be
early but he's a nice horse and worth an extra
star".*

898. RHOSNEIGR (IRE) ★★★
ch.c. Iffraaj – Sadinga (Sadler's Wells).
February 20. Tenth foal. 100,000Y. Tattersalls
October Book 1. BBA (Ire). Half-brother to
the fairly useful 9f (at 2 yrs) and 10f winner
and listed-placed Cool Judgement (by Peintre
Celebre), to the fair 6f winner Showboating
(by Shamardal) and the modest 2-y-o 7f
winner Strictly Art (by Excellent Art). The
dam, a quite useful Irish 12f winner, is a
half-sister to 7 winners including the Group
1 Moyglare Stud Stakes winner Priory Belle
and the Group 1 Premio Lydia Tesio winner
Eva's Request and to the placed dam of the
dual Group 1 winner Chriselliam. The second
dam, Ingabelle (by Taufan), won the Group
3 Phoenix Sprint Stakes and is a half-sister to
4 winners. *"A nice horse, he's one for later on
but he's got a good body on him. Maybe a bit
heavy through the shoulders if you had to crib
him but he's straightforward and he could be
anything".*

899. ROCK OF ESTONIA (IRE) ★★★★ ♣
ch.c. Society Rock – Estonia (Exceed And
Excel). February 19. Second foal. 90,000Y.
Tattersalls October Book 2. Sackville/Donald.
Half-brother to the fair 2016 dual 5f placed
2-y-o Tallinski (by Mayson). The dam, a fair
winner of 5 races over 5f at 3 and 4 yrs, is
a half-sister to 2 winners. The second dam,
Global Trend (by Bluebird), is an unraced half-
sister to 4 winners including the French and
US stakes winner Night Chapter. *"He goes OK*

*and he's done a few bits of work. The lad who
rides him all the times raves about him and
he showed up well this morning doing a half
speed. So he'll be an early 2-y-o". This colt won
first time out at Windsor.*

900. SAFFAH (USA) ★★★★
b.f. More Than Ready – Elghayoor
(Ghostzapper). January 31. First foal. The dam
won over 6f at 3 yrs in the USA and is a half-
sister to 2 winners. The second dam, Hazimah
(by Gone West), a fair 7f and 1m placed
maiden, is a half-sister to numerous winners
including the high-class 2-y-o Mujahid,
winner of the Group 1 7f Dewhurst Stakes
and subsequently third in the 2,000 Guineas.
(Hamdan Al Maktoum). *"A big, lump of a filly
with a lovely temperament, a lovely head on
her and a backside like a table! She's done
a bit of work and she's a nice filly, probably
starting at five furlongs".*

901. SMOOTH SAILING ★★★
b.f. Bated Breath – Royal Confidence (Royal
Applause). February 11. The dam, a useful 5f
(at 2 yrs) and listed 7f winner, was third in the
Group 2 7f Rockfel Stakes and is a half sister
to the quite useful 1m winner Rougette. The
second dam, Never A Doubt (by Night Shift),
a very useful 2-y-o winner of the Group 2 5.5f
Prix Robert Papin, is a half-sister to 3 winners.
*"We've trained all the family and they've all
had knee problems. They all had the ability to
go a bit though, so we'll have to hope this filly
won't have the knee issues. She's done really
well though – so much so that the lady from
the stud came to see her the other day and
didn't recognise her".*

902. SPHERIC ★★★
b.f. Champs Elysees – Starfan (Lear Fan).
March 3. Half-sister to the Group 3 1m Prix
de Fontainebleau winner Glaswegian (by
Selkirk), the quite useful French 2-y-o 1m
winner Fan Club (by Zamindar) and the minor
French 9f winner Phenetic (by Zamindar).
The dam, a useful 6f winner, was fourth in
the Group 1 Prix Marcel Boussac and is a
half-sister to the Group 1 7f Prix de la Foret
winner Etoile Montante. The second dam,
Willstar (by Nureyev), won over 1m in France.
(Khalid Abdulla). *"Not very big, but she's got
something about her. She's very fussy, very*

light mouthed and you have to have the right lad on every time. We'll take our time with her because she won't be early, but she is good-bodied".

903. SPOOF ★★★★
b.c. Poet's Voice – Filona (Motivator). January 26. First foal. €50,000Y. Goffs Orby. Sackville/Donald. The dam, placed 8 times in Italy at 2 and 3 yrs, is a half-sister to 2 winners including the Italian listed winner and Group 3 placed Fanoulpifer. The second dam, Furbeseta (by Danehill Dancer), a fair 1m winner, is a half-sister to 5 winners including the listed winners Pretend and Fiulin. *"He'll be one of our first 2-y-o winners. He goes really well, he was an early foal and he's well-built too – so he's got the scope to train on. He's a man already and at the minute he's the standout".*

904. TAFAWOQ ★★
b.f. Oasis Dream – Raasekha (Pivotal). February 13. Second foal. The dam, a fairly useful listed-placed 1m winner, is a half-sister to 5 winners including the multiple Group 1 winning sprinter Muhaarar, the very useful 2-y-o 7f winner and subsequent UAE Group 3 1m second Tamaathul and the useful 2-y-o listed 6f winner Sajwah. The second dam, Tahrir (by Linamix), a useful dual 7f winner, is a sister to the listed winners Mister Charm and Green Channel and a half-sister to the Group 3 Prix de Guiche winner Mister Sacha. (Hamdan Al Maktoum). *"Temperament issues might arise here because her dam won at Ascot but was very bad tempered in the stalls afterwards. She's a great big filly and she's growing still, so she'll want loads of time".*

905. TAMREER ★★★
ch.f. New Approach – Reyaadah (Tamayuz). April 23. The dam, a useful 6f winner and third in the Group 3 7f Sweet Solera Stakes (both at 2 yrs), was listed-placed over 1m at 3 yrs and is a half-sister to one winner. The second dam, Tafaani (by Green Desert), is an unraced sister to one winner and a half-sister to numerous winners including the high-class 7.3f Hungerford Stakes and Tripleprint Celebration Mile winner and French 2,000 Guineas second Muhtathir. (Hamdan Al Maktoum). *"This filly's done well and she looks*

a million dollars. A little bit upright in her conformation, but she's a nice filly for later on".

906. TARBEYAH (IRE) ★★★
ch.f. Teofilo – Shamtari (Alhaarth). May 12. Fourth foal. Half-sister to the fairly useful triple 6f winner from 2 to 4 yrs Greeb (by Oasis Dream). The dam is an unraced sister to the 2,000 Guineas and Champion Stakes winner Haafhd and a half-sister to numerous winners including the Group 2 Challenge Stakes winner Munir and to the unraced dam of the dual Group 1 winner Gladiatorus. The second dam, Al Bahathri (by Blushing Groom), won the Irish 1,000 Guineas and the Coronation Stakes and is a half-sister to the US Grade 2 winner Geraldine's Store and to the dam of the US Grade 1 winner Spanish Fern. (Hamdan Al Maktoum). *"She's done well because she was only small when she came in, but Teofilo's need time so she'll be one for later in the year. A nice filly though".*

907. WAFY (IRE) ★★★ ♠
b.c. Dubawi – Ghanaati (Giant's Causeway). February 28. Brother to the quite useful 7f to 8.5f winner of 4 races Alnashama and half-brother to the modest 1m winner Almuhalab (by Dansili). The dam, winner of the 1,000 Guineas and Coronation Stakes, is a half-sister to 6 winners including the Group 3 12f Cumberland Lodge Stakes winner and Group 1 Champion Stakes second Mawatheeq and the useful 1m (at 2 yrs) and listed 9f winner Rumoush. The second dam, Sarayir (by Mr Prospector), winner of a listed 1m event, is closely related to the Champion Stakes winner Nayef and a half-sister to Nashwan and Unfuwain. (Hamdan Al Maktoum). *"A great, big horse. Ghanaati's foals seem to take a lot of time to mature, but he's a nice horse, a good mover and has a great temperament. So hopefully the dam has thrown a nice one this time".*

908. WUFUD ★★
b.c. Dubawi – Tahrir (Linamix). May 24. Brother to the 2-y-o 7f winner from two starts Mootaharer and half-brother to 5 winners including the multiple Group 1 6f winner Muhaarar (by Oasis Dream), the very useful 2-y-o 7f winner and subsequent UAE

Group 3 1m second Tamaathul (by Tiger Hill), the useful 2-y-o listed 6f winner Sajwah (by Exceed And Excel) and the fairly useful listed-placed 1m winner Raasekha (by Pivotal). The dam, a useful dual 7f winner, is a sister to the listed winners Mister Charm and Green Channel and a half-sister to the Group 3 Prix de Guiche winner Mister Sacha. The second dam, Miss Sacha (by Last Tycoon), a listed sprint winner, is a half-sister to 6 winners. (Hamdan Al Maktoum). *"He only comes in later this week, so I haven't seen him. He's a late foal but being a Dubawi half-brother to Muhaarar we'll be pleased to see him".*

909. ZUMURUD (IRE) ★★★
gr.c. Zebedee – Thaisy (Tabasco Cat). January 17. Sixth foal. £62,000Y. Goffs UK Premier (Doncaster). Shadwell Estate Co. Half-brother to the modest 6f (at 2 yrs) and 5f winner David's Beauty (by Kodiac) and to the modest 8.5f winner Ice Box (by Pivotal). The dam is an unplaced half-sister to 5 winners including the Group winners Fruits Of Love and Mujadil. The second dam, Vallee Secrete (by Secretariat), a minor French 3-y-o winner, is a half-sister to 6 winners. (Hamdan Al Maktoum). *"We gave him some time off a few weeks ago because he was growing like mad, but he's caught up and he's doing a few bits of work now. He won't be far off a run and his attitude is OK".*

910. UNNAMED ★★★
ch.c. Zoffany – Became (Giant's Causeway). April 20. Third foal. 130,000Y. Tattersalls October Book 1. Sackville/Donald. The dam is an unraced half-sister to two minor winners. The second dam, Encouragement (by Bertrando), is an unraced half-sister to 4 winners including Key Phrase (Grade 1 Santa Monica Handicap). *"Not the most attractive horse in the world with his white eyes, but he's done really well physically. He was very timid when he came in but he's settled down and put on condition, so I wouldn't knock him. He'll be alright later in the year".*

911. UNNAMED ★★★
b.c. Galileo – Bewitched (Dansili). January 11. Third foal. €80,000Y. Goffs Orby. BBA (Ire). The dam, a smart winner of 8 races from 5f to 7f including the Ballycorus Stakes,

the Bengough Stakes and the Renaissance Stakes twice (all Group 3 events) and is a half-sister to 4 minor winners. The second dam, Abbatiale (by Kaldoun), won the Group 3 Prix Penelope, was second in the Group 1 Prix de Diane and is a half-sister to the French listed winner and Group 2 placed Aubergade. *"He was bought by Barry, he's done well and looks a million dollars. He wasn't at all expensive for a Galileo, but he hasn't put a foot wrong here so far".*

912. UNNAMED ★★★
b.f. Red Jazz – Desert Drama (Green Desert). March 30. Eleventh foal. €58,000Y. Goffs Orby. BBA (Ire). Half-sister to the smart 6f (at 2 yrs) and 1m winner and Group 1 Irish 2,000 Guineas second Endless Drama (by Lope De Vega), to the French 5f winner of 5 races (including at 2 yrs) Histoire, the French 4-y-o dual 1m winner Tycoon's Desert (both by Whipper) and a minor winner at 4 yrs in the USA by Honour And Glory. The dam, a French listed 5f winner, was third in the Group 2 Criterium de Maisons-Laffitte and is a half-sister to three other listed winners. The second dam, Tycoon's Drama (by Last Tycoon), won 3 races at 2 yrs in France and the USA including the Grade 3 8.5f Selima Stakes and is a full or half-sister to 4 winners including the dam of the US Grade 1 winner King's Drama. *"She's got a nice pedigree, she's grown and carries herself really well. A very good walker, I think she has a chance this filly".*

913. UNNAMED ★★★
b.f. Oasis Dream – Hidden Brief (Barathea). April 3. Fourth foal. 55,000Y. Tattersalls October Book 1. BBA (Ire). Half-sister to the 2016 2-y-o 7f winner (on his only start) Mushaireb (by Invincible Spirit). The dam, a fairly useful listed-placed 10f winner, is a sister to the Group 3 winner and Group 1 Irish Oaks third Hazarista and a half-sister to 5 winners including the Group 3 winner Hazariya (herself dam of the Derby winner Harzand). The second dam, Hazaradjat (by Darshaan), a 7f (at 2 yrs) and 10f winner in Ireland, is a full or half-sister to 10 winners including the Flying Childers and Middle Park Stakes winner Hittite Glory. *"She's just on the back burner at the minute because of a few niggling problems but she's a nice filly*

with some unusual markings in her tail – like sergeant's stripes. She's done well physically and she'll be alright a bit later on".

914. UNNAMED ★★
b.f. Sea The Stars – Jessica's Dream (Desert Style). May 22. Fifth foal. €190,000Y. Arqana Deauville August. Not sold. Half-sister to the Group 1 1m Prix Jean Prat winner of 5 races Havana Gold (by Teofilo), to the fair 5f winner of 8 races (including at 2 yrs) Rocker (by Rock Of Gibraltar) and minor winners in Hong Kong (by Royal Applause) and Germany (by Montjeu). The dam, a very smart sprinter, won the Group 3 Ballyogan Stakes and the Group 3 Premio Omenoni and is a half-sister to the listed winner and dual Group 1 placed Majors Cast. The second dam, Ziffany (by Taufan), a 2-y-o 7f seller winner, is a half-sister to one winner abroad. *"A late foal, she's done alright and is a butty little filly who's not very big but all there. She's had a few niggling problems, then all the jabs the horses need seemed to catch her out and she never came out from them great. We'll just have to take our time with her, but when she's out you wouldn't know you've got her – she's no problem".*

915. UNNAMED ★★★
b.f. Declaration Of War – La Conquerante (Hurricane Run). February 11. First foal. €90,000Y. Goffs Orby. Sackville/Donald. The dam, a French 10f to 12.5f winner and third in the Group 2 12.5f Prix de Royallieu, is a half-sister to 3 winners. The second dam, Winning Family (by Fasliyev), a French dual 2-y-o winner, is a half-sister to 4 winners including the US dual Grade 3 winner Ballast. *"She had colic around Christmas and she's only just got back into training, but she's turned herself inside out and I think she must be as tough as old boots. I've got to give her full marks for overcoming her illness and she loves the game – she wants to get out and do it".*

916. UNNAMED ★★★
b.f. Oasis Dream – Market Forces (Lomitas). February 17. Sixth foal. 100,000Y. Tattersalls October Book 1. Sackville/Donald. Half-sister to the quite useful 10f winner and subsequent German listed-placed Distain (by Champs Elysees), to the fair dual 10f winner Fast Pace (by Observatory) and the fair 12f winner Limousine (by Beat Hollow). The dam, a fairly useful 12f and 14f winner, was listed-placed and is a half-sister to 5 winners including the useful 2-y-o listed 7f winner Protectress. The second dam, Quota (by Rainbow Quest), a useful 10f winner, is a sister to 5 winners including the Group 1 1m Racing Post Trophy winner and St Leger second Armiger. *"Everybody likes this filly and she hasn't had many hold-ups. She's grown and lengthened, she's a good mover and her rider likes her a lot. She's straightforward too, but on the other hand she doesn't look like a speed merchant and it's not a 2-y-o family either. So the jury's out as to how much of a 2-y-o career she'll have".*

917. UNNAMED ★★★★
b.c. Arcano – Monicalew (Refuse To Bend). April 8. Second foal. £40,000Y. Goffs UK Premier (Doncaster). Half-sister to the fair Irish 2-y-o 7f winner Fire Tree (by Cacique). The dam, a modest 10f winner, is a half-sister to 4 winners including the Group 2 12f Ribblesdale Stakes second Eldalil. The second dam, White House (by Pursuit Of Love), a quite useful 10f winner, is a half-sister to 11 winners including the middle-distance Group winners Little Rock, Whitewater Affair and Short Skirt. *"He's a goer! He's got the type of body to do well as a 2-y-o, he's straightforward and his attitude's good. A five furlong colt to start with, he's definitely one to watch out for".*

918. UNNAMED ★★★
b.c. Cape Cross – Prianca (Diktat). May 6. Fourth foal. €70,000Y. Goffs Orby. BBA (Ire). Half-brother to a winner in Japan by Arch. The dam, a German listed winner, is a half-sister to 3 winners including the useful 2-y-o 7f winner and Group 2 12f Ribblesdale Stakes third Pamona. The second dam, Palanca (by Inchinor), a 2-y-o Group 3 Premio Primi Passi winner, is a half-sister to 3 winners. *"Barry likes this horse but he's got very open knees so he'll need time and he needs to grow a bit too. He has a great temperament and I can see him being a nice little horse if we're just a bit patient with him".*

919. UNNAMED ★★
b.f. Shamardal – Tarfah (Kingmambo). May 12. Half-sister to the Racing Post Trophy (at 2 yrs), 2,000 Guineas, Derby and Irish Derby winner Camelot (by Montjeu) and to the quite useful 10f winner Ideal (by Galileo). The dam, a useful winner of 5 races over 1m and 9f including the Group 3 Dahlia Stakes and the listed Rosemary Stakes, is a half-sister to one winner. The second dam, Fickle (by Danehill), a fairly useful 1m and listed 10f winner, is a half-sister to 7 winners including the useful 11.5f listed winner Birdie and the French middle-distance winner of four listed events Faru. *"This filly was a rat when she came in, but she's done really well although she's not the easiest to ride on a day to day basis because she's a bit 'revvy'. You try to get them into a routine but they need time to mature as well, so you're between two stools in a way. She's done well though, grown and put on condition, so I wouldn't leave her out. Her pedigree speaks for itself".*

920. UNNAMED ★★★
ch.f. Galileo – Withouwithoutyou (Danehill). April 20. €195,000Y. Arqana Deauville August. Not sold. Sister to the fair Irish 2-y-o 7f winner Homeland and half-sister to the Group 1 6f Golden Jubilee Stakes and Group 2 6f Coventry Stakes winner and Group 1 6f Phoenix Stakes second Art Connoisseur (by Lucky Story). The dam, a quite useful 2-y-o 7f winner, is a half-sister to 2 winners. The second dam, Morningsurprice (by Future Storm), is an unraced half-sister to 5 winners including the high-class broodmare Morning Devotion (dam of the Oaks and Irish Derby winner Balanchine and the Group 2 winners Romanov and Red Slippers). *"Quite a nice filly, we haven't had a clear run because it's been 'stop-start' with her, but being a Galileo we knew she needed time anyway. She'll be a nice filly for later on, over seven furlongs plus".*

RICHARD HUGHES

921. ACQUIRER (IRE) ★★
b.c. Zoffany – See Emily Play (Galileo). March 16. Second foal. 130,000Y. Tattersalls October Book 2. Hillen & Hughes. Half-brother to See The Master (by Dutch Art), unplaced in one start at 2 yrs in 2016. The dam is a 2-y-o fourth placed full or half-sister to 4 winners.

The second dam, Tree Tops (by Grand Lodge), a fair 1m to 10f placed maiden, is a half-sister to 3 winners including the US Grade 1 winner Tuscan Evening. (Top Trumps Partnership). *"A fine, big Zoffany colt out of a Galileo mare, he cost plenty of money and he's a strong horse but if I got him out in July I'd be happy. More likely he's a back-end of the season type 2-y-o and I think he'd get a mile and a quarter now".*

922. ADMISSABLE ★★★
b.c. Excelebration – Admirable Spirit (Invincible Spirit). April 9. Second foal. The dam, a quite useful 2-y-o 6f winner, is a half-sister to 3 winners. The second dam, Demi Voix (by Halling), a minor winner at 2 yrs in France, is a half-sister to 3 winners. (Longview Stud & Bloodstock). *"He's come to hand really quickly and he's probably going to be one of our first colts to run. The quickest I've ridden by Excelebration, he was sent to us and we're happy with his progress. He's shown us enough pace to tell us we should start him at five furlongs in April or May".*

923. CARRICKLANE ★★★
b.f. Zoffany – New River (Montjeu). April 23. Second foal. The dam, a fair 10f and 11.5f placed maiden on the flat, won over hurdles and is a half-sister to 2 minor winners. The second dam, Quiet Waters (by Quiet American), ran once unplaced and is a half-sister to 7 winners including French Group 3 winner Summertime Legacy (herself dam of the French Group 1 winners Mandaean and Wavering). (New River Partnership). *"A fine big filly, interestingly my dad trained the dam to win a hurdles race. She's not slow but she's one for the middle of the season so we're in no rush with her but she has an engine. The owners bred her themselves and if they'd had to buy her she'd have cost a lot of money".*

924. ELLEN GATES ★★★★
b.f. Mayson – Mrs Greeley (Mr Greeley). February 6. Second foal. 30,000Y. Tattersalls October Book 3. Hillen & Hughes. The dam, a fair 6f and 7f winner of 3 races at 3 and 4 yrs, is a half-sister to 3 winners including the Group 1 Irish Derby winner and Epsom Derby second Jack Hobbs. The second dam, Swain's Gold (by Swain), won 3 minor races at 3 yrs in the USA and is a half-sister to the US stakes

winner Brazilian. (Peter Makin Syndicate). *"She's the business. A good buy at 30 grand, she's beautiful and she'll be running in May, so despite the stamina influences in the dam's side of her pedigree it seems she takes after her sire".* TRAINERS' BARGAIN BUY

925. EMPRESS ROSE ★★
ch.f. Makfi – Ittasal (Any Given Saturday). February 19. Second foal. €35,000Y. Arqana Deauville August. Private Sale. Half-sister to Classie (by Fastnet Rock), unplaced in one start at 2 yrs in 2016. The dam, a quite useful 2-y-o 7f winner, is a half-sister to 6 winners including the very useful 2-y-o 6f winner and Group 3 Firth Of Clyde Stakes third La Presse. The second dam, Journalist (by Night Shift), a useful 2-y-o 6f winner, was second in the Group 3 6f Princess Margaret Stakes and is a half-sister to the Group 2 Flying Childers Stakes winner Sheer Viking. (Jaber Abdullah). *"A big, tall filly, she's very kind natured and does everything nicely. I won't be in any rush with her because she's one for the second half of the season, starting over seven furlongs".*

926. FUMAROLE ★★
b.c. Maxios – Solar Midnight (Lemon Drop Kid). February 16. Third foal. €60,000Y. Goffs Orby. Richard Hughes. Half-brother to the 3-y-o 7f winner, from two starts, Red Midnight (by Shamardal). The dam, a listed-placed 1m winner in France, is a half-sister to 5 winners including the French listed winner It's Midnight. The second dam, Witching Hour (by Fairy King), a minor winner at 3 yrs in France, is a half-sister to 10 winners including the triple listed winner Party Doll (dam of the dual Group 2 winner and sire Titus Livius). (Flaxman Stables Ireland Ltd). *"A lovely big horse that was sent to me. He's a good, flowing, easy-moving horse and I think the sire is going to suit. This horse has a good, sound mind, he moves well and he has plenty of bone. One for the mid-season to start with, he's nice and agile".*

927. GOLD FILIGREE (IRE) ★★★
gr.f. Dark Angel – Gold Lace (Invincible Spirit). March 10. Second foal. €40,000Y. Goffs Orby. Hillen & Hughes. Half-sister to the modest 2016 dual 5f placed 2-y-o Gold Locket (by Kyllachy). The dam, a quite useful 2-y-o 5f

winner, is a half-sister to 3 winners including the German Group 2 1m and Group 3 9.5f Prix Daphnis winner Emerald Commander. The second dam, Brigitta (by Sadler's Wells), won over 1m and 10f and is a sister to the 2-y-o Group 1 1m Racing Post Trophy winner Commander Collins, closely related to the Grade 1 Breeders' Cup Sprint winner Lit de Justice and the 2,000 Guineas and Derby placed Colonel Collins and a half-sister to the Group 2 Royal Lodge Stakes winner City Leader. (Galloway, Lawrence, Merritt & Mrs Blake). *"One of my early ones, she appears to go well and is very straightforward. For her debut I'll be aiming her for Windsor towards the end of April. An early type and with a good pedigree, I thought she was probably my best value buy".*

928. HAVEN'S VIEW ★★
b.c. Reckless Abandon – Haven's Wave (Whipper). February 12. Third foal. 62,000Y. Tattersalls October Book 2. Hillen & Hughes. Half-brother to the fairly useful 9.5f and 10f winner Wadigor (by Champs Elysees). The dam is an unraced half-sister to 4 winners including the Group 3 St Simon Stakes winner and dual Group 1 placed High Heeled and to the unplaced dam of the Group/Grade 1 winner Just The Judge. The second dam, Uncharted Haven (by Turtle Island), won two Grade 2 events in the USA and is a half-sister to 6 winners. (Top Trumps Partnership). *"Just going through a change at the moment, he was certainly bought to be early but he has a very strong pedigree behind him. On his father's side he's quick and on his mother's side he's a stayer, but he looks like a sprinter. I imagine he'll be racing by May time".* The sire, a son of Exchange Rate, won the Prix Morny and the Middle Park Stakes (both Group 1 6f events at 2 yrs).

929. INUK (IRE) ★★★
b.f. Kodiac – Elkmait (Trade Fair). February 23. Second foal. 55,000Y. Tattersalls October Book 1. Hillen & Hughes. The dam, a quite useful 2-y-o 6f winner, is a half-sister to 8 winners including the Japanese triple Group 3 winner Bounce Shasse and the Irish 2,000 Guineas third Stubbs Art. The second dam, Rich Dancer (by Halling), a moderate 10f placed maiden, is a half-sister to the Group

winners Just James and Blue Jack. (M Hughes & M Kerr-Dineen). *"A petite filly bought from the Book One sale, so she has the £25K bonus going for her. She looks an early type, so I can see her being out in May".*

930. JACK TAYLOR (IRE) ★★★
b.c. Invincible Spirit – Glory Power (Medicean). April 17. Second foal. €42,000Y. Arqana Deauville October. Stephen Hillen. The dam, a listed-placed winner of 3 races in France at 3 and 4 yrs, is a half-sister to 2 winners. The second dam, Sandbox (by Grand Lodge), a listed-placed winner in France, is a half-sister to 6 winners including the Group 3 Prix de Psyche winner Serisia. (Anthony Hogarth). *"If he's not a good buy I don't know what is, because the sire's covering fee is 75 grand and we got him for 42. A beautiful horse, he has a dipped back but that won't stop him and he has a very good pedigree. We'll start him at five or six furlongs".*

931. KENDAR ROUGE (FR) ★★★★
b.f. Kendargent – Lune Rouge (Unfuwain). March 13. €135,000Y. Arqana Deauville October. Stephen Hillen. Half-sister to the Group 1 10f Prix Saint-Alary winner of 5 races Ask For The Moon (by Dr Fong), to the Italian Group 3 7f and German listed 6.5f winner Princess Asta (by Canford Cliffs) and the French 10f winner Mission Apollo (by Lomitas). The dam won once and was listed-placed in France and is a half-sister to 7 winners including the dam of the French Group 3 winner Celimene. (Top Trumps Partnership). *"Probably my classiest filly, I'm in no rush with her but her sister won a Group 1 and she's going to be a mile and a quarter filly next year. She'll be there when I want her, but that won't be before June. A very elegant filly and the best I have".*

932. NOTEWORTHY (IRE) ★★★
b.f. Acclamation – Church Melody (Oasis Dream). March 3. Fourth foal. 120,000Y. Tattersalls October Book 2. Hillen & Hughes. Sister to the quite useful 2-y-o dual 5f winner Al Ghuwariyah and half-sister to the fair 2-y-o 6f winner Indian Pursuit (by Compton Place). The dam is an unraced half-sister to 4 winners including the dual Group 2 winning stayer

Gospel Choir. The second dam, Chorist (by Pivotal), won the Group 1 10f Curragh Pretty Polly Stakes and two Group 3 events and is a half-sister to 9 winners. (Rosenblatt, Mandell & Margolis). *"A fine, big, strong filly. Her pedigree says speed and her sister was speedy but looking at her you wouldn't think she'd be one for five furlongs. She's got quite a bit of size, but at the same time I don't think she's slow and she's definitely one of my nicer fillies with scope. She long and tall, so I don't want to make a call as to when she'll be out".*

933. ODYSSA (IRE) ★★★
b.f. Kodiac – Deliziosa (Iffraaj). April 23. First foal. 43,000Y. Tattersalls October Book 2. Hillen & Hughes. The dam, placed once at 3 yrs in Italy, is a half-sister to 2 winners including the Group 3 Horris Hill Stakes second Pleasant Hill. The second dam, Sunblush (by Timber Country), ran unplaced twice and is a half-sister to 5 winners including the Group 2 Rockfel Stakes winner Cairns. (The Low Flyers). *"She was quite small when we bought her and we thought she was a little bargain, but she's started to grow and she has a fairly late foaling date. Although she's a Kodiac we're not rushing her and I don't think we'll see her out until the end of June onwards".*

934. POLLYISSIMO ★★
ch.f. Nathaniel – Fleurissimo (Dr Fong). January 23. Third foal. 40,000Y. Tattersalls October Book 2. Hillen & Hughes). Half-sister to Fleur Forsyte (by Teofilo), unplaced in one start at 2 yrs in 2016. The dam, a fair 7f (at 2 yrs) and 10f placed maiden, is a half-sister to 3 winners including the listed 1m winner and Group 1 Coronation Stakes third Dolores (dam of the Group winners Duncan, Gretchen and Samuel). The second dam, Agnus (by In The Wings), a winner twice in Belgium at 2 and 3 yrs, is a half-sister to 5 winners including the US Grade 2 San Francisco Mile Handicap winner Wavy Run. (Flitton, Lawrence & Hughes). *"A very nice filly and she's an image of my 3-y-o filly Nathania who's by the same sire. That's the reason I bought her, you'd think she was a clone and if she's half as good as her I'll be happy. She's a back-end filly, but she's not a slob".*

935. POLLY'S GOLD (IRE) ★★★
ch.f. Havana Gold – Keyta Bonita (Denon).
February 3. First foal. €40,000Y. Arqana
Deauville August. Richard Hughes. The dam,
a fair 6f and 7f placed maiden here and a
minor winner abroad, is a half-sister to 4
winners including the Group 3 7f 3 Prix du
Calvados (at 2 yrs), Group 3 Nell Gwyn Stakes
and US Grade 3 9f winner Sandiva and the
useful 2-y-o 7f, 1m and subsequent Danish
listed winner Wentworth. The dam won 6
races in Italy and is a half-sister to 4 winners.
(M Flitton, B Galloway & A Kavanagh). *"She's
going to be really early, I bought her at
Deauville and all being well she'll be running
at Lingfield in early April. She'll go on really
fast ground and she has a great mind, so she'll
be earning her crust and she's a real 2-y-o".*

936. RUSTANG (FR) ★★
b.c. Holy Roman Emperor – Oppamattox
(Munir). May 7. Seventh foal. €67,000Y.
Arqana Deauville October. Stephen Hillen.
Half-brother to the French 7.5f winner,
Group 3 7f Prix Imprudence second and US
5f winner Belle De Lune, to the French 10.5f
winner Evermore (both by Ski Chief) and the
French 5.5f (at 2 yrs) and 6f winner of 4 races
and listed-placed Sorry Woman (by Ivan
Denisovich). The dam is an unraced half-sister
to 2 minor winners in France. The second
dam, Vedeheme (by Miswaki), was unraced.
(White Beech Farm). *"A nice horse for the
back-end, he has a very nice pedigree and I
think he's the best stallion the mare's been to. I
see him as being one for the second part of the
season and if he wins a maiden he'll be worth
a lot of money".*

937. SECRETARIO (FR) ★★
ch.c. Kendargent – Amoa (Ghostzapper).
March 25. €30,000Y. Arqana Deauville
August. Stephen Hillen. The dam, a French
11.5f winner, is a half-sister to 4 winners
including the Group 2 Prix Hocquart winner
and Group 1 Grand Prix de Paris second
Ampere. The second dam, Amorama (by
Sri Pekan), a US Grade 1 John C Mabee
Handicap and Grade 1 Del Mar Oaks winner,
is a half-sister to 5 winners including the
Japanese Group 2 placed Uncoiled and the
French listed 1m winner Table Ronde and to
the unraced dam of the Group 1 Prix Jean
Romanet winner Odeliz. (Mr R Hughes). *"He's*

*a French bred colt and we'll be aiming to win
his maiden over there because of the good
prize money. I thought he was a cheap horse
and he probably wants six furlongs to start
with".*

938. TRAVELLERS JOY ★★
b.f. Equiano – Travelling (Dubai Destination).
March 11. First foal. The dam, a fair 7f (at 2
yrs) to 9.5f winner of 4 races, is a half-sister to
the fair 2-y-o 7f winner Bonfire Knight. The
second dam, Attune (by Singspiel), a useful
listed 7f winner of 4 races, is a half-sister to 3
winners. (Longview Stud). *"The little filly has
done really well since she came to us. She was
a little bit nervous but now she's transformed
and I love the fillies that do that. She's a little
bit weak but she's improved a lot and if she
can improve as much again she'll be a nice
filly".*

939. TWILIGHT WAR (IRE) ★★
b.c. Declaration Of War – Special Assignment
(Lemon Drop Kid). April 27. Third foal.
€70,000Y. Goffs Orby. Andy Smith. Half-
brother to the moderate 2016 7f fourth
placed 2-y-o Speciale Di Giorno (by High
Chaparral). The dam is an unraced half-sister
to 8 winners including the US triple Grade 2
winner Quest Star. The second dam, Tinaca
(by Manila), is an unplaced half-sister to
5 winners including the dual US Grade 2
winner Mariah's Storm (the dam of Giant's
Causeway). (Mr James Langridge). *"A huge
colt, but he's a good mover that covers the
ground well and he'll be a back-end 2-y-o".*

940. UNNAMED ★★★
ch.c. Choisir – Almogia (Gone West). April
1. Third foal. £52,000Y. Goffs UK Premier
(Doncaster). Hillen & Hughes. The dam, a
minor winner at 4 yrs in France, is a half-sister
to the US dual Grade 3 winner Istan. The
second dam, Ronda (by Bluebird), won the
Group 2 Falmouth Stakes and is a half-sister
to 2 winners. (Gallagher Equine Ltd). *"A nice
horse I bought at Doncaster and I think if I'd
bought him in the afternoon he'd have been
twice as dear. He appears to be going really
nicely and he'll be there when I want him –
probably at the end of May. If we can get him
to Ascot we will do, but if not it won't bother
me. He's a very big horse".*

941. UNNAMED ★★★
b.f. Big Bad Bob – Fashionable (Nashwan).
May 5. Eighth foal. €72,000Y. Goffs Orby.
Hillen & Hughes. Half-sister to the 2-y-o
Group 3 Silver Flash Stakes and listed 1m
winner and Group 1 Irish Oaks second Jack
Naylor (by Champs Elysees), to the quite
useful 10f winner Seamless (by Beat Hollow),
the fair 12f and 13f winner Linkable and a
2-y-o winner abroad (both by Rail Link). The
dam, a useful listed 10f winner, is a half-sister
to 6 winners. The second dam, Fine Detail (by
Shirley Heights), a fairly useful 12f winner, is a
half-sister to 8 winners including the US triple
Grade 1 winner Wandesta and the Group 2
12f winner De Quest. (Mr P D Merritt). *"My
owner asked me to buy a filly with a good
pedigree so I picked this one. I rode the half-
sister when she was fourth in the Irish Guineas.
Then she was second in the Irish Oaks. This
filly looks a good buy and she's one for the end
of the season and for seven furlongs".*

942. UNNAMED ★★★
b.f. Iffraaj – Money Note (Librettist). February
15. Third foal. 62,000Y. Tattersalls October
Book 2. Hillen & Hughes. Half-sister to the
fair 2016 2-y-o 5f winner Stringybark Creek
(by Bushranger) and to the fair dual 6f
winner Kyllukey (by Kyllachy). The dam is an
unplaced half-sister to 6 winners including
the very smart Group 1 1m Gran Criterium
winner and 2,000 Guineas second Lend A
Hand. The second dam, Janaat (by Kris), a fair
12f winner, is a sister to the French listed 10.5f
winner Trefoil and a half-sister to 11 winners
including the smart middle-distance winners
Maysoon, Richard of York, Third Watch and
Three Tails (the dam of 3 Group winners).
(Mrs Susan Roy). *"A nice, big, strong girl. I'm
in no rush with her and she looks more of a
seven furlong filly than anything less, but we'll
see. She has loads of scope, so she's going to
make a 3-y-o as well".*

WILLIAM JARVIS
943. BEDIVERE ★★
b.c. Camelot – Foreign Language (Distant
View). May 20. Fifth living foal. 45,000Y.
Tattersalls October Book 2. James Toller. Half-
brother to the modest 2016 2-y-o 6f winner
Ferocity (by Poet's Voice) and to the modest
1m winner Desert Berry (by Green Desert).

The dam, a fair 8.5f winner, is a half-sister to 3
winners including the Scandinavian Group 3
and listed Strensall Stakes winner Binary File
and to the placed dam of the Group/Grade
1 winners Byword and Proviso. The second
dam, Binary (by Rainbow Quest), a French
listed 10f winner, was second in the Group
3 Prix de Psyche and is a full or half-sister
to 10 winners including the listed winners
Bequeath and Bal Harbour. (PCJ Dalby & R
D Schuster). *"A late foal and we won't see
him out until August at the earliest but he's a
likeable colt with a good attitude. He's a good
size, there are middle-distance influences in his
pedigree and he'll probably start his career at
seven furlongs".*

944. CHIEF IRONSIDE ★★★★
b.c. Lawman – Moment Of Time (Rainbow
Quest). February 23. Second foal. 155,000Y.
Tattersalls October Book 2. Jarvis/Washbourn.
The dam, a quite useful 10f listed-placed
maiden, is a half-sister to 7 winners including
the Group 3 10.4f Musidora Stakes winner
and Group 1 Prix de Diane third Time Away
(dam of the Group 2 winner Time On) and the
Group 1 French Oaks second Time Ahead. The
second dam, Not Before Time (by Polish
Precedent), is an unraced half-sister to 7
winners including the very useful Group 3
12f winners Zinaad and Time Allowed and
the dams of the Group 2 winners Anton
Chekhov, First Charter and Plea Bargain. (Mr
Clive Washbourn). *"A particularly nice horse
from the Barnett family, we paid quite a lot
of money for him and the Lawman/Rainbow
Quest cross has worked well before. He's a
little bit behind the others because he had
a setback early on but he's fine now and we
won't lose any time with him because he's a
big horse for the second half of the season.
An exciting colt with the chance of being a
good one".*

945. QUEEN TOMYRIS ★★★★
b.f. Declaration Of War – Caphene (Sakhee).
March 6. Second foal. 85,000Y. Tattersalls
October Book 1. James Toller. The dam
is an unplaced half-sister to 6 winners
including the listed Lingfield Oaks Trial
and subsequent US Grade 3 winner and
Group 1 Nassau Stakes second Cassydora
and the listed 10f winner Classic Remark.
The second dam, Claxon (by Caerleon), a

very useful 1m (at 2 yrs) and Group 2 10f Premio Lydia Tesio winner, is a half-sister to 3 winners including the dual Group 2 placed Bulwark. (Ms E L Banks). *"She's a gorgeous filly, I love her. She's a good size, has a good step to her and a sweet temperament. One of those old-fashioned fillies with big ears and she just looks an honest, really likeable filly. Declaration Of War was a good racehorse and there's no reason why he can't become a successful stallion. Her size suggests she'll be a seven furlong 2-y-o to start with and she's a thoroughly likeable filly".*

946. TILGHMAN (IRE) ★★★

b.c. Lawman – Poppet's Lovein (Lomitas). March 12. Third foal. 72,000Y. Tattersalls October Book 2. Toller/Washbourn. Half-brother to the fairly useful 2016 2-y-o 7f winner Make Time (by Makfi). The dam, a quite useful triple 7f winner at 3 and 4 yrs, is a half-sister to 7 winners including the smart German 6f Group 2 and triple Group 3 winner Overdose and the French listed winner Majestic Mount. The second dam, Our Poppet (by Warning), unplaced in one outing at 2 yrs, is a half-sister to 10 winners including the listed winner and Group 1 third Musicanna. (Mr Clive Washbourn). *"A nice horse, he's very active but different to my other Lawman 2-y-o Chief Ironside. He's got plenty of 'Go' about him, he's forward going and he could easily be out in May. He might even be an Ascot horse if he's good enough, he's enthusiastic and he points his toe well. A six furlong type 2-y-o to begin with".*

947. UNNAMED ★★★ ♠

b.f. Oasis Dream – A Huge Dream (Refuse To Bend). February 8. First foal. 140,000Y. Tattersalls October Book 1. James Toller. The dam, a French listed-placed 6f winner, is a half-sister to 2 winners including the 2-y-o Group 2 7f Vintage Stakes and subsequent Hong Kong dual Group 1 1m winner Xtension. The second dam, Great Joy (by Grand Lodge), won at 3 yrs in Germany and was listed placed and is a half-sister to 4 winners. (Ms E L Banks). *"She was expensive, hasn't grown as much as we'd really like if I'm being critical, but she has a good way of going, she's enthusiastic and I'd imagine she'd be my first 2-y-o runner towards the end of April".*

948. UNNAMED ★★★

b.c. So You Think – Lamanka Lass (Woodman). May 5. Eleventh foal. 6,000Y. Tattersalls October Book 4. William Jarvis. Half-brother to the 7f (at 2 yrs), 1m and subsequent US Grade 2 9f Oak Tree Derby winner Dark Islander (by Singspiel), to the quite useful Irish 2-y-o 7f and subsequent Hong Kong 8.5f winner Billboard (by Big Bad Bob), the quite useful 2-y-o 7f winner Suffolk Punch (by Barathea), the fair dual 12f winner Crocolat (by Croco Rouge) and the modest dual 1m winner Miss Mojito (by Lucky Story). The dam, a fair 1m winner, is a half-sister to 7 winners including Far Lane (Group 3 Darley Stakes). The second dam, Pattimech (by Nureyev), won at up to 7f in the USA and is a sister to the triple US Grade 1 winner Annoconnor and a half-sister to the Grand Prix de Paris and Melbourne Cup winner At Talaq. *"The sire is just beginning to get winners down under now and needs to pick up here in Europe. This colt certainly wasn't an expensive horse, he was a fairly late foal and he's going to need time but he's got a good way of going. He'll be ok over seven furlongs this year, he's a good size and needs to fill out a bit but to look at him he'd make a lot more money if he was at the breeze up sale now. I'm still looking for an owner for him".*

949. UNNAMED ★★★

b.c. Poet's Voice – Xtrasensory (Royal Applause). February 3. Ninth foal. 20,000 foal. Tattersalls December. R G Percival. Half-brother to the 2-y-o 6f winner Responsive (by Dutch Art), to the 2-y-o 5f and 6f winners Tassel and Tishtar (both by Kyllachy), the 6f winner Galvanise (by Bahamian Bounty) – all quite useful, the fair 7f (at 2 yrs) and 1m winner Redsensor (by Redback) and the fair 6f winners Bacall (by Paco Boy) and Fenella Rose (by Compton Place). The dam, a fairly useful 2-y-o 6f winner, is a half-sister to 8 winners. The second dam, Song Of Hope (by Chief Singer), a useful listed-placed 2-y-o 5f winner, is a half-sister to 10 minor winners. (Ms E L Banks). *"He's doing two canters a day, finding life quite easy and looks a straightforward little horse. The type for nurseries later on rather than a Group horse I'd say, but he'll find his mark, he looks to have the right attitude and there's no reason why he shouldn't win. We'll start him at six furlongs".*

EVE JOHNSON HOUGHTON

950. DOMINANT DIVA (GER) ★★
b.f. Jukebox Jury – Dominante (Monsun).
March 10. Seventh foal. €26,000Y. Baden-
Baden. Axel Donnerstag. Sister to the modest
2016 2-y-o 1m winner Dominating and
half-sister to fair 1m winner Savanna Days
(by Danehill Dancer). The dam, a German
listed 10f winner and second in the Group 1
German Oaks, is a half-sister to the German
listed winner Deauville. The second dam,
Dea (by Shareef Dancer), won once at 2 yrs in
Germany and is a sister to the German listed
winner and smart broodmare Dapprima.
(Windmill Racing). *"She's a rangy, well-
balanced filly. I don't think the sire had a
winner until October but since then he's has
13 individual winners. So I don't think she'll be
early, but she will be a 2-y-o in the second half
of the season. I haven't done much with her
yet but I like her".* The sire, a son of Montjeu,
stands in Germany. He won the Irish St Leger
in a dead-heat with Duncan.

951. DOWNTOWN MOMBASA ★★★
br.f. Lord Shanakill – Mattinata (Tiger Hill).
March 31. Sixth foal. Sister to Moreno,
placed over a mile in Germany at 2 yrs
in 2016 and half-sister to the fair 6f and
8.5f winner Reaver (by Sabiango) and two
minor winners in Germany (by Silvano) and
Norway (by Lomitas). The dam, a winner in
the Netherlands at 3 yrs, is a half-sister to
7 winners including the Group 2 12.5f Prix
de Pomone winner Macleya and the Group
3 Prix de Barbeville winner Montclair. The
second dam, Minaccia (by Platini), won a
listed event in Germany over 7f at 3 yrs and
is a half-sister to 4 winners. (Kildaragh Stud).
*"She goes really nicely. A lovely horse, she'll
definitely be a 2-y-o and I love her. I still have
her half-brother the 4-y-o Reaver".*

952. FROSTBITE ★★★
bl.c. Lethal Force – Red Sovereign (Danzig
Connection). February 1. Sixth foal.
£102,000Y. Goffs UK Premier (Doncaster).
Eve Johnson Houghton. Half-brother to the
fair 2016 5f and 6f placed 2-y-o Red Alert (by
Sleeping Indian), to the fair dual 5f winner
Royal Award (by Cadeaux Genereux) and the
quite useful 2-y-o 5f winner Three Crowns (by
Three Valleys). The dam, a fair 6f (including at

2 yrs) and 5f winner of 5 races, is a half-sister
to 2 winners. The second dam, Ruby Princess
(by Mac's Imp), is a placed half-sister to one
winner abroad. (G C Stevens). *"If you'd asked
me a month or so ago I wouldn't have been
complimentary about him because he was
very cheeky and very interested in the girls.
But we have his head pointed in the right
direction now and he goes nice. He's a nice
horse, it won't take long before he's ready to
race and he'll be a sprinter".*

953. GREAT VIZIER ★★
b.c. Sir Percy – Special Green (Sadler's Wells).
March 30. Eighth living foal. 16,000Y.
Tattersalls October Book 4. Highflyer /Eve
Johnson Houghton. Half-brother to the
French 1m winner Pas Mure (by Green Tune)
and to two other minor winners in France
and Italy by Gold Away and Halling. The dam,
a minor French middle-distance winner, is a
half-sister to 4 winners including the listed
15f winner and Group 3 Prix de Lutece third
Double Green. The second dam, Green Bend
(by Riverman), is a placed half-sister to 9
winners including the French Group 3 winner
and smart broodmare Brooklyn's Dance and
to the unraced dam of the Derby winner
Authorized. (Simon Munir & Isaac Souede).
*"He's going to take a bit of time, a lovely horse
but one for the second half of the season and
next year. The sire gets plenty of 2-y-o's but
they tend to progress".*

954. JACK CROW ★★★★
b.c. Bahamian Bounty – Here To Eternity
(Stormy Atlantic). March 11. Third foal.
20,000Y. Tattersalls October Book 2. Highflyer
/ Eve Johnson Houghton. Half-brother to the
quite useful 2016 2-y-o 8.5f winner, from two
starts, Glorious Forever and to the useful 2-y-
o 7f and French listed 8.5f winner Time Warp
(both by Archipenko). The dam, a modest
7f winner, is a half-sister to one winner. The
second dam, Heat Of The Night (by Lear Fan),
a dual 9f winner here, subsequently won a
listed 1m event in Germany and is a half-sister
to one winner. (Mrs Jennifer Simpson Racing).
*"A real nice horse. I love the sire – we have
Cool Bahamian who's now a six year old and
he wins every year and I think this colt will be
much the same. He's tough, he goes well and
he should win this year, but progress next year*

too. I thought he was a good buy and he'll be a six/seven furlong 2-y-o".

955. JUNGLE QUEEN ★★★
ch.f. Leroidesanimaux – Elusive Gold (Elusive City). January 23. First foal. €16,000Y. Tattersalls Ireland September. Eve Johnson Houghton. The dam, a modest 6f winner, is a half-sister to 4 winners including the Group 2 Duke Of Cambridge Stakes winner and triple Group 1 placed Duntle. The second dam, Lady Angola (by Lord At War), a quite useful 12f winner, is a half-sister to 6 winners including the dam of the US Grade 1 winner Honor In War. (Eden Racing). "She's racy and slightly has her own ideas about life but she is a chestnut filly after all. She goes nicely, she's sharp and will be quite early. Sharp enough for five furlongs and then we'll see".

956. LADY MARIGOLD ★★★
b.f. Intense Focus – Peace Lily (Dansili). March 23. Sixth foal. Half-sister to the fair 7f and 1m winner of 4 races Golden Wedding (by Archipenko). The dam, a modest 7f winner at 4 yrs, is a half-sister to 6 winners including Group 2 6f Gimcrack Stakes winner Bannister and the fairly useful 2-y-o 5f and 6f winner and listed-placed Roo. The second dam, Shall We Run (by Hotfoot), placed once over 5f at 2 yrs, is a full or half-sister to 8 winners including the Group 1 6f Cheveley Park Stakes winner Dead Certain. (The Ascot Revellers). "She's very closely related to the Middle Park Stakes winner Astaire because he's also by Intense Focus and their dams are full sisters. She's a home-bred, she isn't very big but give her a squeeze and hopefully there's an engine under the hood. The family is extraordinary, they've done us very well and every generation a good horse comes out. Hopefully she'll be out in May".

957. LADY OF PETRA ★★
b.f. Compton Place – Aqaba (Lake Coniston). May 13. Ninth foal. Half-sister to the quite useful 7f winner Super Talent (by Sakhee's Secret) and to the modest 5.5f and 6f winner of 4 races at 4 yrs Amazing Win (by Marju). The dam, a modest 6f placed 2-y-o, is a half-sister to 4 winners including Alcazar (Group 1 Prix Royal-Oak) and Lady Of Chad (Group 1 Prix Marcel Boussac). The second

dam, Sahara Breeze (by Ela-Mana-Mou), a quite useful 7f and 1m placed maiden, is a half-sister to 5 winners including the Group 1 Fillies Mile winner Ivanka and the dam of the top-class stayer Yeats. (Woodstreet Syndicate & Partner). "A late foal but amazingly she doesn't look as backward as you'd think. She's very 'Compton Place' with a lovely big white face and a lovely big stride on her. She's eager to please, a good type and a nice, solid filly".

958. OPTIMUM TIME (IRE) ★★★
b.c. Manduro – Mypreciousblue (Peintre Celebre). March 10. First foal. €18,000Y. Tattersalls Ireland September. Eve Johnson Houghton. The dam, a 9f winner in France, is a half-sister to four other minor winners in Europe. The second dam, Pony Girl (by Darshaan), a listed-placed winner of 4 races in France, is a half-sister to 3 winners. (The Picnic Partnership). "A lovely horse that goes surprisingly well for one with a pedigree that suggests he ought to be backward at this point. He's beautifully put-together and there's no reason why he shouldn't win as a 2-y-o. I should imagine he'd start at seven furlongs".

959. PERVERSE ★★★
b.c. Farhh – Just Like A Woman (Observatory). March 13. Fifth foal. 24,000Y. Tattersalls October Book 2. Highflyer/Eve Johnson Houghton. Half-brother to the moderate 2016 2-y-o 5f winner Rebel Heart (by Kyllachy), to the quite useful 10f winner Neymar (by New Approach), the fair triple 7f winner Zain Empire (by Dubawi) and the fair 1m and 9f winner Rainbow Beauty (by Manduro). The dam, a fair dual 7f winner at 2 and 3 yrs, is a half-sister to 3 minor winners. The second dam, Always On My Mind (by Distant Relative), a quite useful 6f winner of 4 races, is a half-sister to 7 winners including the listed winner and Group 1 Middle Park Stakes second Red Carpet. "Considering the name of his dam I hope you like the name I gave him! He's a really nice colt but a long-term prospect and one for the back-end as a 2-y-o".

960. RED FOR DANGER ★★★
b.f. Equiano – Red Shareef (Marju). April 18. Twelfth foal. £11,000Y. Goffs UK Premier (Doncaster). Eve Johnson Houghton.

Half-sister to 9 winners including the smart 6f and 1m winner of 10 races and listed-placed Caesar Beware (by Daggers Drawn), the fairly useful 1m (at 2 yrs) to 10.5f winner Collaboration, the quite useful 1m winner Spoke To Carlo (both by Halling), the fair 5f and 6f winner Radio City (by Intikhab) and the modest 6f winners Twice Red (by Intikhab) and Gainshare (by Lend A Hand). The dam won 3 races at 2 and 3 yrs in Italy and is a half-sister to 6 winners. The second dam, Dash Of Red (by Red Sunset), won the listed Silver Flash Stakes in Ireland at 2 yrs and is a half-sister to 7 winners. (Mr G Cosburn & Mr G Everett). *"The mare's had nine winners from nine runners including Spoke To Carlo who I trained and he was the main reason I wanted to look at this filly at the sales. This horse has got bags of boot, I hope she's not a short runner but at the moment she'd be my earliest 2-y-o I think".* TRAINERS' BARGAIN BUY

961. RUNNING CLOUD (IRE) ★★★★
b.c. Cacique – Nimbus Star (Nayef). February 2. Second foal. €40,000Y. Goffs Orby. Highflyer / Shefford Bloodstock. The dam, placed at 2 yrs in France, is a half-sister to 3 winners including the Group 3 1m Prix de Fontainebleau winner Glaswegian. The second dam, Starfan (by Lear Fan), a useful 6f winner, was fourth in the Group 1 Prix Marcel Boussac and is a half-sister to the Group 1 7f Prix de la Foret winner Etoile Montante. (W H Ponsonby). *"A nice horse for mid-to-late summer. Cacique has done very well with his runners but he hasn't had many foals. This is a good-looking colt and he goes nicely".*

962. SAFE WATERS ★★
ch.f. Helmet – Golden Waters (Dubai Destination). March 1. Second foal. 5,000Y. Tattersalls October Book 4. Eve Johnson Houghton. Half-sister to the fair 2017 3-y-o 6f winner Golden Opportunity (by Kheleyf). The dam, a fair 4-y-o dual 10f winner, is a sister to the 1m and listed 10f winner of 4 races and Epsom Oaks second Something Exciting. The second dam, Faraway Waters (by Pharly), a useful 6f winner (at 2 yrs) and listed 10f Pretty Polly Stakes second, is a half-sister to 7 winners including the UAE Group 3 winner Gower Song and the very useful 1m to 10.4f winner and Group-placed Prince Of Denial.

"I thought she was ridiculously cheap because she's a nice filly. The first foal won, the sire is good and she should win races. A strong, well-grown filly with a big backside".

963. SCENERY ★★
ch.c. Elnadim – Widescreen (Distant View). April 7. Eleventh foal. 14,000Y. Tattersalls October Book 3. Highflyer / Eve Johnson Houghton. Half-brother to the fair 2-y-o 7f and subsequent German winner Newnton Lodge (by Rail Link), to the modest 10f and 12f winner Squad (by Choisir) and a minor winner abroad by With Approval. The dam is an unraced half-sister to the champion Zafonic, winner of the 2,000 Guineas, the Dewhurst Stakes, the Prix de la Salamandre and the Prix Morny and to the Group 3 6f Prix de Cabourg winner Zamindar. The second dam, Zaizafon (by The Minstrel), a winner twice over 7f at 2 yrs, was third in the Group 1 1m Queen Elizabeth II Stakes and is a half-sister to the unraced Modena, herself dam of the Eclipse Stakes and Phoenix Champion Stakes winner Elmaamul. *"I like him, he goes nicely and the sire might not be everyone's favourite but if you look at his stats he's done nothing wrong. He'll probably be out around June time I should think, he's cheeky but he'll be alright".*

964. SKYDIVING ★★★
b.c. Al Kazeem – How High The Sky (Danehill Dancer). February 22. Fifth foal. £2,400Y. Doncaster Autumn. Not sold. Half-sister to the quite useful 2016 2-y-o 5f winner Thora Barber (by Rip Van Winkle), to the French 10f winner Rat Pack (by Verglas) and the French 9.5f and 10f winner Across The Sky (by Cape Cross). The dam is an unraced half-sister to 9 winners including the French Group 3 winners Homeland and High Rock. The second dam, Hint Of Silver (by Alysheba), won once at 2 yrs in France and is a sister to one listed winner and a half-sister to another. *"He's really nice, a lovely horse. He'll definitely make a 2-y-o and he's a strong, good-topped colt. Funnily enough he looks similar to my Cacique 2-y-o, he's a lovely mover and he'll be out in mid-season. He was put through the ring at Doncaster and bought in, hence the low auction price".*

965. SO CRAFTY ★★★
ch.f. Mastercraftsman – Mea Parvitas (Oasis Dream). March 27. Second foal. 32,000Y. Tattersalls October Book 2. Highflyer / Eve Johnson Houghton. Half-sister to the fair 2016 dual 5f placed 2-y-o Tiggaliscious (by Acclamation). The dam, a moderate 6f to 1m placed maiden, is a half-sister to 5 winners including the listed winners Foodbroker Fancy and Femme Fatale. The second dam, Red Rita (by Kefaah), a fairly useful 4-y-o 6f winner, was second in the Group 3 6f Cherry Hinton Stakes and the Group 3 6f Princess Margaret Stakes at 2 yrs and is a half-sister to 3 minor winners. (Lionel Godfrey & Peter Wollaston). *"She's nice but she's a bag too and dangerous at both ends! Goes well, she's a bit sharper than I expected so with a bit of luck she should be out by June over seven furlongs. Doing everything asked of her at present".*

966. SUPER FLORENCE (IRE) **★★★**
b.f. Zebedee – Top Of The Ridge (Celtic Swing). April 17. Fourth foal. €9,000Y. Tattersalls Ireland September. Eve Johnson Houghton. Half-sister to the fair 2016 5f and 6f placed 2-y-o Kody Ridge (by Kodiac) and to the moderate 2-y-o 6f winner Black Pudding (by Baltic King). The dam is an unraced half-sister to 4 winners including the useful 2-y-o 6f winner and Group 2 Richmond Stakes second Exhibition. The second dam, Moonbi Ridge (by Definite Article), a winner of 3 races from 10f to 12f in Ireland, was listed-placed twice and is a half-sister to 4 winners. (Mr B Miller). *"We like her, she's a proper Zebedee 2-y-o that'll win races. A lovely filly, not overly big, but there's enough of her and she'll do a job".*

967. TOUR DE PARIS (IRE) **★★**
b.c. Champs Elysees – Disco Lights (Spectrum). April 30. Seventh foal. 20,000Y. Tattersalls October Book 2. Highflyer/Shefford Bloodstock. Half-brother to the fairly useful 2016 Irish 2-y-o 7f winner Branch Line (by Rip Van Winkle), to the quite useful 2-y-o 6f and 7f winner Mutazamen (by Sakhee's Secret), the quite useful 2-y-o 6f winner Tipsy Girl (by Haafhd), the fair 6f winner of four races at 2 and 3 yrs Honcho (by Dark Angel) and the minor US 3-y-o winner Mirror Ball (by Notnowcato). The dam, a fair 1m and 9f

placed 2-y-o, won once at 4 yrs in Germany and is a half-sister to 5 winners including the Ebor Handicap winner Tuning and the useful Group 3 7f Rockfel Stakes second Clog Dance. The second dam, Discomatic (by Roberto), a French 9f winner, is a half-sister to 6 winners including the Group 1 Phoenix Stakes winner Digamist. *"Not in the yard yet, but I've been to see him and he's a real nice horse. He points his toe, has a lovely, big stride on him and he's one for the back-end of the season, but a nice horse".*

968. UNNAMED ★★★
b.f. Camelot – Illandrane (Cape Cross). January 31. Second foal. 32,000Y. Tattersalls October Book 2. Howson & Houldsworth. Half-sister to the modest 2016 7f placed 2-y-o Dahl (by Shamardal). The dam is an unraced half-sister to the US Grade 2 winner and Group 1 Prix Saint-Alary third Arvada and to the Group 3 Craven Stakes winner Adagio. The second dam, Lalindi (by Cadeaux Genereux), a fair middle-distance winner of 7 races, is a half-sister to 5 winners including the useful 2-y-o winner Sumoto (herself dam of the Group 1 winners Summoner and Compton Admiral). *"She's good! For some reason I expected a 2-y-o by Camelot to be backward, but why should they be when he was a champion 2-y-o? There's a bit of quality about this filly and I really like her. I should imagine seven furlongs would be her starting point".*

MARK JOHNSTON

969. DALILEO (IRE)
b.c. Galileo – Snow Queen (Danehill Dancer). March 7. First foal. €150,000Y. Goffs Orby. Mark Johnston. The dam, a useful 2-y-o 6f and 7f winner and third in the Group 3 Brownstown Stakes, is a sister to the Irish triple Group 3 1m winner and US Grade 1 placed Carribean Sunset and a half-sister to 4 winners. The second dam, Bonheur (by Royal Academy), won over 6f at 3 yrs in Ireland and is a half-sister to 7 winners including the German 1,000 Guineas winner Quebrada. (Mr H A Lootah).

970. DREAM TODAY (IRE)
b.c. Dream Ahead – Macheera (Machiavellian). March 9. Sixth foal. 42,000Y.

Tattersalls October Book 2. Mark Johnston. Brother to the 2016 French 2-y-o listed 1m winner Al Wukair and half-brother to the fairly useful Irish listed-placed 7f winner Witches Brew (by Duke Of Marmalade) and to the quite useful Irish 7f (at 2 yrs) and 6f winner Ballyorban (by Cape Cross). The dam, a quite useful 2-y-o 1m winner in France, is a half-sister to 8 winners including the 2-y-o 7f winner and French and Irish 1,000 Guineas placed La Nuit Rose. The second dam, Caerlina (Caerleon), won over 5.5f (at 2 yrs), the Group 1 10.5f Prix de Diane and the Group 3 10f Prix de la Nonette and is a full or half-sister to 8 winners. (The Passionate Partnership).

971. DR RICHARD KIMBLE (IRE)
b.c. Lawman – Aoife Alainn (Dr Fong). March 19. Second foal. 42,000Y. Tattersalls December. Mark Johnston. Half-brother to the fair 2-y-o 7f winner First To Post (by Acclamation). The dam, a winner of 5 races including the Group 1 Premio Lydia Tesio, is a half-sister to 5 winners including the Italian listed winner and Group 2 Italian 2,000 Guineas third Adorabile Fong. The second dam, Divine Secret (by Hernando), is an unraced half-sister to 7 minor winners here and abroad. (Garret J Freyne).

972. ELARQAM
b.c. Frankel – Attraction (Efisio). February 23. Eighth foal. 1,600,000Y. Tattersalls October Book 1. Shadwell Estate Co. Closely related to the useful 10f winner and US dual Grade 3 second Cushion (by Galileo) and half-brother to 5 winners including the useful 5f (at 2 yrs) and Group 3 5f winner Fountain Of Youth, the fairly useful 1m winner of 4 races Huntlaw (both by Oasis Dream), the quite useful 2-y-o 1m winner Devastation (by Montjeu) and the fair 2-y-o 7f winner Elation (by Cape Cross). The dam, a high-class 1,000 Guineas, Irish 1,000 Guineas, Coronation Stakes, Matron Stakes and Sun Chariot Stakes winner, is a half-sister to 4 winners. The second dam, Flirtation (by Pursuit Of Love), ran unplaced and is a half-sister to 4 winners including the French listed 12f winner and Group 2 placed Carmita. (Hamdan bin Rashid Al Maktoum).

973. FAITHFUL PROMISE
b.f. Acclamation – Devotion (Dylan Thomas). February 18. Second foal. 48,000Y. Tattersalls October Book 2. Mark Johnston. Half-sister to the 2016 1m placed 2-y-o from two starts Nick Vedder (by Rip Van Winkle). The dam, a fairly useful 2-y-o 7f winner and second in the Group 3 Irish 1,000 Guineas Trial, is a half-sister to 3 winners. The second dam, Bright Bank (by Sadler's Wells), is an unraced half-sister to 8 winners including the dual Group 1 placed My Branch (herself dam of the Group 1 Sprint Cup winner Tante Rose). (Saeed Manana).

974. FRANCOPHILIA
b.f. Frankel – Lady Jane Digby (Oasis Dream). February 9. Fourth foal. Closely related to the quite useful French 12f winner Galapiat (by Galileo) and half-sister to the modest 2016 10f placed 2-y-o La Vie En Rose (by Henrythenavigator) and the fair 10.5f winner Poniatowski (by Dubawi). The dam, a smart German Group 1 10f and Group 3 11f winner, is a half-sister to 9 winners including the very smart Group 3 7f and 9f winner and Group 1 placed Gateman and the smart 1m Royal Hunt Cup winner Surprise Encounter. The second dam, Scandalette (by Niniski), is an unraced half-sister to 9 winners including the Group 1 July Cup winner Polish Patriot and the Italian listed winner Grand Cayman. (Miss K Rausing).

975. INDIAN ADMIRAL
ch.c. Sepoy – Love And Cherish (Excellent Art). February 16. First foal. 55,000Y. Tattersalls October Book 2. Not sold. The dam, a fairly useful listed-placed 1m (at 2 yrs) and 10f winner, is a half-sister to one winner. The second dam, Party Feet (by Noverre), is an unraced half-sister to the Group 2 Sun Chariot Stakes and Group 3 Matron Stakes winner of 4 races Independence (herself dam of the dual Group 1 winner Mount Nelson and the Group 2 winner Monitor Closely). (Mr A Al Mansoori).

976. JIVE LADY (IRE)
b.f. Exceed And Excel – Fair Sailing (Docksider). May 3. Sixth foal. 82,000Y. Tattersalls October Book 2. Mark Johnston. Sister to the smart listed 6f winner Windfast

and half-sister to the useful 2-y-o 1m winner and Group 3 7f Oak Tree Stakes third Montalcino (by Big Bad Bob) and the quite useful 11.5f winner West Drive (by Sea The Stars). The dam is an unplaced half-sister to 5 winners including the Group 1 Italian Derby winner and King George VI second White Muzzle, the Group 2 German St Leger winner Fair Question and the listed winning dam of the Dubai World Cup winner Almutawakel. The second dam, Fair of the Furze (by Ela-Mana-Mou), won the Group 2 10f Tattersalls Rogers Gold Cup and is a half-sister to four listed winners. (Mr John Brown & Megan Dennis).

977. KITTYLEO (IRE)

b.c. Galileo – Kittens (Marju). February 3. First foal. 140,000Y. Tattersalls October Book 1. Hussain Alabbas Lootah. The dam, a modest triple 12f winner, is a half-sister to 5 winners including the Group 3 7f Prix du Calvados winner and Group 3 1m Ridgewood Pearl Stakes winner Purr Along. The second dam, Purring (by Mountain Cat), a quite useful 7f winner, is a half-sister to the Group 2 1m Falmouth Stakes and Group 3 1m Prix de Sandringham winner Ronda (herself dam of a Group 3 winner) and to the smart 1m (at 2 yrs) and listed 2m winner Silver Gilt. (Mr H A Lootah).

978. LUCKY DEAL

ch.c. Mastercraftsman – Barter (Daylami). May 7. Fifth foal. 85,000Y. Tattersalls October Book 2. Mark Johnston. Half-brother to the fairly useful listed-placed 2-y-o 1m winner Haggle (by Pivotal), to the fairly useful 1m and 10f winner Bermondsey (by Galileo) and the fair 10f winner Petticoat Lane (by High Chaparral). The dam is an unplaced half-sister to 11 winners including the very useful listed 12f winner and good broodmare Puce and the dam of the Group 1 winners Alexandrova and Magical Romance. The second dam, Souk (by Ahonoora), a fairly useful 7f winner, was listed placed over 1m and is a half-sister to 3 winners. (K F Leung).

979. LYNWOOD GOLD (IRE)

b.c. Mastercraftsman – Witch Of Fife (Lear Fan). March 31. Thirteenth foal. €60,000Y. Goffs Orby. Mark Johnston. Closely related

to the 2-y-o Group 3 7f Solario Stakes winner Drumfire (by Danehill Dancer) and half-brother to 6 winners including the quite useful 2016 2-y-o 7f winner Western Duke (by High Chaparral), the very useful 2-y-o Group 3 7f Silver Flash Stakes winner Cabaret (by Galileo), the useful Group 2 6f Gimcrack Stakes second and Hong Kong stakes winner Ho Choi (by Pivotal) and the quite useful dual 1m winner Loreto (by Holy Roman Emperor). The dam, a fairly useful listed-placed 2-y-o 6f and 7f winner, is a half-sister to 6 winners. The second dam, Fife (by Lomond), a fairly useful listed-placed 1m winner, is a half-sister to 5 winners. (Mr J A Barson).

980. MOAKKAD

b.c. Helmet – Generously Gifted (Sakhee). March 31. Fourth foal. 130,000Y. Tattersalls October Book 2. Shadwell Estate Co. Half-brother to the fairly useful 5f and 6f winner of 4 races at 2 to 4 yrs Son Of Africa (by Equiano) and to the fairly useful 2-y-o 5f and 6f winner King Robert (by Royal Applause). The dam is an unraced half-sister to 10 winners including the useful 6f and 7f winner of 3 races Penelewey. The second dam, Peryllys (by Warning), a modest 1m placed maiden, is a half-sister to 6 winners. (Hamdan bin Rashid Al Maktoum).

981. NYALETI (IRE)

b.f. Arch – America Nova (Verglas). May 5. Sixth foal. 40,000Y. Tattersalls October Book 1. Mark Johnston. Half-sister to the 2-y-o 6f and 7f and subsequent Australian Group 2 6f and Group 3 7.5f winner Sir Patrick Moore, to the Group 3 and US Grade 3 1m winner Stellar Path (both by Astronomer Royal) and the quite useful 7f winner War Story (by Myboycharlie). The dam, a French 2-y-o listed 1m winner, is a half-sister to 4 winners including the French listed winner Cat Nova. The second dam, Las Americas (by Linamix), won 5 minor races in France from 3 to 5 yrs and is a half-sister to 2 winners. (3 Batterhams and a Reay).

982. PATRIARCH (IRE)

ch.c. Exceed And Excel – Porto Roca (Barathea). March 4. Half-brother to 7 winners including the 2016 Irish 2-y-o 1m winner Heat Of The Day (by Raven's Pass), the Group

1 10f Dubai World Cup and dual Group 2 12f winner Monterosso, the fair 7f and 8.5f winner Pietrafiore (both by Dubawi), the fairly useful 1m (at 2 yrs) and 12f winner Expert Fighter (by Dubai Destination) and the fair 9f winner Fossola (by Elusive Quality). The dam, an Australian Group 1 7.5f winner, is a half-sister to the Australian Group 1 10f winner Bluebird the Word.

983. RAAYAAT (IRE)
ch.f. Arcano – Maimoona (Pivotal). April 24. Half-sister to the quite useful 7f and 1m winner Red Tea (by Sakhee), to the fair 7f (at 2 yrs) and 1m winner Sahra Al Khadra (by Green Desert) and the moderate 12f winner Ali Bin Nayef (by Nayef). The dam was a useful 5f and 6f winner at 3 yrs. The second dam, Shuruk (by Cadeaux Genereux), a quite useful 2-y-o 6f winner, is a half-sister to the very smart dual listed 10f winner and dual Group 1 placed Volochine and the listed winners Almass, Kahtan, Sakha and Ghataas. (Hamdan bin Rashid Al Maktoum).

984. RAMPANT LION
ch.c. Bahamian Bounty – Mamma Morton (Elnadim). April 7. Seventh foal. Brother to the quite useful dual 6f (including at 2 yrs) Muaamara and half-brother to 4 winners including the 2-y-o listed 6f winner and Group 2 Mill Reef Stakes and Group 2 Richmond Stakes second Master Of War (by Compton Place), the quite useful dual 7f winner Mr McLaren (by Royal Applause), the fair 2-y-o 5f winner Marigot Bay (by Paco Boy) and the Irish 2-y-o 6f winner on his only start Aca Awesome (by Makfi). The dam, a fair 10f and 11f placed maiden, is a half-sister to 10 winners. The second dam, Gharam (by Green Dancer), a very useful 2-y-o 6f winner, was third in the French 1,000 Guineas and is a half-sister to the US Grade 1 9f winner Talinum. (Dr J Walker).

985. RUFUS KING
ch.c. Iffraaj – Mosqueras Romance (Rock Of Gibraltar). March 24. Third foal. £42,000Y. Goffs UK Premier (Doncaster). Mark Johnston. The dam, a quite useful 1m winner, was listed-placed six times and is a half-sister to 5 winners. The second dam, Mosquera (by Acatenango), won 5 races including two listed events in Germany, was third in the Group 3 Prix de Psyche and is a full or half-sister to 8 winners. (Mark Johnston Racing).

986. SEYAADY
b.c. Exceed And Excel – Muwakaba (Elusive Quality). April 11. Fourth foal. Half-brother to the modest 10f winner Just Because (by Mawatheeq). The dam, a quite useful 2-y-o 7f winner, is a half-sister to the fairly useful listed-placed 7f (at 2 yrs) to 10f winner Morghim. The second dam, Saleela (by Nureyev), a quite useful 8.5f winner, is a half-sister to the outstanding filly and broodmare Urban Sea and the 2,000 Guineas winner King's Best. (Hamdan bin Rashid Al Maktoum).

987. SULAFAAT (IRE)
ch.f. Haatef – Elraabeya (Seeking The Gold). March 21. Second foal. The dam was a fair 1m winner. The second dam, Seattle Envoy (by Deputy Minister), is an unraced sister to the Canadian champion 2-y-o and Grade 1 winner Hello Seattle and a half-sister to 3 winners.

988. SUNBREAK
b.f. Dawn Approach – Carry On Katie (Fasliyev). February 11. Sixth foal. Half-sister to the useful 2-y-o dual 5f winner and Group 3 6f Sirenia Stakes second Vocational (by Exceed And Excel) and to the modest 10f winner Sandy's Row (by Street Cry). The dam won 3 races at 2 yrs including the Group 1 6f Cheveley Park Stakes and the Group 2 6f Lowther Stakes and is a half-sister to 2 winners. The second dam, Dinka Raja (by Woodman), a minor French 3-y-o 1m winner, is a half-sister to 3 winners.

989. TAIFBALADY (IRE)
b.c. Dark Angel – Tartiflette (Dr Fong). April 5. First foal. 185,000Y. Tattersalls October Book 2. Shadwell Estate Co. The dam, a quite useful 6f (at 2 yrs) and 7f winner of 3 races, is a half-sister to 3 winners including the Group 3 Chipchase takes and listed winner Aeolus. The second dam, Bright Moll (by Mind Games), a fairly useful 2-y-o 5f and 6f winner, is a half-sister to 7 winners including the Group 2 Mill Reef Stakes second Doctor Brown. (Hamdan bin Rashid Al Maktoum).

990. THE BRITISH LION (IRE)
b.c. Power – Mala Mala (Brief Truce). April 26. Tenth foal. €155,000Y. Goffs Orby. Mark Johnston. Half-brother to 8 winners including the 2016 2-y-o Group 1 6f Middle Park Stakes winner The Last Lion (by Choisir), the very useful dual listed 6f winner and French Group 3 Prix de Meautry second Contest, the fairly useful 5f and 6f winner of 16 races Silvanus (both by Danehill Dancer), the useful UAE listed 5f winner of 11 races Russian Rock (by Rock Of Gibraltar) and the fairly useful 2-y-o 7f winner Horizon Sky (by Duke Of Marmalade). The dam, a very useful 3-y-o 5f winner, was third in the Group 1 Moyglare Stud Stakes and Group 1 Cheveley Park Stakes and is a half-sister to the Group 2 10f winner Mister Monet and the Irish 1,000 Guineas winner Tarascon. The second dam, Breyani (by Commanche Run), was a useful winner at up to 2m. (John Brown & Megan Dennis).

991. VENTURA KNIGHT
b.c. Casamento – Alltherightmoves (Namid). March 22. Second foal. £40,000Y. Goffs UK Premier (Doncaster). Middleham Park. Half-brother to the fair 5f to 7f winner of 3 races at 2 and 3 yrs Smart Mover (by Fast Company). The dam, a moderate 5f fourth placed 2-y-o, is a half-sister to 10 winners including the listed winners and Group 1 placed Crown Of Light and Alboostan. The second dam, Russian Countess (by Nureyev), a useful French 2-y-o 1m winner and listed-placed, is a half-sister to 5 winners. (Middleham Park Racing XXXVII).

992. WASHEEK
b.c. Kodiac – Starring (Ashkalani). April 25. Tenth foal. £85,000Y. Goffs UK Premier (Doncaster). Shadwell Estate Co. Half-brother to 7 winners including the 2-y-o listed 1m winner Letsgoroundagain (by Redback), the fairly useful 2-y-o 7f winner and Group 3 Solario Stakes second Manaafidh, the quite useful 7f to 9f winner of 11 races Spinning (by Pivotal), the quite useful 7f to 12f and hurdles winner Goodwood Starlight (by Mtoto) and the fair 2-y-o 5f winner Daisy Moses (by Mull Of Kintyre). The dam, placed once at 3 yrs, is a half-sister to 5 winners the dual listed 5f winner Watching. The second dam, Sweeping

(by Indian King), a useful 2-y-o 6f winner, is a half-sister to 10 winners. (Hamdan bin Rashid Al Maktoum).

993. UNNAMED
b.f. Intello – Albavilla (Spectrum). January 31. Sixth foal. 42,000Y. Tattersalls October Book 2. Mark Johnston. Half-sister to the fairly useful 10f and subsequent UAE winner of 5 races Antinori (by Fasliyev) and to the quite useful 2-y-o listed 1m winner Pure Excellence (by Exceed And Excel). The dam, a fair 14f winner, is a half-sister to 9 winners including the Irish listed winner Barolo. The second dam, Lydia Maria (by Dancing Brave), a moderate 1m and 10f placed maiden, is a half-sister to 7 winners. (Mr A Al Mansoori).

994. UNNAMED ♠
ch.c. Leroidesanimaux – Caribana (Hernando). April 4. Seventh foal. 16,000Y. Tattersalls December. M Johnston. Half-brother to the Group 3 John Porter and Group 3 St Simon Stakes winner Cubanita (by Selkirk) and to the quite useful 1m winner Camagueyana (by Archipenko). The dam, a fair 9.5f winner, is a half-sister to 2 minor winners. The second dam, Carenage (by Alzao), a quite useful 12 winner, is a half-sister to 6 winners out of the Group 1 Yorkshire Oaks winner Key Change.

995. UNNAMED
b.f. Sea The Stars – Chantilly Pearl (Smart Strike). February 23. Fourth foal. €90,000Y. Goffs Orby. Mark Johnston. Closely related to the useful 2016 2-y-o 6f and listed 1m winner Montataire (by Cape Cross). The dam, a fair 2-y-o 6f winner, is a sister to a US stakes-placed winner and a half-sister to 5 winners including the US listed winner and Grade 2 placed Lemon Chiffon. The second dam, Cataballerina (by Tabasco Cat), was placed in the USA and is a half-sister to 6 winners. (Jaber Abdullah).

996. UNNAMED
b.c. Declaration Of War – Di Moi Oui (Warning). April 24. Twelfth foal. 38,000Y. Tattersalls October Book 2. Mark Johnston. Half-brother to 7 winners including the French listed 10f and listed 12f winner Toi Et Moi (by Galileo), to the French listed 10.5f winner Moi Meme (by Teofilo), the

Italian Group 2 11f second Moi Non Plus (by Singspiel), the French 2-y-o 1m winner Parle Moi (by Montjeu) and the quite useful 1m (at 2 yrs) to 12f winner Latin Charm (by Cape Cross). The dam, a French Group 3 9f and Group 3 10f winner, is a half-sister to 5 winners. The second dam, Biosphere (by Pharly), an Italian listed-placed winner, is a sister to two Italian listed winners. (Mark Johnston Racing).

997. UNNAMED
b.f. Kodiac – Esuvia (Whipper). March 16. Third foal. €105,000Y. Goffs Orby. Mark Johnston. Sister to the 2016 2-y-o Group 2 Norfolk Stakes winner Prince Of Lir. The dam, a quite useful 6f (including at 2 yrs) and 5f winner, is a half-sister to 6 winners including the Group 3 sprint winner Resplendent Glory. The second dam, Aoife (by Thatching), a quite useful dual 6f winner, is a half-sister to 5 winners including the Group 2 5f King's Stand Stakes third My Funny Valentine. (Mark Johnston Racing).

998. UNNAMED
b.c. Pivotal – Field Of Miracles (Galileo). March 6. Second foal. 47,000Y. Tattersalls October Book 2. Mark Johnston. The dam, a very useful 12f winner and second in the Group 2 Ribblesdale Stakes, is a sister to the very useful dual listed 12f winner Cameron Highland and half-sister to 2 winners. The second dam, Landmark (by Arch), a minor 2-y-o winner in the USA, is a sister to the Grade 1 E P Taylor Stakes and Grade 1 Del Mar Oaks winner Arravale. (David Scott & Co).

999. UNNAMED
b.c. Teofilo – Imperialistic Diva (Haafhd). February 25. First foal. 75,000Y. Tattersalls December. Mark Johnston. The dam, a fairly useful listed-placed 2-y-o 5f and subsequent US winner, is a half-sister to 3 winners including the smart Group 2 German 1,000 Guineas winner Electrelane. The second dam, Imperialistic (by Imperial Ballet), a fairly useful 6f (at 2 yrs) to 1m winner of 5 races, was listed-placed and is a half-sister to 3 winners. (Jaber Abdullah).

1000. UNNAMED
b.c. Kodiac – Party Whip (Whipper).

March 9. Third foal. £150,000Y. Goffs UK Premier (Doncaster). Shadwell Estate Co. Half-brother to the 2016 2-y-o Group 3 7f Sweet Solera Stakes winner and Group 2 Cherry Hinton Stakes third Nations Alexander (by Dark Angel). The dam ran once unplaced and is a half-sister to 6 winners including the 2-y-o Group 2 6f Richmond Stakes winner and dual Group 1 6f third Always Hopeful. The second dam, Expectation (by Night Shift), a modest 6f placed 2-y-o, is a half-sister to 5 minor winners here and abroad. (Hamdan bin Rashid Al Maktoum).

1001. UNNAMED
b.f. Teofilo – Winesong (Giant's Causeway). March 10. Seventh foal. 95,000Y. Tattersalls October Book 1. Rabbah Bloodstock. Half-sister to the Group 2 Princess Of Wales's Stakes and Group 2 Jockey Club Stakes winner of 7 races Universal, to the fair Irish 9f and 10.5f winner Windward Passage (both by Dubawi) and the fair Irish 12f winner Madam Mo (by Motivator). The dam, placed third over 10f, is a half-sister to 6 winners including the 2-y-o Group 1 6f Cheveley Park Stakes winner Seazun. The second dam, Sunset Café (by Red Sunset), a minor Irish 12f winner, is a sister to the Group 3 Prix Foy winner Beeshi and a half-sister to 8 winners. (Mr A Al Mansoori).

1002. UNNAMED
b.c. Cape Cross – Wonderous Light (Montjeu). February 1. Second foal. €105,000Y. Arqana Deauville August. Mark Johnston. Half-brother to the French 1m winner Promettre (by Canford Cliffs). The dam, a minor winner at 3 yrs in France, is a half-sister to 3 winners including Ice Queen (Group 3 Noblesse Stakes). The second dam, Wadud (by Nashwan), is a placed sister to the Group 3 Gordon Stakes winner Rabah and to the Group 1 Cheveley Park Stakes third Najiya. (Mr A Al Mansoori).

SYLVESTER KIRK
1003. DORIES DELIGHT (IRE)
b.c. Dandy Man – She's My Rock (Rock Of Gibraltar). March 27. Second foal. 38,000Y. Tattersalls October Book 2. Not sold. The dam, a moderate 2-y-o 8.5f placed maiden, is a sister to the Group 3 Gordon Stakes winner

and Group 1 placed Yellowstone and a half-sister to 10 winners. The second dam, Love And Affection (by Exclusive Era), a winner from 5f to 1m including a minor stakes at 3 yrs, was second in the Grade 1 6f Spinaway Stakes at 2 yrs and is closely related to the Prix d'Ispahan and Budweiser International Stakes winner Zoman. (Michelle Cousins).

1004. GEORGE
b.c. Dragon Pulse – Before The Storm (Sadler's Wells). April 7. Eighth foal. 45,000Y. Tattersalls October Book 2. S Kirk. Half-brother to the fairly useful 2-y-o dual 7f winner Storm Rising (by Canford Cliffs), to the fairly useful 2-y-o 5f and subsequent French 1m winner Mr Majieka (by Oasis Dream) and the fair 9f, 10f and hurdles winner Landau (by Aussie Rules). The dam, a modest 6f and 1m placed maiden, is a half-sister to 4 winners including the dual listed winner Valentine Girl. The second dam, Set Fair (by Alleged), a French 10f winner, is a sister to the Group 2 winner Non Partisan and to the Canadian Grade 3 winner Jalaajel and a half-sister to the dam of the Group/Grade 1 winners Raintrap and Sunshack.

1005. MUSICAL DREAM
ch.f. Dream Ahead – Gift Of Music (Cadeaux Genereux). February 18. First foal. The dam, a modest 2-y-o 6f winner, is a half-sister to 2 winners. The second dam, Loch Verdi (by Green Desert), a useful listed 5f winner of 4 races, is a half-sister to 4 winners including the smart listed 6f winner of 5 races Lochridge. (Jeff Smith).

1006. RIVER CAFE (IRE)
b.f. High Chaparral – Dingle View (Mujadil). February 9. First foal. The dam was a smart winner 11 races including the 2-y-o Group 3 Round Tower Stakes and is a sister to the quite useful 5f to 7f winner of 11 races (including at 2 yrs) and listed-placed Vhujon and a half-sister to 4 winners. The second dam, Livius Lady (Titus Livius), is an unraced half-sister to 3 minor winners. (Neil Simpson & Paul Shanahan).

1007. SHE BELIEVES (IRE)
ch.f. Arcano – African Moonlight (Halling). February 8. Fourth foal. Half-sister to the useful 2016 2-y-o 5f winner Repton (by

Zebedee), to the US Grade 3 9f winner Syntax (by Haatef) and the Italian listed-placed 2-y-o winner Sir Gin (by Moss Vale). The dam ran twice unplaced and is a sister to 2 winners including the Irish dual Group 3 winner of 8 races Mkuzi and a half-sister to 7 winners. The second dam, African Peace (by Roberto), a French listed-placed winner, is s half-sister to 2 winners. (Marchwood Recycling Ltd).

1008. UNNAMED
b.c. Society Rock – Absolutely Cool (Indian Ridge). April 29. Eighth foal. €70,000Y. Goffs Orby. Sylvester Kirk. Half-brother to 4 winners including the Group 2 Railway Stakes and Group 2 Prix Robert Papin winner Kool Kompany, the fair 12.5f and hurdles winner Prussian Eagle (both by Jeremy) and the French winner of 8 races and listed 10f placed Ridge City (by Elusive City). The dam, an Irish 1m placed maiden, is a half-sister to 3 minor winners. The second dam, Absolute Glee (by Kenmare), a 1m (at 2 yrs) and 10f winner, was third in the Group 3 C L Weld Park Stakes and is a half-sister to 4 winners including the US listed winner Step With Style. (Des Kavanagh & Derrick Murphy).

1009. UNNAMED
b.f. Bernardini – Stormy Saturday (Stormy Atlantic). April 28. First foal. 70,000Y. Tattersalls October Book 1. Willie Browne. The dam, placed twice in the USA, is a sister to the US Grade 2 and dual Grade 3 winner Icy Atlantic and a half-sister to the US Grade 3 and triple listed winner Wild Promises. The second dam, Frosty Promise (by Frosty The Snowman), is an unraced half-sister to 7 winners. (Mr G Morin).

WILLIAM KNIGHT
1010. GOODWOOD SHOWMAN ★★★★
b.c. Showcasing – Polly Floyer (Halling). April 20. Fourth foal. 32,000Y. Tattersalls October Book 2. R Frisby. Half-brother to the fair 2016 6f and 7f placed 2-y-o Used To Be (by Kyllachy). The dam, a modest 7f winner, is a half-sister to 6 winners including the US stakes winner and Grade 1 Santa Maria Handicap second Marzelline and the Group 1 Irish Derby third Stellar Mass. The second dam, Juno Marlowe (by Danehill), a fairly useful dual 7f winner, is a sister to the Group/listed winners Leporello, Calypso Grant and

Poppy Carew. (Goodwood Racehorse Owners Group 24). *"He's a nice, scopey colt with a bit of quality about him. A really nice mover, I can see him being ready by July time and contesting seven furlong maidens. He's a nice horse, I like him and I'd like to aim him for the seven furlong maiden at Glorious Goodwood. I don't like going there first time out though, so we'll get a run in him beforehand and see if he's ok. He looks more like a Halling than a Showcasing, so he'll get a mile and a quarter next year".*

1011. KOSHI ★★★ ♠
b.f. Kyllachy – Espagnolette (Oasis Dream). February 4. Second foal. 30,000Y. Tattersalls October Book 3. Will Edmeades. Half-sister to the modest Ashurst Beacon (by Avonbridge), placed twice over 5f at 2 yrs in 2016. The dam is an unraced half-sister to 7 winners including Deportivo (Group 2 Flying Five) and So Beloved (Group 3 Supreme Stakes). The second dam, Valencia (by Kenmare), placed over 1m at 2 yrs on her only start, is a half-sister to 8 winners including the dual US Grade 1 winner Wandesta and the Group 2 12f winner De Quest. (Mrs E Roberts). *"She was a bit gormless to begin with but the penny's just starting to drop. She's a nice-shaped filly and looks a 2-y-o but I've not been able to get on with her. I can see her being ready in July and I would have thought six furlongs would be her trip. A nice mover with a good temperament".*

1012. N OVER J ★★★
b.g. Kodiac – Risk A Look (Observatory). April 16. Third foal. £15,000Y. Goffs UK (Premier). Richard Knight. Brother to the quite useful 1m winner Chenega Bay. The dam is an unraced half-sister to 6 winners including the dual Group 1 winning sprinter Continent. The second dam, Krisia (by Kris), won over 12f and is a half-sister to 6 winners including the French listed 10.5f and 12f winner Short Pause and the dam of the Group 1 Grand Prix de Paris winner Zambezi Sun. (Mr A Hetherton). *"A small, butty 2-y-o, I had to geld him so he was given a short break after that and he should be out by July time over six furlongs".*

1013. QUEEN OF DREAMS (IRE) ★★
b.f. Epaulette – Celestial Dream (Oasis Dream). February 26. Fourth foal. £52,000Y. Goffs UK Premier (Doncaster). T G Roddick. Half-sister to the fair 1m winner Hesbaan (by Acclamation), to the fair triple 5f winner Justice Lady (by Dream Ahead) and a hurdles winner by Marju. The dam, a fair 5f winner, is a half-sister to 3 winners here and abroad and to the unraced dam of the Group 2 winner Norse King. The second dam, Lochangel (by Night Shift), a very smart winner of the Group 1 5f Nunthorpe Stakes, is a half-sister to the champion sprinter Lochsong. (Mr T G Roddick). *"She'll take a little bit of time, she has a nice pedigree and should be quite speedy – she's built that way. So she'll be a nice sprinting type filly for the latter part of the season".*

1014. REMA AL KUWAIT (IRE) ★★★★
b.f. Kodiac – Relinquished (Royal Applause). February 20. Fourth living foal. £100,000Y. Goffs UK Premier (Doncaster). Sheikh Abdullah Al Malek Al Sabah. Half-sister to the fair 6f winner Renounce (by Elnadim). The dam, a fair 2-y-o dual 7f winner, is a full or half-sister to 8 winners including the listed winner Medley and the dam of the Group 1 Australia Cup winner Spillway. The second dam, Marl (by Lycius), a fairly useful 2-y-o 5.2f winner, is a half-sister to 4 winners including the very useful 2-y-o listed 5f National Stakes winner Rowaasi. (Sheikh Abdullah Almalek Alsabah). *"She's done a couple of easy bits of work and she's a nice, straightforward filly with a good temperament. I like her and she should be out in May over six furlongs".*

1015. ROYAL WAVE ★★★★
b.f. Royal Applause – Air Biscuit (Galileo). March 10. Fifth foal. £35,000Y. Goffs UK Premier (Doncaster). Kern/Lillingston. Sister to the fairly useful Irish 7f (at 2 yrs) and 1m winner Warbird and half-sister to the fairly useful 7f (including at 2 yrs) and 1m winner Solar Flair (by Equiano). The dam, a quite useful 1m and 10f winner of 3 races, is a half-sister to 6 winners including the Group 3 5f Prix du Bois and Group 3 5f Prix du Petit-Couvert winner Ziria. The second dam, Surprise Visitor (by Be My Guest), was placed once in France and is a half-sister to

9 winners including the dual German listed winner Mirage (herself dam of the Group 2 winner Swallow Flight) and the champion Scandinavian older horse Red Hero. (Kennet Valley Thoroughbreds VIII). *"We got on with her but she went a bit weak so we gave her a break. She's back in full exercise now and she's sharp, speedy and a nice mover with a good temperament for a Royal Applause. I like her, she's a nice filly and one for five/six furlongs. I train her half-brother Solar Flair who is a six furlong horse despite having won over further".*

1016. SOTO SIZZLER ★★

b.c. Mastercraftsman – Jalousie (Barathea). February 20. Tenth foal. 55,000Y. Tattersalls October Book 2. Richard Knight. Half-brother to 5 winners including the very useful listed 6f winner Van Ellis (by Shamardal), the useful 1m (at 2 yrs) to 12f winner of 5 races King's Destiny (by Dubai Destination), the quite useful 10f and hurdles winner Duroble Man (by Manduro) and the fair dual 1m winner Zubova (by Dubawi). The dam, winner of the listed 10.4f Middleton Stakes and third in the Group 3 Park Hill Stakes, is a half-sister to 5 winners including the Group 3 Horris Hill Stakes second The Deep. The second dam, Duende (by High Top), a fair 2-y-o 6f winner, is a half-sister to 8 winners. (I J Heseltine). *"A big, scopey horse bought to be a staying prospect and that's what he is. He has a lovely action but maybe he'll just have the one run at the back-end".*

1017. UNNAMED ★★★

gr.c. Casamento – Ghedi (Aussie Rules). February 7. First foal. 40,000Y. Tattersalls October Book 2. Richard Knight. The dam, placed four times at 2 yrs in Italy, is a half-sister to 6 winners including the Italian listed winner Lucky Chappy. The second dam, Germane (by Distant Relative), a useful winner of the Group 3 7f Rockfel Stakes and placed in two listed events, is a half-sister to 9 winners including the very useful German 10f winner Fabriano. *"A nice-looking, well-made colt, he's stocky but being by Casamento I don't think he's necessarily precocious. I can see him being out by the end of July over seven furlongs. A nice, straightforward colt".*

1018. UNNAMED ★★★

b.f. Dandy Man – Herful Schnerful (Jeremy). March 3. First foal. €26,000Y. Tattersalls Ireland September. Richard Knight. The dam is an unraced half-sister to 4 winners including the quite useful 2-y-o 5f and subsequent Hong Kong listed-placed winner Final Answer. The second dam, Valandraud (by College Chapel), is an unraced half-sister to 3 winners. *"We've just had to ease off her slightly because she's had a little niggle, but she looks sharp, she's nicely-made, well put together and has a nice way about her. Probably a six furlong 2-y-o".*

1019. UNNAMED ★★★ ♠

br.f. Society Rock – Silk Fan (Unfuwain). February 14. Sixth foal. €19,000Y. Tattersalls Ireland September. Richard Knight. Half-sister to the useful 5f (at 2 yrs) and 6f winner and Group 3 third Haikbidiac (by Kodiac), to the quite useful 5f and 6f winner of 5 races (including at 2 yrs) Fanrouge (by Red Clubs), the quite useful 2-y-o 5f winner Risk Adjusted (by Bushranger), the quite useful 12f and hurdles winner Eagle Rock (by High Chaparral) and the fair 12f winner Widezain (by Chineur). The dam, a fairly useful triple 7f winner (including at 2 yrs), is a half-sister to 5 winners. The second dam, Alikhlas (by Lahib), a fair 3-y-o 1m winner, is a half-sister to 4 winners including the listed winner and Group 2 Lancashire Oaks second Sahool and the dam of the multiple Group winner Maraahel. (Angmering Park Thoroughbreds III). *"We got on with her because we thought she'd be early but she went a bit light on me. So I've eased off her but she's got plenty of natural ability and she's a lovely mover, a little bit temperamental and I think she'll be a nice filly. I think she'll be suited by six furlongs as a 2-y-o and end up being a miler later on. I like her".* TRAINERS' BARGAIN BUY

1020. UNNAMED ★★

b.f. Medicean – Western Pearl (High Chaparral). February 22. Second foal. The dam, a fairly useful 12f winner, was listed-placed three times over middle-distances and is a half-sister to 2 winners. The second dam, Pulau Pinang (by Dolphin Street), a fair 10f to 13f winner of 8 races, is a half-sister to 6 winners including A Smooth One (Group

3 Princess Margaret Stakes). (Mr & Mrs N Welby). *"I trained her mother and she's a dead ringer for her. She's quite narrow and leggy but a lovely-moving filly with a good temperament for a Medicean. I'd say she'll be a stayer in time, but hopefully we'll squeeze a run into her at the back-end".*

DANIEL KUBLER

1021. DAWN COMMANDO ★★
ch.c. Dawn Approach – Dynacam (Dynaformer). March 29. Seventh foal. €10,000Y. Tattersalls Ireland September. Kubler Racing. Closely related to the quite useful 2-y-o 7f and subsequent Hong Kong winner Ensuring (by New Approach) and half-brother to the minor winner abroad by Shamardal. The dam, a quite useful 2-y-o 10f winner, is a half-sister to 3 winners including the champion US 2-y-o colt and Breeders' Cup Juvenile winner Action This Day. The second dam, Najecam (by Trempolino), a winner over 6f at 2 yrs here and later a smart US 1m/9f winner, was placed in two Grade 2 events in the USA, is a full or half-sister to 6 winners including the dam of the Irish Group 3 and UAE Group 2 winner Lord Admiral. (Mr A Stonehill). *"I think he was well-bought. Quite a big horse, he's probably more of a 3-y-o type and he won't be out this year until the autumn".*

1022. DISAPPROVAL (IRE) ★★★
b.f. Approve – Disko (Kodiac). January 9. First foal. €15,000Y. Tattersalls Ireland September. Kubler Racing. The dam, a fairly useful 2-y-o 5f winner, is a half-sister to 2 winners. The second dam, Dissonance (by Rossini), is an unraced sister to the 2-y-o Group 3 Firth Of Clyde Stakes winner Golden Legacy and a half-sister to a winner in Italy. (Diskovery IV). *"The first one we've trained out of a mare we raced! The dam was our first 2-y-o winner and she was very quick. This filly has done some nice work already and she'll be fairly early, so she's sharp and racy. She's done everything easily so far and she's not just an early type. She has enough scope to train on".* TRAINERS' BARGAIN BUY

1023. INVOLVED ★★★
b.c. Havana Gold – Trick Or Treat (Lomitas). March 25. Half-brother to the very useful 7f (at 2 yrs) and listed 11f winner and dual Group 3 third Medrano (by Archipenko), to the quite useful dual 12f winner Guising (by Manduro), the quite useful 2-y-o 1m winner Hollowina (by Beat Hollow) and the fair 8.5f winner Maahir (by Cape Cross). The dam, a winner of 7 races including the Group 3 12f Princess Royal Stakes and the listed Pinnacle Stakes, was third in the Group 1 Yorkshire Oaks and is a half-sister to 3 winners. The second dam, Trick Of Ace (by Clever Trick), a stakes-placed winner of 4 races in the USA over 1m or more, is a half-sister to 5 winners including the US Grade 2 La Prevoyante Handicap winner Prospectress. (Peter Onslow). *"I think this is quite a nice colt and he's a very good mover. As well as breeding this colt the owner bred Havana Gold's dam Jessica's Dream, so this colt has the Onslow his fingerprints all over him! For a horse that's going to get ten furlongs at least next year we have to be pleased with what he's done so far. He'll make a 2-y-o over seven furlongs".*

1024. KIRKSTALL SPIRIT ★★
b.c. Big Bad Bob – Shine Silently (Bering). March 25. Tenth foal. 45,000Y. Tattersalls October Book 2. Kubler Racing. Brother to the Group 3 Dance Design Stakes winner Bible Belt and to the Irish listed winner and Group 3 placed Bob Le Beau and half-brother to 2 winners including the Italian 2-y-o winner and listed Glasgow Stakes second Mac Regal (by King's Theatre). The dam is an unraced half-sister to 3 winners. The second foal, Walliser (by Niniski), a winner of 4 races in Ireland and listed-placed twice, is a half-sister to the dual Group 1 winning stayer Assessor. (Chris Greenall & Partner). *"A nice horse but he's going to need time. The pedigree tells you he won't make a 2-y-o until the back-end and he's much more a 3-y-o type".*

1025. NOT AFTER MIDNIGHT (IRE) ★★★
b.f. Big Bad Bob – Zenella (Kyllachy). April 8. Third foal. €10,000Y. Tattersalls Ireland September. Kubler Racing. Half-sister to the fair 2016 2-y-o 7f winner Dark Crescent (by Elnadim). The dam, a fairly useful 2-y-o listed 1m winner, is a half-sister to 3 minor

winners. The second dam, West One (by Gone West), ran twice unplaced and is a half-sister to 2 winners. (Mr & Mrs Paul and Claire Rooney). *"She seems quite precocious and she's in our most forward bunch. She does things easily and it's not inconceivable to think she could start over six furlongs and then move up in trip".*

1026. UNNAMED ★★

b.f. Vale Of York – Cio Cio San (Dalakhani). January 30. First foal. The dam, a modest dual 6f placed 2-y-o, is a half-sister to the useful 2-y-o 7f and 1m winner and Group 3 third Truth Or Dare. The second dam, Unreachable Star (by Halling), a fair dual 7f placed maiden at 3 yrs, is a half-sister to 2 winners including the 2-y-o Group 1 7f Moyglare Stud Stakes and US Grade 1 placed Necklace. (Ms Vivien O'Sullivan). *"She's only just come into us so we're still getting to know her, but she was an early foal and she has a 2-y-o physique. The breeder has tried the replicate the breeding of the dam's decent half-brother Truth Or Dare who was by Invincible Spirit. Vale of York is a son of Invincible Spirit".*

1027. UNNAMED ★★★

ch.c. Frankel – Riberac (Efisio). February 5. Closely related to the quite useful 10f to 12f winner of 4 races Trimoulet (by Teofilo) and half-brother to 8 winners including the Turkish Group 2 10f and Group 3 11.5f Lingfield Derby Trial winner Dordogne, the listed-placed 1m winner of 5 races Montrachet (both by Singspiel), the 8.5f (at 2 yrs) and 10f winner Gothic (by Danehill Dancer) and the 14f and hurdles winner Cotillion (by Sadler's Wells) – all three quite useful. The dam, a smart winner of 10 races from 5f to 1m including three listed events, was third in the Group 2 Sun Chariot Stakes and a half-sister to 5 winners. The second dam, Ciboure (by Norwick), a fair 6f (at 2 yrs) and 1m winner, is a half-sister to 4 winners. (Mr & Mrs G Middlebrook). *"A great big colt out of a mare who can get 2-y-o winners but they invariably improve with age. It's exciting to have a Frankel, but realistically he won't see the racecourse before late summer at the earliest and he'll want seven furlongs minimum".*

1028. UNNAMED ★★

b.c. Born To Sea – Valluga (Ashkalani). March 21. Tenth foal. €18,000Y. Tattersalls Ireland September. Kubler Racing. Half-brother to the quite useful 1m and 10f winner Ningxai (by Fast Company), to the fair Irish 5f to 7f winner of 4 races from 2 to 5 yrs Slim Chance (by Clodovil), the poor 5f winner Daneglow (by Thousand Words) and 2 winners abroad by Desert Prince and Mujadil. The dam is an unraced half-sister to 7 winners including the Group/Grade 2 winners Royal Touch and Foresee. The second dam, Sovereign Dona (by Sovereign Path), won 4 races including the Group 3 10f Prix de Psyche and is a half-sister to the St James's Palace Stakes winner Don and the French dual Group 3 winner American Prince. (D Blunt & Partner). *"He's a very athletic horse and very light on his feet. He's finding it quite easy at the moment but the conundrum with him is what his trip will be. The pedigree gives mixed messages but if he carries on the way he is doing he'll start at six furlongs. If he starts to grow that'll put things back a bit".*

1029. UNNAMED ★★★

b.f. Intense Focus – Penny Rose (Danehill Dancer). January 17. First foal. £2,400Y. Goffs UK Autumn. Kubler Racing Ltd. The dam, a quite useful 2-y-o dual 7f winner, is a half-sister to 4 winners including the fairly useful 12f winner and listed Cheshire Oaks second Acquainted. The second dam, Love Everlasting (by Pursuit Of Love), a 7.5f (at 2 yrs) and Group 3 12f Princess Royal Stakes winner of 6 races, is a half-sister to 6 winners including the smart Group 3 10f Scottish Classic winner Baron Ferdinand. (Newclose Properties). *"Small and neat, she was an early foal and she's forward. So she's an obvious one for the early months of the season".*

DAVID LANIGAN
1030. APURA (IRE) ★★★★

gr.f. Oasis Dream – Three Mysteries (Linamix). February 5. Half-sister to the triple 10f winner and Group 2 Prix Guillaume d'Ornano second Three Bodies (by Domedriver). The dam, unplaced on her only start, is a half-sister to several winners. The second dam is Maid Of Erin (by Irish River). (Niarchos Family). *"A nice filly, she goes well and hopefully she'll be a*

June/July 2-y-o. She's strong, moves nicely and does nothing wrong".

1031. BALGOWLAH (IRE) ★★★
b.c. Thewayyouare – Rohain (Singspiel). March 28. Seventh foal. €10,000Y. Tattersalls Ireland September. Tom Malone. Brother to the quite useful 1m (at 2 yrs) and 10f winner Noro Lim and half-brother to the useful listed 12f winner of 4 races Aussie Reigns (by Aussie Rules). The dam is an unraced sister to 2 winners including the listed 1m winner of 3 races and Group 3 third Zayn Zen. The second dam, Roshani (by Kris), a fair 1m and 10f winner at 3 yrs, is a half-sister to 8 minor winners here and in the USA. (Diamond Racing). *"He's done very well because he was weak and backward when he came in but he's turned himself inside out. You'd say on pedigree he'd need further but he's done so well I wouldn't be surprised if he was ready for around July time".*

1032. ELAPIDAE ★★★
b.c. Helmet – Al Cobra (Sadler's Wells). March 17. Sixth foal. 45,000Y. Tattersalls October Book 2. Not sold. Closely related to the fair triple 7f and subsequent minor US winner Macaabra (by Exceed And Excel) and half-brother to the fair dual 10f winner Sampera (by Iffraaj). The dam is an unplaced half-sister to 6 winners including the Group 1 12f Prix de l'Arc de Triomphe and dual German Group 1 winner Marienbard. The second dam, Marienbad (by Darshaan), a French 1m winner at both 2 and 3 yrs, is a half-sister to 6 winners including the French and Italian listed winner Kentucky Coffee. (Saif Ali). *"A good, strong colt for later in the summer, he's a nice horse that's much stronger than the dam was. Quite a big horse with a good way of going".*

1033. LEXINGTON EMPIRE ★★★★
ch.c. Intello – Emperice (Empire Maker). January 28. Fifth living foal. 20,000Y. Tattersalls December. David Lanigan. Half-brother to the quite useful 10f winner Empress Adelaide (by Pivotal) and to a minor 5-y-o winner in the USA by Shamardal. The dam is an unraced half-sister to 4 winners including the Group 3 Princess Royal Stakes and Group 3 Lancashire Oaks winner Sacred Song (herself dam of the Group 2 10f Prix Guillaume d'Ornano winner

Multidimensional) and the Canadian multiple Grade 2 winner Strut The Stage. The second dam, Ruby Ransom (by Red Ransom), won a stakes event over 1m in Canada and is a half-sister to 8 winners including the Grade 1 winners Chief Bearheart and Explosive Red. (Middleham Park, Black, Conlon, Delaney). *"A lovely horse, he's very strong, well-made and has a good attitude. He goes very nicely, on pedigree you might think he wants a trip, but he could be a June 2-y-o. We'll probably start him at six furlongs and then he'll be ready to win over seven. A nice, solid horse that'll get better as the year goes on, he's a good size and he's the pick of our 2-y-o's".*
TRAINERS' BARGAIN BUY

1034. PARADOX STATE (IRE) ★★★★
b.c. Camelot – Shine A Star (Oasis Dream). February 13. First foal. The dam was unraced. The second dam, Maid To Believe (by Galileo), a fairly useful 1m (at 2 yrs) to 12f winner of 4 races, is a half-sister to 7 winners including the useful 7f (at 2 yrs) and 10f winner Maid To Perfection (herself the dam of two listed winners). (Niarchos Family). *"He should be ready to start in August or September and he's a strong, good-looking colt. A bit tall, 'on the leg' and feminine looking like a lot of the good colts by his grandsire Montjeu were, but he's going very nicely".*

1035. PURPLEST ★★★
b.f. Iffraaj – Purple Tiger (Rainbow Quest). April 7. Ninth foal. 35,000Y. Tattersalls October Book 3. Not sold. Half-sister to the 2016 5f placed 2-y-o Lightning North (by Mayson), to the very useful 6f (at 2 yrs) and 5f winner of 6 races and Group 2 6f Gimcrack Stakes second Taajub, the quite useful 2-y-o 5f and 6f winner Excel Yourself (both by Exceed And Excel) and the quite useful 5f and 6f winner Polish Pride (Polish Precedent). The dam is an unraced half-sister to 6 winners including the German Group 2 winner and Italian Group 1 second Notability and the French Group 3 winner Simon De Montfort. The second dam, Noble Rose (by Caerleon), won the Group 3 Park Hill Stakes and the listed Galtres Stakes and is a half-sister to Simeon (Group 3 Sandown Classic Trial). (Saif Ali). *"A strong filly that goes very nicely, she's well-made and will make a 2-y-o by mid-summer".*

1036. ROUNDABOUT KITTEN (USA) ★★★
ch.c. Kitten's Joy – Shining Jewel (Gulch).
February 18. Ninth foal. 70,000Y. Tattersalls
October Book 1. Not sold. Brother to the US
2-y-o winner and Group 3 placed Sapphire
Kitten and half-brother to the quite useful
2-y-o 7f and subsequent US winner Gal Aloud
(by War Chant). The dam, a minor winner
of 3 races in the USA, is a half-sister to 7
winners. The second dam, Desert Jewel (by
Caerleon), is an unraced sister to the Group 2
Prix Robert Papin winner Psychobabble and
a half-sister to 8 winners including the US
Grade 1 winner Louis Cyphre. (Ken & Sarah
Ramsay). "*Stronger than the other Kitten's Joys
I have at this stage, he goes nicely and I'd like
to think he'll be ready to run in August over
seven furlongs*".

1037. SUNSET DECISION ★★★
ch.c. Dawn Approach – Sunset Avenue (Street
Cry). March 23. Third foal. Half-brother to the
moderate 1m and 10.5f winner Super Focus
(by Intense Focus). The dam, a fair 2-y-o
7f winner on her only start, is a half-sister
to 6 winners including the listed winner
subsequent US dual Grade 2 second True
Cause. The second dam, Dearly (by Rahy),
won the Group 3 Blandford Stakes and is a
half-sister to 4 winners including Balletto (US
Grade 1 Frizette Stakes). (Saif Ali). "*A nice,
strong colt that will make a 2-y-o despite
coming in late. A nice sized horse, he's coming
along nicely and he goes well*".

1038. TRITONIX ★★
b.f. Nathaniel – Triton Dance (Hector
Protector). March 18. Seventh living foal.
65,000Y. Tattersalls October Book 2. Rabbah
Bloodstock. Half-sister to the very useful
7f (at 2 yrs) and listed 10f Magnolia Stakes
winner Miblish (by Teofilo) and to the useful
Irish dual 6.5f winner and Group 3 Tetrarch
Stakes third Count John (by Intikhab). The
dam, an Irish 2-y-o 5f winner, is a half-sister
to 4 winners including the 2-y-o Group 2 6f
Cherry Hinton Stakes winner Jewel In The
Sand and the German 3-y-o listed 6f winner
Davignon. The second dam, Dancing Drop
(by Green Desert), a useful dual 2-y-o 6f
winner, was listed-placed 5 times and is a
half-sister to 9 winners. (Saif Ali). "*A big filly*

*and probably one for September time. She'll
be better next year but she's a nice, attractive
filly*".

1039. WORTH WAITING ★★★
b.f. Bated Breath – Salutare (Sadler's Wells).
April 18. Ninth foal. 40,000Y. Tattersalls
October Book 2. Rabbah Bloodstock. Half-
sister to 5 minor winners including in France
and Germany by Dalakhani (2), Medicean
and Nayef. The dam won 3 minor races at 3
yrs in France and is a half-sister to 10 winners
including Montare (Group 1 Prix Royal-
Oak). The second dam, Contare (by Shirley
Heights), won two listed events in France over
1m and 9f and is a half-sister to 3 winners.
(Saif Ali). "*Goes well, she's a racy, strong filly
that looks nice and she'll make a 2-y-o by
mid-summer*".

1040. UNNAMED ★★★★
b.f. Shamardal – Althea Rose (Green Desert).
May 10. Fifth foal. Half-sister to the fair 2017
3-y-o 9.5f winner Enfolding (by Fastnet
Rock) and to the modest 6f to 1m winner of
3 races Duke Of North (by Danehill Dancer).
The dam ran once unplaced and is a half-
sister to 9 winners including the top-class
National Stakes, Irish 2,000 Guineas and Irish
Derby winner Desert King and the Group 3
Mooresbridge Stakes winner Cairdeas. The
second dam, Sabaah (by Nureyev), a modest
8.2f placed maiden, is a full or half-sister to
8 winners including the Group 1 1m Queen
Elizabeth II Stakes winner Maroof. (Frank &
Jason O'Malley). "*Typical of the Shamardals,
she's going through a bit of a growing stage
now but she's been nice since day one. I'd like
to think she'll be on the track by August or
September*".

1041. UNNAMED ★★★
b.c. Oasis Dream – Dear Lavinia (Grand Slam).
February 10. Second foal. 20,000Y. Tattersalls
October Book 2. David Lanigan. The dam,
a French 2-y-o 7f and listed 1m winner, is a
half-sister to 2 minor winners in France. The
second dam, Baroness Richter (by Montjeu),
a French listed 10.5f winner, is a half-sister
to 4 winners including the Japanese Group
2 winner Kongo Rikishio. (Saif Ali). "*A cheap
purchase for an Oasis Dream, he's had issues*

but so far he looks ok. He's a good, compact, strong colt and should be ready to go in midsummer".

1042. UNNAMED ★★★
b.f. Cape Cross – Kerrys Requiem (King's Best). March 26. Third foal. 70,000Y. Tattersalls October Book 1. Rabbah Bloodstock. Half-sister to the quite useful 2-y-o 7f winner Lytham St Annes (by Bahamian Bounty). The dam, a fairly useful listed-placed 5f (at 2 yrs) and 6f winner, is a half-sister to 4 minor winners. The second dam, Moonlight Wish (by Peintre Celebre), is an unraced full or half-sister to 7 winners including Group 1 Dewhurst Stakes second Fencing Master and the Group 1 Prix de Diane second Millionaia. (Saif Ali). *"A good, strong filly, she's well-made and should make a 2-y-o".*

1043. UNNAMED ★★★★
b.c. Dansili – Maidin Maith (Montjeu). May 11. Fourth foal. 90,000Y. Tattersalls October Book 1. Rabbah Bloodstock. Closely related to the modest 6f winner Dance Band (by Danehill Dancer) and half-brother to the quite useful 8.5f winner Mezajy (by Makfi). The dam, an Irish 2-y-o 7f winner, is a sister to the winner and Group 1 Gran Criterium third Chinese Whisper and a half-sister to 6 winners including the triple listed 7f winner Modeeroch and the 2-y-o 6f winner and Group 1 6f Cheveley Park Stakes third Danaskaya (herself dam of the 2-y-o Group 1 Dewhurst Stakes winner Belardo). The second dam, Majinskaya (by Marignan), a listed 12f winner, is a half-sister to 6 winners including the dam of the Group 1 5f Prix de l'Abbaye winner Kistena. (Saif Ali). *"A horse that looks like he'll make a 2-y-o, he's a bit light but he'll strengthen up as the year goes on. He goes nicely, he's very straightforward and we'll start him off at seven furlongs".*

1044. UNNAMED ★★★
b.c. Exceed And Excel – Saaboog (Teofilo). March 28. Second foal. 48,000Y. Tattersalls October Book 2. Not sold. Half-brother to the unplaced 2016 2-y-o Big Ego (by Helmet). The dam, a fair 1m and 12f winner, is a half-sister to one winner. The second dam, Saabiq (by Grand Slam), a fairly useful 2-y-o 6f winner, was listed-placed over 6f and 7f

and is a half-sister to two winners in the USA. (Saif Ali). *"He'll want a trip, he's big, strong and does everything nicely. A nice colt, we'll start him off over seven furlongs probably".*

1045. UNNAMED ★★★
b.c. Cape Cross – Satwa Pearl (Rock Of Gibraltar). February 27. Third foal. Half-brother to the unplaced 2016 2-y-o Take A Turn (by Henrythenavigator). The dam, a quite useful 9.5f and 10f winner, is a sister to the French listed-placed 7.5f winner Victoria College and a half-sister to the US Grade 2 third Urban King. The second dam, Uruk (by Efisio), an Italian Group 3 6f winner, is a half-sister to the listed 12f winner All The Aces. (21st Century Farms). *"A lovely horse, the nicest one the mare's produced and he'll be out around September time but be a better 3-y-o. He's attractive, very well-made and a nice strong colt".*

1046. UNNAMED ★★★
b.f. Sayif – Usem (Bahamian Bounty). March 30. Third foal. Sister to the fair 2016 2-y-o 7f winner Sayem. The dam is an unraced half-sister to 2 winners. The second dam, Ripples Maid (by Dansili), won 6 races at 3 and 4 yrs including listed events over 6f and is a half-sister to 7 winners including the very smart 2-y-o Group 3 Horris Hill Stakes winner Peak To Creek. (Saleh Al Homaizi & Imad Al Sagar). *"A nice, attractive filly that's going through a growth stage now, so I'd like to think she'd be out around August time. An athletic filly with a good attitude".*

1047. UNNAMED ★★★
ch.f. Iffraaj – Zacheta (Polish Precedent). March 20. Ninth foal. Half-sister to the Group 2 Joel Stakes and Group 3 Earl Of Sefton Stakes winner Ransom Note (by Red Ransom), to the quite useful 11.5f winner Dawn Sky (by Fantastic Light), the fair dual 1m winner Nice Thoughts (by Shamardal) and the modest 1m winner Shargiah (by New Approach). The dam is an unraced half-sister to 6 winners including Marienbard (Prix de l'Arc de Triomphe). The second dam, Marienbad (by Darshaan), a French 1m winner at 2 and 3 yrs, is a half-sister to 6 winners. (Saif Ali). *"Goes nicely and should make a 2-y-o by midsummer because she's strong, compact and well-made".*

GER LYONS

1048. BUCKY LARSON (IRE) ★★
b.c. Footstepsinthesand – Jessie Jane (Dylan Thomas). March 19. Second foal. 50,000Y. Tattersalls October Book 2. Ger Lyons. The dam, a quite useful 10.5f winner, is a half-sister to 2 winners including the Group 3 Chester Vase second Icon Dream and to the unraced dam of the dual Group 1 winner La Collina. The second dam, Silver Skates (by Slip Anchor), is a placed half-sister to 8 winners including the Group 2 Derrinstown Derby Trial winner Fracas. *"He's backward and in our second yard at the moment. The damline is all about middle-distances".*

1049. CAMELBACK (USA) ★★★
b.c. Exchange Rate – Pick And Choose (Street Cry). February 15. First foal. $60,000 foal. Keeneland November. Alistair Roden. The dam, a minor winner at 3 yrs in the USA, is a half-sister to one winner. The second dam, Pictavia (by Sinndar), a smart Group 3 10f winner, was second in the Group 1 7f Moyglare Stud Stakes and third in the Oaks, is a half-sister to 7 winners including the smart Group 3 10f Royal Whip Stakes winner Maputo. *"He's a forward colt, I like him and he'll probably start at six furlongs. He'll come into his own at seven and he's shown us enough to say he'll win his maiden. A nice colt".*

1050. DALIYAH (IRE) ★★
gr.f. Zoffany – Dalaway (Dalakhani). February 9. First foal. £35,000Y. Goffs UK Premier (Doncaster). Ger Lyons. The dam, a modest 11.5f placed maiden, is a half-sister to 3 minor winners. The second dam, In The Limelight (by Sadler's Wells), an Irish listed 1m winner, is a sister to the Irish listed winner On The Nile, closely related to the triple Group 1 winner Kutub and a half-sister to 3 winners. *"She's doing everything I'm asking of her, but she won't appear until the second half of the season. Quite a number of my 2-y-o's this year are just taking their time".*

1051. DROP THE BEAT (IRE) ★★★
ch.f. Born To Sea – Miss Beat (Beat Hollow). April 27. Second foal. €11,500Y. Tattersalls Ireland September. Ger Lyons. The dam, a quite useful 2-y-o 7f winner, is a half-sister to

3 winners including the 2-y-o listed second Hollow Ridge. The second dam, Bolas (by Unfuwain), a very smart winner of the Group 1 Irish Oaks and the Group 2 Ribblesdale Stakes and is a full or half-sister to 7 winners. *"Early doors I liked her quite a bit, but she had a small setback and I've had to back off her. She'll be fine and although she was a little cheapie I think she was good value".* TRAINERS' BARGAIN BUY

1052. GEORGIE HYPHEN (IRE) ★★★
ch.c. Zoffany – Kathy Best (King's Best). April 5. Fifth foal. €58,000Y. Tattersalls Ireland September. Ger Lyons. Half-brother to the minor Italian winner of 13 races from 3 to 7 yrs Kabestus (by Colossus). The dam is an unplaced half-sister to 10 winners including the Group 3 5f Premio Omenoni winner Kathy College. The second dam, Katy Guest (by Be My Guest), won at 2 and 3 yrs in Italy and is a half-sister to 4 winners. *"He's nice and showing me enough to say he'll be ready to run over six furlongs from May onwards. I'm happy enough with him".*

1053. HYPERLAPSE (IRE) ★★★
ch.c. Casamento – Makheelah (Dansili). March 26. Third foal. €20,000Y. Goffs Sportsmans. Ger Lyons. The dam, a modest 7f and 1m placed maiden, is a half-sister to two listed stakes winners in the USA and Germany. The second dam, Woodlass (by Woodman), won 3 races in France and the USA, was stakes-placed and is a half-sister to 8 winners including the 2-y-o listed Prix Herod winner Vitaba. *"I've been very lucky with the sire and I like this colt. He's typical of the sire in that he's one for the middle of the season onwards".*

1054. INCA'S DAWN (IRE) ★★★ ♠
b.f. Equiano – Up At Dawn (Inchinor). February 12. Seventh foal. 55,000Y. Tattersalls October Book 2. Ger Lyons. Half-sister to the useful 7f (at 2 yrs) and subsequent US 1m Grade 2 and Grade 3 stakes winner Up In Time (by Noverre), to the fair triple 6f winner at 2 and 3 yrs Jimmy's Hall (by Kyllachy) and the modest 12f and hurdles winner Don't Take Me Alive (by Araafa). The dam is an unplaced half-sister to 7 winners including the dam of the Group 3 winner Summer

Fete. The second dam, Up And About (by Barathea), a fair 14.8f winner, is a half-sister to 9 winners including the listed winner and Group 1 placed Musicanna. *"Equiano is another sire I've been lucky with. This is a big filly that's doing everything well and she's one for the middle of the season onwards".*

1055. KODI KOH (IRE) ★★★
b.f. Kodiac – Laywaan (Fantastic Light). February 27. Sixth foal. 52,000Y. Tattersalls October Book 2. Ger Lyons. Half-sister to the quite useful 2-y-o 7f winner Madmoonah, to the modest French 7f winner Electrostatic (both by Invincible Spirit) and the fair 11f winner Nabat Ali (by Nayef). The dam, a fairly useful 1m and 10f winner of 4 races, is a half-sister to 7 winners including the US Grade 3 placed Run Alex Run. The second dam, Electrostat (by Dynaformer), a minor winner in the USA, is a half-sister to 8 winners including the Grade 1 Beldame Stakes winner Weber City Miss, herself dam of the dual Grade 1 winner Slew City Slew. *"A lovely, scopey Kodiac – bigger than normal for the sire. We like her, we bought her off Mark Dwyer and I've always been lucky buying off him. She's very much on the leg at the minute, I like what I've seen but you won't see her before mid-season".*

1056. LETHAL STEPS ★★★
b.c. Lethal Force – Tanda Tula (Alhaarth). April 5. Fifth foal. 28,000Y. Tattersalls October Book 1. Not sold. Half-brother to the quite useful 7f (including at 2 yrs) and 6f winner My Sharona (by Dark Angel). The dam is an unplaced half-sister to 7 winners including the German Group 2 winner Stormont. The second dam, Legal Steps (by Law Society), won once at 3 yrs and is a half-sister to 5 winners including the South African Group 1 winner Super Sheila. *"I like this horse, he's doing everything I'm asking of him and his sire is my tip for the top as far as first season sires are concerned. I'll start him over six furlongs but I should imagine he'll come into his own over seven and you won't see him out before June".*

1057. MASUCCI ★★★
b.c. Zoffany – Meeting In Paris (Dutch Art). February 17. First foal. €90,000Y. Tattersalls

Ireland September. Ger Lyons. The dam, a modest 6f (including at 2 yrs) and 5f placed maiden, is a half-sister to a winner in Germany. The second dam, Sharplaw Star (by Xaar), a fairly useful 2-y-o dual 5f winner, was third in the Group 3 5f Queen Mary Stakes and is a half-sister to 2 winners. *"A colt that's typical of one of mine, he's doing everything asked of him but you won't see him until June/July".*

1058. MAXIMIZER (FR) ★★★
b.c. Maxios – Another Name (Giant's Causeway). February 20. Fifth foal. £42,000Y. Goffs UK Premier (Doncaster). Ger Lyons (private sale). Half-brother to a minor winner abroad by Aussie Rules. The dam is an unplaced half-sister to 3 minor winners. The second dam, Because (by Sadler's Wells), is an unraced sister to the Irish 1,000 Guineas winner Yesterday and the Group 1 Moyglare Stud Stakes winner Quarter Moon. *"Maxios is another first season sire that I rate. This looks a smart colt, I like him and I think he was good value. Likely to be one of our earlier runners".*

1059. MOJAMBO (IRE) ★★★
ch.f. Zoffany – Mojita (Montjeu). April 28. Third foal. £35,000Y. Goffs UK Premier (Doncaster). Ger Lyons. Half-sister to the 2016 Italian listed 7.5f placed 2-y-o Lady Gio (by Kodiac). The dam, a quite useful 11f winner, is out of the modest 7f placed 2-y-o Hatalan (by Mark Of Esteem), herself a half-sister to 6 winners including the Dubai World Cup and Juddmonte International winner Electrocutionist. *"Very similar to our Havana Gold filly in that she'll be a 2-y-o or nothing but at the same time she's not ready to go yet. They need a bit of sunshine and she won't be out before the end of May".*

1060. MY MYSTIQUE (IRE) ★★★★
b.f. Rajj – Imitation (Darshaan). April 7. Ninth foal. Sister to the 2017 3-y-o 10f winner on her second start Insayshable and half-sister to 5 winners including the useful Irish Group 3 6f and 7f winner Ainippe (by Captain Rio). The dam is a unraced half-sister to 4 winners including Darnay (Group 2 Sea World International winner) out of Flawless Image (by The Minstrel). *"She's a lovely-looking filly and I think the world of her. I like*

everything I see, she won't be out before the end of May but I'd like to think she's a nice filly. You might not have heard of the sire but the few I have by him are good". The sire, a son of Danehill, was unraced and is out of Makarova (by Sadler's Wells).

1061. OVERCOMING (IRE) ★★★
b.c. Kodiac – Causeway Charm (Giant's Causeway). April 14. Sixth foal. €340,000Y. Goffs Orby. China Horse Club.
Half-brother to the fairly useful 2-y-o 6f and 7f winner and Group 3 Musidora Stakes second Lily Rules (by Aussie Rules) and to the fair 2-y-o 1m winner D'Niro (by Big Bad Bob). The dam is an unplaced half-sister to 6 winners including the German dual listed winner Chan Chan. The second dam, Candy Charm (by Capote), is an unraced half-sister to 7 winners. *"A very expensive colt, I like what I'm seeing but at the same time I think he's a seven furlong type. He might be out in May at the earliest and he seems to be a nice, precocious type".*

1062. RAGTIME RED (IRE) ★★★
ch.c. Red Jazz – Holly's Kid (Pulpit). April 30. Sixth foal. €46,000Y. Tattersalls Ireland September. Ger Lyons. Half-brother to the quite useful 2-y-o 1m winner Posh Cracker (by Johannesburg), to the quite useful 6f (at 2 yrs) and 1m winner Force (by Raven's Pass) and the fair 5f winner Rawaafed (by Invasor) and a 2-y-o winner in Sweden by Helmet. The dam won 2 minor races in the USA at 2 and 3 yrs and is a sister to the US Grade 1 Del Mar Oaks winner Rutherienne and to the US Grade 3 winner Ruthenia and a half-sister to 6 winners. The second dam, Ruthian (by Rahy), a listed winner of 4 races in the USA, is a half-sister to 3 minor winners. *"He'll be our first runner, so he's the one we'll use to get a line on how our others are doing".*

1063. SHALAILAH (IRE) ★★★
ch.f. Showcasing – Perfect Venture (Bahamian Bounty). February 7. First foal. £48,000Y. Goffs UK Premier (Doncaster). Ger Lyons. The dam, modest dual 6f winner, is a half-sister to 2 other minor winners. The second dam, Perfect Cover (by Royal Applause), is an unplaced half-sister to 6 winners including two listed winners. *"She's a nice filly and I like*

the sire. I don't think you'll see her before the end of May".

1064. SHAPES (IRE) ★★★★
b.f. So You Think – Maskaya (Machiavellian). April 30. Ninth foal. €68,000Y. Goffs Orby. Not sold. Half-sister to 4 winners including the very useful Irish 2-y-o 7f winner and Group 1 Criterium de Saint-Cloud second Drumbeat (by Montjeu), the useful Group 3 14f Lillie Langtry Stakes winner of 4 races California (by Azamour) and the fair 7.6f winner Red Blooded Woman (by Red Ransom). The dam, an Irish 2-y-o 5f winner, is a half-sister to 7 winners including the Group 1 6f Cheveley Park Stakes third Danaskaya (dam of the Group 1 Dewhurst Stakes winner Belardo). The second dam, Majinskaya (by Marignan), a listed 12f winner and Group 3 second, is a half-sister to 6 winners including the dam of the Group 1 5f Prix de l'Abbaye winner Kistena. *"She'll be our first 2-y-o filly to run. She goes to Navan at the end of April and she's showing me plenty of speed and precocity. A tough filly, I'm looking forward to running her".*

1065. TREBLE CONE ★★★
ch.c. Lethal Force – Cardrona (Selkirk). January 26. Third foal. £44,000Y. Goffs UK Premier (Doncaster). Ger Lyons. The dam is an unplaced sister to the useful listed 6f (at 2 yrs) and listed 7f winner Selinka and a half-sister to 3 winners. The second dam, Lady Links (by Bahamian Bounty), a dual listed 6f winner (including at 2 yrs), is a half-sister to 5 winners. *"A mid-season 2-y-o, he's doing everything asked of him and he'll want seven furlongs. No bells and whistles but he's a nice colt".*

1066. WHO'S STEPH (IRE) ★★★
gr.f. Zoffany – Llew Law (Verglas). February 23. Second foal. €40,000Y. Tattersalls Ireland September. Ger Lyons. Half-sister to Thunder Crash (by Footstepsinthesand), unplaced in one start at 2 yrs in 2016. The dam, a moderate Irish middle-distance placed maiden, is a half-sister to the listed Windsor Castle Stakes winner Hototo. The second dam, Harlem Dancer (by Dr Devious), a French listed-placed 10f and 11f winner, is a half-sister to 3 winners. *"A straightforward*

forward filly, doing everything we're asking of her, she's one for the middle of the season".

1067. WOULD BE KING (IRE) ★★★★
b.c. Lethal Force – Smart Coco (Smarty Jones). February 24. Fourth foal. €42,000Y. Goffs Orby. Ger Lyons. Half-brother to the fair 6f winner Cocoa Beach (by Acclamation) and to the modest dual 1m winner Pike Corner Cross (by Cape Cross). The dam, an Irish 2-y-o winner and third in the Group 3 Leopardstown 1,000 Guineas Trial, is a half-sister to 2 winners. The second dam, Djebel Amour (by Mt. Livermore), won 2 minor races at 3 yrs in the USA and is a half-sister to 4 winners including Almushahar (Group 2 Champagne Stakes). *"A smart colt, he'll be top of the class going off what he's showing us at the moment. He shows us plenty, we won't be in any hurry to run him but he's precocious enough"*

1068. ZALZAR ★★★
b.f. Zoffany – Alzaroof (Kingmambo). March 13. Sixth foal. £28,000Y. Goffs UK Premier (Doncaster). Ger Lyons. Half-sister to the fair 10f and hurdles winner Iftiraaq (by Muhtathir). The dam is an unraced half-sister to 4 winners The second dam, Ranin (by Unfuwain), a smart Group 2 14.6f Park Hill Stakes winner, is a half-sister to 9 winners including the very useful 7f and 1m winner Ghalib. *"Typical of all my fillies at the moment, she's doing everything fine but needs some kinder weather to help her. You won't be seeing her out before June".*

1069. UNNAMED ★★★
b.f. Harbour Watch – Fame Is The Spur (Motivator). February 26. Fourth foal. Half-sister to the modest 2-y-o 6f winner Lightning Stride (by Equiano). The dam, a fair 10f winner, is a half-sister to 11 winners including the US dual Grade 2 10f winner Battle Of Hastings and the listed 12f winner Villa Carlotta. The second dam, Subya (by Night Shift), was a very useful winner of 5 races from 5f (at 2 yrs) to 10f including the Lupe Stakes, the Masaka Stakes and the Star Stakes (all listed events). *"I like her but I've just put her away for a month's break. She's done plenty and I'm looking forward to her appearing on the track from mid-season"*

onwards over six/seven furlongs. She's typical of those I had by the sire last year in that they need time".

1070. UNNAMED ★★
b.f. Frankel – Lightening Pearl (Marju). March 10. Second foal. Sister to the 2016 Irish 7f placed 2-y-o Lightening Fast. The dam, winner of the 2-y-o Group 1 6f Cheveley Park Stakes and the Group 3 6f Round Tower Stakes, is a sister to the 3-y-o 11f winner and 2-y-o Group 3 Tyros Stakes third Jolie Jioconde and to the Japanese dual Group 2 winner over 10f and 11f Satono Crown. The second dam, Jioconda (by Rossini), won the listed Silken Glider Stakes and was third in the Group 3 Killavullan Stakes. (Qatar Racing Ltd). *"She's literally only just come into the yard and I don't imagine she'll be on the team to run this year because she's very backward".*

1071. UNNAMED ★★★★
gr.f. Lope De Vega – Missouri Belle (Invincible Spirit). February 4. Second foal. The dam, placed fourth once over 10.5f, is a half-sister to 3 winners including the fairly useful 12f winner Dare To Achieve. The second dam, Mussoorie (Linamix), won over 10f in France, was listed-placed here over 12f and is a half-sister to 5 winners. *"If we have a quality filly it's her. A bit temperamental, there's plenty of size and scope about her and I won't be in any rush to start her".*

1072. UNNAMED ★★★
ch.f. Excelebration – Moriches (Alhaarth). April 1. Fourth foal. €58,000 foal. Goffs November. John Walsh. Half-sister to the moderate 2-y-o 7f winner Steevo (by Dark Angel). The dam is an unplaced half-sister to 8 winners including the very useful Group 3 5f Curragh Stakes and Group 3 5f Molecomb Stakes winner Almaty and the Hong Kong & Singapore Group 1 winner Rave. The second dam, Almaaseh (by Dancing Brave), placed once over 6f at 3 yrs, is a half-sister to 8 winners including Haafhd (2,000 Guineas and Champion Stakes) and Munir (Group 2 Challenge Stakes). *"She looks precocious and is doing everything being asked of her, but I can't see her being out before June. She just needs to grow up".*

1073. UNNAMED ★★★
ch.f. Havana Gold – You Look So Good
(Excellent Art). February 6. First foal. 32,000
foal. Tattersalls December. David Redvers.
The dam, a modest 7f winner, is a sister to the
useful 2-y-o 6f winner and Group 2 Rockfel
Stakes third Gray Pearl and a half-sister to
5 winners including the German Group 2 6f
Goldene Peitsche winner of 5 races Electric
Beat. The dam ran unplaced twice and is a
half-sister to 2 minor winners. *"She's doing
what I'm asking of her but needs to mature,
so she looks like a 2-y-o but she won't be out
before the middle of the season"*.

GEORGE MARGARSON

1074. BLAME CULTURE (USA) ★★★
b.c. Blame – Pearl In The Sand
(Footstepsinthesand). March 19. Second
foal. 40,000Y. Tattersalls October Book 2.
Mangiacapra /Hill/ Hook. Half-brother to
the modest 2016 2-y-o 6f winner Scudding
(by Mizzen Mast). The dam, a fairly useful
Irish maiden, was placed three times at 2 yrs
including in a listed 6f event at the Curragh
and is a sister to one winner and a half-sister
to the useful 2-y-o dual 5f winner and Group
2 5f Norfolk Stakes second Reckless Reward.
The second dam, Champagne Toni (by
Second Empire), ran unplaced twice and is a
half-sister to 9 winners including the smart
Group 3 6f Prix de Meautry winner Andreyev.
(Mangiacapra, Hill, Hook Partnership). *"He's
a big horse and although he shows a lot of
speed he still needs time to fill his frame and
come to hand. A straightforward colt, he's one
of those you wouldn't know was there, but he'll
be a June/July 2-y-o"*.

1075. CITY GUEST ★★★★
b.c. Epaulette – Union City Blues (Encosta
De Lago). March 27. Third foal. 38,000Y.
Tattersalls October Book 2. Amanda
Skiffington. Half-brother to the fair 2-y-o 8.5f
winner Maestro Mac (by Roderic O'Connor).
The dam is an unplaced half-sister to 5
winners. The second dam, Child Prodigy (by
Ballad Rock), a quite useful 2-y-o 6f winner
here and stakes-placed in the USA, is a
half-sister to 5 winners including the triple
Group 1 winner Kutub. (John Guest Racing).
*"The Roderic O'Connor half-brother needed a
trip, but this colt could run and win over five*

furlongs tomorrow. He'll probably have to run
soon because he's very cheeky – a proper colt.
Very athletic and with bundles of talent, I just
have to keep the lid on him without pressing
too many buttons. He finds it all very easy and
he ticks all the boxes to be an early 2-y-o. My
favourite at the moment"*.

1076. HEAVENLY GUEST ★★★
ch.c. Havana Gold – Maid In Heaven
(Clodovil). January 14. Third foal. 55,000Y.
Tattersalls October Book 2. Amanda
Skiffington for John Guest. Half-brother to
the moderate 10f winner Master Of Heaven
(by Makfi). The dam, a fairly useful 6f and
double 7f winner, was listed-placed over 1m
and is a half-sister to 6 winners. The second
dam, Serious Delight (by Lomond), is an
unraced half-sister to 8 winners. (John Guest
Racing). *"A lot of people are tipping Havana
Gold to do well in the first season sires table
and looking at this fella I can see why. He's a
January foal so he's pretty mature but when I
x-rayed his knees it shows they aren't mature
at all yet. He's a solid horse though and he
shows plenty of speed, but I've had to step him
back a bit. He won't be late out though, he'll
be a proper 2-y-o in May or early June"*.

1077. LORD GUEST ★★★
b.c. Lord Shanakill – Webcast (Verglas). March
29. Second foal. €10,000Y. Tattersalls Ireland
September. Howson & Houldsworth / BBA
(Ire). Half-brother to the quite useful 2016
2-y-o 6f winner Anfaass (by Vale Of York). The
dam, a fair Irish 2-y-o 7f winner, is a half-sister
to 3 winners including the fairly useful 2-y-o
triple 7f winner Bunsen Burner. The second
dam, Aeraiocht (by Tenby), a dual Irish 2-y-o
7f winner, is a half-sister to 4 minor winners.
(John Guest Racing). *"I have the 3-y-o out of
the dam and he won last year for us. I bought
this colt in Ireland for €10K and I think if he'd
come to Newmarket the price would have
been three times that. He's had sore shins
so I've backed off him a bit, just as I had to
do with his half-brother last year and it did
him no harm. This is quite a powerful, stocky
horse and he's done nothing wrong. A nice,
average 2-y-o type and there's no reason why
he shouldn't be winning somewhere along the
line"*. TRAINERS' BARGAIN BUY

1078. MAAJMEH DAWN ★★★
b.f. Dawn Approach – Blue Angel (Oratorio).
April 1. Third foal. 20,000Y. Tattersalls
December. Rabbah Bloodstock. Half-sister
to Eagle Creek (by Raven's Pass), unplaced
on his only start at 2 yrs in 2016 and to the
very useful 7f, 9f (both at 2 yrs), listed 10.5f
and UAE 10f winner and Italian Group 3
third Viren's Army (by Twirling Candy). The
dam, a useful dual listed-placed 2-y-o 7f
winner, subsequently won once in the USA
and is a half-sister to 7 winners including the
Group 3 7f Irish 1,000 Guineas Trial winner
Empowering. The second dam, Blue Cloud
(by Nashwan), winner of the listed 7f Prix
Imprudence, is a half-sister to the top-class
miler Bigstone. (Jaber Abdullah). *"She'd
thrown a splint as a yearling before the sales
which affected her price, but we've given
her time, brought her on steady and she's
cantering away nicely. She's a filly the lads
seem to like, she's sensible and looks a nice
filly for the future. On pedigree you'd think
seven furlongs or a mile, but we'll see".*

1079. MACHO GUEST ★★★★
b.c. Camacho – Alabama Grace (Teofilo).
April 10. First foal. 72,000Y. Tattersalls
October Book 2. Amanda Skiffington / John
Guest Racing. The dam is an unraced sister to
the useful 2-y-o 1m winner and dual Group
3 third Havana Beat and a half-sister to 4
minor winners. The second dam, Sweet Home
Alabama (by Desert Prince), placed fourth
over 7f and 1m, is a half-sister to the Group
1 1m Sussex Stakes winner Proclamation and
to the German dual listed winner No Refuge.
(John Guest Racing). *"The most expensive
yearling I bought last year. He takes after
Camacho in as much as he shows me plenty
of speed, looks classy, shows a lot of pace and
has a lovely temperament. He looks like one
for six/seven furlongs in, starting in May or
June".*

1080. MIDNIGHT GUEST ★★★★ ♠
b.f. Acclamation – Midnight Martini (Night
Shift). April 18. Third foal. 45,000Y. Tattersalls
October Book 2. Amanda Skiffington. Sister
to the fair 2016 2-y-o 6f winner Mr Pocket
and half-sister to the quite useful 5f winner
of 4 races at 2 and 3 yrs Midnight Malibu (by

Poet's Voice). The dam, a fairly useful 5f and
6f winner, was second in the Group 3 Firth
Of Clyde Stakes. The second dam, Shaken
And Stirred (by Cadeaux Genereux), is an
unraced half-sister to 3 winners including the
Group 3 Musidora Stakes third Sues Surprise.
(John Guest Racing). *"From a family that Tim
Easterby has had a lot to do with, this filly has
bags of potential. She reminds me a lot of the
good filly I trained, Lucky Kristale, because
from day one she's done everything easily and
yet her coat still looks terrible and it's holding
me back. She won't take long, but I don't want
to run her before May and I'll be surprised if
she's not up to her dam's class. She's not small,
but racy and a proper 2-y-o filly. I'm really
looking forward to her".*

1081. PROTECTED GUEST ★★★ ♠
b.c. Helmet – Reem Star (Green Tune).
February 17. Second foal. 35,000Y. Tattersalls
October Book 3. Amanda Skiffington / John
Guest Racing. The dam, a 1m (at 2 yrs) and
13f winner, is a half-sister to 2 minor winners
abroad. The second dam, Arlecchina (by
Mtoto), a German listed winner at 3 yrs,
was Group 3 placed and is a half-sister to
4 winners including the German Group 2
winner Amico Fritz. (John Guest Racing). *"I
probably wouldn't have looked at him twice
on pedigree, but Amanda put him up to me as
one of the nicest in the catalogue. He's on the
back burner because he needs a bit of time to
develop but he's doing well. Quite an athletic
horse, he was quite light but he's filled out
nicely and I'd expect him to be a mid-to-late
season 2-y-o over seven furlongs and a mile".*

1082. SHYJACK ★★★
ch.g. Archipenko – Coconut Shy (Bahamian
Bounty). May 2. Brother to the unraced 2016
2-y-o Shyarch and to the fair 6f and 7f winner
of 5 races (including at 2 yrs) Shypen and
half-brother to the quite useful 6f and 7f
winner of 7 races (including at 2 yrs) Shyron
(by Byron). The dam, a fair 2-y-o 5.5f and
6f winner, is a sister to one winner and a
half-sister to another. The second dam, Lets
Be Fair (by Efisio), a useful 2-y-o 5f and 6f
winner, is a half-sister to 6 winners including
the listed winner Miss Mirasol. (F Butler).
"We've had most of the family and this fella is

probably the sharpest of them, despite being a May foal. I think you'll see him out before the middle of May and if you look at him he looks like a typical Bahamian Bounty, the damsire. He's a nice little horse".

1083. UNNAMED ★★
gr.c. Universal – Qeethaara (Aljabr). April 14. First foal. The dam was a quite useful 7f and 1m winner of 8 races. The second dam, Agshaan (by Wild Again), is a half-sister to numerous winners including the dual US Grade 1 winner Wild Rush. (Mr A Al Mansoori). *"This colt's sire and dam are both owned by Mr Al Mansoori. This horse is very athletic and he does everything easily, but I think his athleticism may be hiding the fact he's weak, but he doesn't look it. He's strengthened up a lot lately and I should think he'll be out as soon as the seven furlong races come".* The sire, a son of Dubawi, won seven races at up to 12f including two Group 2's and a Group 3.

1084. UNNAMED ★★★
b.f. Farhh – Sweet Lilly (Tobougg). April 24. Fifth foal. 19,000Y. Tattersalls October Book 3. Not sold. Half-brother to the quite useful 2-y-o 7.5f winner Zaina Rizeena (by Shamardal), to the German 7.5f (at 2 yrs) and 1m winner Rosy Blush (by Youmzain) and the fair 1m winner Lilly Junior (by Cape Cross). The dam, a smart triple listed winner and second in the Group 3 Musidora Stakes, is a half-sister to 3 winners. The second dam, Maristax (by Reprimand), a fair 2-y-o 7f winner, is closely related to the useful 2-y-o listed 5f winner Four-Legged-Friend and a half-sister to 6 winners including the dual US Grade 3 winner Superstrike and the dam of the Group 1 winning sprinters Goodricke and Pastoral Pursuits. (Jaber Abdullah). *"The dam was a tail-swisher so I was looking out for that in this filly, but maybe the sire has helped in that regard. She's very athletic, only cantering at the moment but she does everything easily and I'll just train to the pedigree with a view to getting her out in mid-summer. She's got a lot going for her, she's fine in her box but you wouldn't want to be riding her out every day because she's a bit of a madam. I think she's one of the nicer ones that Jaber has sent me".*

P J (CHARLIE) McBRIDE

1085. ALCAVELLA ★★★
gr.f. Worthadd – Albacocca (With Approval). January 31. Second foal. The dam, a moderate 11.5f winner, is a half-sister to 3 winners. The second dam, Ballymac Girl (by Niniski), a modest winner of 5 races in Ireland at up to 15f, is a half-sister to the Nassau Stakes winner Last Second (dam of the French 2,000 Guineas winner Aussie Rules), the Group 3 Doncaster Cup winner Alleluia (dam of the Prix Royal-Oak winner Allegretto) and the Moyglare Stud Stakes third Alouette (dam of the Champion Stakes winner Alborada and the multiple German Group 1 winner Albanova) and to the placed dam of the Group 1 winners Yesterday and Quarter Moon. (Miss K Rausing). *"She's done extremely well since she's been here and done nothing but improve. Her owner gave me a brief that she'd like her to win as a 2-y-o to help advertise the first season sire Worthadd. It's early days yet because she's not galloped yet, but she's a good mover and has a beautiful temperament. She's done really well because she was weak when she arrived but she's strengthened up and physically she's a nice-looking filly now. We like her but we've not pressed any buttons yet and she's probably a seven furlong type 2-y-o".*

1086. BOND STREET BEAU ★★★
ch.c. Dandy Man – Loveleaves (Polar Falcon). March 22. Tenth foal. £20,000Y. Goff UK Premier (Doncaster). Not sold. Half-brother to 6 winners including the very smart Group 2 1m Oettingen Rennen and Group 3 7f Supreme Stakes winner Lovelace (by Royal Applause), the quite useful 12f winner Greyfriars Drummer (by Where Or When), the fair 2-y-o 6f and 7f winner Tussie Mussie and the fair 6f (at 2 yrs) to 1m winner Avonrose (by Avonbridge). The dam, a fairly useful 8.3f winner, is closely related to the South African Group 3 winner Headstrong and a half-sister to 5 winners. The second dam, Rash (by Pursuit Of Love), is an unraced half-sister to 6 winners including the dam of the US Grade 1 winner Stroll. (Mr C M Budgett). *"Potentially a really nice colt although he's just cantering at the moment and hasn't galloped yet. His temperament is good, except he does look at*

the fillies a bit! A strong, well-grown horse and a good mover, he's one for six/seven furlongs in mid-season".

1087. GOLD EAGLE ★★★
b.f. Paco Boy – Fin (Groom Dancer). April 21. Sixth foal. Half-sister to the fairly triple 10f winner Haalan (by Sir Percy), to the quite useful Irish 12f and hurdles winner Fatcatinthehat (by Authorized), the fair 2-y-o 7.5f winner Je Suis Charlie and the minor French 12f winner Seasons In The Sun (both by High Chaparral). The dam won 4 races in France and the USA including a listed stakes and is a half-sister to 5 winners including the listed winner Bonne Etoile. The second dam, Bonne Ile (by Ile de Bourbon), won 7 races here and in the USA including the Grade 1 Yellow Ribbon Invitational Handicap and is a sister to the Group 3 winner Ile de Nisky and a half-sister to the Group 3 winner Hi Lass. (Mr C M Budgett). *"She's sharp, goes up the hill nicely and shows plenty of promise. I think she'll probably be out first 2-y-o runner but that won't be until May over six furlongs. She looks like she'll be ok".*

1088. IMAGE ★★★
b.f. Sepoy – The Terrier (Foxhound). March 6. Seventh foal. 35,000Y. Tattersalls October Book 1. Not sold. Half-sister to the useful triple 2-y-o 5f and Group 3 Flying Five winner Dutch Masterpiece (by Dutch Art), to the quite useful triple 6f winner Dinneratmidnight (by Kyllachy), the quite useful 5f and 6f winner Hilary J (by Mount Nelson), the fair 5f and 6f winner Miss Bunter (by Bahamian Bounty) and the modest 6f and 7f winner Beachwood Bay (by Tobougg). The dam, a fair 2-y-o 5f winner, is a half-sister to 4 minor winners. The second dam, Branston Gem (by So Factual), placed over 5f at 2 yrs, is a half-sister to 3 winners including the dual listed winner Falcon Hill. (Bumble Mitchell). *"A very strong, stocky filly, we were late breaking her in because we've taken our time with her. On pedigree she should be a strong, sharp filly but we've haven't done enough with her yet. Potentially one of the stronger looking 2-y-o's in the yard".*

1089. VAMPISH ★★★
b.f. Sir Percy – Falling Angel (Kylian). March

30. Third foal. Half-sister to the quite useful 2016 2-y-o 6f winner Angel Down (by Kyllachy) and to the moderate 7f winner Ashford Island (by Munnings). The dam, a fair 7f winner, is a half-sister to 6 minor winners here and abroad. The second dam, Belle Ile (by Diesis), a modest 1m winner, is a sister to the listed winner Bonne Etoile and a half-sister to 4 winners. (Mr C M Budgett). *"She's quite a nice, forward-going filly that should be a six furlong type for May or June time. She's showing a fair bit at the moment, so we're very happy with her".*

1090. UNNAMED ★★
b.f. Vale Of York – Little China (Kyllachy). February 16. First foal. 2,000Y. Tattersalls October Book 3. Argamia Bloodstock. The dam was a fair 5f winner of 3 races from 2 to 4 yrs. The second dam, China Beads (by Medicean), is an unraced half-sister to 9 winners. *"Bought very cheaply, she'll take a bit of time and is probably a seven furlong 2-y-o. A nice moving filly, we like her but she'll take time".*

1091. UNNAMED ★★
b.c. Aussie Rules – Native Ring (Bering). February 13. Tenth foal. Half-brother to 7 winners including the fairly useful10f and 12f winner Old Town Boy, the 2-y-o 1m winner My Sebastian (both by Myboycharlie), the 10f, 12f and jumps winner John Louis (by Bertolini) and the 10f and 12f winner Harry Buckle (by Byron) – all three quite useful. The dam won once at 3 yrs in France and is a half-sister to 6 winners. The second dam, Soviet Squaw (by Nureyev), won once at 3 yrs. *"He's a half-brother to a lot of winners that I've trained, most of them stayers, but this one is more of a 2-y-o type than they were. He looks like his half-brother My Sebastian who won for us as a 2-y-o and then was sold to Hong Kong. He hasn't been broken in very long so he's just doing one or two canters up the hill".*

1092. UNNAMED ★★
b.f. Havana Gold – News Desk (Cape Cross) February 9. Second foal. 3,000Y. Tattersalls October Book 3. Argamia Bloodstock. Half-sister to the modest 2017 10f placed 2-y-o Broughtons Story (by Royal Applause). The dam, a modest 10f winner, is a half-sister to

one winner. The second dam, La Presse (by Gone West), a useful 2-y-o 6f winner, was third in the Group 3 6f Firth Of Clyde Stakes and is a half-sister to 6 winners. (Jacqui Barrs). *"One of the most forward 2-y-o's we've got, she travels easily and looks like a 2-y-o, very stocky and probably one for six furlongs to begin with in May, but she'll get further alright".*

1093. UNNAMED ★★★★
b.f. Footstepsinthesand – Sancai (Elusive Quality). March 7. First foal. 2,000Y. Tattersalls October Book 4. Argamia Bloodstock. The dam ran once unplaced and is a half-sister to 6 winners including the listed 10f winner Prince Alzain and the listed 2-y-o 7f winner Echo River. The second dam, Monaassabaat (by Zilzal), a fairly useful 6f (at 2 yrs) and listed 10f winner, is a half-sister to 8 winners including the French 2-y-o Group 2 winner Bitooh. *"She was a cheap filly but she's showing speed. She probably wouldn't be fast enough for five furlongs but she could certainly be a nice six furlong 2-y-o. She's tall and a bit leggy, so we're giving her a bit more time. I like her so I've entered her in all the sales races and the Supersprint, just in case. In effect she's taking the same route as the nice 2-y-o we had last year, Spiritual Lady, so we're excited about her".* TRAINERS' BARGAIN BUY

MARTYN MEADE
1094. CONTRIBUTE ★★★
ch.c. Bahamian Bounty – Myth And Magic (Namid). February 26. Fifth foal. 32,000Y. Tattersalls October Book 2. Kern/Lillingston. Half-brother to two minor winners in Germany (by Duke Of Marmalade) and the USA (by Danehill Dancer). The dam is an unraced half-sister to 11 winners including the Grade 1 9f Matriarch Stakes, Group 2 1m Sun Chariot Stakes and triple Group 3 winner Dress To Thrill and the dam of the Group 1 winner Free Eagle. The second dam, Trusted Partner (by Affirmed), winner of the Group 3 7f C L Weld Park Stakes (at 2 yrs) and the Irish 1,000 Guineas, is a full or half-sister to 10 stakes winners including Easy to Copy (herself the dam of 3 stakes winners). *"He's heading for Newmarket's Craven meeting for his debut because he's quick enough to start off over five furlongs before we step him up in trip. He's*

going very well, we bred him ourselves and I think he's the best we've had from this line. A very good-bodied colt, we've got plenty to work on and we'll be able to go on with him over the next couple of months and see what he's made of".

1095. FASHIONABLESOCIETY (FR) ★★
ch.c. Society Rock – Fabiola (GER) (Medicean). March 31. Second foal. €40,000Y Arqana Deauville October. Private sale. The dam, a minor winner at 3 yrs in Germany, is a half-sister to 9 winners including the German Group 3 winner Felicity (herself dam of the German Group 2 winner Felician). The second dam, Felina (by Acatenango), a German listed winner, is a sister to another German listed winner. *"I was hoping to get him out early but he's still a bit immature at this stage and we won't see him out until August over seven furlongs and a mile".*

1096. GHERARDINI (IRE) ★★★
b.c. Dutch Art – Mona Em (Catrail). March 25. Tenth foal. €52,000Y. Goffs Orby. M Meade / D Farrington. Half-brother to 7 winners including the 2-y-o Group 2 5f Flying Childers Stakes winner and sire Sir Prancealot (by Tamayuz), the French listed 10f winner of 10 races Nice Applause, the quite useful dual 1m winner Stage Attraction (both by Royal Applause), the quite useful 6f winner Catwalk (by Pivotal) and the 2-y-o sprint winners Beau Eile (by Arcano), Monalini (by Bertolini) and Monatora (by Hector Protector). The dam, a listed sprint winner, is a half-sister to 4 winners. The second dam, Moy Water (by Tirol), a 1m (at 2 yrs) and 9f winner, is a half-sister to the listed sprint winners Bufalino and Maledetto. *"He's very forward and was set to run at the Craven meeting but unfortunately he got a corn and that set us back a little bit. He's over it now and he should be racing in late April or early May. He's a typical 2-y-o and doing everything nicely at home".*

1097. MICHAEL CORLEONE (IRE) ★★★★
ch.c. Declaration Of War – Needles And Pins (Fasliyev). January 21. Eighth foal. €105,000Y. Goffs Orby. M Meade / D Farrington. Half-brother to 5 winners including the useful 2-y-o Group 3 7f Oh So Sharp Stakes winner Alsindi (by Acclamation), the fairly useful

UAE 2-y-o 7f winner I Am The Best (by King's Best), the quite useful 7f winner Moonvoy (by Cape Cross), the modest 5f to 7f winner of 14 races Seamster (by Pivotal) and the fair 6f winner Bouyrin (by Invincible Spirit). The dam, a useful 2-y-o listed 5.2f winner and second in the Group 3 5.5f Prix d'Arenburg, is a half-sister to 2 winners. The second dam, Fairy Contessa (by Fairy King), is a 6f placed half-sister to 4 winners including the Group 2 6f Gimcrack Stakes winner River Falls. *"Physically I think this is one of our nicest horses, he looks superb. I should think we'll be able to run him by the end of May because he's done extremely well, really strengthened up and dealt with everything we've given him. So he's a very nice type and I think he'll be a really good racehorse. We'll start him at six furlongs or maybe an easy seven".*

1098. TONY SOPRANO ★★★★
b.c. Lethal Force – Zarkalia (Red Ransom). March 6. Seventh foal. €50,000Y. Goffs Orby. M Meade/D Farrington. Half-brother to the French listed-placed 1m winner Zaridiya (by Duke Of Marmalade), to the French 2-y-o 7f winner Zardaba (by Choisir) and the quite useful Irish 12.5f winner Zarkiyr (by Acclamation). The dam was placed three times in minor races at around a mile and ten furlongs in France. The second dam, Zarkiya (by Catrail), winner of the Group 3 1m Prix de Sandringham and fourth in the French 1,000 Guineas and the Coronation Stakes, is a half-sister to 5 winners and to the unraced dam of the outstanding filly Zarkava. *"He's very forward and we're aiming him for Newbury in mid-to-late April for his debut. Seriously, everything he's done at home has been pretty good and I see no reason why he shouldn't do well. About the most forward of our horses, we'll raise him in trip to six furlongs as soon as we can".*

1099. UNNAMED ★★★
ch.f. Pivotal – Adonesque (Sadler's Wells). March 30. Tenth living foal. 85,000Y. Tattersalls October Book 1. De Burgh / Farrington. Half-sister to 6 winners including the fairly useful 7f to 10f winner and UAE listed-placed Busker (by Street Cry), the French listed-placed winner Bergamask (by Kingmambo and herself dam of the Group 2

Coventry Stakes winner Buratino), the fairly useful 2-y-o 6f winner Alderney (by Elusive Quality) and the quite useful 2-y-o dual 1m winner Fareej (by Kingmambo). The dam, a listed 10f winner, is a half-sister to 6 winners including Danehill Dancer. The second dam, Mira Adonde (by Sharpen Up), ran once unplaced and is a half-sister to 4 winners. *"A lovely filly, but she'll take a bit of time. She's a wonderfully topped filly and one we'll bring out around September time over seven furlongs to a mile".*

1100. UNNAMED ★★★
b.c. Galileo – Breathe (Ocean Of Wisdom). March 26. Seventh foal. €105,000Y. Goffs Orby. M Meade / D Farrington. Brother to the quite useful 2-y-o dual 1m winner and dual listed-placed Magic Of Reality and half-brother to the fair 11f winner Imari Kid (by Pour Moi). The dam is a 1m placed half-sister to the Breeders' Cup, Prix Marcel Boussac and Prix Jacques le Marois winner Six Perfections (herself the dam of two Group winners). The second dam, Yogya (by Riverman), is an unraced half-sister to 5 winners including the outstanding filly Miesque (herself the dam of Kingmambo). *"He's coming on particularly well. I initially expected him to take lots of time because he's by Galileo, but he's actually coming together really nicely and I would have thought we'd be able to get him out in August or September. Hopefully he can do a bit better than his winning sister who was listed-placed".*

1101. UNNAMED ★★
b.c. Camelot – Brigid (Irish River). March 29. Fourteenth foal. 35,000Y. Tattersalls October Book 2. D Farrington. Half-brother to 6 winners including the Group 1 7f Moyglare Stud Stakes winner Sequoyah (dam of the multiple Group 1 winner Henrythenavigator), the Group 1 Fillies' Mile winner Listen, the Irish listed 5.6f winner Oyster Catcher (by Bluebird) and the fairly useful 2-y-o 1m winner Purple Heart. The dam, a minor French 1m winner, is a sister to 2 winners including the dam of the Group/Grade 1 winners Dolphin Street, Insight and Saffron Walden and a half-sister to 5 winners. The second dam, Luv Luvin' (by Raise a Native), won 2 races in the USA and was stakes-placed. *"He'll take time because he's still*

growing and developing and I don't think he'll be running before September time".

1102. UNNAMED ★★★★
b.c. Iffraaj – Childa (Duke Of Marmalade). January 31. First foal. 130,000Y. Tattersalls October Book 2. D Farrington. The dam, a French 2-y-o 9f and 3-y-o listed 10f winner, was second in the Group 2 12f Prix du Conseil de Paris and is a half-sister to 2 winners. The second dam, Chill (by Verglas), won the listed 9.5f Prix Finlande and is a half-sister to the French Group 3 Prix du Lys winner Remus De La Tour. *"One of the nicest horses we brought into the yard this time. A little bit on the small side but he's a wonderful mover and I was hoping to aim him for the Lily Agnes Stakes at Chester in May but he was held up due to sore shins. Hopefully we'll get him out in late May and then find a race at Ascot for him, he's that type of horse. A six furlong type 2-y-o".*

1103. UNNAMED ★★★★
b.c. Teofilo – Distorted Promise (Distorted Humor). March 18. Third foal. €52,000Y. Goffs Orby. M Meade / D Farrington. The dam, a minor winner of 2 races at 3 yrs in the USA, is a half-sister to 3 winners. The second dam, Seba (by Alzao), winner of the listed Chesham Stakes and Grade 1 third in the USA, is a half-sister to 9 winners including Do The Honours (Group 3 6f Prix de Meautry). *"He's got a great future I would have thought. A colt with lots of bone and lots of power, he'll take a bit more time so he's one for September or October but I think he's going places".*

1104. UNNAMED ★★★
ch.f. Raven's Pass – Fabia (Sadler's Wells). February 1. First foal. €38,000Y. Goffs Orby. M Meade / D Farrington. The dam, a quite useful 10f winner, is a half-sister to 3 winners including the Group 3 12f Gordon Stakes winner Rebel Soldier. The second dam, En Garde (by Irish River), a quite useful 2-y-o 5.7f winner, is a half-sister to 7 winners including the top-class Group 1 1m Queen Elizabeth II Stakes and Group 1 9.3f Prix d'Ispahan winner Observatory and the Group 2 Prix de Malleret winner High Praise. *"She's not going to be early but she's done everything we've wanted her to do and I'm very keen on her for later on and as a 3-y-o".*

1105. UNNAMED ★★
ch.c. Raven's Pass – Foundation Filly (Lando). March 16. Third foal. €40,000Y Arqana Deauville October. D Farrington. The dam, a listed-placed winner of 3 races at 2 to 4 yrs in France, is a half-sister to the Group 1 Premio Lydia Tesio winner Floriot. The second dam, Fureau (by Ferdinand), won 3 minor races in Germany and is a half-sister to 5 winners. *"He should be racing in June and he's just a workmanlike colt for six/seven furlongs I should think".*

1106. UNNAMED ★★
b.c. Sea The Stars – Night Fairy (Danehill). March 11. Sixth foal. 80,000Y. Tattersalls October Book 1. De Burgh / Farrington. Brother to the Irish 1m winner Stars So Bright and half-brother to the Group 3 6f Ballyogan Stakes and Group 3 Chartwell Stakes winner of 5 races Majestic Queen (by Kheleyf). The dam, a minor Irish 10f winner, is a sister to the Irish listed 7f winner and smart broodmare Fairy Of The Night and a half-sister to 4 winners including the US Grade 3 and Irish listed winner Dress Rehearsal. The second dam, Sassenach (by Night Shift), a winner over 13f at 4 yrs in Ireland, is a half-sister to 6 winners including the Group 3 2m 2f Doncaster Cup winner Far Cry. *"Hopefully he's my Derby horse for next year but as a 2-y-o he's an October job over a mile. A very strong horse with a big, physical presence, he's tall but has plenty of bone and looks like a 3-y-o now. His pedigree tells you that I really ought to wait with him".*

1107. UNNAMED ★★
b.f. Galileo – Rose Bonheur (Danehill Dancer). May 5. Third foal. 150,000Y. Tattersalls October Book 1. D Farrington. Sister to the fair 9f winner Apres Midi. The dam, a very useful listed 6f and listed 7f winner, was dual Group 3 placed and is a half-sister to the 2-y-o 6f winner and Group 3 7f Silver Flash Stakes third Roseraie. The second dam, Red Feather (by Marju), a Group 3 1m winner in Ireland, was second in the Group 1 Moyglare Stud Stakes and is a half-sister to 3 winners including the smart dual 10f winner and dual Group 3 placed Frankies Dream. *"She was quite weak when she came in but she's getting the hang of things a bit more now. Going the*

right way but still a typical Galileo filly for the back-end".

1108. UNNAMED ★★★
ch.f. Mastercraftsman – Station House (Galileo). February 11. Second foal. 13,000Y. Tattersalls October Book 3. D Farrington. Half-sister to the unplaced 2016 2-y-o Kissinger (by Henrythenavigator). The dam is an unraced sister to the US Grade 1 and dual Grade 3 winner Photo Call. The second dam, Theann (by Rock Of Gibraltar), won the Group 3 6f Summer Stakes and is a half-sister to 5 winners including the triple Group 1 winner Halfway To Heaven and the dual Group 3 winner Tickled Pink. *"Going the right way at the moment, she was a bit weak but in the last few weeks she's strengthened and takes the eye now. She's a tallish filly and although the sire doesn't get them early I should think she'll be ready around July time. I think she was reasonably good value".* TRAINERS' BARGAIN BUY

BRIAN MEEHAN

1109. ALKHALIFA (IRE)
b.c. Kodiac – Bridal Path (Groom Dancer). April 26. Seventh foal. 110,000Y. Tattersalls October Book 2. Shadwell Estate Co. Half-brother to the fair 2016 Irish 2-y-o 5f winner The Mcgregornator (by Bushranger, to the fair dual 7f winner Icy Blue (by Iceman) and the fair triple 7f winner Strike A Light (by Dutch Art). The dam, a fair 2-y-o dual 5f winner, is a sister to one winner and a half-sister to 10 winners including Cupid's Glory (Group 3 7f Horris Hill Stakes) and Clinical (Group 3 Princess Elizabeth Stakes). The second dam, Doctor's Glory (by Elmaamul), a fairly useful 5.2f (at 2 yrs) and 6f winner, is a half-sister to 6 winners. (Hamdan bin Rashid Al Maktoum).

1110. BROTHER RALPH (IRE)
b.c. Redoute's Choice – Fusion (Cape Cross). February 19. First foal. 75,000Y. Tattersalls October Book 1. Angie Loder. The dam, a modest 7f placed 2-y-o, is a half-sister to 5 winners including Attraction (winner of the 1,000 Guineas, Irish 1,000 Guineas, Coronation Stakes, Matron Stakes and Sun Chariot Stakes). The second dam, Flirtation (by Pursuit Of Love), is an unplaced half-sister

to 4 winners including the French Group 2 placed Carmita. (Mr I Parvizi).

1111. CARLINI (IRE)
b.c. Zoffany – Taking Liberties (Royal Academy). April 25. Fourteenth foal. 65,000Y. Tattersalls October Book 2. Sam Sangster. Half-brother to 10 winners including the Qatar listed winner Roman Legend (by Holy Roman Emperor), the listed 1m winner of 7 races here and in Hong Kong Troubadour, the fair 2-y-o 6f winner Danapali (both by Danehill), the fair 2-y-o 7f winner Fistful Of Dollars, the 2-y-o 7f winner Tiptree (by Duke Of Marmalade) and the French 2-y-o winner and 5f listed-placed Agapimou (by Spectrum). The dam ran once unplaced and is a sister to the 2-y-o Group 3 1m Futurity Stakes winner Equal Rights and a half-sister to 6 winners. The second dam, Lady Liberty (by Noble Bijou), was a Group 1 12f winner in Australia. (S P Tucker).

1112. FARAASAH (IRE)
b.c. Arcano – Falsafa (Dansili). March 28. First foal. The dam is an unraced half-sister to 6 winners including the very useful listed 7f Star Stakes (at 2 yrs) and Group 3 7f Nell Gwyn Stakes winner Muthabara. The second dam, Hureya (by Woodman), a quite useful 3-y-o 1m winner, is a half-sister to several winners including the very smart listed 7f (at 2 yrs) and listed 10f winner Muqbil. (Hamdan bin Rashid Al Maktoum).

1113. MINI P (IRE)
ch.c. New Approach – Dawning (War Chant). March 20. First foal. 35,000Y. Tattersalls October Book 2. Angie Loder. The dam, a French 9.5f winner, is a half-sister to 6 winners including the Group 1 Prix Jean-Luc Lagardere winner Karakontie. The second dam, Sun Is Up (by Sunday Silence), is an unplaced half-sister to 7 winners including the South African Group 1 winner Amanee. (Mr I Parvizi).

1114. MOTABASSIM (IRE)
gr.c. Zebedee – Coastal Waters (Halling). February 3. Fourth foal. £75,000Y. Goffs UK Premier (Doncaster). Shadwell Estate Co. Half-brother to the fair 2016 2-y-o 6f winner Monoshka and to a minor winner in Italy

(both by Kodiac). The dam, a fair 7f winner, is a half-sister to 7 winners. The second dam, Gretel (by Hansel), a useful 2-y-o 7f winner and third in the Group 3 1m May Hill Stakes and is a half-sister to 5 winners. (Hamdan bin Rashid Al Maktoum).

1115. MYSAAN (IRE)
ch.c. Havana Gold – Oblique (Giant's Causeway). March 17. Eighth foal. £30,000Y. Goffs UK Premier (Doncaster). Sam Sangster. Half-brother to 5 winners including the quite useful Irish 7f (including at 2 yrs) and 1m winner Obligada (by Beat Hollow), to the French 2-y-o 1m winner Arabian Peninsula (by Dream Ahead) and the fair 10f, 2m and hurdles winner Lady Yeats (by Yeats). The dam, a fairly useful 9f, 10f and listed 12f winner, is a half-sister to 5 winners including the US Grade 2 winner One Off. The second dam, On Call (by Alleged), a useful winner of 7 races at up to 2m, is a half-sister to 6 winners including the fairly useful 5.2f (at 2 yrs) and 6f winner Doctor's Glory (herself the dam of 5 stakes winners). (ARAAM).

1116. PETRUS (IRE)
b.c. Zoffany – Ambrosine (Nashwan). April 26. Sixth foal. £35,000Y. Goffs UK Premier (Doncaster). J O'Brien / Sam Sangster (private sale). Half-brother to the fair 2-y-o 6f winner Cat Patrol (by One Cool Cat). The dam, a fair 10f and 12f winner, is a half-sister to 2 winners. The second dam, Tularosa (by In The Wings), a minor French 3-y-o winner, is a half-sister to 7 winners including the Lockinge Stakes winner Most Welcome. (Mr G P M Morland).

1117. PHOENICIAN STAR (IRE)
ch.c. Mastercraftsman – Place De L'Etoile (Sadler's Wells). May 3. Fourth foal. €60,000Y. Goffs Orby. Sam Sangster. Half-brother to the minor French 12.5f winner Ireland's Teardrop (by Fastnet Rock) and to the minor French 12f and 15f winner Traffic Jam (by Duke Of Marmalade). The dam, a French 1m (at 2 yrs) and 9f winner, is a half-sister to 4 winners including the listed winner and Group 1 Racing Post Trophy second Winged Cupid. The second dam, Sweet Emotion (by Bering), a useful 1m winner and 1m listed-placed, is a half-sister to 4 winners and to the unraced

dam of Lillie Langtry (Group 1 Coronation Stakes and Matron Stakes).

1118. PRINCE CONSORT (IRE)
b.c. Most Improved – Fame And Fortune (In The Wings). April 16. Sixth foal. £30,000Y. Goffs UK Premier (Doncaster). Sam Sangster. Half-brother to 2 minor winners in Italy by Amadeus Wolf and Whipper. The dam won 5 minor races in Italy and is a half-sister to 9 winners. The second dam, Fourth Of July (by Free Round), won once at 2 yrs in France. (Hamdan bin Rashid Al Maktoum).

1119. SHAJI
b.c. Exceed And Excel – Eclaircie (Thunder Gulch). 75,000Y. Tattersalls October Book 2. Shadwell Estate Co. Half-brother to Cape Baba (by Cape Cross), unplaced in two starts at 2 yrs in 2016 and to the useful 2-y-o 6f and subsequent US 4-y-o winner Ginger Goose (by Royal Applause). The dam, a minor French 3-y-o 10f winner, is a half-sister to 5 winners including the 2-y-o Group 1 Racing Post Trophy third Skanky Biscuit. The second dam, Blushing Gleam (by Caerleon), won the Group 3 Prix du Calvados and the listed Prix de Saint-Cyr and is a half-sister to 9 winners including Gold Away (four Group wins in France) and the Group 3 winner and smart broodmare Danzigaway. (Hamdan bin Rashid Al Maktoum).

1120. SPICE WAR
b.c. Declaration Of War – Blast Furnace (Sadler's Wells). May 6. Fourth foal. 40,000Y. Tattersalls October Book 2. Sam Sangster. Half-brother to Bessemer Lady (by Cacique), unplaced in one start at 2 yrs in 2016 and to the fair 11f to 2m winner of 3 races Captain Peacock (by Champs Elysees). The dam is an unplaced half-sister to several winners including the 2-y-o Group 3 6f July Stakes and 3-y-o listed 7f winner Meshaheer and the Group 1 6.5f Prix Maurice de Gheest winner King Charlemagne and the dams of the US Grade 1 winners Albertus Maximus, Daredevil and Here Comes Ben. The second dam, Race The Wild Wind (by Sunny's Halo), won the Grade 1 8.5f Santa Maria Handicap, the Grade 2 Princess Stakes and the Grade 2 Fantasy Stakes. (Mr G P M Morland).

1121. TADBIR (IRE)
b.c. Kodiac – Queen Wasp (Shamardal). March 1. Third foal. £150,000Y. Goffs UK Premier (Doncaster). Shadwell Estate Co. Half-brother to the fairly useful 2016 2-y-o dual 6f winner Rusumaat (by Arcano). The dam is an unraced half-sister to 6 winners including the very smart triple Group 3 winner Naheef. The second dam, Golden Digger (by Mr Prospector), was placed fourth 3 times from 6f (at 2 yrs) to 1m and is a sister to the dam of the triple Group 1 winner Lailani and a half-sister to the high-class Group 2 10f Prince Of Wales's Stakes winner Faithful Son and the very smart Coventry Stakes and Prix Quincey winner Always Fair. (Hamdan bin Rashid Al Maktoum).

1122. UNNAMED
ch.c. Zoffany – Crying Aloud (Street Cry). April 10. Second foal. 40,000Y. Tattersalls October Book 2. Sam Sangster. Half-brother to the modest 2016 6f and 7f placed 2-y-o Mulwith (by Kodiac). The dam, a quite useful dual 6f winner, is a half-sister to 5 minor winners in North America. The second dam, Angelic Deed (by Alydeed), a minor US dual winner at 4 yrs, is a half-sister to 9 winners. (Manton Thoroughbreds II).

1123. UNNAMED
b.c. Helmet – Hearsay (Dubai Destination). February 17. Fourth foal. £42,000Y. Goffs UK Premier (Doncaster). Sam Sangster. The dam, a minor winner at 3 yrs in France, is a half-sister to 9 winners including the Group 3 6f Prix de Meautry winner Do The Honours and the listed 7f Chesham Stakes winner Seba. The second dam, Persian Secret (by Persian Heights), a fairly useful 2-y-o 6f winner here, subsequently won a listed event in France and is a half-sister to 8 winners including the dual Group 2 winning sprinter and smart broodmare Cassandra Go and the Group 3 6f Coventry Stakes winner and sire Verglas.

1124. UNNAMED
b.f. Most Improved – Lady Gray (High Chaparral). January 24. Third foal. €60,000Y. Goffs Orby. Sam Sangster. The dam is an unraced half-sister to the 2-y-o Group 3 7f Prestige Stakes winner Sesmen. The second dam, Poetry In Motion (by Ballad Rock), a

modest 5f winner at 4 yrs, is a half-sister to 5 winners including the German Group 3 winner Neshad.

1125. UNNAMED
b.c. Royal Applause – Precious Secret (Fusaichi Pegasus). January 21. Fifth foal. £38,000Y. Goffs UK Premier (Doncaster). Sam Sangster. Half-brother to the French 7f and 9.5f winner Takbeer (by Aqlaam). The dam is an unplaced half-sister to 11 winners including the very useful 10f winner Shaya and the dam of the US Grade 1 second Tamweel. The second dam, Gharam (by Green Dancer), a very useful 2-y-o 6f winner, was third in the French 1,000 Guineas and is a half-sister to 7 winners including the US Grade 1 9f winner Talinum. (Manton Thoroughbreds II).

1126. UNNAMED
b.c. Acclamation – Viletta (GER) (Doyen). February 20. First foal. 70,000Y. Tattersalls October Book 2. Sam Sangster. The dam, a German lowest 2-y-o 7.5f winner, is a half-sister to 8 winners – mainly in Germany. The second dam, Vallauris (by Surumu), is an unraced half-sister to 6 winners in Germany. (Manton Thoroughbreds II).

1127. UNNAMED ♣
gr.f. Cape Cross – Whatami (Daylami). March 25. Fourth foal. 25,000Y. Tattersalls October Book 2. McKeever Bloodstock. Half-sister to the fair 2-y-o 5f and 7f winner Constantine (by Holy Roman Emperor). The dam, a modest 12f placed maiden, is a sister to the 2-y-o listed Chesham Stakes winner Whazzat and a half-sister to 6 winners including the Italian Group 3 1m winner Whazzis. The second dam, Wosaita (by Generous), a fair 12.3f placed maiden, is a half-sister to 10 winners including the Group 1 10.5f Prix de Diane winner Rafha (dam of the Haydock Sprint Cup winner and sire Invincible Spirit) and the dam of the Group 1 Pretty Polly Stakes winner Chinese White.

ROD MILLMAN
1128. ACHIANNA (USA) ★★★
ch.f. Gemologist – Adoradancer (Danzig Connection). March 31. Thirteenth foal. £26,000Y. Goffs UK Premier (Doncaster).

Half-sister to 7 winners including the US Grade 2 winner Saint Anddan (by A P Indy) and winners in Japan and the USA by Silver Deputy and Tapit. The dam, a US stakes-placed winner, is a half-sister to 3 stakes winners. The second dam, Andora (by Conquistador Cielo), a minor US 2-y-o winner, is out of the US dual Grade 1 winner Sabin. (Mr C Demetriou). *"Quite a tall filly, she's not going to be early but I'd expect her out in mid-summer. A nice filly with a good temperament and well put-together".*

1129. AIRSHOW ★★★ ♠

ch.g. Showcasing – Belle Des Airs (Dr Fong). April 12. Fourth foal. Half-brother to the quite useful 2016 2-y-o 6f winner Scofflaw (by Foxwedge) and to the quite useful 2-y-o 5.5f winner Air Of Mystery (by Sakhee's Secret). The dam, a quite useful 6f (at 2 yrs) and 7f winner, is a half-sister to 3 minor winners. The second dam, Belle Reine (by King Of Kings), is an unraced half-sister to 5 winners. (Mrs H I Slade). *"A sharp 2-y-o, he's already had a run and did well, finishing third. Not over-big but very correct and well-muscled, he'll make a very good first half of the season 2-y-o".*

1130. CRYSTAL CASQUE ★★★

b.f. Helmet – Crystal Moments (Haafhd). May 5. Fifth foal. £5,000Y. Goffs UK Silver (Doncaster). Not sold. Half-sister to the fair 10f winner Al Nasser Alwashik (by Intikhab). The dam, a quite useful 5f, 6f (both at 2 yrs) and 7f winner, is a half-sister to 3 minor winners. The second dam, Celestial Choir (by Celestial Storm), a quite useful 7f to 12f winner of 9 races on the flat, also won 7 races over jumps and is a half-sister to 5 winners. *"A filly that didn't look too special at the sales but she's done very well since. She'll be running by the end of May and she's nice, quite strong and not a bad size either. I think she'll do the job and she'll be a sprinter".*

1131. DADDIES GIRL (IRE) ★★★

b.f. Elzaam – La Cuvee (Mark Of Esteem). March 18. Third foal. £5,500Y. Goffs UK Premier (Doncaster). Howson/Houldworth private sale. Half-sister to a winner in Italy by Alhaarth. The dam, a poor 1m and 9f placed maiden, is a half-sister to 6 winners including the Italian Group 3 winner She Bat and the

listed winner Cask. The second dam, Premiere Cuvee (by Formidable), won the Group 3 Goldene Peitsche and is a half-sister to 4 winners. *"A nice, correct filly, she ticks a lot of boxes because she's a good, correct filly. She's one of those that, however good she is, you'll get 100% out of her because she's so well-mannered. One for five/six furlongs, I think for what she cost she was a bargain".* TRAINERS' BARGAIN BUY

1132. HASTENPLACE ★★★

b.f. Compton Place – Hasten (Lear Fan). March 23. £16,000Y. Goffs UK Silver (Doncaster). Not sold. Half-sister to 7 winners including the quite useful 2016 2-y-o listed-placed 6f winner Hellofahaste (by Hellvelyn), the quite useful 2-y-o 7f winner Great Run (by Compton Place), to the fair 2-y-o 1m winner Clutchingatstraws (by Showcasing), the fair UAE 6f and 7f winner Myownway (by Dubawi), the fair 1m winner Hasty Lady (by Dubai Destination) and the modest 2-y-o 7f winner Gassal. The dam, placed twice in the USA, is a half-sister to 6 winners including the 2-y-o Group 3 Autumn Stakes winner and Group 1 Racing Post Trophy second Fantastic View. The second dam, Promptly (by Lead On Time), a quite useful 6f winner here and subsequently a minor US 1m stakes winner, is a half-sister to 7 winners. (Mr & Mrs Laws). *"A half-sister to a decent 2-y-o last year, Hellofahaste, this filly is probably more racy, so she's an earlier type. Quite nice, she'll be running in April and I think she's good enough to win over five furlongs and then stay further later on".*

1133. LAMB CHOP ★★

b.f. Havana Gold – Mutoon (Erhaab). April 7. Sixth foal. 10,000Y. Tattersalls October Book 4. Not sold. Half-sister to the fair 7f (at 2 yrs) and 6f winner Rattling Jewel (by Royal Applause) and to two minor winners abroad by Rail Link (at 2 yrs) and Barathea. The dam, a moderate 1m and 10f placed maiden, is a half-sister to 10 winners including Ranin (Group 3 Park Hill Stakes). The second dam, Nafhaat (by Roberto), a 12f winner and listed-placed over 2m, is a half-sister to one winner. (Mr R E Pocock). *"Bred and owned by some very good judges, she's a nice filly, not the earliest in the world, but has a bit of class about her. We haven't had her that long but I'd say she'll be racing by the end of May".*

1134. LIVINGSTONES QUEST (IRE) ★★★
b.c. Showcasing – Maramba (Rainbow Quest). May 3. Half-brother to the listed 10f winner Cape Amber (by Cape Cross), to the very useful 2-y-o 5f, 6f listed and 6.5f Watership Down Stud Sales Race winner and Group 3 placed Nyramba (by Night Shift), the quite useful 12f to 2m winner Champagne Champ (by Champs Elysees) and the fair 12f winner Warneford (by Dansili). The dam, a fairly useful 3-y-o 1m winner, is a half-sister to 7 winners. The second dam, Gayane (by Nureyev), a very smart winner of the 6f Sandy Lane Stakes and the 7f Oak Tree Stakes, was second in the Group 1 July Cup and is a half-sister to 7 winners including the Group 2 10f Sun Chariot Stakes winner Ristna and the Group 3 Beeswing Stakes winner Shahid. (Five Horses Ltd). *"The dam has bred stayers but she also had a fast 2-y-o in Nyramba. This colt was a May foal and he won't run before mid-season, but hopefully Showcasing will put some speed into him. I think he'll want seven furlongs this year".*

1135. MASTER GREY (IRE) ★★★★
gr.c. Mastercraftsman – Market Day (Tobougg). April 30. Fifth foal. 90,000Y. Tattersalls October Book 2. Howson & Houldsworth /Rod Millman. Brother to the useful listed 10.5f and listed 12f winner and Group 3 12f third Carnachy (by Mastercraftsman) and half-brother to the fairly useful 7f and 1m winner of 7 races Saucy Minx (by Dylan Thomas) and the moderate 1m seller (at 2 yrs) and 7f winner Coach Montana (by Proud Citizen). The dam, a fairly useful dual 6f winner here at 2 yrs, subsequently won a stakes event in the USA and is a half-sister to 5 winners. The second dam, Makhsusah (by Darshaan), is an unraced half-sister to 9 winners here and abroad. (The Links Partnership). *"The most expensive horse we've ever bought, he's a nice colt that ticks all the boxes. We'll probably wait for six furlongs with him and hopefully he'll be one of our flag bearers for a few years because he'll stay ten furlongs next year. He looks the part, isn't as coarse as a lot of them by Mastercraftsman and he stands out in my yard".*

1136. SPOT LITE ★★★
b.g. Compton Place – High Class Girl (Royal Applause). February 16. Third foal. £28,000Y. Goffs UK Premier (Doncaster). Howson & Houldsworth. Half-brother to the moderate 2016 5f placed 2-y-o Miss Mayson (by Mayson). The dam is an unraced half-sister to 5 winners including the 2-y-o listed winner Janina. The second dam, Lady Dominatrix (by Danehill Dancer), won 4 races including a Group 3 5f event, was second in the Group 2 Flying Five and is a half-sister to 3 winners. (Mr C H Saunders). *"From a family I know quite well, he's typical and will probably run at the end of May. The dam never ran herself but this is quite a nice individual and medium-sized – which means he's quite big for one of mine!"*

1137. UNNAMED ★★★
ch.c. Casamento – Midnight Flower (Haafhd). March 24. First foal. £5,000Y. Goffs UK Autumn (Doncaster). Not sold. The dam, a fairly useful triple 6f winner at 2 and 3 yrs, is a half-sister to 4 winners here and abroad. The second dam, Takawiri (by Danehill), is an unraced half-sister to 2 winners including the French 2-y-o Group 2 second Ascot Glory. *"Not over-big but well put-together, he'll be racing in May and he'll be a five/six furlong 2-y-o. There's a leg for sale in him, which may interest someone who wants to go racing quickly".*

1138. UNNAMED ★★
b.f. Dylan Thomas – Under Milk Wood (Montjeu). April 12. First foal. The dam is an unraced sister to the Group 3 12f St Simon Stakes and listed 10f winner and dual Group 1 placed Clowance and a half-sister to 3 winners out of the German Group 2 11f winner Freni (by Sternkoenig). (Seasons Holidays). *"I trained the mother who was a bit of a handful and she never ran, but this filly is quite nice. I've only had her a short time but she's quite attractive, well-muscled and I'd say she'll want seven furlongs to start with".*

STAN MOORE

1139. AUTUMN LODGE ★★
b.g. Stimulation – Timeless Elegance (Invincible Spirit). February 10. Second foal. £3,000Y. Goffs UK Autumn Doncaster. Not

sold. Brother to the minor 2017 dual 5f placed maiden Darvie. The dam, a fair 6f and 7f winner of 3 races at 3 and 4 yrs, is a half-sister to one winner. The second dam, Tidy Wager (by Catrail), a moderate Irish 4 y o 7f winner, is a half-sister to 10 winners. (The Moore The Merrier). *"He's a tough, hardy horse and will be one to follow in the first part of the season. He could be hard to beat the second or third time out and he's one I really like".*

1140. BOSS FOR A DAY ★★★
ch.c. Mastercraftsman – Santa Agata (Anabaa). April 8. Third foal. 9,000Y. Tattersalls October Book 3. Not sold. The dam, a listed-placed 2-y-o 1m winner in France, is a half-sister to 6 winners including the Irish and German Group 3 winner Common World. The second dam, Spenderella (by Common Grounds), a minor winner at 3 yrs in France, is a sister to the listed winner Raissonable and a half-sister to 6 winners including the US Grade 1 winner Aube Indienne. (Stan Moore Partnership). *"He'll be early enough for one by Mastercraftsman and he could have a run over five furlongs but will be better over six. I think he'll win his maiden handily enough, he's showing good paces and will be a good 2-y-o in the first half of the season but might progress as the year goes on".*

1141. DEBUTANTE'S BALL (IRE) ★★★
ch.f. Society Rock – Query (Distant View). April 28. Sixth foal. £6,000Y. Goffs UK Premier (Doncaster). Stan Moore. Half-sister to the fairly useful 2-y-o 7f winner and listed-placed Sensei (by Dr Fong) and to the modest dual 10f winner Saturation Point (by Beat Hollow). The dam is an unraced half-sister to 8 minor winners here and abroad. The second dam, Questonia (by Rainbow Quest), a useful winner at around 1m, is a half-sister to 2 winners including the listed 10f winner Zante. (Wendy Jarrett & Stan Moore). *"She's showing really nice paces and she'll probably be running by the end of April/ early May. She does everything really well, I like her and she could be quite a progressive filly. She should win her races and I think she was well bought. I would say six furlongs would be her best trip".*

1142. FAS LE FIOS ★★★
b.f. Epaulette – Saffa Garden (King's Best). February 19. Eighth foal. Half-sister to the fairly useful 1m (at 2 yrs) to 12f winner of 3 races Paddys Motorbike (by Fast Company), to the fair 2-y-o 5f winner Blue Lotus (by Elnadim) and a winner in Japan by Singspiel. The dam is an unplaced half-sister to 8 winners including the Group 1 Irish 2,000 Guineas third He's A Decoy. The second dam, Allegheny River (by Lear Fan), won once over 7f at 3 yrs in Ireland and is a half-sister to one winner. (Peter Grimes & Stan Moore). *"She's not very big but she's very sharp and she'll win a race early on. She'll probably want fast ground, she'll be one of our first runners and her half-brother was placed a few times for me last year. Incidentally, the horse's name means 'Pass The Gravy'!"*

1143. ISLAND COURT ★★★★
b.c. Camelot – First Breeze (Woodman). February 10. Tenth foal. Half-brother to 6 winners including the fairly useful Irish 1m (including at 2 yrs) and 11f winner No Strings (by Diesis), the fairly useful listed-placed Irish 6f winner Master Speaker, the 9f winner Be My Storm (by Singspiel) and the Irish 10f and hurdles winner Vital Plot (by Theatrical) – all quite useful. The dam, a minor Irish 7f winner, is closely related to the winner Market Slide (dam of the 2,000 Guineas winner Refuse To Bend and the Melbourne Cup winner Media Puzzle) and a half-sister to the US Grade 1 winner Twilight Agenda and the dam of the Belmont Stakes winner Go And Go. The second dam, Grenzen (by Grenfall), won five Graded stakes events in the USA and was second in the Kentucky Oaks. (Donald Kerr & Sara Moore). *"He seems to do everything well and I'd expect him to win his maiden and then progress. He's well-related and he's showing good paces".*

1144. LADY OF THE COURT ★★★
b.f. Camelot – Caserta (Dansili). January 11. First foal. The dam, a French 1m and 9.5f winner, is a half-sister to 7 winners including the French listed winner Destruct and the Group 3 Musidora Stakes second Quickfire. The second dam, Daring Miss (by Sadler's Wells), won 4 races in France including the Group 2 12f Grand Prix de

Chantilly and is a half-sister to 5 winners including the Group 3 12f Prix de Royaumont winner Apogee. (Donald Kerr & Stan Moore). *"She goes along nicely and her half-sister by Australia cost 300,000 gns as a foal in December. She'll be a six/seven furlong 2-y-o and just like our Camelot colt I have to keep going with her. She'll be ready to run when the six furlong races start and I think she'll have a bit of talent. Hopefully she'll be good enough for Ascot".*

1145. MY GUY ★★
b.g. Lilbourne Lad – Royale Life (Anabaa). February 17. Fourth foal. €7,000Y. Tattersalls Ireland September. Not sold. Half-brother to the Italian winner of 6 races from 2 to 5 yrs Viedma (by Aussie Rules). The dam, a minor French dual 4-y-o winner, is a half-sister to 3 winners including the Italian listed winner Rivabella. The second dam, Royale Highnest (by Highest Honor), a minor French 3-y-o winner, is a half-sister to 3 winners. (Miss A Jones). *"He's sharp and will run in April. He shows good paces and will win a maiden auction, so he's one to follow early on".*

1146. QUICK SKIPS LAD ★★
b.g. Lilbourne Lad – Tallawalla (Oratorio). April 4. Third foal. €1,000Y. Tattersalls Ireland September. Not sold. Half-brother to the unplaced 2016 2-y-o Lady Million (by Frozen Power). The dam, a moderate 1m winner at 3 yrs, is out of the placed Edetana (by Diesis), herself a half-sister to 4 winners. (Quick Steps London and Stan Moore). *"He'll be busy early, he's showing good paces and wasn't expensive but he'll win his races early doors".*

1147. ROSES IN JUNE ★★★
ch.f. Society Rock – Majestic South (Bertolini). March 24. Second foal. €1,800 2-y-o. Goffs February. Not sold. The dam, a moderate maiden, was fourth once over 6f and is a half-sister to the useful 2-y-o Group 3 6f Firth Of Clyde Stakes winner Majestic Dubawi. The second dam, Tidal Chorus (by Singspiel), ran twice unplaced and is a half-sister to 6 winners including the French listed winner South Rock. (Well Fleeced Partnership). *"She was bought cheaply in the February sale so she's not been long broken in, but there's a lot to like about her. She goes really nicely*

and I think she'll come to hand quite quickly". TRAINERS' BARGAIN BUY

1148. SHEILA'S EMPIRE ★★★
b.f. Holy Roman Emperor – Silk Mascara (Barathea). May 3. €8,000Y. Tattersalls Ireland September. Not sold. Sister to Silk King, unplaced in two starts at 2 yrs in 2016. The dam, a quite useful Irish 9f winner, is a half-sister to 4 winners. The second dam, Subito (by Darshaan), a fairly useful 2-y-o 7f winner, is a half-sister to 3 winners. (Ray Styles). *"A tough filly, a typical hardy Holy Roman Emperor and she'll win races. One for six/ seven furlongs and I'll be aiming to run her in May. She hasn't done anything to disappoint and I can see her wanting a bit of cut in the ground".*

1149. SHESGOTTHELOT ★★★
b.f. Finjaan – Noble Nova (Fraam). February 24. Seventh foal. £4,000Y. Goffs UK Premier (Doncaster). Half-sister to the fairly useful 6f winner of 6 races from 2 to 5 yrs New Bidder (by Auction House), to the fair 6f and subsequent German winner Captain Noble (by Captain Rio) and a minor 2-y-o winner abroad by Medicis. The dam, a modest 6f (at 2 yrs) to 8.3f winner, is a half-sister to 7 winners including the useful dual 5f winner Noble One (herself dam of the dual Group 1 winner Peeress). The second dam, Noble Destiny (by Dancing Brave), was a fairly useful 2-y-o 7f winner. (The Geordie Boys & Stan Moore). *"The sire was very quick and this filly shows very good paces, so she should win her races and then hopefully progress. The sire flies a bit under the radar but the way she goes you wouldn't be put off buying another by him".* The sire Finjaan, a son of Royal Applause, won the Group 3 5f Molecomb Stakes at 2 and the Group 2 7f Lennox Stakes at 3.

1150. STYLISH GRACE ★★★
gr.f. Style Vendome – Conciliatory (Medicean). May 8. Third foal. €30,000Y. Goffs Sportsmans. Beechwood Farming (private sale). The dam, a quite useful 1m winner of 3 races, is a half-sister to a minor winner. The second dam, Condoleezza (by Cozzene), was a fair 14f winner. (Mrs J A Newell-Smyth, Wendy Jarrett, Stan Moore). *"She seems to be*

very genuine, would probably be better from the mid-season onwards and really wants to get on with it. She shows plenty and she'll be a tough filly with the option of going for the French premiums, so she could well run over there if she proves she has the ability".

1151. TRIOMPHE (IRE) ★★

b.c. Champs Elysees – Angie And Liz (Spectrum). February 27. Sixth foal. Half-brother to the fairly useful 2-y-o 6f winner and Group 3 Brownstown Stakes second Song Of Time, to the quite useful Irish 2-y-o 7f winner Caprella (both by Kheleyf) and the modest 6f winner Oliveraie (by Dutch Art). The dam, a moderate 6f (at 2 yrs) and 5f winner, is a half-sister to 2 winners. The second dam, Mary Magdalene (by Night Shift), a fair 5f winner, is a half-sister to 2 winners. (Tom & Evelyn Yates, Stan Moore). *"A nice horse for the middle of the season, he came in just before Christmas to be broken so we're still getting to know each other but I think he'll make up into a nice horse".*

1152. UTHER PENDRAGON (IRE) ★★★

b.c. Dragon Pulse – Unreal (Dansili). March 26. Eighth foal. £15,000Y. Goffs UK Premier (Doncaster). Stan Moore. Half-brother to the unplaced 2016 2-y-o Sir Harry Collins (by Zebedee) and to the modest 2-y-o 5f winner Britain (by Manduro). The dam, a fair 2-y-o 5f winner, is a half-sister to 7 winners including the Group 1 Racing Post Trophy third Illustrator. The second dam, Illusory (by Kings Lake), a quite useful 6f winner, is a sister to the Group 2 Lowther Stakes winner Kingscote (the dam of four stakes winners) and a half-sister to 7 winners. (Wendy Jarrett & Stan Moore). *"I like him a lot, he's by a good sire and he'll run early. He's showing good paces and hopefully he'll be good enough to run in the slightly better races. Although he's out of a Dansili mare he seems much more like Dragon Pulse and just wants to go forward all the time. He could be busy in the first half of the season and he'll definitely win races".*

1153. UNNAMED ★★★

ch.f. Rip Van Winkle – Metaphor (Woodman). February 22. Fourteenth foal. €34,000Y. Tattersalls Ireland September. James Mescall. Half-sister to 6 winners including the French

listed-placed 2-y-o 7f winner and smart broodmare Celestial Lagoon (by Sunday Silence), the fairly useful listed 2m winner Justice Belle, the quite useful 7f (at 2 yrs) and 12f winner Blue Hussar (both by Montjeu) and the quite useful 2-y-o 7f winner World's Heroine (by Spinning World). The dam, a listed-placed 2-y-o winner in France, is a half-sister to 5 winners including the Group 3 Craven Stakes and US Grade 3 winner King Of Happiness. The second dam, Mystery Rays (by Nijinsky), a dual Group 3 winner in France, is a half-sister to 6 winners including the Group winners Akraam and Robin des Pins. (The Petticoat Government). *"She's really nice and she'll be ready to run when the six furlong races start. I like her, she seems to have a bit of class and if she won her maiden she could be the type to run at Ascot".*

1154. UNNAMED ★★

b.g. Planteur – Parisian Princess (Teofilo). January 17. First foal. 10,000Y. Arqana Deauville August. Not sold. The dam, a fair 7f and 1m placed 2-y-o is a half-sister to 3 minor winners. The second dam, Night Sphere (by Night Shift), a quite useful Irish 2-y-o 7f winner, is a half-sister to the very useful 2-y-o 6f and subsequent US Grade 2 Providencia Stakes winner and Group 2 7f Rockfel Stakes second Missit. (Mr D G Pryde & Stan Moore). *"A big, strong horse that goes along nicely. He's one for the second half of the season".*

HUGHIE MORRISON

1155. BELLA RAGAZZA ★★

gr.f. Dutch Art – Sell Out (Act One). April 13. 38,000Y. Tattersalls October Book 1. H Morrison. Half-sister to the fairly useful 10f and 11f winner Landwade Lad (by Dansili) and to the minor French dual winner at 4 and 5 yrs Living Desert (by Oasis Dream). The dam, a useful listed 12f winner, was third in the Group 3 St Simon Stakes and is a half-sister to 8 winners including the Group 3 7.3f Fred Darling Stakes winner and Group 2 10f Nassau Stakes third Sueboog (herself dam of the Group 1 Prix d'Ispahan winner Best Of The Bests). The second dam, Nordica (by Northfields), a useful 6f and 1m winner, is a half-sister to 2 winners. (Paul Brocklehurst). *"You're not going to see her before the autumn, her family aren't early 2-y-o's and she'll probably need soft ground. A nice filly by a good sire and from a good family, but I think she'll want a mile or ten furlongs".*

1156. CANDIDATE (IRE) ★★
b.c. Camelot – Miss Mariduff (Hussonet). May 1. Seventh foal. 90,000Y. Tattersalls October Book 1. H Morrison. Half-brother to the Italian listed 1m winner and Group 2 Premio Ribot third Porsenna (by Dylan Thomas), to the Italian dual listed dual 1m winner Basileus (by Dream Ahead), the fairly useful dual 7f winner and Group 3 7f Oh So Sharp Stakes second Astrelle (by Makfi) and the minor Italian winner of 4 races Lawboy (by Lawman). The dam is an unraced half-sister to 6 winners including the Italian listed winner Statue. The second dam, Sopran Mariduff (by Persian Bold), won the Grade 2 Black Helen Handicap and is a half-sister to 9 winners. (M Kerr-Dineen, W Eason, D Fass). *"He's not going to run until the autumn, he was so weak when I bought him but he's developing a lot physically and mentally. He's pretty fragile looking so we're going steady for now, but he's a nice looking horse".*

1157. CORGI ★★★★
b.c. So You Think – Ermyn Express (Selkirk). March 7. Third foal. 85,000Y. Tattersalls October Book 1. Sackville/Donald & Hughie Morrison. The dam, a modest 10f winner, is a half-sister to 6 winners including the US Grade 1 Vanity Handicap winner Byrama and the Group 3 Horris Hill Stakes winner Klammer. The second dam, Aymara (by Darshaan), a fairly useful 12f winner, is a half-sister to 2 winners. (Mr M Kerr-Dineen & Mr M Hughes). *"A lovely horse, he does everything very easily and very confidently. He'll be out in September over a mile probably. A nice big colt with a good attitude and there's a lot to like about him".*

1158. DAME VERA ★★★★
ch.f. Medicean – Some Sunny Day (Where Or When). April 3. Fourth foal. Half-sister to the quite useful 2016 2-y-o 6f winner Dubai Elegance (by Sepoy) and to the fair 12f winner Prospectus (by Sakhee). The dam, a quite useful 10f and 12f winner, is a half-sister to 10 winners including the high-class Group

1 6f July Cup winner Sakhee's Secret and the listed winners Palace Affair and Palace Moon. The second dam, Palace Street (by Secreto), a useful winner over 6f and 7f including the listed John Of Gaunt Stakes and listed Cammidge Trophy, is a half-sister to 7 winners including the listed Extel Handicap winner Indian Trail and the Italian Group 3 winner Sfriss. (Julia Scott & J F Dean). *"A home-bred filly, she's still in pre-training but she should make a summer 2-y-o. I saw her last week and thought she might be my first 2-y-o runner, she seems more like the dam's half-sister Palace Affair than the dam herself".*

1159. DAYBREAK ★★★★
b.f. Dawn Approach – Walk On Bye (Danehill Dancer). April 8. Third living foal. 65,000Y. Tattersalls October Book 2. H Morrison. The dam won the Group 3 Anglesey Stakes at 2 yrs, was third in the Group 1 6f Phoenix Stakes and is half-sister to 2 minor winners. The second dam, Pipalong (by Pips Pride), won 10 races including the Group 1 6f Haydock Park Sprint Cup, the Group 3 Duke Of York Stakes and the Group 3 Palace House Stakes and is a half-sister to 12 winners including the fairly useful 2-y-o 6f listed winner Out Of Africa. (Mr & Mrs G Swire, Mr R Callaghan, Mrs A Scott). *"A similar type to the previous 2-y-o we talked about, Dame Vera, it looks like she'll make a mid-summer 2-y-o. We haven't done a lot with her yet because she grew and developed a lot in the winter, but she looks a nice type. There's plenty of speed in the pedigree, she's a close-coupled filly, growing a bit and everything's in the right place with her".*

1160. DEADLY ACCURATE ★★★
br.c. Lethal Force – Riccoche (Oasis Dream). March 25. Fourth foal. 28,000Y. Tattersalls October Book 2. H Morrison. Half-brother to the fair 6f winner Beauden Barrett (by Dick Turpin) and to the moderate 5.5f and 6f winner Burauq (by Kyllachy). The dam is an unplaced half-sister to 3 minor winners. The second dam, Ammo (by Sadler's Wells), a minor French 3-y-o winner, is a sister to the Group 3 Prix de Royaumont winner Sadler's Flag and a half-sister to 7 winners. (S Malcolm, Tony Pickford, Mrs M Morrison, Mr S de Zoete). *"He's been quite backward*

through the winter but he's just started to come to himself. I won't over-train him on firm ground at this stage, judging by the way he moves. He looks like a sprinter and we'll start to push on with him with the idea of running him in mid-summer".

1161. DORIAN GRAY (IRE) ★★★

b.c. So You Think – Flawless Beauty (Excellent Art). February 21. First foal. 40,000Y. Tattersalls October Book 2. H Morrison & J Toller. The dam, a quite useful 2-y-o 6f winner, is a half-sister to 3 winners including the 2-y-o Grade 1 1m Breeders' Cup Juvenile Turf winner Wrote. The second dam, Desert Classic (by Green Desert), placed fourth over 9f and 12f, is a full or half-sister to 8 winners. (Mr P C J Dalby & Mr R D Schuster). *"We'll look after him for a bit because he's big and a bit of a teenager at the moment but he means well A big, rangy colt, he seems to come from a speedy family but I should think the sharpest we'll start him over is seven furlongs. Well named I think!"*

1162. ESCAPE THE CITY ★★★

b.f. Cityscape – Jasmeno (Catcher In The Rye). April 5. Third foal. Half-sister to the fair 11f winner Pastoral Music (by Pastoral Player). The dam, a modest 12f and 13f winner, is a half-sister to the useful 7f (at 2 yrs) and 1m winner and dual Group 3 placed Sagramor. The second dam, Jasmick (by Definite Article), a quite useful 10f and 14f winner, is a half-sister to 2 winners. *"Not over-big and a bit like her grandam Jasmick who was small and sharp as a 2-y-o and might have won at two but she had an accident. This filly is forward going and wants to do it, so I wouldn't be surprised if she was running over seven furlongs in June".*

1163. GERANIUM ★★★

ch.f. Sakhee's Secret – Kasumi (Inchinor). April 21. Second foal. £3,800Y. Tattersalls Ireland Ascot November. Mary Morrison. The dam, a useful 1m listed winner of 6 races, is a half-sister to 2 winners. The second dam, Raindrop (by Primo Dominie), placed fourth once over 7f, is a half-sister to 5 winners. (Trenchard, Clare, Lady Margadale & Mary Morrison). *"She was cheap but the dam was a listed winner and this filly is quite like her in*

that she's long in the back. Hopefully she'll run later in the year, she hasn't been here long but she does everything quite naturally".

1164. JEDHI ★★★

b.f. Big Bad Bob – Capriolla (In The Wings). January 19. Seventh foal. €43,000Y. Baden Baden. Not sold. Private sale. Half-sister to 5 winners including the useful triple 14f winner and Group 2 Prix Chaudenay second Vent De Force (by Hurricane Run), the useful 12f winner and Group 2 Prix Chaudenay third Marmelo (by Duke Of Marmalade), the quite useful 2-y-o 6f winner Valerius Maximus (by Spartacus) and the fair 2-y-o 1m winner Halling's Quest (by Halling). The dam, a modest 10f placed maiden, is a half-sister to 6 winners including the smart Group 3 11.5f Lingfield Derby Trial winner Saddler's Quest and the French listed middle-distance winners Quiz Mistress and Seren Hill. The second dam, Seren Quest (by Rainbow Quest), was a fairly useful 10f winner. (Tony Pickford, Simon Malcolm, Mrs M Morrison, Mr S de Zoete). *"I bought her in Germany, she's a half-sister to two top stayers but she finds it all quite easy and you wouldn't be surprised if she ran over seven furlongs in July. I think Big Bad Bob may have added a touch of speed to the pedigree".* TRAINERS' BARGAIN BUY

1165. PAMINAH ★★★

b.f. Bated Breath – Starry Sky (Oasis Dream). March 4. Sixth foal. 19,000Y. Tattersalls October Book 2. H Morrison. Half-sister to the quite useful 2016 2-y-o 6f winner Musawat (by Equiano), to the fairly useful Irish 2-y-o 6f winner Blackbriar (by Kyllachy), the Irish 2-y-o 6f winner, from two starts, Tarn (by Royal Applause) and the moderate 6f winner Dutch Dream (by Dutch Art). The dam, a fair 2-y-o 7f winner, is a half-sister to 3 winners. The second dam, Succinct (by Hector Protector), a useful listed 10f winner, is a half-sister to 4 winners including the German listed winner Succession. (M Morrison, S de Zoete, S Malcolm, Tony Pickford). *"She's had a few niggles that have prevented us from getting on with her. She's quite long-bodied and I can see her doing as four of her siblings have done by winning this year, but it won't be until September. She's by Bated Breath which means you can't do too much too soon with her".*

1166. PIPPIN ★★★
ch.c. Intello – Golden Delicious (Cadeaux
Genereux). February 16. Second foal. The
dam, a quite useful 6.5f (at 2 yrs) and dual
7f winner, is a half-sister to one winner. The
second dam, Playgirl (by Caerleon), was
second twice over 10f from three starts and is
a half-sister to 7 winners including the Group
2 10.3f winner Stage Gift. (Mr Nicholas Jones).
*"A nice colt that's fairly straightforward and
looks as though he might be earlier than you'd
expect. He does everything quite naturally and
he's just a nice horse really. I trained the dam
and she won first time out at two over six and
a half furlongs and she progressed as a 3-y-o
and was unlucky not to be listed-placed".*

1167. STARCASTER ★★
b.c. Dansili – Shirocco Star (Shirocco).
February 4. First foal. 60,000Y. Tattersalls
October Book 1. Not sold. The dam, a 2-y-o
1m winner, was second in the Oaks and
the Irish Oaks. The second dam, Spectral
Star (by Unfuwain), a fair 11.8f winner, is a
half-sister to 8 winners including the Group
3 7f Tetrarch Stakes winner and Irish 2,000
Guineas second France. (Castle Down Racing).
*"A weak colt at the moment but he's a nice
mover with a good temperament. He needs
to develop a lot over the coming months and
we'll see him in the autumn, but he's a natural
athlete. I trained the dam to be second in the
Oaks, she came to me in May and was always
a superstar – a class above the rest. This colt
may well develop over the next few months
and you wouldn't recognise him in October".*

1168. UNNAMED ★★★
ch.f. Sea The Stars – Imprecation (First
Defence). January 24. First foal. 60,000Y.
Tattersalls October Book 1. H Morrison.
The dam, a minor French placed 3-y-o, is a
half-sister to 7 winners including the Group 1
1m Prix du Moulin and Group 1 10.5f Prix de
Diane winner Nebraska Tornado, the Group
2 10f Prix Eugene Adam winner Burning Sun
and the US Grade 3 winner Mirabilis. The
second dam, Media Nox (by Lycius), winner
of the 2-y-o Group 3 5f Prix du Bois, is a
half-sister to the Prix d'Aumale, Prix Vanteaux
and Prix de Malleret winner Bonash. (M Kerr-

Dineen, D Fass, G Rothwell). *"A lovely filly that
didn't make as much as should have done at
the sales because she looked like a whippet.
She's developing all the time and hopefully
we'll get her out in the autumn. She's got a bit
of quality about her and she's very light on
her feet".*

1169. UNNAMED ★★
b.f. Exceed And Excel – Rosinka (Soviet Star).
May 4. Fourth foal. Closely related to the fair
12f winner Moshe (by Dansili) and half-sister
to the Group 2 12f Bosphorus Cup and Group
3 12f Cumberland Lodge Stakes winner Move
Up (by Dubawi) and the fair 1m and 10f
winner Jam Jar (by Duke Of Marmalade). The
dam, a useful 2-y-o 6f winner, subsequently
won a US Grade 3 event over 11f and was
Grade 1 placed twice. She is a half-sister to
6 winners including the US Grade 1 12f and
triple Grade 2 winner King's Drama and the
US Grade 1 placed Self Feeder. The second
dam, Last Drama (by Last Tycoon), won and
was listed placed twice over 10f in France
and is a sister to the listed winner and smart
broodmare Tycoon's Drama. (The End-R-
Ways Partnership, & Partner). *"A leggy filly, I
trained two out of the mare and this will be a
late summer 2-y-o. She didn't go to the sales
because she was very weak at the time".*

1170. UNNAMED ★★★
ch.f. Nathaniel – Spicy Dal (Dalakhani). March
29. First foal. The dam, a quite useful 1m
winner and listed 10f second, is a half-sister
to one winner. The second dam, Salsa Steps
(by Giant's Causeway), a fairly useful dual 6f
winner, is a half-sister to 3 winners. (Ben & Sir
Martyn Arbib). *"She's quite similar to the dam
in that she's small, neat and forward-going,
so she could be running in June".*

WILLIAM MUIR
1171. CENT FLYING ★★★
b.c. Sepoy – Sea Of Leaves (Stormy Atlantic).
April 14. Third foal. 30,000Y. Tattersalls
October Book 2. William Muir. Half-brother to
the modest 2016 5.5f placed 2-y-o Le Haule
Lady (by Helmet). The dam, a fairly useful
5f (at 2 yrs) and 6f winner, is a half-sister to
6 winners. The second dam, Dock Leaf (by
Woodman), placed once at 3 yrs in the USA,
is a half-sister to 6 winners including the US
Grade 1 winners Sleep Easy and Aptitude.

(Clarke, Edginton, Niven). *"I love Sepoys although a lot of people don't. The one thing I've learnt about them, particularly through Phijee last year, is not to rush them. This colt is strong and hurdy, he looks like a 2-y-o and he's a lot sharper looking than Phijee. He's stronger and butty, so he looks like a sprinter".*

1172. CHARITY JOY ★★★

b.c. Oasis Dream – Morzine (Miswaki). April 13. Sixth foal. 160,000Y. Tattersalls October Book 1. Jamie Lloyd. Half-brother to the quite useful 9f and 10f winner Ski Lift (by Pivotal) and to the French 12f winner Try Out (by Rail Link). The dam, a quite useful 2-y-o 6f winner, is a half-sister to 7 winners including the 2-y-o Group 3 6f Coventry Stakes and disqualified Group 1 6f Middle Park Stakes winner Three Valleys. The second dam, Skiable (by Niniski), won four times at up to 9f in France and the USA and is a half-sister to 6 winners including the outstanding broodmare Hasili. (Alan Lee Yuk Lun). *"A sharp type of 2-y-o, he may end up going to Hong Kong. I like him, he's a strong, butty, really nice Oasis Dream colt".*

1173. DATA PROTECTION ★★★

b.c. Foxwedge – Midnight Sky (Desert Prince). April 6. Sixth living foal. 12,000Y. Tattersalls October Book 4. Willie Muir. Half-brother to the fair 2-y-o 5f winner Caymus (by Compton Place), the German 2-y-o 5f winner Matchday (by Acclamation), the modest 6f winner Deepest Blue (by Sakhee's Secret) and the moderate 8.5f and 9.5f winner Sarlat (by Champs Elysees). The dam, a moderate 5f winner, is a half-sister to 6 winners including the Group 3 5f Ballyogan Stakes winner Miss Anabaa. The second dam, Midnight Shift (by Night Shift), a fair dual 6f winner, is a half-sister to 8 winners including Owington (Group 1 6f July Cup). (Muir Racing Partnership, Santa Anita). *"He'll probably win first time out, because he's showing all the attributes to say he one of those that could just do something early. We'll wait until his birthday before we set him off, he's grown into a lovely big horse, he's a bit of a 'jack the lad' but he's hardy and he's got ability. He'll win races and he was a good buy".* TRAINERS' BARGAIN BUY

1174. GENERAL ZOFF ★★★

b.c. Zoffany – Aunt Julia (In The Wings). February 18. Seventh foal. 50,000Y. Tattersalls October Book 3. Willie Muir. Half-brother to the very useful 7f (at 2 yrs) to 10.5f winner and Group 2 1m Royal Lodge Stakes third Al Waab (by Danehill Dancer) and to a 4-y-o winner in Germany by Rock Of Gibraltar. The dam, a useful 10f winner, was listed placed three times and is a half-sister to 2 winners. The second dam, Original (by Caerleon), is an unraced half-sister to 5 winners including the listed winner Xtra. (Purple & Lilac Racing X). *"I like him, he looks the part, he's strong and I think he'll turn out to be slightly better than average. I've done all I want with him for now, he moves well and shows a great attitude. Charlie Gordon-Watson was the under-bidder and his plan was to bring him back to the breeze-up sale and hope to get 150 Grand. I'd say that the way this horse has progressed he'd have made that. We'll aim to get him out by early May because he's big, strong and sharp".*

1175. HOLLYWOOD DREAM ★★★★

b.f. Delegator – Royal Obsession (Val Royal). April 28. Half-sister to the quite useful listed-placed 2-y-o 5.5f winner Just Emma (by Bertolini) and to the modest 2-y-o 5f winner Harleys Rocket (by Proclamation). The dam ran twice unplaced and is out of Britique (by Critique). (Mr A A Byrne). *"A really nice filly and one of those that, when you look at horses at this time of year on the gallops, shows she has a bit of class about her. She needs to put on some more condition, but she's very natural – everything is very comfortable for her. I really like her".*

1176. MILLE TANK ★★

b.f. Mastercraftsman – Millevini (Hawk Wing). February 13. First foal. 60,000Y. Tattersalls October Book 2. James McHale. The dam, placed from 2 to 4 yrs in Scandinavia, is a half-sister to the Group 1 Racing Post Trophy and Group 1 St Leger winner Kingston Hill. The second dam, Audacieuse (by Rainbow Quest), won the Group 3 Prix de Flore and is a half-sister to 5 winners including the 2-y-o Group 3 Acomb Stakes winner Waiter's Dream. (Alan Lee Yuk Lun). *"She's going to take time considering the sire but she's quite a nice filly and moves well.*

1177. PREZZIE ★★★★
b.f. Major Cadeaux – Yearbook (Byron).
February 15. Second foal. 45,000Y. Tattersalls
October Book 3. Willie Muir. Brother to
the quite useful 2016 2-y-o 6f winner and
Group 3 Solario Stakes third Mr Wizard. The
dam, a moderate 5f and 6f placed 2-y-o, is a
half-sister to 9 winners including the Group
3 Horris Hill Stakes third Day Of Conquest
and the dam of the Group 1 Gran Criterium
winner Hearts Of Fire. The second dam,
Dayville (by Dayjur), a quite useful triple 6f
winner, is a half-sister to 4 winners including
the Grade 1 Yellow Ribbon Handicap winner
Spanish Fern and to the unraced dams of
the Group/Grade 1 winners Lord Shanakill
and Heatseeker. (Foursome Thoroughbreds).
*"I really like her, I think she's strong, athletic
and shows ability already. A nice filly, her full
brother last year was sold to Hong Kong after
finishing third in a Group 3. We spent enough
money on her, for a Major Cadeaux. This filly
will be sharp, so she's one for five/six furlongs".*

1178. UNNAMED ★★
b.c. Rock Of Gibraltar – Gamra (Green Desert).
April 28. Seventh foal. 6,000Y. Tattersalls
December. W Muir. Brother to the 2-y-o
listed 5f winner and Group 3 Firth Of Clyde
Stakes second Roxan and to the modest
8.5f to 10f winner The Wee Barra and half-
brother to the quite useful 2-y-o 6f winner
Temerity (by Zoffany) and the quite useful 12f
winners Mister Aviation and Boulay (both by
Montjeu). The dam, a fair 3-y-o 1m winner, is
a full or half-sister to 6 winners including the
very smart Group 2 9.7f Prix Dollar winner
Wiorno and the very smart Trusthouse Forte
Mile, Gimcrack Stakes and Earl of Sefton
Stakes winner Reprimand. The second dam,
Just You Wait (by Nonoalco), is an unraced
half-sister to 7 winners including the dam
of the Group winners Ozone Friendly,
Ardkinglass and Soft Currency. (F P Hope).
*"A fairly late foal, he's backward and I haven't
done much with him yet. He's just starting to
put on condition now, I like his action but he'll
take time".*

1179. UNNAMED ★★★
b.f. Teofilo – Kahlua Kiss (Mister Baileys).
April 4. Sixth foal. Half-sister to the smart 6f
(at 2 yrs) and dual listed 10f winner of 6 races

and Group 2 York Stakes third Windhoek (by
Cape Cross), to the quite useful 12f winners
Eager Beaver (by Duke Of Marmalade) and
Spiritoftheunion (by Authorized) and the fair
10f and 12f winner Rahyah (by Acclamation).
The dam, a fairly useful 7f (at 2 yrs) and 10f
winner of four races, was listed-placed twice
and is a half-sister to the 2-y-o winner and
dual Group 3 placed Mister Genepi. The
second dam, Ring Queen (by Fairy King), is
an unraced half-sister to 10 winners including
the US dual Grade 1 winner Special Ring. (M
J Caddy). *"A well-related filly, she's nicer than
Eager Beaver by a long way. I think she's quite
smart".*

1180. UNNAMED ★★★★
b.c. Kodiac – Singed (Zamindar). April 5.
Eleventh foal. 75,000Y. Tattersalls October
Book 2. William Muir. Half-brother to the
useful 2-y-o dual 1m and subsequent Hong
Kong stakes winner and Group 2 1m Royal
Lodge Stakes third Chater Way (by Oasis
Dream), to the 10f and 11f winner On Her
Way (by Medicean), the 7f winner Beauty
Prince (by Arcano) and the 8.5f winner Torch
(by Paco Boy) – all three quite useful. The
dam won once at around 1m in France and
is a half-sister to the French listed winner
and Group 3 placed Inhabitant. The second
dam, Infringe (by Warning), won once at 3
yrs in France and is a half-sister to 7 winners
including the Group 3 winners Ecologist,
Green Reef and Infrasonic. (M J Caddy). *"He
was bought to go to Hong Kong but the owner
has said I can keep him if I think I can get him
rated above 85. He's a big, strong horse and I
think he's a really nice colt. Hopefully when I
step him up he'll show me he is".*

1181. UNNAMED ★★★
ch.c. Intello – Welsh Cake (Fantastic Light).
April 16. Fifth foal. 48,000Y. Tattersalls
October Book 1. Not sold. Closely related
to the fair 2016 2-y-o 7f winner Chica de
la Noche and to the useful 2-y-o 5f winner
Upward Spiral (both by Teofilo) and half-
brother to the quite useful 5f (at 2 yrs) and
6f winner Al Gomry (by Exceed And Excel).
The dam, a fair 7f winner, is a half-sister to
8 winners including the Group 2 1m Prix du
Rond-Point and Group 3 8.5f Diomed Stakes
winner Trans Island. The second dam, Khubza

(by Green Desert), a quite useful 7f winner, is a half-sister to 7 winners including the Group 2 winners Barrow Creek and Last Resort (dam of the US Grade 2 winner Rebellion). (M J Caddy). *"He moves well, he does everything right and I like him but I won't rush him and I haven't done enough with him yet to make my mind up. A nice horse in the making, he's out of a good mare so there's no reason why he shouldn't be a good six/seven furlong horse".*

JEREMY NOSEDA

1182. BETTY F ★★★
ch.f. Frankel – Instance (Invincible Spirit). February 22. First foal. The dam, a fairly useful 6f (including at 2 yrs) and 7f winner, is a half-sister to the Group 1 12f British Champions Fillies and Mares winner Seal Of Approval and the useful listed 2m winner Gale Force. The second dam, Hannda (by Dr Devious), a winner over 10f in Ireland from 2 starts, is a half-sister to 5 winners including the Group 3 7.5f Concorde Stakes winner Hamairi and the listed 6f winner Hanabad. *"I trained the dam who was pretty useful. This is a solid filly, she was a bit on the small side but physically she's done really well since she came into training. She's a good mover, has a nice temperament and is beginning to come forward in the right way. I'm sure there's an engine there and I think she'll be a 2-y-o from July onwards. The dam didn't win as a 2-y-o until October but I think this filly is a bit more precocious. It's nice to have a Frankel 2-y-o and I have a very nice Frankel 3-y-o filly called La Figlia that looks to be of stakes quality".*

1183. BLAZING AWAY (IRE) ★★★
b.c. Declaration Of War – Sahara Sky (Danehill). March 18. Half-brother to the 2-y-o Group 1 6f Phoenix Stakes winner Dick Whittington (by Rip Van Winkle), to the fairly useful 2-y-o 5f winner Sign From Heaven (by Raven's Pass), the fairly useful 2-y-o 5f winner Sign From Heaven (by Raven's Pass), the fair dual 6f winner Lisiere (by Excellent Art) and the fair dual 1m winner Carenot (by Iffraaj). The dam is an unraced half-sister to 9 winners including the Group 1 6f July Cup winner Owington. The second dam, Old Domesday Book (by High Top), a fairly useful 10.4f winner, was third in the listed 10f Sir Charles Clore Memorial Stakes. *"He's a pretty*

set individual and looks like a 2-y-o type. He'll be in fast work by mid-April, I like him and he looks like a six furlong horse that should do his job as a 2-y-o".*

1184. BOLD WARRIOR ★★★
b.c. Declaration Of War – Rochitta (Arch). April 15. Third foal. 105,000Y. Tattersalls October Book 1. Willie Browne. Half-brother to the fair 10f winner Third Rock (by Hat Trick). The dam, a minor US 3-y-o winner, is a half-sister to 6 winners including the UAE Group 2 and Irish Group 3 Ballycorus Stakes winner Lord Admiral. The second dam, Lady Ilsley (by Trempolino), a winner in France and listed-placed twice, is a sister to the winner and Grade 2 second Najecam (herself dam of the Grade 1 Breeders' Cup Juvenile winner Action This Day) and a half-sister to 5 winners. *"A good, solid individual and a good mover that's just cantering at the moment. I'm pleased with him and he's a nice, tough, straightforward colt. A July/August type for seven furlongs".*

1185. CONTRIVE (IRE) ★★
gr.f. Mastercraftsman – Sixpenny Sweets (Dalakhani). April 26. First foal. €40,000Y. Goffs Orby. Brian Grassick Bloodstock. The dam is an unraced half-sister to 5 winners including the Japanese Grade 3 2m winner Cosmo Meadow and the 7f (at 2 yrs) and Group 3 10f Blue Wind Stakes winner Beauty O'Gwaun. The second dam, Angel Of The Gwaun (by Sadler's Wells), is an unraced full or half-sister to 6 winners including the Derby third Let The Lion Roar and the St Leger winner Millenary. *"Quite a backward, tall, leggy filly. She's light on her feet and a good mover but she's going to need some time. A back-end type".*

1186. DELPHINIA (USA) ★★★★
gr.c. The Factor – Ramblin Rosie (Roar). April 13. Fourth foal. $80,000Y. Keeneland September. Kerri Radcliffe. Half-brother to 2 winners including the US 2-y-o 6f winner Mayor Mac (by Discreetly Mine). The dam, a minor winner at 3 and 4 yrs in the USA, is a half-sister to 7 winners including the US Grade 1 Santa Anita Derby winner Buddy Gil. The second dam, Really Rising (by For Really), was a US 2-y-o stakes-placed winner.

"His full-sister is a Graded stakes winner now in America. I'm thrilled with this colt, he's a lovely, good moving, well-balanced horse and I really like him. He goes well now but I'm not rushing him and I'm sure he'll do a good job at two. I always like to buy horses in America when I can. If I can live with the pedigree I can get more horse for my money, for sure".

1187. DUTCHMANS ONE (IRE) ★★★
b.c. Dutch Art – Sentimental (Galileo). March 26. Fourth foal. The dam is an unraced half-sister to four winners including the French listed winners Bermuda Grass and Bermuda Rye. The second dam, Alleluia Tree (by Royal Academy), a French 2-y-o winner, is a half-sister to 7 winners and to the unraced dam of the triple Group 1 winner Scorpion. *"He's the best one I've seen out of this mare to date and he's a good-moving, scopey horse. A July/ August type 2-y-o".*

1188. KAT O'STROPHIC ★★★
b.f. Kodiac – Katevan (Heliostatic). February 19. First foal. 70,000Y. Tattersalls October Book 3. Willie Browne. The dam, a quite useful 2-y-o 1m winner, is a half-sister to 3 winners including the useful 2-y-o 7f winner and dual listed-placed Guilia. The second dam, Lesgor (by Irish River), won over 10f in France, was third in the Group 3 Prix de Psyche and is a half-sister to 3 winners. *"A neat, racy 2-y-o type. She's just gone into fast work and I expect to see her racing by the second half of April. She's fast and should definitely do a job early".*

1189. LAUGHING STRANGER ★★
b.c. Medaglia d'Oro – Laughing Lashes (Mr Greeley). April 6. Third foal. $100,000Y. Keeneland September. Kerri Radcliffe. The dam, a 2-y-o Group 2 7f Debutante Stakes winner, was placed in the Group 1 Moyglare Stud Stakes and the Irish 1,000 Guineas and is a half-sister to 2 winners. The second dam, Adventure (by Unbridled's Song), won 2 minor races in the USA at 3 yrs and is a half-sister to 7 winners including the Group 1 Racing Post Trophy winner Palace Episode. *"A big, scopey colt, he's a nice mover and we'll just have to be a bit patient with him. A back-end 2-y-o, I was astonished he was as cheap as he was".*

1190. MISSY MISCHIEF (USA) ★★★★
b.f. Into Mischief – Ring True (Is It True). February 5. Sixth foal. $195,000Y. Keeneland September. Kerri Radcliffe. Half-sister to a minor US winner and 3 and 5 yrs by Ghostzapper. The dam, a US stakes winner of 4 races at 3 yrs, is a half-sister to 5 winners. The second dam, Notjustanotherbird (by Proud Birdie), won 6 minor races in the USA at 3 and 4 yrs and is a half-sister to 3 winners. *"I just loved her as an individual; she's gorgeous and looked a stone cold runner to me. The pedigree is certainly nothing to shout about, but the sire has made it from nothing and now he's a fabulous stallion. His progeny seem to act on any surface and he's an unbelievable stallion for upgrading his mares. This is a strong filly and a 2-y-o type. Touch wood if everything goes well she'll run in May and I think she's a Royal Ascot filly".*

1191. QUARGENT (USA) ★★★★★
b.f. War Front – Naples Bay (Giant's Causeway). February 6. First foal. $585,000Y. Keeneland September. Marc Keller. The dam was a dual Grade 3 1m winner in the USA at 4 and 6 yrs and is a half-sister to the US dual Grade 1 winner and sire Medaglia D'Oro. The second dam, Cappucino Bay (by Bailjumper), was a US stakes winner of 5 races at 2 to 4 yrs and a half-sister to a stakes winner. *"A lovely filly, I'm delighted with her, she's got size and scope but will be a 2-y-o. I view her as a July type 2-y-o with the speed for six furlongs and she'll stay seven this year. She has a lot of quality and everything about her is positive. I know she cost an awful lot of money but I couldn't believe I got her for that amount. I thought she was a million dollar filly".*

1192. UNNAMED ★★★
b.br.f. Dragon Pulse – Emsiyah (Bernardini). April 23. Third foal. Sister to the fairly useful 2016 6.5f and 7f placed 2-y-o Firefright and half-sister to the quite useful dual 10f winner Absolute Zero (by Cape Cross). The dam ran twice unplaced and is a half-sister to one winner. The second dam, Menhoubah (by Dixieland Band), won the Group 1 Italian Oaks, was third in the 2-y-o Group 1 Moyglare Stud Stakes and is a half-sister to 2 winners. *"She's not here yet but I saw her last*

week and I'm really pleased with her, she's a lovely filly. I view her as a 2-y-o for August time and I'm looking forward to her coming. She's in pre-training in Ireland with a good friend of mine Jim Ryan who does a great job and we've had a lot of luck together".

1193. UNNAMED ★★★
ch.c. Jimmy Creed – Jacqui's Promise (Loup Sauvage). April 27. Seventh foal. $60,000 2-y-o. OBS. Kerri Radcliffe. Half-brother to 3 winners. The dam won 9 races from 2 to 6 yrs in the USA and is a half-sister to 5 winners including the US Grade 3 winner Corporate Jungle and the US stakes winner Followmyfootsteps. The second dam, Lady Carson (by Carson City), was a US stakes winner of 4 races at 3 and 4 yrs. "A good-striding horse, he breezed really well with a great stride on him. I think he's a 2-y-o type and he's in quarantine in America at the moment but I'd expect him to be here in May". The sire, a son of Distorted Humor, was a very fast horse in California .

1194. UNNAMED ★★★★
b.f. Scat Daddy – Me And Miss Jones (Smarty Jones). March 1. Fourth foal. $800,000 2-y-o. Fasig-Tipton. Kerri Radcliffe. Half-sister to a minor US 2-y-o winner by Yes It's True. The dam is an unraced half-sister to 4 winners including the US Grade 3 third Crossbow. The second dam, Forest Heiress (by Forest Wildcat), a US dual Grade 3 winner, was second in a Grade 2 6.5f event at 2 yrs and is a sister to the US Grade 1 6f winner Wildcat Heir and the US stakes winner Forest Heir. "I saw this filly at Niall Brennan's and watched her breeze in the first week in February. I loved her then and having bought La Chunga and Sander Camillo off Niall this filly took me the same way, so please God I'm right. She did a great breeze, looked fabulous and has a great stride on her. I thought she fitted the bill as a possible Royal Ascot 2-y-o. There's a long way to go before that comes to pass and I hope to get her over here soon, so I can race her by the end of May. She looks real fast".

1195. UNNAMED ★★★
b.f. More Than Ready – Music Score (Storm Cat). May 6. Third foal. $600,000 2-y-o. OBS. Kerri Radcliffe. Half-sister to the US dual

3-y-o winner My Music (by Mineshaft). The dam, placed at 3 yrs in the USA, is a half-sister to 4 winners including the champion 2-y-o and Group 1 7f Dewhurst Stakes winner Distant Music and the Group 3 placed New Orchid (dam of the Group 1 Haydock Sprint Cup winner African Rose). The second dam, Musicanti (by Nijinsky), a French 14.5f winner, is a half-sister to 9 winners including Vanlandingham, winner of the Washington D.C. International, the Jockey Club Gold Cup and the Suburban Handicap. "I've had a lot of luck with the sire and brought the first one of his to England, La Chunga, who won the Albany Stakes at Royal Ascot. This filly was a late foal but she did a fabulous breeze and we'd seen her at the farm beforehand and really liked her. She's in quarantine for now, but she's one to make a 2-y-o for July or after. She has size, scope and strength and we like her a lot".

1196. UNNAMED ★★★
b.br.f. Violence – Passion Du Coeur (Distorted Humor). April 22. Sixth foal. $360,000 2-y-o. OBS 2-y-o's. Fiona Shaw, agent for Marc Keller. Half-sister to 3 winners including the Japanese 2-y-o winner Old Bailey (by To Honor And Serve). The dam, a minor US 2-y-o winner, is a sister to the stakes winner and Grade 2 second Distorted Passion (herself the dam of a US Grade 2 winner) and a half-sister to one winner. The second dam, Arianna's Passion (by Unbridled's Song), a stakes winner of 7 races in the USA, is a half-sister to 8 winners including the US Grade 2 winner Warbling. "I loved the way this filly breezed, she looked like she had speed, stretched out and seems to have scope. A gorgeous looking filly, she'll definitely make a 2-y-o, I loved her and she went real fast". The sire, a son of Medaglia D'Oro, won a Grade 1 in the US as a 2-y-o over 8.5f.

1197. UNNAMED ★★★
b.c. Oasis Dream – Que Puntual (Contested Bid). January 16. Sixth foal. 200,000Y. Tattersalls October Book 1. Not sold. Half-brother to the useful 10f (at 2 yrs) to 11f and subsequent Australian Group 3 12f winner Oceanographer (by Sea The Stars), to the quite useful dual 12f winner Enthusiastic and the fair 10f and 12f winner Something

Graceful (both by Galileo). The dam won 5 races from 2 to 5 yrs in Argentina, Canada and the USA including the Canadian Grade 2 Nassau Stakes, was Grade 1 placed and is a half-sister to 5 winners including the Argentine Grade 1 placed Delivery Man. The second dam, Repartija (by Tempranero), a Grade 1 and Grade 2 winner in South America, is a half-sister to the Argentine Grade 1 winner Comisariato. *"He's an August type 2-y-o, well-balanced, a good mover and he's done everything in the right manner. It's a bit early to say anything more than that, but he's a nice, bonny, straightforward colt".*

1198. UNNAMED ★★★
br.c. Hat Trick – Rebuke (Carson City). May 14. Sixth foal. $80,000Y. Keeneland September. Willie Browne. Half-brother to 2 winners in the USA including the 2-y-o 6.5f winner River Dell (by Arch). The dam won 4 minor races a 3 and 4 yrs in the USA and is a half-sister to the US stakes winner Summer Cruise (dam of the US Grade 3 winner Sandbar) and the Group 1 Middle Park Stakes second Rebuttal. The second dam, Reboot (by Rubiano), won four minor races at 3 and 4 yrs in the USA. *"A big, scopey horse who is one for the last third of the season. He's a strong individual and a colt that I like. This is Hat Trick's first crop since he moved to Kentucky and this is a backward colt for now but he's a good mover".*

1199. UNNAMED ★★★
ch.f. Canford Cliffs – Spinning Lucy (Spinning World). February 26. Fourth foal. Half-sister to the 2017 3-y-o 12f debut winner Villette (by Sixties Icon). The dam, a 2-y-o listed 6f winner, is a half-sister to the 2-y-o listed 6f Bosra Sham Stakes winner Midris. The second dam, Dolara (by Dolphin Street), is an unraced half-sister to 4 winners including Idris, a winner of four Group 3 races in Ireland. *"A home-bred of Paul Roy's, the dam's been disappointing so far but this is the nicest one she's produced. She'll be one for the last third of the season over a mile".*

1200. UNNAMED ★★★
b.c. Union Rags – Stylish Storm (Storm Bird). April 1. Twelfth foal. $210,000 2-y-o. OBS. Fiona Shaw, agent for Marc Keller. Closely related to the US Grade 2 6.5f Amsterdam

Stakes winner Most Distinguished (by Dixie Union) and half-brother to 4 winners. The dam, a fair 1m placed maiden, is a half-sister to 3 winners including the US Grade 2 Chula Vista Handicap winner Radu Cool (dam of the Japanese stakes winner Victory Tetsuni). The second dam, Purify (by Fappiano), a minor US winner at 3 and 4 yrs, is a half-sister to 4 winners including the dual Group 3 placed Morning Devotion (the dam of Balanchine). *"I bought him recently at the breeze ups in America and he's still in quarantine there. The grandsire is Dixie Union and from his first crop I bought my good filly Sander Camillo. This is a good type, a good mover and he breezed really well. I saw him about a month before the sales and loved him. He should make a 2-y-o and might get to the racecourse by June. I feel pretty positive about him – he's a nice horse".* The sire, a son of Dixie Union, won the Grade 1 Champagne Stakes and the Belmont Stakes. Sire of two Grade 1 winners in his first crop in 2016.

AIDAN O'BRIEN

1201. ACTRESS
b.f. Declaration Of War – Nasty Storm (Gulch). January 12. Seventh foal. $250,000Y. Saratoga August. Cromwell Bloodstock. Half-sister to the Italian winner and 3 and 4 yrs A Touch Wild (by Touch Gold). The dam won 8 races including two Grade 2's and a Grade 3 in the USA from 2 to 4 yrs and is a half-sister to 9 winners. The second dam, A Stark Is Born (by Graustark), won 4 races in the USA and is a half-sister to 9 winners.

1202. AIRCRAFT CARRIER (IRE)
b.c. Declaration Of War – Strategy (Machiavellian). January 13. Seventh foal. Half-brother to the US Grade 3 winner and Grade 1 placed Justaroundmidnight, to the fairly useful 1m (at 2 yrs) and 11f winner Towerlands Park (both by Danehill Dancer), the useful Irish 2-y-o 5f winner and Group 3 6f Anglesey Stakes third Boris Grigoriev (by Excellent Air) and the fair 1m (at 2 yrs) and 10f winner Havelovewilltravel (by Holy Roman Emperor). The dam, a quite useful 10f and 11f winner, is a half-sister to 2 winners. The second dam, Island Story (by Shirley Heights), a quite useful 10f winner, is a half-sister to 6 winners.

1203. CLEMMIE (IRE)
b.f. Galileo – Meow (Storm Cat). February 14.
Third foal. Sister to the 2016 2-y-o Group 1 7f
Dewhurst Stakes and National Stakes winner
Churchill. The dam, a useful 2-y-o listed 5f
winner, was second in the Group 2 5f Queen
Mary Stakes and is a half-sister to 2 winners
including the Group 3 9f winner Aloof. The
second dam, Airwave (by Air Express), a
champion 2-y-o filly and winner of 6 races
including the Group 1 6f Cheveley Park
Stakes, is a half-sister to 6 winners.

1204. COULD IT BE LOVE (USA)
b.f. War Front – Playa Maya (Arch).
March 17. Seventh foal. Half-sister to 5
winners including the US Grade 1 winner and
champion 2-y-o Uncle Mo. The dam, a stakes-
placed 1m winner in the USA, is out of Dixie
Slippers (by Dixieland Band).

1205. DALI (USA)
b.c. Scat Daddy – Alegendinmyownmind
(Cape Cross). January 31. Third foal.
$525,000Y. Half-brother to the fair 6f
(including at 2 yrs) and 5f winner Absolute
Champion (by Henrythenavigator). The dam
is an unplaced half-sister to 6 minor winners.
The second dam, Midnight Line (by Kris
S), won the Grade 2 Long Island Handicap,
the Group 3 May Hill Stakes and the Group
3 Prestige Stakes and is a half-sister to 5
winners.

1206. MENDELSSOHN (USA)
b.c. Scat Daddy – Leslie's Lady (Tricky Creek).
May 17. Eleventh foal. $3,000,000Y.
Keeneland September. M V Magnier.
Half-brother to 5 winners including the
outstanding multiple US Grade 1 winner
Beholder (by Henny Hughes) and the US
Grade 1 Cash Call Futurity winner and Grade
1 Malibu Stakes second Into Mischief (by
Harlan's Holiday). The dam, a US stakes
winner of 5 races at 2 and 3 yrs, is a half-sister
to 2 winners. The second dam, Crystal Lady
(by Stop The Music), won two minor races at
3 yrs in the USA and is a half-sister to 2 stakes
winners.

1207. MIAMI BEACH
b.c. Invincible Spirit – Interchange (Montjeu).
April 30. Fifth foal. 350,000Y. Tattersalls

October Book 1. M V Magnier / Mayfair /
Peter & Ross Doyle. Half-brother to the fairly
useful 2016 2-y-o 6f winner Tiburtina (by
Holy Roman Emperor) and to the fairly useful
dual 7f winner Bronte (by Oasis Dream). The
dam, a quite useful 12f winner, is a half-sister
to 6 winners, two of them listed-placed. The
second dam, Key Change (by Darshaan), won
the Group 1 Yorkshire Oaks, was second in
the Group 1 Irish St Leger and is a half-sister
to 7 winners.

1208. MOUNT WELLINGTON
b.c. Invincible Spirit – Marvada (Elusive City).
February 10. Second foal. €475,000Y. Arqana
Deauville August. M V Magnier. Half-brother
to 2-y-o Curry (by Acclamation), unplaced in
two starts at 2 yrs in 2016. The dam, winner
of the Group 3 Brownstown Stakes and
second in the Group 3 Ballycorus Stakes, is a
half-sister to 4 winners including the listed-
placed Italian 1m (at 2 yrs) to 11f winner
of 6 races and useful broodmare Paint In
Green. The second dam, Theory Of Law (by
Generous), won 3 races at 3 yrs in France
and is a half-sister to the 2-y-o Group 1 Prix
Morny and triple US Grade 2 winner Charge
D'Affaires.

1209. SEAHENGE (USA)
b.c. Scat Daddy – Fools In Love (Not For Love).
April 10. Third foal. $750,000Y. Keeneland
September. M V Magnier. Half-brother to
the US 2-y-o winner and Grade 3 third Dania
Beach. The dam, a minor US stakes winner
of 5 races, is a sister to a stakes winner and
a half-sister to the US Grade 2 and Grade 3
winner International Star. The second dam,
Parlez (by French Deputy), a minor US winner
of 3 races at 3 and 4 yrs, is a half-sister to 7
winners.

1210. THREEANDFOURPENCE (USA)
b.c. War Front – Liscanna (Sadler's Wells).
May 12. Seventh foal. Brother to the 2016
2-y-o Group 1 6f Cheveley Park Stakes
winner Brave Anna and to the 2-y-o Grade
1 Breeders' Cup Juvenile Turf winner Hit It
A Bomb. The dam, an Irish 2-y-o Group 3 6f
Ballyogan Stakes winner, is a half-sister to the
Irish 7.5f (at 2 yrs) and Group 3 10f Kilternan
Stakes winner and dual Group 2 placed
The Bogberry. The second dam, Lahinch

(by Danehill Dancer), a useful listed 5f (at 2 yrs) and listed 6f winner, was second in the Group 2 Rockfel Stakes and is a half-sister to 7 winners including the smart 2-y-o 5f and subsequent US stakes winner Perugino Bay.

1211. US NAVY FLAG

b.br.c. War Front – Misty For Me (Galileo). February 6. Third foal. Brother to the 2016 2-y-o Group 2 6f Duchess Of Cambridge Stakes and Group 3 6f Grangecon Stakes winner Roly Poly and half-brother to the US Grade 3 1m winner Cover Song (by Fastnet Rock). The dam won the Moyglare Stud Stakes, Prix Marcel Boussac (both at 2 yrs), Irish 1,000 Guineas and Pretty Polly Stakes (all Group 1 events) and is a sister to the Group 1 Prix Marcel Boussac winner Ballydoyle and the useful 7f (at 2 yrs) and listed 9f winner and dual Group 3 placed Twirl. The second dam, Butterfly Cove (by Storm Cat), is an unraced sister to the Group 3 Irish 1,000 Guineas Trial winner Kamarinskaya and a half-sister to 5 winners including the champion 2-y-o colt Fasliyev.

1212. WAR ENSIGN

b.c. War Front – Ventura (IRE) (Spectrum). April 26. Tenth foal. Brother to Cedar Mountain (by Galileo), a winner from 11f to 14f here and subsequently a stakes winner and Grade 2 second in the USA and half-brother to Moonlight Cloud (by Invincible Spirit), a winner of six Group 1 events over 7f and 1m, to the French 2-y-o 1m winner Stars And Clouds (by Makfi) and the fair French 10f winner Lakuta (by Pivotal). The dam won twice over 1m at 3 yrs in Ireland and was listed-placed. The second dam, Wedding Bouquet (by Kings Lake), winner of the Group 3 C L Weld Park Stakes, Group 1 placed twice and a Grade 3 6.5f winner in the USA, is closely related to the Derby, Irish Derby and King George winner Generous.

1213. ZABRISKIE

b.c. Frankel – Moonlight's Box (Nureyev). April 22. Eleventh living foal. €750,000Y. Goffs Orby. BBA (Ire). Closely related to the French 2-y-o 5.5f winner and triple listed-placed Malicieuse (by Galileo) and half-brother to 6 winners including the Prix de l'Arc de Triomphe winner Bago (by Nashwan), the

Group 1 Prix d'Ispahan and Group 1 Prix du Moulin winner Maxios (by Monsun), the French 2-y-o listed 5f winner and Group 3 placed Beta (by Selkirk) and the French 7f (at 2 yrs) and 1m winner Makani (by A P Indy). The dam is an unraced half-sister to the Group 1 Prix Marcel Boussac winner Denebola and to the Group 3 winners Snake Mountain and Loving Kindness. The second dam, Coup de Genie (by Mr Prospector), won the Group 1 6f Prix Morny and the Group 1 7f Prix de la Salamandre and is a sister to the Machiavellian.

1214. UNNAMED

b.c. Galileo – Again (Danehill Dancer). February 4. Third foal. Brother to the 2-y-o listed 7.5f winner Indian Maharaja. The dam won the 2-y-o Group 1 Moyglare Stud Stakes and the Irish 1,000 Guineas and is closely related to 2 winners including the fairly useful 9f winner and Group 3 12f third Arkadina. The second dam, Cumbres (by Kahyasi), is an unraced half-sister to Montjeu.

1215. UNNAMED

ch.f. Galileo – Aleagueoftheirown (Danehill Dancer). March 16. Fifth foal. 2,100,000Y. Tattersalls October Book 1. M V Magnier / Mayfair / Peter & Ross Doyle. Sister to four winners including the Group 1 Falmouth Stakes, Group 1 Sun Chariot and Group 1 Matron Stakes winner Alice Springs, the fairly useful 12f winner and Group 2 12f Ribblesdale Stakes third Criteria and the useful Irish 2-y-o 7f winner and Group 3 Tyros Stakes third Kingston Jamaica. The dam, a useful Irish 9f winner, was listed-placed and is a half-sister to 2 winners. The second dam, Golden Coral (by Slew O'Gold), is an unplaced sister to the Group 1 Coronation Stakes winner Golden Opinion and a half-sister to 7 winners.

1216. UNNAMED

b.c. Galileo – Beauty Is Truth (Pivotal). May 3. Brother to the 2017 Group 3 7f Irish 1,000 Guineas Trial winner Hydrangea, to the 7f (at 2 yrs), Group 3 10f and Australian Group 2 12.5f winner The United States and the useful 2-y-o 9f winner Buonarotti and half-brother to the triple Group 3 6f winner and dual Group 1 placed Fire Lily (by Dansili). The dam, winner of the Group 2 5f Prix de Gros-Chene, is a half-sister to numerous winners including the French listed 9f winner Glorious Sight. The second dam, Zelda (by Caerleon), a French 6.5f winner, is closely related to the dam of the French 1,000 Guineas winner Valentine Waltz and a half-sister to the dual Group 1 winner Last Tycoon and the Group winners Astronef and The Perfect Life.

1217. UNNAMED
b.f. Camelot – Cherry Hinton (Green Desert). January 28. Closely related to the Group 1 Irish Oaks winner Bracelet and to the 2-y-o Group 2 7f Rockfel Stakes winner Wading and half-sister to the fairly useful listed-placed 5f winner Simply A Star (by Giant's Causeway). The dam, a useful maiden, was second in a Group 3 10f Blue Wind Stakes and third in a listed event over 9f in Ireland. She is closely related to the outstanding colt Sea The Stars (winner of the 2,000 Guineas, Derby, Prix de l'Arc de Triomphe etc) and a half-sister to 6 winners including the top-class dual Derby and King George VI winner and sire Galileo, and the dual Group 1 winner Black Sam Bellamy. The second dam, Urban Sea (by Miswaki), won the Group 1 Prix de l'Arc de Triomphe, is closely related to the 2,000 Guineas winner King's Best and a half-sister to numerous winners.

1218. UNNAMED
gr.c. Galileo – Dialafara (Anabaa). February 22. Fourth foal. Brother to the 2016 2-y-o Group 2 Beresford Stakes winner Capri and to the useful 2-y-o 7f winner and Group 3 Acomb Stakes fourth Jamaica. The dam, a minor 3-y-o winner in France, is a half-sister to 5 winners including the 2-y-o 7f winner and Group 3 9f Prix de Conde second Diaghan. The second dam, Diamilina (by Akarad), won the Group 2 Prix de Malleret and the Group 3 Prix de la Nonette and is a sister to Diamonixa (Group 3 Prix Cleopatre) and a half-sister to 7 winners including the Group 3 winner and triple Group 1 placed Diamond Green.

1219. UNNAMED
b.f. Galileo – Green Room (USA) (Theatrical). May 25. Ninth foal. €900,000Y. Goffs Orby. M V Magnier. Sister to the Group 1 Fillies' Mile winner Together Forever and half-sister to the

very smart Group 1 Prix Jean Prat and Group 2 7f Mill Reef Stakes and Group 2 Lennox Stakes winner and triple Group 1 placed Lord Shanakill (by Speightstown), the quite useful 7f and 1m winner Brannagh (by Hennessy) and the quite useful 10f winner Smartie Artie (by Smart Strike). The dam is an unraced half-sister to 5 winners including the US Group 1 winner Spanish Fern and to the unraced dam of the US Grade 1 winner Heatseeker. The second dam, Chain Fern (by Blushing Groom), is an unraced sister to the Irish 1,000 Guineas and Coronation Stakes winner Al Bahathri (dam of the dual Group 1 winner Haafhd).

1220. UNNAMED
b.c. Galileo – Gwynn (Darshaan). February 6. Ninth foal. Brother to the 1m (at 2 yrs) and listed 10f winner Kissed and closely related to the Group 1 Epsom Derby winner Pour Moi (by Montjeu), to the Group 3 1m Prix des Reservoirs and Group 3 10.5f Prix Penelope winner and Group 1 placed Gagnoa and the fairly useful French 2-y-o 1m winner Rendezvous (both by Sadler's Wells). The dam is an unraced half-sister to 2 minor winners. The second dam, Victoress (by Conquistador Cielo), won over 11f and is a half-sister to 7 winners including the dual Group 1 winner Awaasif (dam of the Oaks winner Snow Bride).

1221. UNNAMED
b.f. Galileo – Halfway To Heaven (Pivotal). May 18. Fifth foal. Sister to the 2016 2-y-o Group 1 Fillies' Mile winner Rhododendron and to the very useful Irish 7f (at 2 yrs) and Group 3 10f winner and Group 2 7f Futurity Stakes second Flying The Flag and to the quite useful 12f winner Just Gorgeous. The dam, winner of the Irish 1,000 Guineas, Nassau Stakes and Sun Chariot Stakes winner, is a half-sister to the Group 3 sprint winners Theann and Tickled Pink. The second dam, Cassandra Go (by Indian Ridge), a very smart winner of the Group 2 5f King's Stand Stakes, is a full or half-sister to 7 winners including the smart Group 3 6f Coventry Stakes winner and Irish 2,000 Guineas second Verglas.

1222. UNNAMED
b.c. Galileo – La Traviata (Johannesburg). May 21. Brother to the Group 1 Irish Oaks and Yorkshire Oaks winner Seventh Heaven

and half-brother to the 2-y-o Group 1 6f Middle Park Stakes winner Crusade (by Mr Greeley) and the useful 6f (at 2 yrs) and 1m winner and Group 2 6f Railway Stakes second Cristoforo Colombo (by Henrythenavigator). The dam won 3 races in the USA including the Grade 3 Victory Ride Stakes and is a half-sister to 2 minor winners. The second dam, Piedras Negras (by Unbridled), is an unraced half-sister to 7 winners.

1223. UNNAMED
b.f. Galileo – Lillie Langtry (Danehill Dancer). May 16. Fourth foal. Sister to the top-class multiple Group 1 winner at 2 and 3 yrs Minding and to the Group 3 1m Irish 1,00 Guineas Trial winner Kissed By Angels. The dam, a very smart winner of 5 races including the Group 1 1m Coronation Stakes and Group 1 1m Matron Stakes, is a half-sister to 2 winners including the very useful 3-y-o listed 1m winner and 2-y-o Group 3 6f Anglesey Stakes third Count Of Limonade. The second dam, Hoity Toity (Darshaan), is an unraced half-sister to 5 winners.

1224. UNNAMED
b.f. Fastnet Rock – Madonna Dell'orto (Montjeu). March 3. Third foal. 240,000Y. Tattersalls October Book 2. A Skiffington /M V Magnier / P Shanahan. Half-sister to the quite useful 7f and 7.5f winner of 3 races Viscount Barfield (by Raven's Pass). The dam, a fair 1m and 10f placed maiden, is a half-sister to 9 winners including the French 2,000 Guineas and Grade 1 Keeneland Turf Mile Stakes winner Landseer and the listed 10f winner and Group 1 Prince Of Wales's Stakes third Ikhtyar. The second dam, Sabria (by Miswaki), is an unraced half-sister to 5 winners.

1225. UNNAMED
b.f. War Front – Magical Dream (Galileo). February 23. First foal. The dam, a 2-y-o Group 3 7f C L Weld Park Stakes winner and 3-y-o Group 2 10f Blandford Stakes third, is a sister to the Prix Marcel Boussac (at 2 yrs) Breeders' Cup Turf and 'Arc' winner Found and the Group 3 12f Give Thanks Stakes winner Best In The World. The second dam, Red Evie (by Intikhab), won 9 races including

the Group 1 1m Matron Stakes and the Group 1 1m Lockinge Stakes.

1226. UNNAMED
b.c. Galileo – Massarra (Danehill). March 28. Brother to the 2016 2-y-o listed 6f winner Cuff, to the 2-y-o Group 3 7f Silver Flash Stakes winner Wonderfully, the Irish 2-y-o 7f winner and Group 1 St James's Palace Stakes third Mars and the fairly useful 2-y-o 7f winner Toscanelli and half-brother to 3 winners including the 2-y-o Group 1 1m Gran Criterium winner Nayarra (by Cape Cross). The dam, a useful listed 6f winner and second in the Group 2 Prix Robert Papin at 2 yrs, is a sister to one winner, closely related to the Group 1 6f Haydock Park Sprint Cup winner Invincible Spirit and a half-sister to the Group 3 winners Acts Of Grace and Sadian. The second dam, Rafha (by Kris), won the Group 1 10.5f Prix de Diane, the Group 3 Lingfield Oaks Trial and the Group 3 May Hill Stakes and is a half-sister to 9 winners.

1227. UNNAMED
b.c. Deep Impact – Maybe (IRE) (Galileo). January 26. Second foal. The dam, a 2-y-o Group 1 7f Moyglare Stud Stakes winner and third in the 1,000 Guineas, is a sister to one winner. The second dam, Sumora (by Danehill), a 2-y-o listed 5f St Hugh's Stakes winner, is a sister to the useful Irish 7f winner Fleeting Shadow and a half-sister to the Oaks and German Oaks winner Dancing Rain.

1228. UNNAMED
ch.c. Galileo – Moonlight Cloud (Invincible Spirit). February 25. First foal. The dam, a winner of six Group 1 events over 7f and 1m, is a sister to the US 14f stakes winner and Grade 2 second Cedar Mountain and a half-sister to 2 winners. The second dam, Ventura (IRE) (by Spectrum), won twice over 1m at 3 yrs in Ireland and was listed-placed.

1229. UNNAMED
b.c. Frankel – Moonstone (Dalakhani). April 11. Fifth foal. Closely related to the Group 3 Chester Vase winner US Army Ranger (by Galileo) and half-brother to the 7f (at 2 yrs) and Group 3 12f winner Words, to the useful 1m (at 2 yrs) and listed 11f winner

Nevis (both by Dansili) and the useful 2-y-o listed 6f winner Stubbs (by Danehill Dancer). The dam, winner of the Group 1 Irish Oaks, is closely related to the Breeders' Cup second L'Ancresse, to the Group 1 10f Prix Saint-Alary winner Cerulean Sky (herself dam of the Group 2 Doncaster Cup winner Honolulu) and the useful 10f winner and Group 3 placed Qaatef. The second dam, Solo de Lune (by Law Society), a French 11f winner, is a half-sister to 6 winners including the Grade 2 E P Taylor Stakes winner Truly A Dream and the French Group 2 winner Wareed.

1230. UNNAMED
ch.c. Frankel – Peeress (Pivotal). April 30. Fifth living foal. 1,300,000Y. Tattersalls October Book 1. M V Magnier / Mayfair / Peter & Ross Doyle. Half-brother to the useful listed 7f winner Ladyship (by Oasis Dream), to the quite useful 1m winner Enobled (by Dansili) and the quite useful 7f winner Aristocratic (by Exceed And Excel). The dam, a very smart winner of 7 races including the Group 1 1m Lockinge Stakes and the Group 1 1m Sun Chariot Stakes, is a full or half-sister to 6 winners. The second dam, Noble One (by Primo Dominie), a useful dual 5f winner, is a full or half-sister to 7 winners.

1231. UNNAMED
b.f. Galileo – Prudenzia (Dansili). March 13. Fifth foal. €1,400,000Y. Arqana Deauville August. Peter & Ross Doyle, M V Magnier, Mayfair Speculators. Sister to the minor French 2-y-o 9f winner Sinnamary, closely related to the Group 1 Irish Oaks winner Chicquita (by Montjeu) and half-sister to a minor winner in France by Invincible Spirit. The dam, winner of the listed Prix de la Seine, is a half-sister to 3 winners including the Group 3 Prix du Lutece winner Pacifique. The second dam, Platonic (by Zafonic), a minor winner in France, is a half-sister to 6 winners including the Group 2 Lancashire Oaks winner Pongee.

1232. UNNAMED
b.c. Declaration Of War – Queen Titi (Sadler's Wells). February 25. Half-brother to the smart 2-y-o Group 1 7f Dewhurst Stakes and 3-y-o Group 3 1m Desmond Stakes winner Beethoven (by Oratorio) and to the quite

useful Irish 9f winner King Of The Romans (by Holy Roman Emperor). The dam won the listed 1m Garnet Stakes and is a sister to the Irish Group 3 winner Psalm and a half-sister to 3 winners including the very useful 1m winner and subsequent US stakes-placed winner The Editor. The second dam, Litani River (by Irish River), was listed-placed and is a sister to the top-class broodmare Or Vision (dam of the Group 1 winners Dolphin Street, Insight and Saffron Walden) and a half-sister to the dam of the Group 1 winners Sequoyah and Listen.

1233. UNNAMED
b.c. Galileo – Red Evie (Intikhab). April 7. Fifth foal. Brother to the Prix Marcel Boussac (at 2 yrs) Breeders' Cup Turf and 'Arc' winner Found, to the 2-y-o Group 3 7f C L Weld Park Stakes winner and 3-y-o Group 2 10f Blandford Stakes third Magical Dream and the Group 3 12f Give Thanks Stakes winner Best In The World. The dam won 9 races including the Group 1 1m Matron Stakes and the Group 1 1m Lockinge Stakes. The second dam, Malafemmena (by Nordico), winner of a listed event in Italy and third in the Group 3 Prix du Calvados, is a half-sister to 7 winners including the smart Group 3 5f Prix du Bois and Group 3 6f Prix de Ris-Orangis winner Export Price.

1234. UNNAMED
b.f. Camelot – Rumored (Royal Academy). March 20. Eleventh foal. €320,000Y. Arqana Deauville August. Demi O'Byrne. Half-sister to 5 winners including the Group 1 Prix Morny and Group 1 Prix Jean-Luc Lagardere winner Dabirsim (by Hat Trick), the US stakes-placed winner Preferred Yield (by High Yield), the French 2-y-o 6f winner Pompilius (by Holy Roman Emperor) and the minor French 2-y-o 1m winner Zirgon (by New Approach). The dam is a placed half-sister to 8 winners out of the Italian Oaks winner and Group 1 Moyglare Stud Stakes second Bright Generation (by Rainbow Quest).

1235. UNNAMED
b.f. Galileo – Rumplestiltskin (Danehill). February 20. Sister to the 2-y-o Group 2 7f Debutante Stakes and Group 1 Yorkshire Oaks winner Tapestry, to the 2-y-o Group

3 1m winner John F Kennedy and the fairly useful Irish 2-y-o 7f winners Theatre and Why. The dam won the Group 1 Prix Marcel Boussac and the Group 1 Moyglare Stud Stakes and is a full or half-sister to 5 winners including the Group 2 second Tower Rock. The second dam, Monevassia (by Mr Prospector), is a placed sister to the triple Group 1 1m winner Kingmambo and to the smart Group 3 6f winner Miesque's Son and a half-sister to the high-class triple Group 1 winner East of the Moon.

1236. UNNAMED
ch.c. Galileo – Sant Elena (Efisio). April 30. Sixth foal. 420,000Y. Tattersalls October Book 1. M V Magnier / Mayfair / Peter & Ross Doyle. Half-brother to the 2-y-o Group 1 Prix Morny and Group 1 Middle Park Stakes winner Reckless Abandon (by Exchange Rate), to the fair 7f winner Free Rein (by Dansili) and the modest 8.5f winner of 6 races Jumbo Prado (by El Prado). The dam, a quite useful dual 6f winner (including at 2 yrs) and then listed-placed in Canada, is a half-sister to the US dual Grade 1 winner Ticker Tape and the Group 3 sprint winner Brando. The second dam, Argent Du Bois (by Silver Hawk), placed at 2 and 3 yrs in France, stayed 1m and is a half-sister to 9 winners including the Group 1 Racing Post Trophy winner Crowded House.

1237. UNNAMED
b.c. Galileo – Secret Garden (Danehill). February 1. Tenth foal. Brother to the Group 1 1m Criterium International (at 2 yrs) and Group 1 Irish 2,000 Guineas winner Roderic O'Connor to the useful 1m (at 2 yrs) and listed 10f winner Dazzling and the fairly useful 7f winner Monarch and half-brother to 3 winners including the fairly useful 2-y-o 6f winner and Group 3 6f Sirenia Stakes third Weatherstaff (by Elusive Quality) and the quite useful 2-y-o 1m winner Burnett (by Dynaformer). The dam, a listed 7f winner, is a full or half-sister to 4 winners. The second dam, Chalamont (by Kris), a quite useful 2-y-o dual 6f winner, is a half-sister to the dual Ascot Gold Cup winner Gildoran.

1238. UNNAMED
ch.c. Galileo – Simply Perfect (Danehill). January 26. Sixth foal. Brother to the very

useful listed 9f (at 2 yrs) and Group 3 10f Friarstown Stakes winner of 5 races Mekong River and to the fair 2-y-o 1m winner Really Lovely. The dam won the Group 1 Fillies' Mile and the Group 1 Falmouth Stakes and is a half-sister to 2 winners. The second dam, Hotelgenie Dot Com (by Selkirk), a 7f winner at 2 yrs, was second in the Group 1 7f Moyglare Stud Stakes and third in the Group 1 Fillies' Mile and is a half-sister to 4 winners including the Moyglare Stud Stakes and the Group 2 6f Lowther Stakes winner Bianca Nera.

1239. UNNAMED
b.c. War Front – Together (Galileo). March 7. Second foal. Half-brother to the useful Irish 9.5f winner and Group 2 second and subsequent US 8.5f winner Earring (by Dansili). The dam, 2-y-o Group 3 7f Silver Flash Stakes and subsequent US Grade 1 9f winner, was also Group 1 placed four times in Ireland and is a sister to the listed-placed winner Terrific and closely related to the 2-y-o Group 1 1m Criterium International winner and Irish Derby third Jan Vermeer. The second dam, Shadow Song (by Pennekamp), a French 3-y-o winner, is a half-sister to 7 winners including the Group 3 May Hill Stakes winner Midnight Air (dam of the Group 3 and subsequent US Grade 2 winner Midnight Line) and to the placed dam of the Group 1 Prix de l'Abbaye winner Imperial Beauty.

1240. UNNAMED
b.c. Frankel – Tyranny (Machiavellian). February 3. Ninth foal. 1,100,000Y. Tattersalls October Book 1. M V Magnier / Mayfair / Peter & Ross Doyle. Closely related to the fair Irish 1m winner Knocknagree (by Galileo) and half-brother to 5 winners including the 2-y-o Group 1 6f Phoenix Stakes winner Zoffany (by Dansili), the 2-y-o Group 3 6f Anglesey Stakes winner and Group 2 Gimcrack Stakes second Wilshire Boulevard (by Holy Roman Emperor), the fairly useful 7f to 10.5f winner That's Plenty (by Dr Fong) and the quite useful 6f winner Queen Of Mean (by Pivotal). The dam, a fairly useful dual 7f winner, is a half-sister to 5 winners including the listed 1m and US Grade 2 winner Spotlight. The second dam, Dust Dancer (by Suave Dancer), won the Group 3 Prix de la Nonette and is a

half-sister to 6 winners including the Group 3 Fred Darling Stakes winner Bulaxie (dam of the Group 2 winner Claxon).

1241. UNNAMED
b.c. War Front – Wading (Montjeu). January 29. Second foal. The dam won the 2-y-o Group 2 7f Rockfel Stakes and is a sister to the Group 1 Irish Oaks winner Bracelet. The second dam, Cherry Hinton (by Green Desert), a useful maiden, was second in the Group 3 10f Blue Wind Stakes and third in a listed event over 9f in Ireland. She is closely related to the outstanding colt Sea The Stars (winner of the 2,000 Guineas, Derby, Prix de l'Arc de Triomphe etc) and a half-sister to 6 winners including the top-class dual Derby and King George VI winner and sire Galileo, and the dual Group 1 winner Black Sam Bellamy.

1242. UNNAMED
b.br.f. War Front – Was (Galileo). January 12. First foal. The dam won the Oaks and was placed in three other Group 1's and is a sister to the useful French 2-y-o 7f winner and Group 3 placed Al Namaah and half-sister to the useful listed 7f winner Janood. The second dam, Alluring Park (by Green Desert), a 2-y-o 6f winner and dual listed-placed, is a sister to the Japanese stakes winner Shinko Forest and a half-sister to 6 winners including the champion 2-y-o and Epsom Derby winner and sire New Approach.

1243. UNNAMED
b.f. Galileo – You'resothrilling (Storm Cat). February 27. Sister to the smart 2016 2-y-o 7f winner and Group 3 third Taj Mahal, to the National Stakes (at 2 yrs), 2,000 Guineas, Irish 2,000 Guineas and St James's Palace Stakes winner Gleneagles, the Group 1 Irish 1,000 Guineas winner Marvellous and the 2-y-o Group 3 7f CL & MF Weld Park Stakes winner Coolmore,. The dam, winner of the Group 2 Cherry Hinton Stakes, is a sister to several winners and a half-sister to the multiple Group 1 winner Giant's Causeway. The second dam, Mariah's Storm (by Rahy), won 10 races in the USA including six Graded stakes events from 1m to 9f and is closely related to the Group 2 winner Panoramic.

JOSEPH O'BRIEN

1244. BRIDPORT (IRE)
b.c. High Chaparral – Enharmonic (E Dubai). March 11. First foal. 75,000Y. Tattersalls October Book 1. Joseph O'Brien. The dam ran once unplaced and is a half-sister to 4 winners including the champion 2-y-o and Group 1 7f Dewhurst Stakes winner Distant Music and the dams of the Group 1 Haydock Sprint Cup winner African Rose and the Group 2 winner Canticum. The second dam, Musicanti (by Nijinsky), a French 14.5f winner, is a half-sister to 9 winners including Vanlandingham, winner of the Washington D.C. International, the Jockey Club Gold Cup and the Suburban Handicap. (Lloyd Williams).

1245. DARKOLVA (IRE)
gr.c. Dark Angel – Penolva (Galileo). January 26. Fourth foal. €38,000Y. Tattersalls Ireland September. Joseph O'Brien. Brother to the modest 2016 6f and 7f placed maiden Alfie's Angel. The dam, a moderate 14f winner at 4 yrs, is a half-sister to 8 minor winners. The second dam, Jabali (by Shirley Heights), is an unplaced half-sister to 4 winners including the French Group 2 winner Dadarissime and the French Group 3 winner Floripedes (the dam of Montjeu). (RJB Bloodstock).

1246. DRAPERS GUILD
ch.c. Dutch Art – Euroceleb (Peintre Celebre). April 7. Sixth foal. €90,000Y. Goffs Orby. Joseph O'Brien. Half-brother to the quite useful 10.5f winner Resiliency (by Mastercraftsman), to the minor Italian winner at 2 and 3 yrs Zamiro (by Zamindar) and a minor 3-y-o winner in France by Poet's Voice. The dam, a modest 12f placed maiden, is a half-sister to 10 winners including the listed winners Bowmore and Eurostorm and to the dam of the US Grade 2 winner Pounced. The second dam, Eurobird (by Ela-Mana-Mou), winner of the Irish St Leger and the Blandford Stakes, is a half-sister to the French Derby winner Bikala and to the Irish Derby and French Derby winner Assert. (Calumet Farm).

1247. ESCAMILLO
b.c. Bated Breath – Smart Step (Montjeu). March 12. Second foal. 100,000Y. Tattersalls October Book 1. Not sold. Half-brother to Star Of Doha (by Lawman), unplaced in two

starts at 2 yrs in 2016. The dam, a modest 1m to 10f winner, is a half-sister to 4 winners including the listed-placed This Is The Day and Vanity Rules. The second dam, Miss Pinkerton (by Danehill), a useful 6f (at 2 yrs) and listed 1m winner, is a half-sister to 5 winners including the smart 7f (at 2 yrs) and 10f winner and Group 2 placed Grand Central. (Mrs M O'Brien, Partnership).

1248. FABULAE (IRE)
b.f. Fastnet Rock – Eccentricity (Kingmambo). May 17. Eighth foal. Half-sister to 5 winners including the useful 2-y-o 7.5f winner and Group 3 Irish 1,000 Guineas Trial second Radiantly (by Aussie Rules), the quite useful 12f winner Phosphorescence (by Sakhee) and two minor winners in France by Acclamation and Teofilo. The dam, placed once over 1m at 3 yrs from 2 starts, is a half-sister to 3 winners. The second dam, Shiva (by Hector Protector), winner of the Group 2 10.5f Tattersalls Gold Cup and the Group 3 10f Brigadier Gerard Stakes, is a sister to the Group 2 12f Prix Jean de Chaudenay winner Limnos and a half-sister to 8 winners. (Mrs M O'Brien, Partnership).

1249. HIGH MOUNTE
bl.c. Sea The Stars – Stairway To Glory (Kalanisi). May 7. Fifth foal. 90,000Y. Tattersalls October Book 1. Joseph O'Brien. Closely related to the quite useful 10f, 11f and hurdles winner Cape Of Glory (by Cape Cross) and half-brother to a minor winner in the UAE by Teofilo. The dam, a quite useful Irish 9f winner, is a half-sister to 3 winners including the Group 1 Irish Oaks and Group 1 Prix Vermeille winner Shawanda (herself dam of the St Leger winner Encke) and the dam of the dual Group 1 winner Shareta. The second dam, Shamawna (by Darshaan), won 2 races at 3 yrs in France, was third in the Group 3 Prix de Royaumont and is a half-sister to 2 winners. (Calumet Farm).

1250. INSTINCTIVELY (IRE)
b.f. Cape Cross – Star Express (Sadler's Wells). April 15. Eleventh foal. Half-sister to the quite useful 1m and 9f winner Dubai Sunshine (by Dubawi), to the fair 7f winner Desert Shine (by Green Desert), the modest 5f winner Star Twilight and the moderate 6f winner Haedi

(both by King's Best). The dam, a minor 12f winner, is a sister to the Group 3 Greenham Stakes winner Yalaietanee and a half-sister to the Group 3 Molecomb Stakes winner Sahara Star (dam of the Group 2 winner Land Of Dreams). The second dam, Vaigly Star (by Star Appeal), a smart sprint winner of 3 races and second in the Group 1 July Cup, is a half-sister to the high-class sprinter Vaigly Great. (Mrs A M O'Brien).

1251. LATROBE (IRE)
b.c. Camelot – Question Times (Shamardal). January 28. Third foal. 65,000Y. Tattersalls October Book 1. Joseph O'Brien. Half-brother to the useful Irish 2-y-o 6f winner and US dual Grade 2 placed Diamond Fields (by Fastnet Rock). The dam, a fairly useful listed 6f placed 2-y-o and 6f 3-y-o winner, is a half-sister to the smart Group 3 Sceptre Stakes winner and Group 1 6f Cheveley Park Stakes second Sunday Times. The second dam, Forever Times (by So Factual), a fairly useful 5f (at 2 yrs) to 7f winner, is half-sister to 9 winners including Welsh Emperor (Group 2 7f Hungerford Stakes) and the listed 5f winner Majestic Times. (Lloyd Williams).

1252. MAEWYN (IRE)
b.f. Dream Ahead – Centreofattention (Danehill). March 17. Sixth foal. €80,000Y. Goffs Orby. Not sold. Half-sister to the modest 12f winner Lifting Me Higher (by Sea The Stars). The dam, placed at 3 yrs in Australia, is a sister to the dual Group 1 winner Holy Roman Emperor and to the Australian Group 3 winner Milanova and a half-sister to 5 winners. The second dam, L'On Vite (by Secretariat), is an unraced sister to the Canadian 2-y-o Grade 1 winner Medaille d'Or and the Grade 2 winner D'Accord and a half-sister to the Grade 1 winners La Voyageuse and L'Enjoleur. (Mr Justin Casse).

1253. MEDAL OF HONOUR (IRE)
ch.c. Lope De Vega – Rich Gift (Cadeaux Genereux). May 11. Tenth foal. €340,000Y. Goffs Orby. Joseph O'Brien. Half-brother to 6 winners including the Italian triple listed 5f winner Black Mambazo (by Statue Of Liberty), the Italian 2-y-o listed 5.5f winner Diglett (by One Cool Cat) and the Italian 2-y-o winner and listed 5f second Way To Fly

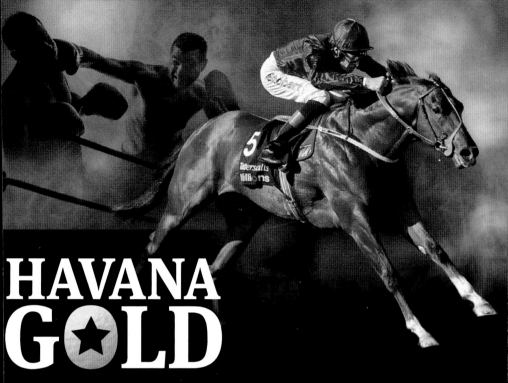

(by Footstepsinthesand). The dam, a quite useful 2-y-o 6f winner, was listed-placed and is a half-sister to 3 minor winners. The second dam, Deep Divide (by Nashwan), a fair 2-y-o 1m placed maiden, is a half-sister to 3 minor winners. (Mr Jeff Fager).

1254. NOW YOU'RE TALKING (IRE)
b.f. Zoffany – Granadilla (Zafonic). February 5. Ninth foal. €185,000Y. Arqana Deauville August. M V Magnier. Half-sister to 7 winners including the French 2-y-o listed 7f winner Aktoria (by Canford Cliffs) and the 2-y-o dual 5f winner Group 3 5.5f Prix d'Arenburg third Galaktea (by Statue Of Liberty). The dam, a fairly useful 7f winner, is a half-sister to 2 winners. The second dam, Epagris (by Zalazl), a useful 6f (at 2 yrs) and 7f listed winner, was second in the Group 3 Nell Gwyn Stakes and is a half-sister to 4 winners. (M V Magnier, Partnership).

1255. PAPARAZZI
b.c. Iffraaj – Columella (Kyllachy). March 17. Second foal. €140,000Y. Goffs Orby. Joseph O'Brien. Half-brother to the fair 2016 2-y-o 1m winner Cirencester (by Sea The Stars). The dam, a fair 2-y-o 5f and 7f winner, is a half-sister to 6 winners including the 2-y-o Group 2 Cherry Hinton Stakes winner Memory and the 2-y-o Group 3 Tyros Stakes winner Remember Alexander. The second dam, Nausicaa (by Diesis), a winner of 3 races in France and the USA over 7f and 1m, was Grade 3 placed and is a half-sister to 3 winners. (Calumet Farm).

1256. ROCKABILL
b.c. Fastnet Rock – Tebee (Selkirk). March 21. Fifth foal. 100,000Y. Tattersalls October Book 2. C McCormack. Half-brother to 4 winners including the fair 2016 2-y-o 9.5f winner Hertford Dancer (by Foxwedge), the quite useful 10f to 12f winner of 4 races Anglo Irish (by Dansili) and the quite useful 10f winner Sunpass (by Pivotal). The dam, a quite useful 10f winner, is a half-sister to 7 winners including the Group 1 Gran Criterium winner Nayarra, the St James's Place third Mars and the 2-y-o Group 3 7f winner Wonderfully. The second dam, Massarra (by Danehill), a listed 6f winner and second in the Group 2 Prix Robert Papin, is a sister

to Kodiac, closely related to the Group 1 Haydock Park Sprint Cup winner Invincible Spirit and a half-sister to the Group 3 winners Acts Of Grace and Sadian. (Demi O'Byrne Partnership).

1257. SEBASTIANO RICCI (IRE)
b.c. Lope De Vega – Dear Dream (Montjeu). February 13. First foal. 80,000Y. Tattersalls October Book 2. Joseph O'Brien. The dam, placed twice at 3 yrs in France, is a half-sister to 3 minor winners. The second dam, Darabela (by Desert King), won once at 3 yrs in France and is a half-brother to 8 winners including the dual Group 2 and dual Group 3 winner Darasim. (Mrs C Regalado-Gonzalez).

1258. SWANSON (IRE)
b.c. Camelot – Conniption (Danehill Dancer). April 10. Third foal. 70,000Y. Tattersalls October Book 1. Joseph O'Brien. The dam, a fairly useful 2-y-o 6f winner, subsequently won a minor race in the USA and is a half-sister to 3 minor winners. The second dam, Showbiz (by Sadler's Wells), a quite useful Irish listed-placed 2-y-o 7f winner, is a half-sister to two listed-placed winners. (Lloyd Williams).

1259. TRUE BLUE MOON (IRE)
gr.c. Holy Roman Emperor – Fancy Intense (Peintre Celebre). February 8. 19,000Y. Tattersalls Ireland September. Not sold. Half-brother to 6 winners including the quite useful 2-y-o 1m winner Kid Suitor (by Choisir), the 2-y-o 7f and subsequent Hong Kong winner Unscripted (by Oratorio), the fair 11f and 12f winner Refractor (by Refuse To Bend), the fair dual 1m winner Fancy Footsteps and to the modest Irish 7f winner Tahitian Pearl (both by Noverre). The dam is an unplaced half-sister to 7 winners including the Group 1 French 2,000 Guineas winner Tin Horse. The second dam, Joyeuse Entrée (by Kendor), won the Group 3 Prix d'Aumale. (Brian Dolan).

1260. UNNAMED
b.c. Camelot – Cinnamon Rose (Trempolino). February 26. Twelfth foal. €55,000Y. Goffs Orby. Joseph O'Brien. Half-brother to 9 winners including the Group 1 7f Moyglare Stud Stakes winner of 5 races Chelsea Rose (by Desert King), the Irish 6f (at 2 yrs) and listed 1m winner and US Grade 3 placed

European (by Great Commotion), the fairly useful 2-y-o 1m winner Hunters Creek (by Cape Cross), the quite useful 7f (at 2 yrs) and 12f winner Woodcutter (by Daylami) and the quite useful 2-y-o 7f winner Next Move (by Tiger Hill). The dam, an Irish 10f winner, is a half-sister to 6 winners including River Warden (Group 2 Prix Eugene Adam). The second dam, Sweet Simone (by Green Dancer), is a placed half-sister to 7 winners. (Mrs M O'Brien, Partnership).

1261. UNNAMED
b.c. Sea The Stars – Kitty Matcham (Rock Of Gibraltar). February 5. Fifth foal. €47,000Y. Goffs Orby. Not sold. Half-brother to the quite useful 1m and 10f winner Sam Missile (by Smart Strike), to the fair 6f to 1m winner Marciano and a minor winner in France (both by Pivotal). The dam, winner of the 2-y-o Group 2 7f Rockfel Stakes, is a sister to the Irish 10f winner and dual Group 1 placed Red Rock Canyon, closely related to the 2-y-o Group 1 7f Prix Jean Luc Lagardere winner Horatio Nelson and a half-sister to the UAE Group 2 winner and Group 1 Eclipse Stakes third Viscount Nelson. The second dam, Imagine (by Sadler's Wells), won the Irish 1,000 Guineas and the Epsom Oaks and is a half-sister to the top-class Generous. (Mrs Diane Nagle).

1262. UNNAMED
b.c. Fastnet Rock – Perihelion (Galileo). April 30. Sixth foal. Brother to the 2-y-o 7f Group 3 7f C.L & M.F Weld Park Stakes winner Qualify and to the very useful 2-y-o 7f winner and Group 2 second Shogun and closely related to the fairly useful 10f winner Satellite (by Danehill Dancer). The dam, a useful 14.7f winner and second in the Group 2 Park Hill Stakes, is a half-sister to 5 winners. The second dam, Medicosma (by The Minstrel), a quite useful 12f and 2m winner, is a half-sister to 5 winners including the Park Hill Stakes winner Eva Luna (the dam of four stakes winners) and the dam of the US Grade 1 winner Flute. (Mrs A M O'Brien Partnership).

JAMIE OSBORNE

1263. BILL CODY ★★★
b.c. Declaration Of War – Call This Cat (One Cool Cat). April 3. Third foal. €165,000Y. Goffs Orby. F Barberini. Half-brother to the fair 10f

and 11.5f winner Cat Royale (by Lilbourne Lad). The dam, a modest 5f placed maiden, is a half-sister to 6 winners including the US Grade 3 winner Pasar Silbano and the 2-y-o listed sprint winners Come To Heel and Gerfalcon. The second dam, Give A Whistle (by Mujadil), a dual 5f winner at 3 and 4 yrs, is a half-sister to one winner. (Michael Buckley & Michael Watt). *"Looking at his pedigree and how he looks he's got a chance of being a 2-y-o in the first half of the season. Obviously the One Cool Cat bit will either make him mad or quick! He seems straightforward in his head and we like him. He wasn't cheap, hopefully we can take a look at him pre-Ascot, he's a nice size for a 2-y-o and he goes OK".*

1264. DUKE OF ALBA ★★★
b.c. Lope De Vega – Royal Alchemist (Kingsinger). March 21. Fourth foal. 75,000Y. Tattersalls October Book 2. Barberini Bloodstock. Half-brother to the quite useful triple 5f winner from 3 to 5 yrs Newton's Law (by Lawman). The dam, a winner over 6f (at 2 yrs) and two listed events over 1m and 9f, was placed in four Group events and is a half-sister to 3 winners. The second dam, Pure Gold (by Dilum), a quite useful 7f winner, is a half-sister to 4 winners. (Michael Buckley & Ballylinch Stud). *"Being by Lope De Vega you'd expect him to be one for the second half of the season, but funnily enough he's showing us a little bit and I wouldn't be surprised if he came earlier. He's typical of the sire, with a plain head with a great physique".*

1265. GOOD KARMA ★★★★
b.c. Kodiac – Turuqaat (Fantastic Light). January 28. First foal. €100,000Y. Goffs Orby. F Barberini. The dam, a winner at 4 yrs in Greece, is a half-sister to 3 winners including the Irish 1,000 Guineas Trial winner Rawaaq. The second dam, Zaqrah (by Silver Hawk), unplaced in two starts, is a half-sister to the very smart Group 3 Greenham Stakes winner Muqbil and to the very useful Group 2 1m second Mostaqaleh. (Michael Buckley & Mrs K Burman). *"A stunning Kodiac, very laid-back and a beautiful mover. He ought to be out before Royal Ascot, the early signs are good and he was an early foal but his dam is by Fantastic Light which adds stamina. He's almost certainly not a five furlong horse but he's a quality Kodiac".*

1266. GOT TRUMPED ★★★
ch.c. Thewayyouare – Madam President
(Royal Applause). March 27. Fourth foal.
60,000Y. Tattersalls October Book 3.
Barberini Bloodstock. Half-brother to the
2-y-o Group 3 6f Round Tower Stakes winner
of 4 races and Group 2 Coventry Stakes
second Cappella Sansevero (by Showcasing).
The dam, a fair 10f winner, is a half-sister
to 4 winners including the Group 2 12f
Ribblesdale Stakes second Eldalil. The second
dam, White House (by Pursuit Of Love), a
quite useful 10f winner, is a half-sister to
11 winners including the middle-distance
Group winners Little Rock, Short Skirt and
Whitewater Affair (herself the dam of two
Japanese Group 1 winners). (Michael Buckley
& Chuck Esserman). *"Probably one of the
more forward we've had by Thewayyouare
and the dam has already bred one to finish
second in the Coventry. He's a bit plain, which
is typical of the sire, but he's a great mover
and quite tall but not weak. Hopefully he'll be
out pre-Ascot because the dam has already
shown she can do it".*

1267. LA LA LAND (IRE) ★★★
br.c. Dark Angel – Taraeff (Cape Cross).
February 20. Second foal. €165,000Y. Goffs
Orby. F Barberini. The dam is an unraced half-
sister to 2 minor winners and to the unraced
dam of the dual listed winner Absolutely
So. The second dam, Tarfshi (by Mtoto), a
winner of 5 races from 7f (at 2 yrs) to 10f
including the Group 2 Pretty Polly Stakes,
is a full or half-sister to 6 winners including
the champion 2-y-o filly and Cheveley Park
Stakes winner Embassy. (Michael Buckley &
Charles E Noell). *"A good-looking horse that
should come in the first half of the season.
He had one small hold-up which has meant
that I don't know quite as much as I should at
this stage. He's good-looking and a nice, solid
2-y-o with plenty of strength but with enough
scope for next year as well".*

1268. PREACHER MAN ★★★
b.c. Lope De Vega – Daniysha (Doyoun).
March 18. Eleventh foal. €70,000Y. Goffs
Orby. F Barberini. Half-brother to the smart
Irish Group 3 1m Amethyst Stakes winner
of 5 races Danak (by Pivotal), to the fair 9.5f
and 10f winner Escape Paradise (by Elusive
Pimpernel), the modest dual 1m winner

Jersey Brown (by Marju) and two winners
over hurdles by Bahhare and Alhaarth. The
dam, a fair 3-y-o 7f winner, is a half-sister to
a hurdles winner. The second dam, Danishara
(by Slew O'Gold), is an unraced half-sister to
4 winners out of the Group 1 Grand Criterium
winner Danishkada. (M.A.C Buckley). *"He's
quite nice and like my other Lope De Vega
2-y-o he's slightly more forward than you'd
expect. A very good-looking horse with plenty
of stamina in his pedigree, he's unlikely to
appear before the seven furlong/mile races
come along. He has a bit of quality and he's a
nice horse".*

1269. SECRET RIO ★★★
b.f. Rio De La Plata – Secret Marks (Echo Of
Light). February 3. First foal. €34,000Y. Arqana
Deauville August. F Barberini. The dam, a
minor winner in France, is a half-sister to
the German Group 2 winner Secret Melody
(herself the dam of two stakes winners in
France). The second dam, Secret Music (by
Dixieland Band), was unraced. (Cordero). *"
A strong filly that looks all 2-y-o, I don't have
much experience of the sire but she's pretty
straightforward and she's as wide as she's tall.
I'll be looking to get her going fairly early".*

1270. SICARIO ★★★
b.g. Thewayyouare – Blessed Beauty
(Alhaarth). April 23. First foal. €5,000Y.
Tattersalls Ireland September. F Barberini. The
dam is an unraced half-sister to 6 winners
including the useful Group 3 7f Prestige
Stakes winner Icicle. The second dam, Blessed
Honour (by Ahonoora), a quite useful 2-y-o 7f
winner, is a half-sister to 6 winners including
the smart Group 2 11.9f Great Voltigeur
Stakes winner Sacrament and to the unraced
dam of the Group 1 winner Chorist. (Michael
Buckley & Jamie Osborne). *"A real little
athlete, he may well be a bit quirky – hence
the gelding op – but he covers the ground
beautifully and looks like he goes well. We like
him and I think it was five grand well spent".*
TRAINERS' BARGAIN BUY

1271. VEGAS BOY (IRE) ★★★
ch.c. Society Rock – Consensus (Common
Grounds). April 30. Eighth foal. €48,000Y.
Goffs Orby. F Barberini. Half-brother to the
fairly useful 2-y-o 5f winner and US Grade 3
1m third Cloneylass (by Verglas), to the quite

useful 6f (including at 2 yrs) to 1m winner of 11 races Al's Memory (by Red Clubs), the fair 2-y-o 5f winner Lucy Parsons (by Thousand Words) and the modest dual 6f winner at 2 and 3 yrs Harmony Bay (by Fast Company). The dam, a fairly useful 6f (at 2 yrs) and 5f winner of 4 races, is a half-sister to 6 winners. The second dam, Kilbride Lass (Lahib), is an unraced half-sister to 4 winners including the triple Grade 1 winner Phoenix Reach. *"He's strong, quite forward, looks quite quick and he's bred that way too. One of the more forward ones, he could easily be our first runner and he's showing a nice bit of pace, so he'll be pre-Ascot".*

1272. ZOFFY (IRE) ★★★★
b.f. Zoffany – Saldenaera (Areion). April 17. Third foal. 95,000Y. Tattersalls October Book 2. Barberini Bloodstock. Half-sister to the fair 2-y-o dual 5f winner Strands Of Silk (by Kodiac). The dam, a minor 3-y-o winner in Germany, is a sister to 2 winners including the German listed winner Saldenart and a half-sister to 4 winners. The second dam, Saldengeste (by Be My Guest), a minor dual 3-y-o winner in Germany, is a half-sister to 9 winners. (M V Magnier, Mrs P Shanahan, Michael Buckley). *"A beautiful filly, I really like her and I've been quite easy on her but she's just starting to show the right signs. I'd be very hopeful that she'll come the right side of Ascot and she covers the ground beautifully. A filly with a lot of quality".*

1273. UNNAMED ★★★
b.c. Pivotal – Aiming (Highest Honor). April 17. Seventh foal. 120,000 foal. Tattersalls December. Kingwood Stud. Brother to the very useful listed 1m winner and Group 1 10f Prix Jean Romanet second Princess Loulou and half-brother to 4 winners including the useful 6f (at 2 yrs) to 9f winner of 5 races and listed-placed Easy Option (by Danehill Dancer), the quite useful 2-y-o 7f winner La Adelita (by Anabaa) and the fair 2-y-o 7f winner Conducting (by Oratorio). The dam was placed over 7f (at 2 yrs) and 1m and is a half-sister to 5 winners including the very smart dual listed 5f winner Watching. The second dam, Sweeping (by Indian King), a useful 2-y-o 6f winner, is a half-sister to 10 winners. (Kingswood Stud). *"He came in quite*

late and he's a big, raw horse with quality, but I wouldn't have too much of an angle on him yet".*

1274. UNNAMED ★★★
b.f. Holy Roman Emperor – Breeze Of July (Cape Cross). March 30. Second foal. €60,000Y. Goffs Orby. Not sold. Half-sister to the fair 1m winner Caution (by Paco Boy). The dam is an unraced half-sister to 4 winners including the Group 3 10f Winter Hill Stakes winner Distant Memories and the listed winners Mutatis Mutandis and Mohedian Lady. The second dam, Amathia (by Darshaan), a listed 9f winner in France and Group 3 placed twice, is a half-sister to 9 winners including the 1,000 Guineas third Hathrah and the smart Group 2 12f Premio Ellington winner Ivan Luis. (Antoinette Kavanagh). *"A neat filly and a typical Holy Roman in that she doesn't have a lot of size to her, but she's as strong as an ox and will almost certainly come pre-Ascot. We're just starting fast work so it's too early to say, but she's got the physique of an early 2-y-o".*

1275. UNNAMED ★★★
b.f. Acclamation – Chincoteague (Daylami). April 22. Fourth foal. 20,000Y. Tattersalls October Book 2. Barberini Bloodstock. Half-sister to the fair 2-y-o 9f winner Maftoon (by Dark Angel). The dam, a modest 10f to 13f placed maiden, is a half-sister to 3 winners including the Group 2 Hardwicke Stakes and Group 3 Earl Of Sefton Stakes winner and triple Group 1 placed Indian Creek. The second dam, Blue Water (by Bering), won 5 races in France including the listed 12f Prix des Tourelles, was third in the Group 3 10.5f Prix de Flore and is a half-sister to 3 winners. *"A typical Acclamation, she's a little bit lengthy but moves beautifully. She shouldn't take too long, although she's out of a Daylami mare which might slow things down a bit. A nice filly with a bit of quality".*

1276. UNNAMED ★★★
b.f. Dream Ahead – Crimson Lass (Dubawi). April 22. Fourth foal. €30,000Y. Goffs Orby. F Barberini. Half-sister to the Irish 2-y-o 5f winner Dancing Zafeen (by Zafeen). The dam, placed at 3 yrs in Germany, is a half-sister to 5 winners including the dual listed 10f

winner Foodbroker Fancy (the dam of 3 stakes winners) and the listed winner Femme Fatale. The second dam, Red Rita (by Kefaah), a fairly useful 4-y-o 6f winner and second in the Cherry Hinton Stakes and the Princess Margaret Stakes, is a half-sister to 3 minor winners. *"The Dream Ahead's I've had before have been rangy-looking but this filly looks more like a Dubawi. She's quite neat, a little bit plain but she gets from A to B quite well and she goes OK. Again, she'll be ready pre-Ascot although I wouldn't go there unless I felt we had a realistic shot of at least getting placed. As with a lot of trainers at this time of the year, although you're not rushing them it's in your mind that you don't want to have an Ascot 2-y-o sitting in its stable".*

1277. UNNAMED ★★★

b.f. Henrythenavigator – Discophilia (Teofilo). February 21. Second foal. €24,000Y. Tattersalls Ireland September. F Barberini. Half-sister to the 2016 Irish 2-y-o 7f winner, from two starts, Escape Clause (by Lawman). The dam, placed once at 3 yrs in France, is a half-sister to 5 winners including the listed winner Etesaal. The second dam, Electric Society (by Law Society), won 6 races including the Grade 2 10f New York Handicap and the Grade 2 9f Diana Handicap and is a half-sister to 6 winners including the Australian Group 3 winner Bourbon Boy. (Michael Buckley). *"She's a strong filly that's done particularly well over the winter and could easily be a 2-y-o for the first half of the season".*

1278. UNNAMED ★★★★

b.f. Camelot – Fanditha (Danehill Dancer). February 9. Second foal. 130,000Y. Tattersalls October Book 1. Not sold. Half-sister to the fair 2016 2-y-o 6f and 7f winner Cuppatea (by Canford Cliffs). The dam, a quite useful 7f (at 2 yrs) to 11f winner of 4 races, was listed-placed over 10f and is a half-sister to 5 winners. The second dam, Splendid (by Mujtahid), placed third once over 6f at 2 yrs, is a half-sister to 3 winners including the very useful 1m (at 2 yrs) and 12f winner Peking Opera. (Kingwood Stud). *"A beautiful moving filly, probably not as backward as you might expect from a Camelot. It wouldn't shock me if she came to hand in the first half of the season. She takes her work well, she's a stunning filly and a great mover".*

1279. UNNAMED ★★

b.c. Showcasing – Molly Mello (Big Shuffle). March 30. Eighth foal. 50,000Y. Tattersalls October Book 1. Not sold. Half-brother to the quite useful 6f to 8.5f winner of 5 races Serenity Sea (by Excellent Art), to the fair 1m to 12f and hurdles winner Brunston (by High Chaparral) and the modest 7f winner Molly Ann (by Medicean). The dam, a listed-placed winner of 4 races from 2 to 4 yrs, is a half-sister to one winner. The second dam, Manitoba (by Surumu), won 2 races at 2 and 3 yrs in Germany and is a half-sister to 2 winners. (Mr M Kurt). *"He's not typical of the sire because he's a lot bigger and stronger than a lot of the Showcasing's I've seen. So there's a lot more of Big Shuffle about him – a sort of German coarseness. But he has a lot of quality, he's a good mover and is one that'll come in the second half of the season".*

1280. UNNAMED ★★★

br.c. Mayson – Scrupulous (Dansili). April 22. Fifth foal. €26,000Y. Goffs Sportsmans. Fourth foal. F Barberini. The dam, a fair 9f winner, is a half-sister to 9 winners including the very useful 6f and 7f (at 2 yrs) and subsequent US stakes winner Steelaninch. The second dam, Mrs Gray (by Red Sunset), a modest 2-y-o 5f winner, is a full or half-sister to 11 winners here and abroad including the German 2-y-o Group 2 6f winner Amigo Sucio and the dam of the Group 2 Prix Robert Papin winner Rolly Polly. *"A strong-looking 2-y-o, he ought to be one of the early runners. The dam's bred nothing but she's basically been to jump stallions and this is the first time she's had a bit of speed. He goes OK and has the look of an early 2-y-o, so he shouldn't be too long".*

1281. UNNAMED ★★

b.c. Oasis Dream – Shaleela (Galileo). March 26. Third foal. €120,000Y. Goffs Orby. F Barberini. The dam is an unraced half-sister to 4 winners including the German Group 2 winner Giant Sandman and the dam of Group 1 Prix de l'Opera winner Shalanaya. The second dam, Sharamana (by Darshaan), winner of the Group 3 12f Prix Minerve, is a half-sister to Shergar. (Michael Buckley & Michael Watt). *"There's plenty of stamina on the dam's side, he's been through a few stages over the winter but he's just starting to pick up well. It's more than likely that he'll not be ready to appear until the second half of the season, but he has a lot of quality".*

1282. UNNAMED ★★
b.c. Pivotal – Side Of Paradise (Sadler's Wells). January 30. Ninth foal. 100,000Y. Tattersalls October Book 1. Barberini Bloodstock. Brother to the Group 1 Coronation Stakes and Group 1 Prix Jacques le Marois winner Immortal Verse and to the French 1m winner Go Lovely Rose and half-brother to 2 winners including the useful 6f (at 2 yrs) to 1m winner Keep Discovering (by Oasis Dream). The dam, a French listed 1m winner and third in the Group 3 10.5f Prix Fille de'Air, is a full or half-sister to 10 winners including Last Tycoon (Breeders' Cup Mile, King's Stand Stakes and William Hill Sprint Championship) and the Group winners Astronef and Perfect Life. The second dam, Mill Princess (by Mill Reef), a French 10f winner, is a half-sister to the Irish Derby winner Irish Ball and to the dam of the classic winners Assert, Bikala and Eurobird. (Mr Charles E Noell). *"A colt with a proper pedigree, not the most beautiful horse in the world but he's a bit like his sire in that respect. He gets from A to B alright and is probably going to want a bit of time. One for the second half of the season, he's got the pedigree of a good horse and hopefully the patience will be rewarded".*

1283. UNNAMED ★★★
b.c. Poet's Voice – Silicon Star (Starborough). March 16. Eighth foal. €48,000Y. Goffs Orby. Not sold. Half-brother to the quite useful 2016 2-y-o 5f and 6f winner Sterling Silva (by Sakhee's Secret), to the fairly useful listed-placed 6f and 7f winner Sacha Park (by Iffraaj), the quite useful 2-y-o 1m winner Pythius (by Lord Shanakill), the minor French winner of 4 races (including at 2 yrs) Silicone Tune (by Green Tune) and the minor French 2-y-o winner Lukes Well (by Shirocco). The dam is an unplaced half-sister to 10 winners including Latona (Group 3 Prix de Saint-Georges). The second dam, Silicon Lady (by Mille Balles), won the Group 3 Prix Thomas Bryon and is a half-sister to 14 winners including the dual Group 3 winner Silicon Bavaria. (Antoinette Kavanagh). *"A lovely,*

quality horse that shouldn't take too long. He's very athletic, strong and well-grown, hasn't been in that long but from what we've seen of him he goes nicely. There's every chance he'll get there in the first half of the year".

1284. UNNAMED ★★★★
b.c. Holy Roman Emperor – Sweet Dreams Baby (Montjeu). March 16. Third foal. €62,000Y. Goffs Orby. F Barberini. Half-brother to the fairly useful 7f (at 2 yrs) to 8.5f winner Roxy Star. The dam is an unraced half-sister to 3 minor winners. The second dam, Shahtoush (by Alzao), won the Oaks and was second in the 1,000 Guineas and is a half-sister to 10 winners including the Group 2 10f Pretty Polly Stakes winner and Epsom Oaks second Game Plan. *"This horse has done particularly well, he was a little bit raw looking as a yearling but he's turned himself inside out and he's a beauty now. A beautiful mover, he's got more scope than a lot of the Holy Roman's, so I like him. I think the dam's second foal has recently won in Japan".*

1285. UNNAMED ★★★
b.c. Oasis Dream – Tavy (Pivotal). January 27. Fourth foal. 150,000Y. Tattersalls October Book 1. Not sold. Half-brother to the fair but lightly-raced 2-y-o 1m winners Nadder (by Notnowcato) and Wylye (by Dalakhani). The dam is an unraced half-sister to 4 winners including the Group 3 Prix du Palais Royal winner Frenchman's Bay. The second dam, River Fantasy (by Irish River), is an unplaced half-sister to 5 winners including the Group 3 Norfolk Stakes winner Romeo Romani. *"A beautiful horse. I've yet to make a decision as to how soon he'll come, but he'll tell me. He's got a great physique and I'd be hopeful for him because he's got the look of a good horse".*

JOHN OXX

1286. DANSEUSE D'ETOILE ★★★
b.f. Pivotal – Walk In Beauty (Shamardal). March 5. Second foal. The dam, placed once over 6f in France, is a half-sister to 8 winners including the 2-y-o Group 2 5.5f Prix Robert Papin winner Zipping and the French Group 3 winner Nipping. The second dam, Zelda (by Caerleon), won once over 6.5f in France at 3 yrs, is closely related to the dam of the

French 1,000 Guineas winner Valentine Waltz and the US Grade 1 winner Sense Of Style and a half-sister to the dual Group 1 winner Last Tycoon. *"A good-looking, athletic filly, she moves very nicely but I haven't had her long. Hopefully a 2-y-o for the second half of the year, she's got a nice pedigree and she's a nice individual so you'd have to be hopeful for her".*

1287. FRIDTJOF NANSEN ★★★
b.g. Kyllachy – Thankful (Diesis). April 12. Fifth foal. 100,000Y. Tattersalls October Book 2. Sackville/Donald. Half-brother to the useful 2-y-o listed-placed 7f winner Morning Post (by Acclamation) and to the fair 7f winner Munfarrid (by Showcasing). The dam is an unplaced half-sister to the listed-placed winner Jo'burg. The second dam, La Martina (by Atraf), a useful 7f winner at 2 yrs in Italy and subsequently a dual stakes winner in the USA, is a half-sister to 5 winners. *"A very good-looking horse, a gelding now, he was a nice yearling and cost a bit of money. He's very fluent, big and strong with a very good action and a nice temperament. We might see him in mid-season and he's starting to work a little bit now, so I'm happy with him".*

1288. IMPOSSIBILITY (IRE) ★★★
b.f. Born To Sea – Chaussons (Indian Ridge). March 21. Fifth foal. €23,000 foal. Goffs November. JBR Global. The dam is an unplaced half-sister to 6 winners including the high-class Irish Oaks, Yorkshire Oaks and Prix de l'Opera winner Petrushka. The second dam, Ballet Shoes (by Ela-Mana-Mou), a fair 3-y-o dual 5f winner, is a half-sister to 5 winners including the Irish 2,000 Guineas and Dubai Champion Stakes winner Spectrum. *"A sharp sort of filly with a nice pedigree and she's starting to do some work. I could see her being out in late spring or early summer and she should show something this year".*

1289. ISAAC WONDER (IRE) ★★★
b.g. Born To Sea – Najaaba (Bahhare). March 31. Tenth foal. Half-brother to the fair 5f winner Dorothy Parker (by Mujadil), to the Scandinavian 2-y-o 6f winner Miss Clodia (by Clodovil) and a 3-y-o winner in Switzerland. The dam, a quite useful 7f to 9.5f winner of 7 races, is a half-sister to 7 winners. The

second dam, Ashbilya (by Nureyev), is an unraced sister to the 2-y-o 7f winner, Group 1 Dewhurst Stakes third and Grade 1 9f Hollywood Derby third Zentsov Street. *"He's a nice horse that would like seven furlongs to start with. A very fluent mover and quite attractive, he's a long striding horse so he'd need a bit of distance but I like him and he should show us something at two. He's quite forward but we'll just have to wait until the seven furlong races start".*

1290. MY SNOWDROP ★★★
b.f. Lilbourne Lad – Khatela (Shernazar). January 31. Tenth foal. €18,000 foal. Goffs November. L Winters. Sister to the fair 2-y-o 6f winner Forgotten Wish and half-sister to 7 winners including the 2-y-o 7.2f and listed 1m Heron Stakes winner and Group 3 9f Prix de Conde second Massive, the quite useful 2m and hurdles winner Busted Tycoon (both by Marju), the French 12f listed-placed Irish Kind (by Cape Cross), the modest 15f winner Khayar (by Refuse To Bend) and the modest 2-y-o 9f winner Khandala (by Soviet Star). The dam won over 1m and 9f in Ireland and is a half-sister to 4 minor winners. The second dam, Khatima (by Relko), won at 3 yrs and is a half-sister to the French triple listed winner Kaldoun. *"A full-sister to a 2-y-o that won at Goodwood, she's well-made, quite nice and hasn't done anything too serious yet but she'll be a 2-y-o for the mid-season onwards. She looks forward enough but was broken a bit late which holds us up a bit, but apart from that she should be able to do something at two".*

1291. SINE PARI ★★★
b.c. Swiss Spirit – Rhagori Aur (Exceed And Excel). April 3. First foal. €40,000Y. Tattersalls Ireland September. John Oxx. The dam, a fair triple 5f winner, is a half-sister to one minor winner. The second dam, Aberdovey (by Mister Baileys), a fair 6f (at 2 yrs) and 1m winner, is a half-sister to 6 winners including the dual 10f and subsequent US stakes winner and Grade 2 placed Solva. *"He's had a little setback which has slowed us down a bit but he's a nice, sharp, racy colt and I like him. As soon as he's ok we should be able to press on and he looks like a 2-y-o winner".*

1292. WAIKUKU (IRE) ★★★★
b.c. Harbour Watch – London Plane (Danehill Dancer). March 20. First foal. €33,000Y. Tattersalls Ireland September. John Oxx. The dam, a fair 7f placed maiden, is a sister to the 2-y-o dual 7f winner and Group 2 1m Royal Lodge Stakes third Al Waab, The second dam, Aunt Julia (by In The Wings), a useful 10f winner, was listed placed three times and is a half-sister to 2 winners. *"A very nice horse but like my other Harbour Watch he'll take a bit of time. A well-grown horse, I like him, he has a good temperament and is a very fluent mover. He takes everything in his stride and I think he's a nice colt".*

1293. WILHELM TELL ★★★★
b.c. Swiss Spirit – Speed Date (Sakhee's Secret). January 31. First foal. 95,000Y. Tattersalls October Book 2. Sackville/Donald. The dam, a modest maiden, was placed fourth twice over 6f at 2 and 3 yrs and is a half-sister to 6 winners including the very useful 5f and listed 6f Cammidge Trophy winner of 6 races from 2 to 4 yrs Aahayson and the useful 5f and 6f winner of 6 races (including a UAE Group 3) Take Ten, See You Later (by Emarati), a dual 5f winner and listed-placed 3 times, is a half-sister to the 2-y-o Group 3 Horris Hill Stakes winner Peak To Creek and the dual listed winner Ripples Maid. *"He's always been a nice colt, he's fairly sharp looking and bred for speed so should be out in mid-season, I have two by Swiss Spirit and they both look sharp".*

1294. UNNAMED ★★★
ch.c. Sea The Stars – History Note (Azamour). February 13. First foal. The dam, a very useful Irish 2-y-o 7f winner, was third in the Group 3 1,000 Guineas Trial and is a sister to 2 winners including the fairly useful dual 1m winner Stepwise and a half-sister to 2 winners. The second dam, Cadence (by Cadeaux Genereux), was a quite useful Irish 9f winner. *"A very nice looking colt and a very fluent mover. He's just been cantering through the winter and he'll take a bit of time like all the sire's stock. We'll be looking forward to him in the autumn".*

1295. UNNAMED ★★★
b.f. Sea The Stars – Loreto (Holy Roman Emperor). March 7. Second foal. €100,000Y. Goffs Orby. Not sold. Half-sister to the very useful 2016 Irish 2-y-o 1m winner Brutal (by Pivotal). The dam, a quite useful dual 1m winner, is a half-sister to 6 winners including the Group 3 winners Cabaret and Drumfire and, the Group 2 6f Gimcrack Stakes second and subsequent Hong Kong stakes winner Ho Choi. The second dam, Witch Of Fife (by Lear Fan), a fairly useful 2-y-o 6f and 7f winner, was listed-placed and is a half-sister to 6 winners. *"A similar type to the previous Sea the Stars 2-y-o we just talked about, she's a lovely, fluent mover. She's growing a bit at the moment so we won't be expecting too much too early with her. We'll be aiming her for a couple of runs in the autumn".*

1296. UNNAMED ★★★★
b.f. Mastercraftsman – Red Feather (Marju). January 30. Eighth foal. €100,000Y. Arqana Deauville August. BBA (Ire). Half-sister to the very useful listed 6f and listed 7f winner and dual Group 3 placed Rose Bonheur (by Danehill Dancer) and to the 2-y-o 6f winner and Group 3 7f Silver Flash Stakes third Roseraie (by Lawman). The dam, a Group 3 1m winner in Ireland, was second in the Group 1 Moyglare Stud Stakes and is a half-sister to the smart dual 10f winner and dual Group 3 12f placed Frankies Dream. The second dam, Galyph (by Lyphard), a modest Irish 10f winner at 4 yrs, is a half-sister to 2 minor winners. *"She's quite a sharp-looking 2-y-o type and it's a 2-y-o family as well. I haven't had her that long, but she's definitely precocious and wants to get on with it. A good-looking filly that should show what she can do at two, probably in mid-season".*

1297. UNNAMED ★★★
b.f. Lord Shanakill – Spirit Watch (Invincible Spirit). February 24. Third foal. Sister to the quite useful dual 7f winner at 2 and 3 yrs Grand Spirit. The dam, placed once over 10f in Ireland, is a half-sister to 5 winners. The second dam, Watch The Clock (by Mtoto), won twice and was third in the listed Sweet Solera Stakes and is a half-sister to 6 winners. *"She's a sharp sort, a good-looker and a good mover. As an individual she's fine, she's done a couple of easy bits of work and goes well. Quite forward-going, hopefully she'll be out*

around June time and she's a full sibling to a 2-y-o winner which is good to see".

1298. UNNAMED ★★★
b.f. Invincible Spirit – What Style (Teofilo). April 5. First foal. The dam, a useful Irish 2-y-o 7f winner, was second in the Group 3 1,000 Guineas Trial and is a sister to one winner and a half-sister to another. The second dam, Out Of Time (by Anabaa), is an unraced half-sister to 4 winners including the Group 2 placed Drill Sergeant and Nobilis. *"She's a good-looking filly and I trained the dam who was stakes-placed. A typical Invincible Spirit in shape and type, but because of a small setback at the farm she was delayed coming in, so she won't be as early as the pedigree might suggest".*

HUGO PALMER
1299. ALBA POWER (IRE) ★★★★ ♠
b.c. Fast Company – Shehila (Zamindar). March 7. First foal. £110,000Y. Goffs UK Premier (Doncaster). Amanda Skiffington. The dam is an unplaced half-sister to 3 minor winners. The second dam, Shehira (by Sendawar), a fairly useful Irish 1m winner, is a half-sister to 5 winners including the Group 1 7f Prix Jean-Luc Lagardere third Shediak. (Carmichael Jennings). *"A smart, speedy colt. He looked like a Royal Ascot type when we bought him at Doncaster and having done a couple of pieces of work he still does. We haven't pushed him seriously yet but I'm impressed with what I'm seeing. He looks like a 2-y-o for the whole year and probably a 3-y-o sprinter next year as well. He's a good size, strong, forward-going and I've found nothing I dislike yet".*

1300. ALPINE PEAK (USA) ★★★
gr.c. Mizzen Mast – Affectionately (Galileo). January 29. Second foal. Half-brother to Asaas (by Distorted Humor), placed fourth on all three of his starts at 2 yrs in 2016. The dam is an unraced half-sister to 11 winners including the Group 1 Sprint Cup winner and good sire Invincible Spirit, the Group 3 12f winners Sadian and Acts O Grace, and the very smart sire Kodiac. The second dam, Rafha (by Kris), won the Group 1 10.5f Prix de Diane and is a half-sister to 9 winners including the Group 2 Blandford Stakes

winner Chiang Mai (dam of the Group 1 winner Chinese White). (Prince A A Faisal). *"He looks like making a 2-y-o of some description and the dam is a sister to two very good stallions. He was light and feminine when he came in but he's doing very well now and my feeling is that he'll be a miler from the high summer onwards. He's done nothing wrong at all".*

1301. ALTERED METHOD ★★★ ♠
ch.c. Dawn Approach – Swift Action (Invincible Spirit). February 13. First foal. £58,000Y. Goffs UK Premier (Doncaster). Oliver St Lawrence. The dam, a quite useful Irish 5f winner, is a half-sister to 6 winners. The second dam, Littlefeather (by Indian Ridge), a very useful 5f (at 2 yrs) and 6f winner of 4 races, was third in the Group 1 7f Moyglare Stakes and is a half-sister to 7 winners including the multiple Group 1 winner Marling and the Group 1 National Stakes winner Caerwent. (Mr J E Dance). *"A strong, forward-going colt, he's done a couple of bits of work and should be running over six furlongs early enough in the season. I like him and considering both his sire and dam won over five he could easily start over that trip."*

1302. AUSSIE WIND ★★★
b.c. Aussie Rules – Ride The Wind (Cozzene). March 11. Third foal. 12,000Y. Tattersalls October Book 3. Bradley/Kelly Bloodstock. Half-brother to the modest 7f winner Bahamian Bird (by Bahamian Bounty). The dam, a modest 1m and 9.5f placed maiden, is a half-sister to one winner. The second dam, Wind Surf (by Lil's Lad), a minor stakes winner in North America, is a half-sister to 3 winners. (Nick Bradley Racing 43 & Partner). *"He's particularly nice, very good-looking and cost nothing. He finds life easy and I can see no reason why he shouldn't be a decent 2-y-o".*

1303. BREAKING RECORDS ★★★
b.c. Kodiac – Querulous (Raven's Pass). January 7. First foal. 110,000Y. Tattersalls October Book 1. Rabbah Bloodstock. The dam is an unraced half-sister to one minor winner in the USA. The second dam, Contentious (by Giant's Causeway), a useful 1m winner and listed placed here, subsequently won in the USA at 4 yrs, was

Group 3 placed in Germany and is a half-sister to the US dual Grade 2 winner Gone Astray. (Dr Ali Ridha). *"He's a speedy horse, but he's not going to be that early. I think he's going to be six/seven furlongs from July onwards. A big horse, but I like him".*

1304. BURFORD BROWN ★★★
br.c. Swiss Spirit – Sareb (Indian Ridge). March 20. Seventh foal. €22,000Y. Tattersalls Ireland September. Amanda Skiffington. Half-brother to the fairly useful 2-y-o 5f winner Chartist (by Choisir) and to the fair 5f winner of four races at 2 and 4 yrs Black Moma (by Averti). The dam ran once unplaced and is a half-sister to 3 minor winners. The second dam, Prends Ca (by Reprimand), a fairly useful 6f (at 2 yrs) to 7.5f winner of 5 races, is a half-sister to 4 winners including the listed Trigo Stakes winner Friendly Persuasion. (Adrian Gott). *"A staggeringly good mover and very good-looking, he's the only horse I bought on spec last year. I'm sure he'll be a fast horse, probably from July/August onwards over five/six furlongs. I really like him".*
TRAINERS' BARGAIN BUY

1305. CENTRAL CITY (IRE) ★★★
b.c. Kodiac – She Basic (Desert Prince). March 28. Third foal. €50,000Y. Tattersalls Ireland September. Sackville/Donald. Half-brother to the fair 2016 2-y-o 8.5f and 10f winner Katebird (by Dark Angel). The dam, a winner in Italy at 3 yrs and third in the Group 2 Premio Regina Elena, is a half-sister to 6 winners including two listed winners in Italy and a minor US stakes winner. The second dam, She Bat (by Batshoof), won the Group 3 Premio Bagutta and is a half-sister to 5 winners. (Mr L L Lee). *"Typical of the sire, he goes and behaves exactly as you'd expect of a Kodiac. When you're given a Kodiac I always think to myself 'Well, that's one winner'. He's a bonny colt, he's done well and I'd be very disappointed if he doesn't end up winning races".*

1306. COLLIDE ★★★
b.c. Frankel – Scuffle (Daylami). March 23. Half-brother to the useful 7f (at 2 yrs) and subsequent US dual Grade 3 winner over 11f and 12f winner Suffused (by Champs Elysees), to the fairly useful listed-placed dual

7f winner Battlement (by Dansili) and the quite useful 5.5f and 6f winner Sleep Walk (by Oasis Dream). The dam, a useful triple 1m winner, was listed-placed and is a half-sister to the high-class Group 1 9f Dubai Duty Free winner Cityscape and the very smart Group 2 5f Temple Stakes and multiple Group 1 placed Bated Breath (both now sires). The second dam, Tantina (by Distant View), a smart winner of 4 races including two listed events over 7f, was Group 3 placed and is a half-sister to 2 winners. (Khalid Abdulla). *"He's gorgeous – a really proper looking colt with a proper pedigree and by a 'buzz' sire. He could be anything, but he's a big horse and he's a long way short of doing anything more than a canter. The pedigree doesn't exactly scream 2-y-o because they all tend to improve and he's a big horse, but with the ease that he finds things I'd be very disappointed if he didn't run at two. My horses either have to be injured or very backward not to run as 2-y-o's so we'll see how he goes. He doesn't look backward and so far he isn't injured!"*

1307. CONFEDERATE ★★★
b.c. Teofilo – Merry Jaunt (Street Sense). February 11. Second foal. 100,000Y. Tattersalls October Book 1. John & Jake Warren. The dam, a modest 10f winner, is a half-sister to 3 winners including the 7f (at 2 yrs) and Grade 1 Hollywood Derby winner Seek Again and the very useful 7f (at 2 yrs) and UAE Group 3 1m winner Treble Jig. The second dam, Light Jig (by Danehill), a US Grade 1 10f Yellow Ribbon Stakes winner, is a half-sister to 10 winners including the 2-y-o listed 1m winner Battle Dore. (Highclere Thoroughbred Racing – Kelly Holmes). *"He's literally just arrived from pre-training but he was a gorgeous looking yearling, really strong. The reports on him are great and I'm looking forward to getting to know him".*

1308. CURIOSITY ★★★
b.c. High Chaparral – Precautionary (Green Desert). March 20. Seventh foal. €65,000Y. Goffs Orby. Willie Browne. Brother to the modest 2-y-o 7f winner Summer Stroll and half-brother to the fair 5f winner of 4 races from 2 to 4 yrs Best Be Careful (by Exceed And Excel). The dam, a modest 2-y-o 6f and 7f placed half-sister to the Group 1 King's

Stand Stakes winner Prohibit, to the French 7f (at 2 yrs) and listed 6.5f winner Prior Warning and the French listed 6f winner and dual Group 3 placed Emergency. The second dam, Well Warned (by Warning), a useful 2-y-o 6f winner, was third in the Group 3 6f Cherry Hinton Stakes and is a full or half-sister to 7 winners. (H Moorhead, C Fahy, J Collins). *"He's had a break, come back in again and he's grown and strengthened. Everything suggests he's one for the second half of the season, but he's not the backward type of High Chaparral that might only have one run this year. You'd think he'd have the chance to be a good 2-y-o, as lots of them have been. We've yet to give him that chance".*

1309. DIEULEFIT (IRE) ★★★
b.f. Oasis Dream – Tereschenko (Giant's Causeway). March 6. Second foal. Half-sister to Fibonacci (by Galileo), unplaced on his only start at 2 yrs in 2016. The dam, unplaced on her only start, is a half-sister to the champion 2-y-o colt Fasliyev and to the Group 3 Irish 1,000 Guineas Trial winner Kamarinskaya. The second dam, Mr P's Princess (by Mr Prospector), is an unraced half-sister to the US Grade 1 winners Menifee and Desert Wine. (Al Asayl Bloodstock). *"Her brother Fibonacci who I train is potentially very exciting, he's working like a good horse at the moment. He only ran once as a 2-y-o in October but he's a big colt and this filly isn't quite so big. Nevertheless I wouldn't think she'd be running before then because she's backward. She'll have every chance to be a good horse but at the moment she has a lot of furnishing to do".*

1310. DRAGON MOUNTAIN ★★★
b.c. Sir Percy – Rouge Dancer (Elusive City). February 1. Fifth foal. £120,000Y. Goffs UK Premier (Doncaster). Amanda Skiffington. Half-brother to the fairly useful 2016 2-y-o dual 6f winner Spiritual Lady (by Pastoral Pursuits), to the fairly useful 10f winner Durand (by Motivator) and the fair 5f and 6f winner Princess Cookie (by Sakhee's Secret). The dam is an unraced half-sister to 2 minor winners. The second dam, Blandish (by Wild Again), placed twice at 3 yrs in the USA, is a half-sister to 8 winners including the Group 3 Prix Perth winner and Group 2 third

Susurration. (Carmichael Jennings). *"A nice colt and I'd like to think he could almost be a Chesham Stakes type horse. He's forward, a lovely mover, hasn't worked yet but he goes well cantering".*

1311. DREAM ASCOT ★★★
b.f. Oasis Dream – World Class (Galileo). March 28. Second foal. 100,000Y. Tattersalls October Book 1. Stephen Hillen. The unraced dam is closely related to the Derby, Racing Post Trophy and Dante Stakes winner Motivator and to the Group 2 12f Hardwicke Stakes winner Macarthur and a half-sister to the smart listed 10f winner Imperial Star. The second dam, Out West (by Gone West), a useful 7.5f (at 2 yrs) and listed 1m winner, is a half-sister to 3 winners. (Lady Mary Manton). *"She's very good-looking and she goes along well but we'll just have to see how we go. She's hard to fault at this stage but I had more Oasis Dream's last year than any other stallion, most of them out of Galileo mares, and I was excited about them all but ultimately they disappointed me".*

1312. DUKHAN ★★★ ♠
b.c. Teofilo – Vedela (Selkirk). April 5. Fourth foal. €260,000Y. Arqana Deauville August. Charlie Gordon-Watson. The dam is an unraced half-sister to 4 winners including Vadamar (Group 2 Grand Prix de Deauville) and the French listed winner Vedouma. The second dam, Vadawina (by Unfuwain), won the Group 1 Prix Saint-Alary and is a half-sister to 7 winners including Vazira (Group 1 Prix Saint-Alary). (Al Shaqab Racing). *"Surprisingly for a Teofilo he's not very big but he's strong, moves well and looks like a 2-y-o. I can't imagine he's going to be running before seven furlongs but at this stage I can see no reason why he shouldn't be running in early July".*

1313. ENCRYPTED ★★★
b.c. Showcasing – Disclose (Dansili). February 16. Third foal. Half-brother to the quite useful 2016 2-y-o 5f winner Impart (by Oasis Dream). The dam, a French listed-placed 1m winner, is a sister to two winners including the useful French 7f (at 2 yrs) and 1m winner and listed placed World Ruler and closely related to the useful French 2-y-o dual 6f winner and

Group 3 1m third Grand Vista. The second dam, Revealing (by Halling), a very useful 2-y-o 1m winner, is a half-sister to the useful 12f winner and dual Group 3 placed Singleton and the useful 6f winner Brevity. (Khalid Abdulla). *"He looks like a proper 2-y-o. He's held up a little at the moment with a sore shin but other than that he's a forward-going sort of colt. He's a nice size, naturally muscular, a good mover and everything about him seems to go well".*

1314. FAJJAJ ★★★★ ♣
ch.c. Dawn Approach – Pleasantry (Johannesburg). March 1. Third foal. 140,000Y. Tattersalls October Book 1. Al Shaqab Racing/Mandore. Half-brother to the quite useful 2016 2-y-o 7f winner Parlance (by Invincible Spirit). The dam is an unraced half-sister to the top-class miler and multiple Group 1 winner Kingman and to the Group 3 Tercentenary Stakes winner Remote. The second dam, Zenda (by Zamindar), won the French 1,000 Guineas, was second in the Coronation Stakes and the Grade 1 Queen Elizabeth II Challenge Cup at Keeneland and is a half-sister to the Middle Park Stakes, July Cup and Nunthorpe Stakes winner and sire Oasis Dream. (Al Shaqab Racing). *"I'm very fond of the sire Dawn Approach, so much so that I've bought a mare and she's just been scanned in foal to him. This is the most expensive Dawn Approach I have and he's the biggest, not all that forward, but he looks like a six furlong 2-y-o. He's very natural and doesn't look like he'll take much getting ready, so he's a horse I'm very keen on. On pedigree he could be anything".*

1315. FORMULA ONE ★★★★
b.c. Frankel – Wizz Kid (Whipper). March 9. Second foal. Half-brother to the fair 2016 5f and 6f placed 2-y-o Spinnaker Bay (by Lawman). The dam, winner of the Group 1 5f Prix de l'Abbaye and the Group 2 5f Prix du Gros-Chene (twice), is a half-sister to the listed 10f winner Mustaheel. The second dam, Lidanski (Soviet Star), a fairly useful Irish 7f winner, was listed-placed and is a half-sister to 5 winners including the listed winner Yaa Wayl. (Carmichael Jennings/ Ballylinch). *"He's only just come in, but hasn't he got a great name? Better still the people who own*

Ballylinch are the people who have bought Formula One from Bernie Ecclestone. It's my good fortune to have him because he picked up a tiny injury at the stud which prevented him from going to the sale. A proper looking horse, he looks like he'll be a 2-y-o from mid-summer onwards and when he fills his frame he's going to be a beast".*

1316. FORGOTTEN PROMISES ★★★
b.c. Iffraaj – Orpha (New Approach). March 1. First foal. The dam, a fairly useful 2-y-o 6f winner, is a half-sister to 4 winners including the Group 1 9f Prix Jean Prat winner Olden Times and the useful 1m (at 2 yrs) and listed 6f winner and Group 1 Cheveley Park Stakes third Festoso. The second dam, Garah (by Ajdal), a very useful winner of 4 races over 6f, was second in the Group 3 5f Duke Of York Stakes and is a half-sister to 6 winners. (Prince A A Faisal). *"He's a big horse, surprisingly so for a first foal. He finds life easy, looks smart and impresses me. I won't put pressure on him too early simply because of his size, but at the moment he's dragging his rider to the top of every hill. So he's doing nicely and might climb the rankings quicker than I anticipated".*

1317. GODODDIN ★★★ ♣♣
b.c. Camelot – Spritza (Spectrum). January 28. Fifth foal. 300,000Y. Tattersalls October Book 1. Amanda Skiffington. Closely related to 2 winners including the quite useful 2-y-o 7f and 10f winner and Group 3 Classic Trial third Rougemont (by Montjeu) and half-brother to a minor winner in Sweden by Pivotal. The dam, a modest 11f and 12f winner, is a half-sister to 3 winners including the fairly useful 12f winner of 4 races and listed-placed Portrait Of A Lady and to the placed dam of the dual Group 1 winner Covert Love. The second dam, Starlight Smile (by Green Dancer), is an unraced half-sister to 4 winners including the dam of the Irish Derby winner Grey Swallow. (Carmichael Jennings). *"A big colt, he's very well-balanced like all the Camelots I have and seems to move beautifully. He's bred to be a Derby colt and physically that's what he looks like – the type to be at his peak in June 2018. But if he's going to be a Derby colt he's probably going to have to do something at two. He's not been here very long but he's done little wrong in that time and he's a nice horse".*

1318. GUELTA ★★★
b.f. Oasis Dream – Canada Water (Dansili).
May 7. Third foal. Sister to the 2016 2-y-o
7f winner, from two starts, Daschas and
half-sister to the fairly useful Group 3 7f Prix
La Rochette second (at 2 yrs) and 3-y-o 6f
winner Lawmaking (by Zamindar). The dam,
a French 1m placed 3-y-o, is a half-sister
to 8 winners including the Prix de l'Arc de
Triomphe and Grand Prix de Paris winner Rail
Link, the French Group 2 12f and dual Group
3 10f winner Crossharbour and the smart
French 1m and 10f performer Chelsea Manor.
The second dam, Docklands (by Theatrical), a
French 1m and 10f performer, is a half-sister
to the smart performer at up to 9f Wharf.
(Khalid Abdulla). *"She's a very attractive
filly, not forward but I think she'll be a 2-y-o
from mid-summer onwards. There are mixed
messages in her pedigree, for example she's
by a fast sire but out of a half-sister to an Arc
winner. I feel Oasis Dream responds better
when he's bred to speed, or at least his most
exciting horses are his speed horses. This is a
nice filly but we're a long way short of finding
out what trip she wants".*

1319. HIGH SEAS (IRE) ★★★
b.f. Henrythenavigator – High Days
(Hennessy). March 15. Fourth foal. Half-sister
to the fairly useful 2016 2-y-o 7f winner
Colibri (by Redoute's Choice). The dam, a fair
2-y-o 6f winner, is a half-sister to one winner.
The second dam, Hi Dubai (by Rahy), won
the listed Pretty Polly Stakes and is a sister
to Fantastic Light, a winner of six Group/
Grade 1 events including the Breeders' Cup
Turf, the Prince of Wales's Stakes and the
Irish Champion Stakes. (Al Asayl Bloodstock).
*"Colibri's sister. He was a decent 2-y-o and
he's a potentially very decent 3-y-o. I like her,
she's not very big and looks like she should be
winning over six furlongs".*

1320. IT'S A WISH ★★★★
b.f. Invincible Spirit – Sun Bittern (Seeking The
Gold). February 26. Fourth foal. €300,000Y.
Arqana Deauville August. Voute Sales Ltd.
Sister to the Group 1 Prix Maurice de Gheest
winner Signs Of Blessing and half-sister to 2
minor winners in France by Pivotal and Oasis
Dream. The dam is an unraced half-sister to
3 minor winners. The second dam, Sunray

Superstar (by Nashwan), a useful 12f winner,
is a sister to the Group 1 10f Prix Saint-Alary
winner Nadia and a half-sister to 5 winners.
(Prince A A Faisal). *"I'm quite excited by her at
the moment, she was very little and narrow
when she came in and whilst she's never going
to be a big filly she's now a proper 2-y-o. She's
really filled out and muscled in every direction,
she's done two bits of work and caught the
eye both times and everything I see about her
looks nice. She looks to me an out-and-out
2-y-o, so we're dreaming that the Prince might
have to dust off his top hat for Royal Ascot".*

1321. LEIGH'S LAW ★★★
b.f. Lawman – Delira (Namid). March 8. Third
foal. 50,000Y. Tattersalls October Book 2.
Amanda Skiffington. Half-sister to the quite
useful 2-y-o 1m winner Wahash (by Dark
Angel). The dam, a modest 5.5f winner, is a
half-sister to 6 winners including Barrier Reef,
a winner of 8 races and second in the Group
3 Beresford Stakes. The second dam, Singing
Millie (by Millfontaine), won twice in Ireland
at 3 yrs and is a half-sister to 7 winners.
(Cityside Electrical Co. Ltd). *"She'll definitely
make a 2-y-o because she's strong, forward
and does everything just right at this stage.
She hasn't worked yet but soon she will and I
like what I've seen".*

1322. LEXINGTON FLAIR ★★★
b.c. Dabirsim – Kyleam (King's Best). April
26. Third foal. 50,000Y. Arqana Deauville
October. F Barberini. The dam is a half-sister
to 2 winners including the French 7f (at 2
yrs) to 10.5f winner and Group 3 placed
Kakofonic. The second dam, Brooklyn Gleam
(by Caerleon), won at 3 yrs and is a half-
sister to 11 winners including the Arc winner
Solemia and the Group 2 Prix Greffulhe
winner Prospect Wells. (Middleham Park
Racing XXVIII). *"This colt is very nice. By a top-
class 2-y-o he's a big, strong, powerful horse".*

1323. MAYASEEN ★★★★
gr.f. Style Vendome – Wing Stealth (Hawk
Wing). March 23. Fifth foal. €200,000Y.
Arqana Deauville August. Al Shaqab Racing.
Half-sister to the Group 1 Irish Oaks and
Group 1 Prix de l'Opera winner Covert Love
(by Azamour) and to the quite useful dual
7f winner at 2 and 3 yrs Stealth Missile (by

Invincible Spirit). The dam, a fair 7f (at 2 yrs) and 12f placed maiden, is a half-sister to 5 winners. The second dam, Starlight Smile (by Green Dancer), is an unraced half-sister to 4 winners including the multiple Irish listed winner Seasonal Pickup and the dam of the Irish Derby winner Grey Swallow. *"I adore this filly, she isn't the prettiest standing up but when I saw her walking at the sale she blew me away. It was the only bright point of the day when Galileo Gold ran so badly in the Prix Jacques le Marois! Interestingly I'm told that the dam has always thrown to whatever stallion she's been covered by. In this instance the sire was a Group One winning 2-y-o and this filly looks like she'll be a 2-y-o too. I think she ought to be running towards the end of June and she might get up to a mile this year".*

1324. MOMENTARILY ★★★★

b.f. Cityscape – Firebelly (Nicolotte). January 25. Sixth foal. 68,000Y. Tattersalls October Book 2. Amanda Skiffington. Half-sister to the useful 6f and 7f winner and Group 3 6f Hackwood Stakes second Firebeam (by Cadeaux Genereux) and to the fair dual 1m winner (including at 2 yrs) Bombina (by Lomitas). The dam, a fairly useful 2-y-o dual 6f and Italian listed 1m winner, is a half-sister to 3 winners including the South African listed winner L'Passionata. The second dam, Desert Delight (by Green Desert), is an unraced half-sister to 9 winners including the Group 3 May Hill Stakes winner Intimate Guest and the dams of the Grade 1 winners Luas Line, Kingsfort and Prince Arch. (TCO Gredley, MV Magnier, Mrs P Shanahan). *"A lovely filly. When they rang me for a quote about the stallion I said that if she was by Galileo she'd have cost a million. Obviously that's idle speculation but she's well-bred, extremely good-looking, moves very well and finds all her work easy. Cityscape is an unproven stallion but a very well-bred one and I think this filly has every chance of putting her sire's name in lights, but we haven't asked any serious questions of her yet".*

1325. MOOTASADIR ★★★★

b.c. Dansili – Mahbooba (Galileo). February 23. The dam was a smart winner of 7 races including the South African Grade 1 7f Golden Slipper Stakes and a UAE Group 2 9f

stakes event. The second dam, Sogha (by Red Ransom), is a half-sister to the French dual Group 3 and dual listed winner Slew The Red. (Sheikh M Bin Khalifa Al Maktoum). *"He's a bit of a 'Wow' horse and I'm told that when the trainers went to see this owner's yearlings he was everyone's number one, so I feel very privileged to have received him. He's a glorious mover and just looks like the sort of horse we should be excited about this time next year. If that's going to happen he's going to have to achieve something this year. From August onwards he'll be racing with one eye on his 3-y-o career. There wouldn't be many better looking 2-y-o's in training at the moment".*

1326. MORNING BEAUTY ★★★

ch.f. Dawn Approach – Extreme Beauty (Rahy). April 19. Ninth foal. 70,000Y. Tattersalls October Book 1. Hugo Palmer. Half-sister to 6 winners including the fair 2016 2-y-o 1m winner, from two starts, Kind Of Beauty (by Helmet), the quite useful 7f and 8.5f winner Poet's Beauty (by Poet's Voice), the quite useful 2-y-o 6f winner Extreme Warrior (by Dubawi) and the fair 6f and 7f winner of 4 races from 2 to 5 yrs Exceeding Power (by Exceed And Excel). The dam, a quite useful 6f (at 2 yrs) and 7f winner, was third in the Group 2 6f Cherry Hinton Stakes is a half-sister to 9 winners including the US Grade 1 winner Go Between. The second dam, Mediation (by Caerleon), won the listed Irish 1,000 Guineas Trial and was Group 3 placed here and in the USA. (Dr A Ridha). *"I'm sweet on the Dawn Approach 2-y-o's. This filly is a bit like her half-sister Kind Of Beauty in that she's a bit 'fizzy' but that didn't stop her winning against all the odds. She was a gawky thing but this filly is stronger and squatter and I think she'll be a 2-y-o for the first half of the season and beyond".*

1327. NEVER BACK DOWN ★★★★

b.c. Kodiac – Steer By The Stars (Pivotal). February 2. First foal. £100,000Y. Goffs UK Premier (Doncaster). Armando Duarte. The dam, a quite useful 2-y-o 6f and 7f winner, is a half-sister to 3 winners including the Group 1 St James's Palace Stakes third Consort. The second dam, Mundus Novus (by Unbridled's Song), a French 1m winner, is closely related to the US Grade 2 Dahlia Handicap winner

Surya (herself dam of the US Grade 2 winner Aruna) and a half-sister to 7 winners. (M M Stables). *"He could be our first runner. He looks speedy and we're only easing the handbrake off at this stage but he looks above average and we might try and win the race that Gifted Master won for us at the Craven meeting. He looks that sort, all speed".*

1328. NEW ORLEANS (IRE) ★★★
b.c. Red Jazz – Agnista (Iffraaj). April 22. Third foal. €24,000Y. Tattersalls Ireland September. Anglia Bloodstock. Half-brother to the modest 6f (at 2 yrs) and 4-y-o dual 7f winner Murdanova (by Zebedee). The dam is an unraced half-sister to 5 minor winners. The second dam, Splendida Idea (by Kenmare), won the listed Premio Baggio in Italy and is a half-sister to 9 winners. (Anglia Bloodstock Syndicate X). *"He looks like he should rock n roll this year. He had a slight lurgy and went out for a month but he's back now and should be running before Ascot".*

1329. PEPPER STREET ★★★ ♠
b.f. Born To Sea – Mindy (Zamindar). February 19. First foal. £34,000Y. Goffs UK Premier (Doncaster). Peter & Ross Doyle. The dam, a fair Irish 4-y-o 11.5f winner, is a half-sister to one winner. The second dam, Scotch Bonnet (by Montjeu), won twice over 11f and 14f in France is a half-sister to the Group 1 Irish Oaks third Sister Bella and to Nicola Bella (dam of the German Group 1 winner Neatico and the US Grade 2 winner Beautyandthebeast). (Anglia Bloodstock Syndicate XI). *"A beautiful mover, she's done a couple of bits of work, goes very nicely and is extremely hard not to like. Very attractive, she points her toe and finds life easy. At the moment she appears much more forward than you might expect from the pedigree".*

1330. PHOTONICS ★★★
b.c. Power – Naval Affair (Last Tycoon). April 9. Eleventh foal. €60,000Y. Goffs Sportsmans. C & S Bloodstock. Half-brother to the 7f (at 2 yrs) and listed 1m Valiant Stakes winner and Group 3 1m Prix de Lieurey second Field Day (by Cape Cross), the quite useful dual 7f winner Czech It Out (by Oratorio), the quite useful 1m and 12f winner War At Sea (by Bering) and 2 minor winners abroad by

Duke Of Marmalade and Green Desert. The dam, a useful 2-y-o 7f winner, is a half-sister to 3 listed winners and to the dam of the dual French Group 2 winner Cut Quartz. The second dam, Sailor's Mate (by Shirley Heights), won the Group 3 Meld Stakes and is a half-sister to 8 winners including the good broodmare Grecian Sea. (Mr J E Dance). *"He was very weak but has done nothing but improve in the whole time he's been here. He ought to be working sometime in April and I think he looks like a proper 2-y-o, so I'm happy with him".*

1331. POWER TO EXCEED ★★★
b.f. Exceed And Excel – Power Of Light (Echo Of Light). February 25. First foal. 60,000Y. Tattersalls October Book 2. Hugo Palmer. The dam, a fairly useful listed-placed 2-y-o 1m winner, is a half-sister to one winner. The second dam, Dubai Power (by Cadeaux Genereux), a quite useful 6f and 1m winner, is a half-sister to 2 winners. (Dr Ali Ridha). *"She's a good-moving filly and pretty typical of what she's meant to be. She looks smart and strong, so I'm very happy with her".*

1332. PULITZER ★★★ ♠
b.f. Kodiac – Solola (Black Sam Bellamy). March 16. Fourth foal. 130,000Y. Tattersalls October Book 1. A C Elliott for Bill Gredley. Half-sister to the 2-y-o Group 3 Horris Hill Stakes winner Smaih (by Paco Boy). The dam won twice at 4 yrs in Germany and is a half-sister to 9 winners including the Group/Grade 1 winners Silvano and Sabiango. The second dam, Spirit Of Eagles (by Beau's Eagle), won 11 minor races in the USA and is a sister to the US Grade 3 winner Big Pal and a half-sister to 9 winners. (WJ & TCO Gredley). *"I think she's quite forward, she's done a couple of bits of work and she's very green but she is out of a Black Sam Bellamy mare after all. She looks like she goes well and being by Kodiac I'd be surprised if she didn't make a 2-y-o".*

1333. RAINBOW HILL ★★★
b.f. Fastnet Rock – Riot Of Colour (Excellent Art). March 26. First foal. 52,000Y. Tattersalls October Book 2. BBA (Ire). The dam, a quite useful 7f winner, is a half-sister to 2 winners including useful 2-y-o listed 6f winner

Invincible Warrior. The second dam, Riotous Applause (by Royal Applause), a fairly useful dual 6f winner (including at 2 yrs), was listed-placed and is a full or half-sister to 8 winners including the 2-y-o Group 1 1m Racing Post Trophy winner Crowded House and to the placed dam of the US dual Grade 1 winner Ticker Tape. (Lady Mary Manton). *"I think she'll be a nice 2-y-o by September. The Fastnet Rocks seem to need a bit of time, but she's well-bred and quite attractive".*

1334. SILVER QUARTZ ★★★★
gr.c. Frankel – Rosamixa (Linamix). February 5. Sixth foal. Half-brother to the useful 2-y-o 1m and 3-y-o listed 1m winner Pearl Mix (by Oratorio), to the quite useful 10f winner Aqualis (by Sea The Stars) and the fair 1m (at 2 yrs) and 12f winner Cartier (by Montjeu). The dam, a winner at 2 yrs in France and fourth in the Group 3 Prix du Calvados, is a sister to the Group 3 Prix de Fontainebleau winner Rajsaman and the French listed 1m winner Rosawa (herself dam of the Group 1 Prix Marcel Boussac winner Rosanara) and a half-sister to 3 winners. The second dam, Rose Quartz (by Lammtarra), won once over 13f at 3 yrs in Ireland. (Al Asayl Bloodstock). *"He was very small and insignificant when he came in, but being grey I suppose it's even more appropriate to blossom from being an ugly duckling to a beautiful swan! But that's what he's doing, he's a cracking looking colt that's beginning to find life easier and easier. I would think a minimum of seven furlongs would suit him from August onwards".*

1335. SOCIETY LILLY (IRE) ★★★ ♠
b.f. Society Rock – Lilly Be (Titus Livius). February 20. Second foal. £32,000Y. Goffs UK Premier (Doncaster). Amanda Skiffington. The dam, a fair 5f and 6f winner of 4 races, is a half-sister to 4 winners. The second dam, Mystery Hill (by Danehill), won at 4 yrs in the UAE and is a half-sister to 3 winners. (Mr C M Humber). *"She looks like an out-and-out 2-y-o but she came in far too late, so her career might be hindered by the fact she should have been in training in November but she only appeared in March. She's not too small, in fact she looks great physically and I can see her being ready in June".*

1336. SWORDBILL ★★★
ch.c. Champs Elysees – Dream Wild (Oasis Dream). January 31. First foal. The dam, a fair 1m winner, is a sister to one winner and a half-sister to the Group 1 Yorkshire Oaks winner Quiff, the useful 10f winner and Group 3 Chester Vase second Arabian Gulf and the useful 12f winner and Group 3 placed Total Command. The second dam, Wince (by Selkirk), won the 1,000 Guineas and is a half-sister to 3 winners including the very smart middle-distance winner Ulundi. (Khalid Abdulla). *"He's a really strong looking horse that's not going to be a five furlong 2-y-o, but I can see no reason why he shouldn't be a seven furlong/mile type from the end of July onwards. He does everything nicely".*

1337. TAOISEACH ★★★★ ♠
b.c. Roderic O'Connor – Munaa's Dream (Oasis Dream). March 7. Third foal. 85,000Y. Tattersalls October Book 2. Amanda Skiffington. Half-brother to the modest 2016 dual 5f placed 2-y-o Affordability (by Bushranger) and to the quite useful dual 6f winner Happy Call (by Kodiac). The dam is an unplaced half-sister to one winner in Germany. The second dam, Munaawashat (by Marju), a fair 6f (at 2 yrs) to 8.5f winner of 5 races, is a half-sister to 9 winners including the Group 3 10f Mooresbridge Stakes winner Windsor Palace, the Irish listed winner Anna Karenina and the useful dual 7f winner and Group 3 Queen Mary Stakes second Al Ihsas. (Mr C M Humber). *"He's got bags of speed and just looks like an out-and-out 2-y-o. A great mover and he goes well".*

1338. THE REVENANT ★★★★★
ch.c. Dubawi – Hazel Lavery (Excellent Art). April 20. Second foal. The dam, a 7f (at 2 yrs) and Group 3 12f St Simon Stakes and listed 10f Aphrodite Stakes winner, is a half-sister to 3 winners including the useful 10f and 12f winner and Group 3 12f second Leo Gali. The second dam, Reprise (by Darshaan), placed fourth once over 10f, is a half-sister to 3 winners. (Al Asayl Bloodstock). *"He excited me so much at the way he was going that I turned him out and that's where he is at the moment. He was finding life so easy that it was all upside down because he's an April foal by Dubawi out of a mare than won her best race over twelve*

furlongs. *This horse shouldn't be looking like my most exciting early 2-y-o. He'll start again in April and he was a little bit light so he needs to furnish, but I hope that spark hasn't been diminished when he comes back. He looks like a bit of a star to me and even though the dam won over seven as a 2-y-o and stayed well, he doesn't look slow. I think he'll be a good 2-y-o from mid-summer onwards".*

1339. THUNDERBOLT ROCKS ★★★
b.c. Farhh – Coquette Noire (Holy Roman Emperor). March 17. First foal. 57,000Y. Tattersalls October Book 1. Bradley /Kelly Bloodstock. The dam, a fair Irish 7f winner, is a half-sister to 3 winners including the 1,000 Guineas second Jacqueline Quest. The second dam, Coquette Rouge (by Croco Rouge), a quite useful Irish 12f and 17f winner, is a half-sister to 5 winners including the dual Group 3 winner Regime and the listed 5f winner and Group 2 Cherry Hinton second Salut d'Amour. (Nick Bradley 45 & Partner). *"He's just having a bit of a break at present. A really nice horse, I liked the sire's yearlings at the sales and I like the way this colt goes. From mid-July onwards I think he'll be a jolly horse, he's no giant so I don't think we'll have to wait too long and everything is easy for him".*

1340. VERVE ★★★ ♠
b.f. Epaulette – Onomatomania (Mr Greeley). February 24. Second foal. €150,000Y. Tattersalls Ireland September. Amanda Skiffington. Half-sister to the quite useful 2016 2-y-o 5f winner Miss Cogent (by Clodovil). The dam is an unraced daughter of the listed-placed Irish 2-y-o 5f winner Seattle Queen (by Seattle Slew), herself a half-sister to 4 winners including the US Grade 2 stakes winner Harissa. (Mr C Humber). *"A big strong filly, she topped the sale in Ireland, I loved her then and still do. She hasn't been in the yard all that long but that probably doesn't matter because she's grown quite a lot. She's probably one to start off over six furlongs from July onwards".*

1341. UNNAMED ★★★★
b.f. Reckless Abandon – Akhmatova (Cape Cross). January 28. Second foal. €120,000Y. Goffs Orby. Blandford Bloodstock. The dam, a quite useful 1m and 10f winner of 4 races,

is a half-sister to 4 winners including the useful Irish 2-y-o 6f winner and Group 3 Anglesey Stakes third Rudolf Valentino. The second dam, Maganda (by Sadler's Wells), a quite useful 10f winner, is a sister to the listed winners In The Limelight and On The Nile and a half-sister to the German and Italian Group 1 winner Kutub. (Sheikh Juma Dalmook Al Maktoum). *"She goes really nicely and it's a shame the sire had so few foals because this filly looks like a bullet, she's big enough to be more than just a bullet and her early bits of work haven't disappointed. She could run in April but at this stage May looks more likely. One of the few we've got that has the chance to be an Ascot filly".* The sire, a son of Exchange Rate, won the Prix Morny and the Middle Park Stakes (both Group 1 6f events at 2 yrs).

1342. UNNAMED ★★★
b.f. Dawn Approach – Al Mahmeyah (Teofilo). March 17. Second foal. Half-sister to the 2016 2-y-o Group 3 5f Prix d'Arenburg winner Afandem (by Vale Of York). The dam, a fair 2-y-o 6f winner, is a half-sister to 4 winners. The second dam, Aguilas Perla (by Indian Ridge), is an unraced sister to the Irish listed 7f winner Cool Clarity and a half-sister to the listed winners Artistic Blue and Queen Of Palms. (Mr H R Bin Ghedayer). *"I like her, she's just a little bit weak and not showing quite as much as her brother Afandem at this stage but she's a bit bigger and we'll see how she goes. Afandem doesn't get a yard over five furlongs".*

1343. UNNAMED ★★★★
b.c. Camelot – Close Regards (Danehill). January 23. Fourth foal. €180,000 foal. Goffs November. Rob Speers. Half-brother to the Australian Group 1 12f winner Magic Hurricane (by Hurricane Run), to the quite useful 7f to 10f winner and listed-placed Maybe Grace (by Hawk Wing) and the fair 5f (at 2 yrs) and 6f winner Fast In The Wind (by Footstepsinthesand). The dam is an unraced half-sister to 7 winners. The second dam, La Luna (by Lyphard), a winner over 9f at 3 yrs in France, is a sister to the Group 3 Prix Daphnis and Group 3 Prix Thomas Bryon winner Bellypha and a half-sister to the Prix Eugene Adam winner Bellman and the Peruvian Grade 1 winner Run And Deliver. (Mr V I

Araci). *"A friend rang me after Rob bought him as a foal and he said that in his opinion he was the best foal at Goffs. The horse has done incredibly well since that point, he moves staggeringly well and there's a huge amount to like about him. You could be tempted to suggest he was a Chesham horse, and indeed he may well be ready to run by that stage, but we'll see how he goes".*

1344. UNNAMED ★★★
b.c. High Chaparral – Garanciere (Anabaa). March 10. Sixth living foal. Half-brother to the fair 2016 1m placed 2-y-o Fujaira Bridge (by Sea The Stars), to the very useful 2-y-o 7f winner and Group 2 7f Rockfel Stakes second I Love Me (by Cape Cross) and the quite useful 1m (at 2 yrs) and 10f winner Ningara (by Singspiel). The dam, a minor 3-y-o winner in France, is a half-sister to 8 winners including the Group 1 Fillies' Mile winner Gloriosa. The second dam, Golden Sea (by Saint Cyrien), won 4 races at 2 and 4 yrs in France and is a half-sister to 8 winners including the French Group 2 winner Glity. (Mr V I Araci). *"He's done very well, he's grown quite a lot but I think he should make into a 2-y-o, I'm happy with him and he looks great".*

1345. UNNAMED ★★★
b.f. Azamour – Green Tambourine (Green Desert). February 15. Twelfth foal. 88,000Y. Tattersalls October Book 2. Hugo Merry. Sister to the quite useful 2-y-o 7f winner Sister of Mercy and half-sister to the quite useful 2-y-o 7f and subsequent US stakes winner Maid For Music (by Dubai Destination). The dam, a quite useful 2-y-o 6f winner, is a half-sister to 7 winners including the useful 2-y-o 7f winners Artistic Lad and Maid To Perfection (herself the dam of two listed winners). The second dam, Maid For The Hills (by Indian Ridge), a useful 2-y-o listed 6f Empress Stakes winner, is a half-sister to 5 winners including the dams of the US Grade 1 winner Stroll and the Group winners Grassy, Lady In Waiting and Savannah Bay. (Ann Black, M Al Qatami & K M Al Mudhaf). *"She only arrived this morning, she was a beautiful filly at the sales and she's hard to dislike now. She looked like to the type to make a 2-y-o, so we'll have to see. I've been so lucky with Azamour because four out of the*

five I've had have won stakes races – I can't believe we're always going to operate at 80% however! These are the last 2-y-o's by the sire and I've been sent a few of them".*

1346. UNNAMED ★★★★
ch.f. Sepoy – Mango Mischief (Desert King). January 17. Fourth foal. 48,000Y. Tattersalls October Book 1. Rabbah Bloodstock. Half-sister to Mango Diva (by Holy Roman Emperor), a very useful winner of 4 races including the Group 2 9f Kilboy Estate Stakes. The dam, a Group 3 10f Daffodil Stakes winner of 5 races, is a half-sister to 4 winners including the useful 2-y-o 6f and 7f and subsequent US Grade 3 winner Eurolink Raindance and the smart 7f (at 2 yrs) and 10f winner Bonecrusher. The second dam, Eurolink Mischief (by Be My Chief), a quite useful 12f winner, is a half-sister to 3 winners including the useful middle-distance colt and listed winner Duke Of Eurolink. (S Ali) *"I like her very much. She's done very well, I thought she was really cheap and I'd be disappointed if she can't win a race that includes the Book One bonus and the Plus Ten bonus. If we also win at a decent track we might get all of her purchase price back in one go. I like all I see of her and I'd say she'd be a six/seven furlong 2-y-o".*

1347. UNNAMED ★★★
gr.c. Dark Angel – Miss Beatrix (Danehill Dancer). April 21. Seventh foal. €370,000 foal. Goffs November. Rob Speers. Half-brother to the French 5.5f (at 2 yrs) to 1m winner of 4 races and Group 3 Prix de Cabourg third Jally (by Tamayuz). The dam won 3 races at 2 yrs including the Group 1 7f Moyglare Stud Stakes and was third in the Group 1 Phoenix Stakes. The second dam, Miss Beabea (by Catrail), an Irish 2-y-o listed 6f winner and second in the Group 1 6f Phoenix Stakes, is a half-sister to 9 winners including the very useful 5f winner Ellen's Lad. (Mr V I Araci). *"A big colt and a late foal, his pedigree suggests he'll be a 2-y-o but I can't believe it's going to be in the first half of the season. From July onwards who knows what he could develop into, but at the moment we're minding him a bit and hoping to aim him at some nice races later on".*

1348. UNNAMED ★★★★
b.f. Cacique – Postale (Zamindar). March 23.
Second foal. 180,000Y. Tattersalls October
Book 1. Al Shaqab Racing. Half-sister to the
fairly useful 2016 2-y-o 1m winner Star Archer
(by Champs Elysees). The dam is an unplaced
sister to the French 2-y-o listed placed Pure
Joy and a half-sister to 5 winners including
the Group 1 Prix Jean Prat winner Mutual
Trust. The second dam, Posteritas (by Lear
Fan), a fairly useful listed 10f winner, is a
half-sister to 7 winners. (Al Shaqab Racing).
*"She's very nice, I hope her 3-y-o half-brother
is going to be a stakes horse and I think she'll
have a similar profile to him. She's a strong
filly, she moves nicely, goes well and she'll be a
seven furlong/mile 2-y-o".*

1349. UNNAMED ★★★
b.c. Clodovil – Vanity's Girl (Compton Place).
April 29. Second foal. 45,000Y. Tattersalls
October Book 1. Seventh Lap. Half-brother
to Golconda King (by Dark Angel), unplaced
in three starts at 2 yrs in 2016. The dam, a
moderate 7f placed 3-y-o, is a half-sister to 5
winners including the Group 3 Ballyogan
Stakes and dual listed winner and Group 1
second Lesson In Humility and the useful
listed 1m winner Boastful. The second dam,
Vanity (by Thatching), a fair 5f and 6f placed
maiden, is a half-sister to 6 winners including
the listed winner Ffestiniog (herself the dam
of 3 stakes winners). (Seventh Lap Racing).
*"He'll definitely be a 2-y-o and a fast one,
but not necessarily early. He's big, he's still
growing and a bit out of shape, so I would
have thought he'd be very much looking to win
a six furlong maiden in August or September".*

AMANDA PERRETT
1350. ASTROMACHIA ★★★★
b.c. Sea The Stars – Fontley (Sadler's Wells).
April 2. Second foal. 80,000Y. Tattersalls
October Book 1. John Connolly / Amanda
Perrett. The dam, a fairly useful 7f (at 2
yrs) and 1m winner, was listed-placed
three times and is a half-sister to 4 winners
including the Group 3 12f Pinnacle Stakes
winner Moment In Time. The second dam,
Horatia (Machiavellian), a 10f winner here,
subsequently won a Grade 3 in the USA and is
a half-sister to 6 winners including the triple
Group 2 winner Opinion Poll. (Mr J Connolly

& Ms Odile Griffith). *"He's a very nice horse
and wasn't expensive all things considered. It's
the same Sea The Stars/Sadler's Wells cross as
three black type winners including Taghrooda.
He won't be particularly early but he goes
really nicely and is one for seven furlongs to
start with. A big, strapping horse, I'm very
pleased with his progress at the moment, his
knees are quite mature and although Ascot
may come too soon he might be around for
Goodwood. We're not usually very busy on the
2-y-o front and last year the winners seemed
to come in November and December, but this
year I think we have got some earlier ones".*

1351. CAPE SUNRISE ★★★
b.c. Cape Cross – Get Happy (Zamindar).
February 15. Second foal. 47,000Y. Tattersalls
October Book 2. Amanda Perrett / Peter &
Ross Doyle. Half-brother to Eternal Dream (by
Dream Ahead), unplaced on his only start at
2 yrs in 2016. The dam, a French listed-placed
winner of two races at 2 and 3 yrs including
over 1m, is a half-sister to 2 winners. The
second dam, Happy At Last (by In The Wings),
a quite useful 2-y-o 1m winner, is a half-
sister to 11 winners including Capal Garmon
(Group 2 Jockey Club Cup). (The Cape Sunrise
Partnership). *"A small, sharp 2-y-o, well-
balanced and the dam was rated 97, so why
not? He should be racing come May time
and he has the make and shape of a 2-y-o.
He'll start at six furlongs but should get seven
furlongs or a mile later on and I'll try aiming
him for the seven furlong Goodwood nursery
we won with Coasting many years ago".*

1352. COGITAL ★★★★
b.c. Invincible Spirit – Galaxy Highflyer
(Galileo). January 30. Sixth foal. 280,000Y.
Tattersalls October Book 1. A Perrett / Peter
& Ross Doyle. Half-brother to the very useful
2-y-o 6f and 7f winner and Group 2 Beresford
Stakes second Oklahoma City (by Oasis
Dream) and to a 2-y-o winner in Russia by
Dansili. The dam is an unraced half-sister to 7
winners including the Group 1 winners Opera
House, Kayf Tara and Zee Zee Top (dam of
the Group 1 winner Izzi Top) and to the dam
of the Group 1 Moyglare Stud Stakes winner
Necklace. The second dam, Colorspin (by
High Top), won the Irish Oaks and is a half-
sister to the Irish Champion Stakes winner

Cezanne and the Group 2 Prix de l'Opera winner Bella Colora (the dam of four stakes winners). (Mr J Connolly & Ms Odile Griffith). *"He's a lovely horse, oozes quality and it's a great family. Seven furlongs should be right for him this year and he should get up to a mile, he doesn't do anything very quickly at home but he's very generous in his work. He's well-built, 16 hands, moves well and he's by Invincible Spirit out of a Galileo mare, so he's got every chance".*

1353. COTTINGHAM ★★★

b.c. Dalakhani – Echelon (Danehill). March 27. Sixth foal. 160,000Y. Tattersalls October Book 1. Amanda Perrett. Brother to the Group 1 Falmouth Stakes and dual Group 2 winner Integral and half-brother to the useful listed-placed 7f and 1m winner Provenance, the modest 12f winner Elysian (both by Galileo), the quite useful dual 10f winner Entity (by Shamardal) and the fair 8.5f winner Jabbaar (by Medicean). The dam won the Group 1 1m Matron Stakes, the Group 2 Celebration Mile and four Group 3 events and is a half-sister to the dual Group 2 Celebration Mile winner Chic. The second dam, Exclusive (Polar Falcon), won the Group 1 1m Coronation Stakes and is a half-sister to 9 winners including the 2,000 Guineas winner Entrepreneur. (Mr George Materna). *"A colt with a wonderful pedigree, he's not over big (15.1 now but growing like a weed) but nevertheless he'll want a bit of time. I wouldn't think we'll see him out much before September time and his full-brother Integral didn't run at all at two. Being by Dalakhani and from that family you'd be tempted to think he wouldn't make much of a 2-y-o, but he looks very similar to our Dalakhani colt You're Hired. He was placed twice at two before winning three races as a 3-y-o for us including over seven furlongs".*

1354. DAGIAN ★★

ch.c. Dawn Approach – Hen Night (Danehill Dancer). February 24. Second living foal. 200,000Y. Tattersalls October Book 1. A Perrett / Peter & Ross Doyle. The dam, a listed 1m winner in Ireland and third in the Group 3 Irish 1,000 Guineas Trial, is a half-sister to 5 winners including the US dual Grade 2 winner and Grade 1 third Amira's Prince (by Teofilo).

The second dam, Twice The Ease (by Green Desert), is an unplaced sister to the 2-y-o listed 6f winner Desert Ease and a half-sister to the triple Group 3 winner Two-Twenty-Two. (Mr J Connolly & Ms Odile Griffith). *"A nice, scopey, strong individual by a first season sire. One for the second half of the season".*

1355. DESERT PATH ★★★

ch.c. Champs Elysees – Desert Image (Beat Hollow). January 29. First foal. The dam, a fairly useful 2-y-o 7f winner and listed 1m second, is a half-sister to 3 winners including the fairly useful 2-y-o 8.5f winner Torrid. The second dam, Western Appeal (by Gone West), a 7f winner at 3 yrs in France, was third in the listed 7f Prix de Saint-Cyr and is a sister to the champion 2-y-o and 3-y-o Zafonic and to the smart Group 3 winner Zamindar. (Khalid Abdulla). *"He's a big 3-y-o type and a good mover from a smart family. The dam won as a 2-y-o and was listed-placed but he's going to want at least seven furlongs later in the season".*

1356. FLIRTARE ★★★★★

b.f. Oasis Dream – Federation (Motivator). January 30. First foal. 105,000Y. Tattersalls October Book 1. A Perrett / Peter & Ross Doyle. The dam, a quite useful 1m winner here and a winner of 3 races in the USA, was Grade 3 placed and is a half-sister to four winners including Attraction (winner of the 1,000 Guineas, Irish 1,000 Guineas, Coronation Stakes, Matron Stakes and Sun Chariot Stakes). The second dam, Flirtation (by Pursuit Of Love), is an unplaced half-sister to 4 winners including the French Group 2 placed Carmita. *"She's speedy, a January foal and she's ready to go. It's a wonderful pedigree and although the dam didn't win until she was three her half-sister Attraction was unbeaten as a 2-y-o and she wasn't bad! This filly will be one of our first runners, she's got bags of speed, a bit of size and scope and if we've got an Ascot 2-y-o she's probably the one".*

1357. GATHER ★★

b.f. Showcasing – Acquisition (Dansili). April 16. Fifth foal. Half-sister to the quite useful 1m winner Recently Acquired (by Beat Hollow). The dam, a quite useful 12f and 14f winner, is a half-sister to 6 winners including the useful 2-y-o listed 7f winner Protectress and the useful 12f to 14f winner and listed-placed Market Forces. The second dam, Quota (by Rainbow Quest), a useful 10f winner, is a sister to 4 winners including the top-class Group 1 1m Racing Post Trophy winner and St Leger second Armiger and the useful 2-y-o 1m and 8.5f winner and Group 1 Racing Post Trophy fourth Besiege. (Khalid Abdulla). *"A nice filly with a bit of size and scope, she's 15.2 now and has been doing her work really nicely. The pedigree is 'speed over stamina' to some extent but she's a nice filly for the second half of the season and into next year I'd say".*

1358. GOOD IMPRESSION ★★★
b.c. Showcasing – Daintily Done (Cacique). March 17. Second foal. The dam is an unraced half-sister to the high-class Group 1 9f Dubai Duty Free winner Cityscape and the very smart Group 2 5f Temple Stakes and multiple Group 1 placed Bated Breath (both now sires) and the useful listed-placed triple 1m winner Scuffle. The second dam, Tantina (by Distant View), a smart winner of 4 races including two listed events over 7f, was Group 3 placed and is a half-sister to 2 winners. (Khalid Abdulla). *"A bit more of a 2-y-o type than our other Showcasing 2-y-o, the dam was unraced but she's a half to Cityscape and Bated Breath so that might just give him a bit of zip. I expect we'll see him over six furlongs in May".*

1359. MASKED DEFENDER ★★★
br.c. First Defence – Costume (Danehill). February 16. Fifth foal. Half-brother to the quite useful 1m winner Epic Voyage (by Empire Maker). The dam, a 1m winner here and subsequently a US dual Grade 2 winner over 1m and 9f, is a half-sister to 3 winners. The second dam, Dance Dress (by Nureyev), a French Group 3 10.5f winner, is a half-sister to 3 winners. (Khalid Abdulla). *"A tall horse, 15.3, he's well-built and a really nice individual. He looks like a 2-y-o for May/June over six furlongs and I like him".*

1360. OVERTRUMPED ★★
b.f. Champs Elysees – Perfect Hand (Barathea). May 12. Sixth foal. Half-sister to the French listed-placed 10f winner Tamelly

(by New Approach) and to the French 11f winner Preempt (by Dansili). The dam, a French 9f winner, is a sister to the French 2-y-o 7f and subsequent US Grade 1 1m Matriarch Stakes winner Price Tag and a half-sister to 2 winners. The second dam, Tarocchi (by Affirmed), a minor French 10.5f winner, is a half-sister to numerous winners including the very useful Group 2 12f Prix de Malleret winner Privity and the Group 3 9f Prix Saint Roman winner Zindari. (Khalid Abdulla). *"She's not over big but she stands over a bit of ground, has a good attitude and is a tough little filly in training. She's going to want seven furlongs plus but she's nice and I really like Champs Elysees fillies – we've had a lot of luck with them".*

1361. PORT OF CALL ★★★
b.c. Harbour Watch – Valiantly (Anabaa). March 26. Eighth foal. 60,000Y. Tattersalls October Book 2. Charlie Gordon-Watson. Half-brother to the quite useful 7f (at 2 yrs) and 1m winner of 4 races Brownsea Brink and to the modest 6f to 1m winner Secret Hero (both by Cadeaux Genereux). The dam, a 6f winner in France, was second in the listed 6f Cecil Frail Stakes and is a half-sister to 2 winners. The second dam, Valbra (by Dancing Brave), is an unplaced sister to the listed winner and Group 3 placed Cheyenne Dream and a half-sister to 6 winners including the dams of the Group 1 winners Continent and Zambezi Sun. (Mr A D Spence). *"He's racy and not over-big but his knees are a bit immature at present. I should imagine we'll see him over six furlongs around June/July time".*

1362. SING A RAINBOW ★★★
ch.f. Frankel – Beatrice Aurore (Danehill Dancer). March 16. First foal. The dam, a Group 3 9f Prix Chloe winner of 4 races, is a half-sister to the Swedish listed 1m winners Ray and Vigelegere. The second dam, Mondschein (by Rainbow Quest), a French listed 12f winner, is a sister to the Group 3 12f winner Jahafil and a half-sister to numerous winners. (Benny Andersson). *"It's nice to have a Frankel of course. She's a lovely specimen, does everything really well, she's athletic, 15.2 and with a nice stride on her. We'll be looking at seven furlongs from Goodwood time onwards with her".*

1363. THRESHOLDOFADREAM ★★
b.f. Camelot – Signella (Selkirk). March 2. Fifth foal. 60,000Y. Tattersalls October Book 2. Amanda Perrett. Half-sister to the fair 6.5f (at 2 yrs) to 7.5f winner of four races Haley's Harley (by Cockney Rebel), to the modest 10f winner Beijing Star (by Dylan Thomas) and a minor winner abroad by Rock Of Gibraltar. The dam, a modest 10f winner, is a half-sister to 5 winners including the Group 3 10.5f Prix de Flore winner Audacieuse (herself dam of the dual Group 1 winner Kingston Hill) and the Group 3 Acomb Stakes winner Waiter's Dream. The second dam, Sarah Georgina (by Persian Bold), a quite useful 2-y-o 6f winner, is a half-sister to 11 winners including the French 1,000 Guineas winner Danseuse du Soir. (Mr D James & Woodcote Stud). *"A filly with a lovely pedigree and Camelot has a lot of nice two-year-olds that everyone seems to be excited about. She's 16 hands so she'll want a bit of time and is a 3-y-o in the making but with a bit of quality".*

1364. UNNAMED ★★★
br.c. Kodiac – Lightwood Lady (Anabaa). May 10. Ninth foal. £18,000 2-y-o Tattersalls Ireland Ascot 2-y-o sales. Amanda Perrett. Half-brother to the fairly useful 1m winner of 4 races Express Himself (by Dylan Thomas), to the quite useful 6f (at 2 yrs) and 5f winner Munshid (by Dutch Art), the quite useful 2-y-o 5f winner (on her only start) Its Alright (by King's Best), the fair 1m and subsequent US winner Totheendoftheearth (by Hurricane Run) and the minor French dual 3-y-o winner Halendale (by Elusive City). The dam, a fair Irish 6f winner, is a half-sister to 6 winners. The second dam, Lyrical Dance (by Lear Fan), a minor winner at 4 yrs in the USA, is a full or half-sister to 7 winners including the Group/Grade 1 winners Black Minnaloushe, Pennekamp and Nasr El Arab. *"He's ready to roll but he was a slightly late foal so that will hold him back a bit. We bought him for a 2-y-o syndicate, so we'll be kicking on with him and he'll running plenty this year".* TRAINERS' BARGAIN BUY

JONATHAN PORTMAN

1365. FOLIES BERGERES ★★★
ch.f. Champs Elysees – May Fox (Zilzal). March 26. Sixth living foal. 22,000Y. Tattersalls October Book 2. J Portman. Half-sister to the very useful Group 3 7f Oak Tree Stakes and US Grade 3 1m winner of 6 races Annecdote (by Lucky Story), to the quite useful 6f (at 2 yrs) to 9f winner of 4 races Meglio Ancora (by Best Of The Bests) and the fair 8.5f winner Down To Earth (by Aussie Rules). The dam is an unraced half-sister to 6 winners here and in Turkey. The second dam, Folly Fox (by Alhijaz), is an unraced half-sister to 5 winners. (Portlee Bloodstock). *"A half-sister to a good filly I trained called Annecdote, but she's not quite as sharp as her. One for the second half of the season, we're not doing much with her yet because being by Champs Elysees she should be given a bit of time".*

1366. GAINSAY ★★★
b.f. Sayif – Pesse (Eagle Eyed). February 24. Sixth living foal. 15,000Y. Tattersalls October Book 3. Kern/Lillingston. Sister to the quite useful 2016 2-y-o 5f to 6f winner of 4 races Sayesse and half-sister to the minor Italian winner of 5 races at 2 and 3 yrs Super Aurora (by Refuse To Bend). The dam, a minor Italian winner of 7 races including at 2 yrs, is a half-sister to 8 winners including the 2-y-o Group 1 1m Racing Post Trophy winner Kingsbarns and the US Grade 3 winner Sweeter Still. The second dam, Beltisaal (by Belmez), placed 5 times at 3 yrs in France, is a half-sister to 6 winners including the listed winner and Group 2 placed Kafhar. (Lambourne, Forbes, Losse). *"She's quite nice, tough and reasonably early. She's just gone 'up behind' a bit, so she's on the grow, which is good because she needed to. I like her, she's tough, could be out from the end of April and has a nice way about her. Before this year I haven't been familiar with the sire but I now have two of them and they just look like horses that have a bit of speed for five furlongs but may get a mile in due course".*

1367. KING OF BURGUNDY ★★
b.c. Holy Roman Emperor – Brilliant Sunshine (Pivotal). February 9. First foal. 240,000Y. Tattersalls October Book 2. Howson & Houldsworth. The dam is an unraced half-sister to the listed winners Ferdoos and Brusco. The second dam, Blaze Of Colour (by Rainbow Quest), a quite useful dual 12f winner, was listed-placed and is a half-

sister to 5 winners. (Tony Wechsler & Ann Plummer). "A big, strong, handsome horse who will need a bit of time. He won't be out before the back-end, he'll want seven furlongs and he has quality about him but he'll be a slow-burner".

1368. MADAM POMFREY ★★★
b.f. Sayif – Miss Poppy (Averti). February 11. Fifth foal. 5,000Y. Tattersalls October Book 4. Linda Sadler. Half-sister to the fair 2016 2-y-o 5f winner Compton Poppy (by Compton Place), to the modest 7f (at 2 yrs) and 1m winner Bon Port (by Major Cadeaux) and the modest triple 6f winner Reflation (by Stimulation). The dam, a modest 6f placed maiden (including at 2 yrs), is a half-sister to 11 winners including the top-class Group 1 5f Nunthorpe Stakes winner and sire Kyllachy. The second dam, Pretty Poppy (by Song), a modest 2-y-o 5f winner, stayed 7.6f and is a half-sister to 4 winners. (Berkeley Racing). *"I loved her at the sales, she has the most marvellous attitude and she's just a nice sort that didn't cost much and could give the partnership some fun".* TRAINERS' BARGAIN BUY

1369. MIREK ★★
gr.g. Zebedee – My Trust (Exceed And Excel). February 20. First foal. €8,000Y. Tattersalls Ireland September. Select Racing. The dam, a moderate dual 6f placed maiden at 2 and 3 yrs, is a half-sister to 3 winners including the dam of the Australian Group 2 and Group 3 winner Astern. The second dam, Alizes (by Rory's Jester), won a Group 2 in Australia and is a half-sister to 4 winners. (Ian Beach). *"He's quite forward and should be running reasonably early. He has a lot of speed but unfortunately he has a lot of anger and impatience in him too, so I'm trying to iron that out. He's very tough, so you'd never beat him in a battle".*

1370. NAUTICA (IRE) ★★★
b.f. Born To Sea – Moynsha Lady (Namid). February 19. Fourth foal. €11,000Y. Goffs Sportsmans. A Skiffington/J Portman. Half-sister to the fair 2016 5f and 6f placed 2-y-o Hamidan's Girl (by Bahamian Bounty) and to the fair 1m winner Hutton (by Lawman). The dam is an unraced half-sister to 9 winners

including the 2-y-o 6f and subsequent US stakes winner and Group 2 6f Coventry Stakes third Luck Money and the 2-y-o Group 3 7f Prix du Calvados winner Charlotte O'Fraise. The second dam, Dundel (by Machiavellian), a quite useful 7f winner, is a half-sister to 6 winners including the Group 3 6f winner Seltitude. (Laurence Bellman & Partners).*"I thought she was going to be pretty early until we x-rayed her knees and the advice was to back off, but she was the one all the lads were talking about. Not a big filly but well-made".*

1371. QUICK BREATH ★★★
b.c. Bated Breath – Shy Appeal (Barathea). April 8. Fifth foal. Half-brother to the 2017 3-y-o 1m debut winner Broad Appeal (by Medicean) and to the fair 8.5f (at 2 yrs) and 12f winner Bold Appeal (by Nayef). The dam, a modest 7f placed 2-y-o in Ireland, is a half-sister to the Group 3 Premio Tudini winner Victory Laurel. The second dam, Special Cause (by Fasliyev), won once over 7f at 3 yrs in France and is a half-sister to 6 winners including the dam of Zafeen (Group 1 St James's Palace Stakes). (Wood Street Syndicate). *"A half-brother to a nice 3-y-o of mine, Broad Appeal, who was a late developer. I'm hoping we'll get this one out a bit earlier, hopefully in mid-summer, but he'll be a 3-y-o as well and I do like him. He looks every bit as nice as his half-brother".*

1372. TOORMAKEADY ★★★
gr.f. Mastercraftsman – Liberally (Statue Of Liberty). February 5. Third foal. The dam, a quite useful 1m to 10f winner of 3 races here, was Grade 3 placed over 9f in the USA and is a half-sister to 9 winners including the 1,000 Guineas and Group 2 Rockfel Stakes winner Speciosa and the US Grade 3 stakes winner of 13 races Major Rhythm. The second dam, Specifically (by Sky Classic), won once at 2 yrs in the USA and is a half-sister to 10 winners including the Group 1 Champion Stakes, Grand Prix de Saint-Cloud and Hong Kong Cup winner Pride. (Whitcoombe Park Racing). *"She's a lovely, big, strong filly and very much more of a 3-y-o type than for this year. All she wants to do is please, she loves being out and just has a bit of quality to her. Seven furlongs in late summer will be fine for her starting point".*

1373. UNNAMED ★★★
b.f. Dawn Approach – Reckoning (Danehill Dancer). March 7. First foal. The dam, a fairly useful 2-y-o 1m winner, was listed-placed three times at around 10f and is a half-sister to 2 winners including the US winner and Grade 3 8.5f second Hope Cross. The second dam, Great Hope (by Halling), a quite useful Irish dual 1m winner, is a half-sister to 5 winners including the dual Group 3 placed Chivalrous. (Maskell Stud). *"A home-bred filly, she's nice but needs time. A bit weak at present, she's quite typical of a lot of home-bred 2-y-o's in that she's a bit backward in condition and didn't come into the yard until late. I should think she'll be starting off at around seven furlongs later in the season".*

1374. UNNAMED ★★★
ch.f. Monsieur Bond – Saphire (College Chapel). March 11. Seventh foal. £46,000Y. Goffs UK Silver Sale (Doncaster). F Barberini. Half-sister to the fairly useful 2-y-o 5f winner and Group 3 5f Cornwallis Stakes second Waffle (by Kheleyf), to the quite useful 7f and 1m winner and subsequent US stakes-placed Byrony (by Byron) and the modest 1m, 12f and hurdles winner King's Road (by King's Best). The dam, a fairly useful 2-y-o 5f and 6f winner, was listed-placed twice and is a half-sister to 4 minor winners. The second dam, Emerald Eagle (by Sandy Creek), a fair 6f to 1m winner of 5 races, is a half-sister to 4 winners. (Clipper Logistics). *"She hasn't arrived here yet. I saw her at the sales and actually bid on her until the bidding went up and up. I thought she looked like one I'd like to train and that she was very racy, so I pestered the people who did buy her to send her to me and they eventually capitulated! They're good owners to have, but this filly is still in a pre-training yard so I can't enlighten you any further".*

1375. UNNAMED ★★★
b.f. Havana Gold – Sparkling Eyes (Lujain). March 29. Fifth foal. 27,000Y. Tattersalls October Book 3. Blandford Bloodstock. Half-sister to the quite useful 6f (at 2 yrs) to 1m winner of 3 races Wimpole Hall (by Canford Cliffs), to the quite useful 6f winner Blurred Vision (by Royal Applause) and the quite useful 5.5f (at 2 yrs) and 6f winner of 5 races

Pea Shooter (by Piccolo). The dam, a fairly useful dual 5f winner (including at 2 yrs), was fourth in the Group 2 5f Queen Mary Stakes, is a half-sister to 3 winners here and abroad. The second dam, Lady Georgia (by Arazi), was a useful 3-y-o 7.8f winner. (Mrs M A Parker). *"A strong-looking type, very nice and a June/July type 2-y-o. There's a lot to like about her and she's quite a big filly that'll start at six or seven furlongs. She came in quite late, so she hasn't done as much as some of the others".*

KEVIN PRENDERGAST

1376. ALGHABRAH (IRE) ★★★
b.f. Tamayuz – Asheerah (Shamardal). March 20. Third foal. Half-sister to the 2016 2-y-o 7f winner from two starts Aneen (by Lawman) and to the 7f (at 2 yrs), Group 1 1m Irish 2,000 Guineas and Group 2 1m Boomerang Stakes winner Awtaad (by Cape Cross). The dam, a fairly useful Irish listed-placed 7f winner, is a half-sister to useful 2-y-o 6f winner and Group 3 7f Killavullan Stakes third Aaraas, to the useful Irish 2-y-o 6f winner and Group 3 7f Silver Flash Stakes third Alshahbaa and the fairly useful listed-placed winner Daymooma. The second dam, Adaala (by Sahm), an Irish 7f (at 2 yrs) and listed 9f winner, is a half-sister to 2 winners. (Hamdan Al Maktoum). *"A half-sister to my Guineas winner Awtaad, she's very nice but she's big and will take a bit of time. We'll aim to get her out around August time over seven furlongs. She's a different type altogether to Awtaad".*

1377. DESERT CHORUS (IRE) ★★★
b.c. Oasis Dream – Harmonic Note (Nayef). March 7. First foal. €140,000Y. Tattersalls Ireland September. Kevin Prendergast. The dam, a quite useful listed-placed dual 1m winner, is a half-sister to 4 winners including the fairly useful 2-y-o 6f winner Haadeeth. The second dam, Musical Key (by Key Of Luck), a fair maiden, was fourth twice over 5f at 2 yrs and is a half-sister to 6 winners including the high-class Hong Kong horses Mensa and Firebolt and the dam of the Group 2 Flying Childers winner Wunders Dream. *"He'll be a colt for seven furlongs to a mile in the second half of the season. He'll want dry ground and I'd say he looks more like Oasis Dream than his damsire Nayef".*

1378. HAWAAM (IRE) ★★★
b.c. Swiss Spirit – Anne Bonney (Jade Robbery). March 26. Fifth foal. €120,000Y. Goffs Orby. Shadwell Estate Co. Half-brother to 4 winners including the Group 3 Sprint Stakes and listed Scurry Stakes winner Waady (by Approve) and the fair 2-y-o 7f winner Pinwood (by Bushranger). The dam, a moderate 9f placed maiden, is a half-sister to 3 winners in Japan and one in France. The second dam, Sanchez (by Wolfhound), a fair 9f placed maiden, is a half-sister to 6 winners including the Group 1 winners Ballingarry, Aristotle and Starborough. (Hamdan Al Maktoum). *"A nice horse, we like him a lot and he'll be racing by the end of April over six furlongs. He looks to go nicely".*

1379. HIMMAH (IRE) ★★★
b.f. Intikhab – Ahaaly (Exceed And Excel). March 8. Second foal. The dam, a quite useful 2-y-o 6f winner, is a half-sister to 4 winners including the useful dual 7f (at 2 yrs), 10f and hurdles winner Nafaath. The second dam, Alshakr (by Bahri), a very useful winner of the Group 2 1m Falmouth Stakes, is a half-sister to 4 winners including the dam of the 1,000 Guineas winner Harayir. (Hamdan Al Maktoum). *"Not too far off a run, we trained the dam who was a winner but quite excitable. This filly should be a six furlong 2-y-o like her dam".*

1380. KHAFFAQ ★★★
ch.c. Helmet – Mujadil Draw (Daggers Drawn). January 31. Fourth foal. €140,000Y. Goffs Orby. Shadwell Estate Co. Half-brother to the 2016 Italian 2-y-o listed 6f winner Mujadil Lachy (by Kyllachy) and to a minor winner in Italy by Champs Elysees. The dam, a listed-placed 2-y-o winner in Italy, is a half-sister to 7 winners including the Italian dual Group 3 winner Titus Shadow. The second dam, Mujadil Shadow (by Mujadil), a minor dual winner in Italy at 2 and 3 yrs, is a half-sister to 4 winners. (Hamdan Al Maktoum). *"A nice, big horse that seems to go well, we haven't had him long but we like him. He moves well and has a good temperament".*

1381. MOGHAMARAH ★★★★
ch.f. Dawn Approach – Shimah (Storm Cat). February 20. Fourth foal. Half-sister to the

useful listed 6f (at 2 yrs), 7f and subsequent UAE sprint winner Mushir (by Oasis Dream) and to the fair 1m winner Estikhraaj (by Dansili). The dam, a listed 6f winner and second in the Group 1 Moyglare Stud Stakes, is a half-sister to 5 winners including the listed 6f (at 2 yrs) and Group 3 7f Athasi Stakes winner Walayef, the Group 2 6f Diomed Stakes winner Haatef and the Irish dual listed 6f winner Ulfah. The second dam, Sayedat Alhadh (by Mr Prospector), a US 7f winner, is a sister to the US Grade 2 7f winner Kayrawan and a half-sister to the useful winners Amaniy, Elsaamri and Mathkurh. (Hamdan Al Maktoum). *"One of our stars. I trained the dam who was a stakes winner and only just got beaten in the Moyglare. I like this filly just as much. She'll be a six furlong 2-y-o".*

1382. MOKTAMEL (IRE) ★★★
b.c. Epaulette – Becuille (Redback). March 28. Third foal. £70,000Y. Goffs UK Premier (Doncaster). Shadwell Estate Co. Half-brother to the fairly useful 7f and 8.5f winner Tony The Gent (by Kodiac) and to the quite useful 7f winner King To Be (by Myboycharlie). The dam, a fair dual 9f winner, is a half-sister to 3 winners including the 2-y-o Group 1 Middle Park Stakes and Group 1 Prix Morny winner Bushranger. The second dam, Danz Danz (by Efisio), is an unraced half-sister to 2 winners. (Hamdan Al Maktoum). *"A nice horse that wants at least six furlongs, he's got a good action so he'll appreciate dry ground".*

1383. MOONLIGHT BAY (IRE) ★★★★
b.c. Pivotal – Naadrah (Muhtathir). February 14. Third foal. €36,000Y. Goffs November. Friarstown Stables. Brother to the quite useful 2-y-o 6f and 7f winner Martini Time. The dam, a 2-y-o 10f winner in France and listed-placed at 3 over 10f, is a half-sister to 3 winners including the Group 3 Prix du Prince d'Orange second Prince Mag. The second dam, Princess d'Orange (by Anabaa), a listed-placed winner at 3 yrs in France, is a half-sister to the dam of the Group winners Irish Wells and Sign Of The Wolf. (Norman Ormiston). *"She won the first 2-y-o race of the season, at Naas on the 26th March. We like her a lot, she'll probably run in the Swordlestown Stakes next. Not a big filly, but quality and a typical Pivotal".*

1384. MY DAYDREAM (IRE) ★★★
b.f. Oasis Dream – Termagant (Powerscourt).
April 18. Second foal. 260,000 foal. Tattersalls
December. Not sold. The dam, a Group 1 7f
Moyglare Stud Stakes winner, is a half-sister
to 5 winners including the fairly useful
1m (at 2 yrs) to 10f winner of 7 races and
listed-placed Splinter Cell. The second dam,
Rock Salt (by Selkirk), placed twice at 3 yrs
in France, is a sister to the Group 2 10f Prix
Eugene Adam winner Kirkwall and a half-
sister to 4 winners. (Mrs Vasicek). *"I trained
the dam who won the Moyglare. This filly is
nice but we'll take our time with her and she's
one for seven furlongs towards the back-end".*

1385. NEW DREAM (IRE) ★★★
ch.f. Exceed And Excel – Asfurah's Dream
(Nayef). March 18. Half-sister to the fairly
useful Irish 2-y-o 6f winner Cool Thunder
(by Shamardal), to the fair Irish 7f winner
Connacht Council (by Haatef) and a hurdles
winner by Marju. The dam, a quite useful 9f
winner, is a half-sister to 8 winners including
the fairly useful 7f (including at 2 yrs) and
1m winner Famous Poet (by Exceed And
Excel). The second dam, Asfurah (by Dayjur),
a very useful winner of the Group 3 6f Cherry
Hinton Stakes, was second in the Group 1
Phoenix Stakes and is a sister to one winner
and a half-sister to 3 winners including the US
dual Grade 3 winner Istintaj. (Hadi Al-Tajir).
*"She hasn't been in long but she's a nice big
filly and a good mover. Hopefully she'll make a
2-y-o in mid-season".*

1386. RAPHAEL (GER) ★★★★
ch.c. Roderic O'Connor – Rusookh (Nayef).
February 25. First foal. £65,000Y. Goffs UK
Premier (Doncaster). Shadwell Estate Co. The
dam is an unraced half-sister to 6 winners.
The second dam, Thamarat (by Anabaa), a
French 2-y-o 6f winner, is a half-sister to 6
winners including the French dual Group 1
winning miler and sire Tamayuz. (Hamdan
Al Maktoum). *"We like him a lot, he's a very
nice horse and probably one of our first colts
to run. I think I'll wait for six furlongs for him,
he's out of a Nayef mare and from the family
of Tamayuz".*

1387. VIVA ITALIA (IRE) ★★★
b.f. Most Improved – Edelfa (Fasliyev).
February 16. Fourth foal. £25,000Y. Goffs

UK Premier (Doncaster). Kevin Prendergast.
Half-sister to the fairly useful 6f (including at
2 yrs) and 7f winner Stamp Hill (by Zoffany)
and to the fair 7f to 8.5f winner Italian Beauty
(by Thewayyouare). The dam won four minor
races in Italy and is a half-sister to 7 winners.
The second dam, Daziyra (by Doyoun), is
an unplaced half-sister to 4 winners. (John
O'Donaghue). *"She goes nicely and as soon
as we get six furlongs and dry ground she'll be
out. We like her".*

1388. RUSSIAN CAMPAIGN (IRE) ★★★
b.f. Declaration Of War – Deep Winter
(Pivotal). April 27. Fourth foal. €30,000Y. Goffs
Orby. K Prendergast. Half-sister to the fair 1m
winner Zabeel Star (by Arcano). The dam, a
quite useful 1m to 10f winner, was listed-
placed in Germany and is a half-sister to 7
winners. The second dam, Russian Snows (by
Sadler's Wells), a smart winner of the Group
2 12.5f Prix de Royallieu and second in the
Irish Oaks, is a sister to the high-class dual
Group 2 winner Modhish and a half-sister to
7 winners including the Group 3 10.5f Prix
de Royaumont winner and good broodmare
Truly Special. (Lady O'Reilly). *"A nice filly, I
know the family well and I actually trained
the third dam Arctique Royale who won the
Guineas. A nice, quality filly and not over-big".*

1389. SIMSIMAH (IRE) ★★★
b.f. Poet's Voice – Aaraas (Haafhd). March
22. Second foal. Half-sister to the fair 2016
7f placed 2-y-o Althiba (by Shamardal). The
dam, a useful 2-y-o 6f winner and third in
the Group 3 7f Killavullan Stakes, is a half-
sister to the useful Irish 2-y-o 6f winner and
Group 3 7f Silver Flash Stakes third Alshahbaa
and the fairly useful listed-placed winners
Daymooma and Asheerah (by Shamardal).
The second dam, Adaala (by Sahm), an Irish 7f
(at 2 yrs) and listed 9f winner, is a half-sister
to 2 winners. (Hamdan Al Maktoum). *"She's
coming along nicely and she'll be ready to run
in early May over six furlongs. Not a big filly
but she has a bit of quality".*

1390. TABAAHY ★★★★
b.c. Kyllachy – Pious (Bishop Of Cashel).
April 14. Twelfth foal. 260,000Y. Tattersalls
October Book 2. Shadwell Estate Co. Brother
to the Group 2 Sandown Mile and Group 2
Joel Stakes winner Penitent and the 2-y-o

Group 2 Mill Reef Stakes winner Supplicant and half-brother to 8 winners including the quite useful 5f winner of 10 races Solemn, the quite useful 7f winners Blithe (at 2 yrs) and Anoint and the fair 5.5f to 7f winner of 7 races Divine Call (all by Pivotal). The dam, a fair dual 6f winner at 2 and 3 yrs, is a half-sister to 5 winners. The second dam, La Cabrilla (by Carwhite), a 2-y-o 5f and 6f winner and third in the Group 3 Princess Margaret Stakes, is a half-sister to the Group 1 Nunthorpe Stakes winner Ya Malak. (Hamdan Al Maktoum). *"A very nice horse, he's a full brother to two Group winners and he's probably one of our better 2-y-o's. A beautiful horse that cost plenty".*

SIR MARK PRESCOTT

1391. BATH AND TENNIS (IRE) ★★★
b.f. Footstepsinthesand – Goldamour (Fasliyev). February 25. Third foal. €65,000Y. Goffs Orby. Amanda Skiffington. Half-sister to the moderate 2016 7f placed 2-y-o Wakened (by Rip Van Winkle) and to the modest 6f winner Big Amigo (by Bahamian Bounty). The dam, placed at 3 yrs in France, is a half-sister to 3 minor winners. The second dam, Glamadour (by Sanglamore), a winner over 11.5f in France, is a half-sister to 11 winners including the outstanding multiple Group 1 winner Goldikova and the Group 1 Prix Vermeille winner Galikova. (Mr T J Rooney). *"She was bought by Amanda Skiffington for Tim Rooney who lives in America but has had horses with us for 30 years. This filly is a sharp sort and will be amongst the first ones to work. A small, solid 2-y-o".*

1392. BOODLEY ★★★
b.f. Acclamation – Galapagar (Miswaki). March 9. Eighth foal. 165,000Y. Tattersalls October Book 1. Kern/Lillingston. Half-sister to the useful 2-y-o 5f and 6f winner and Group 3 7f Solario Stakes second Emirates Flyer (by Acclamation), to the fair 7f winner Tajathub (by Bahamian Bounty), the fair 6f and hurdles winner Magic Jack (by Trade Fair) and the modest 2-y-o 7f winner Inniscastle Boy (Sir Percy). The dam, a French 1m and 9f winner, is a half-sister to 4 minor winners in the USA. The second dam, Runaway Fair Lady (by Runaway Groom), was a minor stakes winner of 5 races in the USA. (Mrs O Hoare). *"She's a forward type and wasn't cheap, but*

the owner has always been lucky with us. A six/seven furlong 2-y-o, she's quite lengthy and Acclamation has been good to me – we've had Athenian who was good and of course Marsha who was very good".

1393. DEAUVILLE SOCIETY (IRE) ★★★★
b.f. Society Rock – Dorothy Dene (Red Ransom). March 5. Fourth foal. 20,000Y. Tattersalls October Book 2. Tina Rau. Half-sister to the fairly useful dual 6f winner at 2 and 3 yrs Navigate (by Iffraaj). The dam is an unraced half-sister to 3 winners including the Group 1 Middle Park Stakes winner Primo Valentino and the Group 2 6f Cherry Hinton Stakes winner Dora Carrington. The second dam, Dorothea Brooke (by Dancing Brave), won over 9f and is a half-sister to 6 winners including Conmaiche (Group 3 Prix Saint-Roman). (Suffolk Bloodstock). *"She'll be fairly forward. A very pleasant filly that should be one of the first ones to work".*

1394. DUTCH MONARCH ★★★★
b.f. Dutch Art – Regal Heiress (Pivotal). March 14. Third foal. Sister to the quite useful 2-y-o dual 7f winner Dutch Heiress and half-sister to the 2016 7f placed 2-y-o, on her only start, Italian Heiress (by Medicean). The dam, a fair 7f to 8.5f placed maiden, is a half-sister to 5 winners. The second dam, Regal Rose (by Danehill), won both her starts including the Group 1 6f Cheveley Park Stakes and is a sister to the Japanese 10f stakes winner Generalist and a half-sister to 8 winners. (Cheveley Park Stud). *"She'll be one of the earlier ones. We had her full sister, Dutch Heiress, who won a couple of 2-y-o races over seven furlongs and this would seem to be a similar sort".*

1395. FLEETING STEPS (IRE) ★★★
b.c. Footstepsinthesand – Breedj (Acclamation). April 13. Third foal. €75,000Y. Goffs Orby. J Brummitt. Half-brother to the quite useful 2016 2-y-o 5f and 6f winner Cuppacoffee (by Intense Focus) and to the fair 3-y-o 5f winner Miss Power (by Zebedee). The dam, a listed 5f placed 2-y-o, is a half sister to 3 minor winners. The second dam, Kildare Lady (by Indian Ridge), is an unraced half-sister to 7 winners including the 2-y-o listed 6f winner and Group 3 placed Shaard. (Mr G Moore (Osborne House). *"A nice, big*

horse that's in a field at the moment and I wouldn't expect him to run before September, but his pedigree suggests he might be quickish".

1396. FROLIC ★★★
b.f. Dutch Art – Jamboretta (Danehill). February 22. Fifth foal. Sister to the promising 2017 3-y-o 1m winner Bowerman and half-sister to the quite useful 7f winner Messila Star (by Pivotal) and the quite useful 2-y-o 7f winner Music And Dance (by Galileo). The dam, a quite useful 9f winner, is a half-sister to the listed winner and Group 3 second Excusez Moi. The second dam, Jiving (by Generous), a fair 6f placed 2-y-o, is a half-sister to the outstanding broodmare Hasili (dam of the Group 1 winners Banks Hill, Cacique, Champs Elysees, Heat Haze and Intercontinental and the Group 2 winner and leading sire Dansili) and to the dams of the Grade/Group 1 winners Leroidesanimaux and Promising Lead. (Cheveley Park Stud). *"She'll be a July type 2-y-o and her brother Bowerman won easily over a mile the other day. A nice, tall, scopey filly that should be able to run in July and I should think six/seven furlongs would be her trip this year".*

1397. GREY SPIRIT (IRE) ★★★
gr.c. Dark Angel – Buttonhole (Montjeu). March 3. Second living foal. 65,000Y. Tattersalls October Book 1. J Brummitt. The dam ran once unplaced and is a half-sister to 5 winners including the Group 1 Fillies' Mile and dual Group 2 10f Blandford Stakes winner Red Bloom and the listed winner Red Gala. The second dam, Red Camellia (by Polar Falcon), winner of the Group 3 7f Prestige Stakes, was third in the French 1,000 Guineas and is a half-sister to 4 winners. (Mr P Bamford – Osborne House). *"Out having a break now, he's a big colt that'll run around September time".*

1398. KINGOFTHESINGERS ★★★
b.c. Leroidesanimaux – Songerie (Hernando). April 11. Seventh foal. Goffs Orby. Sir Mark Prescott. Half-brother to the quite useful 2-y-o 1m winner Valitop (by Pivotal), to the fairly useful 12f and 13f winner Hardstone (by Birdstone) and a winner in Sweden by Mr Greeley. The dam won the Group 3 1m Prix

des Reservoirs at 2 yrs, was third in the Group 2 Park Hill Stakes and is a sister to the German listed winner and Group 1 Italian Oaks third Souvenance and a half-sister to 8 winners including the listed winners Soft Morning and Sourire. The second dam, Summer Night (by Nashwan), a fairly useful 3-y-o 6f winner, is a half-sister to 7 winners including the Group 3 Prix d'Arenburg winner Starlit Sands. (Mr & Mrs Gregson, Fox-Andrews, Hare & Vetch). *"A scopey, 3-y-o type and whatever he does this year you'd expect him to do better next year. Some of the family make back-end 2-y-o's though, for example the dam won the Prix des Reservoirs for us".*

1399. MATCHMAKING (GER) ★★★
ch.c. Mastercraftsman – Monami (Sholokhov). March 20. Second foal. 70,000Y. Tattersalls October Book 1. J Brummitt. The dam, a Group 3 1m winner in Germany and Group 1 placed in Italy, is a half-sister to 8 winners including the Group 1 Italian Oaks winner Meridiana. The second dam, Monbijou (by Dashing Blade), a German listed-placed winner, is a half-sister to 6 winners. (Mr W E Sturt – Osborne House). *"A nice horse, he's turned out having a break now but the dam was a fair 2-y-o in Germany and he could make a nice 2-y-o come September".*

1400. ON THE WARPATH ★★★★
ch.c. Declaration Of War – Elusive Pearl (Medaglia D'Oro). April 1. First foal. $150,000Y. Keeneland September. Oliver St Lawrence. The dam, a US listed stakes winner of 4 races at 2 and 3 yrs, is a half-sister to 2 winners. The second dam, Brazen Bride (by Miswaki), a US stakes-placed winner of 4 races, is a half-sister to 6 winners. (Mr C Walker – Osborne House II & Mr J Gunther). *"He'll start to work in May and he'll be a six/seven furlong 2-y-o. He's always gone nicely".*

1401. RUDE AWAKENING ★★★
b.c. Rip Van Winkle – First Exhibit (Machiavellian). March 12. Seventh foal. 50,000Y. Tattersalls October Book 2. J Brummitt. Half-brother to 5 winners including the 2016 2-y-o 7f winner, on her only start, Goya Girl (by Paco Boy), the fairly useful 7f to 9f winner of 11 races (including at 2 yrs) Prime Exhibit (by Selkirk), the fair 7f winner

Figment (by Acclamation) and the moderate 12f winner Slide Show (by Galileo). The dam is an unraced half-sister to 3 winners including the smart listed 14f winner Moments Of Joy (dam of the dual Group 3 Sagaro Stakes winner Mizzou). The second dam, My Emma (by Marju), winner of the Group 1 12f Prix Vermeille, is a half-sister to 6 winners including the Group 1 St Leger and Group 1 Ascot Gold Cup winner Classic Cliché. (Mr W E Sturt – Osborne House). *"He'll probably start work in May but the sire has been largely disappointing. A nice-going horse from one of the Duke Of Roxburgh's good families, he could make a 2-y-o over seven furlongs or a mile and I thought it fit to keep him in".*

1402. SPECIAL MISSION ★★★
b.f. Declaration Of War – Soft Morning (Pivotal). February 25. Fifth foal. Half-sister to the French listed-placed 2-y-o 6f winner So In Love (by Smart Strike) and to the listed-placed 2-y-o 7f winner Savanna La Mar (by Curlin) and the quite useful 1m winner In The City (by Exceed And Excel). The dam, a useful listed 9.5f winner of 3 races, is a half-sister to 8 winners including the 2-y-o Group 3 1m Prix des Reservoirs winner Songerie and the fairly useful 2-y-o 7.2f winner and Group 3 1m Prix des Reservoirs third Souvenance. The second dam, Summer Night (by Nashwan), a fairly useful 3-y-o 6f winner, is a half-sister to 7 winners including Starlit Sands (Group 3 Prix d'Arenburg). (Miss K Rausing). *"A nice filly, I trained the mother who was a good, rough, tough performer. She got better and better with practice. This filly also looks nice and tough and she'll make a 2-y-o in September over seven furlongs I would think".*

1403. THE NINTH POWER (USA) ★★★★
b.c. Union Rags – Gigahertz (Dynaformer). April 1. First foal. $125,000Y. Keeneland September. Oliver St Lawrence. The dam was placed at 2 and 3 yrs in the USA and is a half-sister to one winner. The second dam, Megahertz (by Pivotal), a US dual grade 1 and multiple Grade 2 winner, is a half-sister to Heaven Sent, twice winner of the Group 3 Dahlia Stakes and second in the Group 1 Matron Stakes. (Bluehills Racing Ltd). *"A nice horse, very good-looking and with a real turf pedigree despite being American-bred.*

He's grown plenty and I've sent him away to mature a bit. He'll make a seven furlong 2-y-o in September and he'll be a nice horse one day. The sire was a very decent first-season American sire and he had a turf pedigree himself, although he was kept to the dirt because he was so good on it".

1404. TRUE NORTH (IRE) ★★★★
b.c. Henrythenavigator – Cosmic Fire (Dalakhani). February 1. Fourth foal. 50,000Y. Tattersalls October Book 2. Axom. Half-brother to the 7f winner (at 2 yrs) and subsequent US winner and Grade 3 placed Ray's The Bar (by Exceed And Excel) and to the French middle-distance winner of 3 races Cosmic City (by Elusive City). The dam, a minor French 3-y-o winner, is a half-sister to 4 winners including the Group 2 Prix d'Harcourt winner Smoking Sun, the French listed winner Zhiyi and the Group 3 second Ikat (dam of the US Grade 1 winner Main Sequence). The second dam, Burning Sunset (by Caerleon), a listed 1m winner and third in the Prix d'Harcourt, is a half-sister to 9 winners including the Oaks winner Light Shift and the Group 2 winners Shiva and Limnos. (Owners Group 018). *"A mid-season 2-y-o, he's a strong, heavy-topped horse bought by Dan Downie who has a very good record buying for us, often not spending much money but doing very well. This horse is fine, he had a sore shin early on but he's resumed now".*

1405. UNNAMED ★★★
b.c. Frankel – Arbella (Primo Dominie). March 23. Seventh foal. Half-brother to the useful listed-placed 7f (at 2 yrs) and 9.5f winner Lat Hawill (by Invincible Spirit), to the quite useful 14f and 2m winner Chocala (by Rock Of Gibraltar), the quite useful listed-placed dual 14f winner Bellajeu (by Montjeu) and the modest 10f winner Primobella (by Duke Of Marmalade). The dam, a useful listed 12f winner at 4 yrs and third in the Group 3 Ormonde Stakes, is a half-sister to 5 winners including the Chester Cup winner and Grade 1 winning hurdler Overturn. The second dam, Kristal Bridge (by Kris), a fair 11f placed maiden, is a half-sister to 7 winners including the dam of Primo Valentino (Middle Park Stakes) and Dora Carrington (Cherry Hinton Stakes). (Qatar Racing Ltd). *"He's not arrived*

yet, but I've seen him at the stud and he's a lovely looking horse. I don't know why he's been delayed and can't tell you much more than that. If anything, when I saw him he looked more of a 3-y-o type than a 2-y-o".

JOHN QUINN

1406. ARCOMATIC ★★★

b.c. Poet's Voice – Natalisa (Green Desert). April 15. Second foal. £30,000Y. Goffs UK Premier (Doncaster). Richard Knight / Sean Quinn. The dam, a quite useful Irish 2-y-o dual 5f winner, is a half-sister to 2 winners. The second dam, Noelani (by Indian Ridge), a Group 3 6f and Group 3 7f in Ireland, is a sister to the Group 1 5f Prix de l'Abbaye winner and smart sire Namid and to the very useful Group 3 6f and 7.5f winner Noelani and a half-sister to 6 winners. (Ontoawinner, J Blackburn & Partner). *"He should be racing at the end of April, he's doing everything nicely, gradually improving and it seems the more we do with him the better he gets. So he'll probably start at five furlongs although six might prove his optimum trip. He comes from a good family of Lady Clague's and the dam won a Premier nursery at Dundalk over five furlongs for John Oxx. If this colt did something similar we'd be happy. There's a lot of speed in the family but being by Poet's Voice he should stay a bit further. A close-coupled, strong, compact colt".*

1407. BLUE HAVANA ★★

b.f. Havana Gold – Labyrinthine (Pivotal). March 26. First foal. €23,000Y. Goffs Sportsmans. Jeremy Glover. The dam, placed at 3 yrs in France, is a half-sister to 3 minor winners. The second dam, Madame Cerito (by Diesis), an Irish 3-y-o 1m winner and listed-placed 2-y-o, is a half-sister to 9 winners including the 1m 2-y-o and subsequent German Group 1 10f winner Ransom O'War. (Fulbeck Horse Syndicate). *"She's done a couple of pieces of work on the grass and seems like a six/seven furlong filly. She's doing all her best work at the top of the gallop which is what you like to see, but we haven't really stretched her yet".*

1408. LORD RIDDIFORD ★★★

ch.c. Zebedee – Beacon Of Hope (Barathea). March 23. Sixth foal. €27,000Y. Tattersalls

Ireland September. Richard Knight / Sean Quinn. Half-brother to 3 minor winners in Italy by Clodovil, Excellent Art and Bahamian Bounty. The dam, placed at 3 yrs in France, is a half-sister to 6 winners including the fairly useful 2-y-o 5f winner and listed-placed All For Laura (herself dam of the Group 2 Cherry Hinton Stakes winner Misheer). The second dam, Lighthouse (by Warning), a fairly useful 3-y-o 8.3f winner, is a half-sister to 4 winners including the Group 1 Middle Park Stakes winner First Trump. (The Jam Partnership). *"One of the sharper 2-y-o's, I think he's a five furlong horse and he's a very good mover so I'd imagine he'd want decent ground. He'll be out pretty soon and he's showing enough for me to be able to say he should win. He could get six furlongs a bit later on, but he does seem quite quick".* TRAINERS' BARGAIN BUY

1409. MR WAGYU (IRE) ★★★

ch.c. Choisir – Lake Louise (Haatef). April 2. First foal. £26,000Y. Goffs UK Premier (Doncaster). Richard Knight / Sean Quinn. The dam, a fair 2-y-o 6f and 1m winner, is a half-sister to 3 winners. The second dam, Emmas Princess (by Bahhare), an Irish dual 10f winner, is a half-sister to 4 winners including the Group 1 10f Premio Presidente della Repubblica and Group 3 8.5f Diomed Stakes winner Polar Prince. (New Century Partnership). *"I would have thought this fella would be our first 2-y-o runner because he's ready to rock n roll. His mother was quite a precocious type, she ran in the first race of the season at the Curragh in the maiden won by Dawn Approach. We'll start this colt off at five furlongs because he's ready to go, but he'll get six and he looks a real 2-yo type in that he's not the biggest. He was bought to be a sharp 2-y-o and he looks exactly that".*

1410. NORTHERN ANGEL ★★★★

b.f. Dark Angel – Muzdaan (Exceed And Excel). February 25. Second foal. €100,000Y. Goffs Orby. Richard Knight / Sean Quinn. Sister to the fair 2016 6f placed 2-y-o Parys Mountain. The dam ran twice unplaced and is a half-sister to 7 winners including the dam of the Hong Kong triple Group 1 winner Lucky Nine. The second dam, Belle Genius (by Beau Genius), won the 2-y-o Group 1 7f Moyglare Stud Stakes and is a half-sister to 3 winners. (Mr David Ward). *"She comes from a good family and her half-brother ran in the Coventry last season. She hasn't yet come in her coat yet but she's doing nice, steady work and I'd hope she'd be a filly that would be out in high summer. It's a family with which Dark Angel has actually done very well because under the second dam there are a few smart performers that were by him. We do like her but we're just not forcing her yet"*.

1411. SEALLA ★★★
b.f. Canford Cliffs – Gems (Haafhd). March 18. Second foal. €14,000Y. Tattersalls Ireland September. Richard Knight / Sean Quinn. Half-sister to the quite useful 2016 2-y-o 6f winner Fayez (by Zoffany). The dam, a modest 12f and 13f winner, is a half-sister to 8 winners including the smart 7f (at 2 yrs) and triple listed middle-distance winner Frank Sonata and the useful 2-y-o listed 7f Sweet Solera Stakes winner Peaceful Paradise. The second dam, Megdale (by Waajib), a fair middle-distance placed maiden, is a full or half-sister to 10 winners including Alhijaz, a winner of four Group 1 events in Italy. (Mr Bill Hobson). *"Her half-brother Fayez won first time up last year and this is quite a sharp type that'll be out at the end of April. We'll start her over five furlongs but she may be better over six, she's very straightforward and given her low purchase price she qualifies for all the maiden auctions up north. That's what we'll stick to in the hope that she can win one"*.

1412. SEEN THE LYTE ★★★
b.f. Kodiac – Highest Praise (Acclamation). April 12. First foal. €24,000Y. Tattersalls Ireland September. Richard Knight / Sean Quinn. The dam is an unplaced daughter of the French listed 10f winner Yarastar (by Cape Cross), herself a half-sister to 5 winners. (Boys of Buckley). *"She had a couple of little niggles that set us back and have prevented us from working her yet. She's cantering every day though and she's a small, racy filly so I don't think it'll take her long to catch up. A five/six furlong 2-y-o, she's a typical Kodiac in that she's all there and once she gets on the track we can race her quite often"*.

1413. SHAHEEN ★★★★ ♠
b.c. Society Rock – La Chicana (Invincible Spirit). February 5. Third foal. 120,000Y. Tattersalls October Book 2. Charlie Gordon Watson / Al Shaqab. Half-brother to the useful listed-placed 11.5f to 14f winner Desert Encounter (by Halling) and to the quite useful triple 6f winner Fast Enough (by Kodiac). The dam, placed once at 3 yrs in France, is a sister to the Group 2 Grand Prix de Deauville winner Allied Powers and a half-sister to 5 winners including the Group 2 Premio Ribot winner Dane Friendly. The second dam, Always Friendly (by High Line), a winner of 3 races including the Group 3 12f Princess Royal Stakes, was second in the Group 1 Prix Royal-Oak and is a half-sister to 5 winners. (Al Shaqab Racing). *"The word is quite good on the first season sire Society Rock and I couldn't say anything but nice things about this lad. His two half-brothers were both decent, he's a very good mover, everything seems to come naturally to him and in the couple of bits of work he's done he's shown natural ability. I'm looking forward to getting him going"*.

1414. WEELLAN ★★★ ♠
ch.c. Mayson – Regal Salute (Medicean). January 24. Second foal. £55,000Y. Goffs UK Premier (Doncaster). Sheikh Abdullah Al Malek Al Sabah. Closely related to the quite useful 6f (at 2 yrs) and 1m winner Worlds His Oyster (by Pivotal). The dam, a fair 1m winner, is a sister to the useful 2-y-o Group 3 6.3f Anglesey Stakes winner Regional Counsel. The second dam, Regency Rose (by Danehill), is an unraced sister to the Group 1 6f Cheveley Park Stakes winner Regal Rose and to the Japanese 10f stakes winner Generalist and a half-sister to 8 winners. (Sheikh Abdullah Almalek Alsabah). *"We train his three-parts brother Worlds His Oyster who is quite a decent handicapper. This colt is fairly forward, he'll make his debut soon but in time I should think he'll get six or seven furlongs. He's a good mover, big and scopey and we like him"*.

1415. UNNAMED ★★★
b.c. Epaulette – Air Maze (Galileo). April 2. Fourth foal. £26,000Y. Goffs UK Premier (Doncaster). Richard Knight / Sean Quinn. Half-brother to the quite useful 7f (including at 2 yrs) and 8.5f winner of 5 races Harlequin Striker (by Bahamian Bounty). The dam, a fair 9f and 10f winner, is a half-sister to 3 winners.

The second dam, Begueule (by Bering), a quite useful 7f and 1m winner at 2 and 3 yrs in France, was listed-placed twice and is a half-sister to 10 winners. (Mr Ross Harmon). *"Probably a horse for the middle part of the season, he's a seven furlong/mile 2-y-o. He hasn't done any fast work yet but he's doing strong canters and he's a good, robust horse – a rugged, hardy type that we'll look to start over seven furlongs".*

1416. UNNAMED ★★★★
b.c. Worthadd – Malayan Mist (Dansili). April 16. Third foal. £130,000 2-y-o. Tattersalls Ireland Ascot Breeze Up. Peter & Ross Doyle. The dam, a quite useful Irish dual 9f winner, is a half-sister to 3 winners including the listed placed Greyfriarschorista. The second dam, Misty Heights (by Fasliyev), an Irish listed 9f winner and second in two Group 3 events, is a half-sister to 11 winners including the multiple South African Group 1 winner Inara and the Group 3 winner Madeira Mist (herself dam of the three times Canadian International winner Joshua Tree). (Al Shaqab Racing). *"I saw him at Willie Browne's Mocklershill Stud a few weeks ago. They're one of the biggest breeze-up consignors and this colt had a very big reputation at that point. He subsequently topped the sale at Ascot, he's a lovely model, physically a very mature horse and ready to go. I'd expect him to be out in May".*

1417. UNNAMED ★★★
b.f. Swiss Spirit – Piranha (Exceed And Excel). April 13. Third foal. €17,000Y. Tattersalls Ireland September. Not sold. Half-sister to the modest 2016 2-y-o 7f and 1m winner Ronnie The Rooster (by Captain Gerrard) and to the fairly useful 6f (at 2 yrs) and 5f winner of 4 races winner Go On Go On Go O (by Medicean). The dam, a quite useful 2-y-o dual 5f winner, is a half-sister to 2 minor winners. The second dam, Mosaique Beauty (by Sadler's Wells), a minor Irish 13f winner, is a full or half-sister to 7 winners including the US Grade 1 Gulfstream Park Breeders' Cup Handicap and Group 2 King Edward VII Stakes winner Subtle Power. (Mickley Stud & Sarah Taylor). *"A filly bought by Richard Kent*

and sent to us, she's a strong filly, hasn't done any fast work yet but she'll be a six furlong filly starting off. So whilst she's not a really sharp type she's not a bad goer and has done nothing wrong".

1418. UNNAMED ★★★★
b.c. Lawman – Polly Perkins (Pivotal). March 15. Eighth foal. £50,000 2-y-o. Tattersalls Ireland Ascot Breeze Up. Richard Knight/ Sean Quinn. Half-brother to the 2-y-o Group 3 Anglesey Stakes winner Final Frontier (by Dream Ahead), to the useful 2-y-o 7f winner and Group 3 7f C L & M F Weld Park Stakes second Lola Beaux (by Equiano) and to the fair triple 7f winner Marmarus (by Duke Of Marmalade). The dam, a useful 2-y-o dual listed 5f winner, is a half-sister to 2 winners. The second dam, Prospering (by Prince Sabo), a moderate 7f winner at 3 yrs, is a half-sister to 6 winners. *"A compact colt who looks sharp and did one of the faster breezes at Ascot. We'll be able to get on with him shortly because he's a real 2-y-o sort and we're looking forward to him".*

1419. UNNAMED ★★★
b.f. Epaulette – Sweet Kristeen (Candy Stripes). April 28. Ninth foal. €47,000Y. Goffs Orby. Richard Knight / Sean Quinn. Half-sister to the useful 8.3f winner and listed 10f second Cliché (by Diktat), to the quite useful 6f (at 2 yrs) and 7f winner Al Shahaniya (by Zoffany), the quite useful 7f and subsequent US winner Rule Breaker (by Refuse To Bend) and the 2-y-o 7f and subsequent minor US winner Learaig (by Diamond Green). The dam, a fair 7f winner at 3 yrs, is a half-sister to 3 winners and the dams of the Group 3 winners Racer Forever and Masta Plasta. The second dam, Aneesati (by Kris), a quite useful 1m winner, is a half-sister to 13 winners including the US Grade 2 winner Magellan. *"A very nice filly, she's big but not backward at all. We trained her half-sister Al Shahaniya who was fairly decent but this filly has more scope than her. She's a very good goer with a good pedigree and the dam has bred some half decent performers by average stallions. She'll probably start over six furlongs but she'll be a seven furlong/miler and we like her".*

KEVIN RYAN

1420. DALAWYNA (FR)
b.f. Kendargent – Dalawysa (Dalakhani). February 5. Third foal. 64,000Y. Tattersalls October Book 2. Not sold. Sister to the minor French dual 2-y-o winner Kendala. The dam, a minor French placed 3-y-o, is a half-sister to the French listed winner Valima - herself the dam of three Group winners including Valyra (Group 1 Prix de Diane). The second dam, Vadlawysa (by Always Fair), a minor French 3-y-o winner, is a sister to the Group 2 Prix Hocquart winner Vadlawys and a half-sister to the Grade 1 Breeders' Cup Mile winner Val Royal. (Mr G Pariente).

1421. ENJOY WELL (IRE)
ch.c. New Approach – Music Show (Noverre). April 28. Second foal. 90,000Y. Tattersalls October Book 1. Not sold. Half-brother to Show Me The Music (by Dubawi), placed over 7.5f and 1m on both his starts at 2 yrs in 2016. The dam won 5 races including the Group 1 Falmouth Stakes, the Group 2 Rockfel Stakes and Group 3 Nell Gwyn Stakes and was Group 1 placed three times. She is a half-sister to the useful winner and triple listed-placed Fantasia Girl. The second dam, Dreamboat (by Mr Prospector), a fair 7f winner, is a sister to the French listed-placed winner Sweetheart and a half-sister to 5 winners including the listed 7f winner and Group 2 placed Stunning. (Jaber Abdullah).

1422. GOLD STONE
b.f. Havana Gold – Slatey Hen (Acclamation). March 31. First foal. £45,000Y. Goffs UK Premier (Doncaster). Hillen & Ryan. The dam, a modest 6f (including at 2 yrs) and 5f winner of 3 races, is a half-sister to 4 winners including the very useful Group 3 6f Norfolk Stakes winner of 6 races Masta Plasta. The second dam, Silver Arrow (by Shadeed), was placed once at 2 yrs and is a half-sister to 4 winners including the listed-placed Ras Shaikh. (Jaber Abdullah).

1423. HAVANA STAR (IRE)
b.c. Havana Gold – Nagham (Camacho). January 21. First foal. €37,000Y. Goffs Sportsmans. Hillen & Ryan. The dam, a fairly useful 2-y-o 5f winner, is a half-sister to 5

winners. The second dam, Happy Talk (by Hamas), an Irish 10f and hurdles winner, is a half-sister to 8 winners including the US Grade 3 winner Storm Dream. (Hambleton Racing Ltd LIII).

1424. HEY JONESY (IRE)
b.c. Excelebration – Fikrah (Medicean). March 23. Third foal. £35,000Y. Goffs UK Premier (Doncaster). Mr & Mrs J Pallister. Half-brother to the fairly useful 7f and 1m winner Loaded (by Kodiac). The dam, a quite useful Irish 2-y-o 1m winner, is a half-sister to 3 winners. The second dam, Justbetweenfriends (by Diesis), was placed over 12f and is a half-sister to 7 winners including the smart dual Group 3 7f winner With Reason and the useful Group 3 1m Curragh Futurity Stakes and listed 7f Sweet Solera Stakes winner Jural. (Pallister Racing).

1425. KINGS FULL (IRE)
b.c. Galileo – Half Queen (Deputy Minister). March 27. Twelfth foal. $500,000Y. Bluesky Bloodstock and Aquis Farm. Brother to Scales Of Justice, unplaced in one start at 2 yrs in 2016 and half-brother to four winners including the US 2-y-o Grade 1 7f and Grade 1 8.5f winner Halfbridled (by Unbridled). The dam, a minor US 3-y-o winner, is a half-sister to the US dual Grade 2 winner Lu Ravi. The second dam, At The Half (by Seeking The Gold), won the US Grade 3 Golden Rod Stakes. (Aquis Farm).

1426. KNIGHTED (IRE)
b.c. Sir Prancealot – Olympia Theatre (Galileo). March 9. Sixth foal. €45,000Y. Goffs Sportsmans. Hillen & Ryan. Half-brother to the fair 2-y-o 7f winner Mandeville and to a minor winner in Italy by Bushranger. The dam is an unraced half-sister to 4 minor winners. The second dam, Opari (by Night Shift), a French 2-y-o 6f winner, is a half-sister to one winner. (Highclere Thoroughbred Racing – Rio Olympics).

1427. MONT KINABALU (IRE)
b.c. Society Rock – Startori (Vettori). March 31. Sixth living foal. €49,000Y. Goffs Sportsmans. Hillen & Ryan. Half-brother to the fair 2-y-o 5f and 6f winner and

Scandinavian listed winner Liber, to the fair 2-y-o dual 5f winner Guru Girl (by Ishiguru) and the modest 2-y-o triple 6f winner White Vin Jan (by Hellvelyn). The dam, a quite useful 2-y-o dual 7f winner, was listed-placed and is a half-sister to 6 winners. The second dam, Celestial Welcome (by Most Welcome), a useful 7f to 12f winner of 8 races, is a full or half-sister to 5 winners including the smart Group 2 12f King Edward VII Stakes second Snowstorm.

1428. MORNING WONDER (IRE)
ch.c. Dawn Approach – Mount Elbrus (Barathea). April 1. Tenth living foal. 65,000Y. Tattersalls October Book 1. Not sold. Half-brother to 6 winners including the useful 2-y-o 7f and 1m winner and Group 1 1m Gran Criterium second Strobilus (by Mark Of Esteem), the useful French listed 11f winner Lava Flow (by Dalakhani), the fairly useful 7f (at 2 yrs) and 12f and hurdles winner Hunterview (by Reset) and the fair UAE 1m winner Baransky (by Green Desert). The dam, a French listed 11f winner, is a half-sister to 4 winners. The second dam, El Jazirah (by Kris), is an unraced sister to the Group 1 Prix de Diane winner Rafha (herself dam of the Group 1 Haydock Park Sprint Cup winner Invincible Spirit) and a half-sister to 9 winners. (Sultan Ali).

1429. PREDICTION (IRE) ♣
b.c. Dream Ahead – Sho Girl (Lawman). January 13. First foal. 31,000Y. Tattersalls October Book 2. Hillen & Ryan. The dam, a fair Irish 4-y-o 11.5 and 14f winner, is a half-sister to 2 winners. The second dam, Shizao (by Alzao), an Irish listed 5f (at 2 yrs) and 7f winner, is a half-sister to 2 winners. (Highclere Thoroughbred Racing – Nick Skelton).

1430. VJ DAY (USA)
b.br.c. War Front – Sassy Image (Broken Vow). April 20. Second foal. $350,000Y. Bluesky Bloodstock and Aquis Farm. The dam won 7 races in the USA including the Grade 1 Princess Rooney Handicap and the Grade 1 Humana Distaff Stakes. The second dam, Ideal Image (by Hennessy), was placed in the USA and is a half-sister to 5 winners including the St Leger third Adair. (Aquis Farm).

1431. WONDERING SPIRIT
b.f. Invincible Spirit – Wonder Why (Tiger Hill). February 28. Seventh foal. 230,000Y. Tattersalls October Book 1. Not sold. Half-sister to 5 winners including the smart Irish 7f (at 2 yrs) and listed 1m winner and subsequent dual Hong Kong Group 1 10f winner Akeed Mofeed, the quite useful 6f and 7f winner Jordan Sport (both by Dubawi), the fairly useful 11.5f and 12f winner Wonder Laish (by Halling) and the quite useful 1m winner Waahy (by Manduro). The dam is an unraced half-sister to 5 winners including two German listed winners. The second dam, Wells Whisper (by Sadler's Wells), placed over 1m and 10f, is a sister to the very useful Group 1 10.5f Prix Lupin and US Grade 2 1m winner Johann Quatz and a half-sister to the top-class middle-distance colt Hernando. (Jaber Abdullah).

GEORGE SCOTT

1432. ADVANCED VIRGO ★★
b.c. Holy Roman Emperor – Amaraja (Galileo). April 1. First foal. The dam, a fairly useful 12f winner, is a sister to the French dual listed 12f winner Launched, closely related to the Group 2 1m Beresford Stakes and Group 3 10f Mooresbridge Stakes winner Curtain Call and a half-sister to the listed 12f winner Nature Spirits. The second dam, Apsara (by Darshaan), is an unplaced half-sister to numerous winners including the Group 1 10.5f Prix Lupin and US Grade 2 1m winner Johann Quatz and the Group 1 Prix du Jockey Club and Group 1 Prix Lupin winner Hernando. (Niarchos Family). *"Henry Cecil trained the dam and this is a big, strong, strapping colt with an economical action. He already seems to favour the grass and I would imagine he'd be mid-summer 2-y-o and make up into a nice 3-y-o next year".*

1433. ARTHUR DALEY (IRE) ★★★★
b.c. Camelot – Nasanice (Nashwan). February 19. Thirteenth foal. €120,000Y. Arqana Deauville August. Elliott & Scott. Half-brother to 8 winners including the Group 2 12f Hardwicke Stakes winner Maraahel, the useful 2-y-o 7f winner and Group 3 third Huja (both by Alzao), the smart 1m Britannia Handicap winner Mostashaar (by Intikhab), the 9f winner Almuktahem (by Green Desert) and

the dual 10f winner Sharedah (by Pivotal), both quite useful. The dam, a fairly useful Irish 9f winner, is a half-sister to 4 winners including the dual Group 2 winner Sahool. The second dam, Mathaayl (by Shadeed), a quite useful 6f and 10f winner, is a half-sister to the Group 3 Princess Margaret Stakes winner Muhbubh (dam of the US Grade 2 winner Kayrawan). (Chelsea Thoroughbreds – Minder). *"He's a beautiful horse, very good looking, athletic and with a very good temperament. He looks identical to his good half-brother Maraahel – I've heard lots of people say that. A very exciting horse, he finds it all easy and the way he's going he'll be ready in July for a seven furlong maiden. I couldn't be more complimentary about him, he's very special at this stage".*

1434. CATHERINE TRAMELL ★★★
b.f. Zoffany – Aine (Danehill Dancer). March 10. Fourth foal. 125,000Y. Tattersalls October Book 1. A C Elliott. The dam, a useful listed 6f winner of 3 races, was listed-placed a further three times and is a half-sister to 2 winners abroad. The second dam, Antinnaz (by Thatching), won the listed Cecil Frail Stakes and is a half-sister to 3 winners. (Lynch Bages & Kings Bloodstock). *"A very attractive, straightforward filly from a very decent racemare. She's done everything easily but she's just started to grow and I should imagine she'll be an early summer type. We'll start her off at six furlongs and she should get a mile later on".*

1435. CRASH HELMET ★★★
b.c. Helmet – Hot Secret (Sakhee's Secret). February 4. Fourth foal. £32,000Y. Goffs UK Premier (Doncaster). Elliott & Scott. The dam, a fair 2-y-o 5f winner, is a half-sister to 6 winners including Temple Meads (Group 2 Mill Reef Stakes). The second dam, Harryana (by Efisio), was a fair 2-y-o dual 5f winner. (Ontoawinner & Saffron Racing 2). *"He's a horse that was showing up really well over the winter but he has a small setback and he won't be seen now until the late summer. Bearing in mind what he was showing early on I think he'll be worth waiting for. He's by a good stallion, it's a fast family and he looks a tough, durable colt".*

1436. ENCRYPTION ★★★
b.c. High Chaparral – Challow Hills (Woodman). February 25. Fifth foal. €50,000Y. Arqana Deauville August. Not sold. The dam, a modest 1m winner, is a half-sister to 5 winners including the US stakes winner and dual Grade 3 placed Teide. The second dam, Cascassi (by Nijinsky), a fair 10f winner here, also won at 4 yrs in France and is a half-sister to 5 winners including Diminuendo (Epsom, Irish and Yorkshire Oaks winner) and the Oaks second Pricket. (The Harnage Partnership II). *"A gorgeous, big, strapping individual. He enjoys his training, covers plenty of ground and has a really low, economical action. He'll be ready for when the seven furlong maidens starts and although he's a big horse he's quite precocious with it. I think he's got a lot of ability and I like him very much".*

1437. GAJA (IRE) ★★★
b.f. High Chaparral – Subtle Charm (Machiavellian). January 18. €70,000Y. Arqana Deauville August. Private Sale. Half-sister to the quite useful 5f winner of 4 races here and UAE 5f and 7f winner Indescribable (by Invincible Spirit) and to the quite useful 1m winner Cipher (by Reset). The dam is an unplaced half-sister to the Oaks winner Snow Bride (dam of the Derby, King George and 'Arc' winner Lammtarra) and the US Grade 3 stakes winner Jarraar. The second dam, Awaasif (by Snow Knight), won the Group 1 Yorkshire Oaks and the Group 1 Gran Premio del Jockey Club and is a half-sister to numerous winners including the 1,000 Guineas second Konafa (herself grandam of Hector Protector, Shanghai and Bosra Sham). (Mrs S Spencer). *"A beautiful filly with a lovely, long raking stride. She's done everything we've asked her to do in her comfort zone and she's quite typical of the stallion in that she's got quite a nice depth to her and a lovely outlook. Realistically she won't be ready until the start of the seven furlong maidens".*

1438. GRAFFITISTA ★★★
b.f. Kodiac – Noble Galileo (Galileo). February 12. Third foal. £42,000Y. Goffs UK Premier (Doncaster). Elliott & Scott. The dam, a quite useful dual 12f winner, is a half-sister to 5 winners including the Group 2 German 1,000 Guineas second Margay. The second

dam, Almarai (by Vaguely Noble), is a placed half-sister to 5 winners including the US Grade 1 winner Buckhar. (M Bartram & J Slade). *"Typical of the stallion, she's very straightforward and shows plenty of speed in her early work. She could be out in April and at this stage like many Kodiacs she's showing a great attitude and plenty of speed. She's out of a staying mare, so hopefully she might be able to train on a bit, but she'll be ready to start over five furlongs".*

1439. HOLY TIBER (IRE) ★★

b.f. Holy Roman Emperor – Quiet Waters (Quiet American). April 27. Seventh foal. 20,000Y. Tattersalls October Book 3. A C Elliott. Half-sister to the fair 12f winner Rivers Run, to the Scandinavian 3-y-o winner Hi Finn (both by High Chaparral) and a hurdles winner by Montjeu. The dam ran once unplaced and is a half-sister to 7 winners including French Group 3 winner Summertime Legacy (herself dam of the French Group 1 winners Mandaean and Wavering). The second dam, Zawaahy (by El Gran Senor), a quite useful 1m winner, is a half-sister to 4 winners including the Derby winner Golden Fleece. *"A compact, likeable filly with a fantastic outlook on life, I think for what she cost she'll give the owner plenty of fun, starting at five furlongs".* TRAINERS' BARGAIN BUY

1440. JAMES GARFIELD ★★★

b.c. Exceed And Excel – Whazzat (Daylami). March 24. Seventh foal. £90,000Y. Goffs UK Premier (Doncaster). Not sold. Closely related to the fairly useful 7.5f (at 2 yrs) and 1m winner and dual listed-placed The Shrew (by Dansili) and half-brother to the quite useful dual 10f winner Trainnah (by Pivotal) and the quite useful 6f (at 2 yrs) and 7f winner Theladyinquestion (by Dubawi). The dam, a useful 2-y-o listed 7f Chesham Stakes winner, is a half-sister to 6 winners including the listed 1m and Italian Group 3 1m winner Whazzis. The second dam, Wosaita (by Generous), a fair 12.3f placed maiden, is a half-sister to 10 winners including the Group 1 Prix de Diane winner Rafha (dam of the Group 1 Haydock Sprint Cup winner and sire Invincible Spirit). (WJ & TCO Gredley). *"He's*

shown a really likeable attitude in everything he's done. I think he'll start off in a six furlong maiden in mid-May. A straightforward colt".

1441. OLYMPIC ODYSSEY ★★★★

b.c. Camelot – Field Of Hope (Selkirk). April 20. Eleventh foal. 170,000Y. Tattersalls October Book 1. Bill Gredley. Half-brother to 8 winners including the UAE Group 3 and French dual listed winner Dormello (by Dansili), the 2-y-o listed-placed 7f winner East India (by Galileo), the 2-y-o 7f winner and 2,000 Guineas third Olympian Odyssey (by Sadler's Wells), the listed 6f and listed 7f winner Field Of Dream (by Oasis Dream) and the dual Italian listed winner Ransom Hope (by Red Ransom). The dam won 6 races including the Group 1 Prix de la Foret and the Group 2 Prix d'Astarte and is a half-sister to 7 winners. The second dam, Fracci (by Raise A Cup), was a listed winner of 4 races in Italy and Group 3 placed twice. (WJ & TCO Gredley). *"A huge colt, an imposing horse with a big white face, he catches the eye and I'm getting very good vibes off my best riders. Everyone that rides him says he's the best two-year-old in the yard, but he came in quite late so physically he's a bit behind the pack. One to look forward to in the second half of the season".*

1442. SIGRID NANSEN ★★★

b.f. Cityscape – Hail Shower (Red Clubs). February 25. First foal. The dam was a modest 7f (at 2 yrs) and 6.5f winner. The second dam, Beat The Rain (by Beat Hollow), won once at 3 yrs in France and is a half-sister to 4 winners including the listed winner Quenched. (S M Smith). *"A neat, good-looking filly that's shown plenty of natural ability over the winter. She's had a minor road bump but I'd expect her to be back and be ready for mid-summer. I'd very much hope she'd be able to win a six furlong maiden".*

1443. SLIPSTREAM (IRE) ★★★★ ♠

b.c. Invincible Spirit – Kiltubber (Sadler's Wells). February 16. Tenth foal. €420,000Y. Arqana Deauville August. Elliott & Scott. Brother to the Group 3 7f Concorde Stakes Anam Allta and half-brother to 6 winners including the UAE and German Group 3 winner Fox Hunt (by Dubawi), the useful 9f to 12f winner and Australian Group 1 second Opinion (by Oasis Dream) and the quite useful 12f winner Kiltara (by Lawman). The dam, an Italian listed 12f winner, is a half-sister to 3 winners. The second dam, Priory Belle (by Priolo), winner of the 2-y-o Group 1 7f Moyglare Stud Stakes, is a half-sister to 7 winners including Eva's Request (Group 1 Premio Lydia Tesio) and the dam of the dual Group 1 winner Chriselliam. (Mrs Michael Spencer & Ballylinch Stud). *"A beautiful individual. His looks match his pedigree and he's finding it all easy so he's about to move into faster work. I wouldn't rule out something like the Coventry Stakes although the results of his family suggest he'll improve as the year goes on. A very strong, straightforward horse and I'm lucky to have a horse of his calibre in the yard".*

1444. STARBOY ★★★
br.c. Camacho – New Magic (Statue Of Liberty). February 16. First foal. £52,000Y. Goffs UK Premier (Doncaster). Elliott & Scott. The dam was a quite useful listed-placed winner of 4 races from 7f to 8.5f. The second dam, Magic Mushroom (by Pivotal), is an unraced half-sister to 6 winners. (Excel Racing Ltd). *"A short-coupled, straightforward colt that should be ready in late May. We'll give him the opportunity to show how good he is. A nice little horse".*

DAVID SIMCOCK
1445. ALACRITAS ★★★ ♠
gr.f. Leroidesanimaux – Albaraka (Selkirk). January 31. Second foal. The dam, a quite useful 8.5f winner, is a sister to the French listed 10.5f winner Alvarita. The second dam, Alborada (by Alzao), winner of the Champion Stakes (twice), the Group 2 Nassau Stakes and the Group 2 Pretty Polly Stakes, is a sister to the triple German Group 1 winner Albanova and a half-sister to 7 winners including the dam of the Derby second Dragon Dancer. *"A very natural filly, she shows up well, never gets tired and we're very pleased with her. She looks the type for one of the early season seven furlong races".*

1446. ALGO MAS ★★★
gr.c. Invincible Spirit – Alla Speranza (Sir Percy). February 12. Second foal. 120,000Y. Tattersalls October Book 1. Not sold. The dam, a useful Irish 1m (at 2 yrs) and Group 3 10f Kilternan Stakes winner, is a half-sister to 4 winners including the listed Noblesse Stakes winner Altesse. The second dam, Alvarita (by Selkirk), a French listed 10.5f winner, is a sister to one winner and a half-sister to the 10f winner and Group 2 10f Prix Greffulhe second Albion. *"A well-bred colt, we've pushed on a little bit with him because both physically and mentally he's good. He hasn't missed a day so we're very pleased with him".*

1447. CUBAN STAR ★★★★
ch.f. Havana Gold – Totally Cosmic (Cozzene). April 12. Eighth foal. £36,000Y. Goffs UK Premier (Doncaster). David Redvers. Half-sister to the minor Italian 2-y-o winner Sopran Cosmic (by Duke Of Marmalade) and to a minor winner in France by Awesome Again. The dam, second in the Group 3 Prix Chloe and the Group 3 Prix Cleopatre, won once at 4 yrs in the USA and is a full or half-sister to 9 winners including the stakes winner Vignette (dam of the St Leger winner Lucarno). The second dam, Be Exclusive (by Be My Guest), won the Group 3 Prix Chloe and is a half-sister to 2 winners. *"She shows plenty of speed, has a good attitude and is probably the most forward of all the 2-y-o's. I'm not sure if she's quick enough to start over five furlongs but she shows up well and we've done plenty with her. Likely to be our first 2-y-o runner, she has a great attitude, wants to please and is thoroughly professional".*

1448. DE MEDICI (IRE) ★★★★
ch.c. Makfi – Bride Unbridled (Hurricane Run). March 1. Second foal. The dam is a half-sister to the fairly useful 2-y-o dual 6f winner and Group 2 Railway Stakes third French Emperor. The second dam, Se La Vie (by Highest Honor), won 2 minor races at 2 and 3 yrs in France and is a half-sister to 4 winners including the Canadian stakes winner and Grade 2 placed Daylight Come. *"A big, powerful horse, he's very mature and has shown up very well. I couldn't be happier with him, there's nothing in his pedigree to suggest*

he should be forward or be good, but he just looks a very natural, good type of horse".

1449. EJTYAH ★★★
b.f. Frankel – Darysina (Smart Strike).
February 5. First foal. The dam, placed over 10.5f at Saint-Cloud, is a half-sister to four stakes winners including Daryakana (Group 1 Hong Kong Vase) and Daramsar (Group 2 Prix du Conseil de Paris). The second dam, Daryaba (by Night Shift), won the Group 1 Prix de Diane and Prix Vermeille. *"A beautiful filly – really quite striking to look at. She's well put together and has trained well. We're about to give her a little break because she's quite stoutly bred on her mother's side and she won't be rushed in any way. Really pretty to look at, nice to watch and I'm very pleased with what she's done so far".*

1450. HIGHLAND SKY ★★★
b.c. Camelot – Healing Music (Bering).
April 22. Ninth foal. €360,000Y. Goffs Orby.
Hugo Merry. Closely related to the quite useful 11f, 12f and hurdles winner Kuda Huraa (by Montjeu) and half-brother to the fairly useful 2016 2-y-o 1m winner Utah and the useful Irish 2-y-o 1m winner and Epsom Derby second At First Sight (both by Galileo). The dam, a French listed-placed 2-y-o winner, is a half-sister to 9 winners including the US Grade 2 winner Herboriste and the French listed winner and subsequent Grade 1 Hollywood Derby second Fast And Furious. The second dam, Helvellyn (by Gone West), a quite useful 2-y-o 8.3f winner, is a half-sister to 6 winners. *"He's not the biggest, he's very mature with a good action and a great attitude. We'll be able to push on with him, he should start at seven furlongs and he's taken everything we've thrown at him, so he's very likeable at this stage. I'd say that the fact he's so mature allows him to show up well".*

1451. IBN AL EMARAT ★★★
b.c. Excelebration – Grace Of Dubai (Dubai Destination). February 2. Second foal. €35,000Y. Arqana Deauville August. Blandford Bloodstock. The dam, a listed-placed 2-y-o winner in France, is a half-sister to 2 minor winners. The second dam, Hill Of Grace (by Desert Prince), was a fair 2-y-o 6f winner. *"A horse that's done very well from*

the sales to now. He showed up well early doors, just went through a little growth spurt and we've just started back up with him. A nice type".*

1452. IMPERIAL ACT ★★★
b.f. Frankel – Victrix Ludorum (Invincible Spirit). March 23. First foal. The dam, a fairly useful 2-y-o 6f and 7f winner, was listed-placed over 6f at 3 yrs and is a half-sister to 2 winners. The second dam, Matikanehamatidori (by Sunday Silence), placed once at 3 yrs in Japan, is a full or half-sister to 7 winners including two listed winners in Japan. (The Victrix Ludorum Partnership). *"Not the biggest, so she's a typical first foal. She's ready to step up now after lots of ground work and we're looking for a bit of speed now. Physically you'd like to think she could run in the first half of the season but whether that's the case I don't know".*

1453. IMPERIAL COURT (IRE) ★ ★
b.c. Zoffany – La Vita Bella (Mtoto). May 2. Second foal. 45,000Y. Tattersalls October Book 2. Blandford Bloodstock. The dam is an unraced sister to a listed-placed winner in Germany and a half-sister to 4 winners including the German Group 3 winner Majoune's Song. The second dam, Majoune (by Take Risks), won 4 races including the Group 3 11f Prix Corrida and is a half-sister to 10 winners including the Group 3 1m Prix des Reservoirs winner and Group 1 10.5f Prix de Diane second Mousse Glacee. *"A horse we bought at the sales and we were very pleased with him, then he went through a massive growth stage very early, so lots changed with him. He's a very good actioned horse with loads of size and scope. Probably one for the second half of the season".*

1454. LOLLYS DREAM (IRE) ★★★
b.f. Declaration Of War – Bunood (Sadler's Wells). April 18. Seventh foal. 130,000Y. Tattersalls October Book 1. David Simcock. Half-sister to the 7f (at 2 yrs) and 1m winner and listed-placed Lanansaak (by Zamindar), to the quite useful 1m winner Estebsaal (by Dansili) and the fair 7f and 1m winner Bakoura (by Green Desert). The dam, a fairly useful 2-y-o 1m winner, was third in

the Group 3 12f Princess Royal Stakes and listed-placed 3 times and is a half-sister to 5 winners. The second dam, Azdihaar (by Mr Prospector), a quite useful dual 7f at 3 yrs, is a half-sister to 5 winners including Shadayid (1,000 Guineas and Prix Marcel Boussac) and the Group 3 winners and sires Dumaani and Fath. *"She's nice, she's done really well and is now ready to step up. I've been very pleased with her, she looks above average and physically she's a good model, so I couldn't be happier at this stage. A six/seven furlong starter I think".*

1455. MAKE MAGIC (IRE) ★★★

b.f. Makfi – Maramba (USA) (Hussonet). April 20. Sixth foal. 19,000 foal. Tattersalls December. David Redvers. Half-sister to the quite useful 6f (at 2 yrs) and 7f winner and Italian Group 3 second Dream Mover (by Dream Ahead), to the quite useful 2-y-o 7f and 8.5f winner Taper Tantrum (by Azamour) and the fair 7f and 1m winner Wakeup Little Suzy (by Peintre Celebre). The dam, a fairly useful 2-y-o listed-placed 6f winner, is a half-sister to 5 winners. The second dam, Coco (by Storm Bird), a fairly useful listed-placed 1m winner, is a half-sister to 5 winners including the US stakes winner and Grade 1 placed Last Romance. *"Not the biggest, but she looks a six furlong filly. She's surprised us, she's shown up well, didn't come in till late but she's very natural".*

1456. MAVERICK OFFICER ★★★

b.c. Exceed And Excel – Gradara (Montjeu). May 3. Third foal. €85,000Y. Arqana Deauville October. Half-brother to the quite useful 1m (at 2 yrs) and 10f winner Gershwin (by Shamardal). The dam won the listed 12f Prix Panacee at 4 yrs and is a half-sister to 6 winners including the Group 1 1m Falmouth Stakes winner Giofra. The second dam, Gracefully (by Orpen), won the 2-y-o Group 3 7f Prestige Stakes and is a sister to the listed winner and dual Group 3 placed Lady Grace and to the 2-y-o Group 3 third Visionist. *"A very natural horse, he shows up well and is a horse that doesn't get tired. He hasn't disappointed me at all and he's one we'll press on with. He's a nice shape, not too big, not too small and he'll be a mid-season 2-y-o".*

1457. MOBHAM (IRE) ★★

b.c. Teofilo – Elegant Beauty (Olden Times). April 6. Seventh foal. 60,000Y. Tattersalls October Book 1. Blandford Bloodstock. Half-brother to the Group 3 1m Prix d'Aumale winner Shahah (by Motivator), to the quite useful dual 6f (at 2 yrs) and 8.5f winner Ligeia (by Rail Link) and the fair 5f and 6f winner Royal Guinevere (by Invincible Spirit). The dam is an unraced half-sister to 8 winners including the champion 2-y-o Grand Lodge and the listed winners La Persiana and Papabile. The second dam, La Papagena (by Habitat), is an unraced half-sister to 7 winners including the listed winners Lost Chord and Eagling. *"A horse that took an age to break and physically he didn't do very well at the start. He just changing now and he's actually a very nice mover, but he will need a bit of time".*

1458. POSTCOMBE ★★★

b.f. Lawman – Postage Stampe (Singspiel). March 5. Sixth foal. Half-sister to the fair 7f winner Postbag (by Three Valleys), to the fair 1m winner Fulney (by Dr Fong) and the moderate 11.5f winner Poste Restante (by Halling). The dam, a quite useful 7f (at 2 yrs) and 10f winner, is a half-sister to 8 winners including the fairly useful 6f (at 2 yrs) to 1m winner of 7 races Kyllachy Star. The second dam, Jaljuli (by Jalmood), a useful 2-y-o 5f and 6f winner, was third in the Group 1 Cheveley Park Stakes and is a half-sister to the multiple Group 1 winner Kooyonga. *"I trained the dam to win a seven furlong maiden as a 2-y-o. This filly was very backward and gawky early doors but she's furnished well, she's training now and she's doing fine. She looks like she'll do the same as her mother and start at seven furlongs in the second half of the season".*

1459. TUM TUM ★★★★

ch.c. Dawn Approach – Lalectra (King Charlemagne). February 6. Seventh foal. 62,000Y. Tattersalls October Book 1. R Frisby. Half-brother to the smart listed 1m winner, Group 1 Racing Post Trophy second and 2,000 Guineas third Van Der Neer (by Dutch Art), to the fairly useful 2-y-o dual 5f winner Showing Character (by Showcasing), the fair 6f (at 2 yrs) and 10f winner Goodwood Treasure (by Bahamian Bounty) and the fair

10f winner Possible Future (by Compton Place). The dam is an unraced half-sister to 9 winners including the listed winner Intense Pink and the Group placed Sir Reginald and Henrik. The second dam, Clincher Club (by Polish Patriot), a fair 5f (at 2 yrs) and 7.5f winner, is a half-sister to 9 winners. *"He's been showing up well, he shows a nice bit of speed and looks like being one of our first seven furlong 2-y-o's. Physically he's done very well and I'm very happy with him".*

1460. UNNAMED ★★★
b.c. Born To Sea – Bibury (Royal Applause). April 5. Third foal. 52,000Y. Tattersalls October Book 3. Blandford Bloodstock. Half-brother to the very useful 6f (at 2 yrs) and listed 10f winner Steel Of Madrid (by Lope De Vega). The dam, a fair 7f winner, is a half-sister to 4 winners including the Group 1 Ascot Gold Cup winner Rite Of Passage. The second dam, Dahlia's Krissy (by Kris S), a listed-placed winner of 5 races in the USA, is a half-sister to 5 winners. *"A tricky little horse that has slight behavioural issues, but he looks mature and because you feel you have to keep on top of him he's actually done plenty. Looks a real early seven furlong 2-y-o type, he's not the biggest but I'm happy".*

1461. UNNAMED ★★★
b.f. Siyouni – Blue Sail (Kingmambo). May 20. Eighth foal. 160,000Y. Arqana Deauville October. Blandford Bloodstock. Half-sister to the French Group 3 10f and listed 12f winner Beautiful Heroine (by High Chaparral) and to the modest Irish 7f winner How Splendid (by Oasis Dream). The dam was placed once at 2 yrs in France and is a sister to the French 1,000 Guineas winner and Coronation Stakes third Bluemamba. The second dam, Black Penny (by Private Account), is a placed half-sister to 7 winners including the Group 1 Prix Morny winner Orpen and the US Grade 3 winner Jules. *"I have two Siyouni 2-y-o's and I like them both. This one is by far the most forward of them, wants to get on with it and I'm pleased with her. The stallion is my tip for the top".*

1462. UNNAMED ★★★
ch.f. Universal – Dance For Georgie (Motivator). February 18. First foal. 20,000Y.

Tattersalls October Book 4. David Simcock. The dam, a modest 7f and 1m winner, is a half-sister to 3 winners including the Italian Group 3 10f winner Wickwing. The second dam, Chetwynd (by Exit To Nowhere), is an unraced half-sister to 4 winners including the listed and subsequent US stakes winner Secret Garden (dam of the dual Group 1 winner Roderic O'Connor). *"I have two by Universal but this is the one to follow as a 2-y-o, she goes well, isn't the biggest but very natural. She's quite sparky and a six/seven furlong filly".* TRAINERS' BARGAIN BUY

1463. UNNAMED ★★
b.f. Galileo – Danehurst (Danehill). April 13. Tenth foal. Half-sister to the fairly useful dual 7f winner Time To Reason (by Kyllachy), to the quite useful 2-y-o 6f winner Ski Slope (by Three Valleys), the fair 2-y-o 5f winner Jamboree Girl (by Bahamian Bounty) and the modest 7f and 1m winner King Pin (by Pivotal). The dam, winner of the Cornwallis Stakes (at 2 yrs), the Curragh Flying Five, the Prix de Seine-et-Oise and the Premio Umbria, is a half-sister to 6 winners including Humouresque (Group 3 10.5f Prix Penelope) and the dual Group 2 third Mighty. The second dam, Miswaki Belle (by Miswaki), second over 7f on her only start, is a half-sister to 9 winners including the Dazzle (Group 3 6f Cherry Hinton Stakes). *"Both my Galileo fillies are very similar, they're not the biggest and they're both slow learners. To look at them you'd be tempted to think they should be 2-y-o runners, but that's not necessarily the case. Doing ok without being spectacular".*

1464. UNNAMED ★★★★
b.c. Blame – Endless Journey (A P Indy). March 22. Fourth foal. $250,000Y. Saratoga August. Blandford Bloodstock. Half-brother to 2 minor winners at 3 yrs in North America by Distorted Humor and Tiznow. The dam is an unplaced sister to the 2-y-o Grade 2 Saratoga Special Stakes winner Jump Start and a half-sister to 5 winners. The second dam, Steady Cat (by Storm Cat), a winner of 5 races and second in the Grade 2 Adirondack Stakes, is a sister to the winner and Grade 3 placed Apollo Cat. *"A really lovely big horse. He has a great action, a great attitude and we have a few Blame's in the yard and I should*

think the jury's out on the stallion. But for his size and his physique he does everything asked of him very well. A really likeable horse and I like him a lot".

1465. UNNAMED ★★★★
b.br.c. Exchange Rate – Istamara (Teofilo). January 19. First foal. $90,000Y. Keeneland September. Blandford Bloodstock. The dam is an unraced half-sister to 3 minor winners. The second dam, Favourable Terms (by Selkirk), won the Group 1 Nassau Stakes the Group 2 Windsor Forest Stakes and the Group 2 Matron Stakes and is a half-sister to 4 winners. *"I'm very pleased with him, he shows up well, he's got a bit of speed and looks a six furlong 2-y-o. Very professional, very mature and a good goer, so you'd love to think he's a May 2-y-o and at the moment he shows up as well as any colt in the yard".*

1466. UNNAMED ★★★
b.f. Dubawi – Meeznah (Dynaformer). March 12. Third foal. 200,000Y. Tattersalls October Book 1. Not sold. The dam, winner of the Group 2 Park Hill Stakes and the Group 3 Lillie Langtry Stakes, is a half-sister to 5 winners including the smart Group 2 12f Princess Of Wales's Stakes second Shahin. The second dam, String Quartet (by Sadler's Wells), a 12.5f listed winner in France and third in the Group 3 Lancashire Oaks, is a sister to the Irish and US listed stakes winner Casey Tibbs and a half-sister to 4 winners. *"A big filly, she has loads of size, loads of scope and a typical Dubawi action – not the most natural. I think the case with Dubawi is that they're happy to tick along and they'll tell you when the time comes to press buttons. That time certainly isn't now, she's one for later in the season".*

1467. UNNAMED ★★★★
b.f. Iffraaj – New Falcon (New Approach). February 10. First foal. 52,000Y. Tattersalls October Book 3. Blandford Bloodstock. The dam, a fair 2-y-o 7f winner, is a half-sister to 5 winners including the Group 3 second Sharnberry. The second dam, Wimple (by Kingmambo), a useful 5f and 6f winner at 2 yrs, was listed-placed and is a half-sister to 3 winners. *"We have two Iffraaj fillies, this is the sharper of the two and the one we've done the most with. She has a good attitude,*

starting to train well now and she's certainly mature enough to carry on. She's shown us a nice bit of speed so she looks like a six furlong type".

1468. UNNAMED ★★★★
b.f. Camelot – Silent Act (Theatrical). February 1. Third foal. 80,000Y. Tattersalls October Book 1. Mark Crossman. Half-sister to the fair 10f winner Harold Lloyd (by Cape Cross). The dam, a modest 11f and 12f winner, is a sister to 2 winners including the US Grade 3 winner Roman Dynasty and a half-sister to one winner. The second dam, Vinista (by Jade Hunter), a US listed stakes winner, was Grade 2 placed twice and is a half-sister to 7 winners. *"A really natural filly with loads of size and scope. She has a good action, finds everything straightforward and wants to get on with it, so I'm very pleased with her. When I bought her I thought she'd need far more time, but the fact she's training like she is doing allows us to carry on. She's one for seven furlongs in mid-season".*

1469. UNNAMED ★★★★
b.f. Camelot – Splendid (Mujtahid). February 3. Twelfth foal. 110,000Y. Tattersalls October Book 1. Demi O'Byrne. Half-sister to 6 winners including the fairly useful 2-y-o 7f winner and Group 3 7f Killavullan Stakes second Lord High Admiral (by Galileo), the quite useful 7f (at 2 yrs) and 11f winner and listed-placed Fanditha (by Danehill Dancer), the quite useful 2-y-o 6f winner Packing Hero (by Black Minnaloushe) and the US stakes-placed winner of 5 races Bohunk (by Polish Numbers). The dam is a placed half-sister to the very useful 1m (at 2 yrs) and 12f winner Peking Opera. The second dam, Braneakins (by Sallust), won 3 races over 12f in Ireland and is a half-sister to the Cheveley Park Stakes winners Park Appeal (the dam of Cape Cross) and Desirable (dam of the 1,000 Guineas winner Shadayid) and the Irish Oaks winner Alydaress. *"Very similar to my other Camelot filly in that she's surprised me. Plenty of size and scope but she's very natural and very pleasing in what she does. They're very similar fillies because they want to get on with it, they don't get tired and mentally they're very good. Both are likely to be seven furlong starters in mid-season".*

1470. UNNAMED ★★
ch.c. Galileo – Walklikeanegyptian (Danehill).
May 21. Sixth foal. Brother to the 2-y-o
Group 3 7f Tyros Stakes and US Grade 1
Belmont Derby Invitational winner Deauville,
to the smart Group 3 11f and listed 10f
winner of 5 races The Corsican and the quite
useful 2-y-o 1m winner Heatstroke. The dam,
a fair 2-y-o 5f and subsequent US winner,
was Grade 3 placed and is closely related to
numerous winners including the Canadian
Grade 2 Nassau Stakes winner Callwood
Dancer and the Group 2 Italian Oaks winner
Contredanse. The second dam, Ahdaab (by
Rahy), placed once over 10f, is a half-sister to
8 winners including the Group 1 1m Queen
Elizabeth II Stakes winner Maroof and to the
placed dam of the Irish Derby winner Desert
King. *"We've had most of the family apart
from Deauville and this colt is a different
type. He's got the most bone of any that
we've had and he's a bigger type. He hasn't
disappointed me in any way and has a good
way of going, but he was a very late foal and
he'll take time".*

1471. UNNAMED ★★★
b.c. Intello – Wild Gardenia (Alhaarth).
February 24. Fifth foal. 120,000Y. Tattersalls
October Book 1. Rabbah Bloodstock. Half-
brother to the fair 8.5f and 9f winner Raheeba
(by Invincible Spirit). The dam, placed fourth
once over 12f, is a half-sister to 5 winners
including Power (Group 1 Irish 2,000 Guineas
and Group 1 National Stakes), Curvy (Grade
1 E P Taylor Stakes) and Thakafaat (Group
2 Ribblesdale Stakes). The second dam,
Frappe (by Inchinor), a fairly useful 2-y-o 6f
winner, is a half-sister to 4 winners including
Footstepsinthesand (2,000 Guineas) and
Pedro The Great (Group 1 Phoenix Stakes).
*"A horse that's done very well over the last
month, he's taking his training well and has
gone forward quickly. He has a good attitude
and a good action, so while he's showing now
I'll carry on with him and he looks like a seven
furlong 2-y-o for mid-summer. I'm very happy
with him".*

1472. UNNAMED ★★★
b.f. Dark Angel – Zallerina (Zamindar). March
24. Second foal. 70,000Y. Tattersalls October
Book 2. Rabbah Bloodstock. Half-sister to

Zenovia (by Invincible Spirit), unplaced in two
starts at 2 yrs in 2016. The dam is an unraced
half-sister to the Italian listed-placed winner
Sgarzulina. The second dam, Zakania (by
Indian Ridge), is an unraced daughter of the
Group 3 Prix de Sandringham winner Zarkiya.
*"A nicer model than her half-sister, she's done
well physically since the sale. She won't be an
early type but she's doing everything in the
right way".*

RICHARD SPENCER

1473. CLUB TROPICANA ★★★
ch.f. Helmet – Twenty Seven (Efisio). February
16. Ninth foal. £25,000Y. Goffs UK Premier
(Doncaster). Bobby O'Ryan / Rebel Racing.
Half-sister to the useful listed-placed 2-y-o
5f winner Beat Seven (by Beat Hollow) and
to the modest 2-y-o 5f winner Kirtling Belle
(by Pastoral Pursuits). The dam, a fair 2-y-o
6f winner, is a half-sister to 5 winners. The
second dam, Naked Poser (by Night Shift),
a quite useful 2-y-o 6f winner, is a half-sister
to 4 winners. (Rebel Racing). *"She was cheap,
largely because she had a problem with a big
haematoma on her back at the sales when
we bought her. She's fine now but a typical
chestnut filly in that she's a bit hot, but she's
a great walker and I like her. She's very leggy
and angular, so we just backed off her a bit to
give her time to grow and do well because it
won't take long to get her fit. She'll be out in
May or June and she's a nice filly".* TRAINERS'
BARGAIN BUY

1474. FLUX CAPACITOR ★★★
b.c. Society Rock – Maleha (Cape Cross).
March 21. Fourth foal. 10,000Y. Tattersalls
December. Richard Spencer. Half-brother
to the fairly useful 2-y-o 6f winner Malilla
(by Red Clubs) and to the fair 7f and 1m
winner Desert Ranger (by Bushranger). The
dam is an unraced half-sister to the useful
listed 1m winner of 7 races Yamal and to
the quite useful 2-y-o 6f winner Trailblazing.
The second dam Pioneer Bride (by Gone
West), is an unplaced half-sister to 7 winners
including Faithful Son (Group 2 10f Prince
of Wales's Stakes) and Always Fair (Group
3 Coventry Stakes and Prix Quincey) and
to the dam of the Irish Oaks winner Lailani.
(Rebel Racing). *"A cheap buy, we have the
half-brother Gustavo Fring who didn't run last*

year but we think a lot of him and as people we're talking up Society Rock at the sales we thought this colt was worth a punt. This is a big horse, he's not going to be doing anything until mid-season but he's a very good-moving horse with a great attitude".

1475. GOWING GOWING GONE ★★★
ch.f. Society Rock – Face The Storm (Barathea). January 30. Ninth foal. £36,000Y. Goffs UK Premier (Doncaster). Bobby O'Ryan / Rebel Racing. Half-sister to the useful 2-y-o 5f and 6f winner and Group 2 7f Superlative Stakes second Roi de Vitesse (by Chineur), to the quite useful 2-y-o 6f winners Rebel Surge, Kojak (both by Kodiac) and Cavort (by Vettori) and the fair 2-y-o dual 5f winner Rise Up Lotus (by Zebedee). The dam, a fair 2-y-o 1m winner, is a half-sister to 3 winners including the listed winner Santa Isobel. The second dam, Atlantic Record (by Slip Anchor), is an unraced half-sister to 4 winners. (Rebel Racing). *"On paper she looks a 2-y-o but she's just going to take time to come to hand. I have two Society Rock 2-y-o's and they're both the same – they're nice but their knees are very immature and they need time to close up and develop. She's cantered and been upsides but we'll have to hold off running her until late May or early June. She's grown a bit and filled out since we bought her and potentially she could be a nice 2-y-o in time".*

1476. LITTLELORDCONFORD ★★★★
b.c. Intikhab – Anna Law (Lawman). February 15. Second foal. £40,000Y. Goffs UK Premier (Doncaster). BobbyO'Ryan / Rebel Racing. Half-brother to the fairly useful 2016 2-y-o 5f winner Battaash (by Dark Angel). The dam is an unplaced half-sister to 9 winners including the 2-y-o Group 2 Champagne Stakes winner and Group 1 July Cup third Etlaala. The second dam, Portelet (by Night Shift), a fairly useful 5f winner of 4 races, is a half-sister to 4 winners. (Rebel Racing). *"He looks a sharp 2-y-o and the 3-y-o half-brother is highly thought of. He's doing everything asked of him and he could be one of our first 2-y-o runners. He's bred for five furlongs, he's a strong 2-y-o, not over-big and hopefully we'll have a lot of fun with him".*

1477. PATTY PATCH ★★★
b.f. Big Bad Bob – Cockney Dancer (Cockney Rebel). April 2. First foal. 42,000Y. Tattersalls October Book 2. P Cunningham. The dam, a quite useful 6f (at 2 yrs) and dual 7f winner, is a half-sister to 6 winners including the very smart 6f (at 2 yrs) and 7f winner and Group 2 Prix Morny second Gallagher and the listed-placed Quick Wit and Roodeye (herself dam of the dual US Grade 2 winner Prize Exhibit). The second dam, Roo (by Rudimentary), a quite useful listed-placed 2-y-o 5f and 6f winner, is a half-sister to the Group 2 6f Gimcrack Stakes winner Bannister. (Rebel Racing). *"A filly from a very good family, she's sharp but I think more mentally than physically. She'll want six furlongs to start with and then we'll step her up to seven. She's still growing but if she stops soon we'll try and get her out from mid-May onwards. A nice filly with a good temperament and she wants to get on with things".*

1478. PESKY WABBITT ★★★
b.c. Compton Place – Good Girl (College Chapel). February 7. Eighth foal. £30,000Y. Goffs UK Premier (Doncaster). Bobby O'Ryan / Rebel Racing. Half-brother to the fairly useful 6f (at 2 yrs) to 1m winner of 4 races Good Again (by Dubai Destination), to the quite useful 6f (at 2 yrs) to 8.5f winner Cruiser (by Oasis Dream) and the quite useful 7f winners Ink Spot (by Diktat) and Destroyer (by Royal Applause). The dam, a useful 2-y-o listed 5f winner and third in the Group 1 6f Cheveley Park Stakes, is a half-sister to 6 winners. The second dam, Indian Honey (by Indian King), is an unraced half-sister to 7 winners. (Rebel Racing). *"At the sale he looked pretty rough, he was messing about, had a big belly and people were raising their eyebrows at him, but we took a punt on him and he was cheaper than he would have been with proper preparation. He's from a fast family, so the pedigree suggests 2-y-o speed and he could be one for June or July. He's doing everything asked so hopefully he's the ugly duckling that's going to turn into a swan".*

1479. PHILAMUNDO ★★★
b.c. Sir Prancealot – Rublevka Star (Elusive Quality). March 29. Fourth foal. £80,000Y. Goffs UK Premier (Doncaster). Bobby O'Ryan

/ Rebel Racing. Brother to the quite useful 2016 2-y-o 7f winner Novoman and half-brother to a minor 3-y-o winner in Germany by Zebedee. The dam, a moderate 2-y-o 5f winner, is a half-sister to 3 winners including the South African listed stakes winner Distance Done. The second dam, Al Desima (by Emperor Jones), a fairly useful 2-y-o 7f winner, subsequently won in the USA, was third in the Grade 1 Yellow Ribbon Stakes and is a half-sister to 9 winners. (Rebel Racing). *"A nice-moving horse, initially he was the pick of our yearlings for me and when we were breaking him in he looked a sharp, early type. In fact he reminded me of Red Jazz at Hills's when we were breaking him in – he was a bit of a playboy. But he's going through a growing phase now and I'd be hoping to get him out in May or June".*

1480. RAJASINGHE ★★★★ ♠
b.c. Choisir – Bunditten (Soviet Star). March 31. Ninth foal. £85,000Y. Goffs UK Premier (Doncaster). Bobby O'Ryan / Rebel Racing. Half-brother to 6 winners including the fairly useful 2-y-o listed-placed 5f winner Kurland (by Kheleyt), the quite useful 2-y-o 5f winner Airborne Again (by Acclamation), the fair 2-y-o 6f winner Star Breaker (by Teofilo) and the fair dual 5f winner Star Fire (by Dark Angel). The dam, a fairly useful 2-y-o 5f winner, was listed-placed and is a half-sister to 3 winners. The second dam, Felicita (by Catrail), won 3 races in France at 2 yrs including two 5f listed events, was Group 3 placed and is a half-sister to 5 winners. (Rebel Racing). *"He could potentially start over six furlongs in May or June because he's very relaxed and we haven't wound him up, but there's nothing to say we wouldn't run him over five if he shows us he's got enough boot for it. He's a well-balanced colt and a nice size with a great attitude. He's bred to do well, he has every chance and he'd be one of my picks".*

HENRY SPILLER

1481. CATCH THE TIDE (FR) ★★
ch.f. Kendargent – Coiffure (King's Best). February 11. Fourth foal. Half-sister to the 2016 French 1m placed 2-y-o Canterbury Quad (by Motivator). The dam is an unraced half-sister to 4 winners. The second dam, Quiff (by Sadler's Wells), won the Group 1

12f Yorkshire Oaks and was second in the St Leger and is a sister to the very useful 10f winner and Group 3 placed Arabian Gulf. (Peter Spiller). *"A home-bred, she's had a bit of time off but she's a fine, big filly that won't be terribly early but has a lovely temperament and the sire's done well. She's one for the end of the season and she'll probably have the odd run here before racing in France for the premiums".*

1482. INITIATIVE ★★
b.c. Excelebration – Viking Fair (Zamindar). February 1. Sixth foal. 20,000Y. Tattersalls October Book 2. Not sold. Half-brother to the moderate 7f winner Beauty's Forte (by Kyllachy). The dam is an unraced half-sister to four winners including the dual Group 3 winner Trade Fair and the listed winner Village Fete (herself dam of the Group 3 Glorious Stakes winner Kings Fete). The second dam, Danefair (by Danehill), a smart winner of the Group 3 12f Prix de Minerve and two 10f listed events in France, is a sister to the Group 3 winners Prove and Vortex and a half-sister to 7 winners including the listed 12f Prix Joubert winner Erudite. (Saville House Racing Club). *"This colt will be our first 2-y-o runner, he's done a bit of work on the grass and he's pleased us very much. We're probably going to wait for six furlongs in mid-May because he's not really sharp enough for five, but he's a really nice horse so I'll try and manage him correctly. He's done nothing but please us, he's just a good size for a 2-y-o, compact, racy-looking and with a good temperament".*

1483. LAUNCESTON PLACE (FR) ★★
b.c. Le Havre – Last Song (Singspiel). February 1. First foal. The dam was placed over 10f in France and is a half-sister to 3 winners. The second dam, Last Rhapsody (by Kris), a 2-y-o 1m winner in France, is a sister to the Group 3 7f Nell Gwyn Stakes winner Lil's Jessy and a half-sister to numerous winners including the smart French 1m listed winner Lone Bid and the useful 1m and 12f winner and listed-placed Love Galore. (Peter Spiller). *"I know he's going to take a bit of time but he's done one piece of work and I'm fairly happy with him so far. A lovely looking horse, he's French-bred so he qualifies for those premiums as well. The grandam won*

her maiden by ten lengths and was bought by Godolphin but she never ran again. I think this colt will be out at the end of May over six furlongs but he'll stay further later on and we have high hopes for him".

1484. UNBRIDLED'S STAR ★★★

b.f. Foxwedge – Celestial Empire (Empire Maker). April 18. Fourth foal. Sister to the 2016 US 2-y-o 5.5f and 6f winner and dual Grade 3 placed Star Empire and half-sister to the fair 2-y-o 7f winner Unnoticed (by Observatory). The dam is an unraced half-sister to 4 minor winners in the USA. The second dam, Script (by Storm Cat), a minor US 3-y-o winner, is a half-sister to 7 winners including three US Graded stakes winners. (Claire Sayer). *"A home-bred, her full-brother Star Empire is trained in the States by Wesley Ward and is on the Kentucky Derby trail at the moment. He won his maiden by six lengths last year and came over here for the Coventry but never ran but he's been graded stakes placed twice since. This is a fine, big filly, she goes nicely and nothing's going to happen too early with her but she's got a lovely stride and she's been pleasing us in her slower paces".*

1485. UNNAMED ★★★

b.c. Foxwedge – Chicklade (Firebreak). February 15. First foal. £4,000Y. Goffs UK Silver (Doncaster). Howson & Houldsworth. The dam is an unraced half-sister to one winner. The second dam, Ballyalla (by Mind Games), a quite useful 2-y-o 6f winner, is a half-sister to 7 winners including the smart 2-y-o dual 6f winner and Group 2 Mill Reef Stakes second Doctor Brown. *"A very nice colt, I think the sire is underrated and although he was cheap this is a fine, big, correct horse".* TRAINERS' BARGAIN BUY

FOZZY STACK

1486. BOOM STAR (IRE) ★★★

b.c. Choisir – Glowing Star (Clodovil). March 1. First foal. £58,000Y. Goffs UK Premier (Doncaster). Hubie de Burgh / C McCormack. The dam is an unplaced half-sister to the 2-y-o 7f winner and Group 1 Irish 1,000 Guineas third Devonshire and to the 2-y-o listed 5f winner Hurryupharriet. The second dam, Nova Tor (by Trans Island), a fair 5f winner of 6 races at 2 and 3 yrs, is a half-sister to 7

other minor winners. *"It looks like he's going to be a sharp, precocious horse and we should get him out in the next few weeks. I'm quite happy with him at the minute, he's not over-big but he's big enough and he'll be a five/six furlong 2-y-o. We have a few by Choisir and I'd say most of them want goodish ground".*

1487. COMMANDER GRIGIO (IRE) ★★★★

b.c. Holy Roman Emperor – Many Hearts (Distorted Humor). April 7. Second living foal. €65,000Y. Goffs Orby. De Burgh Equine. Half-brother to the 2016 Irish 2-y-o 1m winner Galkina (by Pour Moi). The dam is an unplaced half-sister to 4 winners including the listed winner Whitman. The second dam, Sundrop (by Sunday Silence), a smart Group 3 8.5f winner, is a half-sister to 6 winners. *"He's a good, strong-bodied colt that we'll probably set off in a six furlong maiden in May. He seems to go nicely and he'll probably get a bit further too".*

1488. GOODTHINGSTAKETIME (IRE) ★★★

b.f. Canford Cliffs – Addicted To Progress (Holy Roman Emperor). March 1. First foal. €2,200Y. Tattersalls Ireland September. Not sold. The dam ran twice unplaced and is a half-sister to the dual listed winner over 7f and 1m and Group 3 second Lisvale. The second dam, Farthingale (by Nashwan), placed once over 12f in Ireland, is a half-sister to 4 winners including the Group 2 Richmond Stakes third Cedarberg. *"She should be up to running in May and has enough pace for five or six furlongs. Definitely a bargain for what she cost".* TRAINERS' BARGAIN BUY

1489. GOTTARDO (IRE) ★★★★

b.c. Choisir – Chantarella (Royal Academy). April 10. Ninth foal. Brother to the fairy useful 2-y-o 5f winner, listed-placed and Group 2 6f Railway Stakes fourth Another Express and to the fairly useful listed-placed triple 5f winner Celerina and half-brother to the US 2-y-o triple 1m winner Clenor (by Oratorio) and the moderate Irish 6f winner Candy Kiss (by Mull Of Kintyre). The dam is an unplaced half-sister to several winners including the listed 5f Rous Stakes winner My-O-My. The second dam, Maimiti (by Goldhill), is an unplaced half-sister to the useful Irish sprinter Title Roll, winner of the Group 3 King George Stakes and to the listed sprint winner Northern Express. *"He seems quite precocious and typical of the family. He's a bit plain, which is probably typical of the sire, but he'll have enough pace for five/six furlongs and he's a sharp colt".*

1490. ILEX EXCELSA (IRE) ★★★
ch.f. Excelebration – Holly Blue (Bluebird). February 12. Twelfth foal. €160,000Y. Arqana Deauville August. James Stack/C McCormack. Half-sister to 6 winners including the Irish 2-y-o and subsequent South African triple Group 2 winner Gibraltar Blue, the quite useful 10f and 11f winner Pilgrims Rest (both by Rock Of Gibraltar and the Irish 5f (at 2 yrs) and listed 6f winner Scream Blue Murder (by Oratorio). The dam, a useful listed 1m winner, is a half-sister to 6 minor winners. The second dam, Nettle (by Kris), a useful listed 7f winner, is a half-sister to 5 winners. *"A big, scopey filly and a good mover, she should get seven furlongs and she's good looking".*

1491. LADY HEART ★★★
ch.f. Kyllachy – Hightime Heroine (Danetime). March 19. Fifth foal. €30,000Y. Tattersalls Ireland September. Oliver Cooper. Closely related to the useful 2016 2-y-o Group 1 National Stakes fourth and 2017 3-y-o 5f winner Son Of Rest (by Pivotal). The dam, a fair 6f winner, is a half-sister to 5 winners including the listed 1m Heron Stakes winner and Group 1 1m Criterium International third Redolent. The second dam, Esterlina (by Highest Honor), won over 1m at 3 yrs in Ireland and is a half-sister to 3 minor winners in France. *"A half-sister to a 3-y-o we have called Son Of Rest, she wouldn't be as big as him but she's growing and as a result we haven't done a lot with her. As far her trip is concerned, knowing her pedigree (Son Of Rest won over five furlongs the other day) I shouldn't imagine she'd get too far".*

1492. OTTAVA (IRE) ★★★
b.c. Shamardal – Musical Note (Zamindar). January 31. Fifth foal. €190,000Y. Goffs Orby. De Burgh Equine. Half-brother to the fair 8.5f winner Que Sera Sera (by Dansili). The dam is an unraced half-sister to 7 winners

including the French Group 3 winner Short Pause, the French 1m listed winner Cheyenne Dream and to the dams of the Group 1 winners Continent and Zambezi Sun. The second dam, Interval (by Habitat), won four races from 5f to 1m including the Group 2 Prix Maurice de Gheest and is a half-sister to 5 winners including the US Grade 2 winner Interim (dam of the US Grade 1 winner Midships). *"A big, strong horse that seems to go nicely, I'll probably set him off in a six furlong maiden in May. He'll be able to run plenty this year. A good-looking horse and a January foal that cost plenty".*

1493. SHIFTED STRATEGY (IRE) ★★★
b.c. Choisir – Pure Greed (Galileo). March 26. Third foal. €90,000Y. Goffs Orby. C McCormack. The dam, a moderate maiden, was fourth over 10f and 12f and is a half-sister to 3 minor winners. The second dam, Fear And Greed (by Brief Truce), an Irish 2-y-o 6f winner and second in the Group 1 7f Moyglare Stud Stakes, is a half-sister to 5 winners. *"He'll be one that'll set off at six furlongs and he'll definitely stay seven, particularly as he's out of a Galileo mare. A good-looking horse, a bit of good ground wouldn't inconvenience him".*

1494. SIRICI (IRE) ★★★★
ch.f. Choisir – Mironica (Excellent Art). February 1. First foal. The dam, a quite useful Irish 2-y-o 6f winner, is a half-sister to 2 winners. The second dam, Lisfannon (by Bahamian Bounty), placed fourth three times from 5f to 6.5f, is half-sister to 4 winners including the listed 5f winner of 5 races Dazed And Amazed. *"Not over-big, she's had two runs already and won the other day in Dundalk. She won handily enough, she's sharp and we'll certainly be getting on with her in the short term".*

1495. STRANGERINTHENIGHT (IRE) ★★★
b.c. Footstepsinthesand – Headborough Lass (Invincible Spirit). March 20. Fifth foal. €43,000Y. Tattersalls Ireland September. De Burgh Equine. Half-brother to the fair 7f and 1m winner of 4 races Global Leader (by Dark Angel). The dam, a fair 7f winner, is a half-sister to 4 minor winners here and abroad.

The second dam, Snowspin (by Carwhite), a fair 12f winner in Ireland and subsequently a winner in France and Switzerland, is a half-sister to 7 winners including Gulland (Group 3 Chester Vase) and the listed winner Salchow (herself dam of the Oaks third Shadow Dancing). *"A good-looking, good-moving horse that might want a bit of ease in the ground. He's quite sharp so we'll probably set him off over six furlongs and we're happy with what he's done so far".*

1496. TAHILLA (IRE) ★★★
b.f. Holy Roman Emperor – Tarascon (Tirol). April 27. Sister to the useful 2-y-o listed 6f winner High Award and half-sister to four winners including the French listed-placed dual 7f winner (including at 2 yrs) Mayano Sophia (by Rock Of Gibraltar), the quite useful 10f winner Estephe (by Sadler's Wells) and the dual 9f winner Beucaire (by Entrepreneur). The dam, winner of the Group 1 7f Moyglare Stud Stakes at 2 yrs and the Irish 1,000 Guineas, is a half-sister to the Group 2 winner Mister Monet and to the dual Group 1 placed Mala Mala. The second dam, Breyani (by Commanche Run), a useful winner at up to 2m, is a half-sister to 4 winners. *"She's cutting the same shape and size as her brother High Award. Not over-big, seems to move nicely and she'll probably be out by June. A good walker and typical of the sire in that she's not over-big but strong".*

1497. ZIHBA (IRE) ★★★★
b.c. Choisir – Fancy Vivid (Galileo). March 30. Fourth foal. €62,000Y. Tattersalls Ireland September. De Burgh Equine. Half-brother to the moderate Irish 6.5f and 7f winner Double Fast (by Fast Company). The dam, a modest 8.5f placed maiden, is a half-sister 2 winners. The second dam, Starchy (by Cadeaux Genereux), a fair 2-y-o 6f winner, is a sister to the smart Group 2 5f Flying Childers Stakes and Group 3 5f King George V Stakes winner Land Of Dreams (dam of the multiple Group 1 winner Dream Ahead) and a half-sister to 5 winners. *"A good-looking horse, he's one you'd like. A good-mover and very straightforward, he's just starting to grow a bit, shouldn't have any problem having the speed to go six furlongs and then we'll step him up to seven".*

1498. UNNAMED ★★★★
b.f. Fastnet Rock – Annabelle Ja (Singspiel). May 2. Seventh foal. 180,000Y. Tattersalls October Book 1. BBA (Ire). Half-sister to the 2-y-o Group 2 July Stakes, Group 2 Richmond Stakes and Group 2 Park Stakes winner of 8 races Libranno (by Librettist) and the French 2-y-o 6f winner and Group 3 Prix De Cabourg second Al Muthana (by Pastoral Pursuits). The dam, a quite useful 2-y-o 7f winner, is a half-sister to 12 winners in Europe (mainly Germany). The second dam, Alamea (by Ela-Mana-Mou), won 2 minor races at 2 and 3 yrs in Germany and is a half-sister to 8 winners. *"Quite a late foal and she's still a bit unfurnished but she's done a couple of half-speeds. I don't think she's going to be one of those Fastnet Rock's that stay a mile and a half, by any stretch of the imagination. We quite like her and she'll be a nice filly when she comes together. I'm not sure when it'll happen, but it will at some stage".*

1499. UNNAMED ★★★
b.f. Fastnet Rock – Dame Blanche (Be My Guest). February 10. Eighth living foal. 60,000Y. Tattersalls October Book 2. De Burgh Equine. Sister to the quite useful dual 1m winner Fastnet Tempest and half-sister to the quite useful French 10f winner and Group 3 Prix Cleopatre third Excellent Girl, the quite useful 5f to 1m winner of 6 races at 2 to 4 yrs Moon River (both by Exceed And Excel), the minor Italian winner of 4 races Tempesta d'Amore (by Oratorio) and a winner in Qatar by Xaar. The dam, a modest 1m placed 3-y-o, is a half-sister to 6 winners including the US Grade 1 winner and Irish 1,000 Guineas third Luas Line and the Group 2 second Lost In The Moment. The second dam, Streetcar (by In The Wings), fourth once at 2 yrs over 1m, is a half-sister to 9 winners. *"She's a strong, robust filly and a good mover. It wouldn't surprise me if she could run over six furlongs but she'll get up to seven furlongs or a mile in time. Quite a nice filly".*

1500. UNNAMED ★★★
b.f. Scat Daddy – Royal Empress (Holy Roman Emperor). April 17. First foal. 110,000Y. Tattersalls October Book 2. C McCormack. The dam, an Irish 6f winner and third in the 2-y-o Group 3 6f Round Tower Stakes,

is a half-sister to 2 winners including the 2-y-o Group 3 6f Killavullan Stakes winner Craftsman. The second dam, Weekend Fling (by Forest Wildcat), a fair 6f winner at 3 yrs, is a half-sister to 7 winners including the US Grade 1 Arkansas Derby winner Archarcharch. *"She's quite sharp and should be up to running in May over five or six furlongs. What we've seen of her so far we like".*

SIR MICHAEL STOUTE

1501. CRYSTAL KING
ch.c. Frankel – Crystal Star (Mark Of Esteem). May 11. Half-brother to the very smart dual Group 2 12f Pride Stakes, Group 2 12f Princess Of Wales's Stakes and Group 3 10.3f Middleton Stakes winner Crystal Capella (by Cape Cross), to the very smart Group 2 10f winner Hillstar (by Danehill Dancer), the listed 10f winner Crystal Zvezda (by Dubawi) and the fairly useful 1m and 10f winner Sandor (by Fantastic Light). The dam, winner of the listed Radley Stakes and second in the Group 3 Fred Darling Stakes, is a half sister to 6 winners. The second dam, Crystal Capella (by Be My Guest), a fairly useful 2-y-o 7f winner here and subsequently a dual winner in Canada, is a half-sister to 5 winners including the French 1,000 Guineas winner Rose Gypsy.

1502. DESERT SON
ch.c. Dubawi – Russelliana (Medicean). January 28. Second foal. Half-brother to the fair 2016 2-y-o 7f winner Blushing Rose (by Dalakhani). The dam, a useful 2-y-o 6f winner, was second in the Group 2 6f Cherry Hinton Stakes and is a half-sister to 2 winners. The second dam, Rosacara (by Green Desert), a modest 7f and 1m placed maiden, is a half-sister to the high-class triple Group 1 winner Notnowcato.

1503. EXPERT EYE
b.c. Acclamation – Exemplify (Dansili). January 31. Second foal. The dam, a French 2-y-o 1m winner, is a half-sister to the Group 1 Cheveley Park Stakes, 1,000 Guineas and French 1,000 Guineas winner Special Duty (by Hennessy). The second dam, Quest To Peak (by Distant View), ran once unplaced and is a sister to Sightseek, winner of 7 Grade 1 events in the USA from 7f to 9f and a half-sister to the US dual Grade 1 winner Tates Creek.

1504. FINAL SET (IRE)
b.f. Dark Angel – Two Sets To Love (Cadeaux Genereux). March 11. Seventh foal. 700,000Y. Tattersalls October Book 1. Charlie Gordon-Watson. Sister to the fairly useful 5f (at 2 yrs) and 1m winner and Group 3 Sweet Solera Stakes second Midnite Angel and to the fair 7f to 10f winner of 5 races Emman Bee and half-sister to 2 winners including the fair 6f (at 2 yrs) to 1m winner of 4 races Sabatini (by One Cool Cat). The dam is an unraced half-sister to 3 winners including the Group 2 Sandown Mile winner Swallow Flight. The second dam, Mirage (by Red Sunset), a dual listed winner in Germany, is a sister to the multiple listed winner Red Hero and a half-sister to 7 winners.

1505. FOREVER IN LOVE
ch.f. Dutch Art – Ardent (Pivotal). May 9. Third foal. Sister to the useful 2-y-o 7f and 3-y-o listed 7f winner of 4 races Eternally and half-sister to the modest 2016 7f placed 2-y-o Impassioned (by Bahamian Bounty). The dam, a quite useful 6f winner, is a half-sister to 2 winners including the fairly useful 5f (at 2 yrs) and listed 6f winner Irresistible. The second dam, Polish Romance (by Danzig), a minor 7f winner in the USA, is a sister to the US stakes winner Polish Love and a half-sister to 3 minor winners. (Cheveley Park Stud).

1506. HAZARFIYA
b.f. Fastnet Rock – Hazariya (Xaar). April 8. Seventh foal. Half-sister to 5 winners including the Derby and Irish Derby winner Harzand (by Sea The Stars), the 2-y-o Group 3 7f Silver Flash Stakes winner Harasiya (by Pivotal), the useful dual 10f winner and Group 3 second Haziyna (by Halling) and the useful listed 12f winner Hazarafa (by Daylami). The dam, winner of the Group 3 7f Athasi Stakes and a listed event over 7f, is a half-sister to the Group 3 Blue Wind Stakes winner Hazarista and a half-sister to numerous minor winners. The second dam, Hazaradjat (by Darshaan), won twice at 2 and 3 yrs and is a half-sister to 10 winners including the Group 1 Flying Childers Stakes winner Hittite Glory. (H H Aga Khan).

1507. HIDDEN DEPTHS (IRE)
b.c. Dark Angel – Liber Nauticus (Azamour).

March 21. First foal. The dam won the Group 3 10.5f Musidora Stakes and is a half-sister to 2 winners including the useful 2-y-o 7f winner and Group 2 Rockfel Stakes second Thetis. The second dam, Serres (by Daylami), is an unraced half-sister to 6 winners including the Breeders' Cup Turf, King George VI and St Leger winner Conduit and the Group 2 Great Voltigeur Stakes winner Hard Top.

1508. HOMEOPATHIC
b.f. Dark Angel – Holistic (Pivotal). March 20. Second foal. The dam is an unraced sister to 2 winners including the fairly useful listed 6f winner of 5 races Prescription and a half-sister to 8 winners including the smart Group 3 7f Horris Hill Stakes winner of 7 races Cupid's Glory, the listed 1m and 10f winner of 6 races Courting and very useful Group 3 9f and triple listed 1m winner Clinical. The second dam, Doctor's Glory (by Elmaamul), a fairly useful 5.2f (at 2 yrs) and 6f winner, is a half-sister to 6 winners. (Cheveley Park Stud).

1509. LUNAR CORONA
br.f. Dansili – Starscope (Selkirk). January 28. First foal. The dam, a smart 2-y-o 7f winner and second in the 1,000 Guineas and the Coronation Stakes, is a half-sister to the useful listed 1m winner Solar Magic. The second dam, Moon Goddess (by Rainbow Quest), a fairly useful 1m winner, is a half-sister to the Group 1 Eclipse Stakes and Lockinge Stakes winner and sire Medicean. Cheveley Park Stud).

1510. MIDI
b.c. Frankel – Midday (Oasis Dream). January 28. Third foal. Closely related to the very smart 1m (at 2 yrs) and Group 3 10f Classic Trial winner and Group 2 12f Prix Niel second Midterm (by Galileo). The dam was a high-class racemare and the winner of six Group 1 races – Breeders' Cup Filly & Mare Turf, Prix Vermeille, Yorkshire Oaks and Nassau Stakes (three times) and is a full or half-sister to 5 winners including the smart 1m (at 2 yrs) and Group 3 7f winner and Group 1 Nassau Stakes third Hot Snap. The second dam, Midsummer (by Kingmambo), a quite useful listed-placed 11f winner, is a half-sister to the Oaks and Fillies Mile winner Reams Of Verse and the Eclipse Stakes and Phoenix Champion Stakes winner Elmaamul. (Khalid Abdulla).

1511. PROCEDURE
gr.f. Invincible Spirit – Clinical (Motivator). February 19. Second foal. Half-sister to the useful 2016 2-y-o 7f winner and Group 1 National Stakes third Lockheed (by Exceed And Excel). The dam, a very useful Group 3 9f and triple listed 1m winner, is a half-sister to 9 winners including the smart Group 3 7f Horris Hill Stakes winner of 7 races Cupid's Glory, the listed 1m and 10f winner of 6 races Courting and the fairly useful listed 6f winner of 5 races Prescription. The second dam, Doctor's Glory (by Elmaamul), a fairly useful 5.2f (at 2 yrs) and 6f winner, is a half-sister to 6 winners. (Cheveley Park Stud).

1512. REKINDLE
ch.f. Frankel – Hot Snap (Pivotal). January 18. First foal. The dam, a smart 1m (at 2 yrs) and Group 3 7f Nell Gwyn Stakes winner, was third in the Group 1 Nassau Stakes and is a half-sister to 5 winners including the high-class racemare Midday, a winner of six Group 1 races (Breeders' Cup Filly & Mare Turf, Prix Vermeille, Yorkshire Oaks and Nassau Stakes (three times)). The second dam, Midsummer (by Kingmambo), a quite useful listed-placed 11f winner, is a half-sister to the Oaks and Fillies Mile winner Reams of Verse and the Eclipse Stakes and Phoenix Champion Stakes winner Elmaamul. (Khalid Abdulla).

1513. REFRAIN (IRE)
b.c. Dubawi – Folk Opera (Singspiel). February 27. Fifth foal. Half-brother to the fairly useful 2-y-o 7f winner Folk Melody (by Street Cry) and to the quite useful 1m winner Lovely Memory (by Shamardal). The dam, winner of the Grade 1 10f E P Taylor Stakes and the Group 2 10f Prix Jean Romanet, is a half-sister to 4 minor winners. The second dam, Skiphall (by Halling), placed 5 times at 3 yrs in France, stayed 10.5f and is a half-sister to 7 winners including the 2-y-o listed winner Innocent Air and the French and US listed winner and US Grade 1 placed Skipping.

1514. SUN MAIDEN
b.f. Frankel – Midsummer (Kingmambo). April 25. Tenth foal. Half-sister to the high-class racemare Midday, a winner of six Group 1 races (Breeders' Cup Filly & Mare Turf, Prix Vermeille, Yorkshire Oaks and Nassau Stakes

(three times)), to the fairly useful 10f winner Shoal, the quite useful 10f winner Atone, the fair 10f winner Popular (all by Oasis Dream), the smart 1m (at 2 yrs) and Group 3 7f winner and Group 1 Nassau Stakes third Hot Snap (by Pivotal) and the useful listed-placed 10f and 12f winner Midsummer Sun (by Monsun). The dam, a quite useful listed-placed 11f winner, is a half-sister to the Oaks and Fillies Mile winner Reams Of Verse and the Eclipse Stakes and Phoenix Champion Stakes winner Elmaamul. The second dam, Modena (by Roberto), is an unraced half-sister to the dam of Zafonic. (Khalid Abdulla).

1515. VERACIOUS
b.f. Frankel – Infallible (Pivotal). February 17. Half-sister to the Group 2 Summer Mile winner and US Grade 1 Woodbine Mile third Mutakayyef (by Sea The Stars), to the useful Irish listed 1m winner and Group 3 9.5f third Intimation (by Dubawi) and the useful 6f winner of four races Intrinsic (by Oasis Dream). The dam, a very smart 7f (at 2 yrs) and Group 3 7f Nell Gwyn Stakes winner, was second in the Group 1 Coronation Stakes and the Group 1 Falmouth Stakes and is a full or half-sister to 3 winners. The second dam, Irresistible (by Cadeaux Genereux), was a fairly useful 5f (at 2 yrs) and listed 6f winner and is a half-sister to 2 winners.

1516. WEEKDAY
b.f. Dansili – Timepiece (Zamindar). January 16. First foal. The dam, a winner of six races including the Group 1 1m Falmouth Stakes and three listed events, is a half-sister to numerous winners including the Group 1 10f Criterium de Saint-Cloud winner Passage Of Time and the Group 2 King Edward VII Stakes winner Father Time (both by Dansili). The second dam, Clepsydra (by Sadler's Wells), a quite useful 12f winner, is a half-sister to 6 winners including the useful listed 10.5f winner Double Crossed (herself dam of the multiple Group 1 winner Twice Over). (Khalid Abdulla).

1517. WHITEHALL ♠
b.c. Dansili – Majestic Roi (Street Cry). March 31. Sixth foal. 200,000Y. Tattersalls October Book 1. John & Jake Warren. Half-brother

to the German listed 1m (at 2 yrs) and dual Group 3 1m winner Noor Al Hawa (by Makfi), to the fairly useful German listed 9.5f winner of 4 races Majestic Jasmine (by New Approach), the fairly useful 10f winner Long Cross (by Cape Cross) and the quite useful 2-y-o 7f winner Majestic Manner (by Dubawi). The dam won the Group 1 1m Sun Chariot Stakes and the Group 3 Fred Darling Stakes and is a half-sister to 7 winners including the Group 3 Newbury Arc Trial winner Black Spirit. The second dam, L'Extra Honor (by Hero's Honor), a French listed 10f winner, is a half-sister to 11 winners including Montelimar (Group 2 Gallinule Stakes).

1518. UNNAMED
b.f. Frankel – Diary (Green Desert). April 29. Ninth foal. 675,000Y. Tattersalls October Book 1. Joe Foley. Half-sister to the Group 1 5f Prix de l'Abbaye and dual listed 6f winner Total Gallery (by Namid), to the 5f winner (at 2 yrs) and Group 1 Fillies' Mile second Lady Darshaan, the useful listed 13f winner Tempest Fugit (both by High Chaparral) and a winner abroad by Lujain. The dam won 3 races in Greece over 7f at 3 yrs and is a half-sister to 5 winners including the Group 1 Pretty Polly Stakes winner Ambivalent and the Group 1 Gran Criterium third Al Waffi. The second dam, Darrery (by Darshaan), won 3 races at 3 and 4 yrs, was listed-placed and is a half-sister to 3 winners.

1519. UNNAMED
b.c. New Approach – Fallen Star (Brief Truce). February 3. Tenth foal. 420,000Y. Tattersalls October Book 1. John & Jake Warren / Al Shaqab. Closely related to the useful 2-y-o 1m winner and Group 2 12f Lancashire Oaks second Fallen In Love (by Galileo) and half-brother to four winners including the very smart Group 1 1m Coronation Stakes winner Fallen For You and the smart listed 1m winner Fallen Idol (by Pivotal). The dam, a listed 7f winner and Group 3 placed twice, is a half-sister to 6 winners including Fly To The Stars (Group 1 7f Lockinge Stakes). The second dam, Rise And Fall (by Mill Reef), is an unplaced full or half-sister to 7 winners including the listed winners Special Leave, Spring To Action and Laughter.

1520. UNNAMED ♣
b.f. Teofilo – Lady Lahar (Fraam). January 16. Ninth foal. 280,000Y. Tattersalls October Book 1. Blandford Bloodstock. Closely related to the fairly useful listed 1m (at 2 yrs) and 10f winner Classic Legend and to the useful 12f and 14f winner I Have A Dream and half-sister to 4 winners including the very useful Group 3 7f winner of 5 races from 2 to 5 yrs Jallota (by Rock Of Gibraltar), the fairly useful listed-placed 10f winner Popmurphy (by Montjeu) and the fairly useful 7f (at 2 yrs), 1m and hurdles winner Kilburn (by Grand Lodge). The dam, a 2-y-o Group 3 7f Futurity Stakes winner, was third in the Group 2 Cherry Hinton Stakes and the Group 2 Falmouth Stakes and is a half-sister to 4 winners including the listed winner Miss Lahar. The second dam, Brigadier's Bird (by Mujadil), is an unraced half-sister to 3 winners.

1521. UNNAMED
b.c. War Front – Maryinsky (Sadler's Wells). February 16. Eighth foal. Half-brother to the 2016 2-y-o 1m winner on her only start Crimson Rock (by Fastnet Rock), to the Group 1 Pretty Polly Stakes, Irish Oaks, Nassau Stakes and Yorkshire Oaks winner Peeping Fawn (by Danehill) and the 2-y-o Group 1 Criterium International winner Thewayyouare (by Kingmambo). The dam, a 2-y-o 7f winner and second in the Group 1 Fillies Mile, is a half-sister to Better Than Honour (Grade 2 9f Demoiselle Stakes), Turnberry Isle (Group 2 1m Beresford Stakes) and Smolensk (Group 2 1m Prix d'Astarte). The second dam, Blush With Pride (by Blushing Groom), won the Grade 1 9f Kentucky Oaks and the Grade 1 8.5f Santa Susana Stakes and is a half-sister to several smart winners and to the dam of El Gran Senor and Try My Best.

1522. UNNAMED ♣♣
b.c. Al Kazeem – Resort (Oasis Dream). January 26. Fourth living foal. 75,000Y. Tattersalls October Book 1. Charlie Gordon-Watson. Half-brother to the fairly useful 6f to 8.5f winner of 7 races Supersta (by Pivotal) and to the quite useful 1m winner Symbolic (by Shamardal). The dam, a fairly useful 7f and 1m winner, is a half-sister to 8 winners including the smart 2-y-o Group 2 6f Mill

Reef Stakes and Group 2 Lennox Stakes winner Byron. The second dam, Gay Gallanta (by Woodman), a very smart winner of the Group 1 6f Cheveley Park Stakes and the Group 3 5f Queen Mary Stakes, was second in the Group 2 1m Falmouth Stakes and is a half-sister to 11 winners including the smart Group 2 10f Gallinule Stakes winner Sportsworld.

JAMES TATE

1523. BIDDING WAR ★★★★
ch.f. Champs Elysees – Locharia (Wolfhound). April 6. 110,000Y. Tattersalls October Book 2. Rabbah Bloodstock. Half-sister to 8 winners including the fairly useful 2016 2-y-o 5f winner and Group 3 6f second Seafront (by Foxwedge), the quite useful 6f to 9f and hurdles winner of 7 races Credit Swap (by Diktat), the quite useful 7f and 1m winner of 9 races Lochantanks (by Compton Place), the fair 5f winner Yanza (by Bahamian Bounty), the fair 2-y-o 6f winner Woodland Girl (by Kyllachy) and the fair 7f and 10f winner Lady Loch (by Dutch Art). The dam was a fairly useful 2-y-o 5f winner. The second dam, Lochbelle (by Robellino), a fair 10.2f winner, is a half-sister to the champion sprinter Lochsong and the Nunthorpe Stakes winner Lochangel. (Saeed Manana). *"She's a medium-sized filly and very speedy. I don't think she'll be running until May but she's pretty speedy and pretty smart. I train her half-sister the 3-y-o Seafront who is a more relaxed, laid-back type, but this filly is quicker than her".*

1524. BRIGHT ACCOLADE ★★★
b.f. Acclamation – Bright Glow (Exceed And Excel). January 8. First foal. 45,000Y. Tattersalls October Book 2. Rabbah Bloodstock. The dam, a fair dual 7f winner, is a half-sister to 5 winners including the fairly useful listed-placed All For Laura (herself dam of the Group 2 winner Misheer). The second dam, Lighthouse (by Warning), a fairly useful 8.3f winner, is a half-sister to 4 winners including the Group 1 Middle Park Stakes winner First Trump. (Saeed Manana). *"She got held up with a sore shin but she's speedy and goes well. We'll see her out in May over five furlongs, no problem".*

1525. COLLATERAL ★★★★
b.c. Reckless Abandon – May Day Queen (Danetime). March 1. Fourth foal. 200,000Y. Tattersalls October Book 2. Rabbah Bloodstock. Half-brother to the fairly useful dual 5f (including at 2 yrs) and 6f winner and listed-placed Mukhmal (by Bahamian Bounty), to the quite useful 5f and 6f winner of 4 races at 2 and 3 yrs Kingsley Klarion (by Arcano) and the modest 7f winner Abbotsfield (by Sakhee's Secret). The dam, a quite useful 2-y-o 6f winner and Group 3 6f third in Ireland, is a half-sister to 6 winners including the listed winners Accepted and Asidious Alexander. The second dam, Birthday Present (by Cadeaux Genereux), is an unraced half-sister to 3 winners including the Group 1 Moyglare Stud Stakes third Supposition. (Saeed Manana). *"He's our most expensive 2-y-o, he's very relaxed about life but he's working better and better. I'm not sure if you'll see him out in April or May, but I'm sure he'll be a nice horse. It's a sprinting family but he's not buzzy in any way he's quite happy to just eat and sleep!"* The sire, a son of Exchange Rate, won the Prix Morny and the Middle Park Stakes (both Group 1 6f events at 2 yrs).

1526. COMPLIANCE ★★★
b.c. Exceed And Excel – Saadiah (Dubai Destination). March 26. Third foal. 38,000Y. Tattersalls October Book 2. Not sold. Half-brother to the 2016 2-y-o 7f winner, on his only start, Across Dubai (by Cape Cross) and to the fair 9.5f and 10f winner Pivotal Flame (by Pivotal). The dam is an unraced half-sister to 7 winners including the Group 3 Cumberland Lodge and Group 3 September Stakes winner Laaheb and the useful dual 7f winner and Group 3 second Ruwaiyan. The second dam, Maskunah (by Sadler's Wells), is an unraced half-sister to 6 winners including the multiple Group 1 winners Warrsan and Luso, and the Group winners Cloud Castle and Needle Gun. (Saeed Manana). *"In the middle of the pack at the moment, he goes nicely and may not be the best but he's not the worst either. I'm not quite sure what trip he'll want as his Dad was a sprinter but the dam's family all stay, but I'd say he'll start off over six or seven furlongs. A likeable type without being the top of the pile".*

1527. CULTIVATE ★★★
gr.f. Clodovil – Fork Handles (Doyen). February 13. First foal. 35,000Y. Tattersalls October Book 2. Rabbah Bloodstock. The dam, a fairly useful 6f (at 2 yrs) and 10f winner, was third in the Group 3 7f Prix du Calvados and is a half-sister to 3 winners. The second dam, Natalie Jay (by Ballacashtal), a fair winner of 5 races from 6f to 1m, is a half-sister to 3 winners including the listed Sceptre Stakes winner You Know The Rules. (Saeed Manana). *"I'm not sure what she is. She's a little bit lazy and she likes her food. She's showing a bit but quite laid-back about things. I wouldn't put you off, but she's 3-stars at the moment".*

1528. HADDAF (IRE) ★★★★
b.c. Dawn Approach – Deveron (Cozzene). February 1. Seventh foal. 85,000Y. Tattersalls October Book 1. Armando Duarte. Closely related to the modest 2-y-o 1m winner Open Letter (by New Approach) and half-brother to the very useful listed 1m winner of 6 races, from 2 to 5 yrs Lamar (by Cape Cross), the quite useful 2-y-o 6f and 7f winner Hope Cove and the quite useful 2-y-o 7f winner Dffar (both by Shamardal). The dam, a very useful 2-y-o 7f winner and third in the Group 1 1m Prix Marcel Boussac, is a sister to the Canadian dual Grade 2 winner Windward Islands and a half-sister to 5 winners. The second dam, Cruisie (by Assert), a triple US 3-y-o winner, is a half-sister to 4 stakes winners including the dam of the US Grade 1 winner Capote Belle. (Saif Ali). *"A medium-sized, very strong 2-y-o type. He'll start at five furlongs and then we'll take it from there. He goes very well".*

1529. ICONIC SUNSET ★★★★
ch.c. Farhh – Manila Bay (Halling). March 19. First foal. 20,000Y. Tattersalls October Book 2. Not sold. The dam is an unraced half-sister to 4 winners including the very useful 10f (at 2 yrs) to 14f and subsequent Australian Group 1 12f Caulfield Cup winner All The Good. The second dam, Zarara (by Manila), is an unraced half-sister to 10 winners including the Oaks, Irish Oaks and Yorkshire Oaks winner Ramruma and the Lingfield Oaks Trial winner Ausherra (dam of the Group 2 winner Strategic Prince). (Saeed Manana). *"Not bred*

in the purple but goes very well, he's probably a mid-season type but his work is good".

1530. IMMINENT APPROACH ★★★★
b.f. New Approach – Nashmiah (Elusive City). January 21. Third foal. 35,000Y. Tattersalls October Book 1. Bobby O'Ryan. Half-sister to the French listed 6.5f winner Fond Words (by Shamardal) and to the fair 7f winner A Legacy Of Love (by Sea The Stars). The dam, a winner of four listed events at 3 yrs from 7f to 10f and third in the Group 3 Oh So Sharp Stakes, is a half-sister to 6 winners including the useful listed winners Ighraa and Streets Ahead. The second dam, Frond (by Alzao), a quite useful 2-y-o 7f winner, is a half-sister to 8 winners. (Saeed Manana). *"A small, slender type that goes really nicely, she'll probably start over six furlongs rather than five. Not as pretty as her two siblings but smaller and she shows plenty".*

1531. LAST REQUEST ★★★★
b.f. Foxwedge – Royal Pardon (Royal Applause). April 28. Sixth foal. £27,000Y. Goffs UK Silver Sale (Doncaster). James Tate. Half-sister to the fairly useful 2-y-o triple 5f winner and Group 3 third March (by Dutch Art), to the moderate 5f and 6f winner of 9 races from 2 to 5 yrs Lord Buffhead (by Iceman) and the modest 2-y-o 6f winner Secret Applause (by Sakhee's Secret). The dam, a moderate maiden, was placed from 6f to 1m and is a half-sister to 7 winners including Dubai Dynamo and Sadeek (both listed winners). The second dam, Miss Mercy (by Law Society), a modest 2-y-o 6f winner, is a half-sister to 3 minor winners. (Saeed Manana). *"A 2-y-o type, strong, attractive, medium-sized and fast. I hope we'll see her out in April but if not May and she's quite high up in the pecking order. She's got the same head as my nice Foxwedge 2-y-o filly from last year Seafront – and I've put her in the same box!"*
TRAINERS' BARGAIN BUY

1532. LEESHAAN (IRE) ★★★★
b.c. Bated Breath – La Grande Elisa (Ad Valorem). January 26. First foal. £60,000Y. Goffs UK Premier (Doncaster). Rabbah Bloodstock. The dam is an unplaced half-sister to 5 winners including the Sussex Stakes, Queen Elizabeth II Stakes and

Juddmonte International winner Rip Van Winkle. The second dam, Looking Back (by Stravinsky), an Italian winner of 2 races at 2 and 3 yrs and listed-placed, is a half-sister to 2 winners. (Saeed Manana). *"He goes nicely. He's a big, strong colt and I would have thought a six furlong 2-y-o to start with. A 4-star 2-y-o I would say, using your ratings".*

1533. LITIGATION ★★★★
b.f. Foxwedge – Torcross (Vettori). April 27. Eighth foal. 13,000Y. Tattersalls October Book 4. Rabbah Bloodstock. Half-sister to the fair 10f, 12f and hurdles winner Bagber (by Diktat) and to the modest 2-y-o dual 8.5f winner Rural Affair (by Pastoral Pursuits). The dam, a useful 2-y-o 7f winner, is a half-sister to the very useful 6f (at 2 yrs), Group 3 7.5f Concorde Stakes and dual listed winner Sheppard's Watch. The second dam, Sheppard's Cross (by Soviet Star), a quite useful 7f winner of 3 races, is a half-sister to 5 winners including the Irish listed sprint winner Clean Cut. (Saeed Manana). *"She goes very nicely and I'd give her four stars. A good-sized, rangy filly, she has the same head as my Foxwedge 3-y-o Urban Fox who was a triple winner last year and third in the Fillies' Mile, so she's gone in the same box she had!"*
TRAINERS' BARGAIN BUY

1534. MORE SALUTES ★★★
b.c. Acclamation – Champion Place (Compton Place). March 10. Fourth foal. €60,000Y. Goffs Orby. Not sold. Half-brother to the quite useful 5f winner of 5 races from 2 to 5 yrs Desert Ace (by Kheleyf). The dam, a winner of 12 races in Italy including the Group 3 Premio Omenoni, is a half-sister to 4 winners. The second dam, Villa Via (by Night Shift), a fair 5f winner, is a half-sister to 7 winners. (Saeed Manana). *"He was going well but then had a setback so he won't be running until June. A big, strong horse and a speedy type".*

1535. MRASEEL ★★★★
b.f. Sir Prancealot – Suffer Her (Whipper). March 27. Fifth foal. £62,000Y. Goffs UK Premier (Doncaster). Blandford Bloodstock. Half-sister to the quite useful 2016 2-y-o dual 5f winner Tahoo (by Zebedee), to the quite useful 2-y-o 5f winner Sarista (by Kodiac) and the fair dual 5f winner Vodka Chaser (by Baltic

King). The dam is an unraced half-sister to 4 winners including the useful 2-y-o dual 6f winner and listed-placed Campbeltown. The second dam, Jallaissine (by College Chapel), placed twice at 2 yrs in France, is a half-sister to the smart 12f listed winner Riyafa. (Sheikh Hamad Dalmook Al Maktoum). *"Likely to be our first 2-y-o runner, she's smallish, strong and very much a 2-y-o type. A filly that goes nicely, she's not right at the top of my list, but quite high. The dam has already bred three 2-y-o winners and this will be another".*

1536. NEW GENERATION ★★★
b.c. Exceed And Excel – El Manati (Iffraaj). January 28. First foal. 70,000Y. Tattersalls October Book 1. Grove Stud. The dam, a useful 2-y-o 6f winner, was third in the Group 3 5f Cornwallis Stakes and is a half-sister to 5 minor winners. The second dam, Limit (by Barathea), a modest 2-y-o 7f winner, is a half-sister to 5 winners. (Sheikh Rashid Dalmook Al Maktoum). *"I trained the dam and she was very fast. She was buzzy and fiery, but this colt is lazy and still thinks he's on holiday! So at the moment I'd just describe his work as middle of the road".*

1537. ROYAL PARKS ★★★
b.f. Bated Breath – Kensington Gardens (Oasis Dream). February 20. First foal. 50,000Y. Tattersalls October Book 2. Rabbah Bloodstock. The dam, a moderate 9f placed maiden, is a sister to the very smart Group 2 10f Prix Guillaume d'Ornano, Group 2 York Stakes and dual Group 3 winner Sri Putra and a half-sister to 3 winners. The second dam, Wendylina (by In The Wings), is an unraced half-sister to 9 winners including the Group 1 10.5f Prix de Diane winner Caerlina. (Saeed Manana). *"She goes nicely, she's an attractive filly and I think we'll wait for the six furlong races with her. She's in the top half of my 2-y-o's at the moment".*

1538. SHOWDANCING ★★★
b.f. Showcasing – Lady Vermeer (Dutch Art). February 13. First foal. 42,000Y. Tattersalls October Book 2. Rabbah Bloodstock. The dam is an unplaced half-sister to 2 minor winners. The second dam, Classic Vision (by Classic Cliché), a modest 6f and 1m winner, is a half-sister to 5 winners including the dual Group 3 winner Orientor, the Royal Hunt Cup

winner Yeast and the dam of the Irish Group 3 winner Montecastillo. (Saeed Manana). *"She'll be one of our earliest 2-y-o runners and I think she'll win a race, but she's not that good".*

1539. TAKE SHELTER ★★★
b.f. Harbour Watch – Secret Night (Dansili). February 11. Fifth foal. 21,000Y. Tattersalls October Book 3. Rabbah Bloodstock. Half-sister to the modest 7f winner On The Tiles (by Royal Applause). The dam, a fairly useful 5f and 6f winner, was listed-placed and is a half-sister to 8 winners including the useful 2-y-o 7f and listed 10f winner and US dual Grade 2 placed Rosa Grace. The second dam, Night Haven (by Night Shift), a fairly useful 5f (at 2 yrs) and 6f winner and 6f listed-placed, is a sister to 3 winners including the French 2-y-o listed 5f winner Shoalhaven. (Saeed Manana). *"She's a medium-sized 2-y-o type that goes well and she'll be racing in April or May. She should set off at five furlongs and go on from there".*

1540. UNDER OFFER ★★★★
ch.f. Bated Breath – Bailonguera (Southern Halo). March 17. Eighth living foal. 52,000Y Tattersalls October Book 2. Rabbah Bloodstock. Half-sister to 7 winners including the French listed 9.5f winner Bayargal (by Bernstein) and the French listed-placed winners Bulliciosa (by Successful Appeal) and Bargouzine (by Stravinsky and herself dam of the French Grade 3 winner Baghadur). The second dam, Balromana (by Logical), won once in Argentina and is a half-sister to 4 winners. (Saeed Manana). *"A speedy filly that looks almost ready to run, she goes nicely. A medium-sized, nice bodied filly and I'd give her four stars".*

1541. WIDE ACCLAIM ★★★★
b.f. Acclamation – Riynaaz (Cape Cross). February 3. Third foal. 78,000Y. Tattersalls October Book 2. Rabbah Bloodstock. The dam, a quite useful 9f winner, is a half-sister to 4 winners including Riyalma (listed 10f Pretty Polly Stakes). The second dam, Riyafa (by Kahyasi), was a listed 12f winner at Ascot. (Saeed Manana). *"She had a little setback recently but she goes well. She definitely wants to go in the book, there are mixed messages from the pedigree but we like her. She could be out in May or June".*

1542. YAMUNA RIVER ★★★
b.f. Foxwedge – Harryana Too (Compton Place). March 8. Third foal. 22,000Y. Tattersalls October Book 3. Rabbah Bloodstock. The dam, a moderate 7f placed maiden, is a half-sister to 7 winners including the 2-y-o Group 2 Mill Reef Stakes winner Temple Meads. The second dam, Harryana (by Efisio), was a fair 2-y-o dual 5f winner. (Saeed Manana). *"She goes nicely and will definitely be a decent second half of the season 2-y-o. She'll set off at six or seven furlongs".*

1543. ZIARAH ★★★★
b.f. Iffraaj – Ashtown Girl (Exceed And Excel). April 23. Third foal. €140,000Y. Goffs Orby. Rabbah Bloodstock. The dam is an unraced half-sister to 3 winners including the Group 2 Temple Stakes and Group 3 Cornwallis Stakes winner Hot Streak. The second dam, Ashirah (by Housebuster), is an unraced half-sister to the US dual Grade 3 winner Mustanfar. (Sheikh Juma Dalmook Al Maktoum). *"She goes very well! She's big, rangy and a little bit lean like most of the Iffraaj's I've had and she'd be my pick of the 2-y-o's at the moment. She'll make her debut at Newmarket's Craven meeting".*

1544. UNNAMED ★★★★★
b.c. New Approach – Arsaadi (Dubawi). March 5. First foal. 100,000Y. Tattersalls October Book 1. Not sold. The dam, a useful 2-y-o 7f winner here, was second in the Group 3 1m Istanbul Trophy at 4 yrs and in two listed events at Ascot and Sandown and is a half-sister to one minor winner abroad. The second dam, Arsad (by Cape Cross), a modest 11f and 14f winner, is a half-sister to 4 winners including the useful Irish 2-y-o listed 5f winner Flash McGahon. (Sultan Ali). *"A big, rangy colt that goes very well, he'll start off at six furlongs at a good track".*

1545. UNNAMED ★★★
b.f. Mayson – Neyraan (Lujain). April 21. Fifth foal. £28,000Y. Goffs UK Silver Sale (Doncaster). James Tate. Half-sister to the fairly useful 6f (at 2 yrs) and 7f winner Shepherd's Purse (by Pastoral Pursuits) and to the fair 6f and 7f winner Tahchee (by Sleeping Indian). The dam, a minor dual winner at 4 yrs

in Germany, is a half-sister to 4 winners. The second dam, Zaynaat (by Unfuwain), a fair 1m fourth placed maiden, is a sister to the Group 1 Nassau Stakes winner Zahrat Dubai and a half-sister to 4 winners. (Saeed Manana). *"She's showing us a bit, but she's been growing all spring. Goes nicely enough, she's bred to be a sprinter but not necessarily an early one. She'll be out in the summer".*

1546. UNNAMED ★★★★
b.c. Kodiac – Operissimo (Singspiel). May 4. Seventh foal. 57,000Y. Tattersalls October Book 2. Rabbah Bloodstock. Half-brother to the fairly useful 2-y-o 6f winner and Group 3 1m Prix Thomas Bryon second Silver Grey (by Chineur), the fairly useful 1m listed-placed maiden Kodiva (by Kodiac), the quite useful dual 10.5f winner The Character (by Bushranger) and the moderate 7f and 1m winner Free To Roam (by Bushranger). The dam is an unraced sister to the 2-y-o Group 3 1m Prix Thomas Bryon winner Songlark and a half-sister to 5 winners including the dam of the multiple Group 1 winner Sky Lantern. The second dam, Negligent (by Ahonoora), won the 2-y-o 7f Rockfel Stakes, was third in the 1,000 Guineas and is a half-sister to 5 winners. (Sheikh Juma Dalmook Al Maktoum). *"A nice 2-y-o type, but he's a May foal and still has open knees at the moment. I think we'll see him in mid-summer and he's shown us enough to think he'll be decent".*

1547. UNNAMED ★★★★
b.c. Invincible Spirit – Rajeem (Diktat). January 28. Seventh foal. 95,000Y. Tattersalls October Book 1. Dermot Farrington. Half-brother to the dual bumpers winner Master Rajeem (by Street Cry). The dam, a very smart listed 1m (at 2 yrs) and Group 1 1m Falmouth Stakes winner, is a half-sister to one winner. The second dam, Magic Slipper (by Cadeaux Genereux), a modest 3-y-o 7f placed maiden, is a sister to the very smart 2-y-o Group 1 6f Prix Morny and Group 3 5f Molecomb Stakes winner Hoh Magic and a half-sister to 5 winners. (Saeed Manana). *"A big, strong colt who goes very well, he'll start off at six furlongs but will improve with time and distance".* This colt went to the Craven breeze-up but was unsold at £290,000.

1548. UNNAMED ★★★★
ch.f. Dream Ahead – Sweet Nicole
(Okawango). January 29. Fifth foal. 17,000Y.
Tattersalls October Book 2. Rabbah
Bloodstock. Half-sister to the smart Group
2 6f Greenlands Stakes winner of four races
from 2 to 4 yrs Mobsta (by Bushranger), to
the quite useful 6f and 7f winner of 5 races
Cincuenta Pasos (by Footstepsinthesand)
and the Italian 4-y-o winner Mas Fuerte (by
Kyllachy). The dam, unplaced in one start at
2 yrs, is a half-sister to 3 winners including
the Group 2 Betfair Cup and Group 3 Jersey
Stakes winner Tariq. The second dam, Tatora
(by Selkirk), is an unraced half-sister to 3
winners and to the placed dam of the Group
2 Flying Childers Stakes winner Wi Dud.
(Sheikh Hamad Dalmook Al Maktoum). *"This
is a rangy filly and she goes really well. I'm just
holding her back because she's very tall, but
she's bred to sprint and I think she'll be nice.
She'll start off in May or June".*

MARK TOMPKINS

1549. ASTROBLAZE ★★★
ch.f. Havana Gold – Astrodonna (Carnival
Dancer). February 22. Third foal. The dam, a
fair 9f (at 2 yrs) and 1m winner of 4 races, is
a half-sister to 3 winners. The second dam,
Mega (by Petardia), is an unplaced half-sister
to 7 winners including the listed winners
Bolino Star and Don Fayruz. (Mystic Meg Ltd).
*"She's the sharpest of all the fillies, a strong,
forward-going type and I think Havana Gold
will make a useful stallion. She's not very big,
but compact and should be racing in April.
She goes well, so for a change I might have an
early one!"*

1550. HONEY BLOSSOM ★★
b.f. Makfi – Seasonal Blossom (Fairy King).
April 12. Half-sister to 5 winners including
the very useful 6f to 12f winner of 4 races
(including the listed Galtres Stakes) Brushing
(by Medicean), the fair 10f to 14f winner of
6 races Wee Charlie Castle (by Sinndar) and
the fair 1m winner of 4 races Seasonal Cross
(by Cape Cross). The dam is an unplaced
half-sister to 7 winners including the US
Grade 2 winner Wait Till Monday and the
Irish Group 3 winner Token Gesture (dam
of the Grade 1 winner Relaxed Gesture).
The second dam, Temporary Lull (by Super

Concorde), is an unraced sister to the Group 3
Nell Gwyn Stakes winner Martha Stevens. (Mr
John Brenchley). *"She's built like a tank and
puts her head down and tries hard. So I don't
think she'll be long in running. Not very big,
but strong and compact. Makfi's been a bit
in-and-out but he can get an early 2-y-o and
he's doing well down under".*

1551. NESS OF BRODGAR ★★
b.f. Harbour Watch – Missouri (Charnwood
Forest). March 23. Half-sister to 7 winners
including the quite useful 5f to 1m winner of
7 races Captain Cullen (by Strategic Prince),
the fair 1m (at 2 yrs) and 12f winner Battery
Power (by Royal Applause), the fair dual 14f
winner Lost The Moon (by Authorized) and
the modest 9f (at 2 yrs) to 12f and hurdles
winner Dee Cee Elle (by Groom Dancer). The
dam, a quite useful 15f winner, is a half-sister
to several winners. The second dam, Medway
(by Shernazar), a modest 12f winner at 3
yrs, is a half-sister to 8 winners including
the high-class Hong Kong horse Indigenous
and the Cesarewitch winner Old Red. (David
Tompkins). *"A very big filly and the foals out of
this mare win. They need time, but some do
win at two, so this will be a back-end 2-y-o
and I love her".*

1552. ROOF GARDEN ★★
ch.c. Cityscape – Celebrity (Pivotal).
May 12. Third foal. 11,000Y. Tattersalls
October Book 4. Sarabex. The dam, a quite
useful 2-y-o 6f winner, is a half-sister to one
winner. The second dam, Dance Solo (by
Sadler's Wells), placed four times from 7f to
11f here and in Germany, is a full or half-sister
to 6 winners including the Group 1 St James's
Palace Stakes winner Excellent Art. (Sarabex).
*"A strong colt, but he was a late foal, he's
scopey and has something about him. One to
start off in mid-to-late summer, I like him and
he's a nice horse".*

1553. SAINT ANTHONY ★★★
ch.c. Pastoral Pursuits – Mega (Petardia).
April 29. Half-brother to the fair 2-y-o 7f
winner, on her only start, Mystic Winds (by
Shirocco), to the fair 7f (at 2 yrs) to 10f winner
of 5 races Marvo (by Bahamian Bounty),
the fair 9f (at 2 yrs) and 1m winner of 4
races Astrodonna (by Carnival Dancer) and

the fair 1m and 9f winner Mercoliano (by Medicean). The dam is an unplaced half-sister to 7 winners including the listed winners Bolino Star and Don Fayruz. The second dam, Gobolino (by Don), won over 7f in Ireland at 2 yrs and is a half-sister to 4 winners. (Raceworld). *"He was a nightmare to break, possibly the worst I've had, but now we've got him going he's a great mover, very strong, compact, looks like a runner and he should be alright. The dam has bred a few 2-y-o winners and he's a horse with scope".*

1554. TOPAPINION ★★★
b.c. So You Think – Topatoo (Bahamian Bounty). April 28. Half-brother to the fair 12f winner Toptempo (by Halling). The dam, a Group 3 10.3f Middleton Stakes winner, was second in the Group 3 9f Dahlia Stakes and is a half-sister to 5 winners. The second dam, Topatori (by Topanoora), was a quite useful 7f to 11f winner of 4 races. (Mr M Bowring, Dullingham Stud). *"A lovely horse, I love him and you won't see a better mover. Hopefully he'll help put the sire on the map, he's got plenty of scope so he's a 3-y-o type, but I'd like to give him a run this year because we need to do something with him".*

1555. TRUE CALLING ★★
ch.f. Pastoral Pursuits – Trew Class (Inchinor). February 7. Half-sister to the fair 11f and 12f winner of 3 races Kathleen Frances (by Sakhee), to the modest 11f winner Jennifer J (by Motivator) and a bumpers winner Dubai Destination. The dam, a fairly useful 10f winner of 4 races, was listed-placed and is a half-sister to 2 winners. The second dam, Inimitable (by Saveur), a modest 10f winner, is a half-sister to 3 winners. (Raceworld). *"A nice, compact filly that'll grow a bit, she's got plenty of scope and she'll be like the rest of the family. They all need a bit of time and a distance. He sire should put a bit of speed on the mare so I'm hoping she'll be alright. A very attractive filly".*

1556. TTMAB ★★
b.c. Mawatheeq – Astrodiva (Where Or When). March 4. Third foal. The dam, a fair maiden, was placed ten times from 1m to 2m and is a half-sister to one winner. The second dam, Astromancer (by Silver Hawk), a

moderate 4-y-o 14f winner, is a half-sister to one winner. (Dame Judi Dench & Brian Agar). *"A great, big, strong horse by a sire that's now in France but he gets winners. He's a lovely, attractive horse and we like him a lot. More of a 3-y-o type, but he should run in the autumn. The name stands for "To The Moon And Back" and the owner Judi Dench tells me it's what she says to her family when they're leaving!"*

MARCUS TREGONING

1557. BOSTON T PARTY
b.c. Declaration Of War – Sri Kandi (Pivotal). January 7. Fourth foal. 44,000Y. Tattersalls October Book 2. M Tregoning. Half-brother to a winner in Sweden by High Chaparral. The dam, a fair 2-y-o 7.5f winner, is a half-sister to 5 winners including the Group 1 1m Gran Criterium winner Pearl Of Love and the dual US Grade 3 winner Social Charter. The second dam, Aunt Pearl (by Seattle Slew), a winner at up to 7f in the USA, is a half-sister to 7 winners. (Mr R C Villers & Mr J P Cavanagh).

1558. DIVA STAR
ch.f. Siyouni – Kissin Sign (Turtle Bowl). March 12. Second foal. €185,000Y. Arqana Deauville August. M Tregoning. The dam is an unraced half-sister to 5 winners including Irish Wells (Group 2 Grand Prix de Deauville) and Sign Of The Wolf (Group 3 Andre Baboin). The second dam, Sign Of The Vine (by Kendor), is an unplaced half-sister to 3 winners. (FTP Equine Holdings Ltd).

1559. EXCEEDINGLY DIVA
b.f. Exceed And Excel – Anqooda (Oasis Dream). February 17. Second foal. €46,000Y. Tattersalls Ireland September. M Tregoning. The dam, placed fourth over 10f from two starts, is a half-sister to 3 minor winners. The second dam, Atayeb (by Rahy), a fair 12f winner, is a sister to the listed 9f winner Rumoush and a half-sister to the 1,000 Guineas and Coronation Stakes winner Ghanaati and the Group 3 12f Cumberland Lodge Stakes winner and Group 1 Champion Stakes second Mawatheeq. (FTP Equine Holdings Ltd).

1560. MARGUB
ch.c. Bated Breath – Bahamian Babe (Bahamian Bounty). April 24. Fifth foal.

£30,000Y. Goffs UK Premier (Doncaster). Shadwell Estate Co. Half-brother to the modest 2-y-o 7f winner Bahamian Boy (by Paco Boy). The dam, a 2-y-o listed 5f winner of 4 races, is a sister to 5 winners. The second dam, Baby Bunting (by Wolfhound), a modest sprint-placed maiden, is a half-sister to 7 winners including the Group 3 Cork And Orrery Stakes and US Grade 3 Jaipur Stakes winner Atraf and the Group 2 Richmond Stakes winner Son Pardo. (Hamdan bin Rashid Al Maktoum).

1561. MARQUISETTE
b.f. Archipenko – Maria Di Scozia (Selkirk). February 20. Second foal. Sister to the quite useful dual 7f winner Mariee and to the bumpers winner Bentworth Boy and half-sister to the fair 1m and 12f winner Martiniquaise (by Mawatheeq). The dam, a fair 10f and 12f winner, is a half-sister to a winner in Italy. The second dam, Viva Maria (by Hernando), is an unraced half-sister to 9 winners including Polish Patriot (Group 1 July Cup) and the dam of the German Group 1 winner Lady Jane Digby. (Miss K Rausing).

1562. POWER OF DARKNESS
b.c. Power – Summer's Lease (Pivotal). March 29. Fourth foal. 52,000Y. Tattersalls October Book 2. M Tregoning. Half-brother to the modest 1m winner Nancy Astor (by Shamardal) and to the modest 5f winner of 4 races Summer Isles (by Exceed And Excel). The dam, a quite useful 1m winner, is a sister to the smart Group 3 5f Palace House Stakes and US Grade 3 9f winner Needwood Blade and a half-sister to 6 winners including the US Grade 3 winner Islay Mist. The second dam, Finlaggan (by Be My Chief), a quite useful 11f to 2m winner, is a half-sister to 7 winners. (Mr R C Villers).

1563. WATHEER ♠
ch.c. Leroidesanimaux – Sunset Shore (Oasis Dream). January 30. First foal. 15,000 foal. Tattersalls December. Shadwell Estate Co. The dam, a fair 2-y-o 5.5f winner, is a half-sister to 7 winners including the 2-y-o Group 3 1m Prix des Reservoirs winner and Group 2 Park Hill Stakes third Songerie and the useful listed winners Soft Morning, Souvenance and Sourire. The second dam, Summer Night

(by Nashwan), a fairly useful 3-y-o 6f winner, is a half-sister to 7 winners including the Group 3 Prix d'Arenburg winner Starlit Sands. (Hamdan bin Rashid Al Maktoum).

1564. UNNAMED
b.f. Kyllachy – Canukeepasecret (Mind Games). April 5. Third foal. £66,000Y. Goffs UK Premier (Doncaster). Shadwell Estate Co. The dam is an unraced half-sister to 4 winners including the Group 2 Temple Stakes winner and Group 1 King's Stand Stakes third Pearl Secret. The second dam, Our Little Secret (by Rossini), a useful listed 5f winner of 6 races, is a half-sister to 3 winners. (Hamdan bin Rashid Al Maktoum).

1565. UNNAMED
ch.c. Raven's Pass – Loose Julie (Cape Cross). March 31. Fourth foal. 60,000Y. Tattersalls October Book 2. Shadwell Estate Co. Half-brother to the useful 5f (at 2 yrs) and 6f winner of 4 races Banaadeer (by Tamayuz), to the fairly useful 7f (at 2 yrs) and 1m winner Storm Ahead (by Iffraaj) and the modest 7f winner Crystalin (by Arcano). The dam is an unraced half-sister to 4 winners including the 2-y-o listed 6f Silver Flash Stakes winner Desert Sky. The second dam, Badrah (by Private Account), is a placed half-sister to 5 winners including the Group 3 Brigadier Gerard Stakes winner Husyan. (Hamdan bin Rashid Al Maktoum).

1566. UNNAMED
b.c. Dawn Approach – Winds Of Time (Danehill). February 9. Sixth foal. 175,000Y. Tattersalls October Book 2. Shadwell Estate Co. Half-sister to the very useful 2-y-o 6f winner and Group 2 Richmond Stakes second The Paddyman (by Giant's Causeway) and to the quite useful 10f winner Julia Dream (by Montjeu). The dam, a fairly useful 2-y-o 6f winner, subsequently won in the USA and Canada and is a half-sister to 4 winners. The second dam, Windmill (by Ezzoud), a fair 13.8f winner, is a half-sister to 8 winners including the Group 2 12f Ribblesdale Stakes winner Gull Nook (herself dam of the top-class colt Pentire) and the Group 3 winners Banket and Mr Pintips. (Hamdan bin Rashid Al Maktoum).

JOE TUITE

1567. FELSTEAD KNIGHT (IRE) ★★
b.c. Tough As Nails – Fine Day (Fantastic Light). March 27. Seventh foal. €11,000Y. Tattersalls Ireland September. Tuite Racing. Half-brother to 2 winners in North America by E Dubai and Orientate. The dam ran once unplaced and is a half-sister to 5 minor winners. The second dam, Queen's Gallery (by Forty Niner), a French 2-y-o winner and second in the Group 3 7f Prix du Calvados, is a half-sister to 7 winners including the US triple Grade 1 winner Marquetry and the Group 2 Prix du Gros-Chene winner Spain Lane. (Felstead Court Flyers II). *"A lovely horse but he's grown a lot and just isn't coming to hand yet. He'll be a mid-season 2-y-o, looks like he's got a bit of boot and he's a nice type but still backward at present".*

1568. GUINNESS MING ★★★
b.c. Canford Cliffs – Aldora (Magic Ring). April 26. Fifth foal. €36,000Y. Tattersalls Ireland September. Peter & Ross Doyle. Half-brother to the fairly useful 5f and 6f winner of 9 races from 2 to 7 yrs and Group 3 5f third Free Zone (by Kyllachy), to the fairly useful 7f winner Ocean Bay (by Dubai Destination) and the quite useful 1m to 10f winner of 7 races Ocean Applause (by Royal Applause). The dam, a winner of four listed events at around 1m, is a half-sister to 6 winners including the smart 10f performer Polar Red. The second dam, Sharp Top (by Sharpo), won 4 races over 12f, 2m and over hurdles and is a half-sister to 4 winners. (Mr M Geoghegan). *"A lovely colt, he goes about his work in a nice fashion but he's one for the second half of the season. The sire seems to get them that way".*

1569. MANCO INCA ★★★★
b.c. Sir Prancealot – Night Delight (Night Shift). April 10. Sixth foal. £6,000Y. Goffs UK Silver (Doncaster). Tuite Racing. Half-brother to the fair 5f winner of 5 races Landing Night (by Kodiac) and to the modest triple 7f winner Jumbo Steps (by Footstepsinthesand). The dam, a fair 5f and 6f winner at 5 yrs in Ireland, is a half-sister to 9 winners including the stakes winners Air Of Distinction, Kayfa and Rabican. The second dam, Kaysama (by Kenmare), won 2 races at 2 and 3 yrs in France and is a half-sister to 3 stakes winners.

(Mr David Klein). *"He goes well, shows plenty of speed and will be racing in April. We'd expect him to be able to hold his own in the early part of the season. Not the biggest horse, but he works in a nice fashion and he'll be winning".*

1570. MOTHER OF DRAGONS ★★★
ch.f. Society Rock – Queen O'The Desert (Green Desert). April 26. Third foal. €2,000Y. Tattersalls Ireland September. Tuite Racing. The dam, a winner, is out of the placed Al Dhahab (by Seeking The Gold), herself a half-sister to 3 minor winners. (Qatar Racing Ltd). *"She's a very likeable filly and she'll be running in April. Improving all the time, I'm very happy with her and there's a good word for the sire because they look precocious and racy. This is a well-made filly and I've no doubt she was a bargain".* TRAINERS' BARGAIN BUY

1571. RIVENDICATO ★★★★ ♠
b.f. Showcasing – Carsulae (Marju). March 6. Third foal. 120,000Y. Tattersalls October Book 1. Kern/ Lillingston. Sister to the fair 7f winner Strada Di Carsoli and half-sister to Itsakindamagic (by Mount Nelson), placed third over 8.5f on his only start at 2 yrs in 2016. The dam is an unraced half-sister to 8 winners including the listed Cecil Frail Stakes winner Blhadawa. The second dam, Trois Heures Apres (by Soviet Star), is an unraced half-sister to 4 winners including the listed 10f winner and Oaks third Mezzogiorno (herself dam of the Group 2 Blandford Stakes winner Monturani). (Mrs Olivia Hoare & Mrs Paola Hewins). *"The most expensive 2-y-o I have. She's very nice, looks to have a bit of class about her and she's coming to hand reasonably early. She may even start off at the Craven meeting and she shows she's got plenty of ability. Has the speed for five furlongs, but will get six, she's very good-bodied and straightforward".*

1572. UNNAMED ★★★
ch.f. Dutch Art – Crossmolina (Halling). March 12. Seventh foal. 20,000Y. Tattersalls October Book 3. Bathwick. Half-sister to the very smart 6f (at 2 yrs) and listed 1m winner and Group 2 July Stakes second Neebras (by Oasis Dream), to the fair 2-y-o 5f winner Early Bird (by Exceed And Excel) and the fair Irish 7f

winner Jolyne (by Makfi). The dam, a minor winner at 3 yrs in France, is a sister to the dual listed 10f winner Foodbroker Fancy (the dam of three stakes winners) and a half-sister to 3 winners including the listed winner Femme Fatale. The second dam, Red Rita (by Kefaah), a fairly useful 4-y-o 6f winner and second in the Cherry Hinton Stakes and the Princess Margaret Stakes, is a half-sister to 3 minor winners. *"I think she's a nice filly. She was late in but she's a very good-moving, athletic filly and what I've seen so far I like".*

1573. UNNAMED ★★

b.f. Lilbourne Lad – Fritta Mista (Linamix). January 24. Tenth foal. €4,000Y. Tattersalls Ireland September. Not sold. Closely related to the Irish 2-y-o 7f and subsequent Hong Kong Group 3 7f winner Montecchio and to the quite useful dual 1m winner Jimenez (both by Acclamation) and half-sister to the fairly useful 2-y-o 6f and 7f winner and Group 2 May Hill Stakes third Sans Reward (by Barathea) and the fair 5f (at 2 yrs) to 7f winner of 4 races Ursula (by Namid). The dam is a placed half-sister to one minor winner. The second dam, Sea Quest (by Rainbow Quest), is an unplaced half-sister to 9 winners including the Group 1 Yorkshire Oaks winner Hellenic (herself the dam of the Group 1 winners Islington, Greek Dance and Mountain High). *"A nice, scopey sort of filly. I'd hope to be racing her by the end of May. She goes about her work in a nice fashion, has a good attitude and I'd say she'd be a six furlong 2-y-o to start with".*

ROGER VARIAN

1574. ACE VENTURA ★★★

b.c. Mayson – Ventura Highway (Machiavellian). April 13. Tenth foal. 88,000Y. Tattersalls October Book 1. Roger Varian. Half-brother to the smart listed 9f (at 2 yrs) and Group 3 Derby Trial winner Alessandro Volta (by Montjeu), to the fair 2-y-o 6f winner Dylanesque (by Royal Applause) and the moderate 2m winner Venture Capitalist (by Diktat). The dam is an unraced half-sister to 7 winners including the dual Group 3 winner Poet and the dam of the Group 3 winner and Irish 2,000 Guineas second France. The second dam, Hyabella (by Shirley Heights), won three races over 1m at 3 yrs including

the listed Atalanta Stakes and the listed Ben Marshall Stakes and is a half-sister to 6 winners including the high-class Prince of Wales's Stakes winner Stagecraft. (Sheikh Mohammed Obaid Al Maktoum). *"A big, good-looking horse with a good action, I don't think he'll be early but I can see him being a summer 2-y-o over seven furlongs".*

1575. ACT OF BRAVERY ★★★★

b.c. Invincible Spirit – Mama Quilla (Smart Strike). February 7. First foal. The dam, a fair 11.5f winner at 3 and 4 yrs, is a half-sister to 12 winners including the champion 3-y-o filly and multiple Group 1 winner Divine Proportions and the triple Group 1 winner and sire Whipper. The second dam, Myth To Reality (by Sadler's Wells), a triple listed winner of 4 races at 3 yrs in France, was second in the Group 3 Prix de Minerve and is a full or half-sister to 6 winners. (Mr & Mrs G Middlebrook). *"He's a nice type, he moves well, was very immature but he's starting to get a more mature look to him now and he has a good action. He looks sharp enough to be a six or seven furlong 2-y-o and he's a natural athlete".*

1576. AMBIENT ★★★

b.c. Born To Sea – Undulant Way (Hurricane Run). April 2. Third foal. 47,000Y. Tattersalls October Book 2. Armando Duarte. Half-brother to the quite useful 2-y-o 1m winner Newsman (by Makfi). The dam, a fair 11.5f winner, is a half-sister to 3 winners. The second dam, Arietta's Way (by Darshaan), is an unplaced full or half-sister to 10 winners including the Italian Group 1 winners Court Of Honour and Single Empire. (J Collins, C Fahy & S Piper). *"A bit cheeky, but he'll be alright and he's a good-bodied horse with a good action".*

1577. ANGEL'S GLORY ★★★

b.f. Invincible Spirit – Dutch Diamond (Dutch Art). March 1. Second foal. 300,000Y. Tattersalls October Book 1. Roger Varian. Half-sister to the 2016 6f placed 2-y-o, from two starts, Edged In Blue (by Acclamation). The dam, a fair 9f winner, is a half-sister to 7 winners including the Group 1 7f Prix de la Foret and German Group 3 6.5f winner of 16 races Toylsome. The second dam, Treasure

Trove (by The Minstrel), a modest 5f to 7f placed 2-y-o, is a half-sister to 4 winners including the Queen Mary Stakes, Fred Darling Stakes and subsequent US Grade 2 winner Dance Parade (dam of the St Leger and Ascot Gold Cup winner Leading Light). (Sheikh Mohammed Obaid Al Maktoum). *"She's strong, medium-sized, well-made and should make up into a summer 2-y-o. She moves nicely and I quite like her".*

1578. CANVASSED ★★★
b.c. Shamardal – Painter's Pride (Dansili). February 27. First foal. 350,000Y. Tattersalls October Book 1. Roger Varian. The dam is an unraced half-sister to 7 winners including the Prix de l'Arc de Triomphe, French Derby and Grand Prix de Paris winner Peintre Celebre and the French Group winners Peinture Rare and Pointilliste. The second dam, Peinture Bleue (by Alydar), a French listed and US Grade 2 12f winner, is a half-sister to the Group/Grade 3 winners Parme and Provins. (Sheikh Mohammed Obaid Al Maktoum). *"He had a setback in the winter but he's a very good-looking horse with a good action. I think he'll take a bit of time to mature, it's a great pedigree and I'm delighted we bought him, but I couldn't tell you when he'll reach the racecourse. He has a bit of a roman nose, he's very attractive and I like him".*

1579. CAVALRY ★★★
b.c. Exceed And Excel – Queen's Best (King's Best). April 12. Fifth foal. Closely related to the 7f (at 2 yrs) and Grade 1 10f Breeders' Cup Filly and Mare Turf winner Queen's Trust and to the fairly useful dual 7f winner Royal Seal (both by Dansili). The dam, a smart winner of the Group 3 10f Winter Hill Stakes and the listed 12f Chalice Stakes, was second in the Group 2 Blandford Stakes and is a half-sister to 4 winners including the Group 3 Prix de Royaumont third Reverie Solitaire. The second dam, Cloud Castle (by In The Wings), winner of the Group 3 Nell Gwyn Stakes and placed in the Group 1 Yorkshire Oaks and Group 1 Prix Vermeille, is a half-sister to the multiple Group 1 winners Warrsan and Luso, and the dam of the Group 3 winners Tastahil, Hattan, Blue Monday and Laaheb. (Cheveley Park Stud). *"He's tall horse, leggy and athletic at this stage. He's not a typical Exceed And*

Excel, so I don't think he'll be early, but I think he's one for later in the summer and he's a nice mover".

1580. CHARACTER WITNESS ★★★
b.c. Casamento – She's A Character (Invincible Spirit). March 15. Second foal. £38,000Y. Goffs UK Premier (Doncaster). Biddestone Stud. Half-brother to the fair 2016 2-y-o 7f and 8.5f winner Jumping Jack (by Sir Prancealot). The dam, a fair 6f (at 2 yrs) to 9f winner of 4 races, is a half-sister to 4 winners. The second dam, Cavernista (by Lion Cavern), is a placed half-sister to 11 winners including the Group 1 Prix du Cadran winner Give Notice and the triple Group 2 winning stayer Times Up. *"He's quite a nice horse with a very good action. He'll want six or seven furlongs from July onwards, so he's alright".*

1581. DAHIK (IRE) ★★★★
ch.c. Society Rock – Bishop's Lake (Lake Coniston). March 6. Seventh foal. £62,000Y. Goffs UK Premier (Doncaster). Shadwell Estate Co. Half-brother to the fair 2016 2-y-o 5f winner Imdancinwithurwife (by Sir Prancealot), to the Group 3 Blue Wind Stakes winner and Group 1 Tattersalls Gold Cup third Euphrasia (by Windsor Knot), the fairly useful listed-placed 2-y-o 5f winner Langavat (by Bushranger), the modest 6f (at 2 yrs) to 9f winner Lakeman (by Tillerman) and the modest 1m winner Strike A Deal (by Chineur). The dam, a quite useful listed-placed dual 2-y-o 6f winner, is a half-sister to 8 winners including the Group placed 2-y-o's Sir Reginald and Henrik. The second dam, Clincher Club (by Polish Patriot), a fair 5f (at 2 yrs) and 7.5f winner, is a half-sister to 9 winners. (Hamdan Al Maktoum). *"I like this horse, he's quite precocious and could run early. He's a fast horse and should be able to handle himself over five and six furlongs. Not very big, but he's strong and knows his job".*

1582. EKANSE (IRE) ★★★
b.c. Society Rock – Esterlina (Highest Honor). March 19. Tenth living foal. 170,000Y. Tattersalls October Book 1. Roger Varian. Half-brother to the smart 7f (at 2 yrs) and listed 1m Heron Stakes winner and Group 1 1m Criterium International third Redolent (by Redback), to the useful 2-y-o 6f winner and

Group 3 6f Albany Stakes third Illaunglass (by Red Clubs), the quite useful Irish dual 11f winner Klothry (by Marju), the fair 6f winner Hightime Heroine (by Danetime) and the French 2-y-o winners Qatar Dance (by Zebedee) and Zomorroda (by Chineur). The dam won over 1m at 3 yrs in Ireland and is a half-sister to 3 minor winners. The second dam, Shaquick (by Shadeed), won in France and is a half-sister to 8 winners including the dual Group 3 winner and Oaks third Leap Lively (herself dam of the Irish 1,000 Guineas winner Forest Flower). (Sheikh Mohammed Obaid Al Maktoum). *"He's good-looking but he's had a setback and won't train early in the season. I couldn't tell you much about him, but he's well-built and black – so he takes the eye and he's very attractive".*

1583. ELASIA ★★★
b.f. Nathaniel – Elas Diamond (Danehill Dancer). February 1. Second foal. 200,000Y. Tattersalls October Book 2. Roger Varian. Half-sister to the fair 2016 2-y-o 1m winner Elas Ruby (by Raven's Pass). The dam, a fairly useful 2-y-o 1m winner, was listed placed and is a half-sister to 3 winners including the Group 2 Doncaster Cup winner Pallasator. The second dam, Ela Athena (by Ezzoud), a winner of 3 races including the Group 3 Lancashire Oaks, was placed in seven Group/Grade 1 events and is a half-sister to 5 winners. (Sheikh Mohammed Obaid Al Maktoum). *"She's a nice type, a big filly with a good action and plenty of scope. The sire didn't get that many 2-y-o winners last year, so I don't think we'll be expecting too much too soon from this filly, but she's a good prospect and a jolly nice-looking filly. She'll probably emulate her dam and her half-sister and be suited by a mile later in the season".*

1584. FICTITIOUS ★★★
ch.f. Mayson – Fantasize (Groom Dancer). March 24. Eighth foal. Half-sister to the fairly useful 1m winner and listed-placed Illusion (by Anabaa), to the fair 12f winner Visualize (by Medicean) and the modest 8.5f winner Adore (by Oasis Dream). The dam, a useful 7f (at 2 yrs) and 1m listed winner, is a half-sister to the Group 3 6f Cherry Hinton Stakes winner and 1,000 Guineas third Dazzle and to the 2-y-o listed 7f winner Hypnotize.

The second dam, Belle Et Deluree (by The Minstrel), won over 1m (at 2 yrs) and 10f in France and is a half-sister to 5 winners including the US Grade 2 winner Doneraile Court and the Cheveley Park Stakes second Dancing Tribute (herself dam of the Group/Grade 2 winners Dance Sequence and Souvenir Copy). (Cheveley Park Stud). *"She moves well and she's got the look of a summer 2-y-o. She has a good shape and a good action, so I quite like her".*

1585. FLAVIUS TITUS ★★★★
ch.c. Lethal Force – Furbelow (Pivotal). February 22. Second foal. 100,000Y. Tattersalls October Book 2. Roger Varian. Half-brother to the unplaced 2016 2-y-o Go Guarantor (by Medicean). The dam, a quite useful 6f winner, is a sister to the US listed stakes winner Red Diadem and a half-sister to 5 winners including the dam of the Group 2 Richmond Stakes winner Saayerr. The second dam, Red Tiara (by Mr Prospector), a moderate 7.6f fourth-placed maiden, is closely related to the Japanese sprint stakes winner Meiner Love and a half-sister to 4 winners. (Sheikh Mohammed Obaid Al Maktoum). *"I like this horse. He's strong and quite precocious so he could be a May runner over six furlongs and he moves sufficiently well".*

1586. GAME PLAYER (IRE) ★★★★
gr.c. Dark Angel – Lucky Clio (Key To Luck). February 4. Sixth foal. 300,000Y. Tattersalls October Book 1. Roger Varian. Half-brother to the useful dual 5f (at 2 yrs) and 6f winner and dual listed-placed Lucky Beggar (by Verglas), to the useful 1m (at 2 yrs) and 10f winner and Group 3 Dee Stakes third Kingsdesire (by King's Best), the useful triple 10f winner Central Square (by Azamour) and the quite useful dual 1m winner War Of Art (by Tamayuz). The dam was placed 3 times at 3 yrs and is a half-sister to 3 winners including Special Kaldoun, a winner of 9 races including the Group 2 Prix Daniel Wildenstein Casino Barriere (twice). The second dam, Special Lady (by Kaldoun), was placed at 2 yrs in France and is a half-sister to 5 minor winners. (Sheikh Mohammed Obaid Al Maktoum). *"A good, strong horse that's forward in his work, he could be one for six furlongs in May and I quite like him".*

1587. GENERAL MARIUS ★★★
gr.c. Holy Roman Emperor – Megaspiel
(Singspiel). March 23. Second foal. 55,000Y.
Tattersalls October Book 2. Kern/Lillingston.
The dam, a minor US winner at 3 and 4 yrs, is
a sister to the US Grade 2 winner and Grade
1 placed Three Degrees. The second dam,
Miss University (by Beau Genius), ran twice
unplaced and is a half-sister to 9 winners.
*"Not the biggest, but he's well-made and has
a good action. I think there's plenty of stamina
on the dam's side and he'll probably be a six/
seven furlong 2-y-o in the summer".*

1588. GILDED HEAVEN ★★★
ch.f. Medicean – Heavenly (Pivotal). January
26. First foal. The dam, unplaced in two
starts at 2 yrs, is a sister to the listed-placed
7f winner and subsequent Canadian dual
Grade 3 second Endless Light. The second
dam, Celeste (by Green Desert), is an
unraced half-sister to the US triple Grade 1
winner Megahertz and to the dual Group 3
9f winner Heaven Sent. (Cheveley Park Stud).
*"She's nice. She's a tall, leggy filly but she
carries herself well and I think she's got a bit
of quality".*

1589. GOING PLACES (FR) ★★★
b.f. Shamardal – Screen Star (Tobougg).
March 14. Sixth foal. 550,000Y. Tattersalls
October Book 1. Roger Varian. Sister to the
2-y-o Group 1 6f Cheveley Park Stakes winner
and Group 2 6f Lowther Stakes second
Lumiere and half-sister to the fair 2016 2-y-o
8.5f winner X Rated (by Exceed And Excel)
and the quite useful 12f winner Silent Movie
(by Cape Cross). The dam, a 7f winner at 2 yrs
on her only start, is a half-sister to 4 minor
winners. The second dam, Actoris (by Diesis),
a useful French 1m winner, was listed-placed
and is a half-sister to 3 winners. (Sheikh
Mohammed Obaid Al Maktoum). *"A big,
well-made filly with a good action. She's not
an early type but she's a nice prospect and a
different type to her sister Lumiere".*

1590. HERMOSITA ★★★★
b.f. Exceed And Excel – Honorlina (Linamix).
March 28. Fifth foal. 65,000Y. Tattersalls
October Book 2. Not sold. Half-sister to
the fair 12f winner Horseguardsparade
(by Montjeu). The dam, a French 2-y-o

1m winner, is a sister to the French 2,000
Guineas winner Vahorimix and to the French
listed winner Vadalix and a half-sister to
4 winners. The second dam, Vadsa Honor
(by Highest Honor), won the listed Prix de
Thiberville and is a half-sister to 12 winners
including the dam of the Breeders' Cup Mile
winner Val Royal. *"She's a lovely filly and
could be quite smart. She has a good action,
it's a good family and I quite like her. She'll
be a six furlong 2-y-o and will probably stay
seven in time".*

1591. HOWMAN (IRE) ★★★
b.c. Sea The Stars – Hoity Toity (Darshaan).
February 15. Ninth foal. 450,000Y. Tattersalls
October Book 1. Roger Varian. Half-brother
to the Group 1 1m Coronation Stakes and
Group 1 1m Matron Stakes winner Lillie
Langtry (by Danehill Dancer and herself
dam of the top-class filly Minding), to the 7f
(including at 2 yrs) and listed 1m winner of
4 races and dual Group 3 placed Count Of
Limonade (by Duke Of Marmalade) and the
fair 2-y-o 1m winner and US 3-y-o Grade
3 second Danilovna (by Dansili). The dam
is an unraced half-sister to 5 winners. The
second dam, Hiwaayati (by Shadeed), is an
unraced half-sister to 6 winners including
the dual Group 3 winner Great Commotion
and the dual Group 2 winner Lead on Time.
(Sheikh Mohammed Obaid Al Maktoum). *"A
good-looking horse but he'll be a late maturer
I think. There's no rush with him but he moves
well and he's one for the late summer or
autumn".*

1592. IBRAZ ★★★★
b.c. Farhh – Wadaa (Dynaformer).
March 8. First foal. 100,000Y. Tattersalls
October Book 1. Shadwell Estate Co. The
dam, a quite useful 11f winner, is a half-sister
to 8 winners including the Group 3 10f Winter
Hill Stakes and listed 12f Chalice Stakes
winner Queen's Best and the listed winners
Reverie Solitaire and Urban Castle. The
second dam, Cloud Castle (by In The Wings),
winner of the Group 3 Nell Gwyn Stakes
and placed in the Group 1 Yorkshire Oaks
and Group 1 Prix Vermeille, is a half-sister to
the multiple Group 1 winners Warrsan and
Luso, and the dam of the Group 3 winners
Tastahil, Hattan, Blue Monday and Laaheb.

(Hamdan Al Maktoum). *"He really is a nice horse. He moves well, very athletic and we like what we've seen so far. A nice prospect, I was tempted to make him my 5-star pick"*.

1593. KAWASIR (USA) ★★★★
ch.c. Speightstown – Bashful Bertie (Quiet American). February 7. Third foal. $400,000 foal. Keeneland November. Shadwell Estate Co. Half-brother to the US Grade 1 10f Secretariat Stakes winner Beach Patrol (by Lemon Drop Kid). The dam is an unplaced sister to the US dual Grade 2 winner Allamerican Bertie and a half-sister to the US Grade 2 winner Hurricane Bertie. The second dam, Clever Bertie (by Timeless Native), is an unraced half-sister to the US Grade 1 winner Traitor. (Hamdan Al Maktoum). *"He's an attractive colt with a good action, he moves well and catches the eye. Not a bad type at all – he's a nice horse"*.

1594. LA DIVA ★★★
b.f. Helmet – Craigmill (Slip Anchor). February 15. Seventeenth foal. 30,000Y. Tattersalls October Book 2. J Shack. Closely related to the winner Represent (by Exceed And Excel) and half-sister to 11 winners including the Group 2 Bosphorus Cup and listed winner Connecticut (by New Approach), the German listed winner and Group 3 placed Fleurie Domaine (by Unfuwain), the smart listed-placed 1m winner Castleton, the fairly useful dual 10f winner Craigstown (both by Cape Cross), the fairly useful 12f, 2m and hurdles winner Astyanax (by Hector Protector) and the quite useful 2-y-o 1m winner Stirling Castle (by Dubai Destination). The dam, a fair 2-y-o 7f winner, is a half-sister to 6 winners including Coigach (Group 3 Park Hill Stakes). The second dam, Rynechra (by Blakeney), a useful 12f winner, is a half-sister to 6 winners. (Mr J Shack & Mr S Roden). *"Not the biggest, but big enough, she has a good action and she should be racing this summer. Seven furlongs should suit her to begin with I should think"*.

1595. LADY MOMOKA (IRE) ★★★★
b.f. Shamardal – Juno Marlowe (Danehill). May 4. Tenth foal. €470,000Y. Goffs Orby. Roger Varian. Half-sister to 7 winners including the Group 3 12f winner and Irish Derby third Stellar Moss (by Sea The Stars),

the US stakes winner and Grade 1 second Marzelline (by Barathea), the German 2-y-o winner and Group 3 third Sun Of Jamaica (by Cape Cross), the very useful listed-placed 10f and 12f winner of 6 races Fairmile (by Spectrum) and the quite useful 1m winner Shooting Line (by Motivator). The dam, a fairly useful dual 7f winner, is a full or half-sister to 9 winners including the Group 3 Select Stakes winner Leporello. The second dam, Why So Silent (by Mill Reef), is an unraced half-sister to 5 winners. (Sheikh Mohammed Obaid Al Maktoum). *"She's a nice type and a well-made filly with a good action and a good temperament. One for later on in the year but she's quite a nice model. I like her"*.

1596. LAUGH A MINUTE ★★★
b.c. Mayson – Funny Enough (Dansili). April 12. Third foal. 45,000Y. Tattersalls October Book 2. Roger Varian. Half brother to Horroob (by Showcasing), placed third over 6f on his only start at 2 yrs in 2016 and to the fair 2-y-o 7f winner Puzzled Look (by Sakhee's Secret). The dam is an unplaced half-sister to 6 winners including the Lingfield listed winner Oasis Dancer. The second dam, Good Enough (by Mukaddamah), a US 3-y-o winner, was third in the Group 1 Prix Saint-Alary and is a half-sister to the Group 3 Molecomb Stakes winner Classic Ruler. (Sheikh Mohammed Obaid Al Maktoum). *"Quite a feminine horse, he's good-looking and moves well. Should be a summer 2-y-o over six or seven furlongs"*.

1597. LOVEISILI ★★
b.c. Dansili – Loveisallyouneed (Sadler's Wells). March 4. Third living foal. 650,000Y. Tattersalls October Book 1. Roger Varian. The dam is an unraced sister to 4 winners including the Irish 1,000 Guineas winner Yesterday, the Group 1 7f Moyglare Stud Stakes winner Quarter Moon and the smart 10f winner and Oaks and Irish Oaks third All My Loving and a half-sister to 3 winners. The second dam, Jude (by Darshaan), a moderate 10f placed maiden, is a sister to 2 winners including the Irish listed 12f winner Alouette (herself dam of the Champion Stakes winner Alborada and the German triple Group 1 winner Albanova) and a half-sister to the

Group 2 10f Nassau Stakes and Sun Chariot Stakes winner Last Second (dam of the Irish 2,000 Guineas winner Aussie Rules). (Sheikh Mohammed Obaid Al Maktoum). *"This horse had a setback in the winter and he hasn't come back to me yet. You can see from his price tag he was a good-looking horse at the sale, so hopefully he'll come good later on".*

1598. MADELINE (IRE) ★★★
b.f. Kodiac – Madhulika (Marchand De Sable). March 15. First foal. 140,000Y. Tattersalls October Book 2. Roger Varian. The dam won 3 races at 3 yrs in Switzerland and is a sister to the triple listed winner and Group 1 third Dolma (herself dam of the Group 1 Pretty Polly Stakes winner Thistle Bird) and a half-sister to 2 winners. The second dam, Young Manila (by Manila), was listed-placed over 10f and is a half-sister to 9 winners including Fabulous Hostess, a winner of three Group 3 events from 11f to 13f. (Sheikh Mohammed Obaid Al Maktoum). *"She could be one of the earlier ones, she moves well and covers the ground. A speedy type with a good temperament, she's not the biggest but that's not the end of the world with a Kodiac. They're generally runners".*

1599. MASAARR ★★★
ch.c. Distorted Humor – Aryaamm (Galileo). March 28. Eighth foal. Half-brother to the 2016 2-y-o 8.5f winner on his only start Youmkin, to the 2-y-o Group 2 7f Champagne Stakes winner Saamidd, the modest 10f and 11f winner Moayadd (all by Street Cry), the useful listed-placed 12f winner Talmada and the fairly useful 7f and 1m (both at 2 yrs) and 1m winner Yarroom (both by Cape Cross). The dam, a quite useful 10f winner, is a half-sister to the winner and Irish 2,000 Guineas third Oracle and to the winner and French Group 2 1m third Mathematician. The second dam, Zibilene (by Rainbow Quest), a useful listed-placed 12f winner, is a half-sister to the Breeders' Cup Mile, Irish 2,000 Guineas and Queen Anne Stakes winner Barathea and the Fillies Mile and Irish 1,000 Guineas winner Gossamer. (Sheikh Ahmed Al Maktoum). *"He's quite a nice horse, from a good family, he moves well and he'll be running over seven furlongs from July onwards".*

1600. MAZBOON ★★★
ch.c. Sea The Stars – Fresnay (Rainbow Quest). March 15. Sixth foal. Half-brother to the Italian 2-y-o listed 5f winner Freetown (by Speightstown). The dam is an unplaced half-sister to 6 winners including the 2,000 Guineas third Olympian Odyssey and the listed 7f winner Field Of Dream. The second dam, Field Of Hope (by Selkirk), won 6 races including the Group 1 7f Prix de la Foret and the Group 2 1m Prix d'Astarte and is a half-sister to 6 winners. (Hamdan Al Maktoum). *"Typical of the sire, he'll probably take a bit of time but he has a good action. It's encouraging to see the dam has bred a speedy 2-y-o but this colt is going to want much farther I should imagine".*

1601. MOUNTAIN GUARD (IRE) ★★★
b.c. Society Rock – Morinda (Selkirk). February 5. Second foal. 120,000Y. Tattersalls October Book 2. Roger Varian. Half-brother to the modest 2016 6f placed 2-y-o Bizet (by Helmet). The dam is an unplaced half-sister to 6 winners and to the dam of the Group 1 Prix du Cadran winner Molly Malone. The second dam, Morning Queen (by Konigsstuhl), a minor German 3-y-o winner, is a sister to the multiple Group 1 winner Monsun. (Sheikh Mohammed Obaid Al Maktoum). *"I quite like him, he's forward in his work and should be running in May. Quite sharp, I think he's a six furlong horse and he moves well enough".*

1602. MUBHIJ (IRE) ★★★
b.c. Dark Angel – Diva (Oasis Dream). February 28. First foal. £250,000Y. Goffs UK Premier (Doncaster). Shadwell Estate Co. The dam, placed at 3 yrs in Germany, is a half-sister to 5 winners including two German listed winners. The second dam, Dea (by Shareef Dancer), won at 2 yrs in Germany and is a half-sister to 8 winners. (Hamdan Al Maktoum). *"He moves well and he'll be a summer 2-y-o over six/seven furlongs. An attractive horse".*

1603. MUTASAAWY (USA) ★★★
gr.c. Mizzen Mast – Ishraak (Sahm). February 7. Half-brother to the quite useful dual 7f winner (including at 2 yrs) and 10f listed-placed Jabhaat (by Hard Spun), to the fair 7f (at 2 yrs) and 1m winner Kafeel (by First

Samurai) and the Italian 2-y-o 1m listed-placed Motheeba (by Mustanfar). The dam is an unraced half-sister to 6 winners including the US Grade 2 7f winner Kayrawan. The second dam, Muhbubh (by Blushing Groom), won the Group 3 6f Princess Margaret Stakes, was second in the Group 2 6f Lowther Stakes and is a half-sister to Mathkurh (dam of the Group winners Asfurah and Istintaj). (Hamdan Al Maktoum). *"A big horse with a good action and I think he's a racehorse. I don't know how good he'll be but there's nothing wrong with him. He'll make a 2-y-o by July onwards and it's interesting to see the dam's three 2-y-o winners have been over seven furlongs and a mile".*

1604. NARYNKOL ★★★
ch.c. Declaration Of War – Nazym (Galileo). February 16. First foal. The dam is an unraced sister to the Group 1 7f Moyglare Stud Stakes winner Sequoyah (the dam of Henrythenavigator) and to the 2-y-o Group 1 Fillies' Mile winner Listen and a half-sister to the Irish listed 5.6f winner Oyster Catcher. The second dam, Brigid (by Irish River), a minor French 1m winner, is a sister to 2 winners including the French listed winner Or Vision (dam of the Group/Grade 1 winners Dolphin Street, Insight and Saffron Walden) and a half-sister to 5 winners. (N Bizakov). *"A home-bred, the mare cost a fortune as a yearling because it's a very good family. This is a good-looking horse, he has a good step to him, he won't be particularly early but there's plenty to like about him".*

1605. NOBLE EXPRESSION ★★★
b.c. Sir Percy – Disposition (Selkirk). February 15. Second foal. 75,000Y. Tattersalls October Book 2. Roger Varian. The dam was placed and is a half-sister to one winner. The second dam, Far Shores (by Distant View), is a placed sister to one winner and a half-sister to 8 winners including the top-class sprinter and outstanding sire Danehill, the US Graded stakes winners Harpia and Eagle Eyed and the Group 3 Criterion Stakes winner Shibboleth. (Sheikh Mohammed Obaid Al Maktoum). *"Quite a big, good-looking horse that moves well. I'd say he's the type for seven furlongs in July and he'll be alright".*

1606. ORBAAN ★★★★★
b.c. Invincible Spirit – Contradict (Raven's Pass). February 6. First foal. The dam, a fair 10f winner, is a half-sister to two minor winners. The second dam, Acts Of Grace (by Bahri), won the Group 3 12f Princess Royal Stakes and is a half-sister to 10 winners including the Group 1 Sprint Cup winner and good sire Invincible Spirit. (Prince A A Faisal). *"A lovely horse that takes the eye and moves well. He should be a summer 2-y-o, probably over seven furlongs. I like him a lot – he's a smashing horse".* This colt is in-bred 2x3 to the Prix de Diane winner Rafha.

1607. PIVOTAL MAN ★★★★ ♣♣
b.c. Pivotal – Privacy Order (Azamour). February 8. Second foal. 150,000Y. Tattersalls October Book 1. Will Edmeades. Half-brother to the useful 2016 2-y-o listed 6f winner Private Matter (by Mayson). The dam is an unplaced half-sister to the listed winner Red Box and to the French 10f winner and Group 2 Prix Greffulhe second Untold Secret. The second dam, Confidential Lady (by Singspiel), winner of the Group 3 7f Prix du Calvados (at 2 yrs) and the Group 1 10.5f Prix de Diane, is a half-sister to 5 winners. (Arjun & Jai Waney). *"He's a nice horse with a good action and he moves well. I quite like him and I would have thought he'd be a seven furlong 2-y-o".*

1608. PRINCE EIJI ★★★
gr.c. Dubawi – Rose Diamond (Daylami). April 16. Third foal. Half-brother to the quite useful dual 10f and subsequent US Grade 3 10.5f winner Real Smart (by Smart Strike). The dam, a fairly useful 2-y-o 6f winner, was second in the Group 3 7f Prestige Stakes. The second dam, Tante Rose (by Barathea), a winner of 5 races including the Group 1 Haydock Park Sprint Cup, the Group 4 7f Fred Darling Stakes and Group 3 6f Summer Stakes, is a half-sister to several winners including the Sweet Solera Stakes winner Bay Tree. (Sheikh Mohammed Obaid Al Maktoum). *"He's a neat little horse, not very big but typical of the sire, he has a good temperament and a good action. He'll need a bit of time to mature but there's nothing wrong with him and he'll be one for July onwards I should think".*

1609. QAZYNA ★★★★
b.f. Frankel – First (Highest Honor). March 11.
Ninth foal. Sister to the unraced 2016 2-y-o
Future Energy and half-sister to 6 winners
including the smart listed 1m and listed 10f
winner and dual Group 3 third Perfect Stride,
the fairly useful 2-y-o 6f winner Among
Equals, the quite useful 1m winner of 4 races
First Dream (all by Oasis Dream), the French
dual listed 12f and Australian Group 2 12f
winner Au Revoir (by Singspiel) and the
French 2-y-o listed 6f winner Law Lord (by
Diktat). The dam, a French listed 1m winner,
is a half-sister to 12 winners including the
smart Group 3 winners Bluebook and Myself.
The second dam, Pushy (by Sharpen Up), won
the Group 2 Queen Mary Stakes and is a half-
sister to the high-class 2-y-o Precocious and
the Group 1 Japan Cup winner Jupiter Island.
(N Bizakov). *"A nice, big filly with plenty of
scope, she's very much an athlete and I quite
like her".*

1610. QIANLONG ★★★
b.c. Dragon Pulse – Dream Day (Spectrum).
March 31. Fifth foal. 42,000Y. Tattersalls
October Book 2. Armando Duarte. Half-
brother to the modest dual 1m winner
Sooqaan (by Naaqoos) and to a minor
4-y-o 6f winner in Hong Kong by Dark
Angel. The dam, a winner of two races at 2
and 3 yrs in France, was listed-placed over
1m. The second dam, Dream Of Day (by
Machiavellian), a minor French 2-y-o winner,
is a half-sister to 7 winners including the
Group 3 Premio Sergio Cumani winner and
Group 1 Coronation Stakes second Nova
Hawk. (The Qianlong Partnership). *"A neat
little horse that should make a summer
2-y-o. He's got a good action and a good
temperament".*

1611. RICH IDENTITY ★★★
b.c. Intello – Red Bloom (Selkirk). May 3.
Eighth foal. 210,000Y. Tattersalls October
Book 1. Roger Varian. Closely related to
the fairly useful 2016 2-y-o dual 6f winner
Senator (by Frankel) and half-brother to the
fairly useful 10f to 12f winner of 5 races Vasily
(by Sadler's Wells) and the fair 9.5f winner
Sea The Bloom (by Sea The Stars). The dam,
winner of the Group 1 Fillies' Mile and Group
2 10f Blandford Stakes (twice), is a full or half-

sister to 4 winners including the listed winner
Red Gala. The second dam, Red Camellia
(by Polar Falcon), winner of the Group 3 7f
Prestige Stakes, was third in the French 1,000
Guineas and is a half-sister to 4 winners.
(Sheikh Mohammed Obaid Al Maktoum).
*"A nice type of horse with a good shape, he
covers the ground well and moves nicely, so he
could be alright".*

1612. SAM GOLD (IRE) ★★★★
b.c. Iffraaj – Samdaniya (Machiavellian).
February 21. Sixth foal. 120,000Y. Tattersalls
October Book 2. Roger Varian. Half-brother
to the smart 2016 2-y-o dual 7f winner and
Group 1 Prix Marcel Boussac third Dabyah
(by Sepoy) and to the fair 14f and hurdles
winner Samtu (by Teofilo). The dam, a modest
9.7f winner, is a half-sister to 8 winners
including Queen's Best (Group 3 10f Winter
Hill Stakes) and the listed winners Urban
Castle and Reverie Solitaire. The second dam,
Cloud Castle (by In The Wings), winner of
the Group 3 Nell Gwyn Stakes, was placed in
the Group 1 Yorkshire Oaks and the Group 1
Prix Vermeille and is a half-sister to 5 winners
including the multiple Group 1 winners
Warrsan and Luso. (Sheikh Mohammed
Obaid Al Maktoum). *"A nice horse, he's big but
not weak and has a bit of strength to him. He
has a good action and a good temperament,
so I quite like him".*

1613. SHARJA SILK ★★★★
b.c. Dubawi – So Silk (Rainbow Quest).
May 1. Seventh foal. 850,000Y. Tattersalls
October Book 1. Roger Varian. Half-brother
to the 2016 1m placed 2-y-o, from two starts,
So Sleek (by Lawman), to the smart Group
2 14.5f Park Hill Stakes winner and Group 1
British Champions Fillies/Mare Stakes second
Silk Sari (by Dalakhani), the US winner and
listed-placed Fashion Fund and the quite
useful 2-y-o 1m winner Dreamlike (both by
Oasis Dream). The dam is an unraced half-
sister to 6 winners including Ibn Khaldun
(2-y-o Group 1 Racing Post Trophy). The
second dam, Gossamer (by Sadler's Wells),
won the Group 1 Fillies' Mile and the Group
1 Irish 1,000 Guineas and is a sister to the
Breeders' Cup Mile and Irish 2,000 Guineas
winner Barathea. (Sheikh Mohammed Obaid
Al Maktoum). *"A nice horse, probably a late*

maturing colt but he's very handsome and has a good action. I like him and his pedigree suggests he'll want a mile on soft ground in the autumn. It's a very good family".

1614. SOODA (USA) ★★★
b.f. Street Cry – Nayarra (Cape Cross). March 14. Second foal. The dam, a 2-y-o Group 1 1m Gran Criterium winner, is a half-sister to 6 winners including the 2-y-o Group 3 7f Silver Flash Stakes winner Wonderfully, the Group 1 St James's Palace Stakes third Mars and the 2-y-o listed 6f winner Cuff. The second dam, Massara (by Danehill), a useful listed 6f winner and second in the Group 2 Prix Robert Papin at 2 yrs, is closely related to the Group 1 6f Haydock Park Sprint Cup winner Invincible Spirit and a half-sister to the Group 3 winners Acts Of Grace and Sadian. (Prince A A Faisal). *"A nice filly that moves well. She has a good action and is quite forward for a Street Cry because in my experience they take a bit of time but she could make a 2-y-o in the summer".*

1615. STAR SHIELD ★★★
ch.c. Helmet – Perfect Star (Act One). February 8. Fourth living foal. 140,000Y. Tattersalls October Book 1. Roger Varian. Half-brother to the useful 2016 2-y-o Group 3 7f Prestige Stakes winner Kilmah (by Sepoy) and to the fairly useful 1m (at 2 yrs) to 12f winner of 5 races and listed-placed Tears Of The Sun (by Mastercraftsman). The dam, a useful 7f (including at 2 yrs) and listed 1m winner of 5 races, is a half-sister to 4 winners including the listed winner Rewarded. The second dam, Granted (by Cadeaux Genereux), a useful 1m and 8.3f winner, was listed placed three times at up to 9f and is a half-sister to 5 winners. (Sheikh Mohammed Obaid Al Maktoum). *"I really like him but he's had a setback and we might not see him until later in the season. A nice horse".*

1616. TADARAK ★★★
ch.c. Poet's Voice – Sensationally (Montjeu). April 23. Fourth foal. 85,000Y. Tattersalls October Book 2. Shadwell Estate Co. Half-brother to the fairly useful 1m winner of 4 races at 2 and 3 yrs Greatest Journey (by Raven's Pass) and to the fair 1m (at 2 yrs) to 10f winner of 4 races Senza Una Donna (by

Sir Percy). The dam, a fair 9f winner, is a half-sister to 3 winners including the US Grade 2 winner Sun Boat. The second dam, One So Wonderful (by Nashwan), won the Group 1 Juddmonte International and is a half-sister to 8 winners including the Group 2 Dante Stakes winner Alnasr Alwasheek. (Sheikh Ahmed Al Maktoum). *"The sire's a bit cold but this is a good-looking horse and there's nothing wrong with him. He's got a good action and he's from a good family so hopefully he'll be a racehorse one day".*

1617. THE CHEMIST ★★★
ch.f. Dutch Art – Prescription (Pivotal). May 10. Third foal. Half-sister to the moderate 1m winner Dose (by Teofilo). The dam, a fairly useful listed 6f winner of 5 races, is a full or half-sister to 9 winners including the very useful Group 3 9f and triple listed 1m winner Clinical, the smart Group 3 7f Horris Hill Stakes winner of 7 races Cupid's Glory and the fairly useful 7f (at 2 yrs) and listed 1m and 10f winner Courting. The dam, a fairly useful 5.2f (at 2 yrs) and 6f winner, is a half-sister to 6 winners including the useful On Call, a listed winner of 7 races at up to 2m. The second dam, Doctor Bid (by Spectacular Bid), is an unraced half-sister to 9 winners including the smart Group 3 Prix Thomas Bryon winner Glory Forever. (Cheveley Park Stud). *"A big filly and very well-named I think, she has a good action and she's one for the second half of the season. Quite likeable".*

1618. THE LAST EMPEROR ★★★★
b.c. Azamour – Raskutani (Dansili). February 19. Fifth foal. 230,000Y. Tattersalls October Book 2. Roger Varian. Half-brother to the very smart Group 3 13.5f Geoffrey Freer Stakes winner Agent Murphy (by Cape Cross), the fair 1m winner Kylach Me If You Can (by Kyllachy) and the moderate 6f winner Mysterious Wonder (by Oasis Dream). The dam is an unraced half-sister to 7 winners including the Group 2 7f Superlative Stakes and US Grade 3 winner Hatta Fort and the Group 3 Sweet Solera Stakes winner Blue Bayou. The second dam, Oshiponga (by Barathea), a fair 9f winner, is a half-sister to 8 winners including the Canadian Grade 2 winner Miss Keller. (Sheikh Mohammed Obaid Al Maktoum). *"He's a nice horse, quite*

sparky but he's definitely an athlete and covers the ground. He should be running over seven furlongs in the summer and he has a good way of going".

1619. TA ALLAK ★★★
ch.c. New Approach – Nahrain (Selkirk). March 3. Second foal. Half-brother to Benbatl (by Dubawi), an easy 7f winner on his debut at 3 yrs in 2017. The dam, winner of the Group 1 Prix de l'Opera and the US Grade 1 Flower Bowl Invitational, is a half-sister to 5 winners including the very useful dual listed winner Baharah. The second dam, Bahr (by Generous), winner of the listed 7f Washington Singer Stakes (at 2 yrs), the Group 3 12f Ribblesdale Stakes and the Group 3 10.4f Musidora Stakes, is a half-sister to numerous winners. (Sheikh Ahmed Al Maktoum). *"He's a big horse this and he'll take a bit of time I should think. There's nothing wrong with him, he's got a good action and he's a nice horse stood up. The dam was my first Group 1 winner!"*

1620. TALAS ★★★★
b.c. Dansili – Tamarind (Sadler's Wells). March 7. Fourth foal. Brother to the fairly useful 2016 2-y-o 8.5f winner and listed-placed Tansholpan and half-brother to quite useful 10f winner Tamasha (by Sea The Stars) and the fair dual 10f winner Taraz (by Oasis Dream). The dam won the Group 3 12f Give Thanks Stakes and is a sister to the smart German Group 2 8.5f and Italian Group 2 1m winner Crimson Tide and a half-sister to the US Grade 2 and Group 3 Prix de Sandringham winner Pharatta and the US stakes listed stakes winner and Grade 2 placed La Vida Loca. The second dam, Sharata (by Darshaan), is an unraced half-sister to the dual Derby winner Shahrastani. (N Bizakov). *"He's a nice horse this. Good-bodied, well-made and from a good family, he moves well but I should think he'll want a mile this year".*

1621. TO WAFIJ ★★★★
b.c. Kodiac – Rajmahal (Indian Ridge). March 14. Fifth foal. 130,000Y. Tattersalls October Book 2. Shadwell Estate Co. Brother to the very useful 2-y-o listed-placed 6f winner Leaf Clover. The dam is an unraced half-sister to 3 winners including the Group 3 winner and

French 2,000 Guineas third Furner's Green and the listed winners Lady Lupus, Mystical Lady and Palace. The second dam, Lady Icarus (by Rainbow Quest), is an unraced half-sister to 3 stakes winners including the Group 3 7f Supreme Stakes winner Hazaam and Group 3 1m winner Sharman – both very useful. (Sheikh Ahmed Al Maktoum). *"I like this horse. He's a solid, precocious colt and could be a five/six furlong 2-y-o early doors".*

1622. UAE SOLDIER (USA) ★★★
b.c. Dansili – Time On (Sadler's Wells). February 12. Third living foal. 160,000Y. Tattersalls October Book 1. Roger Varian. Half-brother to the quite useful 2-y-o 1m winner Moontime (by Sea The Stars). The dam, a Group 2 Prix de Malleret and listed Cheshire Oaks winner, is a sister to the dam of the 2-y-o Group 1 Moyglare winner Cursory Glance. The second dam, Time Away (by Darshaan), won the Group 3 10.4f Musidora Stakes, was third in the Group 1 Prix de Diane and the Group 1 Nassau Stakes and is a half-sister to 6 winners including the Prix de Diane second Time Ahead. (Sheikh Mohammed Obaid Al Maktoum). *"A nice type, he's late-maturing and still quite babyish in his features but I quite like the way he goes".*

1623. UPFRONT LADY ★★★
b.f. War Front – Maid To Master (Danehill Dancer). February 23. Second foal. 250,000Y. Tattersalls October Book 1. Roger Varian. The dam, a minor French 3-y-o winner and placed over 1m in Ireland, is a sister to the Group 1 Phoenix Stakes, National Stakes and Irish 2,000 Guineas winner Mastercraftsman and to the Group 1 Moyglare Stud Stakes second Famous and a half-sister to 7 winners including the US Grade 3 winner Genuine Devotion. The second dam, Starlight Dreams (by Black Tie Affair), won twice at 3 yrs in the USA and is a half-sister to 5 winners including the listed Zetland Stakes winner Matahif and the dam of the dual Group 1 winner Pressing. (Sheikh Mohammed Obaid Al Maktoum). *"She's alright and she moves well. Should be a summer 2-y-o".*

1624. UNNAMED ★★★
b.c. Mastercraftsman – Ile Deserte (Green Desert). February 15. Sixth foal. 130,000Y.

Tattersalls October Book 2. Charlie Gordon-Watson / M V Magnier. Half-brother to the very useful 2-y-o 6f winner and Group 2 6f Coventry Stakes third St Barths (by Cadeaux Genereux), to the quite useful 2m 1f winner Havisham (by Mount Nelson) and the fair 6f winner Ebony N Ivory (by Equiano). The dam is an unraced half-sister to the dual Group 1 winner (Racing Post Trophy and St Leger) Kingston Hill. The second dam, Audacieuse (by Rainbow Quest), winner of the Group 3 Prix de Flore, is a half-sister to 5 winners including Waiter's Dream (Group 3 Acomb Stakes) and the Irish listed 14f winner Lord Jim. (Mr P D Smith). *"He's a nice type of horse, well-made, with a good action. Mastercraftsman had a good first year at stud and these 2-y-o's are out of the good mares he got off the back of that early success".*

1625. UNNAMED ★★★
b.c. Camelot – Just Wondering (Danehill Dancer). January 29. Second foal. 100,000Y. Tattersalls October Book 2. Roger Varian. The dam, a moderate 7f placed 2-y-o, is a half-sister to 7 winners. The second dam, Ibtikar (by Private Account), a poor 6f (at 2 yrs) and 2m placed maiden, is closely related to the Grade 1 Hollywood Gold Cup, Charles H. Strub Stakes and Californian Stakes winner Desert Wine and a half-sister to 6 winners including the dual Grade 1 winner Menifee and to the unraced dam of the dual Group 1 winner and sire Fasliyev. (Mr Alan Spence). *"A nice horse that moves well and covers the ground, I like him and he'll be a seven furlong 2-y-o to start with".*

ED VAUGHAN
1626. COLOURFIELD (IRE) ★★
b.f. Makfi – Rainbow Desert (Dynaformer). March15. Fourth foal. 21,000Y. Tattersalls October Book 3. Paul Moroney. Half-sister to the unraced 2016 2-y-o The Raven Master by Raven's Pass). The dam, a quite useful 1m winner, is a half-sister to 7 winners including the US Grade 1 Del Mar Oaks winner Dublino. The second dam, Tuscoga (by Theatrical), was unplaced on 2 starts and is a sister to the Grade 1 Matriarch Stakes winner Duda and a half-sister to 5 winners. (Mr Paul Moroney). *"There's plenty of Dynaformer in this filly, she came in a little bit late to us, she's nice but*

she's one for later in the season. A scopey type and more of a 3-y-o really".

1627. PRIME MINISTER ★★★
b.c. Dream Ahead – Logica (Priolo). February 22. Fourteenth foal. 55,000Y. Tattersalls October Book 1. Mark Crossman. Half-brother to the Grade 1 Man O'War Stakes, Group 1 Hong Kong Vase (twice) and Group 2 Grand Prix de Deauville winner Doctor Dino (by Muhtathir), to the Japanese winner and Group 1 third Bande (by Authorized) and a winner in Scandinavia by Okawango. The dam, a minor French 3-y-o winner, is a half-sister to the Irish listed winner and useful broodmare Millie's Choice. The second dam, Salagangai (by Sallust), is an unraced half-sister to 7 winners. (Khalifa Dasmal). *"A lovely, big horse with a nice attitude. He has a bit of a knee action so he may want a bit of juice in the ground. He could be ok to start off at six furlongs but I'd say we'll see him over seven later on".*

1628. UNNAMED ★★
b.c. Nathaniel – Amelia May (Dansili). March 26. First foal. 50,000Y. Tattersalls October Book 2. Rabbah Bloodstock. The dam, a fair 1m and 9.5f placed maiden, is a half-sister to 6 winners including the useful 6f (at 2 yrs) and listed 1m winner Miss Pinkerton. The second dam, Rebecca Sharp (by Machiavellian), winner of the Group 1 1m Coronation Stakes, is a half-sister to 9 winners including the Group 3 11.5f Lingfield Derby Trial winner Mystic Knight. (Abdulla Al Mansoori). *"A lovely moving horse, he's one that will need fast ground and a trip. One for later in the year".*

1629. UNNAMED ★★★
b.br.f. Street Cry – Baghdaria (Royal Academy). April 12. $230,000Y. Keeneland September. Paul Moroney. Half-sister to 3 winners including one in Japan by Curlin. The dam, a US triple Grade 3 winner and Grade 2 placed twice, is a half-sister to 6 winners including the US Grade 1 winners Shackleford and Lady Joanne. The second dam, Oatsee (by Unbridled), was a stakes-placed dual winner at 3 yrs in the USA. (Ballymore Sterling Syndicate). *"A lovely filly with a proper pedigree, she only came in from*

America unbroken in January and came into the yard last week. A lovely filly with a great hip on her, I've only seen her cantering but I like what I see. She still has quite open knees so we'll take our time, but she'll develop into a nice filly for later on and as a 3-y-o. I think having Royal Academy as her broodmare sire is no bad thing".

1630. UNNAMED ★★★
b.f. Sepoy – Dreamily (New Approach). May 5. First foal. The dam, unplaced on both her starts, is a half-sister to 4 winners including the UAE Group 2 Godolphin Mile and listed King Charles II Stakes winner Calming Influence and to the Irish listed and subsequent Canadian Grade 2 winner Steel Light. The second dam, Idilic Calm (by Indian Ridge), a fair Irish 7f winner, is a half-sister to 4 winners. *"She'll take a bit of time as she's only just come in and she was a May foal. She doesn't really bend her knee which suggests she'd want fast ground. She has a good back-end on her, but she still needs to grow a bit in front and I should imagine she'd want seven furlongs. A nice looking filly with a good temperament".*

1631. UNNAMED ★★
gr.f. Champs Elysees – Miss University (Beau Genius). March 13. Thirteenth foal. 70,000Y. Tattersalls October Book 2. BBA (Ire). Half-sister to the US Grade 2 winner and triple Grade 1 placed Three Degrees (by Singspiel), to the useful 7f (at 2 yrs) and listed 6f winner of 6 races, Group 3 Bengough Stakes third and Group 1 Haydock Park Sprint Cup fourth Mehronissa (by Iffraaj) and two minor US winners by Singspiel and Manduro. The dam ran unplaced twice and is a half-sister to 9 winners. The second dam, Gorgeously Divine (by Al Hattab), is an unplaced half-sister to 3 winners. *"A lovely, big filly, she's got a lot of quality about her and covers the ground really well. I trained the half-sister Mehronissa and I think they have a lot of similarities. One for the second half of the season, I should imagine she'd just have a couple of runs this year. It was kind of the owners to send this filly to me".*

1632. UNNAMED ★★★
b.c. Oasis Dream – Roz (Teofilo). April 28. First foal. 180,000Y. Tattersalls October Book

1. Paul Moroney. The dam, a 2-y-o listed 7f Star Stakes winner, was second in the Group 1 Fillies' Mile and is a half-sister to the Australian Group 1 winner Hartnell. The second dam, Debonnaire (by Anabaa), a fair 7f (at 2 yrs) and 1m winner, is a half-sister to 4 winners including the useful 2-y-o 6f winner and listed-placed Proceed With Care and the useful 6f and 7f winner and listed-placed Dramatic Quest. (Sir Owen Glenn). *"He was a late foal and hasn't been in the yard very long. The owner had already bought the mare when Paul Moroney bought him this colt of hers. He's a nice, athletic colt that should be able to make his mark at two over six/seven furlongs".*

ED WALKER
1633. ASSASSINATOR ★★★
b.c. Hurricane Run – Saphira's Fire (Cape Cross). March 3. Fourth foal. 105,000Y. Tattersalls October Book 1. J Brummitt. Half-brother to the very useful 2-y-o Group 3 6f Grangecon Stud Stakes winner Most Beautiful (by Canford Cliffs) and to the modest dual 1m winner Pick Your Battle (by Makfi). The dam, a listed 10f winner, was twice placed third in the Group 2 Pride Stakes and is a half-sister to 2 winners. The second dam, All Our Hope (by Gulch), a winner at 3 yrs and third in the Group 2 Sun Chariot Stakes, is a half-sister to 7 winners. (Mr Bjorn Nielsen & East Wind Racing). *"A very classy colt, he's got a huge amount of the grandsire Montjeu about him, he's lengthy, has a great presence and looks like a Derby horse. At this stage he hasn't done a huge amount but he does everything well and we hope he'll be a nice horse later in the year".*

1634. BLACKHEATH ★★★
b.c. Excelebration – Da's Wish (Sadler's Wells). April 26. Fourth foal. €50,000Y. Tattersalls Ireland September. Sackville/Donald. The dam is an unraced half-sister to 7 winners including the listed winner Katiykha (dam of the Group 2 winner and Oaks third Katiyra). The second dam, Katiyfa (by Auction Ring), won the listed 1m Prix de la Calonne and is a half-sister to 3 winners. (Mr M J Cottis). *"A lovely colt, bred on the same lines as our good 3-y-o Ultimate Avenue, he's exceptionally good-looking and an exciting type for mid-summer onwards. He's a scopey*

but athletic colt that will make a nice 2-y-o but with the emphasis being on his 3-y-o career".

1635. CARADOC (IRE) ★★★ ♣
b.c. Camelot – Applause (Danehill Dancer). March 25. Fourth foal. 270,000Y. Tattersalls October Book 1. Sackville/Donald. Half-brother to the useful 2016 Irish 2-y-o 7f winner and dual Group 2 third Arcada (by Rip Van Winkle), to the fair 6f winner Awjab (by Bahamian Bounty) and the fair 14f and hurdles winner Evening Hush (by Excellent Art). The dam, a fairly useful dual 1m winner, is a half-sister to the listed winner and Group 2 Pretty Polly Stakes second Snippets and to the listed winner Need You Now. The second dam, Sniffle (by Shernazar), is an unplaced half-sister to 5 winners including the Group/Grade 1 winners Frenchpark and Pearly Shells. (Mr P K Siu). *"He's an exceptionally athletic, good-looking son of Camelot who looks to be an exciting first season sire. This colt has all the credentials of a top-class 3-y-o in the making and won't be over-raced this year. Hopefully he'll be a late summer/autumn 2-y-o from seven furlongs onwards".*

1636. DANCE EMPEROR ★★★
b.c. Holy Roman Emperor – Dance Avenue (Sadler's Wells). March 19. Fourth foal. Half-brother to the useful 2016 2-y-o 7f winner Ultimate Avenue (by Excelebration). The dam is an unraced half-sister to 6 winners including the Group-placed Middlemarch and Lady High Havens. The second dam, Blanche Dubois (by Nashwan), is an unraced half-sister to 10 winners including Indian Haven (Irish 2,000 Guineas), Count Dubois (Group 1 Gran Criterium). (Clipper Syndicate). *"A half-brother to our exciting 3-y-o Ultimate Avenue, this colt was sent to us by the breeder. He's a stereotypical son of Holy Roman Emperor in that he's not very big but very compact and strong. He'll be out in May over six furlongs I expect, he's showing up well and should have a busy campaign".*

1637. DANISH DANCER ★★★
ch.g. Sir Prancealot – Daneville (Danetime). February 28. Seventh foal. €42,000Y. Tattersalls Ireland September. Sackville/Donald. Half-brother to the fair 5f (at 2 yrs) and 6f winner of 4 races Dancheur (by

Chineur), to the fair 1m and hurdles winner Jubail (by Redback), the modest 5f winner Danzeb (by Zebedee) and two minor 3-y-o winners in Italy by Tillerman. The dam is an unraced half-sister to 4 winners. The second dam, Loveville (by Assert), is an unplaced half-sister to 9 winners. (Excel Racing). *"A good-looking, athletic son of Sir Prancealot who had a really good first season last year. The dam is a prolific producer of winners and I see no reason why this horse shouldn't follow suit. He's just starting to do a bit more now and should be out in May".*

1638. DESERT DOCTOR ★★★
ch.c. Society Rock – Dorn Hill (Lujain). January 29. Fifth foal. 115,000Y. Tattersalls October Book 2. Donald/Hillen. Half-brother to the smart 2-y-o listed 6f Prix Zeddaan winner and Group 2 Sapphire Stakes second Gracious John, to the modest dual 12f winner Helmsley Flyer (both by Baltic King) and a minor winner of 3 races in Italy by Chineur. The dam, a poor 6f winner at 3 yrs, is a half-sister to 3 other minor winners. The second dam, Benedicite (by Lomond), is an unraced half-sister to 5 winners including College Chapel (Group 2 Prix Maurice de Gheest). (Mrs F H Hay). *"Growing a lot now, he's going to be a 2-y-o for the second half of the season but he does everything very nicely. He's a half-brother to a good horse and he looks like a strong, well-made 2-y-o type that's got enough scope to be more than that in due course. I think he'll probably start over six furlongs".*

1639. ENZO (IRE) ★★★★
b.c. Exceed And Excel – Zamhrear (Singspiel). April 11. Sixth foal. 80,000Y. Tattersalls October Book 1. Sackville/Donald. Half-brother to the quite useful 2-y-o 8.5f winner Rainbow Dreamer (by Aqlaam) and to the quite useful 7f and 1m winner Capelita (by Cape Cross). The dam, a modest 7f and 1m winner, is a half-sister to 9 winners including the triple Group 3 winner Blue Monday and to the unraced dam of the dual Group 2 winning 2-y-o Mehmas. The second dam, Lunda (by Soviet Star), is an unplaced half-sister to 6 winners including the high-class middle-distance horses Luso (winner of the Aral-Pokal, the Italian Derby and the Hong Kong International Vase) and

Warrsan (Coronation Cup and Grosser Preis von Baden). (Mr P K Siu). *"A very athletic, racy type, the pedigree is slightly confusing because it's speed on stamina. I think this colt will start over six or seven furlongs around June time".*

1640. EXRATING ★★★

b.f. Exceed And Excel – Our Little Secret (Rossini). March 21. Seventh foal. 80,000Y. Tattersalls October Book 1. Not sold. Half-sister to the smart Group 2 Temple Stakes and dual listed 5f winner Pearl Secret (by Compton Place), to the quite useful 2-y-o 6f winner Secret Romance (by Sakhee's Secret), the quite useful 3-y-o 6f winner Pearl Bridge (by Avonbridge) and the fair 6f winner Get Up And Dance (by Makfi). The dam, a useful listed 5f winner of 6 races, is a half-sister to 3 winners. The second dam, Sports Post Lady (by M Double M), a fair 5f winner of 4 races, is a half-sister to 5 winners including the useful sprinter Palacegate Episode (a winner of 11 races here and abroad including a Group 3 race in Italy and numerous listed events). (Hot to Trot Racing). *"A lovely filly and a half-sister to Pearl Secret, she's a really exciting filly for later in the year. She's out for a spring break now but she's done plenty and done well. One for the mid-summer, she'll be a sprinter but not an early one".*

1641. FILLE DE REVE ★★★

b.f. Iffraaj – Danehill Dreamer (Danehill). April 7. Seventh foal. 85,000Y. Tattersalls October Book 2. J Brummitt. Half-sister to the fairly useful 6f (at 2 yrs) and 7f winner Sulaalaat (by New Approach), to the fairly useful 2-y-o 1m winner Madeed and the Qatar winner Khudoua (both by Nayef). The dam is an unraced half-sister to 8 winners including Compton Admiral (Group 1 Coral Eclipse Stakes), Summoner (Group 1 Queen Elizabeth II Stakes) and the dam of the multiple Group 1 winner The Fugue. The second dam, Sumoto (by Mtoto), a useful 6f (at 2 yrs) and 7f winner, is a half-sister to 5 winners. (Mr Bjorn Nielsen & Lord Lloyd Webber). *"A good-looking filly, the mare's done well but without producing anything top-class yet. This filly has made giant strides since the yearling sales and looks a nice 2-y-o type for July onwards".*

1642. GLOBAL EXCEL ★★★

b.c. Exceed And Excel – Seta (Pivotal). April 24. Third foal. 120,000Y. Tattersalls October Book 1. Sackville/Donald. Half-brother to the quite useful 2-y-o 6f winner Seastrom (by Oasis Dream). The dam, a very useful triple listed winner over 7f and 1m, was third in the Group 2 May Hill Stakes and is a half-sister to 8 winners including the Group 2 Prix de Pomone winner Armure and the listed winners Gravitas, Berlin Berlin and Affirmative Action. The second dam, Bombazine (by Generous), a useful 10f winner, is a half-sister to 7 winners including the Group 1 winners Barathea and Gossamer (herself dam of the Group 1 winner Ibn Khaldun). (Kangyu International (HK) Ltd & Dr Johnny Hon). *"I know the family very well having been at Luca Cumani's with this horse's dam Seta. He's done very well since the sales and although he won't be that forward he'll be a nice horse in time. We'd very much like to think he could win his maiden later on this season and then we can dream about his 3-y-o career".*

1643. GUNNER JULIUS ★★★

b.c. Lonhro – Peinture Ancienne (Seeking The Gold). February 28. Fifth foal. €200,000Y. Goffs Orby. Half-brother to 2 minor winners in North America by Giant's Causeway and Lemon Drop Kid. The dam is an unraced half-sister to 7 winners including the Prix de l'Arc de Triomphe, French Derby and Grand Prix de Paris winner Peintre Celebre and the French Group winners Peinture Rare and Pointilliste. The second dam, Peinture Bleue (by Alydar), a French listed and US Grade 2 12f winner, is a half-sister to the Group/Grade 3 winners Parme and Provins. (Mr P K Siu). *"He looks a 2-y-o, goes nicely and he's very well-made. All being well he could be out in June/July over six furlongs before stepping up to seven".*

1644. ISOLETTA ★★★

b.f. Oasis Dream – Miss Cap Estel (Hernando). February 25. First foal. The dam, a 1m (at 3 yrs) and listed 10.4f winner of 4 races, is a half-sister to the listed 9f winner St Jean Cap Ferrat. The second dam, Miss Cap Ferrat (by Darshaan), is an unplaced half-sister to 8 winners including the listed winners Miss Corniche and Miss Riviera Golf. (John Pearce Racing). *"A first foal, she's tiny but actually quite speedy and should be one of our first 2-y-o runners".*

1645. MAYGOLD ★★★
b.f. Mayson – Spanish Gold (Vettori). April 26. Eighth foal. Half-sister to 4 winners including the fairly useful listed-placed 6f winner of four races at 2 to 6 yrs Spanish Bounty (by Bahamian Bounty), the quite useful dual 6f winner King Ferdinand (by Tobougg) and the fair dual 6f winner Spanish Acclaim (by Acclamation). The dam, a fair 8.5f winner, is a half-sister to 4 winners. The second dam, Spanish Heart (by King Of Spain), a quite useful winner of 4 races over 7f and 1m, is a half-sister to 7 winners including the Group 3 sprint winner and smart broodmare Northern Goddess. (Sir Charles Hobhouse). *"A really sweet filly, she's very racy and could be a 2-y-o for May/June time over five/six furlongs all being well".*

1646. QUALITY SEEKER (USA) ★★★
b.c. Quality Road – Arravale (Arch). February 3. Third foal. €260,000Y. Goffs Orby. Sackville/Donald. Half- brother to the Canadian winner and Grade 2 Natalma Stakes third Nancy O (by Pivotal). The dam won the Grade 1 Del Mar Oaks and the Grade 1 E P Taylor Stakes and is a half-sister to 4 winners including the Canadian listed stakes winner Hollywood Hideaway. The second dam, Kalosca (by Kaldoun), a winner in France and the USA and Grade 2 third, is a half-sister to 6 winners. (Mr P K Siu). *"A very good-looking, athletic horse by a good American stallion, he won't be that early but he should be out in late summer. An exciting horse, albeit not an early one".*

1647. SIMPSON (IRE) ★★★ ♠
ch.c. Dragon Pulse – Salydora (Peintre Celebre). May 12. Tenth foal. €22,000Y. Goffs Orby. Sackville/Donald. Half-brother to four minor winners abroad by Dubawi, Green Tune, Oasis Dream and Halling. The dam, a listed 9f winner in France, is a half-sister to one winner. The second dam, Silwana (by Nashwan), a French 2-y-o 1m winner, is a half-sister to 7 winners including the French Group 2 Prix de Malleret winner Silver Fun. (Mr R Pegum). *"He was inexpensive but he looks quite smart. He does everything really*

well, especially considering he's out of a Peintre Celebre mare, and I think he'll be much sharper than a lot of his siblings have been. He could run in May over six furlongs". TRAINERS' BARGAIN BUY

1648. SINGING SHERIFF ★★★
b.c. Lawman – La Felicita (Shareef Dancer). April 1. Twelfth foal. 65,000Y. Tattersalls October Book 2. RPG Bloodstock. Half-brother to 8 winners including the Group 1 10f Prix de l'Opera and Group 3 10f Prix de la Nonette winner Lady Marian (by Nayef), the German Group 3 1m winner Lucidor (by Zafonic) and the fairly useful 2m winner of 4 races Lycidas (by Zamindar). The second dam, La Felicita (by Shareef Dancer), a listed-placed winner in Germany, is a half-sister to 4 winners. The second dam, La Concordia (by Surumu), a German listed-placed winner of 4 races, is a half-sister to 6 winners including the dams of the German Group 1 winners Lomitas and Lavirco. (Mr R Ng). *"A big, powerful colt, he's going to take some time but nevertheless he's very exciting. Both the sire and the dam are proven and he could be a really good 3-y-o. He should be able to make an impact at the end of this season and he's got a lot of class".*

1649. SOUMEI ★★★★
b.c. Epaulette – Zoumie (Mark Of Esteem). March 14. Fourth foal. 60,000Y. Tattersalls October Book 2. Sackville/Donald. Half-brother to the quite useful 2-y-o 7f winner Reddot Roman (by Holy Roman Emperor). The dam is an unraced half-sister to 5 winners including the listed 6f winner and multiple Group 3 placed Croisultan. The second dam, Zoudie (by Ezzoud), a fair 10f winner, is a half-sister to 7 winners including the dual Group 3 winner Redback. (Kangyu International (HK) Ltd). *"I really like this horse, he's an exceptionally good mover as I gather quite a few of the Epaulettes are. He's lengthy, does everything well, looks to have a bit of speed about him and could be a 2-y-o for mid-summer".*

1650. STEPHENSONS ROCKET ★★★★
gr.c. Teofilo – Tipperary Honor (Highest Honor). February 4. Seventh foal. €235,000Y. Arqana Deauville October. J Brummitt.

Brother to the French triple 1m winner at 2 and 3 yrs and listed-placed Vaunoise and half-brother to the French triple 1m winner at 2 and 3 yrs and Group 3 10f Prix La Force third Beauvoir (by Footstepsinthesand) . The dam, placed fourth once over 1m at 3 yrs, is a sister to the useful Irish 10f and 12f listed winner Tipperary All Star and half-sister to 5 winners including the US Grade 3 Laurel Dash winner Mayoumbe. The second dam, Moucha (by Fabulous Dancer), a winner of 3 races in France and listed-placed, is a half-sister to 7 winners including the US Grade 3 winner Daloma. (Mr B E Nielsen). *"A seriously nice colt. He's massive but I don't think he's backward and he could be out earlier then I first imagined. He has a very good way of going and he may be one to run before Ascot just in case he's good enough to go for the Chesham Stakes".*

1651. TOSHIMA (IRE) ★★
b.c. Sea The Stars – Sabreon (Caerleon). March 1. Eleventh living foal. 300,000Y. Tattersalls October Book 1. Sackville/Donald. Half-brother to 5 winners including the listed 1m and listed 10f winner and Group 1 Nassau Stakes second Moneycantbuymelove (by Pivotal), the quite useful 1m and hurdles winner Pillar Of Hercules (by Rock Of Gibraltar), the fair 9f and hurdles winner Osgood (by Danehill Dancer) and the fair 1m winner Moon Crystal (by Fasliyev). The dam, a quite useful 10.2f winner, is a half-sister to 8 winners including the French 2,000 Guineas and US Grade 1 winner Landseer and the listed winner and Group 1 placed Ikhtyar. The second dam, Sabria (by Miswaki), is an unraced half-sister to 5 winners. (Mr P K Siu). *"A very expensive colt and he's obviously very good-looking. He's growing, has a lot of class and thinks he's very good – he has a lot of personality. A back-end 2-y-o, he's very much bred to do well next year".*

1652. UNNAMED ★★★
ch.f. Speightstown – Latin Love (Danehill Dancer). March 16. Fourth foal. 110,000Y. Tattersalls October Book 1. J Brummitt. Half-sister to two minor winners abroad by Galileo. The dam, an Irish listed 1m and listed 9f winner and Grade 2 Canadian Stakes second, is a half-sister to two winners. The second

dam, Ho Hi The Moon (by Be My Guest), a minor French 3-y-o 9f winner, is a sister to the French listed winner Diner De Lune and a half-sister to 9 winners including the Group 1 Irish Oaks winner Moonstone, the Group 1 10f Prix Saint-Alary winner Cerulean Sky and the dual Group 1 second L'Ancresse. *"A very nice, racy filly that'll be out in April or early May. She does everything very easily and she's one that could be good enough to get us to Royal Ascot. Not very big but strong and compact, we'll try and make an impact early on with her".*

1653. UNNAMED ★★★
b.c. Swiss Spirit – Nolas Lolly (Lomitas). April 6. Fifth foal. 35,000Y. Tattersalls October Book 2. Sackville/Donald. Half-brother to the German listed 10f winner and Group 2 10f Prix de la Nonette second Holy Moly (by Mount Nelson) and to the fair 2-y-o 6f winner Queenie's Home (by Shamardal). The dam, a winner and Group 3 third in Germany, is a half-sister to 3winners including the US Grade 2 and Grade 3 winner Preachinatthebar and the French listed winner Royal Revival. The second dam, Holy Nola (by Silver Deputy), a stakes winner of 5 races in the USA, is a sister to the triple US Grade 3 winner Bare Necessities and a half-sister to 4 winners. (Mr Philip Afia & Lordship Stud). *"A really strong colt that looks like being a sprinter, I wouldn't be surprised if he was out in May. So far so good".*

1654. UNNAMED ★★★ ♠
b.f. Cape Cross – Oatcake (Selkirk). March 29. Seventh foal. Half-sister to the fairly useful 6f to 1m winner of 4 races Newstead Abbey (by Byron), to the quite useful Irish 6f and 1m and Scandinavian listed winner Coprah (by Bertolini) and the moderate 7f winner Motty's Gift (by Lucky Story). The dam, a moderate 6f placed 2-y-o, is a full or half-sister to 6 winners including the dual Group 3 5f winner Leap For Joy and to the unraced dam of the New Zealand champion King's Chapel. The second dam, Humble Pie (by Known Fact), a listed-placed 2-y-o 6f winner, is a half-sister to the high-class sprinter College Chapel. *"A lovely filly by an exceptional stallion, she still has a lot of growing and changing to do but she has a wonderful temperament and a great*

way of going. Her work will step up in mid-summer and I think she can have a decent crack at some late summer races with a view to having her best days as a 3-y-o".

1655. UNNAMED ★★★
b.c. Oasis Dream – Priceless Jewel (Selkirk). February 17. Second foal. 95,000Y. Tattersalls October Book 1. Not sold. Half-brother to Trilliant (by Dansili), unplaced in one start at 2 yrs in 2106. The dam, a quite useful 6.5f (at 2 yrs) and 6f winner, is a half-sister to 6 winners including the Group 1 6f Haydock Sprint Cup winner Tante Rose, the 2-y-o listed 7f winner Bay Tree and the dam of the Group 1 winners Make Believe and Dubawi Heights. The second dam, My Branch (by Distant Relative), won the listed 6f Firth Of Clyde Stakes (at 2 yrs) and the listed 7f Sceptre Stakes, was third in the Irish 1,000 Guineas and is a full or half-sister to 7 winners. (Mr B E Nielsen). *"A really nice colt, I train his half-brother the 3-y-o Trilliant. This guy is not early but he has a lot of class and is one for back-end maidens".*

CHRIS WALL

1656. BLACK LOTUS ★★★
b.f. Declaration Of War – Ravensburg (Raven's Pass). February 1. First foal. The dam, placed fourth once over 1m from two starts, is a half-sister to 6 winners including the Group 2 12f King Edward VII Stakes and dual Group 3 winner High Accolade. The second dam, Generous Lady (by Generous), a listed-placed middle-distance winner of 4 races in Ireland, is a half-sister to 6 winners including the Italian Group 2 winner Jape. (Raymond Tooth). *"By a first season sire and out of a nice mare I trained who was actually quite nice but only ran twice and got injured, so she wasn't able to race again. We've done quite well with the family, this filly is growing at the moment and I see her as a seven furlong filly in the summer. I quite like her, she's a nice, scopey filly with a good attitude, so I'm hoping she'll do alright for us".*

1657. ECLAIRANTE (IRE) ★★
b.f. High Chaparral – Revealing (Halling). April 13. Twelfth foal. 11,000Y. Tattersalls December. Chris Wall. Half-sister to the useful French 2-y-o dual 6f winner and Group 3 1m third Grand Vista (by Danehill), to the

useful French 7f (at 2 yrs) and 1m winner and listed placed World Ruler, the French 1m winner and listed-placed Disclose and the French 2-y-o 6f winner Concealing (all by Dansili). The dam, a very useful 2-y-o 1m winner, is a half-sister to 6 winners including the useful 12f winner and dual Group 3 placed Singleton. The second dam, Rive (by Riverman), a French 2-y-o 10f winner, is a half-sister to 10 winners. (Hughes, Scott & Mackenzie). *"She'll want a bit of time, we picked her up fairly cheaply at the December sales and she's from an Abdulla family, although the mare is quite old. A nice filly and fairly typical of the sire in many respects physically, she'll want time to grow and strengthen. She'll have a couple of runs later on for experience and be better next year".* TRAINERS' BARGAIN BUY

1658. EQUO ★★★
b.c. Equiano – Catfish (One Cool Cat). April 7. Second foal. Half-brother to Catskill (by Dutch Art), unplaced on her first outing at 3 yrs in 2017. The dam, a quite useful 6f (at 2 yrs) and 5f winner of 3 races, is a half-sister to 3 winners here and abroad. The second dam, Castellane (by Danehill), placed 10 times in France including over 10f, is a half-sister to 9 winners including the dam of the Group 1 Criterium de Saint-Cloud winner Shaka. (Raymond Tooth). *"He ought to be a 2-y-o because he's by a speedy stallion and the mare was fast as well. He's been growing and we haven't done much with him yet, but I'd have thought he'd be a five or six furlong horse in mid-summer. A fairly solid horse that seems to go along ok".*

1659. FOLLOW INTELLO (IRE) ★★
b.c. Intello – Sauvage (Sri Pekan). April 27. Fifth foal. 85,000Y. Tattersalls October Book 2. Not sold. Half-brother to 4 winners including the quite useful triple 1m winner Bassara (by Oasis Dream), the modest 10f and 11f winner Posh Boy (by Duke Of Marmalade) and the modest 7f winner Luang Prabang (by Invincible Spirit). The dam won 5 races at 2 to 5 yrs in France and the USA including the Grade 2 Sheepshead Bay Handicap and is a half-sister to 4 winners including the German Group 3 winner Eyeq. The second dam, Sans Prix (by Caerleon), won over 9f in Ireland and

is a half-sister to 3 winners. (Ms Aida Fustoq). *"He's a big horse, I think we've had them all out of the mare so far and they've all been quite big. He'll be a 3-y-o really, but he's a nice type and I was quite impressed with the sire's yearlings at the sales so I'm hoping he'll be ok one day".*

1660. JUMPING CATS ★★★
ch.c. Champs Elysees – Pivotal Drive (Pivotal). April 15. Sixth foal. 32,000Y. Tattersalls October Book 2. Chris Wall. Half-brother to the 2016 2-y-o 7f winner, from two starts, Private Mission (by Sepoy), to the fairly useful 1m to 14f winner of 6 races Swivel (by Shirocco), the quite useful 6f (including at 2 yrs) and 7f winner Meet Me Halfway (by Exceed And Excel) and the quite useful 6f and 7f winner Courier (by Equiano). The dam is an unraced half-sister to 4 winners including the listed 1m and 10f winner Sublimity and the UAE Group 3 1m winner Marbush. The second dam, Fig Tree Drive (by Miswaki), a fairly useful 2-y-o 6f winner on her only start, is a half-sister to 4 winners. (Des Thurlby). *"He's a half-brother to a filly I trained for the same owner called Meet Me Halfway and she was quite useful. I quite like this colt, he's not going to be a sprinting 2-y-o but that's only to be expected from a Champs Elysees. He's the sort for seven furlongs or a mile later in the season but he creates a favourable impression".*

1661. PENTLAND HILLS (IRE) ★★★
b.c. Motivator – Elle Galante (Galileo). February 26. Seventh foal. 40,000Y. Tattersalls October Book 2. C F Wall. Half-brother to the 1m (at 2 yrs) and Group 2 12f King Edward VII Stakes winner Balios (by Shamardal), to the fair 6f and French 6.5f winner Cersei (by Invincible Spirit) and the modest 10f and hurdles winner Camlann (by Cape Cross). The dam, a German listed-placed 11f winner of 3 races, is a sister to the German listed winner Elle Gala and a half-sister to 9 winners. The second dam, Elle Danzig (Roi Danzig), won the Group 1 Premio Roma (twice) and the Group 1 10f Grosser Preis Bayerisches Zuchtrennen and is a half-sister to 10 winners. (Des Thurlby). *"A nice colt and a half-brother to Balios who was a Group 2 winner for David Simcock. He wasn't expensive but that's*

probably the Motivator factor, he's got plenty of stamina in his pedigree and he'll be a seven furlong/mile horse later on this year. He goes well and does everything right, so hopefully he'll be alright. So far he appears to be one of the sane Motivators – we watched him very closely at the sales just in case".

1662. SPRITZIG ★★★
ch.f. Exceed And Excel – Generous Lady (Generous). April 20. Fourteenth foal. 35,000Y. Tattersalls October Book 2. Not sold. Half-sister to 7 winners including the very smart 7f (at 2 yrs), Group 2 12f King Edward VII Stakes and dual Group 3 12f Cumberland Lodge Stakes winner High Accolade (by Mark Of Esteem), the useful 9f (at 2 yrs) and 13f winner and listed-placed Oasis Knight (by Oasis Dream) and the quite useful 12f to 2m winner Highland Legacy (by Selkirk). The dam, a middle-distance winner of 4 races in Ireland and listed-placed, is a half-sister to 6 winners including the Italian Group 2 and Group 3 winner Jape. The second dam, Northern Blossom (by Snow Knight), was a champion 3-y-o filly in Canada and won two Graded stakes events. (Ms Aida Fustoq). *"She's a three-parts sister to a nice filly we have called Mix And Mingle because she's by the same sire and out of that filly's grandam. The mare is getting quite old, but it's quite a nice family that's done well for the Fustoq stud and we've had a few nice ones out of it. The cross seems to work quite well and this is a nice filly that does everything easily, the dam was a stayer herself but Exceed And Excel does put speed into them. I'd expect this filly to go six/seven furlongs this year, she's very athletic and I quite like her".*

1663. THE FIDDLER ★★
b.c. Big Bad Bob – Strings (Unfuwain). March 18. Ninth foal. 17,000Y. Tattersalls October Book 3. Chris Wall. Half-brother to the fairly useful 2-y-o 1m winner State Opera (by Shamardal), to the quite useful dual 7f (at 2 yrs) and dual 10f winner Bahamian Flight (by Bahamian Bounty), the quite useful 1m and 10f winner of 4 races Qanan (by Green Desert) and a minor winner at 2 and 3 yrs in Germany by Exceed And Excel. The dam is an unraced half-sister to 6 winners including the French 2,000 Guineas winner Victory Note.

The second dam, Three Piece (by Jaazeiro), an Irish placed 2-y-o, is a half-sister to 8 winners including Orchestration (Group 2 Coronation Stakes) and Welsh Term (Group 2 Prix d'Harcourt). (The Equema Partnership). *"We had his half-brother Qanan who was decent but took time. I think this colt will be a bit more forward than he was, but he's growing at the moment and he's a fairly typical Big Bad Bob because he's a dark bay and compact. I should think he'd be more a horse for further down the line, but I'm happy with him, he does everything right and he should be a longer-term prospect for his owners".*

1664. VANTASY ★★
b.c. Rip Van Winkle – Tesary (Danehill). March 22. Seventh foal. 12,500Y. Tattersalls October Book 4. Peter Botham. Half-brother to the quite useful 5f (at 2 yrs) and 6f winner of 4 races Englishman (by Royal Applause), to the quite useful 5f (at 2 yrs) and 6f winner Verbeeck (by Dutch Art), the fair 5f and 6f winner of 4 races Englishwoman (by Acclamation) and the modest 1m winner Merton Lady (by Beat Hollow). The dam, a useful 5f (at 2 yrs) to 7f winner, is a half-sister to 5 winners. The second dam, Baldemara (by Sanglamore), is an unraced half-sister to 5 winners including the Group 1 5.5f Prix Robert Papin winner Balbonella (herself dam of the top-class sprinter Anabaa, the French 1,000 Guineas winner Always Loyal and the useful sire Key Of Luck). (Mr P Botham & Mrs M Tilbrook). *"A cheap purchase and a fairly big colt, he goes along ok, he's a nice mover and pretty sensible. He'll be ok in time but he's a slightly longer-term project I think. The dam has bred sprinters but to speedier sires than Rip Van Winkle and I haven't seen any sprinting speed in him yet".*

ARCHIE WATSON
1665. AMAZING ALICE ★★★★
b.f. Sayif – Dot Hill (Refuse To Bend). February 27. Fourth foal. 20,000Y. Tattersalls October Book 3. Kilbride Equine. Half-sister to the modest 2016 6f placed 2-y-o Mary Brady (by Camacho) and to the fairly useful listed-placed dual 5f winner at 2 and 3 yrs Union Rose (by Stimulation). The dam is an unraced half-sister to 3 winners including the very useful 6f (at 2 yrs) and 5f winner of 4 races

and Group 2 6f Gimcrack Stakes second Taajub. The second dam, Purple Tiger (by Rainbow Quest), is an unraced half-sister to 6 winners including the German Group 2 winner and Italian Group 1 second Notability and the Group 3 7f Prix La Force winner Simon De Montfort. (Mr C R Hirst). *"She's a filly we like a lot and I expect her to be out over five furlongs around late April/early May. She's doing everything right at the moment and she has the scope to be going six furlongs later on. A good-sized, scopey filly".*

1666. ARDEN PEARL (IRE) ★★★
b.f. Swiss Spirit – Music Pearl (Oratorio). February 25. Second foal. 23,000Y. Tattersalls October Book 3. Blandford Bloodstock/ Archie Watson. Half-sister to the fair 6f winner of 4 races at 3 and 4 yrs Born To Finish (by Dark Angel). The dam, a fair Irish 8.5f winner, is a half-sister to 4 winners including the smart 7f (at 2 yrs) and Group 3 1m Desmond Stakes winner Haami. The second dam, Qumaldaaya (by Swain), a very useful filly 7f (at 2 yrs) and Group 2 10f Premio Lydia Tesio winner, is a half-sister to 6 winners including the Derby winner Erhaab. (Jack & Freya Cork). *"Small and racy, she definitely has ability and I think she'll be out over five furlongs in May. She's quick and I like her a lot".*

1667. ARDEN PULSE (IRE) ★★★
b.c. Dragon Pulse – Rose Bourbon (Woodman). April 20. Fifteenth foal. €23,000Y. Tattersalls Ireland September. Blandford Bloodstock / A Watson. Half-brother to 7 winners including the useful 2-y-o listed 7f Acomb Stakes winner and Group 3 7f Vintage Stakes second Bourbonnais (by Singspiel), the French 2-y-o 5f and 6f winner and dual listed placed Princess Roseburg (by Johannesburg), the fair Irish dual 1m winner Georgina (by Polish Precedent) and the North American winner of 10 minor races Artefacto (by Officer). The dam was listed-placed twice in France at up to 1m and is a half-sister to 5 stakes winners including the French 1,000 Guineas winner Baiser Vole, the smart French sprinter Tenue de Soiree and the very smart 1m to 10f colt Squill. The second dam, River Rose (by Riverman), was a listed winner of 5 races over 5f at 2 yrs. (Jack & Freya Cork).

"A nice little colt, he had a little hold-up at the beginning of the year but he shows plenty of speed and he'll be out over six furlongs. He's strong and from what he showed us before Christmas he's got ability".

1668. COME ON BEAR (IRE) ★★★

b.f. Dandy Man – Blusienka (Blues Traveller). March 9. Eleventh foal. £33,000Y. Goffs UK Premier (Doncaster). Blandford Bloodstock / Archie Watson. Half-sister to the very useful 6f (at 2 yrs) and Group 3 7f Tetrarch Stakes winner Energised (by Captain Rio), to the fairly useful 2-y-o 7f winner and Group 3 7f Tattersalls Stakes second Control Zone (by Daggers Drawn), the quite useful Irish 6f winner Urbestchance (by Zebedee) and the moderate Irish 5f and 6f winner Missile Command (by Majestic Missile). The dam, a useful 2-y-o 1m winner, was third in the listed Masaka Stakes and is a sister to 2 winners. The second dam, Pudgy Poppet (by Danehill), unplaced in one start, is a half-sister to 3 minor winners. (M7 Come On Bear LLP). *"A beautiful mover, she has a lovely page and she's a big, scopey filly that'll take a bit of time. I hope to have her out over six or seven furlongs around June time. A filly with a bit of something about her".*

1669. CORINTHIA KNIGHT (IRE) ★★★★ ♣

ch.c. Society Rock – Victoria Lodge (Grand Lodge). January 26. Eight foal. €15,000Y. Tattersalls Ireland September. Blandford Bloodstock / A Watson. Half-brother to 4 winners including the quite useful 5f (at 2 yrs) to 1m winner of 10 races Chiswick Bey (by Elusive City), the minor Italian listed-placed winner North Ireland (by Zebedee) and the fair 2-y-o 6f winner Lady Victory (by Kheleyf). The dam is an unraced half-sister to 2 winners including the French 2-y-o Group 2 second Ascot Glory. The second dam, Lake Victoria (by Lake Coniston), was listed-placed in Ireland and is a half-sister to 5 winners including the US Grade 1 winner Delighter and the Oaks third Oakmead. (Ontoawinner & Partner). *"He might well be the sire's first winner, but it might also be before the book is published. He's a very nice little horse, everything he does is straightforward, he's a January foal, a half-brother to a Brocklesby winner and he does exactly what it says on*

the tin. He's pleased us from day one and definitely has the ability to win races at two". This colt won quite impressively on his debut in April.*

1670. DEADLY REEL (IRE) ★★★

b.f. Pour Moi – Lady Ederle (English Channel). February 23. First foal. €60,000Y. Goffs Orby. Lillingston Bloodstock. The dam, a placed at 2 yrs in the USA, is a half-sister to 7 winners including the Italian Group 3 winner Fathayer and to the placed Dabirsim (dam of the dual Group 1 winning 2-y-o Dabirsim). The second dam, Bright Generation (by Rainbow Quest), winner of the Group 1 Italian Oaks and second in the Group 1 Moyglare Stud Stakes, is a half-sister to 5 winners. (Chasemore Farm LLP). *"She's not the biggest, so I imagine she won't take too long. Doing everything very easily at the moment, she's bred to stay but I'd like to think we can have her out in one of the early seven furlong races in June. She's nice and straightforward, so in that regard she's not typical of some by the sire!"*

1671. HEADLINE ACT ★★★

ch.f. Helmet – Accede (Acclamation). April 2. Fifth foal. £23,000Y. Goffs UK Premier (Doncaster). Blandford Bloodstock / Archie Watson. Half-sister to the fair 2-y-o 6f winner Poster Girl (by Excellent Art) and to the quite useful 7f (at 2 yrs) to 8.5f winner of 5 races Miss Van Gogh (by Dutch Art). The dam, a quite useful 2-y-o 6f winner, is a half-sister to 2 winners. The second dam, Here To Me (by Muhtarram), a fair 6f winner, is a half-sister to 5 winners. (Mr A Watson). *"A lovely filly, she moves beautifully and was looking like being very early but now I think she'll be a six furlong filly around mid-May. She's got talent and the family all perform at two. I like her a lot".*

1672. MERCER'S TROOP (IRE) ★★

b.c. Canford Cliffs – Meek Appeal (Woodman). April 29. Eleventh foal. €32,000Y. Tattersalls Ireland September. Blandford Bloodstock / A Watson. Half-brother to 6 winners including the 2-y-o 1m winner and Group 3 10f Mooresbridge Stakes second Triumphant (by Danehill Dancer) and the fair 10f winners Spinners Ball (by Excellent Art) and Ferdinand Magellan (by Montjeu). The dam won 2 races in Japan and is a half-sister to 9 winners. The second dam, Mozartiana (by Nijinsky), is an unraced half-sister to the champion 2-y-o's El Gran Senor and Try My Best. (Mr G P M Morland). *"A really nice colt, he moves beautifully but he's just been going through a growth spurt and is filling out again now. He'll tell us when he's ready, but he'll kick off over seven furlongs and he's a lovely prospect for his 3-y-o career".*

1673. SAVANNAH DUSK ★★★

b.f. Dream Ahead – First Class Favour (Exceed And Excel). March 14. First foal. €25,000 foal. Goffs November. Richard Knight. The dam, a fair 5f to 7f (at 2 yrs) and 1m winner of 7 races, is a half-sister to 3 winners including the fairly useful 6f and 7f winner and subsequent US Grade 2 second Mister Brightside. The second dam, Lamh Eile (by Lord Shanakill), a quite useful 2-y-o 6f and 7f winner, is a half-sister to 5 winners. (Elaine Chivers & Merlin Racing). *"She arrived in January and has always done everything easily. Out of an Exceed And Excel mare, she shows plenty of speed and I think she's talented. Hopefully we'll have her out over five furlongs in May and she's a nice filly".*

1674. SONG OF SUMMER ★★★

ch.f. Choisir – Height Of Summer (Alhaarth). March 25. Second foal. Half-sister to Aryeh (by Exceed And Excel), placed fourth over 8.5f at 3 yrs in 2017. The dam, a modest 10f winner, is a half-sister to the US Grade 1 9.5f Beverly D Stakes and Group 3 9f Dahlia Stakes winner I'm A Dreamer and to the fairly useful 2-y-o 7f winner and Group 3 Autumn Stakes third Moudez. The second dam, Summer Dreams (by Sadler's Wells), a fair 10f and 14f placed maiden, is a half-sister to the Group 1 German Derby winner All My Dreams. (Al Asayl Bloodstock). *"A home-bred, she had a little hold-up when she was being broken in but she's caught up now and I like her a lot. I've always been a big fan of the stallion, I think this filly is tough and although she's scopey we'll kick her off over six furlongs around May or June time".*

1675. WE ARE THE WORLD (IRE) ★★★★

b.c. Sir Percy – Emerald Sea (Green Desert). February 27. First foal. €22,000Y. Tattersalls

Ireland September. Blandford Bloodstock/ A Watson. The dam, a modest 5f placed maiden, is a half-sister to one minor winner. The second dam, the Canadian stakes winner Wind Surf (by Lil's Lad), is a half-sister to 3 winners in Japan and the USA. (C R Hirst). *"He's a very nice horse – the best I've got. He's got plenty of size and scope and looks like a 3-y-o already, does everything very easily and hopefully he'll turn into a nice seven furlong/ miler at the back end, but he's definitely forward enough to run over six at the end of May. We'll step up to seven fairly quickly after that and hopefully he'll go somewhere nice".* TRAINERS' BARGAIN BUY

DERMOT WELD

1676. ALLANA'A LEANBH (IRE) ★★★

b.f. Lawman – Kartiste (Kalanisi). May 7. Third foal. 50,000Y. Tattersalls October Book 2. BBA (Ire). Half-sister to the quite useful triple 5f winner at 2 and 3 yrs Go Kart (by Intense Focus). The dam is an unraced half-sister to 2 minor winners. The second dam, Kart Star (by Soviet Star), won the listed Prix Coronation and is a half-sister to 5 winners including the listed winner and Group 1 French 1,000 Guineas second Karmifira. (Chanelle Pharmaceuticals). *"A sharp filly, she's quite forward and she'll be out in June. A six/seven furlong 2-y-o".*

1677. ALESSANDRO ALLORI (IRE) ★★★★

ch.c. Dawn Approach – Truly Mine (Rock Of Gibraltar). January 19. Seventh foal. 170,000Y. Tattersalls October Book 1. Chantal Regalado Gonzalez. Half-brother to the listed 6f (at 2 yrs) and Group 3 6f winner Only Mine (by Pour Moi), to the useful 1m, 10f (both at 2 yrs) and 12f winner Miner's Lamp (by Shamardal), the quite useful Irish 10f winner Truthwillsetyoufree (by Dalakhani) and the 2-y-o 7.5f winner Colour Rhapsody (by Rip Van Winkle). The dam, a useful listed 11f winner and third in the Group 3 1m Park Express Stakes, is a half-sister to 3 winners including the listed winner True To Form. The second dam, Truly Yours (by Barathea), a French 2-y-o 1m winner, is a half-sister to the French Group 2 winner Dream Peace and the French 2,000 Guineas second Catcher In The Rye. (Mrs C C Ragalado-Gonzalez). *"A very, very nice colt. I see him as a seven furlong colt from July onwards".*

1678. BETSEY TROTTER (IRE) ★★★
b.f. Camacho – Inourthoughts (Desert Style).
March 18. Fifth foal. 125,000Y. Tattersalls
October Book 2. Bobby O'Ryan / D K Weld.
Half-sister to the quite useful 2016 2-y-o dual
5f winner Tilly Trotter (by Kodiac) and to the
fair 2-y-o dual 6f winner Focusofourthoughts
(by Intense Focus). The dam, a quite useful
Irish 2-y-o 5f winner, is a half-sister to 3
winners including the 2-y-o Group 2 Flying
Childers Stakes winner Green Door. The
second dam, Inourhearts (by Pips Pride), a
useful listed 5f winner of 4 races, is a half-
sister to 2 winners. (Frank Gillespie). *"She's
a sharp filly but she's grown over the past
month. Nevertheless she's a 2-y-o type and
I could see her racing from the end of May/
early June onwards over five and six furlongs".*

1679. CENTROID ★★★
b.c. Dansili – Concentric (Sadler's Wells).
February 13. Fifth foal. Half-brother to the
2016 2-y-o 1m winner on her only start
Enable (by Nathaniel), to the French 1m 7f
winner and Group 2 second Contribution (by
Champs Elysees) and the quite useful triple
1m winner Tournament (by Oasis Dream).
The dam, a useful French listed 10f winner,
was second in the Group 3 10.5f Prix de Flore
and is a sister to the Group 2 12.5f Prix de
Royallieu winner Dance Routine and to the
French 11f winner and Group 3 placed Light
Ballet, closely related to the dual Group 3 1m
winner Apsis and a half-sister to the listed
12f winner Space Quest. The second dam,
Apogee (by Shirley Heights), won the Group
3 12f Prix de Royaumont and is a half-sister
to the Group 2 12f Grand Prix de Chantilly
winner Daring Miss. (Khalid Abdulla). *"He's a
big, powerful colt and one for September or
October".*

1680. CHATEAU LA FLEUR (IRE) ★★★★
b.f. Frankel – Cassydora (Darshaan). February
21. Fifth foal. 900,000Y. Tattersalls October
Book 1. Moyglare Stud. Sister to the 2016
French 2-y-o Group 3 1m Prix d'Aumale
winner Toulifout, closely related to the smart
Group 3 12f Ballyroan Stakes and dual Group
3 14f Curragh Cup winner Ernest Hemingway
and to the hurdles winner Milestone (both
by Galileo). The dam, a useful 7f (at 2 yrs),
listed Lingfield Oaks Trial and subsequent
US Grade 3 winner, was second in the

Group 1 Nassau Stakes and is a half-sister
to 5 winners including the listed 10f winner
Classic Remark. The second dam, Claxon (by
Caerleon), a Group 2 10f Premio Lydia Tesio
winner, is a half-sister to 3 winners including
the Group 2 placed Bulwark. (Moyglare Stud
Farm). *"She's a very, very nice filly, not big but
one for September or October. A small but
quality filly".*

1681. CHIARA LUNA (USA) ★★★★★
b.br.f. War Front – Princess Highway (Street
Cry). March 16. First foal. The dam, winner of
the Group 2 12f Ribblesdale Stakes and third
in the Irish Oaks, is a half-sister to the smart
Irish Group 3 7f Gladness Stakes winner and
multiple Group 1 placed Mad About You and
the smart Group 1 Irish St Leger and dual
Group 3 winner of 9 races Royal Diamond.
The second dam, Irresistible Jewel (by
Danehill), won the Group 2 12f Ribblesdale
Stakes and the Group 3 10f Blandford Stakes
and is a half-sister to numerous winners
including the listed 12f winner Diamond Trim
and the useful Irish 1m winner Legal Jousting.
(Moyglare Stud Farms Ltd). *"A very likeable
filly, I could see her being out over seven
furlongs in July. Add an extra star for her,
because she's one of those I particularly like".*

1682. CHILLED WHITE (IRE) ★★★
b.f. Dawn Approach – Miss Corinne (Mark
Of Esteem). April 20. Eighth living foal.
€140,000Y. Goffs Orby. Moyglare Stud. Half-
sister to 5 winners including the Group 3 7f 3
Prix du Calvados (at 2 yrs), Group 3 Nell Gwyn
Stakes and US Grade 3 9f winner Sandiva
(by Footstepsinthesand), the useful 2-y-o
7f, 1m and subsequent Danish listed winner
Wentworth (by Acclamation), the 5f (at 2 yrs)
to 1m winner and listed-placed Irish Cliff (by
Marju) and the modest 2-y-o 6f and 7f winner
Captain Loui (by Verglas). The dam won 6
races in Italy and is a half-sister to 4 winners.
The second dam, Percy's Girl (by Blakeney),
a useful 10f winner, is a sister to the Group 3
winner Percy's Lass (herself dam of the Derby
winner Sir Percy) and a half-sister to Braiswick
(Grade 1 E P Taylor Stakes). (Moyglare Stud
Farm). *"She's pretty forward and I'd hope to
have her out in June/July over six furlongs.
From a precocious family but early days as far
as the sire is concerned".*

1683. CLIQUE ★★★
ch.f. Bated Breath – Insinuate (Mr Prospector).
February 18. Closely related to the useful
2-y-o 7f winner Convey (by Dansili) and
half-sister to the Group 3 7f Supreme Stakes
winner Stronghold (by Danehill), the listed
10f winner Take The Hint (by Montjeu), the
fairly useful 1m and 10f winner Hanseatic
(by Galileo), the quite useful 8.7f winner Imply
(by Beat Hollow) and the fair 9.5f winner
Indication (by Sadler's Wells). The dam, a
useful listed 1m winner, is a half-sister to
numerous winners including the useful 6f
and 7f winner and listed-placed Imroz. The
second dam, All At Sea (by Riverman), won
the Group 1 Prix du Moulin and was second
in the Oaks, the Juddmonte International and
the Nassau Stakes. (Khalid Abdulla). *"She's
a quality filly and probably one for seven
furlongs in July or August".*

1684. CONTINGENT ★★★★
b.f. Frankel – Proportional (Beat Hollow).
February 7. Second foal. Half-sister to the
listed 12f winner Variable (by Sea The Stars).
The dam, winner of the Group 1 1m Prix
Marcel Boussac, is sister to one winner a
half-sister to 2 winners. The second dam,
Minority (by Generous), won over 11f, was
Group 3 placed twice and is a half-sister to
numerous winners including the 2-y-o listed
7f winner Innocent Air and the French listed
and US stakes winner and US Grade 1 placed
Skipping. (Khalid Abdulla). *"Very much a
quality filly. She's a lovely, big 2-y-o and one
for September or October over seven furlongs
to a mile".*

1685. ENEZA (IRE) ★★★
b.f. Holy Roman Emperor – Eytarna (Dubai
Destination). April 7. Half-sister to the 2016
2-y-o Group 3 7f CL & MF Weld Park Stakes
winner Eziyra (by Teofilo), to the listed 1m
winner Eshera (by Oratorio) and to the fair
12f winner Enzani (by Cape Cross). The
dam, a fairly useful 9f and 12f winner, was
listed-placed and is a half-sister to numerous
winners including the Group 1 Irish Oaks
and Group 1 Prix Royal-Oak winner Ebadiyla,
the smart Group 1 7f Moyglare Stud Stakes
winner Edabiya and the high-class Ascot Gold
Cup winner Enzeli. (H H Aga Khan). *"She's a
sharp filly and I could see her being out in June
or July over six/seven furlongs".*

1686. FALCON EIGHT (IRE) ★★★
b.c. Galileo – Polished Gem (Danehill).
February 20. Seventh foal. Half-brother to
the Group 1 10f Prince Of Wales's Stakes
winner Free Eagle (by High Chaparral), to
the Group 2 12f British Champions Fillies'
and Mares Stakes and dual Group 3 winner
Sapphire (by Medicean) and the very smart
triple Group 2 1m and triple Group 3 winner
Custom Cut (by Notnowcato). The dam, an
Irish 2-y-o 7f winner, is a sister to the Grade
1 9f Matriarch Stakes and Group 2 1m Sun
Chariot Stakes winner Dress To Thrill and a
half-sister to 7 winners. The second dam,
Trusted Partner (by Affirmed), won the Irish
1,000 Guineas and is a sister to the useful
winners Easy to Copy, Epicure's Garden and
Low Key Affair. (Moyglare Stud Farm). *"He's
a nice colt but definitely one for the second
half of the year. Probably September or
October over seven furlongs".*

1687. FILLE DU SEPTEMBRE (IRE) ★★★★
b.f. Choisir – Rocking (Oasis Dream). April 10.
Sixth foal. €130,000Y. Goffs Orby. Moyglare
Stud. Half-sister to the fairly useful 2-y-o 5f
winner and 3-y-o Group 3 6f Ballyogan Stakes
second Boston Rocker (by Acclamation), to
the fairly useful triple 6f winner Mustallib (by
Iffraaj), the fair 2-y-o 5f winner Rocking The
Boat (by Zebedee) and the modest 2-y-o 5f
winner Sleepy Joe (by Jeremy). The dam, a
quite useful 2-y-o 5f winner, is a half-sister to
10 winners including the very smart Group
2 5f Flying Childers Stakes winner Superstar
Leo (herself the dam of two stakes winners).
The second dam, Council Rock (by General
Assembly), a fair 9f and 10f placed 3-y-o, is a
half-sister to 9 winners including the dam of
the Group 1 winners Footstepsinthesand and
Pedro The Great. (Moyglare Stud Farm). *"A
winner already and my only 2-y-o runner so
far. She'll go for a listed race in mid-May over
six furlongs for fillies at Naas. A sharp filly and
a smart one too".*

1688. FLAVIUS (USA) ★★★★
b.c. War Front – Starformer (Dynaformer).
February 16. First foal. The dam, a US Grade 2
10f and triple Grade 3 winner, is a half-sister
to a minor winner in the USA. The second
dam, Etoile Montante (by Miswaki), won
Group 1 7f Prix de la Foret and is a half-sister
to the listed-placed winner Starfan and

to the dam of the French Group 3 winner Glaswegian. (Khalid Abdulla). "He's a very nice colt from a good family and he'll appear in July or August over seven furlongs. He's one I particularly like".

1689. HARBOUR APPROACH ★★★
b.g. Dawn Approach – Portodora (Kingmambo). February 27. Fifth foal. Closely related to the quite useful 9f (at 2 yrs) and 10f winner Dissolution (by New Approach) and half-brother to the fairly useful 2-y-o 7f winner Tempera (by Dansili) and the fairly useful 7f winner of four races Peril (by Pivotal). The dam, a quite useful dual 7f winner, is a half-sister to 2 winners. The second dam, High Walden (by El Gran Senor), a smart 2-y-o 1m winner, was Group-placed and is closely related to the Oaks, Fillies Mile, Musidora Stakes and May Hill Stakes winner Reams of Verse and a half-sister to the Group 1 10f Coral Eclipse Stakes and Group 1 10f Phoenix Champion Stakes winner Elmaamul (by Diesis). (Khalid Abdulla). "He's strong and he'll make a 2-y-o in July or August over seven furlongs".

1690. HAZEL BAY (IRE) ★★★
b.f. Iffraaj – Sadima (Sadler's Wells). April 14. Tenth foal. Half-sister to the Group 1 12f Grand Prix de Saint-Cloud and German Group 1 12f winner Youmzain, to the minor Irish 12f winner Spontaneous (both by Sinndar), the Group 1 1m Lockinge Stakes and dual Group 3 winner Creachadoir, the fair 12f winner Savida (both by King's Best), the Irish Group 3 9.5f winner Shreyas and the Irish 2-y-o 1m winner Sagacious (both by Dalakhani). The dam, a fairly useful Irish 10f winner, is a half-sister to 6 winners abroad. The second dam, Anima (by Ajdal), is a placed half-sister to 8 winners including the multiple Group 1 winner Pilsudski. "A lovely big filly, probably the biggest 2-y-o filly I have. She'll be nice over seven furlongs in August or September".

1691. JASSAAR ★★★
b.c. Dansili – Rasmeyaa (New Approach). February 16. First foal. The dam, a useful 2-y-o 5f winner, was third in the Group 3 7.5f Fairy Bridge Stakes and is a half-sister to the smart 6f, 7f winner and Group 3 1m Desmond Stakes winner Future Generation. The second dam, Posterity (by Indian Ridge), is an

unraced half-sister to 9 winners including the Group 3 6f Prix de Meautry winner Do The Honours and the listed 7f Chesham Stakes winner Seba. (Hamdan Al Maktoum). "A nice, big, powerful colt, I could see him running over seven furlongs to a mile from September onwards".

1692. JEWEL MAKER (IRE) ★★★★
b.c. Invincible Spirit – Sapphire (Medicean). March 1. First foal. The dam, winner of the Group 2 12f British Champions Fillies' and Mares Stakes and two Group 3 events, is a half-sister to the Group 1 10f Prince Of Wales's Stakes winner Free Eagle and the very smart triple Group 2 1m and triple Group 3 winner Custom Cut. The second dam, Polished Gem (by Danehill), an Irish 2-y-o 7f winner, is a sister to the Grade 1 9f Matriarch Stakes and Group 2 1m Sun Chariot Stakes winner Dress To Thrill and a half-sister to 7 winners. (Moyglare Stud Farm). "A bit more forward than some, he's a nice colt and I like him. He could be running by the middle of May over six furlongs before moving up in trip. He's worth an extra star".

1693. LUZUM (IRE) ★★★★
b.c. Epaulette – Empress Ella (Holy Roman Emperor). March 12. Third foal. 130,000Y. Tattersalls October Book 2. Shadwell Estate Co. Half-brother to the modest 2016 2-y-o 7f seller winner Vatican Hill (by Canford Cliffs). The dam is an unplaced half-sister to 2 winners. The second dam, Bella Bella (by Sri Pekan), a quite useful dual 7f winner, is a half-sister to 5 winners including the German listed winner and Group 3 third Silk Petal and the dam of the Group 2 winners Tashawak and Fairy Queen. (Hamdan Al Maktoum). "A strong, powerful individual, he'll be racing in mid-summer. Although we don't know about the first season sire Epaulette yet this is a nice one I can tell you".

1694. MANZIL (IRE) ★★★★
ch.c. Bated Breath – Pointed Arch (Rock Of Gibraltar). April 8. Sixth foal. €75,000Y. Goffs Orby. Shadwell Estate Co. Half-brother to the fairly useful 8.5f (at 2 yrs) to 12f winner Farquhar (by Archipenko) and to the quite useful 2-y-o dual 6f winner Dream Maker (by Bahamian Bounty). The dam, a modest 12f winner, is closely related to the listed 12f

winner Chartres and a half-sister to 7 winners including the dual listed winner Pugin and the dam of the 2-y-o Group 2 Railway Stakes winner and sire Lilbourne Lad. The second dam, Gothic Dream (by Nashwan), won over 7f in Ireland at 2 yrs, was third in the Irish Oaks and is a half-sister to 3 winners. (Hamdan Al Maktoum). *"Now he's a nice colt! Put a star opposite him because he'll be a surprise for them. He's a big colt, but a lovely mover and I would see him running in June or July over seven furlongs. A very good-moving colt".*

1695. MAYAADEEN (IRE) ★★★

b.c. Invincible Spirit – Rose De France (Diktat). February 13. Fifth foal. €750,000Y. Goffs Orby. Shadwell Estate Co. Brother to the Group 2 Challenge Stakes and Group 3 John Of Gaunt Stakes winner and Group 1 7f Dewhurst Stakes second Cable Bay and to the fair 5f winner Tanghan and half-brother to the 2-y-o 5f and 7f winner Sea Wolf (by Amadeus Wolf). The dam, placed four times at 3 yrs in France, is a half-sister to 6 winners including the Group 3 winner and French 2,000 Guineas third Bowman and the dam of the Group 1 winners Kirklees and Mastery. The second dam, Cherokee Rose (by Dancing Brave), won the Group 1 Haydock Park Sprint Cup and the Group 1 Prix Maurice de Gheest and is a half-sister to 4 winners. (Hamdan Al Maktoum). *"He's a very nice colt, a lovely tempered horse and a good mover. I would say we'll see him racing in September or October over seven furlongs".*

1696. MUJID (IRE) ★★★

b.c. Frankel – Bethrah (Marju). February 17. Fourth foal. The dam won 3 races at 3 yrs including the Group 1 Irish 1,000 Guineas and the Group 3 1m Irish 1,000 Guineas Trial. The second dam, Reve d'Iman (by Highest Honor), a minor 3-y-o 9f winner in France, is a sister to the Group 1 Prix Saint-Alary winner Reve d'Oscar, the Group 2 Prix Hocquart winner Numide and the listed French 3-y-o winner Sir Eric. (Hamdan Al Maktoum). *"A strong, powerful individual, he's a nice horse and we'll be looking at August or September for him over seven furlongs to a mile".*

1697. SAPIENS ★★★

b.c. Frankel – Etoile Montante (Miswaki). March 5. Half-brother to the US Grade 2 10f and triple Grade 3 winner Starformer (by Dynaformer). The dam won the Group 1 7f Prix de la Foret and is a half-sister to the listed-placed winner Starfan and to the dam of the French Group 3 winner Glaswegian. The second dam, Willstar (by Nureyev), won over 1m in France and is a half-sister to the US Grade 2 winner Revasser. (Khalid Abdulla). *"A nice colt, he's a little bit immature at the moment and likely to be the type of 2-y-o for September or October over seven furlongs".*

1698. SMILE AHEAD (IRE) ★★★

b.f. Dream Ahead – Instant Sparkle (Danehill). April 4. Fourth foal. Half-sister to the 2016 2-y-o Group 3 7f Killavullan Stakes winner Making Light (by Tamayuz). The dam, a quite useful Irish 12f winner, is a sister to the Group 2 12f Ribblesdale Stakes winner Irresistible Jewel (herself dam of the Group 3 winner Mad About You) and a half-sister to 5 winners including the listed 12f winner Diamond Trim (herself dam of the Group 3 winner Profound Beauty) and the useful Irish 1m winner and Group 3 placed Legal Jousting. The second dam, In Anticipation (by Sadler's Wells), won over 12f and 14f in Ireland and is a half-sister to 6 winners. (Moyglare Stud Farm). *"She's a backward filly at present and one I would see racing in September or October over seven furlongs".*

1699. STELLAR ECLIPSE (IRE) ★★★

b.c. Requinto – Thanks (Kheleyf). April 21. Second foal. 65,000Y. Tattersalls October Book 2. Bobby O'Ryan / D K Weld. Half-brother to Forevertwentyone (by Approve), unplaced in two starts at 2 yrs in 2016. The dam is an unraced half-sister to 6 winners including the French dual listed winner Briviesca. The second dam, Kimono (by Machiavellian), ran twice unplaced and is a half-sister to 4 winners. (Dr Ronan Lambe). *"A sharp colt, he goes well and he'll be racing over five furlongs from the middle of May".*

1700. UNNAMED ★★★★
ch.f. Teofilo – Louve Imperiale (Giant's
Causeway). April 10. Third foal. €120,000Y.
Goffs Orby. Shadwell Estate Co. The dam is
an unplaced half-sister to 5 winners including
Loup Solitaire (Group 1 Grand Criterium),
Loup Sauvage (Group 1 Prix d'Ispahan) and
the Group 3 winner and smart broodmare
Louve. The second dam, Louveterie (by
Nureyev), won the Group 3 Prix Vanteaux and
was second in the Group 1 Prix de Diane and
the Prix Saint-Alary and is a half-sister to 4
stakes winners. (Hamdan Al Maktoum). *"Very
much a quality filly bought from Goffs, she's
lovely and we'll see her out in July or August
over seven furlongs"*.

Sires Reference

This section deals with those sires represented by three or more two-year-olds in the book. All the top British and Irish sires are represented and you will also see some of the best sires standing in America such as Elusive Quality, Kitten's Joy, More Than Ready, Street Cry and War Front.

There are plenty of first-season sires to look out for including Camelot, Cityscape, Dawn Approach, Declaration Of War, Epaulette, Havana Gold, Intello, Lethal Force, Society Rock, Swiss Spirit and Worthadd.

ACCLAMATION (2000) Royal Applause – Princess Athena (Ahonoora). *Racing record:* Won 6 times, including Diadem Stakes. Also placed in King's Stand and Nunthorpe. *Stud record:* This is his eleventh crop and his Group winners to date are Dark Angel (G1 Middle Park Stakes), Equiano (G1 King's Stand Stakes), Marsha (Group 1 Prix de l'Abbaye), Harbour Watch, Saayerr (both winners of the G2 Richmond Stakes), Mehmas (Group 2 July Stakes and Group 2 Richmond Stakes), Lidari (Group 2 in Australia), Lilbourne Lad (G2 Railway Stakes), Aclaim (Group 2 Challenge Stakes), Angels Will Fall (G3 Princess Margaret Stakes), Alsindi (G3 Oh So Sharp Stakes), Attendu (dual Group winner), Hitchens (G3 Greenlands Stakes), Ponty Acclaim (G3 Cornwallis Stakes), Queen Catrine (Group 3 Brownstown Stakes), Talwar (G3 Solario Stakes) and Sparkling Power (G3 in Hong Kong). He also has numerous listed winners to his name. Standing at Rathbarry Stud, Ireland. *2017 fee:* €30,000.

AL KAZEEM (2008) Dubawi – Kazeem (Darshaan). *Racing record:* Won 10 races from 2 to 7 yrs and from 1m to 10.5f including the Tattersalls Gold Cup (twice), Prince Of Wales's Stakes and Eclipse Stakes (all Group 1's). *Stud record:* His first two-year-olds appear this year. Standing at Oakgrove Stud. *2017 fee:* £12,000.

ARAKAN (2000) Nureyev – Far Across (Common Grounds). *Racing record:* Won 6 races including the Group 3 Criterion Stakes, the Group 3 Supreme Stakes (both 7f), the listed Abernant Stakes and the City Of York Stakes (both 6f). *Stud record:* His best winners to date are the dual Group 1 and dual Group 2 winning miler Dick Turpin, the Group 1 National Stakes and triple Group 2 winner Toormore, the dual Group 2 and dual Group 3 winner Trumpet Major and the Irish dual Group 3 winner Sruthan. Ballyhane Stud. 2016 fee: €3,500.

ARCANO (2007) Oasis Dream – Tariysha (Daylami). *Racing record:* Won three races at 2 yrs including the Group 1 6f Prix Morny and the Group 2 6f July Stakes. *Stud record:* This is his fourth crop racing. To date his highest rated offspring are Just Glamorous (Group 3 5f Prix du Petit Couvert), the French winner and Group 2 placed King Genki, the Italian 2-y-o Group 3 winners Kathy Dream and Misterious Boy, the winner and Group 3 placed Mustadeem and the Irish listed-placed winner Tamadhor. Standing in Italy. *2017 fee:* €6,000.

ARCH (1995) Kris S – Aurora (Danzig). *Racing record:* 5 wins including the Super Derby and the Fayette Stakes. *Stud record:* Best winners so far include Arravale (Grade 1 Del Mar Oaks), Archarcharch (Grade 1 Arkansas Derby), Hymn Book (Grade 1 Donn Handicap), Blame (three US Grade 1 wins), Les Arcs (Golden Jubilee Stakes and July Cup), Love Theway Youare (Grade 1 Vanity Handicap), Overarching (South African dual Group 1 winner), Pine Island (dual US Grade 1 winner), Prince Arch (US Grade 1 winner), Montgomery's Arch (Group 2 Richmond Stakes), Pomology (Group 2 Lancashire Oaks), Waterway Run (Group 3 Oh So Sharp Stakes) and the Hong Kong Group 3 winner Art Trader. Standing at Claiborne Farm, Kentucky. *2017 fee:* $40,000.

ARCHIPENKO (2004) Kingmambo – Bound (Nijinsky). *Racing record:* Won the Group 1 10f Audemars Piguet Queen Elizabeth II Cup at Sha Tin and five other Group races including the Group 2 Summer Mile. *Stud record:* His best winners to date are Madame Chiang (Group 1 British Champions Fillies/ Mare Stakes), the South African Group 2 winner Kingston Mines, Group 3 winners Algometer and Va Bank, and the listed winners Lady Penko (also Group 1 third), Algonquin, Medrano, Russian Punch and Time Warp. Standing at Lanwades Stud, Newmarket. *2017 fee:* £10,000.

AUSSIE RULES (2003) Danehill – Last Second (Alzao). *Racing record:* Won four races including the US Grade 1 Shadwell Turf Mile and the Group 1 French 2,000 Guineas. *Stud record:* His best winners to date are Fiesolana (Group 1 Matron Stakes), Djumama (two Group 3 wins in Germany), Duck Feet (Group 3 Premio Guido Berardelli), the Australian Group 3 winner Hard Ball Get and 17 listed winners including the Group placed Aussie Reigns, Bertinoro, Boomerang Bob, Cazals, Chinese Wall, Dinkum Diamond, Grand Treasure, Kramulkie and Private Jet. Died.

AZAMOUR (2001) Night Shift – Asmara (Lear Fan). *Racing record:* Won the St James's Palace Stakes, Irish Champion Stakes, Prince of Wales's Stakes and King George VI and Queen Elizabeth Diamond Stakes. *Stud record:* First runners appeared in 2009. Best winners to date include Covert Love (Group 1 Irish Oaks & Group 1 Prix de l'Opera), Valyra (Group 1 Prix de Diane), Dolniya (Group 1 Dubai Sheema Classic), the Group 2 winners Best Of Days, Eleonora Duse, Hawksmoor, Shankardeh and Wade Giles and ten Group 3 winners including Azmeel, California, Colombian, Liber Nauticus, Native Khan, Thikriyaat and Zannda. Died in 2014.

BAHAMIAN BOUNTY (1994) Cadeaux Genereux – Clarentia (Ballad Rock). *Racing record:* Winner of 3 races at 2 yrs, notably the Prix Morny and the Middle Park Stakes. *Stud record:* Sire of the Group 1 winners Pastoral Pursuits (July Cup) and Goodricke (Sprint Cup), the US Grade 2 winner Mister Napper Tandy, the Group 2 Hungerford Stakes winner Breton Rock, the 2-y-o Group 2 winners Anjaal and Sendmylovetorose, the German Group 2 winner Donnerschlag and the Group 3 winners Blue Bayou, Cay Verde, Coral Mist, Eastern Impact, Life's A Bounty, Naahy, New

Providence and Topatoo. Standing at the National Stud, Newmarket. *2017 fee:* £8,500.

BATED BREATH (2007) Dansili – Tantina (Distant View). *Racing record:* Winner of 6 races over 5f and 6f from 3 to 5yrs, notably the Group 2 Temple Stakes and placed in five Group 1 events. *Stud record:* His first crop were two-year-olds last year. Sire of the winners of 22 races including the dual Group 2 second Al Johrah Standing at Banstead Manor Stud, Newmarket. *2017 fee:* £8,000.

BIG BAD BOB (2000) Bob Back – Fantasy Girl (Marju). *Racing record:* Won 8 races including a Group 3 10f event in Germany and listed races at Ascot (1m) and Deauville (10f). *Stud record:* His first crop appeared on the racecourse in 2010. To date he's had the Irish Group 2 winner Bocca Baciata, the Group 3 winners Berg Bahn, Bible Belt, Brendan Brackan and McCreery, and five listed winners (Backbench Blues, Bible Black and Bob Le Beau, Cherie Good and Tashweeq). Died in 2016.

BLAME (2006) Arch – Liable (Seeking The Gold). *Racing record:* Won three Grade 1 events over 9f and 10f (Stephen Foster Handicap, Whitney Handicap and Breeders' Cup Classic) and three other Graded stakes. *Stud record:* His first crop of runners appeared in 2014 and his best to date include the US Grade 2 and Grade 3 winner March, the US Grade 3 winner Far From Over, Grade 1 placed Going For Broke and several other stakes winners. Standing at Claiborne Farm, Kentucky. *2017 fee:* $25,000.

BORN TO SEA (2009) Invincible Spirit – Urban Sea (Miswaki). *Racing record:* Won a listed 2-y-o event in Ireland and was second in the Group 1 Irish Derby, the Group 2 Royal Whip Stakes and the Group 3 Killavullen Stakes. *Stud record:* A half-brother to Galileo and Sea The Stars, his first two-year-olds appeared last year. Sire of the winners of 22 races including Sea Of Grace (Group 3 Flame Of Tara Stakes) and the listed-placed Born To Be and Star Of Rory. Standing at Gilltown Stud in Ireland. *2017 fee:* €10,000.

CACIQUE (2001) Danehill – Hasili (Kahyasi). *Racing record:* Won 18 races from 3 to 5 yrs including the Grade 1 11f Man O'War

Stakes, Grade 1 10f Manhattan Handicap and the Grade 2 1m Prix Daniel Wildenstein. *Stud record:* From limited books of mares he has the Group 1 winners Dominant (Hong Kong Vase), Mutual Trust (Prix Jean Prat) and Slumber (Manhattan Stakes), along with the Group 2 Prix de Chaudenay winner Canticum, the Group 3 Geoffrey Freer Stakes winner Census and the German 2-y-o Group 3 winner Colomano. Standing at Banstead Manor Stud, Newmarket. *2017 fee:* £12,500.

CAMELOT (2009) Montjeu – Tarfah (Kingmambo). *Racing record:* Won 6 races including the Racing Post Trophy, 2,000 Guineas, Derby and Irish Derby (all Group 1 events). *Stud record:* His first crop are two-year-olds this year. Standing at Coolmore Stud, Ireland. *2017 fee:* €35,000.

CANFORD CLIFFS (2007) Tagula – Mrs Marsh (Marju). *Racing record:* Won 7 races at 2 to 4 yrs and from 6f to 1m including the Irish 2,000 Guineas, St James's Palace Stakes, Sussex Stakes, Lockinge Stakes and Queen Anne Stakes (all Group 1 events). *Stud record:* His first crop of two-year-olds appeared in 2015 and he's bred the winners of 138 races including the Group 2 Railway Stakes winner Painted Cliffs, the Group 3 winners Al Jazi, Most Beautiful and Princess Asta, the Group 1 Oaks and Irish Oaks third Harlequeen, the dual Group 1 placed Salouen and the French listed winner Aktoria. Standing at Coolmore Stud in Ireland. *2017 fee:* €10,000.

CAPE CROSS (1994) Green Desert – Park Appeal (Ahonoora). *Racing record:* Won 4 races including the Lockinge Stakes, Queen Anne Stakes and Celebration Mile. *Stud record:* First runners in 2003. Sire of thirteen Group 1 winners including two outstanding colts in Sea The Stars (2,000 Guineas, Derby, Prix de l'Arc de Triomphe, etc) and Golden Horn (Derby, Eclipse Stakes, Irish Champion Stakes and Prix de l'Arc de Triomphe), the top-class Ouija Board (7 Group 1 wins including the Oaks & the Breeders' Cup Filly and Mare Turf), Awtaad (Irish 2,000 Guineas), Behkabad (Grand Prix de Paris), Nayarra (Group 1 Gran Criterium), the Hong Kong triple Group 1 winner Able One and the Australasian horses Gaze, I'm Your Man, Kindacross, Mikki Street and Seachange. His Group 2 winners include Cape Dollar, Crystal Capella, Halicarnassus, Hatta Fort,

Joviality, Moohaajim, Russian Cross, Sabana Perdida and Treat Gently. Died in April 2017.

CASAMENTO (2008) Shamardal – Wedding Gift (Always Fair). *Racing record:* Won four races including the Group 1 Racing Post Trophy, the Group 2 Beresford Stakes (both at 2 yrs) and the Group 3 Prix du Prince d'Orange). *Stud record:* His first two-year-olds raced last season and to date he's the sire of the winners of 22 races including the Group 3 placed Kings Gift and Stamp Collecting (in Italy). Standing at Dalham Hall Stud, Newmarket. *2017 fee:* £5,000.

CHAMPS ELYSEES (2003) Danehill – Hasili (Kahyasi). *Racing record:* Won the Canadian International, the Hollywood Turf Cup and the Northern Dancer Turf Stakes (all Grade 1). *Stud record:* With three crops to have raced so far he's the sire of the winners of over 160 races including the Group 1 Ascot Gold Cup winner Trip To Paris, the Group 3 Silver Flash Stakes winner and Group 1 Irish Oaks second Jack Naylor, the Group 3 winner and French 1,000 Guineas third Xcellence and the listed winners and Group placed Avenue Gabriel, Eastern Belle, Lustrous and Regardez. Standing at Banstead Manor Stud, Newmarket. *2017 fee:* £8,000.

CITYSCAPE (2006) Selkirk – Tantina (Distant View). *Racing record:* Won 6 races from 2 to 6 yrs including the UAE Group 1 9f Dubai Duty Free and three Group 3 events over 1m. *Stud record:* His first crop of two-year-olds appear this year. Standing at Overbury Stud, Newmarket. *2017 fee:* £4,500.

CLODOVIL 2001 Danehill – Clodora (Linamix). *Racing record:* Won 5 races including the French 2,000 Guineas. *Stud record:* His first crop were two-year-olds in 2007 and his best winners to date are Nahoodh (Group 1 Falmouth Stakes), Moriarty (Group 1 and three Group 2's in Australia), the Group 2 winners Es Que Love, Gregorian, Laugh Out Loud, Shining Emerald and Tuttipaesi, the dual Group 3 winner Beacon Lodge and nine listed winners. Standing at Rathasker Stud, Ireland. *2017 fee:* €8,000.

COMPTON PLACE (1994) Indian Ridge – Nosey (Nebbiolo). *Racing record:* Won 3 races, notably the July Cup. *Stud record:* First runners in 2002. Sire of 11 Group winners and 13 listed winners, notably the dual Group 1 Nunthorpe Stakes winner Borderlescott, the Group 2 and multiple Group 3 winner Deacon Blues, the US Grade 2 winner Passified, the Group 2 winners Godfrey Street, Pearl Secret and Prolific, the Group 3 winners Easy Road, Hunter Street, Intrepid Jack, Minal, Pleasure Place, Champion Place and Shifting Power, and numerous useful performers including Angus News, Boogie Street, Compton's Eleven, If Paradise, Judd Street, Hunter Street, Master Of War, Pacific Pride and Pearl Secret. Died in 2015.

DANDY MAN (2003) Mozart – Lady Alexander (Night Shift). *Racing record:* Won 6 races including the Group 3 5f Palace House Stakes and two listed events. *Stud record:* Has sired the winners of 205 races to date including plenty of 2-y-o's. His best to date are the Hong Kong Group 1 and dual Group 2 winner Peniaphobia, the Group 3 and listed winner Extortionist, the triple Group 2 placed Parbold and the 2-y-o listed Roses Stakes winner Big Time Baby. Standing at Ballyhane Stud. *2017 fee:* €10,000.

DANSILI (1996) Danehill – Hasili (Kahyasi). *Racing record:* Won 5 races in France and placed in six Group/Grade 1 events including Sussex Stakes and Breeders' Cup Mile. *Stud record:* First runners in 2004. Sire of 20 Group/ Grade 1 winners including Rail Link (Arc, Grand Prix de Paris), Harbinger (King George VI), Emulous (Matron Stakes), Fallen For You (Coronation Stakes), Flintshire (Grand Prix de Paris, etc), Foreteller (three in Australia), Giofra (Falmouth Stakes), Miss France (1,000 Guineas), Passage of Time (Criterium de Saint-Cloud), The Fugue (four Group 1's), We Are (Prix de l'Opera), Winsili (Nassau Stakes), Zoffany (Phoenix Stakes), Zambezi Sun (Grand Prix de Paris) and in the USA Dank, Laughing, Price Tag and Proviso. Standing at Banstead Manor Stud, Newmarket. *2017 fee:* £65,000.

DARK ANGEL (2005) Acclamation – Midnight Angel (Machiavellian). *Racing record:* Won four races at 2 yrs including the Group 1 Middle Park Stakes. *Stud record:* First runners 2011. Has built himself an excellent reputation. His best winners to date are Lethal Force (Group 1 July Cup & Group 1 Diamond Jubilee Stakes), Mecca's Angel (Group 1 Nunthorpe Stakes, twice), Alhebayeb (Group 2 July Stakes),

Ardhoomey (Group 2 Flying Five), Birchwood (Group 2 Superlative Stakes), Estidhkaar (Group 2 Champagne Stakes & Group 2 Superlative Stakes), Gutaifan (Group 2 Flying Childers Stakes, Group 2 Champagne Stakes), Harry Angel (Group 2 Mill Reef Stakes) and twelve Group 3 winners including Exogenesis, Heeraat, Lily's Angel, Markaz, Nations Alexander, Realtra, Sovereign Debt and Stormfly and fourteen listed winners. Stands at Yeomanstown Stud, Ireland. *2017 fee:* €65,000.

DAWN APPROACH (2010) New Approach – Hymn Of The Dawn (Phone Trick). *Racing record:* Unbeaten champion 2-y-o, won 8 races from 5f to 1m at 2 and 3 yrs including the National Stakes, Dewhurst Stakes, 2,000 Guineas and St James's Palace Stakes. *Stud record:* His first two-year-olds appear this year. Stands at Kildangan Stud, Ireland. *2017 fee:* €30,000.

DECLARATION OF WAR (2009) War Front – Tempo West (Rahy). *Racing record:* Won 7 races from 2 to 4 yrs and from 7.5f to 10.5f including the Group 1 Queen Anne Stakes and the Group 1 Juddmonte International (both at 4 yrs). *Stud record:* His first two-year-olds appear this year. Stands at Ashford Stud, Kentucky. *2017 fee:* $35,000.

DRAGON PULSE (2009) Kyllachy – Poetical (Croco Rouge). *Racing record:* Won the Group 2 7f Futurity Stakes at the Curragh (at 2 yrs) and the Group 3 1m Prix de Fontainebleau. Second in the Group 1 National Stakes. *Stud record:* His first two-year-olds appeared last year and he had a very good start to his stud career with 21 individual winners including the Italian Group 3 winner Aethos, the Listed Woodcote Stakes winner Legendary Lunch and the Group 2 Duke Of Cambridge second Magical Fire. Standing at the Irish National Stud. *2017 fee:* €8,000.

DREAM AHEAD (2008) Diktat – Land Of Dreams (Cadeaux Genereux). *Racing record:* Won five Group 1 races from 6f to 7f, at 2 and 3 yrs (Prix Morny, Middle Park Stakes, July Cup, Haydock Park Sprint Cup and Prix de la Foret). *Stud record:* From two crops racing his best to date are the Group 2 Criterium de Maisons-Laffitte winner Donjuan Triumphant, the Group 3 Anglesey Stakes winner Final Frontier, the winner and multiple Group placed Raucous and the listed winners Al Wukair (in France), Basileus (Italy) and Ken's Dream (Australia). Standing at Haras de Grandcamp, France. *2017 stud fee:* €12,000.

DUBAWI (2002) Dubai Millennium – Zomaradah (Deploy). *Racing record:* Won the National Stakes at 2 and the Irish 2,000 Guineas and Prix Jacques le Marois at 3. Third in the Derby. *Stud record:* An exceptional sire responsible for 65 Group winners including 28 Group 1 scorers. They include Al Kazeem (three Group 1's), Arabian Queen (Juddmonte International), Dubawi Heights (Gamely Stakes, Yellow Ribbon Stakes), Erupt (Canadian International and Grand Prix de Paris), Happy Archer (two Group 1's in Australia), Hunters Light (three Group 1's in Italy and Dubai), Lucky Nine (Hong Kong Sprint), Makfi (2,000 Guineas, Prix Jacques le Marois), Monterosso & Prince Bishop (both Dubai World Cup winners), New Bay (French Derby), Night Of Thunder (2,000 Guineas and Lockinge Stakes), Poet's Voice (Queen Elizabeth II Stakes), Postponed (four Group 1's including the King George VI), Secret Admirer (two Group 1's in Australia), Sheikhzayedroad (Northern Dancer Turf Stakes), Waldpark (German Derby) and Willow Magic (in South Africa). Standing at Dalham Hall Stud, Newmarket. *2017 fee:* £250,000.

DUTCH ART (2004) Medicean – Halland Park Lass (Spectrum). *Racing record:* Won four races at 2 yrs including the Group 1 Prix Morny and the Group 1 Middle Park Stakes. *Stud record:* Leading first crop sire in 2011 and a consistently good sire ever since. Ten Group winners to date including Slade Power (dual Group 1 6f winner), Garswood (Group 1 Prix Maurice de Gheest), Caspar Netscher (Group 2 Mill Reef Stakes and Group 2 Gimcrack Stakes), Producer (Group 2 in Turkey and the Group 3 Supreme Stakes), Dutch Connection (Group 2 Lennox Stakes, Group 3 Jersey Stakes and Group 3 Acomb Stakes), Dutch Masterpiece (Group 3 Flying Five) and Lady's First (Group 3 Atalanta Stakes), the dual Group 1 second Lightning Thunder and 16 listed winners. Standing at Cheveley Park Stud. *2017 fee:* £25,000.

ELUSIVE QUALITY (1993) Gone West – Touch of Greatness (Hero's Honor). *Racing record:* Won 9 races in USA including Grade 3 events at 7f/1m. *Stud record:* Sire of the Kentucky

Derby/Preakness Stakes winner Smarty Jones, Breeders' Cup Classic and Queen Elizabeth II Stakes winner Raven's Pass, Prix Morny winner Elusive City, dual Group 1 winner Elusive Kate, Australian multiple Group 1 winner Sepoy, the US Grade 1 winners Quality Road and Maryfield, the Group winning two-year-olds Certify, Elusive Pimpernel and Evasive, numerous US graded stakes winners including Chimichurri, Elusive Diva, Girl Warrior, Omega Code, Royal Michele and True Quality, the Group 2 and triple Group 3 winner Shuruq and the smart dual listed winner Baharah. Standing at Jonabell Farm, Kentucky. *2017 fee:* $30,000.

EPAULETTE (2009) Commands (AUS) – Accessories (Singspiel). *Racing record:* Won 3 races in Australia at 3 and 4 yrs including two Group 1 7f events. *Stud record:* His first two-year-olds appear this year. Standing at Kildangan Stud, Ireland. *2017 fee:* €8,000.

EQUIANO (2005) Acclamation – Entente Cordiale (Elä-Maria-Mou). *Racing record:* Won 7 races starting with two wins as a 2-y-o over 7f in Spain, before maturing into a high-class sprinter and twice capturing the Group 1 5f King's Stand Stakes. *Stud record:* His first crop of 2-y-o's appeared in 2014. His best runners to date include The Tin Man (Group 1 British Champions Sprint), Medicine Jack (2-y-o Group 2 Railway Stakes), the Group 3 winners Baciama Piccola (in the USA), Belvoir Bay (in the USA), Dark Reckoning, Fly On The Night and Strath Burn, and the listed winners Alicante Dawn, Valliano (in Australia) and Waipu Cove (in Ireland). Standing at Newsells Park Stud. *2017 fee:* £7,000.

EXCEED AND EXCEL (2000) Danehill – Patrona (Lomond). *Racing record:* Champion sprinter in Australia, won 7 races including the Grade 1 Newmarket H'cap, the Grade 1 Dubai Racing Club Cup and the Grade 2 Todman Stakes. *Stud record:* There are 128 stakes winners to his name so far including the ten Group 1 winners Excelebration (Queen Elizabeth II Stakes, Prix du Moulin, Prix Jacques le Marois), Margot Did (Nunthorpe Stakes), Outstrip (Breeders' Cup Juvenile Turf), Amber Sky (Group 1 Al Quoz Sprint), Guelphe, Helmet, Earthquake, Flamberge, Overreach and Reward For Effort (all in Australia). His sixteen Group 2 winners include Best Terms, Buratino, Fulbright, Heavy Metal, Infamous Angel and Masamah.

Standing at Kildangan Stud, Ireland. *2017 fee:* €50,000.

EXCELEBRATION (2008) Exceed And Excel – Sun Shower (Indian Ridge). *Racing record:* Won eight races from 6f (at 2 yrs) to 1m including three Group 1 stakes – the Prix du Moulin, Prix Jacques le Marois and Queen Elizabeth II Stakes. *Stud record:* His first two-year-olds appeared on the track in 2016 and to date he has the winners of 30 races to his name. They include the Group 3 placed Fulminato (in Germany) and Pellucid. Standing at Coolmore Stud, Ireland. *2017 fee:* €10,000.

FARHH (2008) Pivotal – Gonbarda (Lando). *Racing record:* Won 5 races from 7f to 10f and from 2 to 5 yrs including the Group 1 Lockinge Stakes and the Group 1 Champion Stakes. *Stud record:* His first crop of two-year-olds appear this season. Standing at Dalham Hall Stud. *2017 fee:* £8,000.

FAST COMPANY (2005) Danehill Dancer – Sheezalady (Zafonic). *Racing record:* Ran only three times, all at 2 yrs, winning the Group 3 7f Acomb Stakes and finishing second in the Group 1 7f Dewhurst Stakes. *Stud record:* Sired 26 individual winners from his first crop in 2014 and has now bred the winners of over 200 races to date including Jet Setting (Group 1 Irish 1,000 Guineas), Baitha Alga (Group 2 Norfolk Stakes), Devonshire (Group 3 Ridgewood Pearl Stakes and third in the Group 1 Irish 1,000 Guineas), three listed winners and the Group 3 placed Al Qahwa and Fast Act. Standing at Kildangan Stud. *2017 fee:* €7,000.

FASTNET ROCK (2001) Danehill – Piccadilly Circus (Royal Academy). *Racing record:* Raced in Australia and won two Grade 1's, two Grade 2's and two Grade 3 events over 5f and 6f. *Stud record:* A champion sire in Australia. He's produced over 50 stakes winners to date. His 27 Group 1 winners include Atlante, Atlantic Jewel, Diamondsandrubies (Pretty Polly Stakes), Fascinating Rock (Champion Stakes), Foxwedge, Intricately (Moyglare Stud Stakes), Irish Lights, Lone Rock, Mosheen, Nechita, Planet Rock, Qualify (Oaks), Rivet (Racing Post Trophy), Rock 'N' Pop, Rock Classic, Sea Siren, Super Cool, Wanted and Your Song. The vast majority of them have been in Australasia. Standing at Coolmore Stud, Ireland. *2017 fee:* Private.

FIRST DEFENCE (2004) Unbridled's Song – Honest Lady (Seattle Slew). *Racing record:* Won the Grade 1 7f Forego Handicap and the Grade 3 6f Jaipur Stakes. *Stud record:* With three crops racing he is the sire of the winners of 228 races (to Feb 2017). His best runners have been the US multiple Grade 1 winner and $1.6m earner Close Hatches, Dundonnell (Group 3 Acomb Stakes), Antonoe (Group 3 Prix d'Aumale) and Irish Jasper (US Grade 3 Miss Preakness Stakes). Standing at Juddmonte Farms, Kentucky. *2017 fee:* $7,500.

FOOTSTEPSINTHESAND (2002) Giant's Causeway – Glatisant (Rainbow Quest). *Racing record:* Won all 3 of his starts, notably the 2,000 Guineas. *Stud record:* His best winners include the Chachamaidee (Group 1 Matron Stakes), the Italian and Argentine Group 1 winners Infiltrada, Sand Bijou and Shamalgan, Canadian Grade 1 winner Steinbeck, eleven Group 2 winners including Barefoot Lady, Formosina, Giant Sandman, Living The Life, Minakshi and, in Argentina, King Kon, Sagitariana and Sand Puce, plus twelve Group 3 and 24 Listed winners. Standing at Coolmore Stud, Ireland. *2017 fee:* €10,000.

FOXWEDGE (2008) Fastnet Rock – Forest Native (Forest Wildcat). *Racing record:* Won 3 races in Australia including Group 1 and Group 2 events over 6f. *Stud record:* Having previously stood in Australia where his best runner to date is the Group 2 6f and Group 2 7f winner Foxplay, his first Northern Hemisphere crop were two-year-olds last year. They included the triple winner and Group 1 Fillies Mile third Urban Fox and the Group 3 placed winners King Of Spades and Seafront. Standing at Whitsbury Manor Stud. *2017 fee:* £7,000.

FRANKEL (2008) Galileo – Kind (Danehill). *Racing record:* A champion at two, three and four years of age, he won all 14 of his races, from 7f to 10.5f, including ten Group 1's. *Stud record:* His first crop were two-year-olds in 2016 and he was the leading European first crop sire by worldwide earnings. His six Group winners were Soul Stirring (Group 1 in Japan), Queen Kindly (Group 2 Lowther Stakes) and the Group 3 winners Fair Eva, Frankuus, Mi Suerte (in Japan) and Toolifaut (in France). Standing at Banstead Manor Stud, Newmarket. *2017 fee:* 125,000 Guineas.

FROZEN POWER (2007) Oasis Dream – Musical Treat (Royal Academy). *Racing record:* Won five races from 6f to a mile including the Group 2 German 2,000 Guineas. *Stud record:* From two crops racing he's had 25 individual winners of 80 races, but only one that was stakes-placed. Now standing in Italy. *2017 fee:* €4,000.

GALILEO (1998) Sadler's Wells – Urban Sea (Miswaki). *Racing record:* Won 6 races including the Derby, Irish Derby and King George VI and Queen Elizabeth Stakes. *Stud record:* First runners in 2005. A great stallion and sire of the outstanding champion Frankel, champion 2-y-o's Teofilo and New Approach (subsequent Derby, Champion Stakes and Irish Champion Stakes winner), Derby, Irish Derby and Juddmonte International winner Australia, the triple Group 1 winner Rip Van Winkle, Sixties Icon (St Leger), triple Group 1 winner Noble Mission, Red Rocks (Breeders' Cup Turf), Allegretto (Prix Royal-Oak), Lush Lashes (three Group 1 wins), Soldier Of Fortune (Irish Derby & Coronation Cup), Nightime (Irish 1000 Guineas), Roderic O'Connor (Criterium International, Irish 2,000 Guineas), Cape Blanco (five Group 1 wins), Nathaniel (King George VI & Queen Elizabeth Stakes), Ruler Of The World (Epsom Derby), Treasure Beach (Irish Derby, Secretariat Stakes), dual Guineas and St James's Palace winner Gleneagles, Golden Lilac (French 1,000 Guineas, Prix d'Ispahan and Prix de Diane), Intello (French Derby), dual Group 1 winning 2-y-o filly Minding, triple Group 1 winner Noble Mission, Was (Oaks), Misty For Me (four Group 1 wins), Maybe (Moyglare Stud Stakes) and Galikova (Prix Vermeille). Standing at Coolmore Stud, Ireland. *2017 fee:* Private.

GIANT'S CAUSEWAY (1997) Storm Cat – Mariah's Storm (Rahy). *Racing record:* Won 9 races, 6 of them Group 1 events, including the Prix de la Salamandre, Juddmonte International and Sussex Stakes. *Stud record:* First runners in 2004. The sire of around 100 Group winners including 31 Group/Grade 1 winners including Shamardal (Dewhurst Stakes, St James's Palace Stakes and Prix du Jockey Club), Footstepsinthesand (2,000 Guineas), Ghanaati (1,000 Guineas and Coronation Stakes), Aragorn & Carpe Diem (dual US Grade 1 winners), Eishin Apollon (Group 1 miler in Japan), Heatseeker (Santa Anita Handicap),

Maids Causeway (Coronation Stakes), Intense Focus (Dewhurst Stakes), Eskendereya, First Samurai, My Typhoon, Swift Temper (US Grade 1 winners), Dalkala (Prix de l'Opera) and Rite of Passage (Ascot Gold Cup). Standing at Ashford Stud, Kentucky. *2017 fee:* $75,000.

HARBOUR WATCH (2009) Acclamation – Gorband (Woodman). *Racing record:* Won three races at 2 yrs (all his starts) including the Group 2 6f Richmond Stakes. *Stud record:* His first two-year-olds appeared on the racecourse last year and to date he's sired the winners of 23 races, notably the Group 2 Prix Robert Papin winner Tis Marvellous. Standing at Tweenhills Farm & Stud. *2017 fee:* £6,000.

HAVANA GOLD (2010) Teofilo – Jessica's Dream (Desert Style). *Racing record:* Won 5 races at 2 and 3 yrs from 6f to 1m including the Group 1 Prix Jean Prat and the Group 3 Somerville Tattersalls Stakes. *Stud record:* By a champion 2-y-o and out of a multiple 5f Group winner. His first two-year-olds appear on the racecourse this year. Standing at Tweenhills Farm & Stud. *2017 fee:* £7,000.

HELMET (2008) Exceed And Excel – Accessories (Singspiel). *Racing record:* Won 6 races in Australia at 3 yrs from 6f to 1m including three Group 1's. *Stud record:* His first two-year-olds appeared last season and he's had an excellent start to his stud career. His best two-year-old was the Group 1 Criterium International winner Thunder Snow and he also has the Group 3 placed winners Mur Hiba and Eqtiraan. In Australia he has the Group 3 winners Archives and Limestone. Standing at Dalham Hall Stud, Newmarket. *2017 fee:* £10,000.

HENRYTHENAVIGATOR (2005) Kingmambo – Sequoyah (Sadler's Wells). *Racing record:* Won the Sussex Stakes, St James's Palace Stakes, 2000 Guineas and Irish 2,000 Guineas. *Stud record:* With five crops to have raced he's had 3 individual Group 1 winners – George Vancouver (Grade 1 Breeders' Cup Juvenile Turf), Pedro The Great (Group 1 Phoenix Stakes) and Sudirman (Group 1 Phoenix Stakes). He also has one Group 3 winner in Australia (Lite'n My Veins) and numerous other stakes winners. Standing at Coolmore Stud. *2017 fee:* €7,500.

HIGH CHAPARRAL (2000) Sadler's Wells – Kasora (Darshaan). *Racing record:* Won 10 races, including the Derby, Irish Champion Stakes and Breeders' Cup Turf (twice). *Stud record:* First crop were two-year-olds in 2007. His best performers include the multiple Group 1 winner So You Think, Group 1 Sussex Stakes and Queen Anne Stakes winner Toronado, Group 1 Prince Of Wales's Stakes winner Free Eagle, Australian Group 1 winners It's A Dundeel (six Group 1 wins), Descarado, Monaco Consul and Shoot Out, German Group 1 winner Lucky Lion, Grade 1 Northern Dancer Turf Stakes winners Redwood and Wigmore Hall, Grade 1 Breeders' Cup Turf winner Wrote and High Jinx (Group 1 Prix du Cadran). Died in 2014.

HOLY ROMAN EMPEROR (2004) Danehill – L'On Vite (Secretariat). *Racing record:* Won four races at 2 yrs including the Group 1 7f Prix Jean-Luc Lagardere, the Group 1 6f Waterford Phoenix Stakes and Group 2 6f Railway Stakes. *Stud record:* His best winners so far include Homecoming Queen (1,000 Guineas), Morandi (Group 1 Criterium de Saint Cloud), Hong Kong Group 1 winners Designs On Rome and Beauty Only, New Zealand Group 1 winners Rollout The Carpet and Mongolian Khan, Grade 1 Santa Anita Sprint winner Rich Tapestry, 19 other Group winners including Angelic Light, Banimpire, Charles The Great, Mango Diva, Rich Legacy (all Group 2 winners) and the Group 1 placed Amarillo, Honorius, Ishvana, Leitir Mor, Princess Noor and Sunday Times. Standing at Coolmore Stud, Ireland. *2017 fee:* €17,500.

IFFRAAJ (2001) Zafonic – Pastorale (Nureyev). *Racing record:* Won 7 races including the Group 2 7f Park Stakes (twice), the Group 2 7f Betfair Cup (Lennox Stakes) and the 6f Wokingham Stakes. *Stud record:* His first runners came in 2010 when he had more winners (38) than any first-crop European sire ever. He now has 21 Group winners and amongst the best are Chrisselliam (Group 1 Fillies' Mile and Grade 1 Breeders' Cup Juvenile Fillies), Wootton Bassett (Group 1 Prix Jean-Luc Lagardere), Ribchester (Group 1 Prix Jacques Le Marois), Rizeena (Group 1 Moyglare Stud Stakes and Coronation Stakes), Benvenue (Gran Premio di Milano), the Australasian triple Group 1 winner Turn Me Loose, Hot Streak

(Group 2 Temple Stakes) and the New Zealand Group 2 winners Fix & Serena Miss. Standing at Dalham Hall Stud, Newmarket. *2017 fee:* €27,500.

INTELLO (2010) Galileo – Impressionnante (Danehill). *Racing record:* Won 6 races from 1m to 10.5f at 2 and 3 yrs including the Group 1 French Derby, the Group 3 Prix Messidor and Group 3 Prix du Prince d'Orange. *Stud record:* His first crop of two-year-olds appear this year. Standing at Haras du Quesnay. *2017 fee:* €25,000.

INTIKHAB (1994) Red Ransom – Crafty Example (Crafty Prospector). *Racing record:* 8 wins including the Diomed Stakes and the Queen Anne Stakes. *Stud record:* Sire of 10 Group winners and 14 listed winners including the outstanding racemare and multiple Group 1 winner Snow Fairy, the Group 1 Lockinge Stakes & Group 1 Matron Stakes winner Red Evie, the Group 1 Criterium de Saint-Cloud winner Paita, the Group 2 Yorkshire Cup winner Glen's Diamond and the Group 3 winners Ascertain, Circus Couture, Hoh Mike, Moon Unit, Tell Dad and Toupie. Standing at Derrinstown Stud, Ireland. *2017 fee:* €5,000.

INVINCIBLE SPIRIT (1997) Green Desert – Rafha (Kris). *Racing record:* 7 wins, notably the Group 1 Sprint Cup at 5 yrs. *Stud record:* First runners in 2006. High-class sire of fifteen Group 1 winners namely Charm Spirit (QE II Stakes, Prix Jean Prat & Prix du Moulin), Kingman – four Group 1's including the Sussex Stakes and St James's Palace Stakes), Lawman (French Derby & Prix Jean Prat), Fleeting Spirit (July Cup), Moonlight Cloud (six Group 1's in France), Mayson (July Cup), Hooray & Rosdhu Queen (both Cheveley Park Stakes), National Defense (Prix Jean-Luc Lagardere), Profitable (King's Stand Stakes), Shalaa (Middle Park and Prix Morny), Signs Of Blessing (Prix Maurice de Gheest), Territories (Prix Jean Prat), Vale Of York (Breeders' Cup Juvenile) and Yosai (three Group 1 wins in Australia), plus fourteen Group 2 winners – Ajaya, Allied Powers, Cable Bay, Campfire Glow, Captain Marvelous, Conquest, Impassable, Madame Trop Vite, Muthmir, Our Jonathan, Speaking Of Which, Spirit Quartz, Spirit Song and Zebedee. Standing at the Irish National Stud. *2017 fee:* €120,000.

KITTEN'S JOY (2001) El Prado – Kitten's First (Lear Fan). *Racing record:* Won 9 races including the Grade 1 10f Secretariat Stakes and the Grade 1 12f Turf Classic. *Stud record:* A leading turf sire in the USA. Sire of 32 Graded stakes and 43 Listed stakes winners. His best include Hawkbill (Eclipse Stakes), the 2016 Grade 1 Breeders' Cup Juvenile Turf winner Oscar Performance and other US Grade 1 winners like Admiral's Kitten, Bobby's Kitten, Big Blue Kitten, Chiropractor, Kitten's Dumplings, Real Solution and Stephanie's Kitten. Standing at Ramsay Farm in the USA. *2017 fee:* $100,000.

KODIAC (2001) Danehill – Rafha (Kris). *Racing record:* Won 4 races here and in the UAE over 6f and 7f including the Datel Trophy and Group 3 placed. *Stud record:* His first runners appeared in 2010 and he's a reliable source of decent class winners with 28 Group/Listed winners. They include the champion 2-y-o filly Tiggy Wiggy (Group 1 Cheveley Park Stakes), Group 2 Sandy Lane and Group 2 Hungerford Stakes winner Adaay, Group 2 Flying Childers winner Ardad, Group 2 Lowther Stakes winner Besharah, Group 2 Celebration Mile winner Kodi Bear, Group 2 Norfolk Stakes winner Prince Of Lir and seven Group 3 winners – Bear Cheek, Best Solution, Coulsty, Gifted Master, Jamesie, Shaden and Spirit Of Xian. Standing at Tally Ho Stud, Ireland. *2017 fee:* €50,000.

KYLLACHY (1998) Pivotal – Pretty Poppy (Song). *Racing record:* Winner of 6 races including the Group 1 Nunthorpe Stakes at 4 yrs. *Stud record:* First runners in 2006. Sire of the dual Group 1 Nunthorpe Stakes and dual Group 1 King's Stand Stakes winner Sole Power, the Group 1 6f Golden Shaheen winner Krypton Factor, Group 1 Haydock Park Sprint Cup and Group 1 Diamond Jubilee Stakes winner Twilight Son, Hong Kong Group 1 winner Dim Sum, the Group 2 winners Arabian Gleam, Dragon Pulse, Penitent, Stepper Point, Supplicant and Tariq and numerous smart performers including Awinnersgame, Befortyfour, Corrybrough, Kachy, Mood Music, Gracia Directa and Noble Hachy. Standing at Cheveley Park Stud, Newmarket. *2017 fee:* £15,000.

LAWMAN (2004) Invincible Spirit – Laramie (Gulch). *Racing record:* Won four races

including the Group 1 Prix du Jockey Club and the Group Prix Jean Prat. *Stud record:* First runners 2011. To date he has five Group 1 winners – Harbour Law (St Leger), Just The Judge (Group 1 Irish 1,000 Guineas, E P Taylor Stakes), Most Improved (Group 1 St James's Palace Stakes), Marcel (Racing Post Trophy) and Law Enforcement (Group 1 Premio Gran Criterium), the Group 2 winners Agnes Stewart (May Hill Stakes) and Libran (in Australia) and the Group 3 winners Forces of Darkness (Prix Minerve), Dicton (Prix de Fontainebleau), Loi (Prix de Conde), Lady Wingshot (Fairy Bridge Stakes), Nargys (Sceptre Stakes) and US Law (Prix Thomas Bryon). Ballylinch Stud, Ireland. *2017 fee:* €25,000.

LE HAVRE (2006) Noverre – Marie Rheinberg (Surako). *Racing record:* Won 4 races including the Group 1 10.5f French Derby. *Stud record:* Sire of 26 stakes winners including the French 1,000 Guineas and French Oaks winners Avenir Certain and La Cressonniere, the Group 2 Prix Chaudenay winner Auvray, the 2-y-o Group 3 Prix du Calvados winner Queen Bee, Group 3 Prix de Meautry winner Suedois, Group 3 Prix Vanteaux winner Zghorta Dance and eleven listed winners including the Group 1 Prix Jean Prat third La Hoguette. Standing at Haras de la Cauviniere in France. *2017 fee:* €60,000.

LETHAL FORCE (2009) Dark Angel – Land Army (Desert Style). *Racing record:* Won four races including the Group 1 6f July Cup, the Group 1 6f Diamond Jubilee Stakes and the Group 2 7f Hungerford Stakes. *Stud record:* His first crop of two-year-olds appear this year. Standing at Cheveley Park Stud. *2017 fee:* £10,000Y.

LILBOURNE LAD (2009) Acclamation – Sogno Verde (Green Desert). *Racing record:* Won 3 races including the Group 2 Railway Stakes. Raced only at 2 yrs. *Stud record:* With two crops racing he's sired 47 individual winners including the Group 3 placed Lil's Joy (in France) and Spinamiss (in the USA). Standing at Swordlestown Little Stud in Ireland. *2017 fee:* €5,000.

LOPE DE VEGA (2007) Shamardal – Lady Vettori (Vettori). *Racing record:* Won four races from 7f (at 2 yrs) to 11f including the Group 1 French Derby and the Group 1 French 2,000 Guineas. *Stud record:* His first crop were 2-y-o's in 2014 and he's had an excellent start at stud with 14 Group winners – Belardo (Group 1 Dewhurst Stakes), Jemayel (Group 1 Prix Saint-Alary), the Group 2 winners French Fern (in Australia), Hero Look (in Italy) and Very Special (UAE) and the Group/Grade 3 winners Blue De Vega, Burnt Sugar, Navarra King, Ride Like The Wind, Royal Razalma, Santa Ana Lane (in the USA), South Seas, The Right Man and Vega Magic. He also has ten Listed winners. Standing at Ballylinch Stud, Ireland. *2017 fee:* €50,000.

MAKFI (2007) Dubawi – Dhelaal (Green Desert). *Racing record:* Won four races, notably the 2,000 Guineas and Prix Jacques le Marois. *Stud record:* His first runners appeared in 2014 and his best winners to date include the French 2,000 Guineas and Prix de la Foret winner Make Believe, the Australian Group 1 winner Marky Mark, New Zealand Group 2 winner Sofia Rosa, the dual Group 3 1m winners Miamara and Noor Al Hawa, 2-y-o Group 3 7f winner Mate Story and several listed winners including Cornwallville in France. Standing at Haras de Bonneval. *2017 fee:* €20,000.

MASTERCRAFTSMAN (2006) Danehill Dancer – Starlight Dreams (Black Tie Affair). *Racing record:* Won 7 races, notably the Phoenix Stakes, National Stakes, St James's Palace Stakes and Irish 2,000 Guineas (all Group 1 races). *Stud record:* His first two-year-olds appeared in 2013 and he was the leading European first-crop sire with 28 winners. The best of his winners to date are The Grey Gatsby (Group 1 French Derby and Group 1 Irish Champion Stakes), Amazing Maria (Group 1 Falmouth Stakes and Group 1 Prix Rothschild), Kingston Hill (Group 1 Racing Post Trophy and Group 1 St Leger), Thee Auld Floozie and Te Rapa (Group 1 winners in New Zealand), Group 2 Ribblesdale Stakes winner Even Song, the New Zealand Group 2 winners Mime, Sacred Master and Thunder Lady, thirteen Group 3 winners including Nakuti and Master Apprentice (both here), Craftsman and Iveagh Gardens (both in Ireland). Standing at Coolmore Stud, Ireland. *2017 fee:* €25,000.

MAXIOS (2008) Monsun – Moonlight's Box (Nureyev). *Racing record:* Won 8 races including the Group 1 9.5f Prix d'Ispahan, the Group 1 1m Prix du Moulin and two Group 3's in France. *Stud record:* A half-brother to the multiple Group 1 winner (including the Prix de l'Arc de Triomphe) Bago. His first runners appear on the racecourse this season. Standing at Gestut Fahrhof. *2017 fee:* €10,000.

MAYSON (2008) Invincible Spirit – Mayleaf (Pivotal). *Racing record:* Won five races over 5f and 6f, notably the Group 1 July Cup and the Group 3 Abernant Stakes. *Stud record:* His first runners appeared on the racecourse last season and to date he's the sire of the winners of 32 races including the listed winners Global Applause (also third in the Group 2 Mill Reef Stakes), Private Matter and Rose Briar, plus the Group 3 placed Rosebride. Standing at Cheveley Park Stud, Newmarket. *2017 fee:* £6,000.

MEDICEAN (1997) Machiavellian – Mystic Goddess (Storm Bird). *Racing record:* 6 wins including the Lockinge Stakes and Eclipse. *Stud record:* His first runners appeared in 2005. Sire of 24 Group winners including ten Group 1 winners - Dutch Art (Prix Morny, Middle Park), Nannina (Fillies' Mile, Coronation Stakes), Capponi, Al Shemali (both Dubai Group 1 winners), Siyouma (Group 1 Sun Chariot Stakes and Group 1 E P Taylor Stakes), Almerita & Neatico (both Group 1 German winners), Chevron (Group 1 Raffles International Cup), Bayrir (Grade 1 Secretariat Stakes) and the Hong Kong Group 1 winner Mr Medici. His five Group 2 winners are Sapphire (British Champions Fillies and Mares Stakes), Bankable (in the UAE), Manieree (Blandford Stakes), Dimension & Medici Code (both in North America). Standing at Cheveley Park Stud. *2017 fee:* £6,000.

MORE THAN READY (1997) Southern Halo – Woodman's Girl (Woodman). *Racing record:* Won 7 races in the USA including the Grade 1 7f King's Bishop Stakes and the 2-y-o Grade 2 6f Sanford Stakes. *Stud record:* Sire of 73 Group/Graded stakes winners including 2 Group/Grade 1 winners – Benicio, Buster's Ready, Carry On Cutie, Daredevil, Regally Ready, Room Service, Verrazano (all in North America), Dreamaway, Eagle Way, Entisaar, Gimmethegreenlight, More Joyous, More Than Sacred, Perfectly Ready, Perfect Reflection, Phelan Ready, Prized Icon, Samaready and Sebring (all in Australia/New Zealand). Standing at WinStar Farm, Kentucky. *2017 fee:* $60,000.

MOST IMPROVED (2009) Lawman – Tonnara (Linamix). *Racing record:* Won two of his ten starts, notably the Group 1 St James's Palace Stakes, and was third in the Group 1 7f Dewhurst Stakes. *Stud record:* Half-brother to the Group 1 Criterium International and Grade 1 Turf Classic winner Ectot. His first runners appear on the racecourse this season. Standing at Coolmore Stud. 2017 stud fee: €4,000.

MOUNT NELSON (2004) Rock of Gibraltar – Independence (Selkirk). *Racing record:* Won the Group 1 1m Criterium International at 2 yrs and the Group 1 10f Eclipse Stakes. *Stud record:* His first two-year-olds ran in 2012 and to date he's had the Group 2 Royal Lodge Stakes winner Berkshire, Highlands Queen (Group 2 Prix de Pomone), Boscaccio (Group 2 Oppenheim Union-Rennen), the Group 3 Prix du Calvados winner Purr Along, Group 3 Chartwell Stakes winner Emerald Star and 11 listed winners including the Group 1 placed Elbereth, Mohave Princess and Volume, and the Group 2 placed Holy Moly and Weltmacht. Standing at Boardsmill Stud, Ireland. *2017 fee:* £4,500.

NATHANIEL (2008) Galileo – Magnificient Style (Silver Hawk). *Racing record:* Won four races notably the Group 1 12f King George VI and Queen Elizabeth Stakes and the Group 1 Eclipse Stakes. *Stud record:* His first two-year-olds appeared on the track last year and he had two Group 3 placed horses in Germany and 12 minor winners here and abroad. Standing at Newsells Park Stud. *2017 fee:* £217,500.

NEW APPROACH (2005) Galileo – Park Express (Ahonoora). *Racing record:* Won five group 1 events including the Derby, the Champion Stakes and the Irish Champion Stakes. *Stud record:* His first two-year-olds appeared in 2012. Sire of the champion 2-y-o Dawn Approach (Dewhurst Stakes, National Stakes, 2,000 Guineas, St James's Palace Stakes), Talent (Group 1 Epsom Oaks), Elliptique (German Group 1), May's Dream (Group 1 Australasian Oaks), Sultanina (Group 1 Nassau Stakes), Potemkin (Group 1 Premio Roma), Libertarian (Group 2 Dante Stakes and second in the Derby), Beautiful Romance (Group 2 Middleton Stakes), Connecticut (Group 2 in Turkey), Herald The Dawn (Group 2 Futurity Stakes), Messi (Grade 2 Sky

Classic Stakes), Nearly Caught (Group 2 Prix Kergorlay), New Predator (two Group 2's in Australia) and six Group 3 winners including Cap O'Rushes (Gordon Stakes), Newfangled (Albany Stakes), Montsegure, Sword Of Light and Gamblin' Guru (all in Australia). Standing at Dalham Hall Stud, Newmarket. 2017 stud fee: £30,000.

OASIS DREAM (2001) Green Desert – Hope (Dancing Brave). *Racing record:* Won four races including the Middle Park Stakes, July Cup and Nunthorpe Stakes (all Group 1 events). *Stud record:* His first crop of two-year-olds appeared in 2007 and he's built himself an outstanding reputation. His 15 Group 1 winners are Aqlaam (Prix du Moulin), Arcano (Prix Morny), Charming Thought (Middle Park Stakes), Goldream (King's Stand Stakes & Prix de l'Abbaye), Jwala (Nunthorpe Stakes), Lady Jane Digby (in Germany), Midday (six Group/Grade One's including the Nassau Stakes, Prix Vermeille and Breeders' Cup Filly & Mare Turf), Muarrab (Golden Shaheen), Muhaarar (July Cup, Commonwealth Cup and British Champions Sprint and Prix Maurice De Gheest), Naaqoos (Prix Jean-Luc Lagardere), Power (National Stakes & Irish 2,000 Guineas), Prohibit (King's Stand Stakes), Querari (in Italy) and Tuscan Evening (US Gamely Handicap). His 12 Group 2 scorers include Approve, Frozen Power, Misheer, Monitor Closely, Peace At Last, Quiet Oasis (in USA), Showcasing and Sri Putra. Standing at Banstead Manor Stud, Newmarket. *2017 fee:* £50,000.

PACO BOY (2005) Desert Style – Tappen Zee (Sandhurst Prince). *Racing record:* Won 10 races from 6f to 1m including the Group 1 Prix de la Foret, Queen Anne Stakes and Lockinge Stakes. *Stud record:* From three crops he has the winners of 208 races (to 18th April 2017) including the Group 1 2,000 Guineas and Group 1 St James's Palace Stakes winner Galileo Gold, the Group 2 Flying Childers winner Beacon, the Group 3 winners Smaih and Rainbow Royal (in Italy) and the listed winners Lexington Times, Making Trouble (in Germany), Peacock and Stella Di Paco (in New Zealand). Standing at Highclere Stud. *2017 fee:* £6,500.

PASTORAL PURSUITS (2001) Bahamian Bounty – Star (Most Welcome). *Racing record:*

Won 6 races including the Group 1 6f July Cup, Group 2 7f Park Stakes and Group 3 6f Sirenia Stakes. *Stud record:* His first crop appeared as 2-y-o's in 2009 and his best winners to date are Pastoral Player (Group 3 John of Gaunt Stakes), Rose Blossom (Group 3 Summer Stakes), the listed winners Angel's Pursuit, Catalina Bay (in Italy), Lightscameraction, Marine Commando, Rooke (in France), Spiritual Lady, Terra Di Tuffi (in Germany) and Ventura Mist, and the Group 2 placed Louie de Palma and Kibaar. Standing at Ladyswood & Snailwell Stud. *2017 fee:* £2,500.

PIVOTAL (1993) Polar Falcon – Fearless Revival (Cozzene). *Racing record:* 4 wins including the Nunthorpe Stakes and King's Stand Stakes. *Stud record:* First runners in 2000. An outstanding sire of 132 Group/Stakes winners in all. Among the best of them are African Story (Dubai World Cup), Excellent Art (St James's Palace Stakes), Falco (French 2,000 Guineas), Farhh (Champion Stakes & Lockinge Stakes), Golden Apples (triple US Grade 1 winner), Halfway To Heaven (Irish 1,00 Guineas, Nassau Stakes and Sun Chariot Stakes), Immortal Verse (dual Group 1 winning miler), Kyllachy (Nunthorpe Stakes), Maarek (Prix de l'Abbaye), Regal Parade (Haydock Sprint Cup), Sariska (Oaks and Irish Oaks) and Somnus (Sprint Cup, Prix de la Foret, Prix Maurice de Gheest). Other top performers of his include Beauty Is Truth (Group 2 Prix du Gros-Chene), Captain Rio (Group 2 Criterium des Maisons-Laffitte), Chorist (Group 1 Pretty Polly Stakes), Izzi Top (Group 1 Prix Jean Romanet and Pretty Polly Stakes), Megahertz (two US Grade 1 events), Peeress (Lockinge Stakes, Sun Chariot Stakes), Pivotal Point (Group 2 Diadem Stakes), Saoire (Irish 1000 Guineas), Silvester Lady (German Oaks), Virtual (Lockinge Stakes) and Siyouni (2-y-o Group 1 Prix Jean-Luc Lagardere). Standing at Cheveley Park Stud, Newmarket. *2017 fee:* £40,000.

POET'S VOICE (2007) Dubawi – Bright Tiara (Chief's Crown). *Racing record:* Won 4 races over 7f and a mile, and at 2 and 3 yrs, notably the Group 1 Queen Elizabeth II Stakes, the Group 2 Champagne Stakes (at 2 yrs) and the Group 2 Celebration Mile. *Stud record:* His first crop were two-year-olds in 2015 and to date (11th March 2017) he has the winners of 118 races including the Group 3 Oh So Sharp Stakes winner Poet's Vanity, the Italian Group

3 winners Posta Diletto and Voice Of Love and the listed winners Whitman, Mi Raccomando (in Italy) and My Country (in Australia). Standing at Dalham Hall Stud in Newmarket. *2017 fee:* £8,000.

POWER (2009) Oasis Dream – Frappe (Inchinor). *Racing record:* Won 5 races from 5f to 1m including the Group 1 National Stakes, the Group 2 Coventry Stakes (both at 2 yrs) and the Group 1 Irish 2,000 Guineas. *Stud record:* His first crop were two-year-olds in 2016. He has the winners of 23 races to date (11th March 2017) including four stakes winners in Europe – Peace Envoy (Group 3 Anglesey Stakes), Pleaseletmewin (Group 3 Horris Hill Stakes), Cristal Fizz (listed Radley Stakes) and Biz Power (listed winner and Group 3 placed in Italy). He also has the New Zealand listed winner Gift Of Power. Standing at Coolmore Stud in Ireland. *2017 fee:* €8,000.

RAVEN'S PASS (2005) Elusive Quality – Ascutney (Lord At War). *Racing record:* Won 6 races, notably the Group 1 1m Queen Elizabeth II Stakes and the Grade 1 10f Breeders' Cup Classic. *Stud record:* His first crop of two-year-olds appeared in 2012 and to date (11th March 2017) he has 7 Group winners and 9 Listed winners to his name. The best of them are Steeler (Group 2 Royal Lodge Stakes winner and Group 1 Racing Post Trophy second), Richard Pankhurst (Group 2 Hungerford Stakes), the Group 3 winners Malabar (Prestige Stakes), Secret Number (Cumberland Lodge Stakes), Kataniya (Prix de Royaumont), Greg Pass (in Italy) and Swashbuckling (in Australia), the Group placed listed winners Ibn Malik, Aquila Solitaria (in Italy) and Lovely Pass (in the UAE) and the Group 2 placed winner Mutashaded. Standing at Kildangan Stud, Ireland. *2017 fee:* €12,000.

RED JAZZ (2007) Johannesburg – Now That's Jazz (Sword Dance). *Racing record:* Won 5 races including the Group 2 Challenge Stakes, the Listed Free Handicap and the Listed Spring Trophy. Also placed in nine Group races including when third in the Group 1 Queen Elizabeth II Stakes. *Stud record:* His first crop of two-year-olds appear this season. Standing at Ballyhane Stud in Ireland. *2017 fee:* €4,000.

REQUINTO (2009) Dansili – Damson (Entrepreneur). *Racing record:* Only ran at 2

yrs and won four races including the Group 2 5f Flying Childers Stakes and the Group 3 5f Molecomb Stakes. *Stud record:* His first crop of two-year-olds appeared last season and to date (11th March 2017) he has the winners of 25 races, although only one black-type performer (Broken Stones was third in the Group 2 July Stakes). Standing at Coolmore Stud, Ireland. *2017 fee:* €5,000.

RIP VAN WINKLE (2006) Galileo – Looking Back (Stravinsky). *Racing record:* Won five races from 7f (at 2 yrs) to 10f including the Sussex Stakes, Queen Elizabeth II Stakes and Juddmonte International (all Group 1 events). *Stud record:* His first 2-y-o's ran in 2014 and to date his best have been the Group 1 Phoenix Stakes winner Dick Whittington, the New Zealand Group 2 winner Capella, the Group 3 Renaissance Stakes winner The Magic Prince, the New Zealand Group 3 winners Euro Angel, First Impressions, I Am Beautiful and Magic Dancer, and six listed winners. Standing at Coolmore Stud, Ireland. *2017 fee:* €12,500.

ROCK OF GIBRALTAR (1999) Danehill – Offshore Boom (Be My Guest). *Racing record:* Won seven Group 1 races including the Dewhurst Stakes, 2,000 Guineas, St James's Palace Stakes and Sussex Stakes. *Stud record:* The sire of fourteen Group/Grade 1 winners including the US dual Grade 1 winner Diamondrella, Eagle Mountain (in Hong Kong), Mount Nelson (Eclipse and Criterium International), Samitar (Irish 1,000 Guineas and Garden City Stakes), Prince Gibraltar (Criterium de Saint-Cloud), dual Group 1 winning sprinter Society Rock and Varenar (Prix de la Foret) as well as over 50 other Group winners. Standing at Coolmore Stud, Ireland. *2017 fee:* €9,000.

RODERIC O'CONNOR (2008) Galileo – Secret Garden (Danehill). *Racing record:* Won 3 races, notably the Group 1 1m Grand Criterium (at 2 yrs) and the Group 1 Irish 2,000 Guineas. *Stud record:* His first crop were two-year-olds in 2015 and he his 7 Group winners to his name. They include El Shaklan (Grade 1 in Brazil), Biz Heart (Italian Group 2 Premio Gran Criterium) and Great Page (Group 3 Prix du Calvados). He also has the Lingfield listed winner Haalick. Standing at the National Stud in Newmarket. *2017 fee:* £9,000.

SCAT DADDY (2004) Johannesburg – Love Style (Mr Prospector). *Racing record:* Won four Graded Stakes from 6f to 9f and at 2 and 3 yrs notably the Grade 1 Champagne Stakes (at 2 yrs) and the Grade 1 Florida Derby. *Stud record:* His best winners to date include 11 Group 1 winners in South America, plus Caravaggio (Group 1 Phoenix Stakes), Celestine (US Grade 1 Just A Game Stakes), Harmonize (Grade 1 Del Mar Oaks), Lady Aurelia (Group 1 Prix Morny), No Nay Never (Group 1 Morny and Group 2 Norfolk Stakes), Lady Of Shamrock (US dual Grade 1 winner) and Nickname (US Grade 1 Beldame Stakes), plus numerous Group/Grade 2 winners including Acapulco (Queen Mary Stakes), Daddy Long Legs (Royal Lodge Stakes), Azar, Conquest Daddyo, Dice Flavor, Handsome Mike, El Kabeir, Frac Daddy and Pretty N Cool (all in the USA). Died in 2015 at Ashford Stud, Kentucky after his fee had been raised to $100,000 from $35,000.

SEA THE STARS (2006) Cape Cross – Urban Sea (Miswaki). *Racing record:* Outstanding winner of 9 races including the Derby, 2,000 Guineas, Prix de L'Arc de Triomphe, Irish Champion Stakes, Juddmonte International Stakes and Eclipse Stakes. *Stud record:* His first two-year-olds appeared in 2013 and he's already had five Group 1 winners to his name – Harzand (Derby and Irish Derby), Taghrooda (Oaks and King George VI), Sea The Moon (German Derby) and Vazira (Prix Saint-Alary) and Zelzal (Prix Jean Prat), along with six Group 2 winners – Across The Stars, Cloth Of Stars, Endless Time, Mekhtaal, Mutakayyef and Storm The Stars, plus nine Group 3 and 13 Listed winners. Standing at Gilltown Stud, Ireland. *Stud fee:* €125,000.

SEPOY (2008) Elusive Quality – Watchful (Danehill). *Racing record:* Champion 2-y-o and 3-y-o in Australia. Won four Group 1 sprints at 2 and 3 yrs. *Stud record:* His first northern hemisphere two-year-olds appeared last season and he's had plenty of winners. They include Kilmah (Group 3 Prestige Stakes), the Listed winner and dual Group 3 placed Baileys Showgirl, the Group 1 Prix Marcel Boussac third Dabyah, the Group 3 Oh So Sharp Stakes third Unforgetable Filly and the useful listed-placed Executive Force. Standing at Dalham Hall Stud, Ireland. *Stud fee:* €15,000.

SHAMARDAL (2002) Giant's Causeway – Helsinki (Machiavellian). *Racing record:* Won the Dewhurst Stakes, French 2,000 Guineas, French Derby and St James's Palace Stakes (all Group 1 events). *Stud record:* Has sired 18 Group 1 winners from his first seven crops including Able Friend (four Group 1's in Hong Kong), Baltic Baroness (Prix Vermeille), Casamento (Racing Post Trophy), Dariyan (Prix Ganay), Lope De Vega (French 2,000 Guineas and French Derby), Lumiere (Cheveley Park Stakes), Mukhadram (Eclipse Stakes), Sagawara (Prix Saint-Alary), Speedy Boarding (Prix Jean Romanet and Prix de l'Opera) and Dunboyne Express (renamed 'Dan Excel' in Hong Kong). His 38 Group 2/Group 3 winners include the Group 1 placed Alrahma, Blue Point, Fintry, Ihtimal, Lucida, Mukhadram No Evidence Needed and Puissance de Lune (both in Australia), Elle Shadow and Royal Solitaire (both in Germany). Standing at Kildangan Stud, Ireland. *2017 fee:* Private (was €70,000 in 2015).

SHOWCASING (2007) Oasis Dream – Arabesque (Zafonic). *Racing record:* Won 2 races at 2 yrs including the Group 2 6f Gimcrack Stakes. *Stud record:* Has had an excellent start, with 52 individual two-year-old winners from his first two European crops. Now from three crops he has 9 Group and 5 Listed winners. They include Quiet Reflection (Group 1 Haydock Park Sprint Cup, Group 1 Commonwealth Cup), Prize Exhibit (two Grade 2's and a Grade 3 in the USA), Toocoolforschool (Group 2 Mill Reef Stakes), Showbay (Group 2 in New Zealand), Cappella Sansevero (Group 3 Round Tower Stakes winner and Group 1 third), Caorunn (2-y-o Group 3 in New Zealand), Conselite (Group 3 Italian 1,000 Guineas), Tasleet (Group Greenham Stakes) and five listed winners including Accipiter, Tasleet (also second in Group 2 Richmond Stakes) and Raghu (also Group 1 third in New Zealand). Standing at Whitsbury Manor Stud. *2017 fee:* £35,000.

SIR PERCY (2003) Mark of Esteem – Percy's Lass (Blakeney). *Racing record:* A champion 2-y-o, he won five races notably the Derby and the Dewhurst Stakes. *Stud record:* His first runners appeared in 2011. Sire of six Group winners – Sir John Hawkwood (Group 1 in Australia), Wake Forest (Grade 1 Man O'War

Stakes), Lady Tiana (Group 2 Lancashire Oaks), Sir Andrew (Group 2 in New Zealand), Alla Speranza (Group 3 Kilternan Stakes), Lady Pimpernel (US Grade 3) and 11 listed winners including the Group 2 Royal Lodge Stakes second Nafaqa and the Group 2 Queen Mary Stakes third Newsletter. Standing at Lanwades Stud, Newmarket. *2017 fee:* £7,000.

SIR PRANCEALOT (2010) Tamayuz – Mona Em (Catrail). *Racing record:* Only ran at 2 yrs and won 3 of his 6 sprint races including the Group 2 Flying Childers Stakes and the listed National Stakes. Also second in the Group 2 Prix Robert Papin. *Stud record:* His first runners appeared last season and he had an excellent year in terms of numbers of winners. To date (11th March 2017) he has the winners of 56 races including Madam Dancealot (Group 3 Dick Poole Stakes) and Sir Dancealot (Listed Rockingham Stakes). Standing at Tally Ho Stud in Ireland. *2017 fee:* €8,000.

SIYOUNI (2007) Pivotal – Sichilla (Danehill). *Racing record:* Won four races at 2 yrs including the Group 1 7f Prix Jean-Luc Lagardere. Placed in two Group 1 events in France at 3. *Stud record:* With three racing so far he has sired the winners of 228 races (to the 18th April 2017), notably the triple Group 1 winner Ervedya (Coronation Stakes, French 1,000 Guineas, Prix du Moulin) and the Group winners Volta (Group 2 Prix de Sandringham), Bouree, Finsbury Square, Siyoushake, Souvenir Delondres, Spectre and Trixia. Standing at Haras de Bonneval. *2017 fee:* €45,000.

SIXTIES ICON (2003) Galileo – Love Divine (Diesis). *Racing record:* Won eight races including the Group 1 St Leger, the Group 2 Jockey Club Cup and four other Group events. *Stud record:* His first two year olds appeared in 2012 and his best winners to date include the South American dual Grade 1 winner Sixties Song, the US Grade 2 Royal Heroine Stakes winner Nancy From Nairobi. Group 3 Premio Primi Passi & Listed Woodcote Stakes winner Chilworth Icon, the listed winners Audacia, Cruck Realta, Czabo and Epsom Icon, along with the useful Group 3 placed Harrison and the triple listed-placed Effie B. Sire of the winners of 97 races to March 2017. Standing at Norman Court Stud, Wiltshire. *2017 stud fee:* £5,000.

SOCIETY ROCK (2007) Rock Of Gibraltar – High Society (Key Of Luck). *Racing record:* A winner of 6 races over 6f from 2 to 6 yrs, notably the Group 1 Golden Jubilee Stakes and the Group 1 Haydock Park Sprint Cup. *Stud record:* His first two-year-olds appear this season. Died in 2016, stood at Tally Ho Stud for €6,000.

SO YOU THINK (2006) High Chaparral – Triassic (NZ) (Tights). *Racing record:* Won 14 races in Australia, Ireland and England from 7f to 10.5f including an outstanding ten Group 1's, e.g. the Coral Eclipse Stakes, Prince Of Wales's Stakes, Irish Champion Stakes and the Tattersalls Gold Cup (twice). *Stud record:* His first two-year-olds in the northern hemisphere appeared last season. He has two Group 1 winners in Australia (Inference and La Bella Diosa) and the New Zealand Group 2 winner Gold Rush – all at 3 yrs. Standing at Coolmore Stud, Ireland. *2017 stud fee:* £12,500.

STREET CRY (1998) Machiavellian – Helen Street (Troy). *Racing record:* 5 wins including the Group 1 10f Dubai World Cup and the US Grade 1 9f Stephen Foster Handicap. *Stud record:* First runners in 2006. Sire of the outstanding multiple Grade 1 winning racemare Zenyatta and the Group/Grade 1 winners Street Sense (Breeders' Cup Juvenile, Kentucky Derby, Travers Stakes), Cry And Catch Me (Oak Leaf Stakes), Majestic Roi (Sun Chariot Stakes), Street Boss (Triple Bend Invitational, Bing Crosby Handicap), Seventh Street (Go For Wand Handicap, Apple Blossom Handicap), Street Hero (Norfolk Stakes), Here Comes Ben (Forego Handicap), Victor's Cry (Shoemaker Mile Handicap), Street Hero (Norfolk Stakes), Zaidan (Hong Kong Classic Cup) and the Australian Group 1 winners Long John, Shocking (Melbourne Cup), Winx (four Group 1's) and Whobegotyou (Caulfield Guineas and Yalumba Stakes). Died in 2014.

STYLE VENDOME (2010) Anabaa – Place Vendome (Dr Fong). *Racing record:* Won five races including the Group 1 French 2,000 Guineas, the Group 3 Prix Djebel and two listed events. *Stud record:* His first crop are 2-y-o's this season. Standing Haras de Bouquetot. 2017 stud fee: €5,000.

SWISS SPIRIT (2009) Invincible Spirit – Swiss Lake (Indian Ridge). *Racing record:* A sprint winner of 3 races including the King George V Stakes and the listed Carnarvon Stakes. *Stud record:* A half-brother to the top sprinters Swiss Dream, Swiss Diva and Swiss Franc, His first two-year-olds appear this season. Standing at Whitsbury Manor Stud. *2017 fee:* £4,000.

TEOFILO (2004) Galileo – Speirbhhean (Danehill). *Racing record:* Won 5 races at 2 yrs including the Group 1 Dewhurst Stakes and the Group 1 National Stakes. *Stud record:* His first runners appeared in 2011 and he has 31 Group winners so far, including eleven Group 1 winners – Parish Hall (Dewhurst Stakes), Havana Gold (Prix Jean Prat), Loch Garman (Criterium International), Pleascach (Irish 1,000 Guineas & Yorkshire Oaks), Quest For More (Prix du Cadran), Trading Leather (Irish Derby), Kermadek, Palentino & Sonntag (all in Australia), Special Fighter (Al Maktoum Challenge) and Voleuse De Coeurs (Irish St Leger), plus 8 Group/Grade 2 winners including the US Grade 1 placed Amira's Prince, the Group 1 Sussex Stakes second Arod, the Irish Derby third Light Heavy and Oaks second Tarfasha. Standing at Kildangan Stud, Ireland. *2017 fee:* €40,000.

THEWAYYOUARE (2005) Kingmambo – Maryinski (Sadler's Wells). *Racing record:* Won four races in France including the Group 1 1m Criterium International and the Group 3 1m Prix Thomas Bryon. *Stud record:* Sire of the high-class Group 2 UAE Derby winner and Grade 1 Breeders' Cup Classic second Toast Of New York, the Peruvian Grade 3 winner El Jader, listed winners We Are Ninety (in Ireland), Prince Mambo and Twya (both New Zealand), Group 2 second Thewayyouwish and the Group 3 placed Hug And A Kiss and Tommy Docc. Standing at Haras de Corlay. *2017 fee:* €3,000.

WAR FRONT (2003) Danzig – Starry Dreamer (Rubiano). *Race record:* Won four races at 3 and 4 yrs including the Grade 2 6f Alfred G Vanderbilt Breeders' Cup Handicap at Saratoga. *Stud record:* One of the world's top sires, in his first six crops he has sired twelve Group 1/Grade 1 winners – Air Force Blue, War Command (both winners of the Group 1 Dewhurst Stakes), Brave Anna (Cheveley Park Stakes), Declaration Of War (Juddmonte International, Queen Anne Stakes), Avenge, Data Link, Hit It A Bomb, Jack Milton, Peace

And War, Summer Soiree, The Factor (all in the USA) and Lines Of Battle (in Hong Kong). Also, he has ten Group/Grade 2 winners – Bashart, Departing, On Leave, Pontchatrain, Roly Poly, Soldat, State Of Play, Summer Front, War Dancer and War Decree. Standing at Claiborne Farm, Kentucky. *2017 fee:* $250,000.

WORTHADD (2007) Dubawi – Wigman (Rahy). Race record: Won 9 races from 7f to 11f and from 3 to 5 yrs including the Group 2 Italian Derby, Group 2 Premio Carlo Vittadini, Group 2 Tris Internazionale, Group 3 Premio Parioli (Italian Guineas) and the Group 3 Badener Mele. Second in the Group 1 Lockinge Stakes. *Stud record:* His first 2-y-o's appear this year. Standing at the Irish National Stud. *2017 fee:* €5,000.

ZEBEDEE (2008) Invincible Spirit – Cozy Maria (Cozzene). *Racing record:* Won 6 races over 5f and 6f as a 2-y-o including the Group 2 Flying Childers Stakes, the Group 3 Molecomb Stakes and the listed Dragon Stakes. *Stud record:* First runners in 2014. He has the winners of 311 races (to 11th March 2017) including the dual

Group 2 winner Ivawood, the Group 2 Duke Of York Stakes winner and Group 1 Sprint Cup third Magical Memory, Italian Listed winner and Group 2 Italian Derby second Dee Dee D'Or and the Group 3 placed Manaafidh and Parsley. Sire of the winners of 164 races to date (March 2017). Standing at Tally Ho Stud in Ireland. *2017 fee:* €7,500.

ZOFFANY (2008) Dansili – Tyranny (Machiavellian). *Racing record:* Won 5 races as a 2-y-o including the Group 1 6f Phoenix Stakes and the Group 3 7f Tyros Stakes. *Stud record:* His first crop were two-year-olds in 2015 and he's had a very good start with the winners of 147 races (to 11th March 2017), notably the Group 1 Gran Premio del Jockey Club winner Ventura Storm, the Group 2 winners Foundation, Illuminate, Knife Edge, Waterloo Bridge and Zodiac Ruler (in South Africa), the Irish Group 3 winner Dolce Straga, four Listed winners including the dual Group 1 placed Washington DC and the triple Group 1 placed Architecture. Standing at Coolmore Stud in Ireland. *2017 fee:* €35,000.

Sires Index

Foxwedge	36, 189, 269, 327, 393, 761, 1173, 1484, 1485, 1531, 1533, 1542
Frankel	199, 201, 221, 223, 305, 309, 358, 365, 500, 596, 617, 625, 637, 656, 674, 705, 972, 974, 1027, 1070, 1182, 1213, 1229, 1230, 1240, 1306, 1315, 1334, 1362, 1405, 1449, 1452, 1501, 1510, 1512, 1514, 1515, 1518, 1609, 1680, 1684, 1696, 1697
Galileo	93, 104, 312, 600, 619, 655, 666, 745, 877, 911, 920, 969, 977, 1100, 1107, 1203, 1214, 1215, 1216, 1218, 1219, 1220, 1221, 1222, 1223, 1226, 1228, 1231, 1233, 1235, 1236, 1237, 1238, 1243, 1425, 1463, 1470, 1686
Gemologist	1128
Giant's Causeway	86, 622, 664
Gio Ponti	528
Haatef	987
Harbour Watch	17, 57, 102, 211, 242, 441, 466, 467, 480, 573, 648, 683, 768, 1069, 1292, 1361, 1539, 1551
Hat Trick	1198
Havana Gold	29, 60, 188, 194, 216, 229, 270, 440, 445, 483, 491, 604, 605, 606, 684, 698, 719, 810, 811, 817, 935, 1023, 1073, 1076, 1092, 1115, 1133, 1375, 1407, 1422, 1423, 1447, 1549
Hellvelyn	237
Helmet	172, 179, 232, 257, 293, 342, 350, 391, 422, 450, 461, 474, 562, 868, 962, 980, 1032, 1081, 1123, 1130, 1380, 1435, 1473, 1594, 1615, 1671
Henrythenavigator	321, 352, 478, 1277, 1319, 1404
High Chaparral	88, 117, 129, 241, 855, 863, 866, 878, 892, 1006, 1244, 1308, 1344, 1436, 1437, 1657
Holy Roman Emperor	72, 77, 85, 92, 170, 296, 390, 650, 804, 876, 896, 936, 1148, 1259, 1274, 1284, 1367, 1432, 1439, 1487, 1496, 1587, 1636, 1685
Hurricane Run	1633
Iffraaj	3, 51, 140, 147, 152, 187, 316, 493, 576, 668, 700, 726, 727, 747, 827, 840, 854, 874, 898, 942, 985, 1035, 1047, 1102, 1255, 1316, 1467, 1543, 1612, 1641, 1690
Intello	120, 247, 292, 377, 715, 725, 829, 993, 1033, 1166, 1181, 1471, 1611, 1659
Intense Focus	956, 1029
Intikhab	686, 790, 1379, 1476
Into Mischief	1190
Invincible Spirit	21, 133, 139, 144, 166, 202, 214, 289, 302, 325, 372, 381, 385, 425, 489, 616, 643, 660, 696, 724, 736, 738, 805, 893, 930, 1207, 1208, 1298, 1320, 1352, 1431, 1443, 1446, 1511, 1547, 1575, 1577, 1606, 1692, 1695
Jimmy Creed	1193
Jukebox Jury	250, 950
Kendargent	308, 317, 432, 455, 931, 937, 1420, 1481
Kitten's Joy	99, 149, 197, 735, 1036
Kodiac	18, 64, 98, 135, 138, 253, 258, 271, 283, 297, 311, 324, 348, 367, 369, 434, 439, 494, 495, 518, 522, 524, 563, 658, 685, 691, 718, 722, 734, 746, 762, 785, 789, 795, 801, 818, 820, 830, 838, 839, 843, 849, 882, 929, 933, 992, 997, 1000, 1012, 1014, 1055, 1061, 1109, 1121, 1180, 1188, 1265, 1303, 1305, 1327, 1332, 1364, 1412, 1438, 1546, 1598, 1621

Kyllachy	206, 227, 230, 244, 408, 428, 459, 538, 561, 571, 1011, 1287, 1390, 1491, 1564
Lawman	419, 507, 777, 783, 858, 944, 946, 971, 1321, 1418, 1458, 1648, 1676
Le Havre	629, 1483
Leroidesanimaux	46, 50, 276, 955, 994, 1398, 1445, 1563
Lethal Force	178, 209, 231, 287, 396, 403, 446, 479, 546, 554, 556, 564, 569, 677, 690, 692, 782, 815, 894, 952, 1056, 1065, 1067, 1098, 1160, 1585
Lilbourne Lad	26, 1145, 1146, 1290, 1573
Lonhro	8, 126, 205, 889, 1643
Lope De Vega	34, 41, 295, 378, 386, 514, 765, 1071, 1253, 1257, 1264, 1268
Lord Kanaloa	95
Lord Shanakill	951, 1077, 1297
Major Cadeaux	1177
Makfi	246, 300, 394, 435, 515, 925, 1448, 1455, 1550, 1626
Manduro	958
Mastercraftsman	39, 94, 240, 291, 318, 337, 404, 527, 548, 602, 628, 709, 825, 845, 847, 965, 978, 979, 1016, 1108, 1117, 1135, 1140, 1176, 1185, 1296, 1372, 1399, 1624
Mawatheeq	1556
Maxios	42, 73, 834, 926, 1058
Mayson	186, 340, 355, 363, 516, 568, 584, 680, 730, 835, 924, 1280, 1414, 1545, 1574, 1584, 1596, 1645
Mazameer	447
Medaglia d'Oro	1189
Medicean	184, 541, 545, 654, 742, 1020, 1158, 1588
Mizzen Mast	885, 1300, 1603
Monsieur Bond	1374
More Than Ready	81, 743, 788, 900, 1195
Most Improved	399, 766, 771, 1118, 1124, 1387
Motivator	1661
Mount Nelson	477, 857, 861
Nathaniel	20, 44, 119, 255, 460, 490, 626, 842, 934, 1038, 1170, 1583, 1628
New Approach	9, 10, 30, 141, 157, 225, 364, 379, 421, 444, 688, 905, 1113, 1421, 1519, 1530, 1544, 1619
Norse Dancer	536, 547
Oasis Dream	12, 35, 43, 71, 89, 107, 174, 198, 233, 320, 322, 323, 343, 375, 383, 496, 566, 638, 644, 904, 913, 916, 947, 1030, 1041, 1172, 1197, 1281, 1285, 1309, 1311, 1318, 1356, 1377, 1384, 1632, 1644, 1655
Orfevre	101
Paco Boy	45, 261, 539, 1087
Panis	14
Pastoral Pursuits	62, 1553, 1555
Pastorius	54

Peer Gynt	13
Piccolo	558
Pivotal	203, 243, 523, 713, 714, 897, 998, 1099, 1273, 1282, 1286, 1383, 1607
Planteur	171, 1154
Poet's Voice	130, 356, 371, 454, 594, 678, 681, 844, 903, 949, 1283, 1389, 1406, 1616
Pour Moi	1670
Power	759, 990, 1330, 1562
Quality Road	1646
Rajj	1060
Raven's Pass	25, 220, 517, 565, 651, 871, 1104, 1105, 1565
Reckless Abandon	192, 928, 1341, 1525
Red Jazz	106, 279, 336, 431, 449, 497, 583, 793, 865, 912, 1062, 1328
Redoute's Choice	597, 624, 1110
Requinto	415, 508, 575, 1699
Rio De La Plata	1269
Rip Van Winkle	347, 1153, 1401, 1664
Rock Of Gibraltar	124, 603, 750, 1178
Roderic O'Connor	63, 266, 776, 1337, 1386
Royal Applause	1015, 1125
Sakhee's Secret	28, 1163
Sayif	66, 741, 1046, 1366, 1368, 1665
Scat Daddy	621, 669, 716, 1194, 1205, 1206, 1209, 1500
Sea The Stars	83, 100, 411, 513, 701, 723, 740, 914, 995, 1106, 1168, 1249, 1261, 1294, 1295, 1350, 1591, 1600, 1651
Sepoy	278, 330, 462, 470, 492, 634, 975, 1088, 1171, 1346, 1630
Shamardal	59, 76, 105, 113, 118, 132, 148, 212, 217, 218, 234, 313, 487, 529, 590, 610, 675, 717, 721, 919, 1040, 1492, 1578, 1589, 1595
Showcasing	69, 82, 90, 423, 525, 587, 640, 695, 753, 770, 1010, 1063, 1129, 1134, 1279, 1313, 1357, 1358, 1538, 1571
Sir Percy	24, 251, 354, 376, 402, 953, 1089, 1310, 1605, 1675
Sir Prancealot	406, 526, 550, 593, 784, 1426, 1479, 1535, 1569, 1637
Sixties Icon	53, 249, 256, 273, 281, 285, 306, 505
Siyouni	190, 335, 1461, 1558
Smart Strike	80, 881
So You Think	290, 948, 1064, 1157, 1161, 1554
Society Rock	115, 125, 193, 456, 488, 611, 816, 823, 899, 1008, 1019, 1095, 1141, 1147, 1271, 1335, 1393, 1413, 1427, 1474, 1475, 1570, 1581, 1582, 1601, 1638, 1669
Speightstown	143, 614, 687, 1593, 1652
Stimulation	473, 1139
Street Cry	6, 110, 344, 345, 751, 1614, 1629
Style Vendome	519, 673, 1150, 1323

Swiss Spirit	65, 116, 207, 263, 265, 359, 535, 612, 772, 1291, 1293, 1304, 1378, 1417, 1653, 1666
Tagula	48
Tamayuz	814, 1376
Tapit	645
Teofilo	16, 145, 146, 151, 155, 213, 653, 749, 906, 999, 1001, 1103, 1179, 1307, 1312, 1457, 1520, 1650, 1700
The Factor	1186
Thewayyouare	1031, 1266, 1270
Tough As Nails	1567
Union Rags	635, 1200, 1403
Universal	1083, 1462
Vale Of York	1026, 1090
Violence	1196
Vision D'Etat	468
Vocalised	156
War Front	196, 219, 224, 228, 665, 1191, 1204, 1210, 1211, 1212, 1225, 1239, 1241, 1242, 1430, 1521, 1623, 1681, 1688
Whipper	512
Wootton Bassett	595
Worthadd	131, 329, 401, 1085, 1416
Zebedee	128, 260, 475, 560, 787, 819, 875, 909, 966, 1114, 1369, 1408
Zoffany	159, 239, 338, 463, 532, 585, 618, 703, 733, 778, 792, 910, 921, 923, 1050, 1052, 1057, 1059, 1066, 1068, 1111, 1116, 1122, 1174, 1254, 1272, 1434, 1453

Racing Trends

The following tables focus on those two-year-old races that seem to produce winners that improve the following year as three-year-olds. This type of analysis can enable us to select some of the best of this year's classic generation.

In the tables, the figure in the third column indicates the number of wins recorded as a three-year-old, with GW signifying a Group race winner at that age.

The horses listed below are the winners of the featured races in 2016. Anyone looking for horses to follow in the listed and Group race events this season might well want to bear them in mind. I feel that those in bold text are particularly worthy of close scrutiny.

Boynton	**Lockheed**
Brave Anna	Medieval
Capri	Queen Kindly
Churchill (2)	**Rhododendron**
Coronet	Rivet
Cunco	Spain Burg
Dubai Hero	Syphax
Escobar	**Temple Church**
Larchmont Lad	War Decree

Lowther Stakes
York, 6 furlongs, August.

2001	Queen's Logic	1 GW
2002	Russian Rhythm	3 GW
2003	Carry On Katie	0
2004	Soar	0
2005	Flashy Wings	0
2006	Silk Blossom	0
2007	Nahoodh	1 GW
2008	Infamous Angel	0
2009	Lady of the Desert	1 GW
2010	Hooray	1
2011	Best Terms	0
2012	Rosdhu Queen	0
2013	Lucky Kristale	0
2014	Tiggy Wiggy	0

2015	Besharah	0
2016	Queen Kindly	

This race is not the force it was of old and you have to go back to Nahoodh's Falmouth Stakes win in 2008 for the last Group 1 success. Amazingly, Queen Kindly is the third generation of her family to win this race and therefore appear in the above chart. Her dam being Lady Of the Desert and grandam Queen's Logic. She'll prove best at around six/seven furlongs as a 3-y-o and she should win again.

Dewhurst Stakes
Newmarket, 7 furlongs, October.

2001	Rock Of Gibraltar	5 GW
2002	Tout Seul	0
2003	Milk It Mick	0
2004	Shamardal	3 GW
2005	Sir Percy	1 GW
2006	Teofilo	NR
2007	New Approach	3 GW
2008	Intense Focus	0
2009	Beethoven	1 GW
2010	Frankel	5 GW
2011	Parish Hall	0
2012	Dawn Approach	1 GW
2013	War Command	0
2014	Belardo	0
2015	Air Force Blue	0
2016	Churchill	

The Dewhurst Stakes remains our premier race for two-year-old colts. Frankel proved himself an outstanding champion of course and Rock Of Gibraltar was a real star too. Other outstanding colts to win this in the last twenty years are Shamardal, Zafonic, Dr Devious, Grand Lodge, Sir Percy and New Approach. On the face of it the last three year's results look disappointing, but Belardo came good as a 4-y-o, winning the Lockinge. Last year Churchill won the National Stakes as well as the Dewhurst, just as Teofilo, New Approach and Dawn Approach did before him. He'll prove a tough nut to crack in the Group 1 races over a mile this year.

Zetland Stakes
Newmarket, 10 furlongs, October/November.

2000	Worthily	0
2001	Alexander Three D	2 GW
2002	Forest Magic	NR
2003	Fun And Games	NR
2004	Ayam Zaman	0
2005	Under The Rainbow	0
2006	Empire Day	NR
2007	Twice Over	2 GW
2008	Heliodor	1
2009	Take It To The Max	0
2010	Indigo Way	NR
2011	Mojave	0
2012	Restraint of Trade	NR
2013	Hartnell	2 GW
2014	Crafty Choice	NR
2015	Glamorous Approach	0
2016	Coronet	

Previous winners include the St Leger and Coronation Cup winner Silver Patriarch, the good four-year-olds Double Eclipse and Rock Hopper, Bob's Return (also a St Leger hero), the Ascot Gold Cup winner Double Trigger and of course Twice Over who won four Group 1's during his career with Henry Cecil including as a 6-y-o in 2011. Hartnell went on to win a Group 1 in Australia as a 4-y-o. So there's clearly an emphasis on winners of the Zetland improving with age. Coronet will surely win more races over middle-distances.

Cheveley Park Stakes
Newmarket, 6 furlongs, October.

2001	Queen's Logic	1 GW
2002	Airwave	1 GW
2003	Carry On Katie	0
2004	Magical Romance	0
2005	Donna Blini	1
2006	Indian Ink	1 GW
2007	Natagora	2 GW
2008	Serious Attitude	1 GW
2009	Special Duty	2GW
2010	Hooray	1
2011	Lightening Pearl	0
2012	Rosdhu Queen	0

2013	Vorda	0
2014	Tiggy Wiggy	0
2015	Lumiere	1
2016	Brave Anna	

A number of these fillies have gone on to further Group race success. Indian Ink saved her best day for Royal Ascot, Natagora and Special Duty both went on to win the 1,000 Guineas and Serious Attitude returned to sprinting for another Group race success and the following year she won a Grade 1 sprint in Canada. A half-sister to the Grade 1 1m Breeders' Cup Juvenile Turf winner Hit It A Bomb, more Group race victories await Brave Anna, probably in races at up to a mile.

Denford Stud Stakes (registered as Washington Singer Stakes) Newbury, 7 furlongs, August.

2001	Funfair Wane	1
2002	Muqbil	1 GW
2003	Haafhd	3 GW
2004	Kings Quay	0
2005	Innocent Air	1
2006	Dubai's Touch	2
2007	Sharp Nephew	1
2008	Cry of Freedom	0
2009	Azmeel	2 GW
2010	Janood	0
2011	Fencing	0
2012	Just The Judge	1 GW
2013	Somewhat	0
2014	Belardo	0
2015	Epsom Icon	1 GW
2016	Escobar	

This race can often provide us with Group race or Classic pointers and in that regard the 90's winners Lammtarra and Rodrigo de Triano were outstanding and Haafhd won the 2,000 Guineas and the Champion Stakes. Azmeel trained on to win the Sandown Classic Trial and the Dee Stakes, but the race needed a pick-me-up and Just The Judge did that when winning the Irish 1,000 Guineas. Escobar disappointed in his third and final start of the season, but his sire Famous Name improved with age, so perhaps Escobar can bounce back and win again this year.

Qatar Vintage Stakes Goodwood, 7 furlongs, July.		
2000	No Excuse Needed	1 GW
2001	Naheef	1 GW
2002	Dublin	1
2003	Lucky Story	0
2004	Shamardal	3 GW
2005	Sir Percy	1 GW
2006	Strategic Prince	0
2007	Rio De La Plata	0
2008	Orizaba	0
2009	Xtension	0
2010	King Torus	2
2011	Chandlery	0
2012	Olympic Glory	2 GW
2013	Toormore	1 GW
2014	Highland Reel	3 GW
2015	Galileo Gold	2 GW
2016	War Decree	

All in all this race is very informative in terms of sorting out future stars, with the classic winners Sir Percy, Shamardal, Don't Forget Me, Dr Devious and Mister Baileys, plus the King George hero Petoski being the standouts of the past twenty odd years. Olympic Glory won two more Group 1's as a 4-y-o, so he can certainly be added to that list. Highland Reel won Grade 1's in the USA and Hong Kong and last year Galileo Gold did his connections proud in winning the 2,000 Guineas and St James's Palace Stakes. War Decree is part of Ballydoyle's 3-y-o battalion and although not on top of the pecking order at present he isn't far behind. He can improve and win more races this year.

National Stakes, Curragh, 7f, September.		
2000	Beckett	1
2001	Hawk Wing	1 GW
2002	Refuse To Bend	3 GW
2003	One Cool Cat	1 GW
2004	Dubawi	2 GW
2005	George Washington	2 GW
2006	Teofilo	NR
2007	New Approach	3 GW
2008	Mastercraftsman	3 GW
2009	Kingsfort	1
2010	Pathfork	0
2011	Power	1 GW
2012	Dawn Approach	1 GW
2013	Toormore	1 GW

2014	Gleneagles	2 GW
2015	Air Force Blue	0
2016	Churchill	

As one can see by the list of recent winners, this race is as important as any for figuring out the following year's top performers. For instance New Approach was outstanding when winning the Derby, the Champion Stakes and the Irish Champion, Mastercraftsman and Gleneagles both managed a couple of Group One wins at 3 yrs, and both Power and Dawn Approach notched up Group 1 successes as well. It would be surprising if Churchill couldn't add another Group 1 victory or two to his name this year.

Racing Post Trophy Doncaster, 8 furlongs, October.		
2000	Dilshaan	1 GW
2001	High Chaparral	5 GW
2002	Brian Boru	1 GW
2003	American Post	3 GW
2004	Motivator	2 GW
2005	Palace Episode	0
2006	Authorized	3 GW
2007	Ibn Khaldun	0
2008	Crowded House	0
2009	St Nicholas Abbey	0
2010	Casamento	1 GW
2011	Camelot	3 GW
2012	Kingsbarns	0
2013	Kingston Hill	1 GW
2014	Elm Park	1
2015	Marcel	0
2016	Rivet	

Some notable performers have won this race, including the outstanding colt High Chaparral, the Derby heroes Motivator and Authorized (both by Montjeu – also the sire of St Nicholas Abbey) and of course the 2,000 Guineas and Derby hero Camelot. Rivet took this year's renewal after disappointing in the Dewhurst Stakes. Perhaps if further Group 1 glory is to come his way this year it will be over ten furlongs or more.

Haynes, Hanson and Clark Stakes Newbury, 8 furlongs, September.		
2000	Nayef	4 GW
2001	Fight Your Corner	1 GW
2002	Saturn	0

2003	Elshadi	0
2004	Merchant	NR
2005	Winged Cupid	NR
2006	Teslin	2
2007	Centennial	2 GW
2008	Taameer	0
2009	Ameer	0
2010	Moriarty	0
2011	Cavaleiro	0
2012	Wentworth	1
2013	Pinzolo	1
2014	Snoano	0
2015	Stormy Antarctic	1 GW
2016	Temple Church	

The high-class horses Rainbow Quest, Unfuwain, King's Theatre and Nayef have all won this race and indeed Shergar won it in 1980, but it's been a while since those glory days although Centennial did manage two Group race wins in 2008. A son of Lawman and out of a Dalakhani mare, Temple Church will stay much further than a mile and he'll win more races.

Somerville Tattersall Stakes Newmarket, 7 furlongs, September/October.

2000	King Charlemagne	3 GW
2001	Where Or When	2 GW
2002	Governor Brown	NR
2003	Milk It Mick	0
2004	Diktatorial	0
2005	Aussie Rules	2 GW
2006	Thousand Words	0
2007	River Proud	1
2008	Ashram	2
2009	Sir Parky	0
2010	Rerouted	0
2011	Crius	0
2012	Havana Gold	1 GW
2013	Miracle Of Medinah	0
2014	Maftool	1 GW
2015	Sanus Per Aquam	0
2016	Larchmont Lad	

The Group winners speak for themselves but Milk It Mick also went on to win a Grade 1 in America as a five-year-old. Aussie Rules took the French 2,000 Guineas and also won a Grade 1 event in America. Both River Proud and Ashram won listed races in their 3-y-o season and Havana Gold took the Prix Jean

Prat over a mile. A smart colt, Larchmont Lad won two of his three races last year, he'll stay a mile and will win again.

Rockfel Stakes, 7 furlongs, Newmarket.

2001	Distant Valley	0
2002	Luvah Girl	1 in USA
2003	Cairns	0
2004	Maids Causeway	1 GW
2005	Speciosa	1 GW
2006	Finsceal Beo	2 GW
2007	Kitty Matcham	0
2008	Lahaleeb	2 GW
2009	Music Show	2 GW
2010	Cape Dollar	0
2011	Wading	0
2012	Just The Judge	1 GW
2013	Al Thakhira	1
2014	Lucida	0
2015	Promising Run	1 GW
2016	Spain Burg	

Three Newmarket 1,000 Guineas winners have hailed from the winners of this race since 1999 – Lahan, Speciosa and Finsceal Beo. For good measure Maids Causeway won the Coronation Stakes and Hula Angel won the Irish 1,000 Guineas (a race Finsceal Beo also added to her tally). Lahaleeb, Music Show and Just The Judge all went on to record Group 1 success at 3 yrs. Lucida was Group 1 placed twice but didn't notch up a win. Promising Run won a Group 3 over a mile in Turkey last year and also won a Group 2 this year as a 4-y-o in Dubai. Last year's winner, Spain Burg, is now in the USA.

Beresford Stakes, Curragh, 1m.

2001	Castle Gandolfo	1
2002	Alamshar	3 GW
2003	Azamour	2 GW
2004	Albert Hall	0
2005	Septimus	1 GW
2006	Eagle Mountain	1 GW
2007	Curtain Call	1
2008	Sea The Stars	6 GW
2009	St Nicholas Abbey	0
2010	Casamento	1 GW
2011	David Livingston	0
2012	Battle of Marengo	2 GW
2013	Geoffrey Chaucer	0
2014	Ol' Man River	0

2015	Port Douglas	0
2016	Capri	

Aidan O'Brien generally wins this race, but before Capri's win last year the previous three were disappointing in their 3-y-o seasons. Capri, not surprisingly a daughter of Galileo, was third in the Group 1 Criterium de Saint-Cloud after winning this race. She'll need to improve a few pounds to figure in the top mile/ten furlong events for fillies this year.

Acomb Stakes, York, 7 furlongs, August.

2001	Comfy	NR
2002	Bourbonnais	0
2003	Rule Of Law	2 GW
2004	Elliots World	1
2005	Palace Episode	0
2006	Big Timer	0
2007	Fast Company	0
2008	ABANDONED	
2009	Elusive Pimpernel	1 GW
2010	Waiter's Dream	NR
2011	Entifaadha	0
2012	Dundonnell	1
2013	Treaty Of Paris	NR
2014	Dutch Connection	1 GW
2015	Recorder	NR
2016	Syphax	

There have been a few disappointing seasons since the victories in the 90's of King's Best (2,000 Guineas) and Bijou D'Inde (St James's Palace Stakes), but Rule Of Law turned things around in 2004 with his St Leger victory and Elusive Pimpernel was successful in the Group 3 Craven Stakes Dutch Connection won the Group 3 Jersey Stakes and was second in the Group 1 Prix Jean Prat. Syphax didn't run again last year after winning this race but she remains in training with Kevin Ryan (although now owned by Godolphin). It will be interesting to see how she copes with being upped in class but she should win again.

Two-Year-Old Maiden for Colts Newbury Lockinge Meeting, 6 furlongs, May.

2000	Patsy's Double	1
2001	Amour Sans Fin	0
2002	Cap Ferrat	2
2003	Grand Reward	1
2004	Iceman	0

2005	Championship Point	1
	To Sender	0
2006	Major Cadeaux	1 GW
2007	Coasting	NR
2008	Instalment	1
	Orizaba	0
2009	Canford Cliffs	3 GW
	Meglio Ancora	0
2010	Memen (Div 1)	0
	Strong Suit (Div 11)	3 GW
2011	Wise Venture	0
2012	Sir Patrick Moore	0
2013	Championship	1
2014	Adaay	3 GW
2015	Qeyaadah	0
2016	Medieval (Div 1)	
	Cunco (Div 1)	

One of the season's first six furlong 2-y-o maidens, it regularly attracts a high quality field with plenty of winners going on to future success. Richard Hannon trained winners have regularly gone on to Group success and Canford Cliffs in particular is a standout here. Adaay did well last year, picking up a couple of Group 2's at Haydock Park and Newbury. After this race last year Medieval won again and then was listed placed. He's useful. Cunco is too and was also listed-placed last year. Both these colts should win again at some point this season.

7 furlong 2-y-o maiden at Newmarket's July Meeting (formerly the Strutt & Parker Maiden).

2001	Dubai Destination	0
2002	Tycoon Hall	0
2003	Josephus	0
2004	Belenus	2 GW
2005	Gin Jockey	0
2006	Kalgoorlie	0
2007	Rio De La Plata	0
2008	Soul City	0
2009	Elusive Pimpernel	1 GW
2010	Native Khan	1 GW
2011	Rougemont	0
2012	Ghurair	0
2013	True Story	1
2014	Lexington Times	1
2015	Manaafidh	NR
2016	Dubai Hero	

Although the statistics don't look that

encouraging it should be noted that six out of the last ten winners went on to group success as older horses. Most notably, Dubai Destination took the Group 1 Queen Anne as a 4-y-o and Rio De La Plata was five before he won a pair of Group One's in Italy. Lexington Times won a listed event last year. Dubai Hero only ran the once last season but he remains in training and should win again.

7 furlong Qatar Stallions Maiden. Glorious Goodwood.

2001	Sweet Band	0
2002	Wahsheeq	0
2003	Psychiatrist	0
2004	Jonquil	0
2005	Opera Cape	0
2006	Kilburn	0
2007	Latin Lad	0
2008	Jukebox Jury	3 GW
2009	Stags Leap	1
2010	Pausanias	1 Listed
2011	Nawwaar	0
2012	Steeler	NR
2013	Snow Trouble	0
2014	Dutch Connection	1 GW
2015	Folkswood	1
2016	Lockheed	

This was once a reliable maiden where numerous quality horses made their debuts in 70's, 80's and early 90's. The quality of winners declined markedly but there have been signs of an upturn recently. Dutch Connection won the Group 3 Jersey Stakes as well as finishing runner-up in the Group 1 Prix Jean Prat. Folkswood, a winner over a mile at Newmarket last year, was recently second in a Group 1 on the turf in Dubai over 9f. Lockheed improved after winning this to be placed in the Acomb Stakes and the Group 1 National Stakes. A useful colt that should win again at distances up to a mile.

Superlative Stakes Newmarket, 7 furlongs, July.

2001	Redback	1 GW
2002	Surbiton	NR
2003	Kings Point	0
2004	Dubawi	2 GW
2005	Horatio Nelson	0
2006	Halicarnassus	3 GW

2007	Hatta Fort	2 GW (in USA)
2008	Ole Ole	NR
2009	Silver Grecian	0
2010	King Torus	2
2011	Red Duke	0
2012	Olympic Glory	2 GW
2013	Good Old Boy Lukey	NR
2014	Estidhkaar	0
2015	Birchwood	1
2016	Boynton	

This race was raised to Group 2 from Group 3 in 2006. There are some very decent winners in this list, notably Dubawi and the more recent Olympic Glory who added two more Group 1's as a 4-y-o. Boynton hasn't been out since finishing third in the Vintage Stakes at Goodwood at the end of July. He's a smart colt and should win more races.

Fillies' Mile, Newmarket, 1 mile, October.

2001	Gossamer	1 GW
2002	Soviet Song	0
2003	Red Bloom	1 GW
2004	Playful Act	1 GW
2005	Nannina	1 GW
2006	Simply Perfect	1 GW
2007	Listen	0
2008	Rainbow View	1 GW
2009	Hibaayeb	2 GW
2010	White Moonstone	NR
2011	Lyric Of Light	0
2012	Certify	NR
2013	Chriselliam	Died
2014	Together Forever	0
2015	Minding	5 GW
2016	Rhododendron	

After a tricky five years when results didn't pan out, this race came back with a bang in 2016 with the top-class filly Minding. In previous years, Nannina, Simply Perfect, Rainbow View and Hibaayeb all won Group 1's as 3-y-o's. Soviet Song was a multiple Group 1 winner at 4 and 5 yrs, while Certify didn't run at 3 but won a Group 2 in Dubai at 4 yrs. The O'Brien trained Rhododendron was just one of several very good Ballydoyle 2-y-o fillies last year and in winning this race she probably forced herself to the top of the pack. Whether or not she wins another Group 1 over a mile this year, she could well do so over further.

Horse Index

Order Of Thistle	892	Prince Consort	1118	Rivendicato	1571	Shanghai Elastic	65
Oriental Song	218	Prince Eiji	1608	River Café	1006	Shapes	1064
Ostilio	364	Private Cashier	46	Robinson Crusoe	808	Sharja Silk	1613
Ottava	1492	Procedure	1511	Rock Force	448	Shawwal	648
Our Man In Havana	440	Proschema	443	Rock Of Estonia	899	She Believes	1007
Outlane	380	Protected Guest	1081	Rockabill	1256	Shehasspentthelot	518
Overcoming	1061	Puchita	803	Rocket Man Dan	397	Sheila's Empire	1148
Overtrumped	1360	Pulitzer	1332	Rockin Fella	193	Shesgotthelot	1149
Paint	800	Purplest	1035	Rogue	809	Shifted Strategy	1493
Pak Choi	45	Push n'Pull	572	Roof Garden	1552	Shobrom	577
Paminah	1165	Qazyna	1609	Rose Hip	248	Shootingthebreeze	451
Panophobia	570	Qianlong	1610	Roseau City	537	Short Call	271
Paparazzi	1255	Quality Seeker	1646	Roses In June	1147	Showdancing	1538
Paradox State	1034	Quantatmental	444	Roundabout Kitten	1036	Shuhood	814
Patriarch	982	Quargent	1191	Royal Goldie	270	Shyjack	1082
Patty Patch	1477	Quayside	573	Royal Parks	1537	Sicario	1270
Pentland Hills	1661	Queen Of Dreams	1013	Royal Wave	1015	Sigrid Nansen	1442
Pepper Street	1329	Queen Of Kalahari	894	Rude Awakening	1401	Silca Mistress	272
Perfect Thought	712	Queen Of Rome	804	Rufus King	985	Silver Bullet	452
Perfection	641	Queen Of Salsa	445	Rum Runner	810	Silver Character	453
Perpetrator	313	Queen Penn	574	Rumors Of War	219	Silver Quartz	1334
Persian Rhapsody	314	Queen Tomyris	945	Running Cloud	961	Silver Starlight	525
Perverse	959	Quick Breath	1371	Russian Campaign	1388	Silver Swift	49
Pesky Wabbitt	1478	Quick Skips Lad	1146	Rustang	930	Simmy's Copshop	578
Peter Leonard	571	Raayaat	983	Sabellum	576	Simpson	1647
Petit Palias	642	Ragtime Red	1062	Safe Waters	962	Simsimah	1389
Petrus	1116	Rainbow Hill	1333	Saffah	900	Sinaloa	579
Pheidippides	330	Rajasinghe	1480	Sailing Home	118	Sine Pari	1291
Philamundo	1479	Rampant Lion	984	Saint Anthony	1553	Sing A Rainbow	1362
Phoenician Star	1117	Raphael	1386	Sallab	811	Singing Sheriff	1648
Photonics	1330	Rasan	895	Salty Sugar	644	Sir Derrick	526
Pilot Wings	315	Raven's Song	517	Sam Gold	1612	Siren Song	454
Pink Phantom	343	Reactive	609	Sapiens	1697	Sirici	1494
Pippin	1166	Rebel Streak	47	Sarstedt	249	Sixties Secret	273
Pivotal Man	1607	Recks	192	Sausage Fingers	449	Skydiving	964
Platinum Warrior	745	Recollect	381	Savannah Dusk	1673	Slipstream	1443
Playfull Spirit	643	Reculver	48	Scenery	963	Smart Dart	94
Pleisiur	156	Red Cymbal	713	Scimitar	812	Smart Step	119
Plundered	182	Red For Danger	960	Scooter	316	Smile Ahead	1698
Plunger	342	Red Force One	446	Scriobh Nua	157	Smooth Sailing	901
Point Hope	801	Red Mist	365	Seahenge	1209	Smugglers Top	455
Polar Light	536	Red Roman	896	Sealla	1411	Snaffled	183
Pollyissimo	934	Red Starlight	805	Sebastiano Ricci	1257	So Crafty	965
Polly's Gold	935	Redtedd	447	Secret Eye	344	So Near So Farhh	274
Poppy Love	441	Refrain	1513	Secret Gaze	93	Soar Above	815
Popsicle	802	Regimented	806	Secret Rio	1269	Society Lilly	1335
Porchy Party	442	Regina Nostra	714	Secretario	937	Society Secret	456
Port Lions	746	Rekindle	1512	Seeing Stars	645	Solid Man	95
Port Of Call	1361	Rema Al Kuwait	1014	Seen The Lyte	1412	Song Of Summer	1674
Porth Swtan	893	Requinto Dawn	575	Sensory	646	Sooda	1614
Postcombe	1458	Reshaan	807	Sergio Leone	813	Sopranos Rock	816
Power Of Darkness	1562	Restive Spirit	715	Seyaady	986	Soto Sizzler	1016
Power To Exceed	1331	Revolutionary Man	366	Sha La La Lee	450	Sotomayor	817
Preacher Man	1268	Rewaayat	897	Shaheen	1413	Soumei	1649
Prediction	1429	Rhosneigr	898	Shaji	1119	Sound And Silence	7
Prezzie	1177	Rich Identity	1611	Shakour	647	Sovereign Duke	250
Prime Minister	1627	Richenza	92	Shalailah	1063	Sovrano	50

Dams Index